California's Ultimate Exam-Passing Workbook

for the State of California
Real Estate Salesperson & Broker Test

2015

California's Ultimate Real Estate Exam-Passing Workbook

Published by the
Lumbleau Real Estate School
2015 Edition

Author
John J. Lumbleau

Edited by Derf Fredericks

John Lumbleau
1928-2010

John Lumbleau

John was renowned motivational speaker and sales trainer. His ability to simplify the material you need to know was developed from over 40 years of sales training, motivational speaking, and developing real estate in-session classroom courses - exclusively for the profession of real estate in California. His expertise using videotape education to deliver the highest level of understanding is unsurpassed. Each of John Lumbleau's thirty-three hours of pre-license videotape education begins and ends by giving his students his personal research into the "Essentials of Personal Success".

California Real Estate Licensing

By following each of John's explanations of the subjects covered in state examinations, you have the immediate ability to see, use, repeat and apply all of the material you learned before you proceed to the next step on the way to your real estate license.

Real Estate School

Lumbleau Real Estate School was founded in 1937, making it one of the oldest and best recognized names in approved real estate schools in California real estate education. Over 600,000 students have passed through our courses. The Lumbleau Real Estate School now delivers online real estate classes to students in the comfort and convenience of their home. Your computer has become your personal classroom where you will learn everything you need to know to pass the California state exam and obtain your California Real Estate License.

Today

Management of the Lumbleau Real Estate School is accomplished with a team of dedicated real estate professionals. Our general manager, Derf Fredericks, is a 40 year veteran of real estate sales and education. Derf received his broker's license in 1978, is a past president of his local board of Realtors, former real estate brokerage owner, and a real estate instructor at El Camino College since 1990. Derf is available to answer our students' questions and provides valuable insight into the real estate industry.

Future

Lumbleau Real Estate School strives to stay ahead of technology. With new platforms being released we hope to cater to all future online devices. Live instruction and classroom exam preparation courses coming soon! Stay tuned to see what's in store at Lumbleau.com

"RETAINED UNDERSTANDING"
THROUGH REPETITION, USE, AND APPLICATION

In 1950 while attending Loyola University (now Loyola-Marymount) I had the great privilege of being taught by an educator who changed my life and my concept of level education.

Because this form of education changed my life, it is about to change your life.

The teacher was Father Ferguson, a Jesuit priest. The course was called "Logic." The name was perfect for the course because the teaching was as logical as teaching can be.

I remember the first class as if it were yesterday. Father Ferguson announced to the startled class that this course contained no textbook and that there wouldn't be any homework assignments – no book – no homework! What a great class. Well, that was the first thought.

Father Ferguson then stated that we had fifteen classes and further that he had discerned that there were only twenty-eight basic things to remember out of the entire fifteen weeks of classes.

His method would be simple; he would teach only two things the first day. It would take only ten minutes to teach these two things. The rest of the three hour period would be the testing of each student on the two subjects. He then went on to teach the definition of a syllogism and Universal and Particular thought.

His method was genius of the first order. Though it seamed simple, it was anything but! Each day we would learn two new things. The first day we were quizzed only on two things. The second day-four, the third day-six, the fourth day-eight, on through to the fourteenth day when we were quizzed on all twenty-eight points. The fifteenth day was the final examination consisting of ten of the twenty-eight points. He decided on which ten the day of the final.

First understanding, then repetition and application of that understanding over and over again until it became imbedded into our minds. His method was called "Comprehension and Retention." The technique was, "First understand, then see, use, repeat and apply." I retained more from that course than from any other course from any other source since.

The key to all knowledge is "understanding."

Without understanding, it is difficult to remember and memory is the key to passing the state examination.

The Lumbleau Real Estate School does not teach a "crash course" that provides the answers to questions, the subject matter of which is not fully understood.

The Lumbleau Real Estate School adds to its famous real estate "California Agent Exam-Passing" course Father Ferguson's genius by having every student, see, use, repeat and apply their understanding of the subject matter over and over again.

First understand by viewing a lecture on video, then by the use of existing debriefed state questions – see, use, repeat and apply! This is how we retain understanding.

Father Ferguson's genius has become the method the Lumbleau School uses to have students retain the understanding necessary to correctly answer every question asked in the state exam.

Welcome to Lumbleau Real Estate School. Choosing Lumbleau as your entry point into the great Profession of Real Estate was one of the wisest choices you have ever made.

Sincerely,

Sincerely,
John J. Lumbleau

Table of Contents

An old man, traveling a lonely highway,
Came at the evening cold and gray
To a chasm deep and wide.
The old man crossed in the twilight dim,
For the sullen stream had no fears for him.
But he turned when he reached the other side,
And built a bridge to span the tide.

"Old man,' cried a fellow pilgrim near.
'You are wasting your strength with building here;
Your journey will end with the ending day,
And you never again will pass this way.'

"You have crossed the chasm deep and wide,
Why build you a bridge at eventide.
And the builder raised his old gray head:
'Good friend, on the path I have come.'
 he said, 'There followeth after me today
 A youth whose feet must pass this way.'

"This stream which has been as naught to me,
To this fair-haired boy may a pitfall be;
He too must cross in the twilight dim,
Good friend, I am building this bridge for him."

                              ANONYMOUS

Lesson One

Part One
Understanding Through Video Teaching

Lesson One
VOCABULARY

Each trade and profession has its own vocabulary words peculiar to that particular occupation and real estate is no exception. The "language" of real estate is not difficult to learn; there are no long, seemingly non-understandable phrases as there are in law or medicine. Most of the words are related to common usage, but there are some that have a "real estate" meaning differing from the generally accepted definition, such as the word "several."

In everyday use, "several" retains its familiar definition of meaning of more than two but not many, as when one might say, "I looked at several listings today." In real estate it has a special legal meaning of "separate, distinct, individual" and is used in real estate in that sense to describe ownership of real property by only one person.

From the legal profession we also have some real estate words which we call "or" and "ee" words. These describe the parties to a particular transaction with the two-letter ending indicating which party is being referred to; "or" designates the party performing the action and "ee" indicates the party for or to whom the action is performed. Some of these word pairs are:

assignor - assignee
bailor - bailee
devisor - devisee
grantor - grantee
lessor - lessee
mortgagor - mortgagee
optionor - optionee
pledgor - pledgee
transferor - transferee
trustor - trustee
vendor – vendee

Generally speaking, the word ending in "or" indicates the party doing an act or giving something to the other party; the word ending in "ee" identifies the party receiving something. A mortgagor gives a mortgage to the mortgagee who receives it. A grantor gives a deed to a grantee. A lessor gives a lease to a lessee.

Words are only symbols used to convey an understanding of a situation, condition or object. There is no point in trying to memorize a list of words. If you understand the meaning and purpose you will visualize the situation or object. If you hear only the meaning and purpose you will immediately see the word and be able to use it correctly.

82   Because the real estate housing market is varied in nature and deals with many different types of desires and needs, it is said to be stratified. Stratified means different levels. People acquire property for a specific purpose such as residential, business, investment, agricultural and industrial. Therefore, demands fall within certain definable levels.

85   The "company dollar" is the remainder of the sales commission after the broker has shared with a cooperating broker and the licensed sales agents in his office.

85a   Desk cost includes the total current costs including salaries paid to the office manager and receptionist divided by the number of agents in the office. If you subtract the total desk cost from the "company dollar" total, you get the broker's net income before taxes.

85b   One of a broker's highest cost items is advertising. To be effective, advertising must produce results. The four elements of a successful ad are attention, interest, desire, and action. Although most real estate advertising has been done in the classified section of the newspapers, internet sites are becoming increasing popular.

TRUST FUND HANDLING

86   Previous to the trust fund legislation, irresponsible brokers would often commingle client's money with office money instead of segregating them. Only client's money should be placed into a trust account. This action, in effect, safeguards the client's money in case of a civil action against the broker.

87   Brokers sometimes committed the act of conversion. Conversion is the use of client's or customer's funds for the company or personal needs.

88   Where an agreement specifically authorizes the broker to accept a deposit from the purchaser and the agent at all times holds the deposit as agent of the seller, the risk of loss by the wrongful and negligent act of the broker will rest on the seller.

88a   A broker may accept a deposit in any form provided it is acceptable to the principal. It can be cash, a check, a note or a piece of personal property such as jewelry or title to an automobile. As long as the broker informs the seller of the nature of the deposit and receives consent to the acceptance, it is permissible.

89   A broker places funds accepted on behalf of another:
  (1)   Into the hands of the owner of the funds.
  (2)   Into a neutral escrow depository or
  (3)   Into a trust fund account in the name of the broker as trustee at a bank or other financial institution, for the benefit of the buyer and seller in a sale transaction or the beneficiary and trustee in a loan

transaction, not later than three business days following receipt of the funds by the broker or the broker's salesperson.

The account into which the trust funds are deposited shall not be an interest bearing account for which prior written notice can, by law or regulation, be required by the financial institution as a condition to the withdrawal of funds.

90   A check received from the offeror may be held uncashed by the broker until acceptance of the offer if:

  (1) The check, by its terms, is not negotiable or if the offeror (buyer) has given written instructions that the check shall not be deposited nor cashed until acceptance of the offer.

  (2) The offeree (seller) is informed that the check is being so held before or at the time the offer is presented for acceptance.

In these circumstances, if the offeror's check was held by the broker until acceptance of the offer, the check shall be placed into the trust fund account or into the hands of the offeree if offeror and offeree expressly so provide in writing, not later than three business days following acceptance of the offer unless the broker receives written authorization from the offeree to continue to hold the check.

91   The real estate broker must be designated as trustee of the trust account and all trust fund accounts must provide for withdrawal of funds without previous notice only for the benefit of the principal to whom the funds belong, or for compensation only with the permission of the principal (e.g., withdrawal of a offeror's deposit to be placed into an escrow account following acceptance or withdrawals of monies to pay taxes,

insurance, utilities, repairs, and compensation by a property manager). Like all good accounting practices, voided checks are to be maintained together with cashed checks for the period demanded by the government for income tax verification.

92   Withdrawals from the trust account can be made only upon the signature of the broker or someone authorized by the broker.

93   A broker may authorize the following to withdraw funds from a client's trust account:

(1)   A licensed salesperson in the broker's employ.

(2)   A corporate officer through whom the corporation is licensed as a broker.

(3)   Any unlicensed employee provided such employee is covered by a sufficient fiduciary bond.

TRUST ACCOUNT RECORDS

TRUST ACCOUNT RECORDS

94   The broker must maintain a columnar cash receipts and cash disbursements journal with a separate record for each beneficiary or transaction and a separate record for each property managed by his office. Records must be kept for all money that comes into a broker's possession. Maintenance of journals of account cash receipts and disbursements on automated data processing systems, including computer systems, shall constitute compliance with this subdivision. The broker, given twenty-four (24) hours' notice, shall have these records available for audit by the Real Estate Commissioner

94a   Monies that go directly from the buyer into an escrow account and do not pass through the broker's hands are not required to be accounted for in the broker's records.

94b Trust Account Reconciliation - The balance of all separate beneficiary or transaction records maintained must be reconciled with the record of all trust funds received and disbursed required by Section 2831, at least once a month except in those months when the bank account has no activity.

BROKER & SALESPERSON CONTRACTS

101 The Commissioner's regulations require that every real estate broker shall have a written agreement with each of his salespeople, whether licensed as a salesperson or as a broker under a broker-salesperson arrangement. Though the content of the contract is mandated by law, the contract itself need not be approved by the Commissioner. The agreement shall be dated, signed by the parties, and shall cover material aspects of the relationship between the parties, including supervision of licensed activities, duties and compensation. The broker need not retain a copy of this agreement following the discharge or voluntary transfer of a salesperson or broker associate. However, IRS regulations require any document affecting the determination of tax liability be retained for at least three (3) years. Each broker should set his own retention policy.

LEGAL ACTION TO COLLECT COMMISSION

113 The Bureau of Real Estate has no jurisdiction over action for recovery of commissions. Suit for such recovery must be brought in civil court, and in such suit the broker must first show that he was a duly licensed real estate broker at the time of the transaction.

114 The Bureau of Real estate recognizes that a "finder's fee" commission can be paid to an unlicensed individual as long as the "finder" does nothing more than introduce the parties.

COOPERATING BROKERS

117 Oral agreements between cooperating brokers for a division of commission are legal. It has been ruled that they do not come within the statute of frauds.

(The statute of frauds requires that agreements involving real property or requiring longer than one year to perform must be in writing.) When an assisting broker's services are completed, he is entitled to recover a commission from the cooperating broker in civil court, if necessary. In a case where the listing broker set and agreed compensation at a certain sum, he cannot defeat the assisting broker from receiving a share of the commission by settling with the principal for a lesser sum.

STATE WORKER'S COMPENSATION

118 It is compulsory that every employer who has one or more persons employed shall provide worker's compensation insurance covering accidents or disease contracted in the course of the employee's occupation.

126 The requirements for independent contractor status are:
   (1) The individual must be a licensed real estate agent.
   (2) Substantially all remuneration for services performed must be directly related to sales or output, rather than the number of hours worked.
   (3) The services of the individual must be performed pursuant to a written contract setting forth the individual's status as an independent contractor.
   (4) The contractor must have the final authority as to how the work required to achieve the results is performed.

REALTOR®

131 The term "Realtor®" is the distinctive and exclusive designation for those brokers who are members of the National Association of Realtors®. The beginning words of their Code of Ethics are a well-established basis for the philosophy of our profession. They begin with "Under all is the land. Upon its wise utilization and widely allocated ownership depend the survival and growth of free institutions and our civilization." Because it is an association of equals, all Realtors® agree to arbitrate their disputes rather than go to the expense of litigation

REALTISTS®

133 A Realtist® is a member of a national organization of predominantly African American real estate brokers known as the National Association of Real Estate Brokers.

REAL ESTATE COMMISSIONER

145 It is the principle responsibility of the Commissioner to enforce all the provisions in the real estate law.

164 The Attorney General renders to the Commissioner opinions upon all questions of law that may be submitted to him by the Commissioner. The Attorney General shall act as the attorney for the Commissioner in all actions brought by or against him under any of the provisions of this statute.

165 The Commissioner may adopt, amend, or repeal such rules and regulations for the enforcement of the provisions of this statute. Such rules and regulations shall be adopted, amended, or repealed in accordance with the provisions of the Administrative Procedure Act. In addition to other notices required by law the Commissioner shall notify the Real Estate Advisory Commission of his intention to adopt rules and regulations at least 30 days prior to such adoption and when adopted these shall have the same force and effect as law.

ADVANCE FEE REGULATIONS

169 The Commissioner requires that any materials used in obtaining advance fee agreements be submitted to him at least ten calendar days before they are used.

169a Money received for advance fee promotions must be deposited in the broker's trust account when collected. He must then render an accounting to his principal every calendar quarter. He may disperse the funds when they are expended for the benefit of the principal or five days after the accounting mentioned has been mailed to the principal.

HEARINGS

171 Before denying, suspending or revoking any license, the Commissioner shall proceed as prescribed in the Administrative Procedure Act of the Government Code.

172 An accusation shall be filed not later than 3 years from the occurrence of the grounds for disciplinary action for mistake or incompetence. If the charges involve fraud, misrepresentation or a false promise, the accusation shall be filed within one year after the date of discovery by the aggrieved party or within three years after the occurrence thereof, whichever is later, except that in no case shall an accusation be filed later than 10 years from the occurrence of the alleged grounds for disciplinary action. An accusation called a "statement of issues" as defined in Section 11504 of the Government Code shall be filed and served upon the respondent with the order of suspension. The respondent shall have 30 days after service of the 'order of suspension' and 'statement of issues' in which to file with the commissioner a written request for hearing on the statement of issues filed against him.

suspension (when the license was in force) must be paid. Effectively, the broker under suspension is out of business and, in the normal course of business, the salespeople relocate their licenses with other brokers in the community.

173   It is unlawful for any person to engage in the business, act in the capacity of, advertise or assume to act as a real estate broker or a real estate salesperson within this state (California) without first obtaining a real estate license from the Bureau.

174   The Commissioner may refer a complaint for violation of this section before any court of competent jurisdiction.

175   It is the duty of the District Attorney for each county in the State to prosecute all violations of this section in their respective counties in which the violations occur.

REAL ESTATE BROKER

176 A real estate broker is a person or corporation who in expectation of a commission, does or negotiates to do one or more of the following acts:

177   (1)   Obtains listings of or negotiates the purchase, sale or exchange of real property or a business opportunity.

178   (2)   Leases, rents, or collects rents on real property or a business opportunity.

179   (3)   Assists in filing an application for the purchase or lease of lands owned by the state or federal government (see land locator).

180   (4)   Solicits borrowers or lenders and negotiates loans or collects payments for note owners, on real property or on a business opportunity.

181   (5)   Sells, buys, exchanges, or performs services for the holders of a real property sales contract or a promissory note secured directly or collaterally by a lien on real property, or a business opportunity.

182   The real estate code does not apply to the manager of a hotel, motel, trailer park, or to the resident manager of an apartment building. Should the manager manage more than one building a license is required

184   As used in this section, "in the business" means:

185   (1) The acquisition for resale to the public, and not as an investment, of eight (8) or more real property sales contracts or promissory notes secured directly or collaterally by trust deeds on real property during a calendar year, or

186   (2) The sale to or exchange with the public of eight (8) or more real property sales contracts or promissory notes secured directly or collaterally by trust deeds on real property during a calendar year period. However, any transaction negotiated through a real estate licensee shall be considered to be in compliance with the requirements of this law.

187   Brokers sometimes commit the act of conversion by using client's or customer's funds for the company or personal needs.

188   Where an agreement specifically authorizes the broker to accept a deposit from the purchaser he, at all times, holds the deposit as agent of the seller and the risk of loss by the wrongful and negligent act of the broker will rest on the seller.

188a A broker may accept a deposit in any form. It can be cash, a check, a note or a piece of personal property such as jewelry or title to an automobile, as long as the broker informs the seller of the nature of the deposit and receives consent to the acceptance.

title to an automobile, as long as the broker informs the seller of the nature of the deposit and receives consent to the acceptance.

190   A real estate salesperson is a natural person who, for compensation or in expectation of compensation, is employed by a licensed real estate broker to do one or more of the acts that a broker can do as set forth elsewhere in this law.

191   The acts described in the Real Estate Code are not acts for which a real estate license is required if performed by:

192   A regular officer of a corporation or a general partner of a partnership with respect to real property owned or leased by a corporation or partnership.

203   It is unlawful for any licensed real estate broker to compensate, directly or indirectly, any persons who are not licensed real estate brokers, or real estate salespersons licensed under that broker.

204 The offering of premiums, prizes, merchandise discounts or other inducements to list or sell is not, in itself, unethical even if receipt of the benefit is contingent on listing or purchasing through the broker making the offer.

205   No real estate salesperson can be employed by or accept compensation from any person other than the broker under whom he or she is licensed. The act of a salesperson becomes the act of their broker. All listings obtained by a salesperson, while under the jurisdiction of a broker, become the property of that broker.

213   A real estate broker shall not place any form of advertising which does not contain a designation disclosing that the broker is licensed. Any such advertisement is described as a "blind ad."

216   Within one month after the closing of a transaction in which title to real property or the sale of a business is conveyed through a licensed real estate broker, the broker must inform both seller and purchaser, in writing, of the final selling price. If the transaction is closed through escrow and the escrow holder renders a closing statement which reveals such information that shall be deemed in compliance with this section on the part of the broker.

217   Within one week after the closing of a sale involving the creation of a new deed of trust secured by real property, the broker who negotiated such sale must cause the new deed of trust to be recorded, or deliver it to the beneficiary with instructions to record it, unless written instructions not to record are received from the beneficiary, or it is delivered to the escrow holder with instructions not to record.

219   A "land locator" must report to the Commissioner the names and addresses of all persons to whom they render such service and the amount of compensation received. The report shall be filed quarterly within ten days after the end of each calendar quarter.

ADVANCE FEE REQUIREMENTS

228   Any real estate broker who collects an advance fee from any other person shall deposit such amount in a trust account. Such funds are trust funds and not the funds of the agent (see Sections 169 & 169a).

229   Amounts may be withdrawn by the agent only when actually expended for the benefit of the principal or five days after the verified accounts mentioned have been mailed to the principal. Each principal shall be furnished a verified accounting, in a form prescribed by the Commissioner, at the end of each calendar quarter and when the contract has been completely performed by the licensee.

230   A licensed real estate broker shall retain for three years copies of all listings, deposit receipts, canceled checks, trust records, and other documents executed by him or obtained by him in connection with any transaction for which a real estate broker license is required. The retention period shall run from the date of the closing of the transaction or from the date of the listing if the transaction is not consummated.

233   The commissioner may require any other proof he or she may deem advisable concerning the truthfulness of any applicant for a real estate license (e.g., fingerprints may indicate a criminal background requiring a further investigation of an applicant).

249 A restricted license issued, as the Commissioner in his discretion finds advisable in the public interest, may be restricted:
   (1) By term.
   (2) To employment by a particular real estate broker, if a salesperson.
   (3) By conditions to be observed in the exercise of the privileges granted.

250   When issued, a restricted license does not confer any property right in the privileges to be exercised thereunder, and the holder of a restricted license does not have the right to renewal of such license. The Commissioner may, without hearing, issue an order suspending the licensee's right to further exercise any privileges granted under a restricted license pending final determination made after formal hearing.

254   Each officer of a corporation through whom the corporation is licensed to act as a real estate broker must be a broker and can only act for and on behalf of the corporation. No salesperson may become a director.

BUSINESS AND RESIDENCE ADDRESSES

258 A real estate salesperson shall maintain on file with the commissioner his current mailing address and the address of the principle business office of the broker to whom the salesperson is licensed. Notice of changes in license information or status is required to be submitted to the Bureau and shall be given on forms prescribed by the Bureau not later than five days after the effective date of the change. Whenever there is a change in the location or address of the principle place of business or of a branch office of a broker, he shall notify the Commissioner not later than the three business days following the change.

259   Whenever a real estate salesperson enters the employ of a real estate broker the broker must immediately notify the Commissioner in writing or by such other means as may be allowed. The salesperson must also notify the Commissioner if the transfer is from an inactive status. The salesperson may start working for the broker immediately.

260   Whenever employment of a real estate salesperson is terminated, the broker must notify the Commissioner in writing within three business days following the termination.

263   Every licensed real estate broker, either natural or incorporated, shall maintain a place of business in the State of California The "place of business" can be from a broker's residence as well as from a commercial space. The only requirement is that it has an address and not be a post office box. If a broker has branch offices, all salesperson's licenses will be at the main office.

PREPAID RENTAL LISTING SERVICE

267   It is a violation of real estate law if licensees in this business refer a property to a prospect knowing that:
   (1)   The property does not exist or is unavailable for rent.

(2) The property has been represented in a false, misleading and deceptive manner.

(3) The licensee has not confirmed the availability of the property for tenancy during the four day period immediately prior to making the referral

(4) The licensee had not obtained permission, oral or written, to list the property from the property owner, manager or other authorized person.

268 The prepaid rental listing service licensee, other than a real estate broker, is required to refund the entire prepaid (advance) fee if the licensee fails to supply the prospective tenant with at least 3 suitable rental properties within 5 days of executing their agreement. If no rental is obtained by the prospect within the agreement period, all money above the sum of $25 must be refunded. The prospective tenant must demand the refund in either case within ten (10) days of the termination of the contract.

DISCIPLINARY ACTION

279 The Commissioner may upon his own motion and shall, upon the verified complaint in writing of any person, investigate the actions of any person engaged in the business or acting in the capacity of a real estate licensee within this state and he may temporarily suspend or permanently revoke a real estate license at any time where the licensee while a real estate licensee has been found guilty.

286 It is a recognized fact that the compensation paid to a real estate broker may be in the form of money or any other item of value (e.g., the broker may receive land, a trust deed or other personal property). It is also recognized that once received, any gain or loss in value of the commission received belongs to the broker.

287 The use by a licensee of any provision n a listing allowing the licensee an option to purchase, except when such licensee prior to or coincident with election to exercise such option to purchase, reveals in writing to the principal the full amount of licensee's profit and obtains the written consent of the principal approving the amount of such profit.

289 Obtaining the signature of a prospective purchaser to an agreement which provides that such prospective purchaser shall either transact the purchasing, leasing, renting, or exchanging of a business opportunity property through the broker obtaining such signature, or pay a compensation to such broker if such property is purchased, leased, rented or exchanged without the broker first having obtained the written authorization of the owner of the property concerned to offer such property for sale, lease, exchange, or rent.

295 Willfully used, the term "Realtor" or any trade name or insignia of membership in any real estate organization of which the licensee is not a member (e.g., "Realtist").

307 When any real estate salesperson is discharged by his employer for a violation of any of the provisions of this article, a certified written statement of the facts with reference thereto shall be filed forthwith with the Commissioner by the employing broker and if the employing broker fails to notify the Commissioner as required, the Commissioner may suspend or revoke the real estate broker's license.

315 The required application and fee for the license must be submitted and paid within one year from the date of the examination.

REAL ESTATE RECOVERY PROGRAM

328 There shall be separate accounts in the Real Estate Fund for purposes of real estate education and research and for purposes of recovery which shall be known respectively as the Education and Research

Account and the Recovery account. The section "No portion of the amount of any license fee collected is credited to the Education and Research Account" has been added effective as of November 1996.

APPLICATION FOR PAYMENT FROM RECOVERY FUND

330   When an aggrieved person obtains a final judgment against a real estate broker based upon the broker's fraud, misrepresentation, deceit, or conversion of trust funds, the aggrieved person may, upon the judgment becoming final, and after exhausting all attempts to personally recover the amount due from the broker's personal assets, file an application with the Bureau of Real Estate for payment from the Recovery Account.

343   The maximum recovery allowed for causes of action is fifty thousand dollars ($50,000) for any one transaction and two hundred fifty thousand dollars ($250,000) for one licensee.

LICENSE SUSPENSION

344   The law establishes that should the Commissioner pay any amount from the fund in settlement of this type of claim, the license of the accused broker and/or salesperson is automatically suspended upon the date of payment. No license suspended for such a cause can be reinstated until the amount of the payment has been repaid in full plus interest at the prevailing legal rate for such matters. A discharge in bankruptcy will not relieve the licensee from these penalties and disabilities.

MOBILEHOMES

345   Notwithstanding any other provision of law, a person licensed as a real estate broker may: sell or offer to sell, buy or offer to buy, solicit prospective purchasers, solicit or obtain listings of, negotiate the purchase, sale or exchange of, any mobile home only if the mobile home has been registered under the Health and Safety Code for at least one year.

 It is unlawful for any licensee to:

353   Advertise no down payment when in fact one is required, inducing the buyer to finance such down payment by separate financing.

355   Mobile home license administration is under the jurisdiction of the Department of Housing and Community Development. Real estate licensees are permitted to negotiate the sale of mobile homes that are less than a year old, provided the requirements of Section 18551 of the Health and Safety Code for transforming a mobile home to real property have been satisfied.

Lesson One
Part Two - Study Questions

_____(Lesson One - Paragraph 82 – Question 1)_____

Because the real estate housing market, as you have just seen, is varied in nature and because the housing market deals with many different types of desires and needs, it is said to be:

(A) Structured.   (B) Stratified.   (C) Fractured.   (D) Fractionated.

(B) Because the real estate housing market, as you have just seen, is varied in nature and because the housing market deals with many different types of desires and needs, it is said to be stratified. Stratified means different levels. People acquire property for a specific purpose such as residential, business, investment, agricultural and industrial. Therefore, demands fall within a certain definable level.

_____(Lesson One - Paragraph 85a – Question 1)_____

The desk cost for a broker is:

(A) The cost of equipment and telephone divided by the number of desks in the office.
(B) The cost of equipment and telephone plus the rent divided by the number of desks
(C) The office rent and telephone expense divided by the number of desks in the office.
(D)   The total current costs including salaries paid to the office manager and receptionist divided by the number of agents in the office.

(D) This is a precise definition of the trade term "desk cost."

_____(Lesson One - Paragraph 86 – Question 1)_____

Commingling is most nearly the opposite of:

(A) Trust fund.   (B) Mingle.   (C) Segregate.   (D) Neutral depository.

(C) Commingling" is the act of mixing or blending. "Segregate" means to set apart to isolate.

_____(Lesson One - Paragraph 87 – Question 1)_____

A real estate broker found guilty of conversion would be subject to a heavy penalty. The following act best illustrates conversion:

(A) The broker receives a cash deposit together with a signed offer from a buyer. He deposits the cash into his personal account after the offer is accepted and after the seller instructs him to keep the deposit money as part of his commission.
(B) The broker receives a check from a buyer together with a signed offer and deposits the check in his personal account and commingles it with his own money.
(C) The broker receives a check from a buyer together with a signed offer with instructions from the buyer to hold the check until the offer is accepted, and the offer is accepted and the broker places the check in his office safe.
(D) A salesperson receives $500 cash from a buyer, together with a signed offer and before the offer
    is accepted, the licensee spends the $500 on a vacation in Nevada.

(D) "Conversion" in the sense implied by the question is the misappropriation and use of money or property of another, and should not be confused with "commingling." Conversion is a far greater offense. Commingling is the mixing or blending of a principal's money or property with that of the agent. Conversion is the appropriation of the principal's money for agent's use.

_____(Lesson One - Paragraph 88 – Question 1)_____

A broker was authorized to accept a deposit in his listing agreement with the seller. The broker accepts an offer with a deposit in the form of check made payable to the seller. The broker lost the check prior to his presenting the offer. In this case:
(A)   The buyer has no recourse because he should have made the check payable to a title or escrow
        company.
(B)   The broker has sole liability because of his negligence.
(C)   The seller and broker share liability for the buyer's loss.
(D)   Because the seller had authorized the broker to accept the deposit as his agent, the risk of
        its loss by the wrongful or negligent act of the broker rests upon the seller.

 (D) Legal experts offer this opinion: Where an agreement specifically authorizes the broker to accept a deposit from the purchaser he, at all times, holds the deposit as agent of the seller and the risk of loss by the wrongful and negligent act of the broker will rest on the seller. This point is the only one raised in the question.

_____(Lesson One - Paragraph 88a – Question 1)_____

The following could be used by a buyer as an earnest money deposit in purchasing real property:
(A)   Postdated check.   (B) Unsecured promissory note.
(C)   Promissory note secured by a deed of trust. (D) All of the above.

(D) The buyer is said to put up an earnest money deposit. The deposit is not required in a contract; it just shows that this buyer is in earnest and is putting a deposit up to reveal his true interest in the property. This deposit can be in any form. The form of the deposit, however, must be disclosed to the seller before the seller accepts the offer.

_____(Lesson One - Paragraph 88a – Question 2)_____

When using a note as a deposit from a buyer in making an offer:
(A)   The note would be the same as cash.
(B)   The agent should inform the seller that the deposit is in the form of a note before the seller accepts the offer.
(C)   A note cannot be used as a deposit for an offer.
(D)   The note must be cashed before opening escrow.

 (B) A licensee may accept a note from the buyer as a deposit. This often is in the form of a deposit given by builders. However, the licensee must inform the seller that the deposit is a note before the seller accepts the offer.

_____(Lesson One - Paragraph 89 – Question 1)_____

If a broker maintains a trust account, such an account:
(A) Must have a balance of at least $300.
(B) Must have at least 5% over the average balance of the account.

(C) Must receive interest on the amount in the trust account the same as if it were a savings account.
(D) Benefits both the beneficiary and the trustor.

(D) No minimum balance is required in a trust account and normally does not draw interest. It is maintained for the benefit of the person to whom the money belongs and is for the benefit of all parties to a transaction should a civil action occur.

_____(Lesson One - Paragraph 90 – Question1)_____

On July 10, 1998 the buyer executes a deposit receipt and gives the agent a check. In doing so, he instructs the agent to hold the check until July 30,1998. Under these circumstances the agent should:
(A) Refuse to take the check.   (B) Hold the check uncashed and inform the seller accordingly.
(C) Open escrow the next day and deposit the seller's check into it   (D) None of the above.

(B) The broker holds the check as the agent of the buyer until the offer is accepted. A broker may take such a check and hold it uncashed, but he must inform the seller and obtain the seller's consent to hold the check uncashed.

_____(Lesson One - Paragraph 90 – Question 2)_____

As a broker you receive an offer to purchase with the buyer's personal check for $1,000 as a deposit. The buyer's offer states the check is to be held uncashed until the close of escrow. You should:
(A) Refuse to accept the offer as it would be a violation of agency.
(B) Accept the offer, however, deposit the check in your trust account.
(C) Take the offer and inform the seller of the conditions on the deposit before his acceptance.
(D) Accept the offer; however do not present it to the seller until buyer authorizes deposit of his check.

(C) A broker may take a note or uncashed check as a deposit; however, he must inform the seller of the form of the deposit before the seller accepts the offer.

_____(Lesson One - Paragraph 90 – Question 3)_____

Sam Smith, the owner of Blackacre, lists the property for sale with Broker Brown. Sam fails to authorize the agent to accept a deposit on his behalf. Charles Cable makes an offer on Blackacre and gives Broker Brown a check for $5,000 as a deposit. Under these circumstances, Broker Brown:
(A) Cannot accept the deposit because of the wording of the listing agreement.
(B) Can accept the deposit as the agent for Buyer Cable and place the monies in the broker's trust fund.
(C) Can accept the check if he immediately gives it to Seller Smith.
(D) None of the above are correct.

(B) The question states the owner did not authorize Broker Brown to accept a deposit on his behalf. However, the law of agency demands an agent to accept all offers unless specifically instructed by his principal not to do so. Under these circumstances, Broker Brown should take this offer. However, he would accept the deposit as the agent of Charles Cable, and hold the deposit as the agent of the buyer.

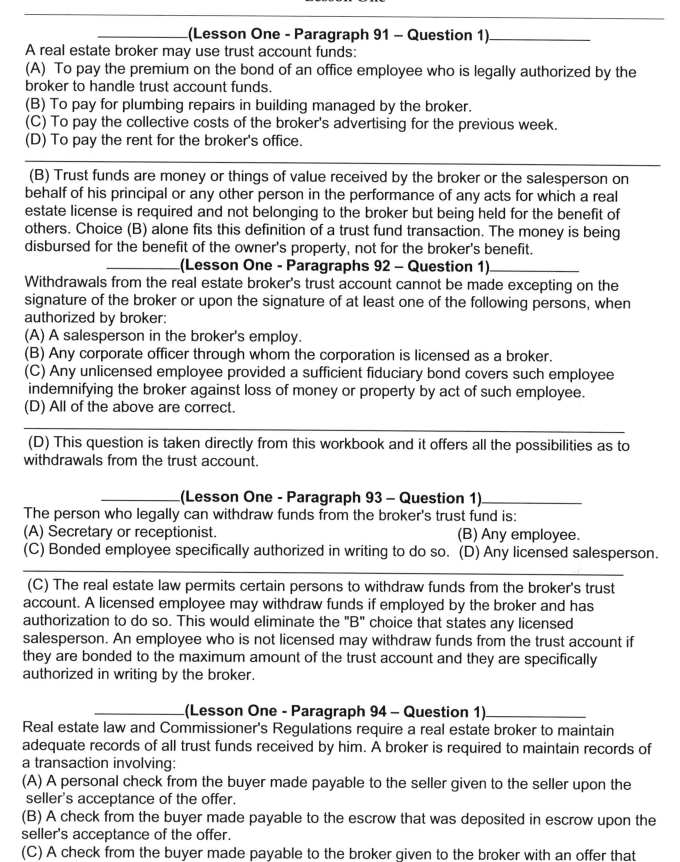

_____(Lesson One - Paragraph 91 – Question 1)_____

A real estate broker may use trust account funds:

(A) To pay the premium on the bond of an office employee who is legally authorized by the broker to handle trust account funds.

(B) To pay for plumbing repairs in building managed by the broker.

(C) To pay the collective costs of the broker's advertising for the previous week.

(D) To pay the rent for the broker's office.

___

(B) Trust funds are money or things of value received by the broker or the salesperson on behalf of his principal or any other person in the performance of any acts for which a real estate license is required and not belonging to the broker but being held for the benefit of others. Choice (B) alone fits this definition of a trust fund transaction. The money is being disbursed for the benefit of the owner's property, not for the broker's benefit.

_____(Lesson One - Paragraphs 92 – Question 1)_____

Withdrawals from the real estate broker's trust account cannot be made excepting on the signature of the broker or upon the signature of at least one of the following persons, when authorized by broker:

(A) A salesperson in the broker's employ.

(B) Any corporate officer through whom the corporation is licensed as a broker.

(C) Any unlicensed employee provided a sufficient fiduciary bond covers such employee indemnifying the broker against loss of money or property by act of such employee.

(D) All of the above are correct.

___

(D) This question is taken directly from this workbook and it offers all the possibilities as to withdrawals from the trust account.

_____(Lesson One - Paragraph 93 – Question 1)_____

The person who legally can withdraw funds from the broker's trust fund is:

(A) Secretary or receptionist.   (B) Any employee.

(C) Bonded employee specifically authorized in writing to do so. (D) Any licensed salesperson.

___

(C) The real estate law permits certain persons to withdraw funds from the broker's trust account. A licensed employee may withdraw funds if employed by the broker and has authorization to do so. This would eliminate the "B" choice that states any licensed salesperson. An employee who is not licensed may withdraw funds from the trust account if they are bonded to the maximum amount of the trust account and they are specifically authorized in writing by the broker.

_____(Lesson One - Paragraph 94 – Question 1)_____

Real estate law and Commissioner's Regulations require a real estate broker to maintain adequate records of all trust funds received by him. A broker is required to maintain records of a transaction involving:

(A) A personal check from the buyer made payable to the seller given to the seller upon the seller's acceptance of the offer.

(B) A check from the buyer made payable to the escrow that was deposited in escrow upon the seller's acceptance of the offer.

(C) A check from the buyer made payable to the broker given to the broker with an offer that was to remain open for 5 days. The offer was not accepted and the broker returned the check to the buyer.

(D) All of the above.

(D) Do not confuse trust fund records and trust fund accounts. Brokers will probably need a trust account at their bank if they receive any cash or checks that must be held by them. If they pass the money on to someone else, they may not need an account, but still must keep a record of every nickel that passes through their hands.

_____(Lesson One - Paragraph 94 – Question 2)_____

A broker:
(A) Must maintain a trust account
(B) Must keep a record of who paid and received funds only if they go into escrow.
(C) Must keep a record of everything going through his hands even though deposited in escrow.
(D) May not disburse funds directly to his principal.

(C) Even though a broker is not required to maintain a trust account, he must keep trust records of all trust money that come into his possession.

_____(Lesson One - Paragraph 101 – Question 1)_____

A written agreement between the broker and salesperson is required:
(A) By the National Association of Realtors.
(B) If both parties believe it is a good idea.
(C) By the Real Estate Commissioner's Regulations.
(D) By the California Association of Realtors.

(C) The Real Estate Commissioner's regulations require a written employment agreement between brokers and salespersons. This contract need not be kept after termination of employment.

_____(Lesson One - Paragraph 101 – Question 2)_____

After termination of employment, a real estate broker must retain the written agreement he/she has with each salesperson in his office for:
(A) 2 years. (B) 0 years. (C) 3 years. (D) 5 years.

(B) The broker following the employment period need not retain employment agreements.

_____(Lesson One - Paragraph 112 – Question 1)_____

A real estate broker license is required to handle the initial sale of:
(A) A lot in a subdivision. (B) Land, which contains mineral, oil and gas.
(C) Any federal land.   (D) A unit in a condominium.

(B) A real estate broker can handle mineral oil and gas property transactions. (Law updated 1998)

_____(Lesson One - Paragraph 113 – Question 1)_____

To secure a commission a real estate agent would:
(A) File a civil suit in court against the person owing him the commission.
(B) File a lien on the property for the commission.

(C) Seek the assistance of the Real Estate Commissioner
(D) Seek the assistance of the National Association of Realtors

(A) In a suit for a commission, it is strictly a civil matter between the principal and the agent. The best answer to this question is to file a suit in court.

_____(Lesson One - Paragraph 117 – Question 1)_____
A broker with an open listing contract on a property agrees orally with another broker to share a commission upon the sale of the property. The property sells. The listing broker is paid a commission, but he refuses to share the commission as promised.
(A) The statute of frauds prevents the selling broker from seeking recovery of the commission he believes he has earned.
(B) The selling broker would have a good chance to secure a judgment against the listing broker in court.
(C) The selling broker is prevented from securing a commission because the listing broker had an open listing.
(D) The selling broker is prevented from securing a commission because of the statute of limitations.

(B) The essential point of this question is that an agreement between brokers to share a commission does not come under the statute of frauds. An oral agreement between brokers is enforceable. The selling broker would have a good chance in arbitration or court to sue for his share of the commission.

_____(Lesson One - Paragraph 117 – Question 2)_____
Assume a broker took an open listing to sell a parcel of real property. Later, this same broker made an oral agreement with another broker to share any commission should the second broker procure a buyer for the listed property. The second broker did in fact submit an offer which resulted in the sale of the property. The listing broker refused to share the commission for the sale. In this case:
(A) He need not share commission, as it was an open listing.
(B) He need not share commission because of the statute of frauds.
(C) Second broker would stand a good chance of winning a court suit for his share of the commission.
(D) Second broker could not sue seller for his share of the commission.

(C) Agreements between brokers to split a commission due on the conclusion of a sale completed through their joint efforts need not be in writing to be enforceable. Such agreements are no longer interpreted to come under the statute of frauds.

_____(Lesson One - Paragraph 126 – Question 1)_____
When a person works for another and is responsible only as to the results of his work, and not as to the means by which the result is accomplished, he is classified as:
(A) An employee. (B) A servant. (C) A master. (D) An independent contractor.

(D) In general, an individual who is subject to the control and direction of another as to the result of his works and not as to the means is an independent contractor and not an employee. However, if the person for whom the services are performed has the right to control and direct the individual who performs the services, not only as to the result but also as to the details and means by which the result is accomplished an employer-employee relationship exists.

_____(Lesson One - Paragraph 131 – Question 1)_____
"Under all is the land. Upon its wise utilization and widely allocated ownership depend the survival and growth of free institutions and our civilization." This quotation is from the:
(A) U.S. Constitution.
(B) Bill of Rights.
(C) Preamble to the Code of Ethics of the National Association of Realtors.
(D) None of the above.
_____

(C) This is a direct quote from the preamble to the Code of Ethics of NAR.

_____(Lesson One - Paragraph 131 – Question 2)_____
Should a dispute regarding a commission arise between two licensees who are members of the National Association of Realtors, by the provisions of that organization's Code of Ethics, they will settle the matter by:
(A) Litigation. (B) Estoppel. (C) Arbitration. (D) Mandamus.
_____

(C) The N.A.R. Code of Ethics states that brokers should settle matters between two licensees through arbitration, not by litigation.

_____(Lesson One - Paragraph 133 – Question 1)_____
In 1947, a national organization was formed as the National Association of Real Estate Brokers (predominantly African American). This group of brokers has adopted the name of:
(A) Realtist. (B) African American Realtors. (C) Realtors. (D) African American Brokers.
_____

(A) This group of predominantly African American brokers adopted the title "Realtist."

_____(Lesson One - Paragraph 145 – Question 1)_____
The following regulates real estate brokers and their employees.
(A) The California Association of Realtors.   (B) The Real Estate Commissioner.
(C) The National Association of Realtors.   (D) None of the above is correct.
_____

(B) Real estate brokers and their licensed employees are regulated by the Real Estate Commissioner.

_____(Lesson One - Paragraph 164 – Question 1)_____
The Attorney General of California would become involved in which of the following situations:

(A) The legality of licensing procedures.
(B) A broker whose license has been suspended brings court action against the Real Estate Commissioner to overturn the decision.
(C) Investigations into fraudulent real estate subdivisions.
(D) All of the above.
_____

(D) The Attorney General acts as legal adviser to and represents in court all state departments. He also has the power to investigate fraudulent practices involving consumers.

_____(Lesson One - Paragraph 169 – Question 1)_____

How far in advance of use must advance fee advertising material, including contract, forms, letters or cards used to solicit prospective sellers, radio and TV advertising, be submitted to the Commissioner?
(A) 5 days. (B) 7 days. (C) 10 days. (D) Not at all.

(C) The Real Estate Commissioner's Rules and Regulations (No. 2970) require that any or all materials used in obtaining advance fee agreements shall be submitted to the commissioner at least ten (10) days before they are used

_____(Lesson One - Paragraph 171 – Question 1)_____

The formal hearing procedure followed when a complaint is filed against a real estate licensee is conducted in accordance with the provisions set forth in the:
(A) Real estate law.   (B) Rules and regulations of the Real Estate Commissioner.
(C) Administrative Procedure Act.   (D) Business and Professions Code.

(C) Paragraph #10100 of the B & P Code States, "Before denying, suspending or revoking any licensee issuable or issued under the provisions of this law, the Commissioner shall proceed as prescribed by the Administrative Procedure Act of the Government Code."

_____(Lesson One - Paragraph 172 – Question 1)_____

The Real Estate Commissioner can be stopped from taking disciplinary action against a broker licensee on an accusation of incompetence:
(A) If the broker moves out of the State of California.
(B) If the broker's license has just recently expired.
(C) If the broker closes his office.
(D) If the Commissioner's action had not commenced within 3 years of the event in which the licensee is accused.

(D) Paragraph No. 10101 of the B and P Code states that the accusation .... shall be filed no later than 3 years from the occurrence of the grounds for revocation or suspension with which the accused is charged.

_____(Lesson One - Paragraphs 176 to 182 – Question 1)_____

Under the authority of a valid California real estate license, you may:
(A) Negotiate in Nevada the sale of a ranch located in California.
(B) Negotiate the sale of a note and collect a fee for doing so.
(C) Sell a business.
(D) Do all of the above.

(D) Possession of a California real estate license enables its holder to perform all of the acts listed. However, a California licensee could not go to the State of Nevada (or any other state) and offer real property for sale to the residents of that state. Whereas a number of years ago a separate license was required to sell a business opportunity (which is personal property), today this is one of the acts authorized to be done by holders of real estate salesperson and real estate broker licenses.

_____(Lesson One - Paragraph 179 – Question 1)_____

Certain activities performed for compensation require a person to hold a real estate license. The following would require a real estate license, providing compensation was received:
(A) The negotiation of the sale of real property by a person holding a duly executed power of attorney.
(B) A trustee named in a trust deed, selling real property 120 days after a notice of default was recorded.
(C) A corporation officer with a fixed salary who sells the corporation's own real property without
receiving any extra compensation.
(D) Assisting in the filing of an application for the purchase or lease of lands owned by the state
or federal government.

(D) Some brokers charge a fee to aid persons in locating government lands still open for homesteading. Those engaged in this activity are known as "land locators" and are required to have a real estate license. Activities mentioned in the three other choices may be carried out without having a license.

_____(Lesson One - Paragraph 179 – Question 2)_____
Mr. Tilton aids Mr. Barton in filing an application for a homestead on federal government land and Mr. Barton agrees to pay a fee to Mr. Tilton for the aid. Mr. Tilton must hold:
(A) A real estate broker's license.
(B) A real estate broker's license endorsed with a real property securities dealer's endorsement.
(C) Both A & B.
(D) Neither A nor B.

In this question you are to see the difference between the need to have a real estate license and a "permit" or "endorsement". Mr. Tilton is acting as a "land locator." To accept a fee for this service he is required to hold a real estate broker's license.

_____(Lesson One - Paragraph 182 – Question 1)_____
A man owns three apartment buildings in different parts of town. He hires a manager to manage the three apartment buildings in exchange for free rent for one of the apartments. This manager must have:
(A) A broker's license. (B) A salesperson's license. (C) A property manager's license. (D) No license.

(A)   With respect to leasing, the real estate law (§101,31.01) exempts from the licensing requirement the manager of a hotel, motel, auto and trailer park, the resident manager of an apartment building, apartment complex, court, or the employees of such manager. This question does not meet the requirements for the exemption. The owner of the property can only hire a broker as his representative. If the manager had only a salesperson's license he could not receive compensation directly from the property owner, but only through his employing broker.

_____(Lesson One - Paragraph 185 – Question 1)_____
In some circumstances private persons are required to have a real estate license to sell their own property. The following would be one of those instances:

(A) The owner of four residential properties.
(B) The owner of notes secured by trust deeds.
(C) The owner of four lots in a land subdivision.
(D) The owner of business opportunities.

(B) Real Estate Law (B. & P. Code #10131. 1) establishes that a person who buys or sells 10 or more notes in a calendar year must be a licensee to handle the transactions or they must handle the transactions through a licensed real estate broker.

_____(Lesson One - Paragraph 203 – Question 1)_____

You are a California real estate broker. An out-of-state broker refers a prospect to you and you consummate a sale. You want to split your commission with the cooperating broker. Under the California Real Estate Law:
(A) You may pay a commission to a broker of another state.
(B) You cannot divide a commission with a broker of another state.
(C) You can pay a commission to a broker of another state only if he is also licensed in California.
(D) None of the above.

(A) California Law permits a California broker to share a commission with an out-of-state broker.

_____(Lesson One - Paragraph 204 – Question 1)_____

A real estate broker advertises that if a buyer buys from him or a seller lists with him he will pay the party $50 from the fee or commission he receives from the transaction. The following is the best statement concerning this situation:
(A) This is illegal, being in violation of Business and Profession Code § 10176.
(B) He can give a rebate of commission to the seller, but he cannot pay the $50 to the buyer.
(C) He can credit the buyer's escrow account with $50, but he could not compensate the seller.
(D) He can do this.

(D) This states what constitutes a finder's fee. A finder's fee may be paid to unlicensed persons, as long as the fee remains a finder's fee.

_____(Lesson One - Paragraph 204 – Question 2)_____

A real estate broker advertises that he will give a television set valued at $500 to any buyer who purchases a property listed for sale with his office. This type of advertising is considered to be:
(A) Legal only if the gift value is $100 or less.
(B) Legal if the seller of the property is mailed a copy of the advertisement.
(C) Legal if proper disclosure is made to all interested parties.
(D) Illegal for sales incentive even if disclosure is made to all interested parties.

(C) Advertising incentives are legal if proper disclosure is made to all interested parties.

_____(Lesson One - Paragraph 205 – Question 1)_____

Assume a listing was secured by one of Jones' salespersons and this salesperson transferred to another broker during the term of the listing:
(A) The listing is salesperson's property and he may take it with him to his new broker.
(B) The salesperson should not have taken the listing if he planned to transfer, but should have arranged with owner of the property to pick up the listing later when he had transferred.
(C) The listing is the property of the first broker.
(D) The salesperson's transfer to another broker canceled the listing.

(C) The listing is an employment contract between the seller and the broker and not the salesperson who acts for the broker. All listings secured by real estate sales licensees belong to the employing brokers.

_____(Lesson One - Paragraph 205 – Question 2)_____

Broker Lamb operates his own real estate office and has no salespeople. Broker Hall also operates a real estate office and employs John Maple as a full-time salesman. Salesman Maple could receive compensation directly from broker Lamb for performing which of the following acts for broker Lamb:
(A) Selling a home listed by broker Lamb that was placed in the multiple listing service.
(B) Negotiating a loan for one of broker Lamb's clients, enabling broker Lamb to realize a 10% commission on the loan transaction.
(C) Managing commercial properties for broker Lamb.
(D) None of the above.

(D) A real estate salesperson cannot receive a commission directly from anyone except through his employing real estate broker for performing any act for which a real estate license is required.

_____(Lesson One - Paragraph 213 – Question 1)_____

When advertising listed property for sale, real estate licensees may identify themselves in the advertisement by using the designation:
(A) Agt.   (B) Bro.   (C) Either (A) or (B).   (D) Neither (A) nor (B).

(C) When an agent is advertising property for sale, the ad must indicate that he is acting as an agent, and that he is not the principal owner of the property. Otherwise it is said to be a "blind ad." The Commissioner's regulations specifically state that in declaring one to be an agent in an ad, the terms "Agt." and "Bro." are acceptable.

_____(Lesson One - Paragraph 213 – Question 2)_____

A mortgage company that is soliciting loans secured by real property must include in its advertising the:
(A) Name of the broker or mortgage company and license number.
(B) The telephone number of the broker or mortgage company.
(C) The address of the broker or mortgage company.
(D) The real estate license number of the broker or mortgage company.

(A) Lack of the name of the broker in any advertisement is illegal. It is often referred to as "blind advertising." A mortgage company must be licensed as a real estate broker.

_____(Lesson One - Paragraph 216 – Question 1)_____

When selling a property without use of an escrow, the broker must, within 30 days, inform the buyer and seller of:
(A) His name, address, and real estate license number.
(B) The exact amount of the commission received by the broker.
(C) The exact amount of the purchase price paid by the buyer.
(D) All of the above.

(C) The real estate law specifies that it is the broker's responsibility to cause the information about selling price to be given to both seller and buyer within one month after the close of the transaction.

_____(Lesson One - Paragraph 216 – Question 2)_____
Within one month after the closing date of a sale of a home negotiated by a licensed real estate broker, such broker must inform the seller and buyer in writing of the:
(A)   Name of the escrow company.   (B)   Selling price of the property.
(C)   Commission received.   (D)   Amount of taxes and time necessary to pay off the loan.

(B) Section 10141 of the Real Estate Law states in part: "Within one month after the closing of a transaction in which title to real property, or the real or personal property of a business, is conveyed from a seller to a purchaser through a licensed real estate broker, such broker shall inform or cause the information to be given to the seller and purchaser in writing of the selling price thereof. If the transaction is closed through escrow and the escrow holder renders a closing statement which reveals such information, which shall be deemed compliance with this section on the part of the broker."

_____(Lesson One - Paragraph 217 – Question 1)_____
A real estate broker negotiated the sale of a home and acted as escrow holder for this transaction. As part of the purchase price, the buyer executed a note and deed of trust in favor of the seller. The beneficiary of the trust deed indicated he wanted the broker to record all pertinent instruments. The time limit allowed the broker to record the trust deed is:
(A) One week after close of the transaction.
(B) Two weeks from close of the transaction.
(C) Thirty days from close of the transaction.
(D) He must record it by the next business day after close of the transaction.

(A) Real Estate Law (B & P Code No. 10141.5) requires that the broker involved in any transaction in which a new lien is created against the property being sold must see to the proper recording of the lien within one week of the close of the transfer of title.

_____(Lesson One - Paragraph 217 – Question 2)_____
When is a broker not responsible for the recording of a trust deed?
(A) When instructed by the trustee not to do so.   (B) When instructed by the trustor not to do so.
(C) When instructed by the beneficiary not to do so.   (D) Never.

(C) Within one week after the closing of a sale involving the creation of a new deed of trust secured by real property, the broker who negotiated such sale must cause the new deed of trust to be recorded or deliver it to the beneficiary with instructions to record it, unless written instructions not to record are received from the beneficiary.

_____(Lesson One - Paragraph 230 – Question 1)_____

Real Estate Law requires that a real estate broker retain for three years copies of all documents executed by him or obtained by him in connection with any transaction for which a real estate license is required. The retention period shall be from:
(A) The date of the listing.
(B) The date of acceptance of the offer.
(C) The date of closing of transaction or from date of listing if the transaction is not consummated.
(D) The date the deed is recorded.

(C) The question is a direct quote from paragraph #10148 of California Real Estate Law.

_____(Lesson One - Paragraph 230 – Question 2)_____

Copies of all listings, deposit receipts, canceled checks, and trust records must be retained by a licensed real estate broker for:
(A) One year. (B) Two years. (C) Three years. (D) Five years.

(C) The Real Estate Law of California requires a broker to keep copies of his real estate related records for three years. Remember that an exception is the broker loan statement that must be kept for four years.

_____(Lesson One - Paragraph 233 – Question 1)_____

The Commissioner can deny a real estate license if the applicant cannot show that he:
(A) Has a reputation of honesty, truthfulness, and integrity.
(B) Has been found not guilty of any violations of law with which he has been charged.
(C) Has never declared bankruptcy.
(D) Has never had complaints filed.

(A) Paragraph 10152 of the Real Estate Law provides that the Commissioner may require such other proof as he may deem advisable concerning the honesty, truthfulness, and good reputation of any applicant for a real estate license.

_____(Lesson One - Paragraph 254 – Question 1)_____

Broker Smart represents the owner of a large tract of new homes and hires attractive young women to act as hostesses at the model homes location, paying them a fixed weekly salary. The hostesses are permitted to quote prices and financing from the brochure, do their best to get callers interested, but do not write up any offers or sign any documents. Interested buyers are turned over to a regular salesperson to write up the purchase agreement. In your opinion:
(A) The type of duties performed by the hostesses would require a real estate license.
(B) A real estate license is never required when an individual is paid a fixed weekly salary.
(C) A real estate license is not required for the hostesses since they are only quoting prices
(D) No one employed by a broker on a subdivision tract requires a license.

(A) Anyone acting in the capacity of a real estate agent must have a real estate license. The showing of property, quoting of prices and discussion of financing are acts of a real estate agent.

_____(Lesson One - Paragraph 263 – Question 1)_____

The Real Estate Commissioner will issue a broker's license to a corporation. If a corporation has a broker's license, the following is true:

(A)   The payment of one license fee entities any officer of the corporation to engage in the business of real estate for the corporation.

(B)   Each officer of a corporation through whom it is licensed may engage in real estate activities the scope of the corporation under the authority of the corporation license.

(C)   When a disciplinary action is invoked against the corporation licensee the individual licenses

of the corporate officers are simultaneously revoked.

(D)   Every corporation to which a real estate broker license is issued must maintain a place of

business in California.

(D) Every active real estate broker license must have a place of business in the State of California. This is a matter of Real Estate Law (B & P Code #10 162)

_____(Lesson One - Paragraph 263 – Question 2)_____

Mr. Jones was a licensed real estate broker who maintained his office in one room of his residence. He maintained a large sign on the premises with substantial lettering stating "Harry Jones, Realtor." The broker had no licensed sales people but hired a high school student to obtain listings and paid him for the service. The nearest bank or escrow office was approximately 25 miles from Jones' office. Because of the trouble involved, the broker placed deposit money he received in his office safe until he made his weekly trip to the escrow office or bank. Broker Jones was not a member of any real estate association nor did he belong to any established multiple listing service. This broker has violated real estate law and regulation in all of the following instances, except:

(A) Commingling of funds.   (B) Use of non-licensed personnel.
(C) Location of place of business.   (D) Illegal sign.

(C) Except for possible local ordinances there is no provision in the Real Estate Law or Commissioner's Regulations about the situation of the place the broker conducts his business. If he does use a portion of his residence for business purposes, it must be maintained in such a way as to deal with his clientele in a professional and businesslike manner. All the other choices identify violations of some law.

_____(Lesson One - Paragraph 286 – Question 1)_____

A real estate broker negotiated the sale of a real property and acted as agent for the seller. By agreement, the licensee can be paid his commission in the form of:

(A) Assignment by seller of first monies due seller from buyer on a mortgage.
(B) Assignment of a note.
(C) Buyer's personal note.
(D) Any of the above.

(D) Any of the above. The licensee can accept compensation for his/her services in any manner of form agreed upon with the seller or the buyer.

_____(Lesson One - Paragraph 286a – Question 2)_____

Handley sold Price a parcel of land and, as he had agreed, gave his broker 30 acres of land as compensation for his services. The land had recently been valued by a fee appraiser to be worth $200 per acre. On the day following completion of this transaction, a complete stranger offers the broker $500 per acre for his land. If the broker sells this property to the stranger for $15,000, the following is true:
(A) The broker has done nothing morally or ethically wrong.
(B) The broker is guilty of taking a secret profit from the buyer.
(C) The broker would be subject to disciplinary action by the Real Estate Commissioner.
(D) The buyer should file an interpleader action in court.

(A) The broker has done nothing morally or ethically wrong in this situation. He earns the benefit of the bargain that he fell heir to in serving the needs of the seller originally and in selling the property at a profit.

_____(Lesson One - Paragraph 287 – Question 1)_____
A broker has a provision allowing him to purchase property in an agreement employing him, for compensation, to sell the property for the owner. He tells the owner that he will buy the property. To do this he must:
(A) Disclose all facts known about the property to the seller.   (B) Present any pending offers.
(C) Have the written consent of the principal to exercise the option. (D) Do all of the above.

(D) This is required by reason of section 10176(h) of the Real Estate Law. In this situation the licensee is acting simultaneously as an agent and a principal with the same person. To act as a principal (exercise the option) the law requires the licensee to reveal anticipated profit to the seller in writing and obtain the seller's written consent to such profit for the licensee.

_____(Lesson One - Paragraph 295 – Question 1)_____
John Smith, a licensed real estate broker, is not a member of the California Association of Realtors or the National Association of Realtors. In advertising he indicates that he is a Realtor. The following is the best statement concerning this situation:
(A) There is nothing wrong with this.
(B) It is a felony. A district attorney for doing this may prosecute him.
(C) He is subject to discipline by the Real Estate Commission for using the word "Realtor."
(D) A listing of a property obtained because of the advertisement would be void.

(C) The term "Realtor" is a registered term. Real estate law provides that a broker who uses the term and is not a member of the National Association of Realtors is subject to discipline and may lose his license.

_____(Lesson One - Paragraph 295 – Question 2)_____
Jim Johnson is a California licensed real estate broker. He is not a member of the National Association of Realtors, the California Association of Realtors, or his local realty board. In advertising homes that he has listed for sale, Jim indicates that he is a "Realtor." This act:
(A) Is unethical and morally wrong.
(B) Is improper because he is not a member of the local board of Realtors.
(C) Could subject Jim to disciplinary action by the Real Estate Commissioner.
(D) Is acceptable because he is a licensed California real estate broker.

(C) The real estate law specifically states that a broker who is not a member of the National Association of Realtors or of the California Association of Realtors, may not use the term "Realtor', otherwise his license may be suspended. He is in violation of law.

_____(Lesson One - Paragraph 307 – Question 1)_____

A bank gave $500 to a licensed real estate salesperson for referring his buyer to the bank for a new loan. When the salesperson's broker became aware of the $500 referral fee, the broker immediately fired the salesperson, notified the Real Estate Commissioner and warned all other salespeople never to accept such a fee. In this situation:
(A) The bank is subject to disciplinary action be the Real Estate Commissioner
(B) The salesperson is subject to disciplinary action by the Commissioner, but not the broker.
(C) The salesperson and the broker are subject to disciplinary action by the commissioner
(D) The broker overreacted, the salesperson and the bank did nothing illegal or unethical because
this type of a referral fee is legal.

(B) A lender cannot give "kickbacks" to real estate licensees for referring customers or clients. The Real Estate Commissioner does not have jurisdiction over banks but can discipline any licensee involved in this type of activity. The broker does not have to be disciplined because he notified the Real Estate Commissioner immediately and used reasonable supervision of his licensees.

_____(Lesson One - Paragraph 307 – Question 2)_____

When a salesperson leaves a broker's employ, the broker is required by real estate law to notify the Commissioner in writing. When a salesperson is discharged by his/her employer for possible violation of the real estate law, the employing broker must:
(A) Immediately notify the Commissioner by telegram.
(B) Forthwith file with the Commissioner a certified written statement of the facts in the case.
(C) Notify the Commissioner in writing within three business days.
(D) Return the salesperson's license to the Commissioner.

(B) Real Estate Law (B and P Code 10178) requires such handling of a situation in which a licensed employee has allegedly and knowingly violated a provision of the law.

_____(Lesson One - Paragraph 315 – Question 1)_____

For the person who has qualified in an examination for a real estate license, the maximum time allowed to file the required application would be:
(A) One year from the date of taking the test.
(B) One year from being notified of the results of the test.
(C) Two years from the date of taking the test.
(D) Five years from being notified of the results of the test.

(A) Please remember this important rule. After you successfully pass your state exam you will have one year from the date of taking it to apply for your real estate license. After you pass your college equivalent courses there is no time limit within which you must take the state exam.

_____(Lesson One - Paragraph 330 – Question 1)_____

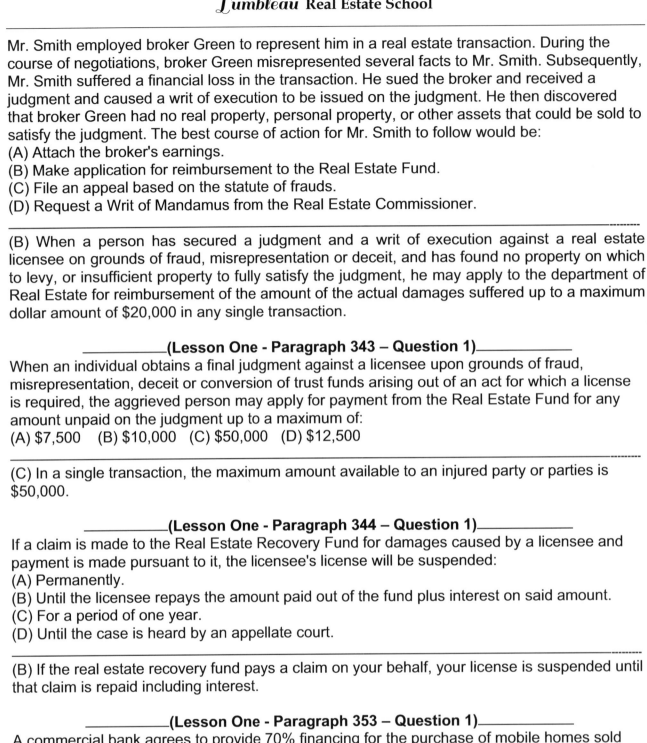

Mr. Smith employed broker Green to represent him in a real estate transaction. During the course of negotiations, broker Green misrepresented several facts to Mr. Smith. Subsequently, Mr. Smith suffered a financial loss in the transaction. He sued the broker and received a judgment and caused a writ of execution to be issued on the judgment. He then discovered that broker Green had no real property, personal property, or other assets that could be sold to satisfy the judgment. The best course of action for Mr. Smith to follow would be:
(A) Attach the broker's earnings.
(B) Make application for reimbursement to the Real Estate Fund.
(C) File an appeal based on the statute of frauds.
(D) Request a Writ of Mandamus from the Real Estate Commissioner.

(B) When a person has secured a judgment and a writ of execution against a real estate licensee on grounds of fraud, misrepresentation or deceit, and has found no property on which to levy, or insufficient property to fully satisfy the judgment, he may apply to the department of Real Estate for reimbursement of the amount of the actual damages suffered up to a maximum dollar amount of $20,000 in any single transaction.

_____(Lesson One - Paragraph 343 – Question 1)_____
When an individual obtains a final judgment against a licensee upon grounds of fraud, misrepresentation, deceit or conversion of trust funds arising out of an act for which a license is required, the aggrieved person may apply for payment from the Real Estate Fund for any amount unpaid on the judgment up to a maximum of:
(A) $7,500   (B) $10,000   (C) $50,000   (D) $12,500

(C) In a single transaction, the maximum amount available to an injured party or parties is $50,000.

_____(Lesson One - Paragraph 344 – Question 1)_____
If a claim is made to the Real Estate Recovery Fund for damages caused by a licensee and payment is made pursuant to it, the licensee's license will be suspended:
(A) Permanently.
(B) Until the licensee repays the amount paid out of the fund plus interest on said amount.
(C) For a period of one year.
(D) Until the case is heard by an appellate court.

(B) If the real estate recovery fund pays a claim on your behalf, your license is suspended until that claim is repaid including interest.

_____(Lesson One - Paragraph 353 – Question 1)_____
A commercial bank agrees to provide 70% financing for the purchase of mobile homes sold through broker Potts real estate office. Broker Potts also has an agreement with Southern Pacific Loan Co. to finance the remaining 30% down payment for qualified buyers. In his advertising the sale of these mobile homes, broker Potts states that they can be purchased with "no down payment." The "no down payment" statement in his advertising is:
(A) Lawful, since the buyer is, in effect, obtaining 100% financing.
(B) Unlawful, since the buyer must apply for the second loan to make the down payment.
(C) Lawful, since there is nothing in California laws forbidding this kind of financial arrangement.
(D) Unlawful since real estate law expressly forbids this kind of advertising.

(D) Real estate license law states that it is against the law for a real estate licensee to advertise the sale of a mobile home in the manner described.

_____(Lesson One - Paragraph 354 – Question 1)_____
The document used to transfer the title to a mobile home is:
(A) A vehicle certificate of registration.
(B) A bill of sale.
(C) A deed.
(D) A compliance agreement.

(B) When mobile homes were transferred from the Department of Motor Vehicles to the jurisdiction of the Corporations Commissioner the transfer document was changed from a vehicle registration to a bill of sale.

_____(Lesson One - Paragraph 355 – Question 1)_____
Manning, a real estate broker, maintains an office at the same location where he displays 18 transportable mobile homes which he offers for sale. To legally negotiate the purchase, sale or exchange of these mobile homes, Manning must also be licensed:
(A) As a business opportunities broker by the Bureau of Real Estate.
(B) As a securities dealer by the Department of Corporations.
(C) By the Department of Housing and Community Development.
(D) None of the above.

(C) The Department of Housing and Community Development has been given jurisdiction in matters involving mobile home sales.

Lesson One
Part Three
Understanding Through Question Testing

 Log into your course at www.lumbleau.com.

STUDENT LOGIN

Login: [   ]
Password: [   ]

 On your student home page, click on the "State Exam Preparation".

STATE EXAM
PREPARATION

 Under the "Guided Lesson" tab click on the first of fourteen links: "Regulation and Control of the Real Estate Practitioner".

Real Estate Salesperson Course

| Guided Lessons | Practice Exams | Progress Report | Success Video |

Print	Questions
Click	HERE>>> 1. Regulation and Control of the Real Estate Practitioner

Here you will be tested on all of the questions you have been studying and learn the most recently added questions. It is essential, for maximum retention, that you eliminate all of the questions you can easily answer and "TAG" for study the questions with which you have difficulty.

Lesson Two
Part One
Understanding Through Video Teaching

Lesson Two
THE AGENT

19   The laws of agency govern the rights and duties of principal to agent, principal to a third party, and agent to a third party. Anyone other than the principal and agent is a third party to the agency relationship. All employees of the agent act under the agency position and are, in effect, agents of the principal.

AGENT AND PRINCIPAL CONSIDERED AS ONE

25   The law imposes this vicarious liability on the principal based on the unique nature of the relationship between the principal and agent. The agent and the principal are, to a substantial degree, considered by the law to be one party; the agent is, in a manner of speaking, the clone of the principal, one and the same. The two take on a mutuality of identity. The acts of an agent, in terms of legal consequences become, in effect, the acts of the principal. The principal, it follows, has liability for the acts of the agent.

28   Many court cases speak out on the distinction between a principal agency relationship and that of a principal independent contractor. These cases universally agree that the existence of right of control and supervision is required to establish agency. If the one who performs service is not subject to control but is engaged to produce results by means and a manner of his own choosing, he is an independent contractor

THE AGENT AS FIDUCIARY

29   The establishment of an agency relationship in California gives rise to a second legal relationship between the same parties. Under California law, upon being appointed an agent by operation of law, one also becomes the fiduciary of the principal. The licensee thus occupies two separate and distinct offices vis-à-vis the principal's agent and fiduciary. The fiduciary relationship is separate and apart from the agency relationship, although the former is a result of the latter. A fiduciary relationship, as does that of agency, imposes on the individual so denominated an extraordinary standard of performance as well as specific duties owed by the fiduciary to the principal.

35 The agent deals with the property of the principal whether that property is real property, as in an agent/seller agency, or money in an agent/buyer relationship. The word fiduciary means trust or a thing held in trust. The principal places trust in the agent to protect and promote the interests of the principal. The agent is required to keep the principal fully informed at all times during the period of agency and cannot reveal anything negative about his or her principal to a third party. A trustee/beneficiary is another example of a fiduciary relationship.

DUTIES OWED TO PRINCIPAL

37 Pursuant to the California Civil Code, an agent must specifically disclose to the principal all facts material to the transaction known by the agent, or which should be known by the agent. As to the measure of what is and what is not "material," case law indicates that information is material if it would in any way affect a decision of the seller made during the course of the transaction. If the fact in question is likely to affect the judgment of the principal in assenting to a transaction, the fact is "material" and must therefore be disclosed. In other words, any information which could

result in a decision as to the sale, or which would in any way change the way in which the principal would negotiate the terms of the transaction, must be disclosed.

DUTY OF LOYALTY

43 This duty of loyalty also requires that the agent not benefit from the relationship other than from the agreed upon compensation. Neither may the agent obtain any advantage over the principal by the slightest misrepresentation, concealment, duress, or adverse pressure of any kind.

DUTY TO USE SKILL, CARE AND DILIGENCE

66 The problem agents confront most often within the context of this duty, in the typical transaction, is what to do with deposit money. If the deposit is in the form of a promissory note, the agent has the simple duty of informing the principal of this fact prior to the principal's consideration of an offer.

69 If there is any question whatsoever in the mind of an agent when he cannot obtain an agreement between the parties as to whom a deposit belongs, the best practice would be to hold the deposit. By doing so, the agent must recognize that he risks breaching his fiduciary duty to account to the principal. Another solution to such a problem would be to initiate an interpleader action and have a court determine the disposition of the deposit money.

DUTY TO OBEY REASONABLE INSTRUCTIONS

70 Provided that the instructions of the principal to the agent are relevant to the transaction for which the agent was retained and provided that those instructions are reasonable and nondiscriminatory, the agent has an obligation to obey those instructions. This duty has been interpreted to include the duty of the agent not to exceed the authority granted by the principal. It is also interpreted as the right of a principal to control the duties of an agent. When an agent acts without the authority or in excess of his authority, he may be held liable for damages suffered by the principal.

DUTIES OF A FIDUCIARY

72 These specific fiduciary duties are often described as trust, confidence and competence. In order for there to be a fiduciary relationship the principal must have a reasonable expectation that the agent will carry out the task subject to the agency (trust) and that any information given the agent by the principal, whether seller, buyer or both, which if disclosed would work to the disadvantage of the principal, must be kept confidential (in confidence) by the fiduciary agent. The agent must act throughout the transaction in a competent and professional manner.

DUTIES OWED BY AGENT TO THIRD PARTIES

73 The duties owed by the agent to the party opposite the principal (in the real property context, usually the buyer) are restricted to honesty and fair dealing.

CIVIL CODE PROVISIONS

79 It is the duty of a real estate broker, to a prospective purchaser of residential real property comprising one to four dwelling units, including a manufactured home (mobilehome), to conduct a reasonably competent and diligent visual inspection in accessible areas of the property offered for sale and to disclose to that prospective purchaser, on an approved disclosure form, all facts materially affecting the value or desirability of the property that such an investigation would reveal. This obligation becomes the obligation if that broker has a written contract with the seller to find or

obtain a buyer or is a broker who cooperates with such a broker to find and obtain a buyer.

86 This disclosure must be in written form and must be made by the seller, by the seller's agent and by the buyer's agent, if agents are involved in the transaction.

86a It is the intent of the Legislature that the delivery of a real estate transfer disclosure statement may not be waived in an "as is" sale.

89 If the prescribed disclosure is delivered subsequent to the execution of the offer to purchase, a recessionary period, as to the offer, is created. In this event, the buyer, if delivery is made in person, has three days from the date of the delivery and in the event delivery is made by mail, then the buyer has five days from the date of the deposit into the mail, to rescind his offer to purchase by written notice to the seller.

DISCLOSURE OF AGENCY REPRESENTATION

93 A license is required to disclose the licensee's understanding as to whom his or her representation as agent extends. This must be accomplished in a format prescribed by the law as soon as possible.

94 The Civil Code requires all licensees to sign a statement setting out the "agency relationship" involved. The purpose of the statute is to inform the parties involved, usually the buyer and the seller, which licensee represents their interests as their agent in the transaction at hand.

MISREPRESENTATION

101 Mistake - A valid contract implies a mutual agreement of the parties. When there is a substantial mistake as to a material fact that caused the complaining party to enter into the agreement, the contract may be void or voidable. The fact that the injured party

was negligent does not in itself preclude release from mistakes, unless this negligence is gross, such as the failure of the injured party to read the agreement. If the negligence is on the part of the agent, the injured party may have a right to rescind the agreement.

102 Negligent Fraud - When an agent makes a positive statement of fact about which he or she does not have sufficient information to justify such an assertion, the agent's good faith is no defense to a charge of fraud. In other words, fraud does not necessarily imply that the person charged with its commission acted with a malicious intent to defraud others and cause them damage. Persons may act "fraudulently" because they were careless or negligent in their words or acts. Negligent fraud subjects a licensee to disciplinary action, civil action and possibly criminal action.

103 Known False Statement - If an individual does make a statement, intentionally, with knowledge of its inaccuracy, or makes the statement having cause to doubt its accuracy, then the statement is fraud.

104 Failure to Disclose - The failure to disclose a fact material to the transaction whether to buyer or seller, is fraud in California.

104a If the seller makes a known false statement that is relied upon by both the broker and the buyer and as a consequence the transaction falls out of escrow and the buyer sues the seller and broker, the seller would be responsible for both the commission plus damages for defending against buyer's suit.

105 The Alquist-Priolo Special Studies Act regulates development in earthquake fault areas in California. It is concerned with fault ruptures, not shaking damage. A geologic report must be obtained for all new construction after 1975 that is within ¼ mile

of an active fault. This information must be disclosed to the buyer.

WAIVER

109 It may be possible as well that a principal will be allowed to waive the protection afforded by the law, even if the relationship satisfies the definition of agency. This waiver, if to be made effective, must be in writing and must be intelligently made by the principal. It is suggested that if this waiver be the intent of the parties, the specifics of the circumstances resulting in this waiver should be explained in the writing by recital.

110 Any party contemplating such a waiver should be aware, however, that there exists a public policy in this state disfavoring this type of waiver. Such a waiver will likely be found unenforceable if the result of the waiver would be unfair as to the principal, or if the waiver was entered into by the principal lacking an understanding of the consequences of that action.

DUAL AGENCY

111 "Dual Agency" is the concept that holds that under certain circumstances, an individual can act as the agent for both parties to a transaction. In the context of real property practice, this would involve a licensee acting as the agent for both the buyer and the seller. If dual agency does not exist, then the duty of the agent and the compensation paid to the agent are of consequence only between the agent and the single principal involved.

111a Though numerically speaking there are more dual agency agreements created in the sale of houses, an exchange agreement invariably creates a dual agency. This contract form involves two principals in trading real properties. In the terms of the standard form in use both parties agree to pay compensation to the licensee named for services rendered.

CONSENT REQUIRED

112 Regarding dual agency, California law provides that under no circumstances may a licensee act as a dual agent without the knowledge and consent of all parties to the transaction. No matter the degree of honesty displayed by the agent in the transaction, without this consent, the licensee will be allowed to recover compensation from neither seller nor buyer. Further, by case law, an undisclosed dual agency provides the ground for rescission by either party without having to make a showing of financial loss or other damage.

THE GRATUITOUS AGENT

115 Consideration is not required for the relationship. An agent who works without compensation is called a gratuitous agent.

CREATION OF THE AGENCY RELATIONSHIP

120 An agency may be created by one of three methods:
  (1) By express agreement
  (2) By ratification
  (3) By conduct and estoppel (ostensible agency)

EXPRESS CONTRACT

121 In real property practice, the agency relationship is normally established by the execution of an express agreement between the seller and broker. This contract is commonly referred to as a "listing agreement" or "authorization to sell." The listing agreement is a contract governed by general contract law. The statute of frauds requires that all agency contracts, such as a listing agreement, be based upon a written agreement. The agency created in this manner is referred to as an "actual agency."

123 The most important thing that occurs when the listing agreement is signed, in terms of legal consequences, is the written appointment of the broker as agent by the seller. As agent, from the time that the broker is authorized to act as the seller/principal's agent, the specific duties discussed above attach to the broker in his relationship to the seller.

RATIFICATION

124 It is also possible to create an agency relationship by what is called "ratification." In the absence of circumstances requiring an authorization in writing, if one individual holds himself or herself out as being another's agent and in so acting bestows upon that individual some benefit which is accepted by the latter, such an acceptance will generally prompt the courts in California to recognize the relationship between the two as being one of agency.

124a Ratification is often how a real estate broker becomes the agent of a buyer. The agent is showing a buyer property that is listed through the multiple listing service. This normally creates a sub-agency. However, if the buyer asks about a property on a corner that is not listed for sale, agency is created. The broker asks the buyer if he or she would like to make an offer on the unlisted property. If the broker accepts a check from the buyer the broker becomes the agent of the buyer. This creates a fiduciary relationship with the buyer.

125 Note that any third party dealing with the purported agent will not in any way become bound until such time as the conduct in question is ratified. This relationship is not revocable under this rule if the agent, separate and apart from the status of agent, maintains an interest in the subject matter of the transaction. It is often characterized as an "agency coupled with an interest."

OSTENSIBLE AGENCY

126 A third method by which the agency relationship can be created is based on the theory of "estoppel." If an owner, through his conduct or by want of ordinary care, leads a third party to believe that a broker is in fact authorized to act as that owner's agent and if that third party does indeed rely on that representation, the purported principal will be estopped from denying that agency. Ostensible agency cannot be created solely by the conduct of the agent. The most important consideration in the concept of ostensible agency is the conduct of the principal.

FACTS INVOLVING AGENCY

(1) A listing always creates a fiduciary relationship.

(2) The fiduciary relationship created by a listing is similar to a trustee relationship.

(3) Under a listing agreement with the seller, the broker owes his fiduciary obligation to the seller only.

(4) Though his fiduciary obligation is to the seller, the licensee still has an obligation of honesty and fairness to the buyer.

(5) The laws of agency are concerned with three relationships:
    (a) Agent to principal - (fiduciary)
    (b) Agent to 3rd party - (honesty, fairness)
    (c) Principal to 3rd party (seller responsible for agent's actions)

(6) Consideration is not required for a valid agency. An agent working without compensation is termed a "gratuitous agent."

(7) Generally, either party can revoke an agency relationship with possible liability.

(8) When an agency is coupled with an interest, it is irrevocable.

(9) An agent must present all offers. If more than one offer is received, he must present all offers at the same time. Without instructions to the contrary, all offers must be presented.

(10) If an agent discovers termites in a structure, he must inform the seller and buyer.

SUMMARY OF AGENCY

140. An agent must present all offers. When an agent receives more than one offer, he must present all offers at the same time. Without instructions to the contrary, all offers must be presented.

TERMINATION OF THE AGENCY RELATIONSHIP

142 As with most relationships created by contract (as well as by ratification and by estoppel), the agency relationship can be terminated upon the agreement of the parties. In addition, under California law the principal, because of the unique character of the agency relationship, is given the power to unilaterally revoke the agency at any time. The principal, while having the power to so revoke but not necessarily the right may, under proper circumstances, be liable to the agent as the result of the breach of the contract. Another method by which agency contracts may be terminated is based upon the contact itself.

143 Agency contracts, such as listing agreements, fall into a category of contracts called "personal service contracts." Personal service contracts such as listing agreements automatically terminate on the death or incompetency of either party.

Lesson Two
Part Two - Study Questions

_____(Lesson Two - Paragraph 19 – Question 1)_____
The law of agency concerns itself with the rights, duties, and liabilities between and among:
(A) Agent and a third party with whom the agent deals.
(B) Principal and agent.
(C) Principal and third party introduced by the agent.
(D) All of the above.

(D) The laws of agency have been described as a vast body of rules governing the rights and duties of principal to agent, principal to a third party, and agent to a third party.

_____(Lesson Two - Paragraph 28 – Question 1)_____
In order for the relationship between two parties to become a valid agency relationship, there must be evidence of:
(A) A written contract.   (B) Consideration.
(C) Power being vested in the principal to direct the actions of the agent. (D) None of the above.

(C) For a relationship to be classified as "agency," there must be some control by the principal over the actions of the person acting for him. This kind of relationship must exist for an agency to be created. The other choices are not essential to the relationship.

_____(Lesson Two - Paragraph 35 – Question 1)_____
The phrase which best describes the nature of a broker's duty to keep a principal fully informed is:
(A) Ethical conduct.   (B) Continuing responsibility.
(C) Fiduciary obligation. (D) Trustworthy business principles.

(C) The statement presents a description of a fiduciary obligation.

_____(Lesson Two - Paragraph 34 – Question 2)_____
The position of trust assumed by the broker as an agent for a principal is described most accurately as:
(A) A gratuitous relationship. (B) A trustor relationship.
(C) A fiduciary relationship.   (D) An employment relationship.

(C) The position of trust that exists between an agent and principal is a "fiduciary" relationship.

_____(Lesson Two - Paragraph 35 – Question 1)_____
In a real estate sales transaction you are the agent of the buyer and not of the seller. Considering California's agency laws, the duty(s) you owe the buyer is/are:
(A) Honesty and fair dealing. (B) Fiduciary. (C) Secondary liability. (D) Subrogation.

(B) The question states: "...you are the agent of the buyer." Therefore, under agency laws, you have a fiduciary relationship with the buyer. The distracting choice "honesty and fair dealing" is owed to all parties in every transaction. It is not classified as a fiduciary duty.

_____(Lesson Two - Paragraph 37 – Question 1)_____

Broker Henley lists some vacant property for sale with an exclusive listing. Another broker finds a buyer at the listed price and a sales agreement is signed by the buyer and seller and placed in escrow. Two days before the close of this escrow, broker Henley learns that the buyer has purchased other similar vacant properties in the same area at a much higher price. In this circumstance broker Henley should do the following:

(A) Advise the seller to negotiate a better contract with the buyer.
(B) Say nothing since the escrow is so near closing.
(C) Disclose the facts to the seller.
(D) Advise the seller to refuse to go through with the sale.

(C) Disclose the facts to the seller. The broker could not do what choices (A) and (D) suggest, as this would be interpreted to be practicing law without a license. The broker by acting in such a manner would also be inducing the seller to breach a binding contract which would be illegal. If he says nothing he would be violating his fiduciary responsibility to the seller. He must disclose the pertinent facts to his principal - the seller.

_____(Lesson Two - Paragraph 37 – Question 2)_____

A buyer makes a written offer on March 10th and gives the broker a check for $500.00. The buyer instructs the broker to hold the check until March 30th regardless of when the offer is accepted. In this situation, the broker should:
(A) Refuse to accept the offer and the check under these terms
(B) Give the check to the seller if the offer is accepted regardless of the date.
(C) Present the offer and inform the seller that the check is to be held uncashed until March 30th.
(D) Deposit the check into escrow or the brokers trust account by the next business day following acceptance of the offer.

(C) The broker must follow all lawful instructions and present all material facts to his client.

_____(Lesson Two - Paragraph 43 – Question 1)_____

The property manager receives compensation for all of the following acts, except:
(A) Collecting rentals.
(B) Leasing space to new tenants.
(C) Obtaining discounts on supplies used.
(D) Supervising major repairs or alterations to the property.

(C) The discounts earned on the supplies used should benefit the owner of the property being managed. The property manager is paid in relation to the manner in which the property performs. This would be the rental income stream and the activities that relate to the production of that income.

_____(Lesson Two - Paragraph 69 – Question 1)_____

Johnson entered into a contract with Jackson for the purchase of Jackson's real property. Johnson gave a deposit to broker Agnew in part payment for the property. The broker places

the money in his trust account. A dispute arises between Johnson and Jackson regarding the transaction and both claim the deposit money as their own. Since the broker could not bring the parties to agree on a solution and because he cannot be certain as to how the matter could be equitably settled, he initiates a court action to end the dispute. This court proceeding is known as:
(A) An interpleader action. (B) An assignment. (C) A condition subsequent. (D) A surrender.

(A) An interpleader. Interpleader describes an action available to a person who holds property about which others are in dispute and in which he claims no legal interest. Such a person may, on depositing the disputed property in court, be relieved of any further liability to the persons disputing the matter.

_____(Lesson Two - Paragraph 70 – Question 1)_____
A real estate agent refuses to show a single family residence to a member of a minority group. The following is the best statement of the law in regard to this situation:
(A) The salesperson can refuse to show the property if the seller is exempt from the law.
(B) The salesperson should show the property even if the seller orders him not to show unless the owner is physically present on the property.
(C) If the owner has directed the agent to show the property only when he is physically present, the salesperson should not show the property if the seller is not home.
(D) The salesperson wants to show it only on sunny days.

(C) An agent must obey the lawful instructions of the principal. If the principal gives an instruction not to show the property to anyone when he is not present, it is a legal instruction and not discriminatory. The agent must follow this instruction.

_____(Lesson Two - Paragraph 70 – Question 2)_____
A broker who has a signed listing to sell a property can refuse to submit an offer:
(A) In circumstances in which he also has obtained a back-up offer.
(B) Whenever the offer is for less than the listed price.
(C) If in the listing agreement he also has an option to purchase the property.
(D) When expressly instructed to do so by the owner.

(D) Instructed not to present certain offers or if the offer is patently frivolous. The normal rule is a broker or salesperson must submit all offers to the seller, except when instructed otherwise.

_____(Lesson Two - Paragraph 72 – Question 1)_____
A selling agent is the exclusive agent of the buyer only. The following is the best statement concerning what he cannot do:
(A) Present an offer to seller and the seller's agent with the seller's permission.
(B) Personally present offer to seller.
(C) Reveal anything negative regarding the buyer to the seller.
(D) Represent the seller, because he is paying the fee.

(C) You are the exclusive agent of the buyer only, therefore you do have a fiduciary relationship with the buyer: one of honor, trust and loyalty. You should not reveal negative facts concerning the buyer to the seller, such as "...my buyer is under divorce proceedings," or "...he's lost his job," or "...he is under great pressure to sell." Facts such as these are part of your loyalty to the buyer. As you are not the agent of the seller, you do not disclose them to the seller.

_____(Lesson Two - Paragraph 72 – Question 2)_____

Fenton listed his home for sale with broker Hamilton. The listing price was $40,000 and Fenton told Hamilton that a quick sale was imperative. Hamilton showed the home to Martin and told Martin that Fenton was financially insolvent and would accept $38,000 for the property. Based on Hamilton's statement, Martin offered to purchase Fenton's home for $38,000. Fenton accepted the offer. Regarding Hamilton's action the following is true:

(A) Hamilton did not violate his fiduciary obligation to Fenton because Fenton did accept the offer.
(B) Hamilton did not violate his fiduciary obligation because he was employed to sell the property and he fulfilled his obligation.
(C) Hamilton violated his fiduciary obligation to Fenton because he acted in excess of his authority.
(D) Hamilton was unethical and violated his fiduciary obligation to Fenton; however, since Fenton
accepted the offer, no harm was done.

(C) Broker Hamilton exceeded his fiduciary duty in telling Martin what he did regarding the seller's (Fenton) financial situation.

_____(Lesson Two - Paragraph 73 – Question 1)_____

A young, newly married couple contact broker Able regarding the purchase of a home. He shows them a home that meets their needs in every respect. In discussing financing, it is revealed that they have a limited amount of cash and are $2,000 short of the required down payment. In order to purchase the home they will have to execute a large second trust deed and borrow money on their automobile to complete the down payment. The broker should:
(A) Strongly recommend against the purchase of the home.
(B) Since it is the home they want, recommend the purchase.
(C) Advise them of the pitfalls of over-extending their credit and allow them to make their own decision.
(D) Do not concern himself with the financial problems of buyer as he is only representing the seller.

(C) An ethical broker will not take advantage of inexperienced clients but will point out the risks involved in over-extending credit, and make sure they understand the obligations they are assuming.

_____(Lesson Two - Paragraph 73 – Question 2)_____

If the broker is the agent of the seller, he owes the buyer:
(A) The duty of honesty and fair dealing.
(B) The same fiduciary obligations he owes to the seller.
(C) Only the duty to answer questions honestly.
(D) Only a duty to disclose any item which relates directly to the sales price of the property.

(A) The question deals with the responsibility the agent owes the buyer as the seller's agent. He owes fiduciary obligations to the seller, but to the buyer he owes the duty of honesty and fair dealing.

_____(Lesson Two - Paragraph 79 – Question 1)_____
On the real estate transfer disclosure form, the broker must:
(A) Make a visible inspection of accessible areas and report his findings on the form.
(B) Inspect all areas, including inaccessible areas, and report his findings to the buyer.
(C) Inspect accessible areas and inaccessible areas and inform buyer and seller.
(D) Inspect all common areas.

(A) On a real estate transfer disclosure form, the broker must also make an inspection of the property with the seller, and make a visual inspection in the accessible areas. He must report his notes on the form.

_____(Lesson Two - Paragraph 79 – Question 2)_____
Regarding the real estate transfer disclosure form, the broker must:
(A) Inspect the property and make notes concerning his findings on the form
(B) Inspect all common areas.
(C) Inform the buyer concerning the financing on the property.
(D) Inspect the accessible and inaccessible areas.

(A) The real estate transfer disclosure form is the responsibility of the seller. However, the law requires the listing agent to make a visual inspection also. The notes of his inspection must be placed on the form.

_____(Lesson Two - Paragraph 86 – Question 1)_____
The person that must prepare the transfer disclosure statement is:
(A) An administrator in probate.
(B) One spouse to another in a divorce proceeding.
(C) The transferor.
(D) A trustee in an REO sale.

(C) The transferor disclosure statement must be prepared by the seller (the transferor). The real estate broker also inspects the property and makes his notes concerning a visual inspection on the form.

_____(Lesson Two - Paragraph 86a – Question 1)_____
If a private person lists his home for sale "as is":
(A) He is obligated to provide a real property disclosure statement to prospective buyers.
(B) He is not obligated to provide a real property disclosure statement to prospective buyers.
(C) There is no warranty on the property.
(D) This implies "buyer beware" (caveat emptor).

(A) It is the intent of the legislature that the delivery of a real estate transfer disclosure statement may not be waived in an "as is" sale.

_____(Lesson Two - Paragraph 86a – Question 2)_____

A private party offers a single family residence for sale without the services of a real estate salesperson or broker. He advertises the property in "as is" condition. In this situation the seller:
(A) Does not have to disclose any known defects in the property.
(B) Does not have to provide the buyer with a real estate transfer disclosure statement.
(C) Is required inspect the property and provide a disclosure report on all observable areas.
(D) Is required inspect the property and provide a disclosure report on all unobservable areas.

(C) When an owner sells in "as is" condition, he is still required to give a real estate transfer disclosure statement to the buyer. The seller can disclose only on the observable areas. The seller is not required to report on areas that cannot be seen (unobservable).

_____(Lesson Two - Paragraph 89 – Question 1)_____
Assume Harry Jones alone made an offer. Within the time limit set by the buyer, the owner signed the acceptance. However, it developed that the buyer, without knowledge on the part of broker or seller, had died before the seller accepted. In such circumstances:
(A) Since seller had accepted the offer within the time limit, the estate of the deceased person is
liable for completion of the contract.
(B) The contract would, by its terms, be unenforceable.
(C) Death cancels all real estate contracts.
(D) None of the above answers is correct.

(B) If you will read the deposit receipt carefully you will note that a delivery of a signed copy of the acceptance must be made to the buyer within five days; otherwise "the offer shall be deemed revoked." Under the circumstances stated in the question, no delivery had been or could be made to the buyer, therefore, the terms of the contract apply.

_____(Lesson Two - Paragraph 89 – Question 2)_____
The word "rescind" means:
(A) Changed. (B) Terminated. (C) Substituted. (D) Subordinated.

(B) Rescind means to annul or repeal, thereby terminating a contract.

_____(Lesson Two - Paragraph 93 – Question 1)_____
Which of the following forms became mandatory in the sale or leasing of improved residential property consisting of one to four units in the year 1988?
(A) The seller transfer statement.
(B) The buyer-agent relationship statement.
(C) The agency disclosure statement.
(D) The broker disclosure statement.

(C) An agency disclosure statement is required to disclose to the purchaser and seller the choices available to them concerning the role of the agents within the transaction.

_____(Lesson Two - Paragraph 94 – Question 1)_____
John Smith is the agent of the buyer. He should disclose this relationship to other persons involved in a sales transaction:
(A) After he secures the listing.   (B) Before escrow is opened.

(C) Immediately after escrow has closed. (D) As soon as possible.

(D) Your relationship with the parties must be disclosed as soon as practical.

_____(Lesson Two - Paragraph 94 – Question 2)_____
A California law effective in January 1988 requires a/an:
(A) Truth in lending disclosure.   (B) Agency disclosure.
(C) Financial disclosure.   (D) Regulation disclosure.

 (B) The question asks about a new California law effective in January 1988 which in the standards of agency legislation over the last 300 or 400 years is considered to be a relatively new law. The law that was effective on that date was the real estate agency disclosure law, wherein the licensee must elect, disclose and confirm his agency relationship, seller only, buyer only, or a dual agency involving seller and buyer.

_____(Lesson Two – Paragraph 101 - Question 1)_____
A broker has obtained a listing on an income property. He prepares and presents a projection on this property to a prospective buyer. The projection does not include an allowance for vacancy and other reserves applicable. On the basis of the broker's projection the property shows a net return of 12%. Under these conditions the broker may be guilty of:
(A) He has done nothing wrong.
(B) Misrepresentation.
(C) Negligence or incompetence.
(D) Real estate law does not concern itself with such matters.

(C) There is no evidence of the broker's attempt to consciously mislead his prospective buyer. It appears that the broker dealt with a property which was unfamiliar to him. He should have recognized his inability to deal with this situation and have sought proper advice or training to be able to represent properties of this type.

_____(Lesson Two - Paragraph 102 – Question 1)_____
Salesman Allen, while showing a house to a prospective buyer in a subdivision under construction, told the buyer: "If you buy this property you will be taking advantage of a great bargain. I guarantee that in four years it will double in value." Four years later the buyer could not sell the property even for the same price that the developer was asking at the time he bought it. In this situation the following is true:
(A) Salesman Allen could not be disciplined because he was merely "puffing" and it is well established that "puffing" is an accepted way of life in sales.
(B) Salesman Allen was not responsible for the fact that the general economy had worsened during the four years, so he could not be disciplined.
(C) Salesman Allen would have to make good on his guarantee.
(D) Salesman Allen could lose his license.

(D) There are numerous court cases in which it has been determined that such conduct is misleading, fraudulent and a kind of misrepresentation. Such conduct would put the licensee in danger of losing the real estate license.

_____(Lesson Two - Paragraph 102 – Question 2_____

A real estate licensee who misrepresents a property to a buyer while acting as agent for a seller may subject himself to:
(A) Disciplinary action by the licensing authority.   (B) Civil action.
(C) Criminal action.   (D) all of the above.

(D) All of the above. Such misrepresentation is a violation of real estate law, subject to disciplinary action. The licensee, in misrepresenting something, is committing a criminal act and is civilly liable to the persons that such action would injure.

_____(Lesson Two - Paragraph 103 – Question 1)_____

In listing a single family residence for sale, a broker promises to advertise it regularly, on a weekly basis, until it sells. Contrary to his agreement with the owner, the broker has no intention of advertising the property weekly. This would constitute:
(A) Deliberate fraud. (B) Constructive fraud. (C) Actual fraud.   (D) Negative fraud.

(C) Actual fraud has several types of fraud under its definition. Actual fraud includes an act called promissory fraud. If a person makes a promise with no intent to keep it, this is a form of actual fraud. Deliberate fraud is not a legal term. Constructive fraud is defined by a breach of any agency duty and is also an act of fraud. For example, failure to supply the 12 day notice in the sale of a business opportunity is defined by law as fraudulent. The fraud would be in the form of constructive fraud. Negative fraud is also a type of actual fraud. Negative fraud occurs when one does not disclose a material defect that is not apparent by a visual inspection of the property.

_____(Lesson Two - Paragraph 104 – Question 1)_____

Baker accepted an offer from Able to purchase Blackacre. During the negotiations Able inquired and was assured that the property was connected to the sewer. After the contract was accepted and before escrow closed, Able learned that the property was not connected to the sewer but that a new septic tank had been installed on the parcel. Able could:
(A) Demand a percolation and soils test.
(B) Require and automatically receive a reduction in the price of the property.
(C) Require a partial release.
(D) Rescind the contract.

(D) Under this circumstance, the buyer has the right to rescind the agreement as escrow has not closed.

_____(Lesson Two - Paragraph 104 – Question 2)_____

A real estate broker secured a listing on a property for $10,000. Knowing that the owner was anxious to sell, the broker had another party buy it for him without disclosing this fact to the seller, at a price of $8,000. Under the circumstances, the broker is violating Section 10176(g) of the Real Estate Code and would be guilty of:
(A) Commingling. (B) Dual agency. (C) Earning a secret profit. (D) None of the above.

(C) It is unlawful for an agent to acquire the property of his principal without the principal's consent.

_____(Lesson Two - Paragraph 105 – Question 1)_____

A broker is listing a home that lies on an earthquake fault. The owner of the home tells the broker not to disclose this fact to the buyer. The broker should:
(A) Tell the seller to sell the home himself.
(B) Take the listing and inform the buyer orally regarding the facts.
(C) Take the listing and not disclose the facts.
(D) Refuse to take the listing.

(D) In the circumstances posed by this question, the owner is instructing the agent to violate the law. The Alquist-Priolo Special Studies Act regulates development in earthquake fault areas in California. It is concerned with fault ruptures, not shaking damage. A geologic report must be obtained for all new construction after 1975 that is within 1/4 mile of an active fault. This information must be disclosed to the buyer, therefore the agent should refuse to take the listing and leave the house immediately.

_____(Lesson Two - Paragraph 115 – Question 1)_____
All of the following are needed to create an agency relationship, except:
(A) Consideration. (B) Competency of parties. (C) Legality. (D) Fiduciary.

(A) This is a negative question and asks for what is not needed to create an agency. Consideration is not required to be an agent. One can become a gratuitous agent, meaning working without consideration for their actions.

_____(Lesson Two - Paragraph 120 – Question 1)_____
The relationship of principal and agent can be created in all of these ways, except:
(A) By express contract. (B) By oral agreement. (C) By ratification. (D) By subornation.

(D) Subornation has to do with entering into a conspiracy to commit perjury. The term has nothing to do with agency. The other choices suggest ways in which an agency can be created.

_____(Lesson Two - Paragraph 123 – Question 1)_____
The best way to establish an agency relationship is by:
(A) An oral agreement. (B) Voluntary by agent. (C) Implied contract by law. (D) Written contract.

(D) To avoid a dispute, the best way to establish agency is with a written contract.

_____(Lesson Two - Paragraph 124 – Question 1)_____
A property is not listed for sale. A person, who wants to buy the property, executes an offer to purchase it via a real estate agent. In doing so, he gives the broker a $5,000 check as a deposit. Under these circumstances, the broker:
(A) Can accept the check as the exclusive agent of the buyer.
(B) Cannot accept the check.
(C) Can accept the check on behalf of the property owner provided he presents the offer directly

to the seller as the seller's agent.
(D) None of the above.

_____

(A) When you approach a property which is not listed for sale, and you have a buyer who agrees to buy this home, the buyer gives the broker a $5,000 check to act for him. You can accept this check as the exclusive agent for the buyer. You have no listing with a seller.

_____(Lesson Two - Paragraph 124 – Question 2)_____
"A" acts for "B" in agency without authorization. "B" chooses to accept the agency. This is:
(A) Estoppel. (B) Expressed contract. (C) Ratification. (D) Application.

(C) Ratification is the adoption or approval of an act performed on behalf of a person without previous authorization. If "B" accepts the act of agency, he would do so in writing to ratify. Estoppel is the doctrine which bars one from asserting rights which are inconsistent with a previous position or representation.

_____(Lesson Two - Paragraph 126 – Question 1)_____
Armour has given Bailey the impression that Chappel is Armour's agent even though Chappel was never given the authority to represent Armour. From Bailey's standpoint the agency is:
(A) Actual. (B) Ratified. (C) Special. (D) Ostensible.

(D) An example of an ostensible agent would be where a store owner must leave his place of business for a few minutes and asks a friend to watch the counter. A customer enters, makes a purchase thinking the friend is the owner. The owner's friend is ostensibly the owner's agent.

_____(Lesson Two - Paragraph 140 – Question 1)_____
At noon Buyer Byrd made an offer to purchase a single family residence. In doing so, he instructed the real estate broker not to present his offer until 6:00 p.m. By 6:00 p.m. three more offers are submitted. The real estate broker should:
(A) Present the offers to the property owner in the order that they were submitted.
(B) Wait until the seller acts on the first offer before presenting the other offers.
(C) Present all offers simultaneously as soon as possible.
(D) Ignore the other three offers.

(C) The rule of agency is that all offers must be presented to the seller and let the seller make the decision as to which offer to accept.

_____(Lesson Two - Paragraph 140 – Question 2)_____
Real estate broker Garvey presented an offer to purchase residential property to owner Smith at 12:00 noon on September 29. Smith requested that he be given until 8:00 PM to make his choice. At 5:00 PM on the same day, Garvey received two other offers from different buyers submitted by one of his salespeople. Garvey fully expects that the owner will reject all three offers. By law the broker must:
(A) Present the two new offers to Smith in the exact order in which the salesperson received them.
(B) Hold the two new offers received at 5:00 PM until after 8:00 PM before submitting to the owner.
(C) Present the two new offers to the owner at the same time as soon as he is available.

(D) Do none of these.

(C) The agent must submit all offers to the principal as soon as it can reasonably be done. Agents should so conduct themselves that their principals are put in the position to make the most beneficial decision for themselves.

_____(Lesson Two - Paragraph 143 – Question 1)_____

The owner of an apartment building appointed a real estate broker as his agent to collect the monthly rents on all of the apartments. Rents were due on the first of the month and on January 1st. The broker had collected all the rents except one. On January 2nd, the owner died. On January 3rd the broker called on the one remaining tenant to collect the rent and the tenant refused to pay it saying that the death of the owner had revoked the agent's authority to collect it. The same tenant had previously paid rent to the agent. Under the circumstances, the tenant:

(A) Was right.

(B) Could not refuse to pay the rent since the authority of the agent continued until the appointment of an administrator or executor.

(C) Could not refuse on the legal theory that once he has recognized the agency and paid rent he

cannot thereafter refuse until he has received notice from the true owner.

(D) Could not refuse since the rent became due on January 1, prior to the death of the owner.

(A) Since an agency agreement is a personal service contract, it automatically terminates upon the death or incompetence of either party. In this case, the broker's principal died and the broker's agency is terminated.

Notes

Lesson Two
Part Three
Understanding Through Question Testing

 Log into your course at www.lumbleau.com.

STUDENT LOGIN

Login:

Password:

 On your student home page, click on the "State Exam Preparation".

STATE EXAM
PREPARATION

 Under the "Guided Lesson" tab click on the second of fourteen links: "The Laws of Agency".

Real Estate Salesperson Course

| Guided Lessons | Practice Exams | Progress Report | Success Video |

Print	Questions
Click	HERE>>> 2. The Laws of Agency

Here you will be tested on all of the questions you have been studying and learn the most recently added questions. It is essential, for maximum retention, that you eliminate all of the questions you can easily answer and "TAG" for study the questions with which you have difficulty.

Lesson Three
Part One
Understanding Through Video Teaching

Lesson Three
PROPERTY

77   The California Civil Code defines property as "the thing of which there may be ownership." Ownership is defined as "the right of one or more persons to possess and use property to the exclusion of others."

78   Property is divided in two classes:
   (1) Real Property - that which is immovable.
   (2) Personal Property - that which is movable.

REAL PROPERTY

79   Real property, or real estate as it is often called, consists of:
   (1) Land.
   (2) Anything affixed to it so as to be regarded as a permanent part of the land (fixtures).
   (3) That which is incidental or appurtenant to the land (e.g. stock in a Mutual Water Company, easements).
   (4) That which is immovable by law.

80   Real property is land and all that which is attached thereto or contained therein. It includes rights in the minerals that are beneath the surface of the earth, water flowing upon it, and things of a permanent nature attached to the earth, such as buildings, trees and unsevered, unripened fruits of the soil.

81   Land is thought of primarily as the ground or soil upon which we walk or upon which we place structures. It also includes the air space above as a right to build to the height allowed by law and the right to defend against the encroachment of neighboring properties. The ownership of land also includes the right to sub-adjacent support from adjoining land. The ownership of land is absolute and unconditional in the owner from the center of the earth to the outer reaches of space, except as against the right of the State to purchase land for public use by the power of eminent domain, and to enact regulations by virtue of its police powers.

PERSONAL PROPERTY

82   According to the Civil Code, "Every kind of property that is not real property is personal property."

82a   Personal property provides difficulties for real estate brokers because it can be hypothecated, alienated, and may become real property.

83   Therefore, when personal property becomes immovable, it must become real property. Often documents become confused (e.g. although mortgages and trust deeds are legally tied to real property the instruments themselves are considered to be personal property).

FIXTURES

84   Anything is considered affixed to the land when it is attached to it by roots, as in the case of trees, vines or shrubs; or imbedded in it as in the case of walls; or permanently resting upon it, as in the case of buildings; or permanently attached to that which is permanent by means of cement, plaster, nails, bolts and screws. Items thus permanently attached are called fixtures. Rights by others to use real property are called easements (including easements in gross). These are also a form of real property. Another name you need to know is fructus naturales. It defines crops that are a product of nature alone generally classified

as real property trees, whether deciduous leaf shedding or evergreen, bushes

87   The method by which it was attached. Here the degree of permanence is important. If attached by cement, plaster, nails, or bolts, it is likely to be classed as a "fixture."

91   These five tests can be remembered by using the following memory tool - MARIA:
 M ethod of attachment
 A daptability of the property
 R elationship of the parties
 I ntention of the parties
 A greement between the parties

TRADE FIXTURES

94   Personal property affixed to real property for the purpose of trade, manufacture, business, etc., such as showcases permanently attached in a store, is a "trade fixture" and does not "run with the land" (become real property). A trade fixture may be removed by an owner or a tenant. If the removal causes damage or injury, the premises must be restored to their original condition. Trade fixtures which have been installed by a tenant as necessary for his particular use to earn income, or which have been so designated by an agreement between the parties, should be removed from the rented premises before the expiration of the lease. Those fixtures, which are not removed as prescribed, may become the property of the landlord as "abandoned."

MINERAL, OIL & GAS RIGHTS

95   Things contained in the land, such as coal, oil, minerals, etc., are real property until they are taken from the ground when they become personal property. A landowner may convey the land containing, or thought to contain, such materials without reservation, in which event the person to whom the parcel is conveyed acquires the right to such substances. Alternatively, the landowner may convey the land and reserve, in the grant deed, the right to all minerals contained therein, including oil, by a provision in the deed often referred to as a reservation or an exception.

96   When such rights have been reserved by the grantor in the conveyancing instrument, the "reserving" party has an implied easement to enter upon the conveyed land for the purpose of extracting the substances which he reserved, unless the reservation specifically states "without right of surface entry."

EMBLEMENTS

97   Emblements can be identified as fructus naturales or fructus industriales. Fructus naturales would be trees, shrubs, vines and crops that are produced by nature alone, and are ordinarily considered to be a part of the land to which they are attached until they are removed, at which time they become personal property. Fructus naturales can be owned separately from the land. California Law provides that for purposes of sale, things attached to the land that are agreed to be severed before sale, or are under contract of sale, are to be treated as goods, and governed by the rules regulating the sale of goods, which are personal property.

98   The term "emblements" is more frequently applied to crops such as grain, garden vegetables, fruit from orchards, and other growing crops that are the fruit or result of annual labor and industry. The latter are classed as fructus industriales and may be either real or personal property depending upon the circumstances in each case. When considering the buyer and seller of land where there are such crops, these crops are a part of the land until they are removed either physically or by agreement and their ownership will pass to the grantee (buyer) by a conveyance of the land to another. An agreement between the seller and buyer could change this understanding. Such

industrial crops are sold ordinarily by abiding by the code provisions regulating the sale of goods.

99   Between tenant and landlord, emblements are owned by the tenant, since they are the result of efforts of the tenant.

ACQUISITION & TRANSFER OF PROPERTY

99a   Throughout the years of growth in our capitalistic society, the relative nonliquidity of real estate as a form of capital continues to be the economic Achilles' heel of real estate investments. A person investing in real estate accepts such a fact and pays much more attention to the amount of his investment, to the cash flow the venture will produce, and the protection offered by urban land holdings and their capital improvement through inflationary trends. Downturn in California real estate prices does not affect the long-term investor who has a 10 to 15 year goal of either holding or exchanging the property.

103   The principal rights an owner has in property is:
   (1) The right to occupy and use
   (2) To sell in whole or in part
   (3) Refuse to sell, rent or lease
   (4) Grant easements
   (5) Give, abandon, improve
   (6) Devise by will
   (7) Exclude others from using it
The owner of the title also has the right not to take any of these actions. All of the above rights are commonly known as the "bundle of rights."

DEED AND DELIVERY

105   When ownership of real property, or an interest in it, is transferred from one person to another, it is usually accomplished through a document called a deed. A deed is not a contract. It is a conveyancing instrument.

106   There are many kinds of deeds including: grant deed, quitclaim deed, gift deed, tax deed, etc. Whatever the type, the purpose of a deed is to pass or "convey" title to real property. A deed is often referred to as a "conveyance." To "alienate" the title also means to transfer it, as by deed. The opposite of alienation is acquisition.

107   In addition to the obvious need for competent parties, a valid deed must:
   (1) Be in writing.
   (2) Contain the identity, by name or designated in such a way that it can be determined with certainty who the (grantor and grantee) are.
   (3) Have a granting clause.
   (4) Give a proper description of the property.
   (5) Be signed by the grantor. However, a deed need not be acknowledged to be valid.

109   Identity of the Parties - the grantor must be competent to convey and the grantee capable of receiving the grant of the title and the identity of these parties must be included in the deed. Should the name of the grantor change during the course of holding title the new deed must be signed identifying the grantor as both.

109a   A deed to a fictitious person is void. However, a deed to an actual person by a name that he has assumed is valid. Thus, a distinction must be made between a fictitious name (valid), and a fictitious person (void). A deed is also valid even though the grantee is not named, but is adequately described. A deed to "the wife" of a named person is valid; to a person by the name of his office such as "the pastor" of a named church is valid; a conveyance to "all the children" of a specified person is valid.

110   Granting Clause - A deed must contain an action word or phrase denoting the intent of the grantor to convey the

property to the grantee. A deed may read: "I hereby convey," "transfer," "quitclaim," "deed," or "grant." On the other hand, in a gift deed, "give" serves this purpose. These are words of transfer and each kind of deed has its own special granting clause.

112a An ambiguity in a legal description of land on the face of a deed would be described as a patent ambiguity or defect. If the defect can be discovered only by reference to something other than the instrument, the ambiguity would be called latent. The ambiguity could create a cloud on the title to the property and could negate the effectiveness of the deed. Parole or extrinsic evidence referring to admissible verbal evidence to clarify the ambiguity could cure it. There are numerous court cases where additional evidence has been accepted to remove an uncertainty in the description in a deed.

113 Signature of Grantor - The person signing the deed is known as the grantor. The party or parties making the conveyance of the premises must sign a deed. If there is more than one owner all must sign. Both man and wife must sign deeds to community property. All owners in a joint tenancy must sign to convey title to the entire holding. The same is true of tenants in common or partnership holdings, except that one may be appointed to act for the others and thus convey the property. If corporate property is sold the corporation bylaws and constitution would indicate the names of the grantees who received the deed and who would become the grantors upon a sale of the corporate property.

114 A forged deed is always void, even in the hands of an innocent purchaser.

DELIVERY

115 A deed, even though valid, is of no effect unless delivered and accepted. Government deeds such as tax deeds and trustee's deeds as well as reconveyance deeds that clear the record must be recorded thus providing constructive notice of the transaction or event.

116 Generally speaking, signing and delivery of a deed transfers title. Whether or not there has been a delivery sufficient to pass title depends upon the intention of the grantor. Delivery, used in this connection, means more than simply turning over physical possession of the deed. The grantor must have the intention to pass title. Lacking intention to deliver title does not pass.

119 Recording the deed in the county recorder's office, thus putting the title of record in the grantee's name, even though the grantee may not have seen the document, would ordinarily be interpreted as evidence of a valid delivery of the deed and the title. Keep in mind that such a presumption is refutable in court with the presentation of sufficient evidence for the court to determine otherwise. The legal principle is, "an unrecorded deed is valid between the parties but invalid as to any subsequent recorded interests without notice."

126 Consideration - It will be noted that consideration is not listed as one of the essentials to a valid deed. The law presumes some kind of consideration for the transfer. Frequently a deed will state "for one dollar and other valuable consideration" to avoid mentioning the actual purchase price, but even this is not required to make the deed valid. However, lack of consideration could be of material concern where the rights of third persons are involved and lack of consideration may adversely affect the conveyance.

128 Acknowledgement - A county recorder's office will not accept a deed for recording unless it has been acknowledged. This means that the person who executes (signs) the deed transferring his property to another, must appear before a duly

authorized officer and acknowledge (admit) he signed the deed of his own free will. The law requires this acknowledgment to protect the owner from having unwarranted or unauthorized instruments filed against his title, without his knowledge or consent.

ASSIGNMENT PROHIBITED

131   A deed is non-assignable. It is not a contract. It is a conveyancing instrument. It can only be used once and therefor cannot be assigned to another party. If the property is sold a new deed must be made. The reason for this is that a deed must be signed by the grantor. If a person has received a deed in which he is named as the grantee, he cannot hand that deed to another person to affect a transfer. He becomes a grantor and must sign a new deed. This rule applies even where the title is being conveyed back to the original grantor.

GRANT DEED

133   A deed in which the grantor uses only the words "I grant" as the action or transfer word is called a grant deed. A grant deed is used only once. It is not an assignable or negotiable instrument. By reason of the magic word "grant" exclusively this deed carries certain implied warranties as to the condition of the title which is not carried by other types of deeds. When a grantor uses the words "I grant" he is in effect warranting (guaranteeing) that:
    (1) He has not already conveyed the title to the property to any other person.
    (2) That the estate conveyed is free from encumbrances, except for those disclosed to the grantee.

A grant deed also conveys any after-acquired title, if any involved. This means that if the grantor subsequently acquires any title or claim of title to the real property which the grantor has by implication claimed to grant in fee simple, any acquired interest passes by operation of law to the grantee or

the grantee's successors in interest. The after acquired title would pass to the trustee as additional security. Note that the grantor does not warrant that he owns the title. In California the title insurance policy is generally demanded by the buyer for this assurance of receiving title.

QUITCLAIM DEED

135   In this type of deed the grantor merely relinquishes any right or claim he has to the property. If he has absolute ownership he conveys absolute ownership. If he has no actual claim or right in the property the quitclaim deed transfers nothing. The granting clause contains the words "I quitclaim", meaning I quit any claim I have on the title to this property.

136   Usually, quitclaim deeds are used to clear a land contract or some "cloud", "color of title", lis pendens action, or some minor defect which needs to be removed in order to perfect the title. The party of record signs a quitclaim deed.

137   A lis pendens is a Latin expression meaning "litigation pending." It is recorded to cloud the title in a lawsuit affecting real property. The lis pendens is effective until judgment has been rendered and the appeal period has expired or the plaintiff rescinds it by quitclaim deed, or the court dismisses it. To record a lis pendens action there must be evidence of litigation.

138   Any conditions revealed by a title search which affect the title to property (usually relatively unimportant items) but which cannot be removed without a quitclaim deed or court quiet title action is a "cloud on the title".

140   A court action brought to establish title or to remove a cloud on title is called a quiet title action. In the event a quiet title action is necessary, it may take a considerable length of time for the court proceedings should the

purchaser choose to contest the action (e.g., a contestant claiming title under adverse possession).

141   There are no implied warranties in a quitclaim deed. It guarantees nothing, not even that the grantor owns the property or any interest in it. It does not convey after-acquired title. It is often used as a quick solution to a quiet title action.

GIFT DEED

142   A grantor may make a gift of the property to the grantee using a grant deed or quitclaim deed. He may, but need not, say the transfer is made in consideration of "love and affection." A gift deed is valid unless made to defraud creditors in which event it may be voided by the creditors. The granting clause contains the word "give" or some similar word.

OTHER TYPES OF DEEDS

149   Warranty Deed - A deed used to convey real property, which contains express warranties of title and quiet possession. The grantor agrees to defend title to the premises against apparently lawful claims of third persons. It is used commonly in other states but not in California, where it has been supplanted by the grant deed. The modern practice of securing title insurance has reduced the importance of warranty deeds.

150   Trust Deed - Conveys bare legal title (but no possession) of a property to a trustee (third party) as security for a loan and differs from other deeds in that only "legal title" is conveyed. A trust deed is a "security device", in the nature of a lien, but differs from other deeds in that the trust deed, and the note for which it was given as security, may be assigned.

152   Patent - A grant from a sovereign. In American law, the instrument by which a state or government grants public land to an individual.

QUESTIONS ON GRANT DEEDS

1. Does the fact that the amount of consideration is not stated make the deal invalid?
   No - A statement of consideration is not essential to a deed.

2. Is the property description sufficient to be recorded as a valid deed?
   Yes - The deed may be valid for recording purposes, but not for title insurance purposes.

3. Can this deed be recorded?
   Yes - Under recording laws, where two or more persons execute an instrument by which property rights are affected, such instruments are entitled to be recorded if acknowledged by any one of such persons.

4. What would be the effect if buyers do not record?
   Title would remain of record in the grantor's name. The buyer runs the risk of losing title to an innocent third party.

5. Is the deed properly signed?
   Yes - Both grantors, husband and wife, have signed. Ordinarily, grantees do not sign.

6. How is title vested by this deed?
   As community property if not stated.

RECORDING REQUESTED BY:

WHEN RECORDED MAIL TO:

Jonathan and Margaret Brown
P.O. Box 515
San Bernardino, California

SPACE ABOVE THIS LINE FOR RECORDER'S USE

APN: 1234-567-890   **GRANT DEED**

THE UNDERSIGNED GRANTOR(S) DECLARE(S):
    DOCUMENTARY TRANSFER TAX is $22.00   CITY TAX is $22.00
    ☒ computed on the full value of the property conveyed, or
    ☐ computed on full value less value of liens or encumbrances remaining at the time of sale,
    ☐ Realty not sold
    ☐ Unincorporated area   ☐ City of   , and

FOR A VALUABLE CONSIDERATION, receipt of which is hereby acknowledged,
Five Hundred Thousand Dollars ($500,000)

hereby GRANT(S) to JOHNATHAN and MARGARET Brown, husband and wife

the following described real property in the County of San Bernardino State of California:

As shown in Exhibit "A" attached hereto and made a part hereof, and commonly known as The Norton Ranch, situated in Section 16. Twp In. Range IE, San Bernardino B&M

Dated: 1/1/2014

STATE OF CALIFORNIA   }
COUNTY OF San Bernardino   }ss

On January 1, 2014   before me

John Doe   , Notary Public,

personally appeared Sam Smith

Sam Smith
Sam Smith
Sally Smith
Sally Smith

who proved to me on the basis of satisfactory evidence to be the person(s) whose name(s) is/are subscribed to the within instrument and acknowledged to me that he/she/they executed the same in his/her/their authorized capacity(ies), and that by his/her/their signature(s) on the instrument the person(s), or the entity upon behalf of which the person(s) acted, executed the instrument.

I certify under PENALTY OF PERJURY under the laws of the State of California that the foregoing paragraph is true and correct.

WITNESS my hand and official seal.

Signature *Joe Doe*

SPACE BELOW RESERVED FOR NOTARY SEAL

JOHN DOE
COMM. #9999999
NOTARY PUBLIC - CALIFORNIA
SAN BERNARDINO COUNTY
My Comm. Expires Jan 12, 2009

OTHER METHODS OF ACQUIRING
TITLE WITHOUT A DEED

ADVERSE POSSESSION

153   Adverse Possession - a method of acquiring title to property without a deed. Before this law was codified and written into the California statutes, title could be obtained by adverse possession by the adverse possessor using the property for 20 years.

156   Open and Notorious Occupancy - Physical occupation and use of the property as if it were owned by the adverse possessor is required. If it is a residence, he must live in it. If a farm, he must farm it, fence it, etc. Personal occupation is not essential. Possession may be by a tenant of the person claiming adverse possession. In any case, the occupancy must be adverse and hostile to the owner.

158   Payment of Property Taxes - During the preceding five-year period, the adverse possessor must pay the real property taxes on the property as they become due. The fact that the record owner is also paying the taxes would not mean that the adverse possessor had not complied with this requirement.

159   Over a period of years the laws of California have been interpreted that land held for public use cannot be taken under a claim of adverse possession.

161   Accession - Acquisition of title by accession may also be in the form of accretion where, from natural causes, land forms by imperceptible degrees upon the bank of a river or stream caused by the action of the water in washing up sand, earth, and other materials on the shore. The added land becomes the property of the owner of the waterfront property.

DEDICATION

168   Recordation - The last act required to accomplish statutory dedication is the recording of the map with the offer and acceptance attached. If not recorded, dedication has not taken place.

ESCHEAT

171   The state may acquire the property of persons dying without a will and without heirs by a method called escheat. The title is said to "revert to the state." The deceased must leave no heirs or have only alien heirs who do not reside in this country and who are citizens of a country which does not allow United States citizens to inherit property located in that country. However, the process of escheat is not automatic. Legal proceedings must be held, instituted either by an action filed by the Attorney General, or by decree or distribution by the probate court. Once there has been such legal action, the distribution or decree does not become final for five years, during which time a claimant may bring legal proceedings to recover or "redeem" the property. Where the state gains title by escheat and later sells the property, the grantee receives   a   State   Comptroller's   deed.

175   Public buildings which have been acquired through eminent domain action occasionally must be disposed of by public authority. Such sales are usually conducted by sealed bids.

Public notice is given inviting sealed bids for the purchase of excess public lands. The notice sets a date on which the bids will be opened. The sale will be concluded with the person submitting the highest sealed bid.

BANKRUPTCY PROCEEDINGS

178 A liquidation proceeding, ordinarily referred to as a "straight bankruptcy", is introduced under Chapter 7 of the Bankruptcy Act. Such proceedings can be initiated voluntarily by the bankrupt party or involuntarily by the action of the bankrupt's creditors. In these proceedings, debtors disclose all the assets they own (the bankruptcy estate) and deliver them to the bankruptcy trustee. The ownership of these assets passes to the trustee. The trustee identifies certain property which the debtor can retain and then administers, liquidates and distributes the remaining assets to the benefit of the creditors.

179   Bankruptcy law provides a means for establishing the relative rights of creditors, for recovering any preferential payments made to creditors or improper transfers of property to others, and for setting aside any preferential liens obtained by creditors. What normally happens is that if bankrupt parties have been honest in their business dealings and in the bankruptcy proceedings, and there are no objections from creditors, they are usually given a discharge (relieved) of their debts. This relief is effective as of the date of the discharge by the bankruptcy court.

180   The filing of a bankruptcy petition operates as an automatic stay (effective as of the date of filing to certain kinds of creditors' actions against the bankrupt debtors or their property. Some of these would be:

181   (1) Actions to begin or continue judicial proceedings against the debtor.

182   (2) Actions to create, perfect, or enforce a lien against the debtor's property (foreclosure actions) without court permission.

183   (3) Actions to set off indebtedness owed the debtor that arose before the start of the bankruptcy proceeding.

184   You should recognize that certain obligations are not affected by the discharge of a bankrupt debtor. Among non-dischargeable debts would be:

185   (1) Debts due as a tax or fine to any federal, state or local government unit.
186   (2) Debts which result from liabilities for obtaining money by false pretenses and misrepresentation.

187   (3) Debts which are due for alimony or child support.

188   (4) Debts not scheduled in time for proof because the creditor was not notified of the bankruptcy proceeding even though the debtor knew that he owed the money to the creditor.

188a (5) Debts incurred after the bankruptcy proceeding was initiated.

189   Should bankrupt debtors transfer property or incur obligations with intent to hinder, delay, or defraud creditors, such transfers are voidable by the bankruptcy trustee. Examples of this would be transfers of property for less than its reasonable value within a year of filing the petition in bankruptcy.

Lesson Three
Part Two
Study Questions

_____(Lesson Three - Paragraph 77 – Question 1)_____

Legally, property is:
(A) Real that is tangible. (B) Personal fixtures. (C) Personal, if not real. (D) All of the above.

(C) Property is defined in California Civil Code as "the thing of which there may be ownership." Items capable of ownership that are fixed in character are identified as real property. Everything other than real property is identified as personal property.

_____(Lesson Three - Paragraph 77 – Question 2)_____

The right to use, possess, enjoy, transfer and dispose of a thing to the exclusion of others best defines:
(A) An estate. (B) Real estate.   (C) Ownership.   (D) Equity.

of consideration is not essential to a deed. of consideration is not essential to a deed.
(C) Identifies ownership.

_____(Lesson Three - Paragraph 78 – Question 1)_____

The principal difference between real property and personal property is:
(A) Value. (B) Permanence. (C) Length of life. (D) Mobility.

(D) The principal difference between real and personal property is mobility.

_____(Lesson Three - Paragraph 79/3 – Question 1)_____

The following is generally classified as real property:
(A) Unpicked fruit sold on a contract.   (B) Stock in a mutual water company.
(C) Minerals that have been extracted from the ground. (D) Cultivated annual crops.

(B) That which is appurtenant to the land is classified as real property. A mutual water company is owned by the land owners it serves and the stock in the company represents water rights of the land. This stock runs with the land, meaning that when the land is transferred, the stock must be transferred with the land.

_____(Lesson Three - Paragraph 79/3 – Question 2)_____

Stock in a mutual water company:
(A) Requires a separate written contract to convey to the buyer.
(B) Is appurtenant to land and thus automatically transfers to the buyer.
(C) Must be mentioned in the deed in order to transfer it to the buyer.
(D) Must be owned as tenants in common.

(B) Stock is evidence of ownership. Stock in a mutual water company is evidence of ownership of water rights. When a property that has stock in a water company appurtenant to it, the stock transfers with the ownership transfer.

_____(Lesson Three - Paragraph 80 – Question 1)_____

Property may be real or personal. An example of property that is classified as real is:
(A) Wheat growing on leased land.　　　(B) A grape crop that has been mortgaged.
(C) Kitchen cabinets in a mobile home.　　(D) A stand of virgin timber.

(D) "Standing timber," that is, trees attached to the ground by roots, is real property answers (A), (B), and (C) are examples of personal property.

_____(Lesson Three - Paragraph 80 – Question 2)_____

The following is real property:
(A) Leasehold.　　(B)　Chattel real.　　(C) Debts.　　(D) Planted trees.

(D) In the four choices, there are personal property, leasehold, and chattel real. Chattel real is another name for a leasehold indicating it is a personal property interest in real property. In real property, debts such as those evidenced by a note and deed of trust are personal property. Planted trees indicate the tree has been affixed to the land; therefore, it is real property.

_____(Lesson Three - Paragraph 81 – Question 1)_____

The legal concept of the limits or boundaries of real property is defined as:
(A) The surface of land and the material of the earth whether soil roots, or other substance.
(B) The surface of land and sufficient of the sub-surface to construct improvements on the land.
(C) The surface of land, material of the earth and sufficient air space to construct buildings on the land.
(D) From the center of the earth upward to the limits of the sky.

(D) Real property consists of not only the surface of the land, but also includes the airspace above and the materials of the earth below the surface. One classic definition of the boundaries of real property is: "the boundaries of any parcel of land extend in the shape of an inverted pyramid from the center of the earth upward to the limits of the sky." Courts in modern times have permitted the public use of the air above private land, as a highway in the sky, so long as such use does not interfere with the landowner's use of his property.

_____(Lesson Three - Paragraph 82 – Question 1)_____

An example of personal property is:
(A) Fructus naturales. (B) A load of gravel. (C) A fixture. (D) An easement appurtenant.

(B) All property that is not real property is personal property. A load of gravel has been removed from the land, is moveable, and consequently is classified as personal property. All of the others are real property. (A) Fructus Naturales defines crops that are a product of nature alone generally classify as real property - trees, bushes, etc. (C) A fixture is attached to the land and is real property.

_____(Lesson Three - Paragraph 82a – Question 1)_____

Personal property provides difficulties for real estate brokers because it:
(A) Can be hypothecated. (B) Can be alienated. (C) Could become real property. (D) All of the above.

(D) Personal property can be hypothecated, alienated, and can become real property. It can be placed as security, sold, and it can become a fixture when affixed to real property.

_____(Lesson Three - Paragraph 83 – Question 1)_____

Mortgages and trust deeds are:
(A) Personal property without exception. (B) Chattels real.
(C) Real property in most cases.   (D) Always real property.

(A) Although mortgages and trust deeds are legally tied to real property the instruments themselves are considered to be personal property.

_____(Lesson Three - Paragraph 83 – Question 2)_____

The following is generally considered personal property:
(A) A land appurtenance.   (B) Mineral rights. (C) An existing mortgage. (D) Growing trees in a forest.

(C) A mortgage is a contractual agreement and is always considered to be personal property. The other choices suggest examples of items that are generally considered real property.

_____(Lesson Three - Paragraph 84 – Question 1)_____

John Smith adds some cabinets to the home that he owns. The method of construction he uses permanently attaches the cabinets to the home. The cabinets become real property because John has:
(A) Created an encumbrance.   (B) Incorporated the cabinets into the land.
(C) Created a lien.   (D) Attached the cabinets to the chattel real.

(B) A fixture is defined as anything that becomes attached to the land. A tree, fence, or home becomes a fixture when attached to the land. When items are attached to the home, such as garbage disposals, kitchen fixtures, bathroom fixtures, or cabinets, they too become attached to the land.

_____(Lesson Three - Paragraph 84 – Question 2)_____

When personal property is made a part of real property, it becomes a:
(A) Fixture. (B) Appurtenance. (C) Inclusion. (D) Attachment.

(A) A fixture is a tangible thing that previously was personal property and which has been attached to land or a structure attached to land in such a way as to become a part of the real property.

_____(Lesson Three - Paragraph 87 – Question 1)_____

An investor purchased a property that had a well with a pump. For purposes of real property taxation
the well and pump would be assessed as:

(A) Personal property. (B) Improvements to real property. (C) Exempt from taxation. (D) Part of the land.

(B) When the pump is installed it is no longer personal property but becomes a fixture. Consequently, it would be assessed as an improvement to the land.

_____(Lesson Three - Paragraph 91 – Question 1)_____
The following is not a test of a fixture:
(A) Agreement. (B) Intention. (C) Cost of the item. (D) Annexation.

(C) Remember the tests of a fixture: The adaptability of the item, the intention of the person attaching, the method of attachment, and agreement between the parties. The cost of an item is not the test of a fixture.

_____(Lesson Three - Paragraph 91 – Question 2)_____
All of the following are factors that can be used in determining that personal property becomes real property, except:
(A) Agreement between the parties involved. (B) Permanence of annexation of the item.
(C) Cost of the item.   (D) Relationship between the parties involved.

(C) Agreement between the parties involved, the method of attachment effecting permanency and the relationship between the parties are standard tests used to determine the intention of the person attaching the property.

_____(Lesson Three - Paragraph 94 – Question 1)_____
All of the following are considered to "run with the land", except:
(A) Fences. (B) Buildings. (C) Trade fixtures. (D) Stock in mutual water company.

(C) Trade fixtures are articles affixed by a tenant "for purposes of trade, manufacture, ornament, or domestic use," and may be removed unless by nature or by agreement they have become part of the premises. They, as such, are not appurtenant to real property.

_____(Lesson Three - Paragraph 94 – Question 2)_____
Upon the termination of a lease, trade fixtures can usually:
(A) Be removed by the tenant if removal can be effected without damage.
(B) Be removed only by written consent of the lessor.
(C) Be sold by the lessor.
(D) Be removed by the tenant only if he reimburses the lessor for their value.

(A) The tenant may remove personal property affixed to real property for the purpose of trade, manufacture, business, etc., if the removal can be effected without damage to the property, or if such damage is repaired and the property restored to its original condition.

_____(Lesson Three - Paragraph 95 – Question 1)_____
Unless otherwise specified, the rights to minerals which lie beneath the surface of land:
(A) Are automatically transferred with the sale of the real property.
(B) Cannot be leased.
(C) Are kept by the original owner.
(D) Cannot be conveyed apart from the real estate surrounding the minerals.

(A) Minerals are defined as real property while they remain un-mined. They are transferred with the real property unless specifically reserved in the deed.

_____(Lesson Three - Paragraph 95 – Question 2)_____

An exception in a grant deed:
(A) Withdraws part of the property from the grant.
(B) Gives the grantee special privileges.
(C) Has no effect on the value of the property.
(D) Would make the deed invalid as to future grantees.

(A) When a grantor retains the mineral, oil and gas rights in a property he is conveying, or when he retains an easement over a portion of the property, he reserves or excerpts (withdraws) a part of that property from the grant. The grantee then would not have full use of the property, and this could, in some instances, affect its value.

_____(Lesson Three - Paragraph 98 – Question 1)_____

Johnson owned a farm property on which he was growing a crop of corn. Before the harvest he sold the property to Hanson. It was his intention to harvest the crop after the sale even though this was not stated in the sales agreement. The following would most likely be true regarding the corn crop:
(A) Johnson would have the right to harvest the crop, as this was his intention.
(B) The crop would go with the land as it is considered real property.
(C) Johnson's intent would take precedence over the sales agreement.
(D) Hanson cannot claim the crop as it would be considered personal property.

(B) Growing crops on land are presumed to go with land when the land is sold unless other agreements have been made.

_____(Lesson Three - Paragraph 98 – Question 2)_____

The following may not always be classified as real property:
(A) Land. (B) Improvements affixed to the land. (C) Seasonal crops. (D) Appurtenant easements.

(C) Seasonal crops even when still on the vine or tree are often sold before harvested and would be considered personal property. These same crops are often mortgaged before the growing season and would be considered personal property.

_____(Lesson Three - Paragraph 103 – Question 1)_____

You may do which of the following with real property when you have the complete "bundle of rights."
(A) Possess, sell or lease.   (B) Enter into an enforceable listing contract, not in writing.
(C) Give away, will or anything else. (D) Both A and C.

(D) The "bundle of rights" is the exclusive right of a person to own, possess, use, enjoy and dispose of personal or real property consistent with the law.

_____(Lesson Three - Paragraph 103 – Question 2)_____

The active operation of residential income property generally is controlled by the:
(A) Trustee's interest. (B) Creditor's interest. (C) Vendor's interest. (D) Equity interest.

(D)   The owner would control the property. The owner is the equity interest mentioned in this question.

_____(Lesson Three - Paragraph 105 – Question 1)_____
The primary purpose of a deed is to:
(A) Move title.   (B) Encumber a property.
(C) Secure a lien on a property. (D) Grant a person the use of a property, but not to have title to it.

(A) The primary purpose of the deed is to move title.

_____(Lesson Three - Paragraph 105 – Question 2)_____
In the following instance, title is passed to the buyer of real property when there already is a first trust
deed lien against the property:
(A) With the recording of a reconveyance deed.
(B) With the permission of the beneficiary for the assumption of the existing loan.
(C) With the grantor issuing a grant deed to the buyer.
(D) None of the above.

(C) The owner issuing the new owner a proper instrument in writing --- a grant deed in this case normally passes title.

_____(Lesson Three - Paragraph 106 – Question 1)_____
To alienate title to real property one would:
(A) Encumber it. (B) Cloud the title. (C) Place a homestead on the property. (D) Convey the title.

(D) The term "alienate" means to transfer or convey. To alienate title means to convey it.

_____(Lesson Three - Paragraph 106 – Question 2)_____
The following word is most nearly the opposite of alienation:
(A) Acceleration. (B) Amortization. (C) Acquisition. (D) Avulsion.

(C) "Alienate" means to transfer property to another. "Acquisition" means to acquire - to come into possession.

_____(Lesson Three - Paragraph 107 – Question 1)_____
An inventory of the buildings and improvements to real property are required in:
(A) A deed.   (B) A land contract/installment sales contract.
(C) A title insurance policy. (D) None of the above.

(D) In all of the above instruments the land is described, not the improvements. When title to land is conveyed, the fixtures (items attached to the land) and appurtenances (easement rights, water rights) run with the land, even though not described in the conveyance instrument.

_____(Lesson Three - Paragraph 107 – Question 2)_____

Concerning a deed used in the transfer of title from the seller to buyer, the following would be effective to convey title, except:
(A) A deed made to Jeb Stuart under his assumed name of Chauncey Cartwright.
(B) A deed made to Franklin and Dolly Madison.
(C) A deed made to Andrew Jackson and his wife.
(D) A deed made to John Hamilton or Harry Winkler.

___

(D) A deed must be made to a specific grantee. The "or" found in this choice makes it too indefinite.

_____(Lesson Three - Paragraph 109 – Question 2)_____

Mary Thomas, a single woman, bought an apartment building in her name only. Three years later, she married Bill Jones and they purchased a home in their names as joint tenants. Mary then sold the apartment building to Barnie, signing the deed as "Mary Jones." This could result in:
(A) Bill becoming the owner of the apartment building due to the right of survivorship.
(B) Bill becoming the owner of half of the apartment building due to community property.
(C) A cloud on the title.
(D) Mary still owning the apartment building.

___

(C) The record shows the recorded owner of the property to be Mary Thomas, a single woman. If Mary Jones attempts to transfer title, there would be a cloud on the recorded title. Signing the deed "Mary Jones, formally Mary Thomas," could avert this.

_____(Lesson Three - Paragraph 114 – Question 1)_____

A deed would not be valid if:
(A) A person serving time in prison executed it. (B) It is a forged deed held by equitable buyer.
(C) The grantee is 18 and unmarried.   (D) Consideration was not paid.

___

(B) A person serving time in prison has the capacity to deed their interest in real property, consideration is presumed in a deed, and the status of the grantee has no effect on the validity of a deed. A forged deed always is void, regardless of who holds it.

_____(Lesson Three - Paragraph 114 – Question 2)_____

The following would cause a deed to be void from its inception:
(A) An incompetent grantee.   (B) A grantee using an assumed name.
(C) A legal description was not used to describe the property. (D) A forged deed.

___

(D) The conditions stated in choices (A), (B), & (C) do not result in void deed. With reference to (A), a grantee must be capable of receiving title, but need not be competent. For example, a deed to a deceased person is void.

_____(Lesson Three - Paragraph 115 – Question 1)_____

All of the following must be recorded to be effective, except:
(A) Reconveyance deed. (B) Tax deed. (C) Trustee's deed. (D) Trust deed.

___

(D) To be effective a trust deed must be properly delivered to the person to whom it is directed. Recording of a trust deed would be good evidence that a proper delivery has been made but it is not a necessary requirement. All of the other suggested documents must be recorded to be effective.

_____(Lesson Three - Paragraph 115 – Question 2)_____

A grant deed passes title when it is:
(A) Executed. (B) Delivered. (C) Recorded. (D) Acknowledged.

(B) The grant deed passes title upon delivery. Delivery may be manual or recorded. A manual delivery would convey title and the deed could be recorded several weeks later. The purpose of the recording would be to create constructive notice of the prior delivery.

_____(Lesson Three - Paragraph 116 – Question 1)_____

For the delivery of a deed to be effective, it must have clear evidence of:
(A) Recordation. (B) Intention. (C) Acknowledgment. (D) The legal description of the property.

(B) To be effective it must be shown that the grantor intended to pass title to the grantee.

_____(Lesson Three - Paragraph 116 – Question 2)_____

Effective delivery of a deed depends upon the:
(A) Knowledge of its existence by the grantee. (B) Mere physical transfer of the deed to grantee.
(C) Intention of the grantor.   (D) Prior acknowledgment of grantor's signature.

(C) When a deed is delivered by mistake or without authority, there is no intention to transfer the title and therefore, no title is transferred.

_____(Lesson Three - Paragraph 119 – Question 1)_____

A quitclaim deed was executed by Mr. Smith and delivered to Mr. Brown. Mr. Brown did not record
his deed. The failure to record would most probably make the deed:
(A) Invalid as between the parties, and valid as to third parties with constructive notice.
(B) Invalid as between the parties and invalid as to third parties with constructive notice.
(C) Valid as between the parties and valid as to subsequent recorded interests without notice.
(D) Valid as between the parties and invalid as to subsequent recorded interests without notice.

(D) The legal principle involved is, "an unrecorded deed is valid between the parties but invalid as to any subsequent recorded interests without notice."

_____(Lesson Three - Paragraph 119 – Question 2)_____

A grantor executed a deed. He acknowledged and recorded the deed. Later, he changed his mind and wanted to rescind the transaction. Considering these circumstances, the following is the correct statement:
(A) He may withdraw from the transaction, as the deed was not delivered.
(B) Recordation implies delivery.
(C) The deed was not valid, as it was not recorded by the grantee.
(D) The grantee may withdraw if the deed is still in his possession.

(B) This question illustrates the principle that recording presumes delivery. A refutable presumption is a rule of law that the court will draw a particular conclusion from a particular fact unless the truth of that conclusion is disproved. In this case, the court would conclude the deed to have been delivered unless the grantor could prove it was not his intention to deliver title.

_____(Lesson Three - Paragraph 128 – Question 1)_____
The following is not required for a valid deed:
(A) A grantor. (B) A grantee. (C) Property description. (D) An acknowledgment.

(D) The question is a negative question. An acknowledgment is not required for a deed to be valid. Acknowledgment is required for recording a deed. A deed is valid between the parties even though not recorded. The other choices are requirements for a valid deed.

_____(Lesson Three - Paragraph 128 – Question 2)_____
All of the following are essential to a valid deed, except:
(A) It must be in writing.
(B) Parties must be competent to convey and capable of receiving the grant of the property.
(C) There must be a granting clause.
(D) It must be acknowledged.

(D) A deed does not have to be acknowledged to be valid. It must be acknowledged to be recorded. The other choices suggest items that are necessary for a valid deed.

_____(Lesson Three - Paragraph 131 – Question 1)_____
The following is not assignable:
(A) A trust deed. (B) A grant deed. (C) A broker's commission. (D) A real property sales contract.

(B) Full title instruments are not assignable. A trust deed is assignable because it is a security device only and not specifically a title instrument.

_____(Lesson Three - Paragraph 135 – Question 1)_____
A quitclaim deed conveys only the present right, title, and interest of the:
(A) Grantor. (B) Servient tenement. (C) Grantee. (D) Property.

(A) A quitclaim deed conveys only the present rights of the owner, not the future rights he may obtain. The person signing the quitclaim deed is known as the grantor. The person receiving any rights is the grantee.

_____(Lesson Three - Paragraph 136 – Question 1)_____
Blackacre is sold on a land contract. The seller records the contract of sale. Later the buyer defaults. If a quitclaim deed is used to clear title, the person signing it would be the:
(A) Buyer. (B) Seller. (C) Trustee. (D) Beneficiary.

(A) The question deals with a sale of land on a recorded contract of sale. A quitclaim deed is used to clear the title. The buyer would give the quitclaim deed to all of his interest in the property to the seller. The buyer's interests would be removed from the record by the recording of the quitclaim deed.

_____(Lesson Three - Paragraph 137 – Question 1)_____
A lis pendens is effective until:
(A) The plaintiff rescinds it. (B) Dismissed. (C) Final judgment by the court. (D) Any of the above.

(D) A lis pendens is a Latin expression meaning "litigation pending". It is recorded to cloud the title in a lawsuit affecting real property. It is effective until judgment has been rendered and the appeal period has expired, or the plaintiff rescinds it, or the court dismisses it.

_____(Lesson Three - Paragraph 137 – Question 2)_____
Regarding a lis pendens all of the following are true, except:
(A) If the owner of property is not involved in the litigation, the filing of a lis pendens would have no   effect on title to the property.
(B) May effect a change of title depending on the outcome of the lawsuit.
(C) May be removed only by court action.
(D) Lis pendens can be recorded on a property by anyone.

(D) Again this is a negative question. We are looking for the false statement and "D" is false. A lis pendens can be recorded only by the parties involved in a pending lawsuit involving title to real property. It is a common misconception that one may record a lis pendens involving such things as commission disputes.

_____(Lesson Three - Paragraph 138 – Question 1)_____
Vernon is a vendee in a recorded land contract of sale. He can no longer make the required monthly payments so he abandons the property. This most likely would result in:
(A) A cloud on title.   (B) The vendee would get his down payment back.
(C) No effect on the marketability of the title. (D) The vendor has no recourse.

(A) When a land contract of sale is recorded, it gives constructive notice to the world that the vendee has the right to the title to the property. If he abandons the property, the record continues to show that he has the right to the title and it could not be sold to someone else. This cloud on the title must be removed before sale by a quit claim deed from the former vendee or a court quiet title action.

_____(Lesson Three - Paragraph 138 – Question 2)_____
Vendor sells real property to vendee using a land contract of sale. The vendee records this instrument. The vendee has a poor record of making payments on the contract and is successful in avoiding the vendor. One night the vendee moves out and establishes residence in another state. The following would be correct:
(A) Negotiability of the instrument is not impaired.
(B) There is a cloud on vendor's title.
(C) A future purchaser would not be concerned about the disposition of this matter.
(C) None of the above.

(B) The recorded land contract would appear as a cloud on title until removed either by recording a quitclaim deed from vendee or by recording a judgment as the result of a quiet title action.

_____(Lesson Three - Paragraph 141 – Question 1)_____
A quiet title action usually refers to the following:
(A) Foreclosure on property.   (B) Foreclosure on a trust deed.
(C) Eminent domain.   (D) Removing a cloud on title or establishing title.

(D) A quiet title action is a court action filed to remove a cloud (or claim) or to establish title. This action must specifically involve title to real property.

_____(Lesson Three - Paragraph 141 – Question 2)_____
A properly executed quitclaim deed conveys:
(A) Two implied warranties.   (B) Any after-acquired title.
(C) A mere possibility not coupled with an interest. (D) Any existing interest in the property.

(D) Any existing interest in the property is conveyed by the use of a quitclaim deed. There are no implied warranties in the quitclaim deed. A grant deed conveys after-acquired title but not a quitclaim deed. You cannot convey the mere possibility of an interest.

_____(Lesson Three - Paragraph 149 – Question 1)_____
The following has generally brought about the infrequent use of the warranty deed in California:
(A) The abstract of title. (B) Title insurance. (C) The quitclaim deed. (D) The certificate of title.

(B) In states other than California, the grantor in the warranty deed specifically guarantees certain matters regarding title to the grantee. In California where the grant deed is used with its implied warranties, the additional protection of title insurance policy is in widespread use. The title insurance company, with approved financial stability, gives more adequate assurance to the grantee of the title that he is receiving than any individual grantor could give.

_____(Lesson Three - Paragraph 152 – Question 1)_____
A government land patent is:
(A) A deed. (B) A protection against copies. (C) A grant from the sovereign. (D) An original deed.

(C) A government patent is an instrument used by the government to transfer or convey real property title to individual owners.

_____(Lesson Three - Paragraph 156 – Question 1)_____
The following is not necessary to successfully acquire title of unimproved land by adverse possession:
(A) Minimum of five years occupancy. (B) Open and notorious use.
(C) Color of title or claim of right.   (D) Live on the property.

(D) If land is unimproved, it is difficult to live on the property unless it would be in a tent or trailer. This requirement is therefore waived when establishing a claim under adverse possession. You might use the property for farming or grazing and still satisfy the other requirements.

_____(Lesson Three - Paragraph 158 – Question 1)_____

All of the following are requisites of gaining title to real property by adverse possession, except:
(A) Must occupy the property hostile to the record owner.
(B) Must possess the property continuously for 5 years.
(C) Must pay the taxes for five years before they become delinquent.
(D) Must possess the property under some evidence of color of title or claim of right.

(C) Real estate taxes must be paid for the five years period of occupancy but not necessarily before they become delinquent each year.

_____(Lesson Three - Paragraph 161 – Question 1)_____

An example of acquiring real property by accession is:
(A) Adverse possession.   (B) Eminent domain.   (C) Police power.   (D) Accretion.

(D) Accession is the addition to property by improvement or by natural growth. Accretion is an addition to land by natural causes and would be an example of the application of the doctrine of accession.

_____(Lesson Three - Paragraph 168 – Question 2)_____

Proceedings to create an easement over a parcel of land by statutory dedication have been initiated.
The last act to be accomplished is:
(A) Eminent domain.   (B) Recordation of the final map.
(C) Acceptance by the governing body. (D) Approval of the planning commission.

(B) Statutory dedication proceedings follow this order:
    1. Submit a preliminary map.
    2. Make an offer of dedication.
    3. Receive an acceptance of offer of dedication.
    4. Record the final map.

_____(Lesson Three - Paragraph 168 – Question 1)_____

A statutory dedication of land for public use that gives the governmental body acquiring the parcel an easement, becomes effective by:
(A) Prescription.   (B) The government's power of eminent domain.
(C) Recording a subdivision map with the certificate of dedication & acceptance. (D) Reservation.

(C) The steps required to accomplish a dedication consist of a signed certificate of dedication executed by all parties of interest. This is submitted to the local governing body with a copy of the map. The local governing body signs an acceptance and all the documents are recorded. Dedication becomes effective at that point.

_____(Lesson Three - Paragraph 179 – Question 1)_____

Other than non-dischargeable debts, all provable debts of a bankrupt debtor are cut off (discharged) as of the date:
(A) Of filing the petition in bankruptcy. (B) Of the first meeting of creditors.
(C) Of the discharge in bankruptcy. (D) Of the publication of the notice of the petition in bankruptcy.

(C) In a bankruptcy, the debts are cut off or discharged as of the date the bankruptcy court issues

_____(Lesson Three - Paragraph 181, 182 – Question 1)_____
A person and his property that is encumbered by a first deed of trust are in Chapter 7 bankruptcy.
Under these circumstances the:
(A) Debtor can sell the property.
(B) Debtor need not make payments on the promissory note secured by the first deed of trust.
(C) Holder of the first deed of trust can foreclose.
(D) Court can sell the property and use the proceeds there from to pay debts owed to unsecured creditors.

(C) The trust deed is a voluntary lien, specifically naming a beneficiary. In bankruptcy, the court will release the property for foreclosure by the trustee named in the deed of trust. These funds will go to the beneficiary named in the trust deed.

Notes

Lesson Three
Part Three
Understanding Through Question Testing

Log into your course at www.lumbleau.com.

STUDENT LOGIN
Login: [   ]
Password: [   ]

On your student home page, click on the "State Exam Preparation".

STATE EXAM
PREPARATION

Under the "Guided Lesson" tab click on the third of fourteen links: "Acquisition and Transfer of Real Property".

Real Estate Salesperson Course

Guided Lessons   Practice Exams   Progress Report   Success Video

Print	Questions
Click	HERE>>> 3. Acquisition and Transfer of Real Property

Here you will be tested on all of the questions you have been studying and learn the most recently added questions. It is essential, for maximum retention, that you eliminate all of the questions you can easily answer and "TAG" for study the questions with which you have difficulty.

LESSON 4

PROPERTY AND ESTATES

Lesson Four
Part One
Understanding Through Video Teaching

Lesson Four
INTERESTS IN ESTATES

19   The term "estate" signifies the degree, quantity, nature, and extent of interest which a person may have in real property.

FEE SIMPLE ESTATE

22   This is the greatest ownership a person may have in real property. The outstanding characteristics of a fee simple estates are that it is inheritable, freely transferable and of indefinite duration.

24   When the owner of the fee (title) holds it without any qualification, it is called an estate in fee simple absolute. A fee simple absolute is free of any deed restrictions.

25   When the owner of the fee holds it with a qualification it is called a fee simple subject to a condition subsequent. The grantor has conveyed the land for "so long as" it is not used for the sale of alcoholic beverages. The former grantor must institute a court action before this condition can be enforced.

LIFE ESTATE

26   This is an estate in real property created by deed or devise (will) by which the grantee has all the rights of possession, use, and income during his life or the lives of other designated persons.

27   A life estate is a freehold estate. If the person giving the life estate designates that the title is to go to some other person upon the death of the life estate holder, the person so designated is said to be the "remainderman" and has an estate in remainder. If no designation of a remainderman is made, the estate that remains is called an estate in reversion and goes back to the previous owner or heirs.

28   A lease given, or a sale made on property which is held as a life estate, terminates upon the death of the holder of the life estate. It is not binding upon the holder of the estate in reversion or in remainder.

29   It is also possible for a life estate holder to encumber the property by making it security for a loan but such encumbrance would not be effective against the property when he dies. A lender (if one could be found) would probably require the additional security of a life insurance policy to insure repayment of the loan. The holder of a life estate may sell his interest. He cannot convey more than he has, and upon his death, the rights of any buyer would terminate.

LESS THAN FREEHOLD ESTATES

31   There are other interests in real property which, although possibly of great value, do not involve title to property. These interests are mainly leases. A lease is personal property. It is sometimes referred to as "chattel real."

32   Sale-leaseback - When a company wants to create an immediate cash flow but does not want to give up the occupancy of a building they own, a sale-leaseback may be arranged. The investor buys the building from the owner who, in the same escrow transaction, leases back the building over a long period of time.

33   A lease or leasehold is a contract between an owner or landlord (lessor) and the tenant or renter (lessee). The lease must include the names of parties, description of

the property, amount of rent, method of payment, and length of term.

34   The term "demise" means to convey an estate such as a lease. The term "alienate" means to convey.

35   There are two basic types of leases:
   (1) An estate for years, ordinarily called a term lease.
   (2) A periodic tenancy, also referred to as definite and indefinite leases.

36   Estate for years - Has a label that is somewhat misleading because the period may be for less than a year if measured in days, weeks, or months. An estate for years ends at the expiration of the term and without notice.

37   Periodic tenancy - Continues from period to period which can be year-to-year, month-to-month, or week-to-week. The periodic tenancy continues until either the landlord or the tenant terminates the agreement. Usually, the rental period determines the length of time for the required notice of termination. In the absence of a written document, there is a presumption that it is a month-to-month tenancy in the lease of a single-family residence.

38   Estate at will – One which is terminable at the will or unilateral decision of the lessor and also at the will of the lessee with no agreed upon period of duration. California requires a written notice of not less than 30 days to vacate to be served upon the tenant. The 30-day notice may be served on the tenant at any time during the rental period.

39   Estate at sufferance - An estate in which the lessee who has rightfully come into possession of the property retains possession after the expiration of the term of the agreement without the lessor's consent. A notice of termination is not necessary.

40   A lease for agricultural purposes is normally limited to 51 years. Leases for all other purposes may not exceed 99 years.

41   The statute of frauds requires that leases for more than one year must be in writing to be enforceable.

43   A written lease must be signed by the lessor. It is not necessary that the lessee sign the lease. The fact that he enters into possession and pays the rent is evidence of the acceptance of the agreement even though he has not signed the instrument.

43a   The commission charged by a broker for negotiating the terms of a lease agreement is usually based upon a percentage of the rents for the full term of the lease. Commission for the entire period of the lease is normally paid at the time the lease is signed.

ASSIGN OR SUBLET

46   In California, unless specifically prohibited by the terms of the lease, property can be sublet by the lessee or he may assign the lease. There is a distinct difference. If the lessee sublets, he is still the lessee and an interested party. If he assigns, he transfers all of his rights to the new tenant (assignee) and his obligation to pay rent comes to an end when the landlord consents to the assignment. Any easement or other rights given by a lessee or sublessee are limited in time to the term of the original lease.

46a   An index lease is tied to a recognized national index (the cost of living index or CPI, as an example) and the rental is adjusted in accordance with the movements of this index.
$1,080 Rental x (108/104) Index
(104 is the index level at the time the lease is signed.)

46b The graduated or step-up lease provides that the rent shall be increased at various stipulated times in the future.

46c A lease of land only would not be a depreciable investment and would be somewhat like an annuity returning a fixed amount each period over the lease term.

47 A net lease is a rental agreement in which, in addition to the rental charge, the tenant pays some or all of the property taxes, the fire insurance premiums, and property maintenance expenses. If all three are paid by the tenant, this arrangement produces net income to the landlord. It is often referred to as a triple net lease or a "net, net, net" lease.

48 A gross lease on the other hand is a lease which obligates the lessor to pay all or part of the expenses of the leased property, such as utilities, fire insurance, maintenance, and real property taxes.

49 When a lessee or sublessee sublets the property, he is said to hold a sandwich lease and would be both a lessor and lessee at the same time.

50 Many leases are for a stated period with an option for an additional period on the same terms and conditions or at an increased rent amount. Others provide for the purchase of the property by the lessee during the term of the lease, if he so desires, at a stated price and terms. The latter is known as a lease with option to purchase. If the lease with an option to purchase were assigned by the lessor, in the absence of an agreement prohibiting the assignment, the option would "follow with the sale." The buyer would take title subject to the lessee's exercise of his rights of purchase.

54 In the event that a landlord should evict a tenant unjustly, the tenant may sue for damages for wrongful eviction, sue for restoration of possession of the premises, or stop possession and pay no further rent.

56 If a tenant fails to pay rent, the landlord may serve a "three-day notice to pay rent or quit," or if tenant violates some other lease condition, a "three-day notice to quit" is used. Failure to comply with such a notice entitles the landlord to start an "unlawful detainer" action in court.

57 As a result of such unlawful detainer suit, the court may issue a "writ of possession" which, when served by the sheriff, results in eviction of the tenant from the premises within 5 days after service. At the time the writ is issued, the court also may render judgment for the amount of damages and rent found due, or for three times the amount of rent. Death of either party does not cancel a lease. The heirs and assigns of the lease have full rights until the lease is terminated either by action of law or by its terms.

58 If a lessee abandons the premises, the landlord cannot immediately consider a loss of rent for the remaining term. He may, after notice of default to the lessee, re-rent the property, keeping the right to collect from the original lessee the difference between the agreed upon total rental and what he actually received or he may leave the property vacant and sue for each month's rent as it becomes due and remains unpaid. He may also accept the abandonment and take possession terminating the lease.

61 In every lease, the law implies a covenant on the part of the lessor for the quiet enjoyment and possession of the property by the lessee during the term of the lease. It is a warranty by the lessor against lessor's own acts, not those of strangers.

62 The law requires that the lessee takes reasonable care of the premises and not commit any damages beyond ordinary wear and tear.

LESSEE MAY MAKE REPAIRS

63   Within a reasonable time after notice to the lessor of dilapidations the lessor ought to repair, and the lessor neglects to do so, then the lessee may repair the same himself if the cost of such repairs does not require expenditure of greater than one month's rent. The lessee may deduct these expenses from the rent or vacate the premises and be relieved from his obligations as a lessee.

66   The lessor is liable for injuries resulting form a defective condition in an area over which the lessor retains control, such as stairs and common hallways. This is true in every case except when a private dwelling house is leased for occupancy by one family only.

66a Security deposit - An amount of money deposited with lessor to secure the performance of the lease terms and/or "clean-up" of premises. It is not rent and belongs to lessee. The law (California Civil Code 1950.5) establishes that the tenant has a priority claim on it. A deposit is refundable by definition. It is not a fee. The landlord holds the deposit only as security against any money that might be due to him after the tenant vacates the property. If the tenant damages the property or is behind in his rent, for example, the landlord may apply the deposit towards those amounts. Any unused portion of the deposit must be returned to the tenant within twenty-one day after he vacates the premises.

67   Rent is the consideration paid for use of property. In either an oral or written agreement, it is important to state specifically when the rent is to be paid to the landlord. Without written conditions to the contrary, rent is payable at the termination of the respective periods as it becomes due whether the holding period is by the day, week, month, quarter or year.

PERCENTAGE LEASE

68   A percentage lease is usually employed when leasing retail business property and makes use of a percentage of the gross receipts of the business to determine rental payment. Such lease agreements should also require that there be a fixed minimum rental for each payment period ([$1200 + (.05 x Income)], where income may be defined as gross or net of expenses).

69   The term "run with the land" refers to the right off a person that is not eliminated simply by transfer of the title. Leases continue after the transfer of title as do mineral rights, unless exempted, stock in a Mutual Water Company, and easements.

Lesson Four
Part Two
Study Questions

_____(Lesson Four - Paragraph 19 – Question 1)_____

A landlord, an apartment owner, an owner of a residential condo unit, and a tenant of an apartment have the following in common:
(A) Each have an estate.
(B) Each have a fee interest.
(C) Each have a less-than-freehold interest.
(D) All of the above.

(A)   The term "estate" means ownership of an interest in real property. All these parties have a form of an estate or interest in real property. The landowner or apartment owner has a fee simple interest. An owner of a residential condominium has a fee simple interest in common in the common areas and a separate interest in space. A tenant of an apartment has a leasehold estate which is called a less than freehold estate. Each has an estate.

_____(Lesson Four - Paragraph 22 – Question 1)_____

Fee simple estate most closely refers to:
(A) The greatest interest a person can own in land.
(B) An easy way to transfer title to land.
(C) An expensive way to transfer title to land.
(D) A common way to hold title to land.

(A)   Fee simple estate is often defined as the greatest interest a person can own in land. The next estate would be a life estate. One could own a leasehold estate which involves possession solely.

_____(Lesson Four - Paragraph 22 – Question 2)_____

A distinguishing feature of a fee simple estate is that it:
(A) Is free of encumbrances.
(B) Is freely transferable.
(C) Is of definite duration.
(D) None of the above.

(B)   The fee simple estate has distinguishing features from a life estate or a leasehold estate. One of these distinguishing features is that it is "freely transferable." Fee simple does not mean free of encumbrances. Another characteristic of fee simple is indefinite duration.

_____(Lesson Four - Paragraph 25 – Question 1)_____

A buyer agrees not to sell alcoholic beverages on the property being acquired. This fact is noted in the deed granting him title. In common law, the buyer has an estate defined as:
(A) Property subject to a condition subsequent.
(B) Taken fee simple defeasible title to the property.
(C) A cause of action against the seller for unlawful restraint of title.
(D) None of the above.

(A)   The buyer does acquire the property subject to a condition subsequent. The condition is that no liquor be sold on the property. Several years ago the term fee simple defeasible, which is a common law definition of title, was removed from California legislation. In earlier days, such a condition automatically removed title if you violated the restriction. Now this restriction is called a fee simple subject to condition subsequent. A court action must be instituted by the former grantor before this condition can be exercised.

_____(Lesson Four - Paragraph 25 – Question 2)_____

A grant deed given in the purchase of a property contained a clause that stated, "The property conveyed may never be used for the sale of liquor, and if so used title will revert to the original grantor." The type of title received by the grantee is:
(A) Fee simple.
(B) Fee simple absolute.
(C) Subject to a condition subsequent.
(D) Estate for years.

(C) Freehold estates are twofold: Estates in fee (or fee simple) and estates for life. An estate in fee simple is the highest type of interest a person can have in land. It is of potentially indefinite duration and is freely transferable and inheritable. Fee simple may be absolute (exists completely in the holder of the estate). Fee simple estates may also be subject to a condition subsequent. Such an estate can be lost or defeated by the happening of some event subsequent to the creation of the fee.

_____(Lesson Four - Paragraph 26 – Question 1)_____

The following would possess an "estate" in real property:
(A) A beneficiary. (B) A mortgagee. (C) A life tenant. (D) All of these.

(C) An estate is an ownership interest in real property. The life tenant owns possession and use of the property for life. A beneficiary and a mortgagee own a security interest in the property. They would have only a lien against the property.

_____(Lesson Four - Paragraph 26 – Question 2)_____

An estate in real property is held by a:
(A) Life tenant. (B) Beneficiary. (C) Mortgagee. (D) All of the above.

(A)   A life tenant holds an estate in real property. He holds it for the duration of the life of a certain person, including that of the holder of the life estate. A beneficiary is the party for whose benefit the trustee holds bare naked title when a trust deed is created. A mortgagee is a lender who has loaned money for which the security is real property that has been hypothecated for the payment of the debt.

_____(Lesson Four - Paragraph 27 – Question 1)_____

Grace willed the use of her home to Franklin for the balance of his life; thereafter the home was to go to her William. The following statement is incorrect:
(A) Franklin has a freehold estate.
(B) Franklin would have a fee simple estate.
(C) The duration of this estate is only for the length of the life of Franklin.
(D) The estate can be encumbered by Franklin, but only for the life of Franklin.

(B) Franklin has a life estate which is a freehold estate. A fee simple estate is the greatest interest one can hold in real property. The question asks for the incorrect answer which is (B).

_____(Lesson Four - Paragraph 27 – Question 2)_____

"A future interest in property arising by operation of law to take effect in possession in favor of a grantor after the termination of a prior estate" defines a:
(A) Estate in fee. (B) Estate in reversion. (C) Estate for years. (D) Estate in remainder.

(B) An exact definition. An example would be a life estate that reverts to the grantor upon the termination of the life estate.

_____(Lesson Four - Paragraph 28 – Question 1)_____

Able leased a property from Baker for a period of five years. Three years after signing the lease, Baker died and it was determined that Baker held only a life estate. Able was asked to vacate the property. If Able contested the action, a court would find:
(A) The leasehold was valid for 5 years.   (B) The leasehold was invalid from the beginning.
(C) Able's leasehold expired upon Baker's death. (D) None of the above.

(C) A lease given on property which is owned as a life estate terminates upon the death of the lessor, and is not binding upon the holder of the estate in reversion or remainder.

_____(Lesson Four - Paragraph 28 – Question 2)_____

The holder of a life estate entered into a lease as lessor of the property which she owned. The lease was for a period of five years, and the holder of the life estate died after two years. The owner of the estate in remainder said the lease was invalid and told the tenant to leave. The following is correct:
(A) The lease was valid only during the life of the lessor
(B) The lease was valid for the remainder of the five years
(C) The lease was invalid because a life tenant may not lease the property
(D) The lease was invalid as it was for longer than the statutory one-year period.

(A) This is one of the instances where a lease is canceled automatically, without the consent of the original parties to the contract. Since the lessor held only a life estate, he can exert no control over it after his death. Lessee has no recourse and must vacate the premises.

_____(Lesson Four - Paragraph 29 – Question 1)_____

Jones holds a life estate in Blackacre. He grants his life estate to Baker. The following is a correct statement regarding this sale:
(A) The grantor has an estate in remainder.
(B) The grantee holds a reversionary interest in Blackacre.
(C) The grantee has an estate for the life of the life tenant.
(D) The grantor can expect to regain title to Blackacre.

(C) The holder of a life estate is designated as a life tenant. A life tenant, unless expressly restrained, may sell, lease encumber, or otherwise dispose of his interest. He cannot transfer an interest beyond the duration of his life estate.

_____(Lesson Four - Paragraph 29 – Question 2)_____

"0" sells Blackacre to "A" and in doing so retains a life estate in Blackacre and remains in possession. Later "0" sells his interest in Blackacre to "B" and grants "B" possession. "A" is disturbed by this turn and sues for immediate possession. "A's" position is described as:
(A) Possession of Blackacre reverts to "A."

(B) "B" can retain possession of Blackacre for the life of "0."
(C) "A" could legally demand immediate possession.
(D) "A" could demand his money back.

(B)   This question asks, "Can a life estate be sold to another?" This answer is yes. "B" in this instance will hold a life estate to Blackacre until the death of "0". On "O's" death, "B" would be legally required to leave Blackacre unless he came to a separate agreement with "A".

_____(Lesson Four - Paragraph 31 – Question 1)_____

All of the following are real property, except:
(A) Realty. (B) Air space. (C) Leasehold interest in real property. (D) Easements appurtenant.

(C) The leasehold estate is an interest in land of the lessor, but it is personal property to the lessee.
A lease is often referred to as a "chattel real" for this reason.

_____(Lesson Four - Paragraph 31 – Question 2)_____

All of the following are classified as real property, except :
(A) Mineral, oil and gas rights   (B) A leasehold on a residence.
(C) Uncultivated fruit trees.   (D) An easement appurtenant.

(B) A lease is classified as personal property and is treated according to the laws of personal property. A lease creates an estate in real property; however, it is classified as a chattel real - an item of personal property that consists of an interest in real property.

_____(Lesson Four - Paragraph 32 – Question 1)_____

The following action taken by the owner of a fee simple estate would cause his interest to be converted to that of less-than-freehold estate:
(A) A grant of the mineral rights therein to a third party.
(B) A lease of the land for agricultural purposes to a third party for a period of five years.
(C) A grant of life estate.
(D) A sale and leaseback.

(D) In each of the suggested choices (A), (B) and (C), the person granting still retains an ownership interest in the property. However, in selling it to another and leasing it from the new owner, the freehold estate (fee) is given up and a less-than-freehold estate (lease) is acquired.

_____(Lesson Four - Paragraph 33 – Question 1)_____

The owner of a leasehold estate is the:
(A) Remainderman. (B) A lessor. (C) Reversionor. (D) Lessee.

(D) The lessor, the owner of the property, grants the use of the property to the lessee. Thus, the lessee is the owner of the leasehold estate created by this grant. The terms remainderman and reversioner refer to life estates. The remainderman is the person who receives the portion of the life estate remaining after the death of the holder of the life estate when said life estate was determined by the life of a person other than the holder of the life estate and that other person is still alive. The reversioner is the person to whom the estate would revert upon the death of the person upon whose life the life estate was created.

_____(Lesson Four - Paragraph 33 – Question 2)_____

of the landlord, the estate of the landlord, or whoever is the successor to the landlord, must honor the rental agreement for its full term.

_____(Lesson Four - Paragraph 36 – Question 2)_____
A landlord does not have to give notice of termination to a tenant in:
(A) A month-to-month tenancy. (B) A periodic tenancy.
(C) An estate from year to year. (D) An estate for years.

(D) Notice of termination of the estate for years is implied in the contract because it is established for a definite period of time. It requires no notice of termination by its very nature.

_____(Lesson Four - Paragraph 39 – Question 1)_____
A tenant holding over after expiration of a lease without the consent of the lessor holds a:
(A) Periodic tenancy.   (B) Tenancy in common.
(C) Tenancy at sufferance.   (D) Month-to-month tenancy.

(C) The word "sufferance" as used in this connection is defined as "consent or sanction implied by a lack of interference or failure to enforce a prohibition." When a tenant remains over at the expiration of a lease without the express consent of the lessor, he is said to have a tenancy at sufferance.

_____(Lesson Four - Paragraph 40 – Question 1)_____
An owner of a residence located in a rural area may lease the home for:
(A) A maximum of 51 years. (B) 99 years. (C) An unlimited period of time. (D) None of the above.

(B) The maximum term for a non-agricultural lease is 99 years. Agricultural land can be leased for only 51 years.

_____(Lesson Four - Paragraph 41 – Question 1)_____
Which of the following is not required to create a lease for more than one year?
(A) It must be in writing.   (B) Lessor and lessee must both sign it always.
(C) A termination date.   (D) The amount of rent and the method of payment.

(B) In the case of a written lease, the lessor must sign it. It is not necessary that the lessee sign the lease. The fact that he enters into possession and pays the rent is evidence of the acceptance of the agreement, even though he has not signed the instrument.

_____(Lesson Four - Paragraph 46 – Question 1)_____
If a lessee assigns his interest to another, the party receiving such interest is known as:
(A) Sublessor. (B) Tenant. (C) Master lessor. (D) Assignor.

(B) The party holding the, right of possession of someone else's property is called a tenant. In this case he would be a sublessee which is not a listed choice.

_____ (Lesson Four - Paragraph 46 – Question 2)_____
A sublessor is:
(A) One who assigns his rights and his duties for the unexpired term of the lease.
(B) One who transfers his rights but not his duties with right of return if the terms are breached.

of the landlord, the estate of the landlord, or whoever is the successor to the landlord, must honor the rental agreement for its full term.

_____(Lesson Four - Paragraph 36 – Question 2)_____
A landlord does not have to give notice of termination to a tenant in:
(A) A month-to-month tenancy. (B) A periodic tenancy.
(C) An estate from year to year. (D) An estate for years.

(B) Notice of termination of the estate for years is implied in the contract because it is established for a definite period of time. It requires no notice of termination by its very nature.

_____(Lesson Four - Paragraph 39 – Question 1)_____
A tenant holding over after expiration of a lease without the consent of the lessor holds a:
(A) Periodic tenancy.   (B) Tenancy in common.
(C) Tenancy at sufferance.   (D) Month-to-month tenancy.

(C) The word "sufferance" as used in this connection is defined as "consent or sanction implied by a lack of interference or failure to enforce a prohibition." When a tenant remains over at the expiration of a lease without the express consent of the lessor, he is said to have a tenancy at sufferance.

_____(Lesson Four - Paragraph 40 – Question 1)_____
An owner of a residence located in a rural area may lease the home for:
(A) A maximum of 51 years. (B) 99 years. (C) An unlimited period of time. (D) None of the above.

(B) The maximum term for a non-agricultural lease is 99 years. Agricultural land can be leased for only 51 years.

_____(Lesson Four - Paragraph 41 – Question 1)_____
Which of the following is not required to create a lease for more than one year?
(A) It must be in writing.   (B) Lessor and lessee must both sign it always.
(C) A termination date.   (D) The amount of rent and the method of payment.

(B) In the case of a written lease, the lessor must sign it. It is not necessary that the lessee sign the lease. The fact that he enters into possession and pays the rent is evidence of the acceptance of the agreement, even though he has not signed the instrument.

_____(Lesson Four - Paragraph 46 – Question 1)_____
If a lessee assigns his interest to another, the party receiving such interest is known as:
(A) Sublessor. (B) Tenant. (C) Master lessor. (D) Assignor.

(B) The party holding the, right of possession of someone else's property is called a tenant. In this case he would be a sublessee which is not a listed choice.

_____ (Lesson Four - Paragraph 46 – Question 2)_____
A sublessor is:
(A) One who assigns his rights and his duties for the unexpired term of the lease.
(B) One who transfers his rights but not his duties with right of return if the terms are breached.

(C) One who assigns his rights to one who accepts his duties with right of return if the terms are breached.

(D) One who assigns and records a short form lease containing terms and conditions of the new lease.

(B) Read this question carefully and you will find a one-word clue. What is the difference between assigning and transferring? When you assign your liability, your responsibility passes. When you transfer, your responsibility remains.

_____(Lesson Four - Paragraph 47 – Question 1)_____

The clause in a rental agreement that provides that the tenant pays the property taxes ordinarily is found in:

(A) A net lease. (B) A percentage lease. (C) A sandwich lease. (D) None of the above.

(A) A net lease is usually on business property when the tenant agrees to pay the taxes and insurance on the property in addition to the rent. A percentage lease bases the rent on a percentage of the gross income with a minimum fixed rent.

_____(Lesson Four - Paragraph 47 – Question 2)_____

A net lease is:

(A) A lease arrangement where the lessee share his profit with the lessor.
(B) Guarantees income to the lessor.
(C) Provides a net income to the lessee.
(D) Insures that the lessor will pay taxes and insurance.

(B) In a net lease the lessor receives the lease payment out of which he would have to pay little or no expense. This is so because the lessee agrees to pay the real property taxes and the fire insurance expense necessary for the property in addition to the agreed upon lease payment.

_____(Lesson Four - Paragraph 49 – Question 1)_____

Owner leases to Kent and Kent subleases the property to Smith. The holder of the sandwich lease would be:

(A) Owner. (B) Kent. (C) Smith. (D) Owner and the one who occupies the property.

(B) Kent holds the sandwich lease. He is the party who holds the leasehold interest from the owner but has transferred a part of his interest to a third party. Kent is sandwiched, so to speak, between the owner and the user of the property.

_____(Lesson Four - Paragraph 49 – Question 2)_____

When real property is subleased, the interest held by the sublessor is commonly called:
(A) A double lease. (B) A freehold lease. (C) An assignment. (D) A sandwich lease.

(D) The lessor holds the original lease. If the lessee sublets the property he would be the sublessor and the person subletting would be the sublessee. Since the lessee is still primarily liable for the lease and is in between the lessor and sublessee, the lessee is sandwiched.

_____(Lesson Four - Paragraph 56 – Question 1)_____

An unlawful detainer action is used by the:

(A) Lessee. (B) Debtor. (C) Beneficiary. (D) Lessor.

(D) An unlawful detainer action is an action in court to regain possession of leased property. The lessor takes the action.

_____(Lesson Four - Paragraph 56 – Question 2)_____

The person who most likely would make use of the remedy called "unlawful detainer" is:
(A) The trustor. (B) The holder of a note in default. (C) The lessor. (D) The grantor.

(C) The summary procedure to remove someone unlawfully in possession of property is called "unlawful detainer." The lessor would most likely have recourse to such action to regain possession from a defaulting lessee.

_____(Lesson Four - Paragraph 58 – Question 1)_____

Mr. Roamer entered into a two-year written lease with the owner of a residence. Mr. Roamer occupies the home for one year and then abandons the property. Under these circumstances the lessor can do all except one of the following:
(A) Leave the premises unoccupied and sue for the entire rent due for the remaining term.
(B) Leave premises unoccupied and sue for each installment as it becomes due.
(C) Re-occupy the premises and re-rent the home on behalf of the tenant.
(D) Re-enter and occupy the premises and forget the original lease.

(A) If a lessee abandons the premises, the landlord cannot immediately consider a loss of the rent for the remaining term. He may, after notice of default to the lessee, re-rent the property keeping the right to collect from the original lessee the difference between the agreed upon total rental and what he actually received, or he may leave the property vacant and sue for each month's rent as it becomes due and remains unpaid. He may also, if he so desires accept the abandonment and take possession, in which case the lease is terminated and the lessee released from his obligation.

_____(Lesson Four - Paragraph 61 – Question 1)_____

A "covenant of quiet enjoyment" refers to:
(A) Title. (B) Possession. (C) Personal occupancy. (D) None of the above.

(B) In every lease there is an expressed or implied covenant by the lessor of quiet enjoyment and possession by the lessee during the term of the lease. This would be true whether or not the lessee personally occupies the property.

_____(Lesson Four - Paragraph 61 – Question 2)_____

The person hiring real property from its owner is given an exclusive right to use. He is a:
(A) Tenant. (B) Licensee. (C) Lodger. (D) None of the above.

(A) Payment for the use or possession of another property is the renting or hiring of the property.

_____(Lesson Four - Paragraph 62 – Question 1)_____

All of the following would make it possible for a tenant to vacate his leasehold without any liability for the remainder of the agreement, except:
(A) Unlawful damage to the property by the tenant.

(B) The landlord makes unwarranted changes in the character of the property to the tenants detriment.
(C) Expulsion by the landlord.
(D) Harassment and threats by the landlord to cancel the lease.

(A) In every lease there is an implied covenant by the lessor of quiet enjoyment and possession by the lessee during the term of the lease. This warranty is breached by an eviction, whether actual or constructive. Answers (B) and (D) are examples of constructive eviction. Answer (C) is an example of actual eviction. Answer (A) is a violation of the lease committed by the lessee, not by the lessor.

_____(Lesson Four - Paragraph 63 – Question 1)_____

An apartment is rented on a month-to-month basis. The water pipes suddenly develop a major leak and the tenant demands that the owner fix the pipes immediately or he has the right to terminate the lease and vacate the premises:
(A) The tenant must fix the pipes and deduct the cost of repairs from the next month's rent.
(B) The tenant is correct.
(C) The tenant may terminate any month-to-month tenancy without notice.
(D) The tenant must give at least a 4-day notice.

(B) The lessee has the option of either fixing the pipes and deducting the cost from the rent to the extent of one month's rent or terminating the lease and vacating the premises immediately.

_____(Lesson Four - Paragraph 66 – Question 1)_____

A landlord is obligated to keep in good and safe condition all of the property in commonly used areas in every case but one of the following:
(A) A high rise apartment building with extensive lobby and hallways.
(B) A theater building containing an extensive lobby and restroom facilities.
(C) A private dwelling house leased for occupancy by one family only.
(D) A commercial rental property with certain commonly used areas for convenience of all tenants.

(C) In the absence of fraud or concealment or a covenant in the lease, a landlord is not liable to a tenant or his invitees for defective conditions on leased property. An exception to this rule is where injuries result form a defective condition in the area which the lessor retains control, such as stairs, common hallways, the lessor is liable and not the lessee.

_____(Lesson Four - Paragraph 67 – Question 1)_____

"A" negotiated a rental agreement on January 20 to start February 1 and obtained the first month's rent in advance. However, there was no mention of the due dates of subsequent payments. On February 20, the lessor had not received a rental payment. The lessor may:
(A) Serve a 4-day notice to quit or pay rent. (B) Institute a court action.
(C) Sue for triple damage.   (D) Do nothing as the rent is not yet due.

(D) According to the law the rent is not due until the rental period has expired. In order for the rent to be payable in advance, a specific agreement to this effect must be executed. In the circumstances stated, there was no such agreement; consequently, the rent for the second month is not due until March 1.

_____(Lesson Four - Paragraph 67 – Question 2)_____

The term "rent" is best defined as:

(A) A month-to-month tenancy.　(B) Consideration paid for the right of possession.

(C) An oral lease.　　　　　　　(D) A tenancy-at-will

(B) "Rent" when used as a noun means the consideration paid by a tenant for the use or occupancy of real property. When used as an infinitive as in "I am going to rent an apartment" we have a tendency to interpret it as a meaning to secure an oral lease or month-to-month tenancy. Choice (B) is the best definition of the term.

_____(Lesson Four - Paragraph 68 – Question 1)_____

The following best defines "rent":

(A) The annual return of revenue from a capital investment.

(B) The periodic payment of consideration for a contract where the parties lend a sum of money   which they agree not to recall.

(C) The consideration given for the use and possession of a specific property under stated conditions.

(D) The month-to-month tenancy of a contract not reduced to writing.

(C) Rent is consideration given for use and possession of property.

_____(Lesson Four - Paragraph 68 – Question 2)_____

In a typical percentage lease, rent is calculated as a percentage of:

(A) Assets of the lessee's business.　　　(B) Net sales of the lessee's business.

(C) Gross sales of the lessee's business.　(D) Net taxable income of the lessee's business.

(C) A percentage lease is typified by the rent being calculated as a percentage of gross.

_____(Lesson Four - Paragraph 69 – Question 1)_____

Which of the following "run with the land"?

(A) Easements appurtenant

(B) Covenants

(C) Stock in a Mutual Water Company

(D) All of The Above

(D) That which "runs with the land" is permanently affixed to the title and is always automatically transferred with the title upon sale.

Lesson Four
Part Three
Understanding Through Question Testing

Log into your course at www.lumbleau.com.

STUDENT LOGIN

Login: [ ]

Password: [ ]

On your student home page, click on the "State Exam Preparation".

STATE EXAM
PREPARATION

Under the "Guided Lesson" tab click on the fourth of fourteen links:
"Property and Estates".

Real Estate Salesperson Course

Guided Lessons	Practice Exams	Progress Report	Success Video

Print	Questions
Click	HERE>>> **4. Property and Estates**

Here you will be tested on all of the questions you have been studying and learn the most recently added questions. It is essential, for maximum retention, that you eliminate all of the questions you can easily answer and "TAG" for study the questions with which you have difficulty.

Lesson Five

Part One
Understanding Through Video Teaching

Lesson Five
TENANCY

28 Tenancy denotes "a holding" of something. In a lease "a holding" is the possession of the property. Joint tenancy is a joint holding of the title.

SEVERALTY

37 "Severalty" is the technical name given to ownership by one person only.

38 The "person" owning the property in severalty may be a natural person (any human) or a legal person (a corporation). All government property is owned in severalty.

TENANCY-IN-COMMON

45 Tenants-in-common own individual undivided interests. These interests need not be equal in quantity and duration. These interests may be acquired at different times with different instruments and may be sold or willed separately. Each tenant-in-common holds a separate deed to their interest. Because of this, there is no right of survivorship.

46 The tenant-in-common co-owners have only one unity, possession.

47 This equal right to the possession provision allows each to use the total property without interference from the others.

JOINT TENANCY

48 The law establishes specific requirements for this type of holding. Among the requirements are four unities – time, title, interest and possessions. All parties must create joint tenancy at the same time by one instrument conveying the title. All parties must enjoy the same proportional interest, and all enjoy equal rights to the possession of the property.

49 The right of survivorship is the distinguishing characteristic of a joint tenancy. Whole title is vested in each of the tenants and the one who dies simply drops out of the estate. The survivors do not take the property by inheritance because they already owned the whole. Joint tenants may not will their interests in the tenancy although they may sell or otherwise dispose of their interests before death.

50 If there are only two people in a joint tenancy and one of them conveys his interest to a third party, it breaks the joint tenancy and makes both new and old owners tenants-in-common. If three or more people hold title as joint tenants and one conveys his interest, the grantee becomes a tenant-in-common with the others who remain joint tenants to each other.

51 A joint tenant may execute a deed of trust against his interest or a judgment lien may be placed against it. This does not terminate the joint tenancy but in case of his death before he has repaid the loan or satisfied the judgment, the survivors of the joint tenancy are not liable to the creditors of the deceased. At death, the property belongs to the joint tenancy survivors, not the heirs of the deceased.

53 The creation of a joint tenancy must be by deed or will. It may be created by a sole owner deeding the property to him and others, or by tenants-in-common deeding to themselves or to themselves and others.

54 In whatever way created, there must be only one deed and the words "as joint

tenants" or "in joint tenancy" must appear in the deed to establish this estate.

55   The major advantage of holding property "as joint tenants" is the simplicity of clearing title upon the death of one joint tenant. Termination by death is automatic and the survivor becomes the owner at that time. For title record purposes, the surviving joint tenant must record a court decree establishing the fact of death or an "affidavit of death of a joint tenant(s)" together with a death certificate.

61   Community property basically consists of equal interests in all property acquired by a husband and wife during a valid marriage, excepting specific types of separate property. Under the Civil Code of California, as interpreted by the courts, the excluded separate property of the husband or wife consists of:

62   All property owned by either husband or wife before marriage is separate property.

68   A husband and wife taking title in their names by a deed describing them as husband and wife would take title in community property. If they wish to take title as joint tenants, the deed must so describe them. For the purpose of division of property on dissolution of marriage or legal separation, any property acquired by the husband and wife during marriage as joint tenants or by any other form of title holding, is the community property of the parties.

70   Neither spouse may make a gift without the consent of the other. Neither spouse may encumber the furniture, furnishings, fittings of the home, or clothing of the spouse or minor children without the written consent of the spouse. Both must join in the conveyance, encumbrance, or leasing (for more than a year) of community real property.

71   Each spouse has the right to dispose of his one-half of the community property by will. If either spouse dies intestate (without a will) the survivor succeeds to the decedent's half interest.

71a   The law that governs the distribution of property after dissolution of marriage is contained in the Civil Code.

TENANCY-IN-PARTNERSHIP

73   The partnership may be one of two kinds: A general partnership or a limited partnership. A general partner may be entered into verbally; however, it is highly advisable that it be in writing. A limited partnership must be in writing and the "articles of partnership" must be filed with the Secretary of State of California and the county clerk of the county where the business operates. The usual form of a partnership agreement is called "articles of partnership."

74   All general partners are personally liable to third parties for all partnership debts. This would mean that each partner is liable for the entire obligations of the partnership even though they may be greater than his original investment in the business.

75   A limited partner is not liable for any amount other than the sum he has invested in the partnership. Syndications usually take the form of a limited partnership because of this fact. Because of this insulated liability of the limited partner, he may take no part in the management or operation of the business and his name may not be used in connection with the business

77   A partnership may own real property. Each partner is a co-owner with the other partners of a specific property, holding title as a tenant-in-partnership. The title to the real property may be held in the names of all the partners or under a fictitious firm name, commonly called a "D.B.A." (doing business

as). A fictitious business name is good for five years from the last day of the year in which it was recorded.

80 The statute of frauds lists those contracts that must be in writing if either of the parties finds it necessary to take a dispute to court. A partnership agreement is not included in the list, and is therefore not required to be in writing.

81 A partner may not will his interest in specific partnership property. On the death of a partner, a form of survivorship arises in the surviving partners. This right of survivorship is only for the purpose of controlling the business until such time as the partnership can be dissolved and the interest of the deceased partner is distributed to his heirs.

EASEMENTS

83 An easement may be defined as the right to use land owned by another person for a specific purpose. As such, it is an encumbrance on the property on which it is placed. Easements may be for a definite or indefinite duration. Generally speaking, whereas a lease is an exclusive right, an easement is usually a non-exclusive right to use. The use may be varied, extending from a right-of-way to gain access to land owned by the holder of the easement, or the right to have flood water flow across a person's land, to rights to take minerals from the land of another, or to use such land for public streets, or for installing public utilities. An easement granted for ingress and egress, to be valid, does not need to be specifically located in the deed.

83a Simple permissive use never grants, transfers, or creates an easement no matter how many years would be involved.

APPURTENANT EASEMENTS

85 Whatever the reason for its existence, an easement creates a "servitude" on the land. It serves the purposes of another who is not the owner of the land. The land upon which the easement is imposed is known, legally, as the "servient tenement" while the land which is benefited by the easement is called the "dominant tenement." Easements are considered appurtenant to the dominant tenement and pass automatically upon transfer so that subsequent owners of the dominant tenement also have the rights granted under the easement. Buyers of the servient tenement buy the property subject to the easement.

EASEMENTS IN GROSS

86 Easements, which by their nature are not appurtenant to a particular parcel of land or "dominant tenement," are known technically as "easements in gross." In such instances, there is no dominant tenement. An example is rights given to utility companies to erect poles or string wires upon private land.

89 By grant - Easements created by grant must comply with the general requirements of a deed and may arise either by express grant, giving the right of use, or by express reservation, whereby the grantor of the land reserves the use of a portion of the land being transferred for himself. The grant of an easement or easements is often included in the provisions of a deed. The deed must, like the description of the property, properly describe the location of the easement. A deed to an unlocated easement is valid. The fact that an easement is unlocated may give rise to legal questions; however, if it is recorded, it is a valid easement.

89a Recording of an easement is not necessary to give notice to a subsequent purchaser.

90 By dedication - Most often easements by dedication are created by subdividers when obtaining approval from local government agencies.

91 By necessity - Easements by necessity generally are recognized whenever a transfer occurs which truly "land locks" a parcel of land. A land locked parcel is entirely surrounded by land of adjoining owners so that the new owner has no access to his property without the easement. Both the dominant tenement and the servient tenement must have had a private common owner at one time. Though no actual easement is created by written document, use becomes the identifying factor

92 By prescription - An easement also may be acquired by prescription, essentially as one would acquire land by adverse possession that is by open and notorious use for a period of five years without protest or recorded notice of consent. Payment of taxes is not required. This type of easement may be lost by mere non-use continuing over a five-year period.

92a An easement gained by prescription is not usually recorded because the owner would not normally acknowledge the instrument.

TERMINATION OF EASEMENTS

99 Easements by prescription are the only kind which are lost by non-use, with the exception of those created by dedication where it is expressly stated that if they are not used for the dedicated purposes, the use of the land shall revert to the owner.

100 All other easements are terminated only by express written release (quitclaim deed) from the holder of the easement or by merger of the dominant and servient tenements. Those granting use of a property for public utilities, rights-of-way, etc., generally remain in force indefinitely. Often, property owners are not aware of easements and restrictions which are recorded and are dismayed to find that the gas company, for instance, may come in and dig up their lawns to lay new pipes.

LICENSE

101 A license is a revocable right for a person to use real property belonging to another. It is personal to the holder and cannot be assigned by the holder without the consent of the owner of the real property affected. A license, as a general rule, is synonymous with an "invitation."

CAPACITY - REAL PROPERTY & MINORS

105 Minors are all persons under 18 years of age. Although minors may acquire title to property at any time since the law presumes that they accept it, they may not dispose of property except as provided by law.

106 Everyone 18 years of age or over has the rights of an adult, including the right to vote, make enforceable contracts, marry, etc. The only prohibitions affecting an 18 to 21 year old are those regarding alcoholic beverages.

107 California law now identifies emancipated minors. Such minors are persons under the age of 18 years who either:

108 (1) Have entered into a valid marriage, whether or not the marriage has been dissolved.

109 (2) Are on active duty with any of the armed forces of the United States of America.

110 (3) Have received a declaration of emancipation by petitioning the superior court of the county where they reside.

117 Anyone dealing with minors does so at their own peril. In a real estate transaction, it would be the real estate broker's responsibility to determine the proper status of the buyer or the seller. Generally, the safest method of dealing with minors is to do

so through a court appointed guardian unless it has been determined that the minors have been legally emancipated. If a client is a minor, whether emancipated or not, it is reported to the escrow company to enable the title company to do proper research and provide protection within their policy of title insurance.

UNDER CONSERVATORSHIP (INCOMPETENT)

119   A person who officially has been adjudged to be incompetent is incapable of entering into contracts, concerning any matter, and such contract would be void. Persons of unsound mind but not entirely without understanding, whose capacity has not been determined officially, may enter into contracts, but such contracts and transfers are voidable upon proof of incapacity. As with minors, incompetents may acquire property (such as by gift or inheritance) but cannot dispose of it except through proper procedure by appointment of a conservator whose actions are subject to court approval.

CORPORATIONS

120   A corporation is a "legal person". It is an entity created by law, having a personality and existence distinct and apart from that of the shareholders. Property owned by a corporation is held in severalty, by one legal person, the corporation. Since the government is considered as one entity it, like a corporation, holds title in severalty. While the shareholders own the corporation, the continuation of its business is not affected by the death of any one of them as a corporation is said to have the capacity for perpetual succession. It does not die. It logically follows, that a corporation cannot hold property in joint tenancy as it would always outlive an individual.

121   Corporations have the capacity to issue bonds, collateralized by the real property they own, to raise capital that would

ordinarily be done through trust deed financing.

122   The details of forming a corporation are a matter for an attorney. Articles of incorporation must be filed with the Secretary of State and a corporation franchise secured. Permission to issue stock is received from the Corporations Commissioner. Foreign corporations (those outside of the state) must register with the Corporations Commissioner before they can do business in California. Officers of the corporation do not have the power to contract on behalf of the corporation without authorization of the board of directors, which has the governing power.

125   Small "family owned" corporations are sometimes created as Chapter S corporations. This feature allows all of the protections of a corporation except that the income is not double taxed. It is taxed as individual income to the stockholders.

126   The most important characteristic of a corporation is the fact that income is subject to corporate tax first and, if given as dividends to the shareholders, to individual income tax.

132   Though it is a tax reporting entity and must file an income tax report for income tax purposes, a partnership is not treated as a separate entity. Each partner must report their share of income and expenses on their individual income tax returns.

ADMINISTRATORS AND EXECUTORS

139   On the death of a person, the title of all his property, both real and personal, is transferred to the persons entitled thereto under the will of the deceased, or by the law of intestate succession, except that property held under joint tenancy. The control of the title comes under the jurisdiction of the Probate Department of the Superior Court. The court will appoint an administrator or an administratrix. The deceased may have

appointed an executor or executrix in his will for the purpose of conserving the estate, paying all debts, and distributing the property.

140   The probate code limits the capacity of the administrator or executor to enter into contracts or conveyances. Generally speaking, before they may bind the estate they must have approval of the probate court. This rule applies also to listing any probate property with a real estate broker. It is possible for the court to approve an exclusive real estate listing for a period not to exceed 90 days. In the event the listing is approved, the broker is required to procure a purchaser for at least 90% of the appraised value and secure court confirmation of the sale before the court would order payment of any commission. The court sets the commission rate to be received by the real estate broker.

141   Once such an offer has been accepted by the administrator or executor it is subject to confirmation by the court and a hearing date is set for such confirmation. This hearing date must be published in a newspaper of general circulation. At the time of the hearing, the law provides that any person wishing to enter an overbid on the property may do so. The first overbid must be in an amount equal to the original bid plus 10% of the first $10,000 and 5% of any amount over $10,000 of the original bid. Thus, if the original bid is for $36,000, the first overbid must be at least $38,300 [$36,000 + $1,000 (10% of $10,000) + $1,300 (5% of $26,000)]. Thereafter, additional overbids may be in any increased amount set by the court. The court may confirm whichever bid is for the best interest of the estate.

142   The court also gives serious attention to any sale of the deceased's property within one year prior to death.

143   It is well established in law that the relatives and business associates of a seriously ill person may take advantage of that person by forcing the sale of property at a less than market price. The court may set aside such a sale.

ESCHEAT

162   The state may acquire the property of persons dying without a will and without heirs or with only alien heirs who do not reside in this country and who are citizens of a country which does not allow United States citizens to inherit property located in that country. The title is said to "revert to the state."

WILLS

166   In the event a person dies without leaving a will, the law provides for the disposition of the estate of the deceased. This is called "intestate succession." A large number of special rules are found in the laws that deal with this circumstance. These rules depend upon the character of the property and the relationship of the next of kin or the heirs at law of the deceased person.

167   Certain words and phrases occur with regard to the willing of property. The common beginning to a will states, "Being of sound mind, I hereby devise and bequeath to my heirs and assigns all of my real and personal property." Devise is defined as the testamentary disposition (willing) of land or realty. A bequest is the gift of personal property by will.

168   Other words used in wills are executor or executrix who is appointed in the will to administrate the disposition of the estate. Ambulatory - a changeable will or a will subject to change. Codicil - an addition or supplement altering a will. A legacy - personal property received by will. Lineal - pertains to the direct line of descendants.

HOMESTEADS

180   To provide against loss of the home because of legal action, the law permits a person to protect his home by recording a declaration of homestead which will exempt his property from any after-secured judgment or after-recorded involuntary lien with the exception of mechanic's liens and, as a specific provision of California Civil Code, sections dealing with condominium assessments.

181   If the homestead declaration is filed by the judgment debtor or his spouse, as a member of a family unit of the dwelling in which they reside, is protected from a writ of execution (court order to have the property sold after judgment) to the extent of $75,000 of equity. Only one homestead at a time is valid on a given residence.

182   The term "family unit" in this instance means the judgment debtor and spouse if the spouses reside together in the dwelling.

186   For instance, a person may be supporting his mother, grandmother, a minor brother or sister, a minor child or children of the deceased brother, or sister and be recognized as a member of a "family unit" and secure the exemption of $75,000. The members of the "family unit" must be named in the declaration of homestead.

188   The homestead does not prevent a creditor from forcing the sale of the homesteaded residence if the equity in the property exceeds the homesteaded amount. The first monies from the sale would satisfy the court costs, then trust deeds or mortgage liens, then the debtors (homeowners) exemption. The balance would go to the creditors. If there is excess, it would go to the homesteader.

189   Homestead means the principal dwelling:

190   (1) In which the judgment debtor or spouse resided on the date the judgment creditor's lien attached to the dwelling

191   (2) In which either or both resided continuously until the date of the court determination that the dwelling is a homestead.

192   The dwelling may consist of community or separate property held in joint tenancy or tenants-in-common and may be a condominium, planned development, stock cooperative, community apartment project, or a lease for 30 years or longer. It may also be an apartment in an apartment house that is occupied by the owner of the entire building. Only the rooms actually occupied will constitute the homestead.

193   A declaration of homestead is of no effect until it is recorded.

195   To terminate the homestead, a declaration of abandonment may be prepared and recorded. The homestead is also broken if the property is sold to others or transferred to others by foreclosure of the property under mortgage or trust deed. Destruction by fire does not indicate abandonment.

STATUTE OF FRAUDS

202   The statute of frauds provides that certain contracts must be in writing to be enforceable. Most contracts involving the sale and leasing of real estate fall into this classification. A lease for a term of one year or less need not be in writing, but the law then presumes a month-to-month tenancy and the burden is upon the renter to prove otherwise.

203   A broker's authorization to sell real property must be in writing or he cannot sue for a commission. If the contract is signed by one party but is ratified by the conclusion of

the sale, the court would most probably rule that the contract was valid.

203a A trust deed or lien that is recorded must be in writing. If a purchaser of a property assumes an existing trust deed, the assumption must be in writing.

PROVISIONS OF THE STATUTE

204 The statute provides that certain contracts are invalid unless the agreement, or some note or memorandum, is in writing and signed by the parties. Contracts that are required to be in writing are:

205 An agreement that, by its terms, is not to be performed within a year from the making thereof.

212 It should be noted from the reading of the provisions of this statute that a contract employing a broker to find a purchaser, to effect an exchange, lease property for more than a year, or a management contract which extends beyond the period of a year, must be in writing to be enforceable against the principal. Such a contract would also have to be in writing to give the agent the ability to bring an action in court for payment of a commission.

213 On the other hand, a contract to negotiate a loan or lease for one year or less, need not be in writing to be enforced by the courts.

214 If a real estate broker works under a verbal real property sales listing, it is not an illegal contract, but if the seller refuses to pay the commission there is no way the broker may enforce his right to collect it. If the seller keeps his verbal promise to pay, the broker has the right to keep that commission. The use of the statute of frauds to enforce all oral agreements that have been executed is not valid. If a party to an oral agreement, after the contract is complete and all terms met, at a later date decides to rescind the agreement, the statute cannot be used.

215 The statute of frauds has the purpose of preventing a suit on a contract that is oral when it is required to be in writing. It cannot be used as a defense after the contract has been performed (executed). The courts have also held that an oral listing creates a principal-agent fiduciary relationship even though the agent has no enforceable contractual claim for a commission.

STATUTE OF LIMITATIONS

216 "Laches" is a doctrine based upon the inequity of permitting a claim to be enforced because the claimant has delayed too long in pursuing his rights. It is upon this doctrine of laches that the statute of limitations is based, allowing given time periods in which to bring court actions.

WITHIN THREE YEARS

226 An action for the relief on the ground of fraud or mistake. Such cause of action is not deemed to have accrued until the discovery by the injured party of the facts constituting the fraud or mistake.

WITHIN FOUR YEARS

227 An action upon any contract, obligation, or liability founded upon an instrument in writing.

WITHIN FIVE YEARS

232 An action for "mesne profits" of real property. An action for the recovery of real property.

WITHIN TEN YEARS

233 Only for an action upon a judgment or decree of any court of the United States or of any state within the United States.

POWER OF ATTORNEY

234   A   power-of-attorney   is   an acknowledged written instrument which authorizes one person to act for another in his stead.

235   The person who confers this right upon another is called the principal and the person so authorized to act for the principal is called his attorney-in-fact.

239   Any person capable of contracting may act as an attorney-in-fact. When he signs any instrument on behalf of his principal, he should sign in this manner: John Smith, by William Jones, his attorney-in-fact.

240   Due to title insurance requirements, the power-of-attorney should be recorded with the county recorder of the county in which the power conferred is to be used. If not recorded, the title company is unaware that the attorney-in-fact has the legal authority to act if selling real estate.

241   The principal may revoke the power-of-attorney at any time by recording a properly acknowledged declaration revoking the authority in the same county in which the original   agreement   was   recorded.   The power-of-attorney   is   a   personal   service contract, hence, the death of either party, or the incapacity of the principal, will terminate the agreement.

242   There are certain things an attorney-in-fact cannot do: He cannot give away his principal's property, convey or mortgage it without receiving adequate consideration. He may not deed or mortgage it to himself or otherwise use the property of the principal for his own benefit. Such acts are voidable. He must have no interest adverse to his principal in order to act as an attorney-in-fact.

243 An attorney-in-fact is prohibited from mortgaging   or   conveying   property   upon which a homestead exemption has been recorded.

Lesson Five
Part Two
Study Questions

_____(Lesson Five - Paragraph 37 – Question 1)_____

A person holding title to real property in severalty would most likely enjoy:
(A) A life estate. (B) An estate for years. (C) Ownership in common with others. (D) Sole ownership.

(D) The word "severalty" in real property law means one person. Holding title in severalty would be sole ownership.

_____(Lesson Five - Paragraph 37 – Question 2)_____

Sole ownership of real property by an individual is ownership:
(A) Of an undivided interest in common. (B) In gross. (C) In severalty. (D) In joint tenancy.

(C) The legal term "severalty" as used in real estate is defined as "the quality or state of being individual or particular - distinctness, separateness" and a, "sole, separate and exclusive possession, dominion or ownership." An estate "in severalty" indicates sole ownership - by one person only.

_____(Lesson Five - Paragraph 45 – Question 1)_____

When title to real property is held by someone as a tenant in common:
(A) Such an owner may not will his interest. (B) The surviving owner receives the total interest.
(C) Each owner may sell his undivided interest. (D) All interests must be equal.

(C) Each owner of an undivided interest as a tenant in common may sell his interest, may will his interest and need not have an equal interest. The only unity required of a tenancy-in-common is equal right of possession.

_____(Lesson Five - Paragraph 45 – Question 2)_____

One of the features of owning real property as tenants-in-common is:
(A) Each co-owner must have equal interest.
(B) Each owner may not will his interest.
(C) Each co-owner may acquire interest at different times in different instruments.
(D) The sole survivor owns the property in severalty.

(C) In tenancy-in-common, interests can be acquired at different times and different documents may be involved. Requirements of acquisition at the same time, equal interests which cannot be willed and that passes to the last survivor, apply to joint tenancy and not tenancy-in-common.

_____(Lesson Five - Paragraph 46 – Question 1)_____

Under a tenancy-in-common relationship:
(A) There is only one unity required for its existence - possession.
(B) The rights of survivorship exist.
(C) Each party has one-half interest in the rights of the other.
(D) A co-owner, while in possession, can be charged rent for his use of the land.

(A) This should be a part of your fundamental understanding of tenancy-in-common.
_____(Lesson Five - Paragraph 46 – Question2)_____
Tenants in common share in the matter of:
(A) Time. (B) Title. (C) Interest. (D) Possession.

(D) Tenants-in-common possess one unity or equality, and that is the right of possession.

_____(Lesson Five - Paragraph 47 – Question 1)_____
Tenancy-in-common would involve all the following, except:
(A) Undivided interest.   (B) Equal or unequal interests.
(C) Interest passes to devisees or heirs upon death. (D) An arrangement for rights of possession.

(D) All tenants-in-common have equal rights of possession even though they have unequal interests.
Therefore, an arrangement for possession would not be required.

_____(Lesson Five - Paragraph 47 – Question 2)_____
Three people hold an undivided interest in real property as tenants-in-common. From this information, the following would always be a true statement:
(A) Each person has an equal interest.
(B) Each person has an unequal interest.
(C) Each person acquired their interest at the same time.
(D) Each person cannot identify their particular part of the property.

(D) Holding in tenancy-in-common requires only one unit (equality) - that of possession. The tenants-in-common may have equal or unequal interests and may acquire their interests at different times. The term undivided interest indicates owning a part interest in the whole title without the property being partitioned (divided) into separate parcels.

_____(Lesson Five - Paragraph 48 – Question 1)_____
The unities of possession, title, time and interest are necessary in order to create the following types of ownership:
(A) Tenancy-in-common. (B) Joint tenancy. (C) Community property. (D) Severalty.

(B) Remember T.T.I.P. are unities of joint tenancy. (Time, title, interest, possession).

_____(Lesson Five - Paragraph 48 – Question 2)_____
For a man and a woman to hold title as joint tenants:
(A) A clause in the deed must provide for a right of survivorship.
(B) They each must have equal ownership.
(C) They must be husband and wife.
(D) All of the above.

(B) For anyone to hold title as joint tenant, all joint tenants must have equal interest.

_____(Lesson Five - Paragraph 49 – Question 1)_____
The terms "time, title, interest, and possession" are related to:
(A) Adverse possession. (B) Subdivisions. (C) Leaseholds. (D) Survivorship.

(D) Time, title, interest and possession are the four unities present in joint tenancy. The distinguishing characteristic of joint tenancy is survivorship.

_____(Lesson Five - Paragraph 49 – Question 2)_____
The unities of time, title, interest and possession relate to:
(A) Devisees of heirs acquiring status as tenants in common. (B) The theory of survivorship.
(C) The presumption of a tenancy in partnership.   (D) An estate at will.

(B) The question states the four unities that are essential to a joint tenancy. The theory of survivorship is the distinguishing characteristic of a joint tenancy.

_____(Lesson Five - Paragraph 50 – Question 1)_____
Small conveyed a farm to his three sons, A, B and C, as joint tenants. B sold his interest in the farm to W. After this sale, A died leaving a sole heir, S. The ownership interests in the farm following A's death would be:
(A) S will inherit 1/3 share as tenant in common.
(B) C owns 2/3 share as tenant in common with W.
(C) C, W and S will be joint tenants following probate of A's estate.
(D) All three shares are now subject to probate.

(B) A + B + C as joint tenants. B sells to W, which removes that undivided 1/3 interest in the tenancy but this does not destroy the relationship between A and C. They are still joint tenants. When A dies his will does not affect the interest in this holding and A's interest immediately passes to C. Hence, C holds a 2/3 interest together with W who has a 1/3 interest as tenants-in-common.

_____(Lesson Five - Paragraph 51 – Question 1)_____
Hayes owned a parcel of real estate with Jones who borrowed $10,000 using his interest in the property as security for the debt. In the event Jones died before repaying the debt, the property would no longer be subject to this lien if the two of them held title to the property:
(A) As tenants-in-common. (B) As joint tenants.
(C) As general partners.   (D) None of the above is correct.

(B) One of the features of joint tenancy is that if one of the joint tenants has encumbered his portion of the joint tenancy property then dies, the remaining joint tenants receive the deceased joint tenant's interest unencumbered with the debt.

_____(Lesson Five - Paragraph 51 – Question 2)_____

A brother and sister owned an income property together as joint tenants. The brother died and at the time of his death it was discovered that he was heavily in debt. The following statements would be correct:
(A) The creditors of the deceased brother now hold title with the sister as a tenant-in-common.
(B) Title to the income property must go through probate proceedings to protect the creditor's interests.
(C) The sister is now the fee owner and holds title free and clear of the lien.
(D) The deceased brother's wife and his sister now hold title as joint tenants.

(C) Where there are only two people in a joint tenancy holding and one dies, the joint tenancy is immediately terminated and the interest of the deceased passes to the survivor free and clear of all liens placed on the property by the deceased joint tenant.

_____**(Lesson Five - Paragraph 54 – Question 1)**_____

Three venturesome investors take title to a parcel of industrial real property in the following manner:
"The Ajax Engineering Company, a joint venture made up of Henry Dole, James Colby and Hal Smith." Title to this property vests:
(A) The individual investors as joint tenants to each other.
(B) The entity "The Ajax Engineering Company."
(C) The individual ventures as tenants-in-common.
(D) None of the above.

(B) The statement that title is to be placed as the "Ajax Engineering Company, which is a joint venture made up of Henry Dole, James Colby and Hal Smith." This type of a title description would preclude a joint tenancy. Title would require the expression "As joint tenant." Title expressing that it is a "joint venture" would preclude the title to be presumed to be tenants-in-common.

_____**(Lesson Five - Paragraph 55 – Question 1)**_____

Assume this property is held in joint tenancy by the sellers and the day after the purchase agreement acceptance was signed and delivered to buyer, Mr. Doe died of a heart attack. In your opinion:
(A) This would automatically cancel the contract.
(B) Mrs. Doe could sign the escrow instructions and complete the transaction.
(C) Mrs. Doe could take no action until after Mr. Doe's will is probated.
(D) The transaction could not be placed in escrow without Mr. Doe's signature on the escrow.

(B) Upon the death of one of the two parties in a joint tenancy, the interest of the deceased tenant passes immediately to the survivor and probate is not required. Mrs. Doe need only establish the fact of Mr. Doe's death and, as sole owner, may sign the escrow instructions and complete the transaction.

_____**(Lesson Five - Paragraph 61 – Question 1)**_____

Community property is property owned by:
(A) Churches. (B) Husband and wife. (C) The municipality. (D) A neighborhood complex.

(B) Community property is a title holding that is held by a husband and wife. If a married couple takes title to real property as husband and wife, the title holding is presumed to be community property.

_____(Lesson Five - Paragraph 61 – Question 2)_____

Two single persons may own real property in each of the following ways, except:
(A) Tenancy-in-common. (B) Joint tenancy. (C) Community property. (D) Tenancy in partnership.

(C) Community property is a title holding available only to a husband and wife.

_____(Lesson Five - Paragraph 61, 62 – Question 1)_____

The following statement would always be false:
(A) The husband may not sell personal community property for value without the consent of the wife.
(B) Damages collected as a result of injury to a husband are community property.
(C) A surviving spouse is entitled to one-half of the community property, the balance may be willed to others.
(D) Separate property of either spouse becomes community property of the survivor upon the death of one spouse.

(D) Separate property of a deceased spouse could never become community property as the community ceases to exist upon death of a spouse.

_____(Lesson Five - Paragraph 62 – Question 1)_____

Two people each acquire real property while they are single. After marriage, the property:
(A) Becomes community property.   (B) Becomes joint tenancy property.
(C) Remains their separate property. (D) Cannot be disposed of without the consent of the other.

(C) Property acquired prior to marriage is separate property.

_____(Lesson Five - Paragraph 68 – Question 1)_____

Mary and John Root, husband and wife purchased a house in Fresno. The deed reads "I hereby grant to John Root all the real property located at 501 Elm Street in the City of Fresno." In California we are to assume:
(A) That the property is community property.   (B) It is John's separate property.
(C) It is Mary's separate property - held in trust for her by John. (D) That it is held in joint tenancy.

(A) All property purchased by the husband while married is assumed (presumed) to be community property. If it is to be the separate property of the husband, he must substantiate that it was purchased with his separate funds and not community money.

_____(Lesson Five - Paragraph 68 – Question 2)_____

If the purchasers of real property have the title to the property placed in the name of, "John Little and
Mary Little, as husband and wife", it is presumed that they hold title as:

(A) Joint tenants. (B) Community property. (C) Tenants-in-common. (D) Severalty.

(B) The fact that marital status is given as husband and wife and is not further designated joint tenancy, places the holding as community property. You cannot have a joint tenancy unless the designation is spelled out in the deed.

_____(Lesson Five - Paragraph 70 – Question 1)_____

When real property is held by husband and wife as community property, an agreement to sell that property which has been signed by only one spouse would be considered to be:
(A) Illegal. (B) Unenforceable. (C) Binding. (D) A violation of the statute of frauds.

(B) Neither spouse may make a gift without the consent of the other. Neither spouse may encumber the furniture, furnishings or fittings of the home, or the clothing of the other spouse or minor children without the written consent of the other spouse. As in prior law, both must join in the conveyance, encumbrance, or leasing (for more than a year) of community real property.

_____(Lesson Five - Paragraph 70 – Question 2)_____

If only one spouse signs a contract to sell community real property, the contract is:
(A) Unenforceable. (B) Illegal. (C) Enforceable. (D) Valid.

(A) The sale of community real property requires the consent of both spouses. If signed by only one spouse, the contract is voidable at the option of the other spouse. The purchaser would be unable to enforce the contract in court; therefore, it is also described as unenforceable.

_____(Lesson Five - Paragraph 71 – Question 1)_____

A husband and wife consult their attorney concerning a method of taking title to real property that would enable each of them to will their one-half interest in the property to whomever they wish; however, if one of them should die without a will, they wish the surviving spouse to receive the deceased spouse's interest without probate. The attorney would most likely recommend:
(A) Joint tenancy. (B) Community property. (C) Tenancy-in-common. (D) Tenancy by the entireties.
(B) Community property vesting permits each spouse to will his one-half interest to others. However if the spouse should die intestate, the surviving spouse receives the deceased spouse's interest without probate. (Tenancies by the entireties is a title vesting that is not recognized in California.)

_____(Lesson Five - Paragraph 71 – Question 2)_____

A married spouse can will:
(A) None of the community property.   (B) One-half of the community property.
(C) The separate property of her husband. (D) All property held in joint tenancy.

(B) Either husband or wife can will their half of community property. The wife has no control over her husband's separate property and property held in joint tenancy cannot be willed because of the right of survivorship.

_____(Lesson Five - Paragraph 71a – Question 1)_____

The law which governs the distribution of property after dissolution of marriage is contained in the:
(A) Code of Civil Procedure.   (B) Civil Code.
(C) Business and Professions Code. (D) Commissioner's Rules and Regulations.

(B) The law that governs the distribution of property after dissolution of marriage is contained in the Civil Code.

_____(Lesson Five - Paragraph 74 – Question 1)_____

In the event of financial difficulties, the creditors can look to the personal assets of a:
(A) General partner in a partnership venture. (B) Corporation officer.
(C) Limited partner.   (D) None of the above.

(A) A partner in a general partnership is individually liable for any and all obligations of the partnership. A limited partner is liable only to the amount of his investment. Officers of a corporation have immunity from creditors of the corporation since the corporation is considered to be a legal person.

_____(Lesson Five - Paragraph 75 – Question 1)_____

Under current federal income tax law, the ownership holding for multiple investors which would both minimize the tax obligation for the individual and also limit their personal liability would be:
(A) A general partnership. (B) A limited partnership. (C) A corporation. (D) A proprietorship.

(B) The question asks for a type of investment that would both minimize tax obligations and limit personal liability. A general partnership is incorrect because there is liability for the debts of the partnership to the general partner. A corporation is incorrect because corporations have limited liability but there is double taxation. The profits of the corporation are taxed and the remaining dividends are taxed when received by the shareholder. A proprietorship does not afford limited liability.

_____(Lesson Five - Paragraph 77 – Question 1)_____

Once the proprietor of a business has filed a fictitious business name statement in the office of the county clerk, it will expire:
(A) Never, unless abandoned. (B) 10 years from July 1 in the fiscal year in which it is filed.
(C) 5 years from December 31 in the year in which it is filed. (D) 10 years from the date it is filed.

(C) A fictitious business name is valid for five years from the last day of the year in which it is filed. If filed on May 1, it would be good for five years from December 31.

_____(Lesson Five - Paragraph 80 – Question 1)_____

The statute of frauds does not apply to:
(A) A listing contract to sell real property.
(B) A partnership formed to invest in real property.
(C) A commission agreement concerning the sale of real property.
(D) A lease of real property for a two-year period.

(B) The statute of frauds does not apply to partnership agreements, even if formed to invest in real property. However, any agreements executed by the partnership to purchase real property would require written instruments binding the partnership to other principals.

For the protection of all parties, every contract should be in writing. However, the statute of frauds lists those contracts that must be in writing if either of the parties finds it necessary to take a dispute to court. A partnership agreement is not included in the list and is not required to be in writing.

_____(Lesson Five - Paragraph 83 – Question 1)_____

An acquired legal privilege for right of use or enjoyment, short of an estate, which one may have in the land of another, is known as:
(A) An easement. (B) A riparian right. (C) A devise. (D) A lease.

(A) An easement. The statement presents a clear-cut description of an easement. The key to your understanding should be the comment: "short of an estate."

_____(Lesson Five - Paragraph 83 – Question 2)_____

An easement is always:
(A) A general restriction. (B) A specific restriction. (C) An encumbrance. (D) An equitable restriction.

(C) Anything that affects the title to or limits the use of real property is considered an encumbrance.

_____(Lesson Five - Paragraph 83a – Question 1)_____

An easement by prescription can be acquired following permissive use of land for the following number of years:
(A) 5. (B) 1. (C) 20. (D) None of the above.

(D) An easement by prescription can never be acquired through permissive use. The use must be hostile to the owner - without consent.

_____(Lesson Five - Paragraph 85 – Question 1)_____

Mr. Plumber owned a lot that held an appurtenant easement over the neighboring property of Mr. Marty, giving him the right to run a sewer line across Mr. Marty's property. If Mr. Plumber sells the lot to Mr. Sano, but does not mention the easement in his deed, the easement:
(A) Remains with Plumber. (B) Transfers to Sano. (C) Reverts to Marty. (D) Is lost by escheat.

(B) An appurtenance is defined as: "an incidental right attached to a principal property right and passing in possession with it." When Mr. Plumber transferred title to his lot to Mr. Sano, he also transferred the appurtenant easement.

_____(Lesson Five - Paragraph 85 – Question 2)_____

Property owned by Andrews has an easement from Brown over Brown's property. This easement would be:
(A) Restrictive. (B) Appurtenant. (C) In gross. (D) Selective.

(B) An easement that is over another's property is said to be appurtenant to the property with the right to cross. It runs with the land.

_____(Lesson Five - Paragraph 86 – Question 2)_____

The Northern California Telegraph Company has secured the right to place telegraph lines across the back of various residential properties. They have acquired an easement:
(A) By prescription.   (B) In gross.
(C) That can be canceled if not used in five years.   (D) Known as an utility encroachment.

(B) This easement is known as an easement in gross and is usually acquired through a dedication or by eminent domain. Easements in gross are not attached to any particular parcel but to some person, natural or legal (a company).

_____(Lesson Five - Paragraph 89 – Question 1)_____

If a man sold his property and reserved a right in the deed to cross over the property to get to some other land he owned but did not use this right for a period of five years:
(A)   He would have lost his right by non-use.
(B)   His right would continue to be valid, as he reserved it in the deed.
(C)   He would lose his right as it is evident he no longer needs it.
(D)   He would lose the right if his purchaser resold the property.

(B)   The only type of easement that can be lost through non-use is one acquired by prescription or by dedication where it is expressly stated that if not used for the purposes for which dedicated the use of the land will revert to the owner. Easements acquired by reservation are valid indefinitely.

_____(Lesson Five - Paragraph 89 – Question 2)_____

With regard to easements, all of the following statements are correct, except:
(A) A lessee can give an easement for a driveway to a third person; however, the easement is valid
only for the duration of the lease.
(B) An easement may be created by dedication.
(C) A deed granting an unlocated easement is invalid.
(D) An easement may be created by prescription in the State of California by open and hostile use for a continuous period of 5 years.

(C) There is an important distinction with respect to the description contained in an easement and a description in a deed. A deed conveying the fee title to an indefinite strip of land would be void for uncertainty, but a deed to an unlocated easement is valid. The fact that an easement is unlocated may give rise to legal questions. However, if it is recorded, it is a valid easement. The other choices are all correct.

_____(Lesson Five - Paragraph 90 – Question 1)_____

An easement by dedication may be created by:
(A) eminent domain. (B) the filing of a subdivision map. (C) police power. (D) U.S. patent.

(B) A subdivider offers to dedicate an easement when he submits a subdivision map. The government accepts the offer and the subdivider records the map thus dedicating the easement.

_____(Lesson Five - Paragraph 92 – Question 1)_____
An interest in real property may be acquired by either prescription or by adverse possession. The interest resulting from prescription would be:
(A) the right to use another's land (B) a possessory title (C) an equitable interest (D) a private grant.

(A) A right to use another's land by prescription is an easement called a prescriptive easement. When one claims the full title to land, it is called adverse possession.

_____(Lesson Five - Paragraph 92 – Question 2)_____
All of the following pertain to easements gained by prescription, except:
(A) taxes must be paid. (B) open and notorious use for five continuous years.
(C) use hostile to the title holder's intention. (D) use is under some claim of right or color of title.

(A) Prescriptive easements do not require payment of taxes. Someone perfecting such an easement must act upon some claim of right to do so.

_____(Lesson Five - Paragraph 99 – Question 1)_____
An easement that has been acquired by prescription may be terminated or extinguished by:
(A) Merger of the ownership of the easement and the servient tenement. (B) By written agreement.
(C) Non-use for five years. (D) Any of the above.

(D) An easement that has been acquired by prescription may be terminated or extinguished by merger of the ownership of the easement, by written agreement, and by non-use.

_____(Lesson Five - Paragraph 99, 100 – Question 1)_____
The following is an incorrect statement regarding an easement:
(A) It can be protected against third party interference.
(B) It can be removed.
(C) It is a non-possessory interest in land.
(D) It can be terminated at will by the possessor of the burdened land.

(D) The possessor of the land over which the easement passes is not the owner of the easement. He is the owner of the servient tenement. Only the owner of the easement, the dominant tenement, or the court can terminate an easement. An easement is an encumbrance on title that is non-possessory in nature.

_____(Lesson Five - Paragraph 99, 100 – Question 2)_____
An easement on real estate would terminate if the holder of the dominant tenement recorded:
(A) Deed of Reconveyance. (B) Notice of non-responsibility.
(C) Defeasance clause.   (D) Quitclaim deed.

(D) The usual instrument used to eliminate an easement would be a quitclaim deed from the owner of the dominant tenement.

_____(Lesson Five - Paragraph 100 – Question 1)_____

To eliminate an easement, one typically would use a/an:
(A) Lease. (B) Trust deed. (C) Quitclaim deed. (D) Injunction.

(C) How to eliminate an easement on one's property? An easement belongs to the land and runs with the land; therefore, if a neighbor has an easement across your property you must get a quitclaim deed from that neighbor giving up any right he has to cross your land.

_____(Lesson Five - Paragraph 100 – Question 2)_____

Two adjoining lots have an easement between them with one owner holding a dominant tenement and the other a servient tenement. Under these circumstances:
(A) The dominant tenement cannot use the easement for ingress and egress
(B) The burdened property is owned by the holder of the dominant tenement.
(C) The easement can be eliminated by merging the two properties under one owner.
(D) This type of easement can only be created by prescription.

(C) Where the dominant and servient tenement come under one ownership, the lesser (servient) merges into the greater thus terminating the easement. The same effect would take place, for example, if an owner of property acquired a lease on his own property. The lease would merge into the greater estate. This type of easement can be created in many ways other than by prescription.

_____(Lesson Five - Paragraph 101 – Question 1)_____

The following best illustrates the difference between an easement and a license:
(A) A license is a personal right.   (B) A license may be revoked.
(C) A license may not be assigned. (D) All of the above.

(D) Easements and licenses both give authority to use another person's land within.

_____(Lesson Five - Paragraph 101 – Question 2)_____

A license is similar to an easement in the following way:
(A) It may be in writing.   (B) It may be terminated by the grantor.
(C) It may be assigned by the holder. (D) Revoked at any time.

(A) A license is defined as a personal, revocable, and non-assignable permission or authority to enter upon the land of another person for a particular purpose, but without possessing any interest in the land. An easement is assignable but not revocable and generally cannot be terminated by the grantor. Both may be in writing.

_____(Lesson Five - Paragraph 105 – Question 1)_____

A minor can do the following without court approval:
(A) Convey title of real property to another.
(B) Receive title to real property by gift or inheritance.
(C) Convey real property to another through a guardian.
(D) Delegate another to act as agent in their behalf.

(B) Any of the other acts would require court approval.

_____(Lesson Five - Paragraph 105 – Question 2)_____

A licensed real estate broker is successful in securing a buyer for a property who is ready, willing and able to buy. The offer is accepted and signed by both parties and escrow is

opened. During the escrow period the title company discovers that the seller is an unemancipated minor and notifies the broker and escrow holder. Under these circumstances, the contract is:
(A) Valid. (B) Void. (C) Voidable. (D) Outlawed.

(B) A real estate contract signed by an unemancipated minor is not really a contract at all since it lacks one of the essentials, capacity. We usually refer to this as a void contract, not voidable. A contract that is void is not a contract at all.

_____(Lesson Five - Paragraph 106 – Question 1)_____
A contract signed by an unmarried woman over the age of 18 is:
(A) Valid. (B) Void. (C) Unenforceable. (D) Illegal.

(A) An unmarried person is one that was previously married. Once a person attains the age of 18 he may enter into a valid contract

_____(Lesson Five - Paragraph 106 – Question 2)_____
Generally, a single person does not have capacity to sign a valid and binding real estate contract until the age of:
(A) 18. (B) 19. (C) 20. (D) 21.

(A) A single person must have reached the age of 18 to sign a valid real estate contract. The exception to the rule is an emancipated minor.

_____(Lesson Five - Paragraph 108 – Question 1)_____
A lease of real property executed by a married minor under 18 years of age is:
(A) Void. (B) Voidable by lessor. (C) Voidable by lessee. (D) Valid.

(D) A person under the age of 18 who is married is said to be "emancipated," that is, treated as an adult. A contract by a married minor is valid.

_____(Lesson Five - Paragraph 108 – Question 2)_____
A 17-year-old divorcee wishes to sell her real property. She contracts a licensed real estate broker to give a listing for the sale. In such circumstances, the broker:
(A) Can accept the listing.
(B) Cannot accept the listing because it could be community property.
(C) Cannot accept the listing until the courts declare the man to be emancipated.
(D) Cannot accept the listing until the minor becomes 18 years of age.

(A) This divorcee is an emancipated minor and is to be treated as an adult. Hence, she can employ a broker to act as her agent.

_____(Lesson Five - Paragraph 117 – Question 1)_____
An unmarried person under the age of 18 can make a valid conveyance of real property they own:
(A) When using an agreement of sale as the instrument of conveyance.
(B) When guardianship proceedings have been established for the minor.
(C) When a lessor in a written lease for less than a year.

(D) When selling unimproved land for which a final public report has been issued by the real estate
commissioner.

(B) A minor may acquire real property without a guardianship; however, guardianship proceedings are essential for obtaining a valid conveyance from the minor. In this question, no mention is made of an emancipated minor.

_____(Lesson Five - Paragraph 117 – Question 2)_____

Spencer, a 15-year-old emancipated minor, desired to sell real estate he owned and has presented evidence of his emancipation to the listing broker. When the broker sells the property he should submit the proof of emancipation to:
(A) The title insurer. (B) The escrow company. (C) The buyer's lender. (D) The buyer.

(B) The title insurer may also want to see this. The broker will give it to the escrow and they will submit it to the title insurer.

_____(Lesson Five - Paragraph 119 – Question 1)_____

The following would make subsequent contracts entered into by an affected person void:
(A) A person commits himself to a mental institution voluntarily
(B) A person becomes disabled physically and is unable to live a normal life style
(C) A conservator has been appointed for a person in formal conservatorship proceedings
(D) A person is formally committed to a mental institution.

(D) The Civil Code provides that when a person is formally adjudged insane and committed to a mental institution, their future contracts are void by law. The distracting answer is (C). When a conservator has been appointed, this does not by statute make subsequent contracts void. A conservator may be appointed for the person or appointed to preserve the person's property. A conservatorship does not automatically make subsequent contracts void.

_____(Lesson Five - Paragraph 120 – Question 1)_____

A corporation cannot hold title to real property as a:
(A) Joint tenant. (B) Tenant-in-common. (C) Partnership. (D) None of the above methods.

(A) A corporation may not hold as a joint tenant. The purpose of a joint tenancy is for survivorship and, as a corporation does not die, it may not hold title in this fashion. However, a corporation being a legal person may hold title as a tenant-in-common or as a partner.

_____(Lesson Five - Paragraph 122 – Question 1)_____

Quack Corporation has been in the business of operating 22 franchise outlets in various states continuously for the past five years. The corporation's most recently audited financial statement shows a net worth of $3,000,000. Should Quack Corp. decide to expand their operation into California, the following is true:
(A) It would have to register with the State Corporations Commissioner.
(B) It would have to post with the Commissioner a $10,000 fidelity bond.
(C) It would only have to register in the counties in which it was to operate.
(D) It has enough past experience and sufficient assets to be exempt from filing.

(A) State law exempts from registration those corporations with a net worth of not less than $5,000,000 and have had at least 25 franchisees conducting business at all times during the five year period immediately preceding the offer to sell. Quack Corp. does not meet these.

_____(Lesson Five - Paragraph 125 – Question 1)_____

The presence of a corporate seal on a deed:
(A) Means that consideration was paid.
(B) Implies that the proper or authorized person signed the deed.
(C) Would indicate that title is being conveyed to a corporation.
(D) Is needed for recording the instrument.

(B) Years ago a corporate seal represented real authority. Today, however, a seal is said to have only "evidentiary value" that the document was executed in a proper manner. A document so executed by virtue of a resolution of the board of directors would be valid without the seal.

_____(Lesson Five - Paragraph 126 – Question 1)_____

You are one of a number of people considering the purchase of an income-producing real property. In taking title to this property as a group, the following title holding would subject the income produced by the property to double taxation:
(A) Joint tenancy. (B) Tenancy-in-common. (C) Tenancy-in-partnership. (D) Corporation.

(D) If title is taken by a corporate entity or in the name of a corporation the income would be taxed to the corporation and again as the income remaining is distributed to the stockholder. Hence, double taxation.

_____(Lesson Five - Paragraph 132 – Question 1)_____

For federal income tax purposes the following would be incorrect with respect to partnership entities. The partnership:
(A) Must file an income tax return each year.
(B) Income, gains and losses, and other deductions on credit are allocated to the individual partners.
(C) Need not file an income tax return.
(D) Earnings are taxable to the individual partners, whether they are distributed, accumulated or reinvested in the partnership venture.

(C) This is an incorrect statement. The partnership itself is not a tax paying entity. It is an income reporting entity that is not subject to tax. All the income and deductions on the partnership property, including depreciation, will be attributed to the partners for inclusion in their respective individual tax returns.

_____(Lesson Five - Paragraph 139 – Question 1)_____

The court given jurisdiction over all probate matters in California is the:
(A) Superior court. (B) Municipal court. (C) Supreme court. (D) County court.

(A) Every county has a Superior Court and the State Constitution gives this court jurisdiction over probate proceedings.

_____(Lesson Five - Paragraph 139 – Question 2)_____

A person who acquires title to real property by intestate succession does so by:
(A) A holographic will.   (B) A nuncupative will.
(C) Appropriate court action. (D) Action for declaratory relief.

(C) When one dies intestate, he leaves no will. The estate of the deceased who is intestate is distributed according to a court decree.

_____(Lesson Five - Paragraph 140 – Question 1)_____

The executor of a decedent's estate petitioned and received approval from the probate court for the sale of the real property in the estate. The property:
(A) Must be sold at public auction. (B) Must be advertised and sold to the highest bidder.
(C) May be sold at any price and on any terms approved by the court. (D) Must be sold for cash.

(C) An executor's or an administrator's method of disposal of the estate of a decedent, be it auction or regular sale, and the amount received, must usually be approved by the court before it can become final.

_____(Lesson Five - Paragraph 140 – Question 2)_____

When a person dies, an administrator or an executor may become involved in settling the affairs of the deceased. If the sale of real property is completed during the probate period and a real estate broker is instrumental in concluding the sale, the following would be correct concerning commissions to be paid to licensed real estate agents:
(A) The heirs set the commission.
(B) The probate court sets the commission.
(C) The administrator or executor sets the commission.
(D) The buyer sets the commission.

(B) A California Appellate Court decision held that the probate court has exclusive jurisdiction to set a broker's claim to a real estate commission.

_____(Lesson Five - Paragraph 141, 142 – Question 1)_____

Concerning the court-administered sale of property while in probate, all of the following are correct statements, except:
(A) The price offered must be at least 90% of court appraised value.
(B) Commission for a sale is based upon a schedule of commissions maintained by the courts and
based upon selling prices.
(C) The first overbid must be at least 10% higher on first $ 10,000 and 5% on the balance.
(D) Property may be sold at public auction or private sale; however, the sale is subject to confirmation by the court.

(B) There is no schedule of commissions established by courts or by law. The probate judge approving the sale will establish the amount of commission payable to the broker who procured the buyer.

_____(Lesson Five - Paragraph 141, 142 – Question 2)_____

In a probate sale, the following would least likely affect the judge's final decision:
(A) Recently concluded sales of comparable properties during the preceding six-month period.

(B) Involuntary sales during the past year.
(C) Sales of properties in like areas with similar characteristics.
(D) Sale of a comparable property in the same neighborhood allowing for noticeable differences.

(B) The court would be concerned with determining the current "market value" of the property. The "willing buyer - willing seller" requirement would not be supported by evidence of forced sales (involuntary sales).

_____(Lesson Five - Paragraph 162 – Question 1)_____
An individual would not gain legal title to real property with the following:
(A) A patent. (B) Prescription. (C) Escheat. (D) A grant deed.

(C) An individual does not gain title by the process of escheat. This is a right of the state.

_____(Lesson Five - Paragraph 162 – Question 2)_____
Jackson dies leaving no will and no heirs. His estate (real property):
(A) Would pass to his next of kin following the determination of the probate court.
(B) Would revert to the State of California.
(C) Would transfer to the county where the property is located.
(D) Would, after a five-year redemption period, escheat to the county where it is located.

(B) California law carefully protects the interests of possible successors in interest to the estate of a deceased person who dies intestate. Within the limits of these legal safeguards the estate would revert, escheat, to the State of California should a person die intestate and without heirs.

_____(Lesson Five - Paragraph 166 – Question 1)_____
The word "bequeath" is most opposite to which of the following:
(A) Intestate. (B) Devise. (C) Will. (D) Grant.

(A) The word "bequeath" means to give or leave personal property by will. The choice with the most opposite meaning would be "intestate" - to die without leaving a will.

_____(Lesson Five - Paragraph 166 – Question 2)_____
The following would be related to intestate succession:
(A) A holographic will.   (B) Dying without a will.
(C) A will which does not specify all possible heirs. (D) None of the above.

(B) When a person dies without leaving a valid will, that person's property passes to his heirs at law. When a person dies and leaves a valid will, the property passes to the testator's devisees.

_____(Lesson Five - Paragraph 167 – Question 1)_____
A person who receives personal property under the terms of a will is referred to as the:
(A) Grantee. (B) Legatee. (C) Devisee. (D) Claimant.

(B) A legatee is one who takes title to personal property as the beneficiary in a will (educationally defined).

_____(Lesson Five - Paragraph 167 – Question 2)_____

Land is passed in a will by:
(A) Devise. (B) Bequest. (C) Legacy. (D) Intestate succession.

(A) Devise is defined as the testamentary disposition (willing) of land or realty. A bequest is the gift of personal property by will. A legacy is personal property received by will. Intestate succession is the legal right of an heir to the property when the deceased did not leave a will.

_____(Lesson Five - Paragraph 167 – Question 3)_____

The following term does not belong with the others:
(A) Executor. (B) Sale. (C) Will. (D) Devise.

(B) Choices (A), (C), and (D) are concerned with the subject of wills.

_____(Lesson Five - Paragraph 168 – Question 1)_____

The terms "ambulatory," "devise," "codicil," would relate to:
(A) Accession. (B) Community real property. (C) Wills. (D) Intestate succession.

(C) These legal terms are used in connection with wills and are defined, briefly, as follows: Ambulatory - a changeable will or will subject to change. Devise - a gift of real property by will. Codicil - an addition or supplement altering a will.

_____(Lesson Five - Paragraph 180 – Question 1)_____

As a "member of a family unit" a husband recorded a declaration of homestead on the family residence that was encumbered by an $82,000 first trust deed. The wife did not sign the declaration. The property was worth $108,000. The owner had a new roof put on the building but did not pay the roofing contractor who then filed a mechanic's lien. The lien was:
(A) Not enforceable because homestead property is protected from any liens.
(B) Enforceable because the wife did not sign the declaration of homestead.
(C) Enforceable because mechanic's liens take priority over homestead exemptions.
(D) Not enforceable because with a 1st TD of $12,000 there is no equity above the exemption.

(C) A homestead exemption does not protect the owner against mechanic's liens or trust deed foreclosures. If both spouses reside on the premises, either spouse may declare the homestead.

_____(Lesson Five - Paragraph 180, 181 – Question 1)_____

A man and wife own a residence that is presently valued at $123,000 and has an existing first trust deed of $99,000. In 1956, the wife had recorded a homestead on behalf of her family but without the consent or knowledge of her husband. A creditor who secured a judgment of $2,000 and now wants to execute the judgment by forcing the sale of the home after recently suing them. Under these circumstances:
(A)   The homestead would be ineffective since it was recorded without the consent of the husband.
(B)   The judgment creditor could collect the $2,000 since the maximum limit on the wife's exemption is $30,000.
(C)   The execution of the judgment would not be possible at this time.

(D)   The creditor must first obtain permission from the 1st trust deed holder since it is a prior lien.

(C) The wife can homestead a residence as a member of a family unit and obtain the exemption without the consent of the husband. In this case they are protected and the court will not permit a sale of the home since there would be no proceeds available for the judgment creditor.

_____(Lesson Five - Paragraph 180, 181 – Question 2)_____

Mr. and Mrs. Booker purchased a home for $120,000 and secured a new first trust deed and note at that time. Within two months after the purchase, the Bookers' recorded a homestead on the home. One year later they had a judgment lien levied against them for $5,500. Subsequently, they listed the property and sold it for $121,000, at which time the trust deed and note balance was $105,500. Under these circumstances, the holder of the judgment lien would receive the following amount from escrow out of the proceeds of the sale:
(A) $5,550. (B) $4,500. (C) $6,000. (D) Nothing.

(D) If the property sells for $121,000 and the lien is $105,500, their equity is only $15,500 and the judgment lien holder would receive nothing.

_____(Lesson Five - Paragraph 181 – Question 1)_____

All of the following are requirements of a valid homestead, except:
(A) Type and description of the property.
(B) Identify by name claimant's spouse, if any.
(C) A statement that person claiming is married.
(D) A statement that the claimant is residing on the property at the time of the filing.

(C) A person need not be married to file a homestead. Thus, married status is not a requirement.

_____(Lesson Five - Paragraph 186 – Question 1)_____

A single woman who maintains a household as "head of the family," properly filed a declaration of homestead on her residence. A judgment of $12,000 is obtained against her. The present value of the residence is $83,000 against which a $59,000 first trust deed is recorded. In the event of an attempt to execute the judgment on her residence, the creditor could successfully obtain:
(A) Any amount from the equity above the $25,000 homestead exemption.
(B) One-half the judgment amount.
(C) Nothing, as the homestead exemption would prevent execution on the judgment.
(D) The full $12,000 judgment claim.

(C) Any person qualifying as a "head of a family," no matter what their marital status, would qualify for the exemption under California Law.

_____(Lesson Five - Paragraph 188 – Question 1)_____

The first priority in the distribution of funds in the judicial sale of homesteaded property would go to:
(A) Discharge of prior encumbrances. (B) Execution of judgment.
(C) Homestead claimant.   (D) Court costs.

(D) A homestead exemption does not protect the claimant against trust deeds, mortgages, mechanic's liens, nor any lien recorded before the homestead. In a sale, these prior encumbrances would be satisfied following the court costs.

_____(Lesson Five - Paragraph 188 – Question 2)_____

A homeowner's equity in his residence exceeds the amount of his homestead exemption. In the event of an execution sale to satisfy a judgment:
(A) Judgment creditor could purchase the property for the exemption amount.
(B) Judgment creditor could satisfy his judgment for the exemption amount only.
(C) Judgment debtor would have no prior claim because of his excess equity.
(D) Judgment debtor would receive the exemption amount prior to judgment.

(D) The judgment debtor (homeowner) is entitled to the exemption amount from his equity prior to satisfaction of the judgment.

_____(Lesson Five - Paragraph 189 to 191 – Question 1)_____

A claimant could record a homestead declaration on all of the following properties, except:
(A) A multiple residence dwelling where the owner claimant lives in one unit.
(B) A residence with a second house in the rear of the lot.
(C) A property with a house under construction in which the claimant plans to live.
(D) A residence held in joint tenancy.

(C) Choices (A), (B), and (D) suggest circumstances in which the owner in residence would be able to claim the homestead exemption. The homestead claimant must actually reside on the property to be able to file a declaration of homestead. In choice (C), this is not the case.

_____(Lesson Five - Paragraph 189 to 191 – Question 2)_____

A claimant could record a homestead declaration on all of the following properties, except:
(A) A single-family residence.
(B) A farm where the claimant lives.
(C) A single family residence under construction.
(D) A two story unit in a multi-unit structure.

(C) Homestead means the principal dwelling: (a) In which the judgment debtor or spouse resided on the date the judgment creditor's lien attached to the dwelling and, (b) in which either or both resided continuously until the date of the court determination that the dwelling is a homestead. Obviously, a home under construction is not being lived in.

_____(Lesson Five - Paragraph 193 – Question 1)_____

A search of the records at the county recorder's office will always indicate a current and valid:
(A) Easement. (B) Homestead declaration. (C) Land sales contract. (D) Lease.

(B) A declaration of homestead is one of the documents that must be recorded to be effective; therefore, a search of the records would show this fact. The requirement of recording does not apply to the choices suggested in (A), (C) or (D).

_____(Lesson Five - Paragraph 193 – Question 2)_____

The following document must be recorded to be effective:

(A) Grant deed. (B) Mortgage. (C) Trust deed. (D) Declaration of homestead.

(D) A declaration of homestead is one of the documents that must be recorded to be effective.

_____(Lesson Five - Paragraph 195 – Question 1)_____

A man homesteaded his house and later sold it conveying title by grant deed but did not file a declaration of abandonment. He then purchased another dwelling and proceeded to homestead the new property. The second homestead was:

(A) Valid, as he sold the property by grant deed and did not need to file a declaration of abandonment.
(B) Valid, even if he had not sold the first property, as the head of a family may have several   homesteads at the same time.
(C) Void, as he failed to file declaration of abandonment on first home.
(D) Void, as only one homestead is ever permitted for the same reason.

(A) A declaration of homestead can be cleared from the records in two ways, by filing a declaration of abandonment, or by recording a deed transferring title to another. In the latter case, the filing of a declaration of abandonment becomes unnecessary as the transfer of title automatically abandons the homestead. Upon purchase of another property, the man was entitled to homestead it. A person cannot homestead two properties simultaneously, but may homestead one after another as he transfers title or files a declaration of abandonment on the previous one.

_____(Lesson Five - Paragraph 203 – Question 1)_____

The statute of frauds requires that the following must be in writing to be enforceable:
(A) The sale of stock and goodwill of a business.
(B) A lease of one year.
(C) A listing for one year on a business opportunity.
(D) A commission agreement on the sale of real property.

(D) The statute of frauds requires any commission agreement between a seller and the broker concerning the sale of real property to be in writing. A business opportunity is classified as personal property and does not come under the statute of frauds. A lease more than one year must be in writing.

_____(Lesson Five - Paragraph 205 – Question 1)_____

John and Sam enter into a one-year lease agreement calling for monthly payments of $910. This instrument was executed October 31, 2012, to become effective December 1, 2013. To be enforceable, it:
(A) Need not be in writing.   (B) Must be in writing.
(C) Must be acknowledged.   (D) Is subject to review by the court.

(B) More than one year will pass between the date the instrument is executed and the date that the agreement is completed. Section 1624 of the Civil Code (statute of frauds), requires "an agreement that by its terms is not to be performed within a year from the making thereof," must be written to be enforceable.

_____(Lesson Five - Paragraph 205 – Question 2)_____

Evidence established that an owner and a new tenant orally entered into a ten-month lease, payable $155 per month. Two months after the tenant moved in, he changed his mind. Which of the following is correct?
(A) Valid even though it was oral.   (B) Valid as month-to-month tenancy.
(C) Invalid as it was not in writing. (D) Invalid because it was not delivered.

(A) A lease of one year or less does not have to be in writing to be enforceable. The fact that the tenant acknowledges moving in and paying the agreed upon rent would be sufficient to substantiate the lease. A ten-month lease is not a month-to-month tenancy.

_____(Lesson Five - Paragraph 212 Question 1)_____

It would be most difficult for a broker to collect a commission in the following circumstance:
(A) Leasing real property seven months with no written authorization.
(B) Selling personal property with no written authorization.
(C) Leasing real property one year with no written authorization.
(D) Exchanging real properties with no written authorization.

(D) Property may be leased for one year or less without written authorization and personal property may be sold without written authorization, so you could collect a commission on these transactions. To collect a commission on an exchange you must have the commission agreement in writing

_____(Lesson Five - Paragraph 214 – Question 1)_____

If a broker accepts an oral contract to earn a commission on the sale of real property and the seller actually pays him the money:
(A) The broker can accept the commission
(B) It is illegal if not in writing
(C) It is against the rules of the Real Estate Commissioner
(D) The broker may lose his license

(A) The statute of frauds states that one may not enforce an oral contract with the principal in court for a commission. This is not a bar to a mutual agreed payment of commission.

_____(Lesson Five - Paragraph 214 – Question 2)_____

A sells the property to B by grant deed for an "all cash" purchase price of $5,000. There was no other written memorandum of the transaction. Six months later B attempts to rescind the sale on the basis of the statute of frauds. Concerning the legal basis of B's claim:
(A) The statue of frauds applies because of the lack of written memorandum.
(B) B may void the sale but must restore the property to its original condition.
(C) B may rescind the sale because the statute of frauds defines this transactions as fraudulent.
(D) The statue of frauds does not apply.

(D) The statute of frauds does not apply to an executed oral agreement as we have in this question.

_____(Lesson Five - Paragraph 216 – Question 1)_____

The legal term "laches" principally involves:
(A) A delay that justifies presumption that a party has waived his right. (B) Fraud and deceit.

(C) Neglecting to reduce an agreement to a proper writing. (D) A presumption of validity.

(A) "Laches" is a doctrine based upon the inequity of permitting a claim to be enforced because the claimant has delayed too long in pursuing his rights, thereby waiving his rights or making it difficult to arrive at a safe conclusion of the truth. It is upon this doctrine of laches that the statutes of limitations are based allowing given time periods in which to bring court actions.

_____(Lesson Five - Paragraph 226 – Question 1)_____

A broker innocently misrepresents a property because of information given him by the seller. Some time later the buyer discovers the misrepresentation. The buyer has to bring this to court within:
(A) Two years from the event.   (B) Three years from discovery of the misrepresentation.
(C) Four years from the event. (D) Five years from discovery of the misrepresentation.

(B) Three years from the discovery of the misrepresentation. In this instance, the licensee is the innocent victim of the seller's deception and misrepresentation and would be guilty of no wrongdoing. The action suggested in this question is against the seller who perpetrated the fraud. In cases of fraud, the injured party must act within three years of the discovery of the fraud as provided by the statute of limitations.

_____(Lesson Five - Paragraph 227 – Question 1)_____

In an action against the seller for payment of a commission, the following is a true statement:
(A) A listing agreement signed by the seller but not by the broker is unenforceable by the broker.
(B) The seller and buyer may mutually agree to rescind their agreement and effectively relieve the   seller from payment of a commission.
(C) Such action must be commenced within four years from the time the commission was earned.
(D) A commission earned but not paid creates a lien on the subject property.

(C) The statute of limitations provides that a default in agreements dependent upon a written instrument must be acted upon within 4 years of the due date of the instrument. In the matter of choice (A), should a sale take place within time established by the terms of a listing agreement signed by the owner (seller) and in the possession of the broker named in the agreement, a court would normally uphold the agreement.

_____(Lesson Five - Paragraph 227 – Question 2)_____

A contract to sell is drawn up between a buyer and seller. The contract is properly and legally executed in every detail. Four months later with the contract still in force, the seller changes his mind and decides not to sell thinking he can now get more for the property. Under the statute of limitations the buyer must bring action against the seller in civil court within:
(A) 90 days. (B) 2 years. (C) 4 years. (D) 10 years.

(C) An action upon any contract obligation or liability founded upon an instrument in writing must be brought to court within four years of the date of breech.

_____(Lesson Five - Paragraph 232 – Question 1)_____

After Mr. Gardner purchased his home he discovered by survey that his neighbor's fence was three feet on his newly acquired property. This disturbed him greatly. For remedy, if a friendly settlement cannot be reached, he should bring civil suit against:

(A) The broker, for failure to disclose the encroachment

(B) His neighbor, for removal of the encroachment on the grounds of trespass if less than five   years have elapsed since the encroachment was created.

(C) His neighbor, under the law of adverse possession.

(D) The title company, for failure to show encumbrance on the standard form title report.

(B) The action taken for removal of the encroachment would be an action for trespass. The broker is not required to be a surveyor. The (C) choice is incorrect as this does not involve adverse possession. Adverse possession is a claim to title to property by open and notorious use, adverse to the owner, and with payment of taxes. Answer (D) is incorrect. The standard title policy does not insure against such off-record risks such as encroachment. This risk to be insured requires the extended coverage or the ALTA policy.

_____(Lesson Five - Paragraph 234 – Question 1)_____

If the buyer limited the time for acceptance in a purchase agreement to only three days and the sellers were away on a weekend and could not be contacted by the broker, the broker could legally sign the seller's name to the acceptance if:

(A) The sellers had told him before they left that if he got a good offer he should accept it for them.

(B) The sellers had given him a properly executed and recorded power of attorney.

(C) He signs the seller's name and adds "by John White, Broker"

(D) He had his signature notarized.

(B) A properly executed and recorded general power of attorney would allow the broker to act for the seller in signing the acceptance, escrow instructions, and even the grant deed.

_____(Lesson Five - Paragraph 235 – Question 1)_____

A private person authorized by another to act in his place and stead, either for some particular purpose or for the transaction of business in general, not of a legal character, is known as:

(A) An attorney-in-fact. (B) An affiant. (C) A conservator. (D) An attorney at law.

(A) The statement of the question provides an exact definition of an attorney-in-fact. Do not confuse the person - the attorney-in-fact - with the written instrument in which the authority to act for another is set forth - the power of attorney. With respect to the other choices: (B) An affiant is one who makes an affidavit, (C) A conservator is appointed by the court when a person is found incapable of managing his affairs.

_____(Lesson Five - Paragraph 235 – Question 2)_____

The person who has been given the right to act on behalf of another is known as:

(A) An affiant. (B) A principal. (C) An attorney-in-fact. (D) An executor.

(C) The power of an attorney is the piece of paper and the one with the right to act is the attorney-in-fact.

_____(Lesson Five - Paragraph 241, 242 – Question 1)_____

Mr. "B" gave Mr. "A" a power of attorney to sell his home. Under which of the following conditions may it not be exercised:
(A) Mr. "A" conveyed title with a gift deed. (B) Mortgaging his principal's property to himself.
(C) Death of his principal.   (D) All of the above.

(D) All of these circumstances prevent the sale of real property by the attorney-in-fact

_____(Lesson Five - Paragraph 241 to 243 – Question 1)_____

Mr. "B" gave Mr. "A" a power of attorney to sell his home. Under which of the following conditions may it not be exercised:
(A) A court ruling that Mr. "B" was incompetent. (B) When mortgaging "Bs" property to himself.
(C) The property had a declaration of homestead recorded on it by Mr. "B." (D) All of the above.

(D) All of the above are restrictions on the authority of an attorney-in-fact.

_____(Lesson Five - Paragraph 242 – Question 1)_____

An attorney-in-fact cannot do the following:
(A) Record the power of attorney, if notarized. (B) Do specific acts under a general power of attorney.
(C) Mortgage the principal's property to himself. (D) None of the above.

(C) An attorney-in-fact is a person who has been authorized to act for another, in his stead. He cannot act adversely to the interest of his principal. By mortgaging the principal's property to himself, he would be signing the principal's name to a promissory note made out to him.

_____(Lesson Five - Paragraph 242 – Question 2)_____

W, who has been properly designated "attorney-in-fact" for S, cannot do the following with "B's" property:
(A) Mortgage "B's" interest in the property for a valuable consideration.
(B) Deed "B's" property to "B's" favorite nephew without valuable consideration.
(C) Lease the property to a tenant for a reasonable consideration.
(D) Deed the property to another for a valuable consideration.

(B) An attorney-in-fact is forbidden by law from making a gift of his principal's property to anyone.
The agent must always seek to protect the interest of his principal.

Notes

Lesson Five
Part Three
Understanding Through Question Testing

 Log into your course at www.lumbleau.com.

STUDENT LOGIN
Login: [　　　]
Password: [　　　]

 On your student home page, click on the "State Exam Preparation".

STATE EXAM
PREPARATION

 Under the "Guided Lesson" tab click on the fifth of fourteen links: "Legal Aspects".

Real Estate Salesperson Course

Guided Lessons	Practice Exams	Progress Report	Success Video

Print	Questions
Click	HERE>>> 5. Legal Aspects I

Here you will be tested on all of the questions you have been studying and learn the most recently added questions. It is essential, for maximum retention, that you eliminate all of the questions you can easily answer and "TAG" for study the questions with which you have difficulty.

Lesson Six
Part One
Understanding Through Video Teaching

Lesson Six

Encumbrances

60   The word "encumbrance" as used in real estate is a general term denoting anything that affects the title or limits the use of real property. It means any right or interest in land possessed by someone other than the owner.

61   Encumbrances fall into two general categories. Those for money called liens affect the title by making it security for the payment of a debt and non-money encumbrances, such as easements and deed restrictions.

61a   Encumbrances can be voluntary or involuntary. If the owner by contractual agreement allows the encumbrance to be placed against his title, it is voluntary. If the city or county places a tax lien or an easement in gross for utilities on the property without the owner's approval, it is involuntary.

62   Since most property is encumbered with some type of restriction, easement, or lien, it is common practice for a buyer to accept a deed on encumbered property. Title companies always insure encumbered property.

MONEY ENCUMBRANCES - LIENS

63   A lien is defined as a charge imposed upon property by which it is made security for the performance of an act, usually the payment of a debt, and is known as a money encumbrance.

65   Liens may be specific or general. A specific lien is imposed on a single property. A general lien is one imposed upon all non-exempt property owned by the debtor in the county where the lien is properly recorded.

VOLUNTARY LIENS

67   When a borrower voluntarily encumbers his property by giving an interest in it as security for a loan, the instrument used for this purpose is known as a "security device." A lien is not an estate. It simply encumbers an estate.

SECURITY DEVICES IN GENERAL

72   Anyone holding a mortgage or trust deed note may borrow against it and use it as security. The note is considered to be intangible personal property and may be pledged as collateral to a lender. It is also referred to as a pledge agreement.

MORTGAGE WAREHOUSING

72a   When one lender places a number of trust deeds or mortgages with another lender as security on a large loan, the practice is referred to as "mortgage warehousing." Warehousing operations also refer to mortgage bankers when they make a short term loan from a bank to acquire funds for several take-out loans for buyers of homes. They then use this as security for large short-term loans. When they collect a number of these individual take-out loans, they will sell them as a "portfolio of loans" either to Fannie Mae or to some other organization that buys bank loans.

72b   Mortgage bankers who build a "portfolio of loans" will often receive a "line of credit" as their business builds in an ethical manner.

74   Financing requires both a note and a security device (mortgage or trust deed). Should a discrepancy arise as to the maturity date, the discrepancy would be resolved in favor of the note which is the actual evidence of the debt. The lien itself is the "security device" and is incidental to the debt.

CREATION OF MORTGAGES

76   A mortgage is a written contract by which specific property is hypothecated to secure a debt or obligation. "Hypothecate" means to make a property security for a loan without delivering possession of the property to the lender. Because the mortgage conveys no right of possession it is not an estate in real property. Since the instrument itself is a lien on real property, it is transferable by the lender (mortgagee) but is not a negotiable instrument in the true sense of the word.

77   There are two parties to a mortgage, the mortgagor (borrower) and the mortgagee (lender).

79   The mortgage contract creates a lien on the property of the borrower so that if he does not repay the note the lender may take steps to have the property sold to pay the debt.

CREATION OF TRUST DEEDS

80   The mortgage and trust deed (deed of trust) have the same purpose. They make real property security for a loan. They are also similar in the fact that the borrower retains possession of the physical property. The procedure employed in using the trust deed differs from that of the mortgage.

81   The security given is not a contract, but a special form of deed used to hypothecate the title. It differs from a mortgage in that a deed places a lien against the title. It is also a trust instrument.

82   There are three parties to a trust deed, the trustor (borrower), the beneficiary (lender), and the trustee (a third disinterested party, a sort of "stake holder").

82a   The beneficiary under a trust deed, mortgagee under a mortgage, and owner under a land contract are all similar with regards to the fact that they are all lenders.

83   The bare legal (naked) title to the property is conveyed by the trust deed from the borrower (trustor) to the trustee upon the signature of the trustor. Title is held in trust until the loan is repaid. The lender holds the actual trust deed and note as evidence of the loan.

83a   The relationship between the beneficiary and the trustee is fiduciary in nature because the trustee can only act on the direct orders of the beneficiary.

84   For a trust deed to be valid, it must:
(1) Be in writing.
(2) Be signed by the trustor.
(3) Name the trustee.
(4) Have a granting (trusting) clause.
(5) Have a sufficient description of the property.

85   The trust deed creates a lien against the property. If the borrower does not repay the note as agreed, steps can be taken to sell the property to repay the debt.

87   There are many clauses found in mortgage and trust deed instruments but such agreements are not concerned with the validity of the trust deed. The recording of note and security evidences the validity, not by the legal rights and defenses inserted into the instruments.

PACKAGE MORTGAGE

88   The growing popularity of the practice of selling in one package not only the land and the structure erected thereupon, but a number of the fixtures for comfortable living including stoves, refrigerators, air conditioners, and dishwashers has brought about the use of what is called the package mortgage. It contains the statement that such articles, "are and shall be deemed to be fixtures" and considered in all respects as a part of the real estate which serves as the security.

FICTITIOUS MORTGAGE
OR TRUST DEED

89   The full length form of a mortgage or trust deed is generally two pages of closely set print. To avoid duplication in the recorder's office and to reduce the forms to one page, the law allows the recording of a basic set of provisions as a "Fictitious" mortgage or trust deed. This permits

these provisions to be incorporated into any short form mortgage or trust deed by reference to the recorded fictitious document giving the book, page, and date of the recording in the county.

90 Open-end mortgage - One which provides that the outstanding balance can be increased in order to advance additional funds to the borrower, up to the original sum of the note.

91 Wrap-around trust deed (Also called an all-inclusive trust deed) - Wrap-around financing is financing in which the trust deed is subordinate to, yet includes the encumbrance or encumbrances to which it is subordinated.

91a One of the facts that should be remembered when using this form of financing is that for federal income tax purposes the buyer is not considered to have assumed the existing first loan in the year of the sale.

REQUEST FOR NOTICE OF DEFAULT

97 Different liens upon the same property have priority according to the time of their recording. A "first trust deed", as the name implies, has first claim on the property with the exception of taxes or previously recorded liens, such as mechanics' liens, judgments, etc. At a foreclosure sale, if there are no such previous liens, the proceeds go first to pay the cost and expenses of sale then to pay off the holder of the first trust deed. Any amount left over is applied to the pay off a second trust deed note, or other subsequent liens, in the order of their recording. Should the funds be exhausted before the last recorded trust deed note is paid the beneficiary of that note will loose their money. Should funds still remain, the trustor receives any balance remaining after all other claims have been paid.

98 Any person interested in a particular deed of trust, such as a junior lien holder, may make sure of being informed of a notice of default and notice of sale. The holder of a second trust deed, for instance, would be vitally interested in knowing of any default on the first trust deed. The holder of the second trust deed has the right during the default period to make up all past payments and cure the default on the first trust deed. The monies used to accomplish the cure are then added to the monies due to the second trust deed holder and become in default to that individual, or institution. The second trust deed holder then proceeds to begin a new foreclosure and unless there is a "due on sale" clause, preserve all rights to maintain the first trust deed in place upon, during, and following the foreclosure sale. To make certain that such default does not occur without his knowledge, the holder of a junior trust deed may record a "request for notice of default" with the county recorder in that county in which the property is located. The trustee or other person authorized to record the notice of default or notice of sale must, within 10 days after recording, inform the person named in the request of notice of any such recorded document by mailing to that person a copy of the document.

REFINANCE

103 Should a seller want to refinance a first trust deed or mortgage loan and the secondary financing is not subordinate to the creation of a new first loan the second trust deed must be paid in full.

BENEFICIARY'S STATEMENT

104 A beneficiary is a lender involved in a trust deed. When an individual or an escrow wishes to determine the exact balance of a loan as of a given date, together with accrued interest, interest rate, and other items of the loan, they ask the beneficiary (the lender) for a "beneficiary's statement." A lender must provide such a statement, but may charge a fee for this service.

BENEFICIARY'S RIGHTS

105 The beneficiary has a clause in the trust deed that approval must be obtained by the lender before you adjust the boundary lines of a property serving as security. You would also need approval to consolidate the property with other properties and before signing any agreements in the neighborhood regarding restrictions on the use of the property.

AFTER-ACQUIRED TITLE

106   Because a grant deed conveys any after-acquired title (additions of fixtures to the real property or improvements to the land), it follows that because of the use of a deed in trust deed financing the after-acquired title would pass to the trustee as additional security.

RELEASE OF MORTGAGES & TRUST DEEDS CLEARING THE RECORD

111   When any mortgage has been satisfied, the mortgagee is required to record a certificate of discharge.

112   When any deed of trust loan has been satisfied, the beneficiary is required to execute and deliver to the trustee a request for a full reconveyance. The trustee is required to execute and record, or cause to be recorded, a full reconveyance. The instrument is called a reconveyance deed.

BLANKET FINANCING

112a When financing the construction of many homes in a subdivision, a contractor will use one trust deed to finance all of the homes. The trust deed is called a blanket trust deed and contains a provision that as each home is sold, that lot will be given a partial release from the blanket trust deed and a new trust deed will be created on that one lot to finance the purchase.

113   When exercising the provisions of a release clause in a blanket encumbrance by paying off a part of the lien, the borrower will receive and record a partial reconveyance deed, releasing part of the property held as security.

117   With respect to a mortgage; the mortgagee, within 30 days of the satisfaction, must execute and record or cause to be recorded, a certificate of discharge in the office of the county recorder in the county in which the mortgage is recorded.

118   With respect to a deed of trust, the beneficiary is required to execute and deliver to the trustee the original note, deed of trust,

request for full reconveyance, and any other documents needed to reconvey the deed of trust. The law does not establish any time limit within which the beneficiary must deliver these documents.

119   Following the repayment of a debt secured by a trust deed, the trustee must sign and execute the full reconveyance and record it, or cause it to be recorded, in the office of the county recorder in which the deed of trust is recorded. The trustee has 21 calendar days after receipt to record the full reconveyance.

FORECLOSURE - MORTGAGE

127   Generally, there is only one remedy or method by which to enforce payment of the debt in the event the mortgagor fails to make payment as agreed and that is to institute an action in court called a foreclosure suit. When court trial is held and the default established, the court orders a sale of the property to be held by the sheriff or court commissioner. "Notice of Sale" must be posted in a public place for 20 days and published once a week for 20 days before the sale can take place.

128   At the sale the property is sold to the highest responsible bidder. The bidder does not at this time receive a deed or possession of the property. He receives a certificate of sale that states if the mortgagor does not redeem his property within one year, the buyer will then receive a sheriff's or court commissioner's deed.

129   Right of redemption - The period during which the mortgagor has the right to redeem his property by paying off the debt, interest, and costs incurred within one year after the foreclosure sale is known as the "Period of Redemption." During this period, the mortgagor retains possession. He may sell his "Right of Redemption" and the grantee would have the right to redeem.

TRUST DEED

130   If the property is a home, the mortgagor may live in it during the year. If he redeems, the buyer cannot collect rent, but if he fails to redeem, the mortgagee may sue him for reasonable rent. If the foreclosed property is

business or income property, the buyer at the foreclosure sale is entitled to the rent and profits. If the mortgagor redeems, the money is applied toward the redemption amount.

131 Deficiency judgment - If the foreclosure sale does not bring enough to pay the mortgage and costs, the mortgagee may ask for a deficiency judgment except in the case of a purchase money mortgage.

134 A trust deed may be foreclosed in two ways: as a mortgage or by a trustee's sale.

135 Mortgage foreclosure - In this type of foreclosure, the procedure is identical with a mortgage foreclosure in court except that if a deficiency judgment is not asked in the foreclosure, the trustor has no right of redemption after the sale. If a deficiency judgment is asked for in the foreclosure, the trustor has one year to redeem the same as in a mortgage.

135a In the judicial foreclosure of a trust deed when the price bid at the sale is for a sum less than the amount of the judgment, the period of redemption for the trustor would be one year. Should the bid price be equal to or greater than the judgment sum, the redemption period would be 3 months.

136 Trustee's sale - This type of foreclosure action provides the reason for the almost exclusive use of trust deeds in California. The security (real property) can be sold outside of court in a comparatively short time and there is no redemption period for the trustor (borrower).

137 It should be recognized that a beneficiary appoints a trustee. In institutional financing, the trustee is usually a corporation owned by the lending institution. No state or federal law governs directly the licensing or activities of a trustee.

DEFAULT

138 When a borrower defaults in payments or otherwise jeopardizes the "security," the beneficiary notifies the trustee in writing of the default and requests him to take steps to foreclose. The trustee prepares and records a "Notice of Default" setting forth the identification of the trust deed, the nature and extent of default, and stating that the beneficiary has elected to sell, or cause a sale of the property, to satisfy the obligation. A copy of the notice is sent to the trustor. This notice states that three months after its recording, the trustee may advertise the property for sale. It also states that until five business days before the sale takes place, the trustor has the legal right to reinstate his loan in good standing by paying all past due payments plus costs and expenses.

139 In the event of default on a first trust deed, the holder of the second lien may make the payments on the first lien (reinstate it) and then foreclose under his own lien. This action will require another three month and twenty-one day waiting period after the filing of the notice of default by the holder of the second or any other junior lien. The reinstatement of the first lien by the junior lien holder is known as making an "advance."

NOTICE OF SALE

140 If the trustor takes no action during the three month waiting period, the trustee executes a "Notice of Sale" which must be published in a newspaper of general circulation at least once a week for at least three weeks, with the first date of publication being at least 20 days before the date of sale. The notice must state the time and place of sale describe the property to be sold and the occasion for the sale. A copy must be posted for the same period of time in a public place in the city or judicial district where the property is to be sold and also in some conspicuous place on the property itself. A copy of this notice must be mailed to all lien holders whether or not a "Request for Notice" was recorded.

141 During the 20-day period of publication, the trustor may reinstate the loan by paying all past-due payments plus permitted costs and expenses prior to five business days before the sale is to take place. During the five business days immediately prior to the sale, the trustor

must pay off the entire loan plus permitted costs and expenses to prevent the sale from taking place. During the foreclosure, the trustor may stay in possession of the foreclosed property. Following the sale, the trustor has no recourse. All rights, including possession, are terminated. The total process takes about four months.

142   Upon default of a mortgage or trust deed, most standard forms provide that the beneficiary or mortgagee may reserve the right to collect the rents.

144   The money paid at the sale is dispersed as follows: After the trustee's cost of sale, normal priority distribution is first trust deed, second trust deed, etc. Any remainder would go the trustor.

145   To prevent an owner from having a negative impact on his credit, an offer can be made to the holder of the note in default to provide a "deed in lieu of foreclosure." If this deed is accepted by a lender from a defaulting borrower, both lender and borrower avoid the necessity and expense of foreclosure proceedings. The lender would, under these conditions, become responsible for the payment of any liens recorded after the lien he holds.

EXPIRATION OF LIEN

147   "Unless the lien of a mortgage, deed of trust or other instrument that creates a security interest of record in real property to secure a debt or other obligation has expired earlier or as provided in other law, such a lien expires: (1) Either ten years after the last date fixed for payment or performance of the obligation is ascertainable from the record; or (2) if this cannot be determined from the record, then sixty years after the instrument that created the security interest or other obligation was recorded. Hence, it can no longer be stated that a trust deed never outlaws.

149   It is also a matter of law that a deficiency judgment may not be obtained in the foreclosure of residential (1 to 4 units) purchase money encumbrances.

PURCHASE MONEY ENCUMBRANCES

151   A "purchase money" trust deed or mortgage can arise only when there is the extension of credit to a buyer by the seller, or an actual loan of money by a third party, for the purpose of enabling the buyer to purchase and reside in certain types of property. In California, a purchase money trust deed is advantageous in the eyes of the lender because it would take priority over buyer's liens at the time of purchase

157   Regardless of the classification of the encumbrance, if the money was actually loaned by a third party, it is known as a hard money encumbrance.

PROMISSORY NOTES

160   A note, or promissory note, is the primary evidence of the obligation to pay money. The obligation or promise is secured by the mortgage or trust deed.

163   A note may be signed by more than one person as a "joint note," indicating that each is equally liable for its payment; or as a joint and several note, making them jointly and individually liable for the entire amount.

TYPES OF NOTES

164   Today, most real estate loans are fully amortized. The note provides for repayment in equal installments over a period of years. A portion of each payment covers the interest earned up to that point and the remainder is a repayment of the principal. Some loans require a set amount to be paid on the principal in each installment plus any accrued interest.

165   It should be noted that the vast majority of conventional real estate loans utilize simple interest. Simple interest is defined as interest calculated on the principal amount of the loan only. You should understand other forms of calculating interest. Compound interest is defined as calculating interest on principal and accrued interest. Compound interest normally involves savings for investments. Add-on interest is generally used in automobile loans where the interest for the full principal for a three-year loan would be added to the loan. That

amount would be divided by 36 and paid off in those installments. Savings accounts normally pay compound interest while real estate lenders charge simple interest.

168   You should also recognize that in addition to fully amortized loans, partially amortized loans are used a great deal in real estate circumstances. In a partially amortized loan agreement there will be a final payment that is larger than any of the other installment payments that must be paid to clear the debt. This final and larger payment is most often referred to as a "balloon payment."

169   Graduated payment mortgages have a fixed interest rate and payments that increase during the loan. This kind of mortgage note often creates a negative amortization increasing the amount of the loan instead of paying it off.

STRAIGHT LOANS

170   A straight note (often used in "alternative financing" arrangements and in seller financing arrangements) provides for repayment of the entire amount of principal and interest in a lump sum at maturity. It may also provide for periodic payments of interest only, with the principal all due and payable at a specified date.

171   "Or more" clause - By agreement between the parties it may be arranged that the borrower elects to pay an amount greater than the specified monthly payment, or even to pay off the entire amount of the loan before maturity, without penalty.

172   Prepayment penalty clause - Generally speaking, financial institutions and other lenders dependent upon earned interest for income do not wish to have loans paid before maturity. The unexpected pay off of a loan would mean that the money would have to be reinvested and or it would not be earning interest. To provide time for such reinvestment without loss of interest, the note will state that if the borrower wishes to pay off the debt in full before the due date, he must pay the lender an additional sum as penalty for such prepayment. This clause is

often waved if the buyer obtains financing from the same lender.

173   Any loan for residential property of four units or less executed on or after January 1, 1980, may be prepaid in whole or in part at any time without penalty after 5 years. However, prepayment made within 5 years of the date of execution may be subject to a prepayment penalty. An amount not exceeding 20% of the original principal amount may be prepaid in any 12-month period without penalty. A prepayment charge may be imposed on any amount prepaid in any 12 month period in excess of 20% of the original amount of the loan. The penalty shall not exceed an amount equal to the payment of six months interest in excess of 20% of the original principle amount. After such loans have been in existence more than 5 years, no prepayment penalty may be charged.

174   Acceleration clause - An acceleration clause in a mortgage, trust deed, or land contract, causes the entire balance of the note to become immediately due and payable upon the happening of a certain stated event. This event may be a default in payments, destruction of the improvements, transfer of the property, or any reason agreed upon. The event must be stated.

175   Alienation or "Due on sale" clause - The event which causes a note to "accelerate" (become immediately due and payable), is the sale or transfer of the property which is the security for the note. Such provision is known as an "alienation clause." When such a clause is in a mortgage or deed of trust secured by one to four residential units, it must be stated in the note. To "alienate," means to transfer title.

175a A seasoned note is a note that has a history of prompt payments.

UNIFORM NEGOTIABLE INSTRUMENTS ACT

180   There are various types of endorsements including:

181   Blank - Where the holder simply signs his name on the back of the note.

182 Special - Where the holder writes, "Pay to the order of (named transferee)," and then signs.

183 Restrictive - Where the holder restricts future negotiation by writing, "Pay to the order of State Bank for Deposit only," and then signs.

184 Qualified - Where the holder adds the words, "Without Recourse," to what would otherwise be a blank or special endorsement

185 A "holder in due course" is one who takes a note by negotiation, that is, by endorsement by the original payee. The holder in due course is the person who, under the Uniform Negotiable Instruments Act may have a greater right to collect the note from the maker than the original payee may have. To be a holder in due course this third person must not only acquire the note by negotiation (endorsement) but must acquire it in the ordinary course of business, in good faith (without knowledge of any defects), before maturity (due date), and for value.

186 When it is said that the holder in due course has a greater right to collect from the maker than the original payee, it is really meant that the maker has fewer defenses against payment to a holder in due course than he has against the original payee. The maker of a note may have a variety of defenses (legal reasons for not paying) against payment. All of these legal defenses are available against the original payee. Not all of them are available against a holder in due course.

186a In order to determine which defenses are available against the original payee and/or against the holder in due course, defenses are separated into two categories: (1) Personal defenses and (2) real defenses. Both types are good against the original payee, but only real defenses are good against the holder in due course. A recent Federal Trade Commission regulation rule limits the use of the holder in due course doctrine in consumer transactions. Thus, personal defenses may be available against both the original payee and the holder in due course.

187 Personal defenses are:
(1) Fraud in the inducement.
(2) Lack or failure of consideration.

(3) Prior payment or cancellation.
(4) Set off.

188 Real defenses are:
(1) The maker is a minor or incompetent.
(2) Note was given for illegal conduct.
(3) Forgery.
(4) Material alteration.

INVOLUNTARY LIENS

191 Liens other than security devices are involuntary liens placed on the title against the expressed will of the owner. These liens are:
(1) Real property taxes.
(2) Personal property taxes (generally).
(3) Special assessments.
(4) Attachments.
(5) Judgment liens.
(6) Mechanic's liens.
(7) State or federal income tax liens.

ATTACHMENTS (SPECIFIC LIEN)

194 To create an attachment, the creditor at the time he files a lawsuit, obtains from the court a writ of attachment. This is an order for the sheriff or other official to seize and hold the property. If the debt is paid or sufficient property is sold to satisfy the debt, the attachment lien must be removed as an encumbrance. This is done by a release of attachment. An attachment is a specific lien and is good for three years or until final judgment, whichever occurs first.

JUDGMENTS (GENERAL LIEN)

195 A judgment is an involuntary, general lien and is a final order of a court as the result of a lawsuit. The details of the judge's determination of the rights of the parties, is called an "abstract of judgment." Until such an abstract is recorded, it has no effect upon the property of the debtor. When recorded it becomes a general lien on all non-exempt real property of the debtor that he owns in the county in which the abstract is recorded or property which he may acquire in that same county in which the judgment is effective.

196 If the losing party to a lawsuit pays voluntarily, there is no need for further action. If

the judgment is not paid and the winning creditor wishes to force payment, he must take court action to secure a "writ of execution" which authorizes the sheriff or other official to seize and sell the property to satisfy the judgment.

MECHANIC'S LIENS (SPECIFIC LIEN)

200 California law expressly provides that where a person who furnishes labor or material for the improvement of real property is not paid for such labor or material, he may file a lien upon the property which has been improved by his effort. Under the theory that improvements contribute additional value to the land, it is equitable to charge such land with the cost of the improvement.

204 The right to file a mechanic's lien extends to all persons and laborers of every class who perform labor or services and to persons who furnish material or service, such as equipment suppliers, architects, artisans, etc.

205 A mechanic's lien is of no effect unless it is recorded. Such liens must be "verified" before they can be recorded. "Verification" is a sworn statement before a duly qualified officer as to the correctness of the contents of an instrument.

216 After a notice of completion has been recorded, original contractors must file within 60 days and other claimants, such as sub-contractors, workmen and material suppliers, must file within 30 days for a mechanic's lien.

221 The "scheme of improvement" is the entire project from the very beginning of work to the very end. A mechanic's lien takes effect as if recorded at the beginning of the scheme of improvement; therefore, the time of beginning of the work is of great importance especially when a question arises as to whether a trust deed or mechanic's lien has priority. For instance, if there was an original contract and the foundation, or even the preparation for the foundation of a building, then a lien filed by a workman who performed his services weeks or months later (as would be the case with a painter, for example), would come ahead of and have priority over the mortgage or trust deed

recorded after the scheme of improvement commenced. For this reason, lending agencies or anyone else making construction loans, check and photograph the property to see and prove that no work has been started or materials delivered, before recording the trust deed.

227 Notice of Non-responsibility - This is a device used by a person having an interest in real property and who wishes to protect himself against certain mechanic's liens or other claims. A tenant or occupant may order work done to a property without the knowledge of the owner. If within 10 days after he discovers work is being done, the owner posts a proper "Notice of Non-responsibility" on the premises and records a copy with the County Recorder, he can protect himself against claims from workmen and others who have not been paid for such work. It is most important that the notice be both posted on the premises and recorded. If such posting has not been made, the recorded notice affords no protection.

228 General liens affect all the property of the owner in the county where recorded.

Examples:
229 (1) Judgment liens, state and federal income tax liens are treated similarly.
230 (2) Lien for a decedent's debts.
231 (3) Inheritance tax liens (state and federal).
232 (4) Corporation franchise tax liens.

233 Specific liens affect only a certain piece of property. Examples:

234 (1) Mortgage liens and/or trust deed liens.
235 (2) Attachment liens.
236 (3) Property taxes and assessment liens.
237 (4) Mechanic's liens.
238 (5) Vendee's liens.
239 (6) Vendor's liens.
240 (7) Surety bail bond liens.

RESERVATIONS, RIGHTS OF WAY

242 The expression "CC&Rs" is used frequently in real estate practice. It is an abbreviation for covenants, conditions, restrictions, reservations, rights, rights-of-way

and easements of record. Title to property usually is taken "subject to the CC&Rs."

243 Covenants, conditions, and restrictions refer to deed restrictions on the title.

244 Reservations indicate that a portion of the title is reserved or an easement is reserved for the benefit of the grantee; for example, in mineral rights.

245 Right - refers to the possible circumstance where a grantor has retained or given a personal right to enter upon the property for some specific purpose, such as a right to obtain water, cut wood, or fish.

246 Rights-of-way - refers primarily to a privilege to pass over the land of another and is the same as an easement unless the title to the right-of-way has been granted. A right-of-way may be granted (as an easement or title) for the passage of a railway or to lay pipelines.

DEED RESTRICTIONS

248 Restrictions on real property control the use of the land. They may be imposed by the owner of the land at the time the title is conveyed or they may be imposed by the government under police powers. If imposed by the exercise of police powers, the restriction is termed "zoning" and is not an encumbrance. A restriction imposed by the owner at the time title is conveyed is an encumbrance. The restriction may be enforced by a person or persons who do not hold title to the restricted land. These are called deed restrictions. There are no restrictions that the law prevents an owner from placing in a deed. The law may make some unenforceable, such as those that discriminate or prevent the new owner from placing a "for sale" and "for lease" sign in attempting to resell to others as it infringes on the owner's right to alienate the property. California Civil Code specifically provides that such a covenant is unenforceable, but the owner may still include them.

249 There are two general kinds or types of deed restrictions:

(1) A restriction in the nature of a condition subsequent.
(2) A restriction in the nature of a covenant.

250 A restriction in the nature of a condition subsequent can be imposed only by deed and usually has a forfeiture clause that states that the property shall, upon violation of the restriction, automatically revert to the original grantor or maker of the restriction. For example: If the grantor deeds property to the grantee "so long as it is never used as a cocktail lounge" and the grantee did so use the land, it would revert to the grantor who had originally imposed the restriction.

251 A restriction in the nature of a covenant is more or less an agreement or promise between all lot owners under the restriction. Each lot owner has the right to enforce the restriction by requesting an injunction from the court prohibiting the violation or bring suit for damages. This type of restriction often makes the property unmarketable.

252 A deed restriction may be imposed upon one or more parcels at the same time. If imposed upon one parcel only, the restriction would be written into the deed at the time the title is transferred. If imposed upon a number of parcels at the same time as in a subdivision, the grantor would record a "Uniform Declaration of Restrictions" in the county recorder's office. When such restrictions are imposed upon a number of parcels at the same time, they are imposed for the benefit of all of the owners of the individual parcels and the restrictions may be enforced by any one or any group of the owners of the other affected parcels. They are most often used in exclusive guarded subdivisions and control the lot size, minimum square footage, type of building, etc.

256 Restrictions may cover a multitude of matters including:
(1) Use - for residential or business.
(2) Character of buildings – single-family or multiple units.
(3) Cost and minimum area - requiring construction to cost no less than a certain sum when erected on a lot in a specified area.

(4) Location of structure on the lot - specifying setbacks and side lines.

(5) Architectural approval of proposed buildings by a local group designated for that purpose by the declaration.

Because of inflationary and deflationary periods in the economy, the dollar amount of construction is the most difficult restriction to impose.

257   Deed and private contract restrictions may be removed by:

(1) Securing a quitclaim deed from the person who originally imposed the restriction on a single parcel.

(2) By quiet title action in court.

(3) By recording a notice of cancellation signed by a given percentage of the lot owners, if such is provided for in the contract.

If not so provided, it might be that all lot owners would have to give releases or quitclaim deeds before restrictions can be lifted. Noncompliance by a high percentage of other owners having the same restriction would tend to have a court lean toward allowing the restriction to become invalid.

258   Should an owner refuse to comply with a deed restriction, the action of the court is called an "injunction." By definition, an injunction is a writ or order issued under the seal of a court to restrain one or more parties to a suit or proceeding from doing an act which is deemed to be inequitable or unjust in regard to the rights of some other party or parties to the suit.

GOVERNMENTAL RESTRICTIONS

261   Changes in zoning or other restrictions of this nature require application to the planning commission, which follows an administrative procedure in handling such applications. City and county planning commission members are delegated the authority to make recommendations to the city council or the Board of Supervisors.

ENCROACHMENTS

265   If there is an encroachment for which there is no justification, the owner of the land encroached upon has the right to bring a proper action in court to have the encroachment removed (such as a "quiet title" or "ejectment" suit). If not barred by the statute of limitations, he may also collect damages for trespass. The statute of limitations indicates that any action for trespass must be taken within three years.

Lesson Six
Part Two
Study Questions

_____(Lesson Six - Paragraph 60 – Question 1)_____

Following is a group of words commonly used in real estate. The one word which does not fall into the same category as the rest is:
(A) Easement. (B) Property tax lien. (C) Judgment. (D) Claim.

_____

(D) An easement, a judgment, and property taxes would be encumbrances. A claim would not fall into this category. It sounds appropriate and is a good distraction.

_____(Lesson Six - Paragraph 60 – Question 1)_____

The following is a correct statement regarding an encumbrance on real property:
(A) Specific liens always are voluntary.
(B) Federal income tax is an encumbrance, not a lien.
(C) All encumbrances are liens, but not all liens are encumbrances.
(D) It is not unusual for a buyer to accept a deed on a property with previous encumbrances.

_____

(D) Regarding encumbrances, we can say generally that all liens are encumbrances but we cannot say that all encumbrances are liens. We can say all leases are encumbrances, but we cannot say that all encumbrances are leases. Encumbrances are defined as anything that affects or limits your title to real property. Choices (A), (B), and (C) are all incorrect. (D) is the correct choice because we must accept recorded encumbrances on property when we buy a home. We have utility easements called gross easements. We have to take title subject to the easements granted to the telephone, power, gas, and water company. We also take property with tax liens on it. Title is subject to existing tax liens which are encumbrances.

_____(Lesson Six - Paragraph 61 – Question 1)_____

"A charge upon specific real property by which it is made security for the performance of an act," defines a/an:
(A) Lien. (B) Encumbrance. (C) Attachment. (D) Condition.

_____

(A) The statement defines a lien. An encumbrance is any burden on a parcel of real property. It is any right or interest in land possessed by someone other than the owner. All liens are encumbrances but not all encumbrances are liens. Attachment is a process by which real or personal property of a party to a lawsuit is seized and retained in the custody of the court to compel appearance before the court or to furnish security for a debt or costs arising out of the litigation. A condition (subsequent) is attached to an already vested estate or to a contract whereby the estate is defeated by failure or non-performance of the condition. The significant feature of it is that the property owner could forfeit title to the property if he violated the condition.

_____(Lesson Six - Paragraph 65 – Question 1)_____

A lien on real property cannot be:
(A) Specific.   (B) General.   (C) Performance.   (D) Voluntary.

(C) A lien is an encumbrance that makes the property security for the payment of a debt. It can be specific, general, or voluntary but cannot be performance, a physical act.

_____(Lesson Six - Paragraph 65 – Question 1)_____

When a levy is made on all the property owned by the debtor in a county, it is:
(A) An attachment. (B) A specific lien. (C) A general lien. (D) A judgment.

(C) When the court places a levy on all property owned by a debtor, it is a general lien.

_____(Lesson Six - Paragraph 67 – Question 1)_____

The following is not an estate:
(A) Reversion. (B) Remainder. (C) A trust deed. (D) All of the above are estates.

(C) A trust deed is not an estate, it is a lien. An estate defines an interest in real property. (A) Defines an estate in reversion. (B) Defines an estate in remainder. (D) Incorrect as it says all are estates. This is a negative question; therefore (C) is the correct answer.

_____(Lesson Six - Paragraph 72 – Question 1)_____

In the sale to or exchange with the public of ten (10) or more real property sales contracts or promissory notes secured directly or collaterally by liens on real property during a calendar year, a broker's license is required.   As used in this sense in Real Estate Law, the term "collaterally" nearly means:
(A) A purchase money loan.   (B) A junior type loan.
(C) A loan secured by another loan.   (D) A blanket encumbrance.

(C) A loan secured collaterally by real property is a loan being made against the security of an already existing trust deed or mortgage. A pledge agreement loan is an example of this type loan.

_____(Lesson Six - Paragraph 72 – Question 2)_____

A man sold his home for $125,000 and took back a first trust deed and note for $99,000. He is now in need of some cash and wants to use the trust deed as security for the loan with the bank. This second type of loan transaction would be known as a:
(A) Pledge agreement.   (B) Mortgage.   (C) Reconveyance.   (D) Severalty.

(A)   Using personal property (the trust deed) as security for a loan is considered a pledge, similar to the pawnbroker holding property (a wrist watch) for loan security.

_____(Lesson Six - Paragraph 72a – Question 1)_____

If a person mentions a "warehousing operation" in relation to real property financing, he is referring to a:
(A) Long term loan.
(B) Mortgage banker collecting loans before reselling them.
(C) Mortgage broker holding long-term debentures secured by real property.
(D) Storage facility for physical items.

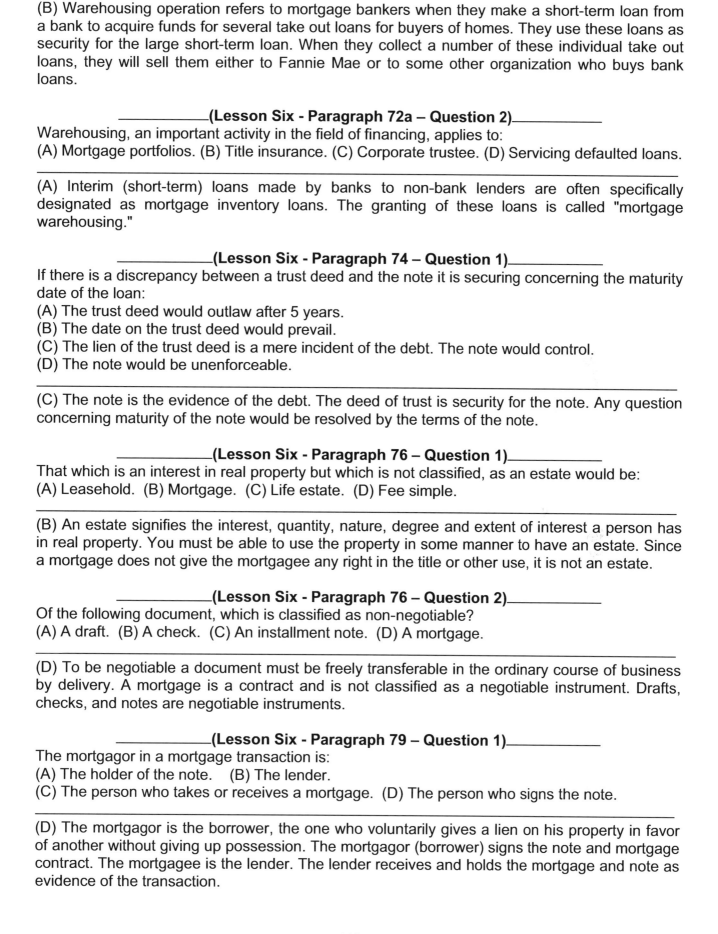

(B) Warehousing operation refers to mortgage bankers when they make a short-term loan from a bank to acquire funds for several take out loans for buyers of homes. They use these loans as security for the large short-term loan. When they collect a number of these individual take out loans, they will sell them either to Fannie Mae or to some other organization who buys bank loans.

——————(Lesson Six - Paragraph 72a – Question 2)——————
Warehousing, an important activity in the field of financing, applies to:
(A) Mortgage portfolios. (B) Title insurance. (C) Corporate trustee. (D) Servicing defaulted loans.

(A) Interim (short-term) loans made by banks to non-bank lenders are often specifically designated as mortgage inventory loans. The granting of these loans is called "mortgage warehousing."

——————(Lesson Six - Paragraph 74 – Question 1)——————
If there is a discrepancy between a trust deed and the note it is securing concerning the maturity date of the loan:
(A) The trust deed would outlaw after 5 years.
(B) The date on the trust deed would prevail.
(C) The lien of the trust deed is a mere incident of the debt. The note would control.
(D) The note would be unenforceable.

(C) The note is the evidence of the debt. The deed of trust is security for the note. Any question concerning maturity of the note would be resolved by the terms of the note.

——————(Lesson Six - Paragraph 76 – Question 1)——————
That which is an interest in real property but which is not classified, as an estate would be:
(A) Leasehold. (B) Mortgage. (C) Life estate. (D) Fee simple.

(B) An estate signifies the interest, quantity, nature, degree and extent of interest a person has in real property. You must be able to use the property in some manner to have an estate. Since a mortgage does not give the mortgagee any right in the title or other use, it is not an estate.

——————(Lesson Six - Paragraph 76 – Question 2)——————
Of the following document, which is classified as non-negotiable?
(A) A draft. (B) A check. (C) An installment note. (D) A mortgage.

(D) To be negotiable a document must be freely transferable in the ordinary course of business by delivery. A mortgage is a contract and is not classified as a negotiable instrument. Drafts, checks, and notes are negotiable instruments.

——————(Lesson Six - Paragraph 79 – Question 1)——————
The mortgagor in a mortgage transaction is:
(A) The holder of the note.   (B) The lender.
(C) The person who takes or receives a mortgage. (D) The person who signs the note.

(D) The mortgagor is the borrower, the one who voluntarily gives a lien on his property in favor of another without giving up possession. The mortgagor (borrower) signs the note and mortgage contract. The mortgagee is the lender. The lender receives and holds the mortgage and note as evidence of the transaction.

_____(Lesson Six - Paragraph 80 – Question 1)_____
Mortgages and trust deeds differ in all of the following, except:
(A) Parties. (B) Security. (C) Statute of limitations. (D) Title.

(B) In both mortgages and trust deeds, the "security" for the loan is the real property.

_____(Lesson Six - Paragraph 81 – Question 1)_____
A trust deed differs from a mortgage in which of the following respects:
(A) Possession. (B) Recording. (C) Title. (D) Amortization.

(C) Mortgages and trust deeds are alike with respect to choices (A), (B) and (D). With both instruments the borrower retains possession of the property. Both may be recorded and both may be paid off in installments. With a trust deed, however, the title is transferred to the trustee. Under a mortgage, title remains vested in the borrower.

_____(Lesson Six - Paragraph 81 – Question 2)_____
A gives title to B to hold a security for a loan of $22,000 from C. It follows, logically, that the instrument used was a:
(A) Grant deed. (B) Trust deed. (C) Quitclaim deed. (D) Mortgage.

(B) If re-read carefully, you will find an indirect description of what takes place when a trust deed is used to secure a note when real property is the security.

_____(Lesson Six - Paragraph 82 – Question 1)_____
An owner who gives a trust deed as security for a debt has borrowed money from the:
(A) Trustee. (B) Mortgagee. (C) Beneficiary. (D) Trustor.

(C) The parties to a trust deed relationship are: the trustor (the borrower), the trustee (the third party with the power of sale), and the beneficiary (the lender).

_____(Lesson Six - Paragraph 83 – Question 1)_____
When executing a trust deed, power of sale is given in the event of a default and granted by the:
(A) Trustor to the beneficiary. (B) Trustor to the trustee. (C) Buyer to seller. (D) Buyer to lender.

(B) When a borrower (trustor) signs a trust deed (executes it), he transfers to the trustee with power of sale the bare legal title to be held in trust to insure repayment of the loan.

_____(Lesson Six - Paragraph 83 – Question 2)_____
In a properly executed deed of trust, the power of sale that is created is a result of the relationship between the:
(A) Trustor to beneficiary. (B) Trustor to trustee. (C) Trustee to beneficiary. (D) Grantor to grantee.

(B) In the agreements found in a deed of trust, the trustor (borrower) gives the trustee (third party) the power to sell the property given as security for the note in the event trustor defaults in his payments to the lender. There are many additional agreements in such a trust deed establishing the conditions under which the trustee can exercise this power of sale.

_____(Lesson Six - Paragraph 84 – Question 1)_____

For a trust deed to be valid, the trustor must:

(A) Agree to pay the taxes.   (B) Agree to pay the fire insurance.

(C) Agree not to encumber the property. (D) None of the above.

(D) For a trust deed to be valid, it must (a) be in writing; (b) be signed by the trustor; (c) name the trustee; (d) have a granting (trusting) clause; (e) have a sufficient description of the property. None of these are suggested in the question.

_____(Lesson Six - Paragraph 85 – Question 1)_____

Recording the following creates a lien on real property:

(A) Easement. (B) Restriction. (C) Trust deed. (D) Notice of non-responsibility.

(C) A lien is an encumbrance involving money. Trust deeds create liens. Regarding answer (A), an easement is an encumbrance but it is not a lien type of encumbrance. Regarding (B), a restriction is an encumbrance because it limits your use of the property but it is not a lien. (D), a notice of non-responsibility prevents a mechanic's lien from being created.

_____(Lesson Six - Paragraph 87 – Question 1)_____

In order for a deed of trust to be valid and enforceable, it must contain a clause requiring the trustor to:

(A) Have property insured against fire and other hazards.

(B) Pay tax assessments before they become delinquent.

(C) Comply with health laws and police regulations.

(D) None of the above

(D) The clauses suggested in choices (A), (B), and (C) are often found in trust deed instruments but such agreements are not concerned with the validity of the trust deed.

_____(Lesson Six - Paragraph 88 – Question 1)_____

A "package mortgage" is:

(A) A mortgage on real property and personal property including household goods of an individual.

(B) A mortgage on real property on which there are unlimited funds available with periodic payments at any time.

(C) A number of mortgages grouped together on a number of parcels.

(D) A mortgage shared by a conventional lender and FHA or VA.

(A) The growing popularity of the practice of selling in one package not only the land and the structure erected thereupon, but a number of the fixtures for comfortable living (stoves, refrigerators, air conditioners, dishwashers, carpets, etc.). This has brought about the use of what is called the package mortgage. Some lending institutions undertake to sanction the financing of these articles as a part of the security for the real estate mortgage. The security device usually contains the statement that such articles, "shall be deemed to be fixtures," and are to be considered in all respects as a part of the real estate which serves as a security for the mortgage.

_____(Lesson Six - Paragraph 89 – Question 1)_____

At the county recorder you will find that the recorded deed of trust refers to standard clauses contained in a previously recorded trust deed. The previously recorded trust deed is known as a:
(A) Prima facie deed of trust.　　(B) Short term deed of trust.
(C) Master deed of trust.　　(D) Fictitious deed of trust.

(D) Nearly all deeds of trust used by banks, escrow, and title companies are the "short form." This document recites the trustee's name, describes the property, and has a place for signatures. The complete terms of the trust deed are not printed in the short form but refer to an original deed of trust recorded in each county. It is identified as a fictitious deed of trust. This document lists all the terms and conditions in detail.

_____(Lesson Six - Paragraph 89 – Question 2)_____

Mr. Smythe recently purchased a property and upon receipt of a copy of his trust deed discovered that it made reference to certain previously recorded agreements affecting his new property. These previously recorded matters would most likely be found in:
(A) A prima facie deed of trust. (B) A short form deed of trust.
(C) A fictitious deed of trust.　　(D) A master deed of trust.

(C) The standard forms of trust deed in general use contain lengthy and detailed general provisions which are common to all of the security instruments used by each institutional lender or title company. To avoid the necessity of repetitious recordation of these general provisions, a "fictitious" document, usually a trust deed in California, is recorded. This recordation gives constructive notice of the provisions in the instrument and reference is made to this document in later title transfer instruments.

_____(Lesson Six - Paragraph 90 – Question 1)_____

The type of mortgage loan that permits borrowing additional funds at a later date is called a/an:
(A) Equitable mortgage. (B) Junior mortgage. (C) Open-end mortgage. (D) Extendible mortgage.

(C) A loan that permits one to add to the unpaid balance of the loan, without rewriting the note, is said to be an open-end loan.

_____(Lesson Six - Paragraph 90 – Question 2)_____

Harrison borrowed $30,000 from A to Z Savings and Loan Association. The security instrument used was an open-end mortgage. This would mean that:
(A) The rate of interest due on the loan is "open" and can be changed periodically.
(B) This is an open line of credit for Harrison.
(C) The balance due on the mortgage can be increased or decreased by Harrison at any time.
(D) The parties can agree to extend more money without rewriting the mortgage.

(D) This is a matter of fact. An open-end mortgage contains an agreement that permits the mortgagor to borrow more money after the loan has been reduced without rewriting the mortgage.

_____(Lesson Six - Paragraph 91 – Question 1)_____

A wrap-around deed of trust will always:
(A) Be the most senior lien.　　(B) Be a junior lien.
(C) Secure a non-purchase money debt. (D) Be for a term not to exceed 10 years.

(B) Because it includes all superior liens, it will always be subordinate to those liens. In establishing such a loan, the buyer is counseled to ask for an agreement that he will not be liable for any of the penalties if the underlying loan must be paid in full.

_____(Lesson Six - Paragraph 91 – Question 2)_____

A purchase money trust deed loan which is subordinate to, but includes the amount of the encumbrance or encumbrances to which it is subordinated is known as:
(A) An all-inclusive trust deed loan. (B) A hold-harmless trust deed loan.
(C) An overriding trust deed loan.   (D) Any of the above.

(D) All of these terms have been used to identify what is normally called a wrap around loan. In establishing such a loan the buyer is counseled to ask for an agreement that he will not be liable for any of the penalties if the underlying loan must be paid in full.

_____(Lesson Six - Paragraph 98 – Question 1)_____

The following party benefits most from the recordation of a request for notice of default:
(A) Trustor of the 2nd trust deed. (B) Trustee of the 1st trust deed.
(C) Trustee of the 2nd trust deed. (D) Beneficiary of the 2nd trust deed.

(D) Any beneficiary is anxious to know if a foreclosure is going to take, place so that they can step in and protect the security for their loan. Since the trustor is the borrower, he already knows of the default as he/she did not make the payment(s) and the trustee notified him.

_____(Lesson Six - Paragraph 98 – Question 2)_____

The following should record a request for notice of default:
(A) The note holder. (B) The holder of a junior trust deed. (C) The trustor. (D) The mortgagor.

(B) A request for notice of default is a request recorded with a junior loan that in the event the borrower receives a notice of default on his first trust deed, the same notice of default is to be sent to the junior T.D. holder. This way, even thought the junior is current and the first is in default, the holder of the junior will know forthwith if the borrower is delinquent on the first. This permits the holder of the junior trust deed to reinstate the delinquency on the first, add this amount to his lien, and begin his own foreclosure. In his proceedings he has the legal right to assume the first rather than make a bid for all cash. All other bidders at the foreclosure sale would be required to overbid him with an all cash bid.

_____(Lesson Six - Paragraph 103 – Question 1)_____

"A" owns real property encumbered with both a first trust deed and note and a second trust deed and note. He sells this property to "0" who obtains a new first trust deed to finance the purchase. In this situation the second trust deed:
(A) Will become a first trust deed. (B) Will retain the same priority.
(C) Will have to be paid off.   (D) Will become a prior lien.

(C) In reading the statement carefully you will note that "0" obtains a new first trust deed loan. To be able to do this, the second trust deed and note must first be paid.

_____(Lesson Six - Paragraph 104 – Question 1)_____

In a beneficiary statement the:
(A) Lender shows the profit made on the specific loan. (B) Lender shows the loan balance.
(C) Lender shows the profit made on all loans.   (D) Trustor shows the loan balance.

(B) A beneficiary is a lender involved in a trust deed. When an individual or an escrow wishes to determine the exact balance of a loan as of a given date, together with accrued interest, interest rate, and other items of the loan, they ask the beneficiary (the lender) for a beneficiary statement. A lender must provide such a statement, but may charge a fee for this service.

_____(Lesson Six - Paragraph 105 – Question 1)_____

Trust deed beneficiaries would insist that they give approval for any:
(A) Boundary line adjustment agreements. (B) Consolidation agreements.
(C) Restriction agreements.   (D) All of the above.

(D) The term "trust deed beneficiaries" mean lenders. The lender has a clause in the trust deed that the lender must obtain approval before you were to adjust the boundary lines of the property serving as their security. You would also need approval to consolidate the property with other properties. You would also need approval before signing any agreements in the neighborhood regarding restrictions on the use of the property. Therefore, all of those would require approval.

_____(Lesson Six - Paragraph 106 – Question 1)_____

After-acquired title is conveyed in many trust deeds for the benefit of the beneficiary. It conveys:
(A) Additional land acquired afterwards by the trustor.
(B) Personal property later affixed to the real property so as to become real property.
(C) Improvements built on the land after title is acquired.
(D) All of the above.

(D) "After-acquired title" refers to title to fixtures or other real property items that become part of the land that is securing the existing trust deed. If a lot serving as security for a loan made ten years ago has land affixed to it, that land becomes encumbered with the trust deed lien made ten years ago. If personal property becomes part of the real property that is described as a fixture, such as kitchen fixtures, or newly installed bathroom fixtures, they too become encumbered with the lien made ten years ago. If additional improvements such as a swimming pool, added bedroom, or new landscaping are added to the real property, they too become encumbered with a trust deed lien made ten years ago.

_____(Lesson Six - Paragraph 111 – Question 1)_____

The document used to release a loan secured by a mortgage is the:
(A) Deed of reconveyance. (B) Certificate of discharge.
(C) Certificate of sale.   (D) Mortgagee's statement.

(B) When any mortgage has been satisfied, the mortgagee or the assignee of the mortgagee is required to execute and record or cause to be recorded a certificate of discharge.

_____(Lesson Six - Paragraph 112 – Question 1)_____

Able made his final payment on a note secured by a deed of trust. To clear this item from the county records, Able should:

(A) Obtain the original note and trust deed from lender and have him write "paid in full" across the face of document.

(B) Record a deed of reconveyance obtained from the trustee that has been executed by the trustee.

(C) Record a deed of reconveyance obtained from the beneficiary that has been executed by the beneficiary.

(D) Record deed of reconveyance obtained from beneficiary and trustee that has been executed by both parties.

(B) When a trust deed is used, the trustee holds the bare naked title as security for debt. The trust deed is recorded. When the debt has been paid in full, the trustor (borrower) would want to remove the lien that had been created by the recording of the trust deed. Recording a deed of reconveyance that has been executed by the trustee does this. This instrument conveys back to the trustor/borrower the bare naked title that the trustor had granted for the trustee to hold as security.

_____(Lesson Six - Paragraph 112 – Question 2)_____

A reconveyance deed is signed by the:

(A) Grantee. (B) Beneficiary. (C) Trustor. (D) Trustee.

(D) The transfer of title to real property cannot be accomplished by assigning the deed by which the present owner gained title to the property. The person issuing the deed must sign a new deed. A reconveyance deed signed by the trustee conveys back to the trustor the bare naked title that the trustee was holding as security.

_____(Lesson Six - Paragraph 119 – Question 1)_____

An owner of a single-family residence has made his final payment on his first trust deed and wants to clear this encumbrance from the records. The reconveyance deed must be signed and recorded by the:

(A) Trustor. (B) Beneficiary. (C) Escrow officer. (D) Trustee.

(D) When requested by the beneficiary, the trustee executes and records a reconveyance deed.

_____(Lesson Six - Paragraph 119 – Question 2)_____

A deed of reconveyance would be signed by the:

(A) Beneficiary. (B) Trustor. (C) Trustee. (D) Lender.

(C) When a trustor (borrower) signs a trust deed as security for a loan, he transfers his title to the trustee. When the loan is paid off, the beneficiary (lender) notifies the trustee that the debt has been satisfied and requests him to issue a reconveyance deed, transferring title back to the trustor. The trustee, as grantor, must sign this deed because title is in his name.

_____**(Lesson Six - Paragraph 127 – Question 1)**_____

A mortgagee who finds it necessary to foreclose a mortgage would:
(A) Notify the trustee of the default.
(B) File an attachment.
(C) Notify the mortgagor of the default, wait 90 days, and then publish a notice of default in a newspaper of general circulation.
(D) File an action in court.

(D) Mortgages are foreclosed by court action. This is the reason most lenders prefer the use of trust deeds as security for loans. Trust deeds generally are foreclosed in a trustee's sale, outside of court.

_____**(Lesson Six - Paragraph 129 – Question 1)**_____

Who retains custody of the property for one year after a mortgage foreclosure?
(A) Court. (B) Bailiff. (C) Sheriff. (D) Mortgagor.

(D) The borrower (mortgagor) retains custody of the property secured by the mortgage for the statutory period of redemption, which in California is one year from the date of the certificate of sale given the purchaser at the court sale.

_____**(Lesson Six - Paragraph 129 – Question 2)**_____

Following a court foreclosure sale, should the beneficiary request a deficiency judgment, the trustor can retain possession of the property for approximately:
(A) 90 days. (B) 120 days. (C) 1 year. (D) 5 years.

(C) Notice the question refers to a court foreclosure and a deed of trust (trustor). The certificate of sale on foreclosure passes title to the purchaser; however, it is a conditional title, subject to being defeated by redemption and does not carry the right of possession prior to expiration of the period of redemption. In California, this is one year when the lender requests a deficiency judgment. This twelve-month period is shortened to three months if a deed of trust or a mortgage with power of sale is foreclosed and if the full amount of the judgment is bid at the sale.

_____**(Lesson Six - Paragraph 129 & 141 – Question 1)**_____

The main difference between a trust deed and a mortgage is:
(A) Redemption. (B) Possession. (C) Hypothecation. (D) Amortization.

(A) A mortgage has a one-year statutory redemption period after the court has sold the property. There is no statutory redemption period after a trustee's sale. The trustor loses all rights he possessed prior to the sale. Analysis of answers: (B) Rights of possession are the same under both. (C) Hypothecation means: "to place a security without giving up possession." (D) The amortization would be similar in both documents.

_____**(Lesson Six - Paragraph 135 – Question 1)**_____

When a deed of trust is foreclosed by court sale, the action:
(A) Is the same as a foreclosure by trustee's sale.
(B) Under certain circumstances would allow the trustor a redemption period.
(C) Is not legal in California.
(D) Prevents a deficiency judgment.

(B) In this type of foreclosure the procedure is identical with a mortgage foreclosure in court except that if a deficiency judgment is not asked in the foreclosure, the trustor has no right of redemption after the sale. If a deficiency judgment is asked for in the foreclosure, the trustor has one year to redeem the same as in a mortgage.

—————————(Lesson Six - Paragraph 135 – Question 2)—————

A foreclosure of a trust deed by court action:

(A) Is the same procedure as foreclosure by trustee's sale.
(B) Usually establishes a "right of redemption" period.
(C) Is not legal in California.
(D) Bars all possibility for a deficiency judgment.

(B) A foreclosure by court action will generally create a right of redemption of the debtor in the property for a period of time. The purpose of going to court to foreclose the trust deed is usually to establish a judgment for deficiency. In choosing court foreclosure you might create this redemption period. There are two methods of foreclosing trust deeds: foreclosure by sale and foreclosure by court. Foreclosure by sale is a private sale and the sale is final; however, you cannot obtain a deficiency judgment. A foreclosure by court is treated the same as a mortgage foreclosure and there is a redemption period unless waived or if one is not available because the loan was purchase money.

—————————(Lesson Six - Paragraph 136 – Question 1)—————

Mr. "A" sells his house for $10,000 and takes back a trust deed and note for $5,000. Needing cash he immediately sells the trust deed and note at a discount to "B" for $3,500, assigning the trust deed and endorsing the note "without recourse." If trustor defaults before making any principal payments and disregarding costs of collection, the buyer of the first trust deed could obtain the greatest amount of money in the shortest period of time in this way:

(A) Foreclosure by trustee's sale to collect $3,500.
(B) Sue for specific performance.
(C) Recover from Mr. "A" as the transaction was usurious.
(D) Foreclosure by trustee's sale to recover $5,000.

(D) The fact that Mr. "A" sold this encumbrance at a discount in order to obtain ready cash does not change the face value of the note. The reason Mr. "B" bought the discounted trust deed was to obtain a higher percentage yield on his investment and, hopefully, over the term of the note to recover the full face value. In this case the trustor has defaulted. Mr. "B," who is now the beneficiary, will notify the trustee of the default and ask him to proceed with foreclosure. Since the property is worth $10,000 and is only encumbered with the purchase money trust deed, it is safe to assume that proceeds from the trustee's sale will be sufficient to pay Mr. "B" the $5,000 represented by the note. A request recorded with a junior loan that in the event the borrower receives a notice of default on his first trust deed, the same notice of default is to be sent to the junior T.D. holder. This way, even thought the junior is current and the first is in default, the holder of the junior will know forthwith if the borrower is delinquent on the first. This permits the holder of the junior trust deed to reinstate the delinquency on the first, add this amount to his lien, and begin his own foreclosure proceedings. All other bidders at the foreclosure sale would be required to overbid him with an all cash bid.

_____(Lesson Six - Paragraph 136 – Question 2)_____

Should the trustor default in making payments on a note secured by a deed of trust, the most expedient way for the beneficiary to proceed in seeking recovery would be:
(A) Judicial sale.
(B) Foreclosure by sale.
(C) Lien sale.
(D) Sheriff's sale.

_____

(B) Foreclosure by sale. This is the manner in which a trustee's sale is usually described.

_____(Lesson Six - Paragraph 137 – Question 1)_____

The trustees who are designated by lenders and borrowers in creating loans secured by trust deeds come under the supervisory jurisdiction of:
(A) The Secretary of the State of California.   (B) The Real Estate Commissioner.
(C) The California Corporations Commissioner. (D) None of the above.

_____

(D) No regulatory agency has yet been created to supervise the activity of trustees.

_____(Lesson Six - Paragraph 138 – Question 1)_____

A trustee has legally begun the process to sell property secured by a trust deed. After the notice of default is recorded, the trustee must wait at least three months before:
(A) The foreclosure in final.   (B) Issuing the reconveyance deed.
(C) Publishing the notice of sale. (D) Conveying title to the beneficiary.

_____

(C) The trustee prepares and records a "notice of default" setting forth the identification of the trust deed, the nature and extent of default, and stating that the beneficiary has elected to sell, or cause a sale of the property, to satisfy the obligation. A copy of the notice is sent to the trustor. This notice states that three months after its recording, the trustee may advertise the property for sale.

_____(Lesson Six - Paragraph 138 – Question 2)_____

If a borrower is unable to make payments and falls two months behind in submitting required trust deed loan payments, he:
(A) Has a right of redemption. (B) Has a right of reinstatement.
(C) Has no rights.   (D) Loses the security property.

_____

(B) Reinstatement can be made for 3 months following the notice of default and until 5 days prior to the date of the trustee's sale.

_____(Lesson Six - Paragraph 139 – Question 1)_____

The owner of a single family residence sells his home for a price of $126,000, receiving $12,000 cash, having the buyer assume an existing first deed and note of $98,000 and takes back a 2nd trust deed for the balance. The buyer is making regular payments on the 2nd trust deed but defaults on the 1st trust deed. The most logical procedure for the seller would be to:
(A) Refinance the 1st trust deed and foreclose on his 2nd trust deed.
(B) Reinstate the 1st trust deed and foreclose on his 2nd trust deed.
(C) Do nothing at this time since the 2nd is not in default.
(D) Do nothing on his 2nd trust deed but foreclose on the 1st trust deed.

(B) To protect his interest, the seller should make up the back payments (reinstate) on the first trust deed and foreclose on his second. The second trust deed is in default by reason of his payment to reinstate the first trust deed, even though he is receiving payments on the second. The seller cannot foreclose on the first since he was not a party to the first deed loan.

_____(Lesson Six - Paragraph 140 – Question 1)_____

When selling under a power of sale in a trust deed, the trustee must wait three (3) months after recording notice of default before:
(A) Taking possession.   (B) Foreclosure is final.
(C) Transferring title to beneficiary. (D) Publishing notice of sale.

(D) A notice of sale can be published in a newspaper of general circulation only after the prescribed 3-month waiting period in the foreclosure action. The 3-month waiting period commences with the recordation of the "notice of default."

_____(Lesson Six - Paragraph 141 – Question 2)_____

When a trust deed is in default, the party with possession of the property is the:
(A) Mortgagee. (B) Beneficiary. (C) Trustee. (D) Trustor.

(D) The parties to a trust deed are the trustor (the borrower), the trustee (the titleholder), and the beneficiary (the lender). When the beneficiary asks the trustee to record a notice of default and to send a copy of the notice of default to the trustor, this begins a three-month period of default, followed by at least a 21-day sale period. During this default and sale period, the trustor (the borrower) remains in possession of the property.

_____(Lesson Six - Paragraph 142 – Question 1)_____

The following is true regarding an "assignment of rents" clause that is frequently made a part of a mortgage contract on a deed of trust. This clause:
(A) Protects the trustor or mortgagor.
(B) Benefits the beneficiary or mortgagee.
(C) Provides that the borrower pays rent in the event he defaults.
(D) Provides that the buyer pays rent until the title to the property passes.

(B) The "assignment of rents" clause provides that upon default by a borrower the lender will receive any rents collected from use of the property until the default is corrected or the property is sold in foreclosure.

_____(Lesson Six - Paragraph 144 – Question 1)_____

A foreclosure sale of a property brought $7,000. The first trust deed note is for $8,000 and the second trust deed has a remaining balance of $2,000. The holder of the second trust deed will receive the following amount in settlement:
(A) 2/7ths. of the proceeds. (B) $2,000 less costs. (C) $ 1,000. (D) Nothing.

(D) The holder of a first trust deed has "first" claim on the proceeds derived from a foreclosure sale after court costs, etc. have been paid. In this case, with only $7,000 available, there will be nothing left to satisfy the claim of the second trust deed holder as the entire amount will go to the holder of the first trust deed.

_____**(Lesson Six - Paragraph 144 – Question 2)**_____

Regarding the foreclosure of property, if the property is sold at a trustee's sale and there was enough money to cover the encumbrances against the property, which of the following would be correct as to the priority of distribution of the funds received:

(A) First money would go for cost of sale, then 1st trust deed, 2nd trust deed, then trustor.
(B) First money would go for 1st trust deed, then 2nd trust deed, cost of sale, balance to trustor.
(C) First money to 1st trust deed, then 2nd trust deed, trustor and remainder to cost of sale.
(D) All monies go to the first trust deed holder.

(A) The first money would have to go to cover the cost of the sale. This would be a nominal amount. After the cost of sale, there would be normal priority distribution such as 1st trust deed, 2nd trust deed, etc. Any remainder would go the trustor.

_____**(Lesson Six - Paragraph 145 – Question 1)**_____

If the beneficiary is given a deed in lieu of foreclosure, the beneficiary:
(A) Receives equitable title but not legal title to the property.
(B) Takes responsibility for any junior loans that might be on the property.
(C) Always receives the property free and clear.
(D) Is hypothecating the property to secure a loan.

(B) When the lender (beneficiary) accepts a deed instead of foreclosing on the property, he does take the property with the encumbrance of junior loans on the property. The buyer at a foreclosure sale, however, would receive the property free from liens that are junior to the one being foreclosed.

_____**(Lesson Six - Paragraph 147 – Question 1)**_____

The right to foreclose on a trust deed by trustee's power of sale outlaws by statute in:
(A) 3 years. (B) 4 years. (C) 90 days. (D) None of the above.

(D) Recent law provides that a trust deed lien expires in either in 10 years after the last date fixed for payment or performance of the obligation is ascertainable from the record or if this cannot be determined from the record, 60 years after the instrument that created the security interest or other obligation was recorded. Hence, none of the above.

_____**(Lesson Six - Paragraph 149 – Question 1)**_____

If there is a default in the payments on a purchase money loan on a residence, after a period of time the holder of the purchase money trust deed will be able to:
(A) Get a deficiency judgment.
(B) Get an attachment.
(C) Get a deed of reconveyance.
(D) None of the above.

(D) If there is a default on a purchase money trust deed on a residence, the only course of action for the holder of the trust deed is to foreclose. He could not get a deficiency judgment and an attachment is used to "legally hold" property until judgment is rendered.

_____(Lesson Six - Paragraph 149 – Question 2)_____

If the seller loaned a buyer money and subsequently the buyer defaulted in his payments and the seller foreclosed:

(A) If foreclosure action was in court, a deficiency judgment would be awarded if the sale did not bring enough to pay amount due seller.

(B) The seller could not recover the property as title would pass to the first trust deed holder.

(C) A deficiency judgment could be secured as a result of the trustee's sale.

(D) If property did not bring enough at the sale to pay the beneficiary in full, he could not get a deficiency judgment through any method of foreclosure.

(D) Money loaned for the purpose of purchasing a residence of four units or less, or credit extended by the seller to the buyer to enable him to purchase, are considered "purchase money encumbrances" and no deficiency judgment can be secured regardless of the method of foreclosure.

_____(Lesson Six - Paragraph 151 – Question 1)_____

Mr. Harden purchased a residence for $85,000 and paid $17,000 cash down. He executed a trust deed and note for the balance of the purchase price. Such a note and trust deed would be considered purchase money if:

(A) It was a hard money transaction. (B) Seller extends credit to the buyer.
(C) The loan was made by an institutional lender. (D) Any of the above.

(D) A purchase money mortgage or trust deed includes both the extending of credit by a seller on any type of real property purchase and the lending of money to purchase a residential property of less than five units where the borrower occupies one unit.

_____(Lesson Six - Paragraph 157 – Question 1)_____

In the sale of real property a hard money loan, it is best described as:
(A) A purchase money loan. (B) A promissory note.
(C) A cash loan. (D) A note secured by a deed of trust or mortgage taken by the seller.

(C) A "hard money" loan involves the giving of cash money to the borrower by the lender. The best description would be a cash loan.

_____(Lesson Six - Paragraph 157 – Question 2)_____

An example of a "hard money" loan is a:
(A) Second trust deed loan. (B) Purchase money loan. (C) Cash loan. (D) First trust deed loan.

(C) A "hard money" loan is one in which the lender actually gives cash to the borrower as contrasted with the situation in which the seller only extends credit to a purchaser. A "hard money" loan could be a secured by a first deed of trust or by a junior lien. It could include funds that were used to purchase the property or money secured later to refinance it.

_____(Lesson Six - Paragraph 160 – Question 1)_____

A promissory note:
(A) May not be executed in connection with a loan on real property.
(B) Is an agreement to do or not to do a certain thing.
(C) Is the primary evidence of a loan.
(D) Is one which is guaranteed or insured by a governmental agency.

(C) Do not confuse the definition of a contract with that of a promissory note. A note is a promise to pay, and is the primary evidence of a loan.

_____(Lesson Six - Paragraph 160 – Question 2)_____

The following is correct regarding a promissory note:
(A) Always used in a real estate transaction.   (B) Always used to secure a trust deed.
(C) Recorded as proof of debt.   (D) Evidence of debt to lender.

(D) A promissory note is a promise to pay back a sum of money. The note is said to be evidence of the debt. The trust deed is said to be security for the note. The note states the debt. The trust deed puts property into trust as security for payment of that note.

_____(Lesson Six - Paragraph 163 – Question 1)_____

In the situation in which a loan is made to several unrelated persons, the following words would be included in the note for the lender's protection:
(A) Severally. (B) Joint and severally. (C) Jointly. (D) Severally and individually.

(B) The lender is best protected if not only the group is liable for payment of the obligation but also each person is individually liable for the entire obligation. This is accomplished by including the words "jointly and severally" in the proper place in the terms of the note.

_____(Lesson Six - Paragraph 163 – Question 2)_____

When a loan is created with more than one borrower, the following usually is added to the promissory note for the protection of the lender:
(A) Unconditionally. B) Universally. (C) Jointly and severally. (D) Beneficially.

(C) When there is more than one borrower on the note, the promise and obligation to pay that balance is the responsibility jointly of all the co-borrowers. Each individual is severally liable for the full debt. Again, "severally" in law means individually.

_____(Lesson Six - Paragraph 164 – Question 1)_____

A loan that is completely repaid, principal and interest, by a series of regular equal installment payments is known as a:
(A) Straight loan. (B) Balloon payment loan. (C) Fully amortized loan. (D) Variable rate mortgage loan.

(C) The question states the loan is completely repaid principal and interest by a series of equal installment payments. This describes the loan as fully amortized rather than having a balloon payment at the end. A balloon payment is defined as the last payment being more than twice the smallest payment. A straight loan has no principal payments. The principal is all due and payable when the note becomes due.

_____(Lesson Six - Paragraph 164 – Question 2)_____

When a loan is fully amortized by equal monthly payments of principal and interest, the amount applied to principal:
(A) And interest remains constant.   (B) Decreases while the interest payment increases.
(C) Increases while the interest payment decreases.   (D) Increases by a constant amount.

(C) When amortizing a loan by equal monthly payments, the amount applied to the principal gradually increases while the amount applied to interest gradually decreases.

_____(**Lesson Six - Paragraph 165 – Question 1**)_____

When a lender loans money to a homeowner secured by the home, the interest charged is:
(A) Simple interest. (B) Add-on interest. (C) Compounded monthly. (D) Compounded daily.

(A) Interest on home loans is calculated by simple interest. Compound interest is when interest is paid on interest and normally involves savings for investments. Add-on interest is generally used in automobile loans where the interest for the full principal for a three-year loan would be added to the loan. That amount would be divided by 36 and paid off in those installments.

_____(**Lesson Six - Paragraph 165 – Question 2**)_____

The method of calculating interest on real estate mortgages that is used by most large conventional lenders is:
(A) Compound interest. (B) Annuity interest. (C) Simple interest. (D) Discount interest.

(C) Simple interest is defined as interest calculated on the principal amount of the loan only. The vast majority of conventional real estate loans utilize this method. Compound interest is defined as calculating interest on principal and accrued interest. Savings accounts normally pay compound interest while real estate lenders charge simple interest.

_____(**Lesson Six - Paragraph 168 – Question 1**)_____

A balloon loan is:
(A) A standing loan. (B) An amortized loan. (C) A partially amortized loan. (D) A self-liquidating loan.

(C) A balloon loan is a final payment that is more than twice the smallest payment. Therefore, this would be classified as a partially amortized loan. It was not completely amortized over the length of the loan and left a large payment at the end.

_____(**Lesson Six - Paragraph 168 – Question 2**)_____

A balloon payment is associated with a:
(A) Partially amortized loan. (B) Final payment made on any loan secured by a trust deed.
(C) Fully amortized loan.   (D) None of the above.

(A) A balloon payment is defined as the final payment when it is an amount more than twice the smallest payment. Such a loan would be classified as partially amortized as opposed to fully amortized.

_____(**Lesson Six - Paragraph 169 – Question 1**)_____

A graduated mortgage payment permits a lower initial monthly payment, thus enabling some otherwise unqualified buyers to purchase a property. Usually this results in:
(A) Higher portion of the monthly payment being applied toward reduction of the loan principal.
(B) Larger down payment.
(C) Negative amortization.
(D) None of the above.

(C) Negative amortization occurs when unpaid interest is added to the principal balance of the loan. With lower initial monthly payments it is common for the payment not to cover the entire interest owed. Consequently, this unpaid interest is added to the loan.

_____(Lesson Six - Paragraph 170 – Question 1)_____
A straight note is best defined as:
(A) Principal is all due at one time.   (B) Sometimes used to finance real property.
(C) Sometimes secured by a trust deed. (D) All of the above.

(A) A straight note is one that has no principal payments. The principal is due all at one time.

_____(Lesson Six - Paragraph 171 – Question 1)_____
Many installment notes include an "or more" clause. Such a provision in the note:
(A) Allows the borrower to accelerate payoff of the note by without penalty.
(B) Makes it possible for the lender to advance additional loan funds to the borrower.
(C) Provides for a moratorium on the note payments in the event of a natural disaster.
(D) Indicates that the note has several makers.

(A) Allows an accelerated payoff of the note by the borrower without penalty. The inclusion of the term "or more" in the language of the note gives the borrower some flexibility in dealing with the repayment of the note. If economic conditions change and interest rates drop, the borrower could pay off the existing loan and refinance the obligation with a loan at a lower interest rate.

_____(Lesson Six - Paragraph 172 – Question 1)_____
When selling his home Able learns that the existing loan contains a penalty clause that requires six months interest to be paid if the loan is paid off prior to maturity. However, he should be made aware that a lender often waives the prepayment penalty if:
(A) The purchaser obtains his financing at the current interest rate from the lender holding the existing loan.
(B) The loan contains an acceleration clause.
(C) The seller gives 30 days notice of intention to prepay.
(D) A "tight money market" exists in the economy.

(A) In most cases the lender will waive his right to a prepayment penalty if the buyer finances his purchase through the existing lender at the current rate of interest.

_____(Lesson Six - Paragraph 172 – Question 2)_____
When financing real property, a prepayment penalty often is:
(A) Charged when applying for a loan.
(B) A clause in a deed of trust that protects the trustor.
(C) Charged for late payments on the loan.
(D) Demanded from a trustor who pays off a loan prematurely.

(D) A prepayment penalty is assessed against the trustor/borrower when he pays off a loan prematurely. This protects the beneficiary, not the trustor.

_____(Lesson Six - Paragraph 173 – Question 1)_____
If money is borrowed from a California chartered savings and loan association secured by a home and the borrower wants to pay it back early (prepay), a prepayment penalty would not be due if:
(A) The loan includes an acceleration clause.
(B) The loan has been in existence for more than 5 years.
(C) The loan is a secured by a second deed of trust.
(D) The loan is secured by a first deed of trust.

(B) California Civil Code prohibits a pre-payment penalty on a loan secured by a one-to-four family residence after the loan has been in existence for five years.

_____(Lesson Six - Paragraph 174 – Question 1)_____

Property is being sold whereby the purchaser is to continue the payments of an existing amortized loan secured by a first mortgage. In order for the buyer to assume the existing mortgage without penalty, the agent should check to be sure the existing mortgage does not include:
(A) An acceleration clause. (B) A release clause.
(C) A subordination clause. (D) A practical release clause.

_____

(A) An acceleration clause. This type of clause identifies an event that, should it occur, the note becomes due and payable at once.

_____(Lesson Six - Paragraph 174 – Question 2)_____

If a negotiable note has an acceleration clause, it:
(A) Loses negotiability.   (B) Reduces negotiability.
(C) Does not affect negotiability. (D) Does not affect negotiability but has no benefit.

_____

(C) Negotiability of a note is not affected by the inclusion of an acceleration clause in the terms of the note.

_____(Lesson Six - Paragraph 175 – Question 1)_____

In a tight money market with no relief in sight, a loan with a low interest rate has an alienation clause. Concerning the alienation clause, the following is a correct statement:
(A) The owner must refinance the property.
(B) It is of benefit to the lender.
(C) A buyer may assume the loan without the lenders approval.
(D) A buyer may take title subject to the loan without the lenders approval.

_____

(B) An alienation clause requires that the existing loan be paid off in the event of the resale of the property. In a tight money market interest rates tend to rise. It would be a definite advantage to the lender to be able to demand payoff on a low interest loan and place the money at a higher interest rate loan.

_____(Lesson Six - Paragraph 175 – Question 2)_____

The 2nd TD to be executed by the buyers will contain an "alienation clause." This means:
(A) That the second trust deed would always remain in second place even if the first were paid.
(B) That the entire remaining balance would become due and payable in the event the buyers were delinquent in payments on the second.
(C) That the property could not be resold until after the due date on the second trust deed.
(D) That the remaining balance would become due upon resale or transfer by the buyers.

_____

(D) This choice is a good explanation of an alienation clause.

_____(Lesson Six - Paragraph 184 – Question 1)_____

When a person endorses a note without warranty to the person receiving it or to any other person, he signs it:
(A) In blank. (B) With protest. (C) With recourse. (D) Without recourse.

_____

(D) When a person endorses a note "without recourse" he is, in effect, notifying the party taking the note he is not responsible for its eventual payment.

_____(Lesson Six - Paragraph 185 – Question 1)_____
A holder who takes a promissory note for value in good faith without notice that it is overdue or has been dishonored and without notice of any defense against it or claim to it on the part of any person is:
(A) An endorser without recourse.   (B) A bona fide assignee for value.
(C) A holder through a holder in due course. (D) A holder in due course.

_____

(D) The statement of the question describes a "holder in due course."

_____(Lesson Six - Paragraph 187 – Question 1)_____
A holder in due course would be successful against a defense of:
(A) Failure of consideration to the maker.   (B) Incapacity of the maker.
(C) The interest rate of the note is usurious. (D) Maker denies the alleged signature on the note.

_____

(A) A "personal defense" is never good against a holder in due course. Lack of consideration is a personal defense. A holder in due course would be successful against a defense of this type. The other answers are "real defenses" and can be good against a holder in due course.

_____(Lesson Six - Paragraph 187 – Question 2)_____
In a court suit against the maker of a dishonored note, a holder in due course would be most successful against a defense of the maker involving:
(A) Failure of consideration to the maker. (B) A usurious interest rate.
(C) Incompetency of the maker.   (D) An alteration in the amount of the note.

_____

(A) Lack of consideration to the maker would be a personal defense. Usurious interest rates, incompetency, or material alteration would be real defenses that would stand against the world, including the holder in due course.

_____(Lesson Six - Paragraph 194 – Question 1)_____
The following would involve a court action:
(A) An attachment. (B) A homestead declaration. (C) A mechanic's lien. (D) All of the above.

_____

(A) An attachment is that process by which real or personal property of a party to a lawsuit is seized and retained in the custody of the court for the purpose of acquiring jurisdiction over the property to compel an appearance before the court or to furnish security for a debt or costs arising out of the litigation.

_____(Lesson Six - Paragraph 194 – Question 2)_____
A writ of attachment when issued by the court will be effective, without extension, for a period of:
(A) 5 years. (B) 3 years. (C) I year. (D) 10 years.

_____

(B) The attachment is a lien upon all real property attached for a period of three years after the date of the levy. This period may be extended by appropriate court order. Note the question states without extension.

_____(Lesson Six - Paragraph 195 – Question 1)_____

In distinguishing between an "attachment lien" and a "judgment lien":
(A) The first type must cover all property held by an owner.
(B) The first type is recorded after a court decision.
(C) The second type is recorded prior to court decision to await the outcome of a lawsuit.
(D) The latter type is recorded after a court has rendered a decision.

(D) "Attachment" is a process by which real or personal property is seized and held in the custody of the law as a security for the satisfaction of a judgment yet to be secured. Recording the final judgment of a court as the result of a lawsuit creates a judgment lien after the court has rendered its decision.

_____(Lesson Six - Paragraph 195 – Question 2)_____

An attachment may be released or discharged in all of the following ways, except:
(A) By a release of attachment signed by the plaintiff.
(B) By an order of the court discharging the writ.
(C) By the rendering of a judgment in favor of the plaintiff.
(D) By a release of attachment signed and acknowledged by the officer who levied the writ.

(C) An attachment will be effective up until the point the holder receives satisfaction of his judgment lien. The rendering of the judgment is not enough to terminate the writ of attachment.

_____(Lesson Six - Paragraph 196 – Question 1)_____

The sale of real property which takes place under the direction of a court-appointed official to satisfy a judgment lien takes place as the result of:
(A) A foreclosure action.   (B) A writ of attachment.
(C) An unlawful detainer action. (D) A writ of execution.

(D) After a judgment has been obtained it becomes a lien on all nonexempt real property when recorded. In order to foreclose on the lien, it is necessary to obtain a writ of execution from the court. A writ of attachment is obtained before court proceedings begin in order to prevent disposal of assets before rendering of a judgment.

_____(Lesson Six - Paragraph 196 – Question 2)_____

An order of a court to an official to sell property to pay a judgment is called:
(A) A foreclosure. (B) A writ of execution. (C) A deficiency judgment. (D) An attachment.

(B) The statement gives a proper description of a writ of execution.

_____(Lesson Six - Paragraph 200 – Question 1)_____

A mechanics lien differs from a judgment in that:
(A) A mechanic's lien is derived from a statute.
(B) A mechanic's lien need not be recorded.
(C) A mechanic's lien becomes unenforceable after a lapse of time.
(D) Anyone having an interest in the property has the right, after the claim is due and before the right of redemption has expired, to discharge a mechanic's lien by satisfying the claim.

(A) The source of a mechanic's lien is not from common law. It is part of statutory law created by the state of California. A judgment evolves from common law. Analyzing other choices, (B) states a mechanic's lien need not be recorded. This is false. (C) states a mechanic's lien becomes unenforceable. This is not a difference, as a judgment also becomes unenforceable after ten years. (D) is false because there is no right of redemption concerning a mechanic's lien. The mechanic's lien involves a contract between two parties, the owner and the mechanic. If it is not paid, the mechanic has the right to start court action to satisfy his claim.

_____**(Lesson Six - Paragraph 204 – Question 1)**_____
A mechanic's lien may be filed by:
(A) Mechanics. (B) Materialmen. (C) Architects. (D) All of the above.

(D) The right to file mechanic's liens extends to all persons and laborers of every class who perform labor or services on the property and to persons who furnish materials and services.

_____**(Lesson Six - Paragraph 204 – Question 2)**_____
Which of the following would have the right to file a mechanic's lien on a new building?
(A) The architect of the structure.
(B) A carpenter working for the general contractor.
(C) A handyman who built a patio 75 days after the notice of completion was filed by the owner.
(D) All of the above.

(D) A mechanic's lien exists in favor of every person who contributes to a work of improvements, from the architect to the landscape gardener. All of the persons indicated in the question have a right to act upon the lien. A new lien arises with each "work of improvement" so the handyman has such a lien right.

_____**(Lesson Six - Paragraph 205 – Question 1)**_____
A verification is required prior to recording a:
(A) Title report. (B) Trust deed. (C) Notice of non-responsibility. (D) Mechanic's lien.

(D) Verification is required prior to recording a mechanics lien.

_____**(Lesson Six - Paragraph 205 – Question 2)**_____
The following lien must be verified and recorded to be valid:
(A) Trust deed. (B) Homestead. (C) Easement. (D) Mechanic's lien.

(D) A mechanic's lien to become effective must be recorded. Before it can be recorded, the mechanic must verify it as a truthful statement under the penalty of perjury, indicated by the term "verified."

_____**(Lesson Six - Paragraph 216 & 227 – Question 1)**_____
The following recorded document might have an effect on a mechanic's when:
(A) A notice of non-responsibility. (B) A notice of cessation.
(C) A notice of completion.   (D) All of the above.

(D) Each of the choices listed will affect a mechanic's lien. The notice of non-responsibility will protect the owner from such a lien if he did not order the work done. The notice of cessation sets up a time limit for filing a lien. The notice of completion also sets a time period during which the lien can be filed.

_____**(Lesson Six - Paragraph 216 & 227 – Question 2)**_____
Which of the following must be recorded to be effective?
(A) A notice of cessation.   (B) A notice of completion.
(C) A notice of respor;sibility. (D) All of the above.

(D) All of these documents must be recorded to be effective.

_____(Lesson Six - Paragraph 221 – Question 1)_____
Mr. Destructo was hired by the owner of a parcel of real property to remove an old dwelling on the property in preparation for the erection of a new 10-unit apartment building. After the property was cleared, the owner obtained a construction loan for the new apartment building and commenced with the new work. If Destructo is not paid for the demolition work and files a mechanic's lien, his lien would:
(A) Not take priority over the construction loan.
(B) Commence from the beginning date of his work.
(C) Be rejected since he did not file his claim prior to the new construction.
(D) Be added to the new construction loan and paid by the lender.

(B) The priority for mechanic's lien always dates back to the beginning date of construction or date when the scheme of improvements began. The removal of the old structures is considered part of the construction work.

_____(Lesson Six - Paragraph 221 – Question 2)_____
Mr. Oak, working as a sub-contractor, installs a hardwood floor in a new custom built home at the request of the general contractor. Mr. Oak's right to file a mechanic's lien dates back to:
(A) Beginning date of construction. (B) Starting date of hardwood floor installation.
(C) Completion date of his job.   (D) Completion date of all construction.

(A) The right to file a mechanic's lien dates back to the beginning date of construction. Such date is of great importance in determining whether a trust deed or mechanic's lien has priority. For instance, if material is delivered to the construction site in preparation for the foundation of a building before a construction loan is recorded, a lien filed by a workman who performed his services weeks, or even months later, would come ahead of and have priority as a claim against the property.

_____(Lesson Six - Paragraph 227 – Question 1)_____
The Constructo Company obtained a loan to buy land. They demolished several old houses on the land then applied for a construction loan. The lender on the second loan would least likely protect his interest by:
(A) A physical inspection of the property. (B) A subordination agreement.
(C) An ALTA policy.   (D) Recording a notice of non-responsibility.

(D) A notice of non-responsibility is used when the owner discovers unauthorized work being conducted on his property. The lender would not use it.

_____(Lesson Six - Paragraph 229 – Question 1)_____
The following are examples of specific liens when properly recorded, except:
(A) Real property taxes delinquent for two years.
(B) Mechanic's liens for labor or supplies furnished on an improvement.
(C) A blanket mortgage on a subdivision without a release clause.
(D) A judgment for punitive damages.

(D) A judgment becomes a general lien on all of the property of the debtor in the county where the judgment is recorded.

_____(Lesson Six - Paragraph 229 – Question 2)_____
According to the provisions of the "Subdivided Lands Law" in California, which of the following would least likely be determined to be a blanket encumbrance:
(A) Real property taxes. (B) Mechanic's liens. (C) Construction loans. (D) Mortgages and trust deeds.

(A) Taxes, assessments and water rates levied according to law become a specific lien on real property. If the charges are not paid the taxing body may take action to enforce them which can result in the sale of the property. The other suggested choices, though generally classified as specific liens, may affect more than one property. For example, a contractor or lender working on a project of 50 homes may take action against the entire project with an appropriate legal action resulting from the lien rights he holds.

_____(Lesson Six - Paragraph 229 to 232 – Question 1)_____
All of the following would be general liens:
(A) Mortgage, attachment, vendee's liens.
(B) Deed of trust, judgment, vendor's liens.
(C) Lien for decedent's debts, federal income tax lien, corporation franchise tax lien.
(D) Attachment, judgment, mechanic's lien.

(C) In choices (A), (B), and (D) you can recognize at least one specific lien attachment, the deed of trust. Title to property of a deceased person passes to the devisees or heirs subject to liens as existed at the time of the decedent's death. This property is also subject to the lien of all just debts against the estate. A federal income tax lien is a general lien against all property of a person subject to such a lien. The corporation franchise tax lien is a general lien on the property of the corporation and can be enforced against it. Franchise tax is levied on the corporation's right to do business within the state or states.

_____(Lesson Six - Paragraph 237 – Question 1)_____
Mr. Bee employed the Dolphin Pool Construction Company to install a swimming pool at his home. After completion, the contractor filed a lien to obtain payment of the contract price. The encumbrance created was:
(A) A general lien. (B) A voluntary lien. (C) A specific lien. (D) None of the above.

(C) A specific lien. A mechanic's lien is a lien upon a single property where the work was done.

_____(Lesson Six - Paragraph 242 – Question 1)_____
Private restrictions on the use of land may be created by:
(A) Private land use controls.   (B) Written agreement.
(C) General plan restrictions in subdivisions. (D) Any of the above.

(D) The question deals with private restrictions as opposed to public restrictions such as zoning laws. Private restrictions, often called deed restrictions, can be created between a group of people either by contract, a written agreement, or restrictions in the original subdivision. All of the choices are correct.

_____(Lesson Six - Paragraph 242 to 246 – Question 1)_____
Deed restrictions, easements, leases, and mortgages are limitations on ownership described as being:
(A) Contractual. (B) Involuntary. (C) Both A and B. (D) Neither A nor B.

(A) Some texts identify limitations on the ownership of real property as 1. Governmental - such as eminent domain, police power, etc. 2. Contractual - such as deed restrictions, easements, leases, mortgages, trust deeds. As used here, contractual would have the sense of a covenant in a legal instrument.

_____(Lesson Six - Paragraph 242 to 246 – Question 2)_____

A deed restriction:
(A) Must be for the public welfare.   (B) Is always a burden on the landowner.
(C) May not be for aesthetic value only. (D) None of the above.

(D) A deed restriction is a private restriction or limitation on property. It need not be for the public welfare. Most deed restrictions are designed to benefit the landowner. Deed restrictions often deal only with aesthetic considerations - color of homes, landscaping, type of architecture, odors and fumes.

_____(Lesson Six - Paragraph 248 – Question 1)_____

A deed restriction:
(A) Must be for esthetic value.   (B) Must be for general welfare
(C) Must be for the common good.   (D) May benefit the land.

(D) Deed restrictions, also known as private restrictions, need not be for the general welfare or for the common good, as must zoning laws. However, deed restrictions often benefit the value of the land by prohibiting uses of the property that might lower its value.

_____(Lesson Six - Paragraph 248 – Question 2)_____

The following would never be considered to be liens on real property:
(A) Mortgages. (B) Judgments. (C) Deed restrictions. (D) Property taxes.

(C) Legitimate deed restrictions limit the use of private property in some manner. However, they are never liens.

_____(Lesson Six - Paragraph 250 – Question 1)_____

A distinction between a restriction of a covenant and a restriction of a condition is:
(A) A condition runs with the land.   (B) Covenants may be created by deed.
(C) A covenant may bind successors in ownership. (D) A condition is only created in a grant.

(D) Restrictions that are in the form of conditions can only be created as a qualification of an estate granted in a conveyance. However, covenants may be created by an agreement among property owners as well as in the original conveyance. The other choices do not reflect differences. Conditions and covenants may run with the land. Covenants may be created by a conveyance as well as by agreement. Covenants as well as conditions may bind succeeding owners.

_____(Lesson Six - Paragraph 250, 251 – Question 1)_____

Covenants differ from conditions because:
(A) A condition can be conveyed only by the grant of an estate.
(B) A covenant cannot be conveyed by the grant of an estate.
(C) Only conditions run with the land.
(D) Only covenants can restrict the use of the land by the owner.

(A) A condition can only be created by deed or by contract of an owner. A covenant may be created either by granting an estate, by mutual consent, or agreement of a group of owners for their benefit. Conditions always "run with the land" while covenants may do so. Both conditions and covenants may restrict the use of land by the owner.

_____**(Lesson Six - Paragraph 250, 251 – Question 2)**_____
Private restrictions may be created by appropriate clauses:
(A) In deeds. (B) In written agreements. (C) In neither A nor B. (D) In either A or B.

(D) Private owners create restrictions typically by appropriate clauses in deeds, in agreements, or in the general plans of entire subdivisions.

_____**(Lesson Six - Paragraph 256 – Question 1)**_____
Of the following restrictions, which would be the most difficult to enforce?
(A) Minimum dollar value of improvements. (B) Minimum lot size.
(C) Minimum square feet of improvements. (D) Type of improvements to be constructed.

(A) The physical characteristics of real property are more easily controlled than are aesthetic or amenity values. The other choices are physical in nature. Dollar value of improvements is to some degree a matter of opinion, hence more difficult to control.

_____**(Lesson Six - Paragraph 256 – Question 2)**_____
Of the limitations imposed by subdivision restrictions, the least effective is shown by experience to be:
(A) Minimum dollar cost for the improvements on each lot.   (B) Minimum lot size.
(C) Maximum height of the improvements. (D) Minimum area of the improvements.

(A) The other choices relate to matters that are physical in nature and could be policed readily. An owner could more easily disguise the costs involved in improving his property.

_____**(Lesson Six - Paragraph 257 – Question 1)**_____
A man is buying lot #8 in a subdivision of 9 lots that has a deed restriction affecting all 9 lots limiting the use of the property to a single-family residence. He will buy lot #8 if he can use it for a barbershop. He can, most likely, buy under these circumstances if:
(A) The area was recently rezoned C-4.
(B) Seven of the nine owners agree to such use.
(C) Seven of the nine owners already operate similar businesses on their lots.
(D) The one man who objects had not received architectural approval of his residence.

(C) The use by the seven owners contrary to the deed restriction would be strong evidence in court that the character of the neighborhood had changed. This would support the buyer's action. Even though seven owners gave their written consent to use in this manner, a single owner's objections might make it necessary for the court to uphold the restriction.

_____**(Lesson Six - Paragraph 258 – Question 1)**_____
A court order restricting a party from doing an act is known as:
(A) A judgment lien. (B) A restriction. (C) An injunction. (D) An indenture.

(C) The statement in the question is a good, simple definition of an injunction.

_____(**Lesson Six - Paragraph 258 – Question 2**)_____

Mr. Crawford has been burning rubbish on his own property. The neighbors have complained and have secured a court order to have Mr. Crawford stop the offending practice. That court order would be known as:

(A) An indenture. (B) A general lien. (C) A writ of habeas corpus. (D) An injunction.

(D) Injunction - A writ or order issued under the seal of a court to restrain one or more parties to a suit or proceeding from doing an act which is deemed to be inequitable or unjust in regard to the rights of some other party or parties to the suit.

_____(**Lesson Six - Paragraph 265 – Question 1**)_____

After Mr. Gardner purchased his home he discovered by survey that his neighbor's garage was three feet over his newly acquired property. This disturbed him. For remedy, if a friendly settlement cannot be reached, he should bring a civil suit against:

(A) The broker, for failure to disclose the encroachment.
(B) His neighbor.
(C) The Real Estate Commissioner.
(D) The title company for failure to show the encumbrance on the standard form title report.

(B) If there is an encroachment for which there is no justification, the owner of the land encroached upon has the right to bring a proper action in court to have the encroachment removed (such as a "quiet title" or "ejectment" suit).

Lesson Six
Part Three
Understanding Through Question Testing

 Log into your course at www.lumbleau.com.

STUDENT LOGIN
Login:
Password:

 On your student home page, click on the "State Exam Preparation".

STATE EXAM
PREPARATION

Under the "Guided Lesson" tab click on the sixth of fourteen links: "Legal Aspects II".

Real Estate Salesperson Course

Guided Lessons	Practice Exams	Progress Report	Success Video

Print	Questions
Click	HERE>>> **6. Legal Aspects II**

Here you will be tested on all of the questions you have been studying and learn the most recently added questions. It is essential, for maximum retention, that you eliminate all of the questions you can easily answer and "TAG" for study the questions with which you have difficulty.

LESSON 7
LAND
MEASUREMENTS
CONSTRUCTION
TERMS
ARITHMETIC

Lesson Seven
Part One
Understanding Through Video Teaching

Lesson Seven
VOCABULARY

1 Base and Meridian - In the U.S. Government Survey System, imaginary lines used in the system to identify the location of public lands.

2 Commercial Acre - A term applied to the remaining portion of a full acre of newly subdivided land after allowances for public streets, roads and alleys. Approximately 40,000 square feet.

3 Contemporary Architecture - Modern or functional design, as distinguished from traditional or stylistic.

4 Contiguous - To touch upon, border upon, in physical contact, touching near or adjoining. A term used to describe the relative position of lots or parcels of land (Abutting).

5 Cul-de-sac - A street open at one end only. A dead-end street. A blind alley (French: "bottom of sack").

6 Front Foot - Property measurement for sale or valuation purposes. Property measured by the front foot on its street line with each foot extending the depth of the lot. Usually used for commercial lots and special tax assessments.

7 Legal Description - A written description by which property can definitely be located by reference to government surveys or approved recorded maps.

8 Megalopolis – Greek word meaning "Great city." The dictionary describes it as an extensive, heavily populated, continuously urban area that includes any number of cities.

9 Metes and Bounds - A type of legal description of a parcel of land which identifies the boundaries of the parcel.

10 Monument - A fixed object and point established by surveyors to establish land locations.

11 Plat - A major plan of a certain parcel of land.

12 Plat Book - A book showing the lots and legal subdivisions of an area.

13 Range - A strip of land six miles wide as determined in the U.S. Government Survey, which runs north and south and which is parallel to meridian lines used in the survey system.

14 Tier (Township lines) - A strip of land six miles wide as determined by the U.S. Government Survey, which runs east and west and which is parallel to the base lines used in the survey system.

15 Township - In the survey of public lands of the United States, a territorial subdivision six miles long, six miles wide, and containing 36 sections. Each one mile square, located between two range lines and two township lines.

16 Anchor Bolt - A bolt that securely binds the mud sill to the foundation wall.

17 Backfill - Dirt and other matter that is filled in around retaining walls, foundations, or other excavations.

18 Baseboard - A board placed against the wall around a room next to the floor.

19 Base Molding - Molding used at top of baseboard.

20 Base Shoe - Molding used at junction of baseboard and floor. Commonly called a carpet strip.

21 Batten - Narrow strips of wood or metal used to cover joints, internally or externally. Also used for decorative effect.

22 Beam - A structural member transversely supporting a load. A beam is supported by a post as in, "Post A and B" construction. A pier also supports a beam. If post or pier is not used, several studs are nailed together to support the beam.

23 Bearing Wall - A bearing wall is a wall that supports weight of the structure. It is intact during remodeling. You do not remove it. A bearing wall can be at any angle to a door that one wishes as in certain entry halls. Normally, your bearing wall is required to be of stronger construction than would be a partition that does not bear weight.

24 Bench Mark - A fixed marker from which differences in elevation are measured by surveyors.

25 Blacktop - Asphalt paving used in streets and highways.

26 Board Foot - A measure of lumber, one foot square by one inch thick (12" x 12" x 1" = 144 cu. in.).

27 Bracing - Framing lumber nailed at an angle in order to provide rigidity.

28 Bridging - Small wood or metal pieces used to brace floor joists.

29 B.T.U. - British thermal unit, a standard used for measuring heating and air conditioning capacity.

30 Building Line - A line set by law at a certain distance from a street line in front of which an owner cannot build on his lot (setback line).

31 Building Paper - A heavy waterproofed paper used as sheathing in wall or roof construction as a protection against air and moisture (tar paper).

32 Built-in - Cabinets or similar features built as part of the house.

33 Casing - A frame of a window or door.

34 Casement Widow - Frames of wood or metal which swing outward.

35 Circuit Breaker - An electrical device which automatically interrupts an electric circuit when an overload occurs. May be used instead of a fuse to protect each circuit and can be reset.

36 Clapboard - Boards usually thicker at one edge used for siding.

37 Collar Beam - A beam that connects the pairs of opposite roof rafters above the attic floor.

38 Combed Plywood - A grooved building material used primarily for interior finish.

39 Compaction - Whenever extra soil is added to a lot to fill in low places or to raise the level of the lot. The added soil is often too loose and soft to sustain the weight of buildings. It is necessary to compact the added soil so that it will carry the weight of buildings without the danger of their tilting, settling, or cracking. Expensive to a contractor.

40 Conduit - Usually a metal pipe in which electrical wiring is installed.

41 Counter Flashing - Flashing used on chimneys at roofline to cover shingle flashing and to prevent moisture entry.

42 Crawl Space - Distance between ground level and the first floor of a structure built on a foundation (18" minimum height).

43 Deck - Usually an open porch on the roof, ground, or lower floor, porch, or wing.

44 Dry Rot - A fungus decay causing seasoned lumber to become brittle and

crumble to powder. Of all the woods, redwood is the least susceptible to this condition.

45 Dry Wall - A wall constructed with dry panels of plywood, fiberboard, gypsum board, etc., which are nailed to the studs, as opposed to a wet or plastered wall.

46 Eaves - The lower part of a roof projecting over the wall.

47 EER - When an air conditioning unit has a higher energy efficiency ratio (EER), it means that the unit is more efficient.

48 Expandable House - Home designed for further expansion and addition in the future.

49 Expansion Joint - A bituminous fiber strip used to separate units of concrete to prevent cracking due to expansion as a result of temperature changes.

50 Façade - Front of a building.

51 Fire Stop - A solid, tight closure of a concealed space, placed to prevent the spread of fire and smoke through such a space.

52 Flashing - Sheet metal or other material used to protect a building from seepage of water.

53 Footing - The base or bottom of a foundation wall, pier, or column.

54 Foundation - The supporting portion of a structure below the first floor construction, or below grade including the footings.

55 Frost Line - The depth of frost penetration in the soil. Varies in different parts of the country. Footings should be placed below this depth to prevent movement.

56 Furring - Strips of wood or metal applied to a wall or other surface to even it, to form an air space, or to give the wall an appearance of greater thickness.

57 Gable Roof - A pitched roof with two sloping sides.

58 Gambrel Roof - A curb roof, having a steep lower slope with a flatter upper slope above.

59 Girder - A large beam used to support beams, joists and partitions.

60 Grade - Ground level at the foundation.

61 Header - A framing member, usually of one or more pieces of lumber, placed over an opening in a wall.

62 Hip Roof - A pitched roof with sloping sides and ends.

63 Indirect Lighting - The light is reflected from the ceiling or other object external to the fixture.

64 Jamb - The side post or lining of a doorway, window or other opening.

65 Joint - The space between the adjacent surfaces of two components joined and held together by nails, glue, cement, mortar, etc.

66 Joist - One of a series of parallel beams to which the boards of a floor and ceiling laths are nailed, supported by large beams, girders, or bearing walls.

67 Kiosk - A freestanding booth in a parking lot or a shopping mail. Film processing booths and key shops located in these areas are examples of kiosks.

68 Lath - A building material of wood, metal, gypsum, or insulating board fastened to the frame of a building to act as a plaster base.

69 Lintel - A horizontal board that supports the load over an opening such as a door or window. Can also be metal if supporting brick or masonry. Similar to a header.

70 Live Load - Floor joists are required to support a live load of at least 40 pounds per

square foot and a roof must support a live load of at least 20 pounds per square foot.

71 Louver - An opening with a series of horizontal slats set at an angle to permit ventilation without admitting rain or sunlight.

72 Minimum Areas - In every dwelling at least one room must have no less than 120 square feet of superficial floor area. Every other habitable room except the kitchen or breakfast room must have 90 square feet of floor area.

73 Molding - Usually patterned strips used to provide ornamental variations of outline or contour. Such as cornices, bases, window and door jambs.

74 Overhang - The part of the roof extending beyond the walls to shade buildings and cover walks.

75 Penny - Size of nails such as one-penny, three-penny, etc.

76 Party Wall - A wall erected on the line between two adjoining properties which are under different ownership for the use of both properties. Example: a fence, which both "parties" use.

77 Parquet Floor - Hardwood flooring laid in squares or patterns.

78 Pier - A column of masonry, usually rectangular in horizontal cross section, used to support a beam or other structural members.

79 Pitch - The incline or rise of a roof (4" to every foot for wood shingles). Longest life for steepest pitch.

80 Plate - A horizontal board placed on a wall or supported on posts or studs to carry the trusses of a roof or rafters directly. A shoe or base member of a partition or other frame. A small flat board placed on or in a wall to support girders, rafters, etc.

81 Prefabricated House - A house manufactured and sometimes partly assembled before delivery to building site.

82 Purlin - A piece of timber laid horizontally to support the common rafters of a roof.

83 Quarter Round - A molding that presents a profile of a quarter circle.

84 Radiant Heating - A method of heating usually consisting of coils or pipes placed in the floor, wall, or ceiling.

85 R-Rating - A system which has been developed by authorities to measure the relative ability of building insulation materials to resist cold or to retain heat. R9. R15, and R19 are examples of these ratings. The higher the number, the greater the protection.

86 Rafter - One of a series of boards on a roof designed to support roof loads. The rafters of a flat roof are sometimes called roof joists.

87 Ridge - The horizontal line at the junction of the top edges of two sloping roof surfaces. The rafters at both slopes are nailed at the ridge.

88 Ridge Board - The board placed on edge at the ridge of the roof to support the upper ends of the rafters. Also called roof tree, ridge piece, ridge plate and ridge pole. Highest board in a wood frame house.

89 Sash - Wood or metal frame containing one or more window panes.

90 Scribing - Fitting woodwork to an irregular surface.

91 Shake - A hand-split shingle.

92 Sheathing - Structural covering. Usually boards, plywood, or wallboards, placed over exterior studding or rafters of a house.

93 Sill - The lowest part of the frame of a house resting on the foundation and supporting

the uprights of the frame (studs). The board or metal forming the lower part of an opening as a door or window sill.

94 Soil Pipe - Pipe carrying waste out from the house to the main sewer line.

95 Sole or Sole Plate - A member, usually a 2" x 4", which wall and partition studs rest.

96 Studs - Vertical structural lumber, normally 2" x 4" x 8', used in framing a building. Usually required to be 16 inches or less on center.

97 Termites - Ant-like social insects of various types which is destructive to wooden structures. Most destructive type is the subterranean termite.

98 Treads - Horizontal boards of a staircase used as the steps.

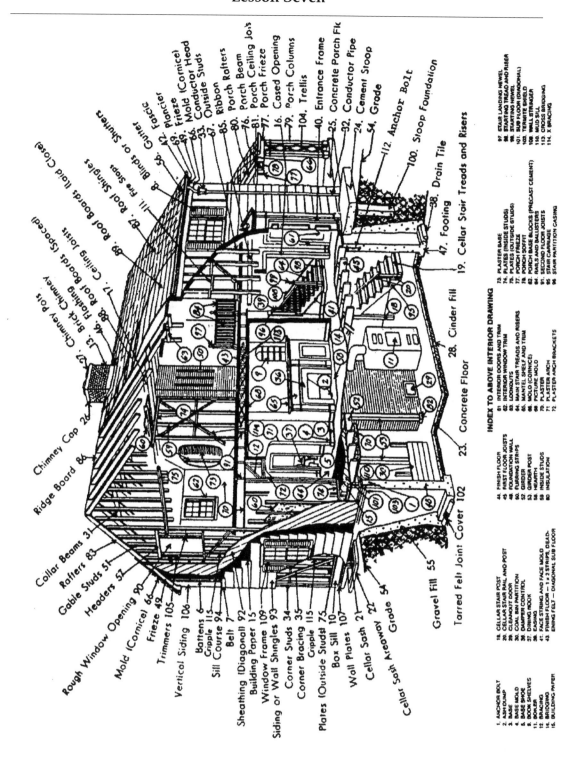

Chimney Pots
13. Brick Chimney
86. Flashing
82. Roof Boards (Spaced)
17. Ceiling Joists
85. Roof Boards (laid Close)
87. Roof Shingles
111. Fire Stops
56. Blinds or Shutters
96. Gutter
42. Fascia
69. Frieze
58. Mold (Cornice)
66. Conductor Head
33. Outside Studs
67. Ribbon
85. Porch Rafters
80. Porch Beam
76. Porch Ceiling Joists
81. Porch Frieze
16. Cased Opening
79. Porch Columns
104. Trellis
40. Entrance Frame
25. Concrete Porch Floor
32. Conductor Pipe
24. Cement Stoop
54. Grade
112. Anchor Bolt
100. Stoop Foundation
38. Footing
47. Drain Tile
19. Cellar Stair Treads and Risers
28. Cinder Fill
23. Concrete Floor

Chimney Cap 26
Ridge Board 31
Collar Beams 31
Rafters 83
Gable Studs 51
Headers 52
Rough Window Opening 90
Mold (Cornice) 66
Frieze 49
Trimmers 105
Vertical Siding 106
Battens 6
Cripple 115
Sill Course 94
Belt 7
Sheathing (Diagonal) 92
Building Paper 15
Window Frame 109
Siding or Wall Shingles 93
Corner Studs 34
Corner Bracing 35
Cripple 115
Plates (Outside Studs) 75
Box Sill 10
Wall Plates 107
Cellar Sash 21
Cellar Sash Areaway 22
Grade 54
Gravel Fill 55
Tarred Felt Joint Cover 102

INDEX TO ABOVE INTERIOR DRAWING

1. ANCHOR BOLT
2. ASH DUMP
4. BASE
5. BASE MOLD
6. BASE SHOE
8. BOOK SHELVES
9. BOILER
12. BRACING
14. BRIDGING
16. BUILDING PAPER
18. CELLAR STAIR POST
20. CELLAR STAIR RAIL AND POST
29. CLEANOUT DOOR
30. COAL BIN PARTITION
36. DAMPER CONTROL
37. DINING NOOK
39. EASING
41. FACE STRING AND FACE MOLD
43. FINISH FLOOR — 1 x 2 STRIPS, DEADENING FELT — DIAGONAL SUB FLOOR
44. FINISH FLOOR
45. FIRST FLOOR JOISTS
48. FOUNDATION WALL
50. FURRING STRIPS
52. GIRDER
53. GIRDER POST
58. HEARTH
59. INSIDE STUDS
80. INSULATION
61. INTERIOR DOORS AND TRIM
62. INTERIOR WINDOW TRIM
63. LOOKOUTS
64. MAIN STAIR TREADS AND RISERS
65. MANTEL SHELF AND TRIM
68. MOLD (CORNICE)
69. PICTURE MOLD
70. PLASTER
71. PLASTER ARCH
72. PLASTER ARCH BRACKETS
73. PLASTER BASE
74. PLATES (INSIDE STUDS)
75. PLATES (OUTSIDE STUDS)
77. PORCH FRIEZE
78. PORCH SOFFIT
82. PORCH BASE BLOCKS (PRECAST CEMENT)
83. PORCH BASE BALUSTERS
84. RAILS AND BALLISTERS
91. SECOND FLOOR JOISTS
95. STAIR CARRIAGE
98. STAIR PARTITION CASING
97. STAIR LANDING NEWEL
98. STARTING TREAD AND RISER
99. STARTING NEWEL
101. SUB FLOOR (DIAGONAL)
103. TERMITE SHIELD
108. WALL STRINGER
110. MUD SILL
113. CROSS BRIDGING
114. X BRACING

CONSTRUCTION
TYPE V SHEET — WOOD FRAME BUILDINGS
TYPICAL ONE & TWO STORY CONSTRUCTION DETAILS

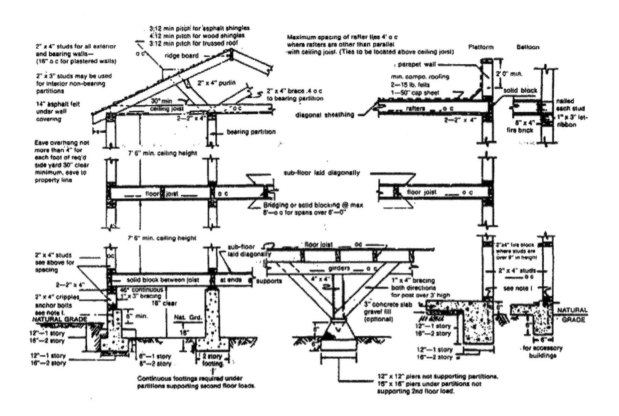

ARCHITECTURAL STYLES

607

CONTEMPORARY

CAPE COD

DUTCH COLONIAL

FRENCH PROVINCIAL

CALIFORNIA RANCH

ARCHITECTURAL AND ROOF STYLES

608

HIP ROOF

GEORGIAN COLONIAL

GAMBREL ROOF

DUTCH COLONIAL

HIP ROOF

SPANISH

GABLE ROOF

NEW ENGLAND COLONIAL

GABLE ROOF

SOUTHERN COLONIAL

GABLE ROOF

MONTEREY

COMPOUND GABLE ROOF

CALIFORNIA BUNGALOW

GABLE ROOF

CAPE COD

COMPOUND GABLE ROOF

CALIFORNIA RANCH

LAND DESCRIPTIONS
SECTION, TOWNSHIP AND RANGE

100   Legal descriptions usually fall into one of three general categories:

(1) United States Government survey in which the description refers to section, township, and range.

(2) A running description outlining the boundaries of a parcel of land called "metes and bounds." Used in describing irregularly shaped parcels.

(3) Reference to a recorded map, usually used in describing land subdivided into lots, known as a lot and book description.

101   Legal descriptions are absolutely necessary in any instrument to be recorded that affects the transferability of the title to real property as used in deeds, mortgages and trust deeds, easements etc. Instruments that are not needed by a title insurance company, such as property tax statements, often do not call for a complete legal description.

102   Land in the United States is surveyed into tracts bounded by lines conforming to the true meridian and baseline. The largest of these tracts, called a township is six miles square. Each row of townships running north and south parallel to a true meridian is called a range. Each row of townships running east and west parallel to the principal base line is called a tier.

102a Every township might not have the same land area. Adjustments in land area must be made because of the curvature of the earth. This results in what are identified as "fractional sections."

106   In Northern California, the Humboldt Base Line and Meridian.

107   In Central California, the Mount Diablo Base Line and Meridian.

108   In Southern California, the San Bernardino Base Line and Meridian.

PROBLEM NUMBER ONE

Shade out on the map the following land description:

The E1/2 of the NW1/4 of the SE1/4 of Section 17 and the SW1/4 of the SE1/4 of the NE1/4 of Section 17, and the N1/2 of the NE1/4 of the SE1/4 of Section 17, and the NW1/4 of the SW1/4 of Section 16.

How many acres? What is the value at $47.50 per acre?

ANSWER TO PROBLEM NUMBER ONE

PART 1.
<u>E1/2 - NW1/4 - SE1/4 - SEC. 17</u>
20   40   160   640   Acres

PART 2.
<u>SW1/4 - SE1/4 - NE1/4 - SEC. 17</u>
10   40   160   640   Acres

PART 3.
<u>N1/2 - NE1/4 - SE1/4 - SEC. 17</u>
20   40   160   640   Acres

PART 4.
<u>NW1/4 - SW1/4 - SEC. 16</u>
40   160   640   Acres

(90 ACRES @ $47.50 PER ACRE - $4,275.00)

PROBLEM NUMBER TWO

Shade out on the map the following land description:

The SW 1/4 of the NE 1/4 of Section 20, and the S 1/2 of the SW 1/4 of the SE 1/4 of the N.E. 1/4 of Section 20, and the N 1/2 of the NE 1/4 of the SE 1/4 of Section 20, and the NW 1/4 of the NW 1/4 of the SW 1/4 of Section 21, and the SW 1/4 of the NW 1/4 of Section 21, and the S 1/2 of the SE 1/4 of the NW 1/4 of Section 21 and the SE 1/4 of the NE 1/4 of the SE 1/4 of Section 20.

How many acres in this tract?

PART 1.
<u>SW 1/4 - NE 1/4 - SEC. 20</u>
40   160   640   Acres

PART 2.
<u>S1/2 - SW1/4 - SE1/4 - NE1/4 - SEC.20</u>
5   10   40   160   640   Acres

PART 3.
<u>N1/2 - NE1/4 - SE1/4 - SEC.20</u>
20   40   160   640   Acres

PART 4.
<u>NW 1/4 - NW1/4 - SW1/4 - SEC.21</u>
10   40   160   640   Acres

PART 5.
<u>SW1/4 - NW1/4 - SEC.21</u>
40   160   640   Acres

PART 6.
<u>S1/2 - SE1/4 - NW1/4 - SEC. 21</u>
20   40   160   640   Acres

PART 7.
<u>SE1/4 - NE1/4 - SE1/4 - SEC. 20</u>
10   40   160   640   Acres

(145 acres in this tract.)

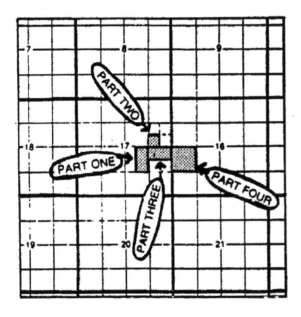

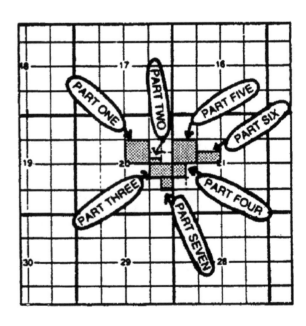

TOWNSHIP PLAT

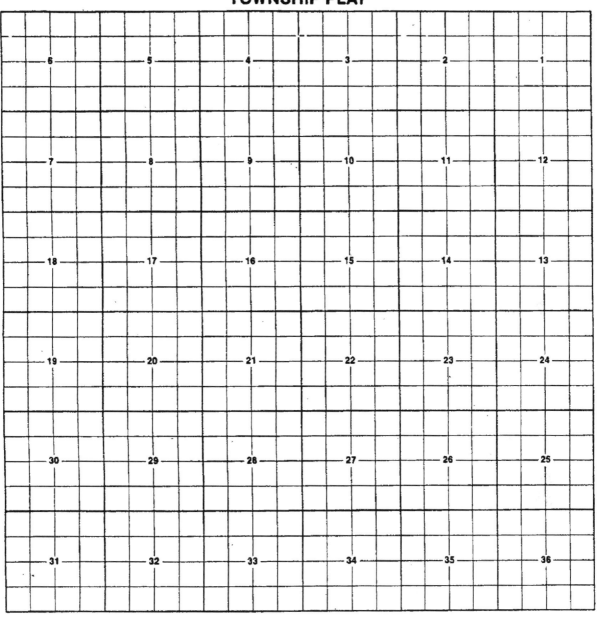

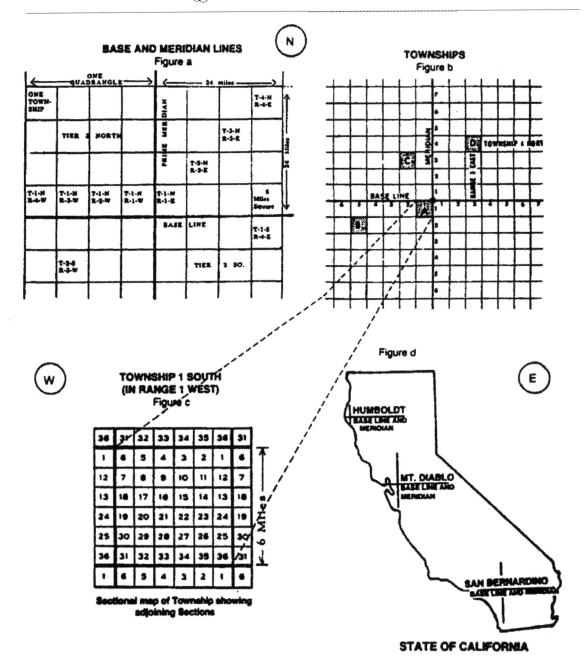

BASE AND MERIDIAN LINES
Figure a

TOWNSHIPS
Figure b

TOWNSHIP 1 SOUTH
(IN RANGE 1 WEST)
Figure c

Sectional map of Township showing
adjoining Sections

Figure d

STATE OF CALIFORNIA

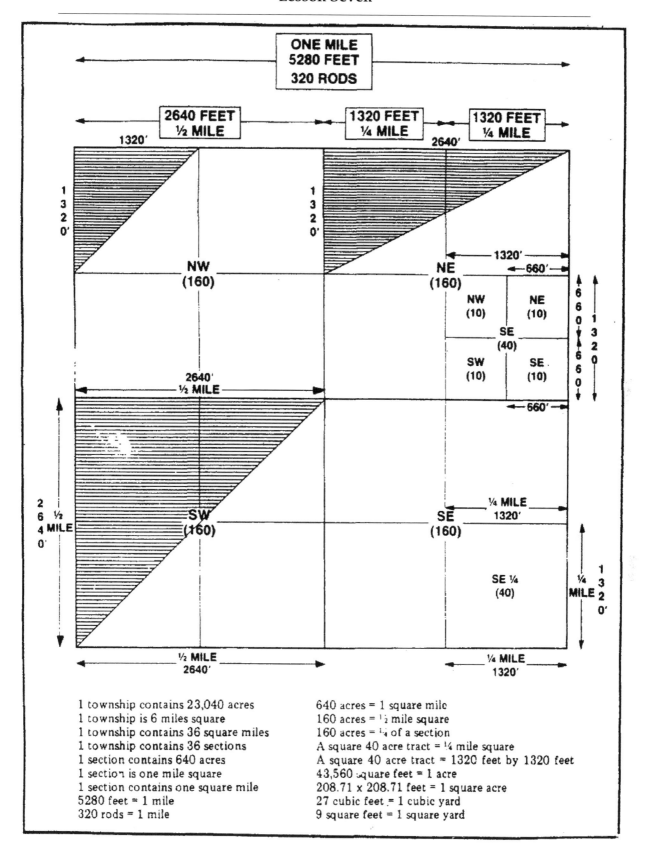

1 township contains 23,040 acres
1 township is 6 miles square
1 township contains 36 square miles
1 township contains 36 sections
1 section contains 640 acres
1 section is one mile square
1 section contains one square mile
5280 feet = 1 mile
320 rods = 1 mile

640 acres = 1 square mile
160 acres = ½ mile square
160 acres = ¼ of a section
A square 40 acre tract = ¼ mile square
A square 40 acre tract = 1320 feet by 1320 feet
43,560 square feet = 1 acre
208.71 x 208.71 feet = 1 square acre
27 cubic feet = 1 cubic yard
9 square feet = 1 square yard

Video Page 614

METES AND BOUNDS

➡ **110** Metes and bounds simply means "the measurement of the boundaries" it is usually used in the description of irregularly shaped parcels and always begins with a north or south direction from the starting point. The original settlers in California described their property by the use of natural boundaries (rivers or streams) and monuments (piles of rocks). This description is, compared to United States Government survey is less desirable because the streams can change their course and the monuments destroyed. Most of these original; descriptions have since been converted to government surveys.

110a The seaward boundary of an ocean front lot is the mesne (average) high title line.

111 NOTE: To determine acreage in METES AND BOUNDS problems (irregularly shaped parcel) you must remember that a diagonal line cuts any square or rectangle in half. You square up the diagonal line (the WHOLE line, not just a portion of it). (See diagram below) Now you need only to count the number of acres in the squared up area and divide by two.

LOT BOOK DESCRIPTION
(Known as "RECORDED MAP")

112 Lots sold from recorded maps carry a description referring to the map and giving the book and page number of the recordation. A typical description of this kind would be:

Lot 7, Block B, Tract 6447, as recorded in Book 8 1, pages 100- 105 of Maps, Records of Los Angeles County.

113 Lot Book descriptions may be by FRACTIONAL description or by METES AND BOUNDS. Any type of description which is sufficient to locate a parcel of land, or a lot, or a part of a lot, on the county recorder's books, or

in the field, is considered a good description. The less complicated it is, the better for all concerned. However, the record books are filled with wordy, detailed descriptions which a real estate broker or salesperson may be called upon to locate, so it is necessary to understand how to read them.

114 FRACTIONAL descriptions are used when the property can be described by a certain fraction of the lot, such as "the south twenty feet" or "the east one-half." A whole lot and a portion of another would be described as "All of Lot 1, and the east one half of Lot 2" followed by the Lot Book description locating it in the county records. Such descriptions are not possible where the lot is irregular in shape. These must be described by METES AND BOUNDS. Regularly shaped lots may also be described by metes and bounds, but a fractional description is less complicated, and the simplest method is usually the best.

115 A typical FRACTIONAL description problem might read like this:

Below is a portion of the Smith Tract; Lots 1 to 8 as recorded in Book 72, pages 1314, Maps and Records of Los Angeles County. Describe the various parcels.

Correct legal description of each of the three parcels below:

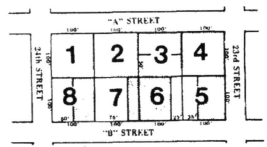

1. The E- 1/2 of Lot 8 of the Smith Tract, as recorded in Book 72, pages 13-14, Maps and Records of the Los Angeles County.

2. The east 25 feet of Lot 7 and the West 75 feet of Lot 6 of the Smith Tract, as recorded in Book 72, pages 13-14, Maps and Records of Los Angeles County.

3. The north 50 feet (or the N-1/2) of Lot 3, all of Lot 4, and the east 65 feet of Lot 5, of the Smith Tract, as recorded in Book 72, pages 13-14, Maps and Records of Los Angeles County.

TEST ASSIGNMENT

Plot the following legal descriptions on the survey map reproduced below:

1. Starting at a point located at the SE corner of the intersection of A and 24th Streets, draw a line due east 150 feet; thence south 200 feet; thence due west 150 feet; thence in a northeasterly direction to the NE corner of Lot 12; thence to the point of beginning; being a portion of Tract 985, as recorded in Book 87, pages 17-18, Maps and Records of Ventura County.

2. The east 25 feet of Lot 2; the west 50 feet of Lot 3; and all of Lot 10, of Tract 985, as recorded in Book 87, pages 17-18, Maps and Records of Ventura County.

3. AR of Lot 5; the north 50 feet of Lot 8; and the east 50 feet of Lot 9, Tract 985, as recorded in Book 87, pages 17-18, Maps and Records of Ventura County.

4. Starting at a point located 50 feet west of the SE corner of Lot 7, of Tract 985, as recorded in Book 87, pages 17-18, Maps and Records of Ventura County, draw a line 200 feet due north; thence 50 feet east; thence 150 feet due south; thence to the point of beginning.

This is a portion of Tract 985, as recorded in Book 87, pages 17-18, Maps and Records of Ventura County.

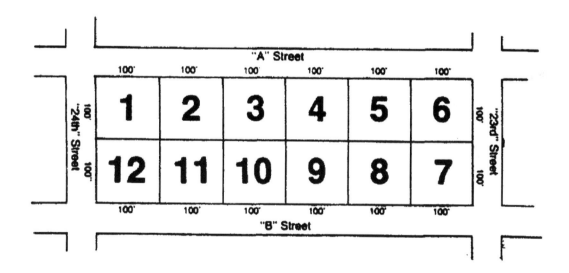

ANSWERS TO TEST ASSIGNMENT

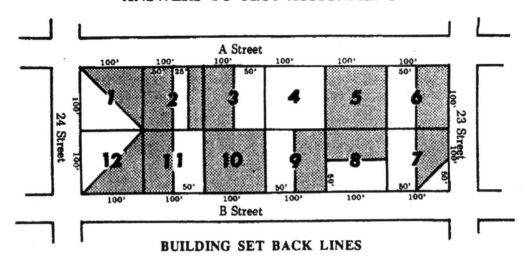

BUILDING SET BACK LINES

To preserve a view, or for other purposes such as uniformity in the placement of buildings on the various lots fronting upon a street, deed restrictions and city or county building ordinances usually contain a provision that the house or other structure be set back from the lines of the lots a certain distance. Thus, every time a building is constructed, the builder is forced by law to keep the substantial parts of the structure within the set back lines scheduled for that particular lot, as illustrated below.

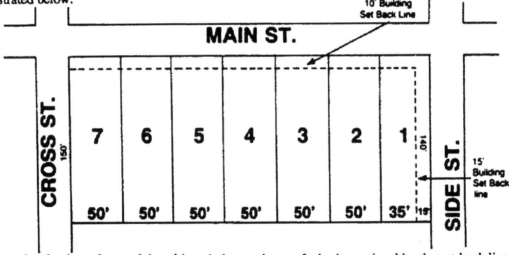

It must be clearly understood that although the purchaser of a lot is restricted by the set-back lines as to the area upon which he may erect a structure, he must purchase the entire lot. Thus, on the map above, for building purposes Lot No. 1 is 35 feet by 140 feet or 4,900 square feet of buildable area (35 x 140 = 4,900 sq. feet); Lots No. 2 thru No. 7, are each 50 feet by 140 feet or 7,000 square feet of buildable area (50 x 140 = 7,000 sq. feet). If the property is sold by the front foot, the width of all lots for sales purposes is 50 feet; if sold by the square foot the price of each lot would be based on 7,500 sq. feet (50 x 150 = 7,500 sq. feet).

AT THE BOTTOM OF THE PAGE IS A MAP SHOWING THE PRE-SUBDIVISION OF LOTS INTO FIVE IRREGULARLY-SHAPED PARCELS WHICH CAN ONLY BE DESCRIBED BY METES AND BOUNDS.

These problems concern the description of these problems and the correct answers will be found on the following page:

1. QUESTION - Legally describe the shaded area in Lots 1-2-3-6-7-8. How many square feet are there in this parcel?

2. QUESTION - Describe the shaded area of lots 4 and 5. How many square feet are there in this area?

3. QUESTION - Describe the shaded area of lot 9. How many square feet are there in this area?

4. QUESTION - Describe the shaded area of lots 10-11-14-15. How many square feet are there in this area?

5. QUESTION - Describe the shaded area in lots 12 and 13. How many square feet are there in this area?

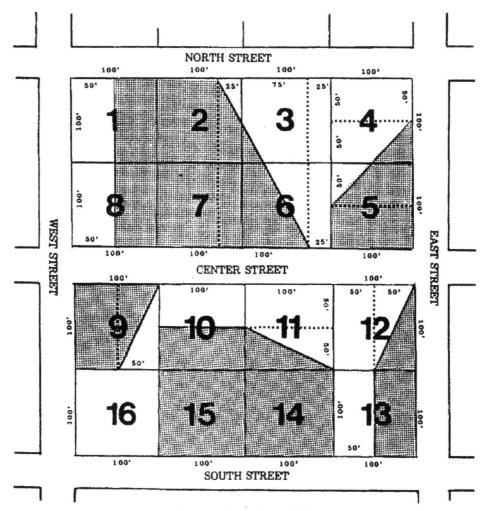

Lots 1 through 16 of Tract 1147, as per map recorded on Page 64, Book 27, Official Maps and Records of the County of Los Angeles, State of California

187

ANSWERS

1. Starting at a point 25' due west of the S.F. corner of Lot 6, draw a line 25' due west; thence 200' due north; thence 125' due east; and thence to the point of beginning. The shaded area contains 35,000 sq. ft.

Calculation to determine square footage:

Divide the entire parcel into two separate areas as shown by the dotted line running vertically through lots 2 & 7. To the west (left) is a rectangular area 125' wide by 200' deep containing 25,000 square feet. To the cast (right) is a triangular area. "Square up" the diagonal line as shown by the dotted line running vertically through lots 3 & 6. This becomes a rectangular parcel 100' wide by 200' deep containing 20,000 square feet. One-half of this, or 10,000 square, is in the shaded area. 25,000 square feet added to 10,000 square feet gives us 35,000 square feet.

2. Starting at a point 50' due south of the N.E. corner of lot 4, draw a line 150' due south; thence 100' due west; thence 50' due north, thence to the point of beginning. The shaded area contains 10,000 sq. ft.

Calculation to determine square footage:

Divide the described parcel into two separate areas shown by the dotted lines running horizontally through lots 4 and 5. To the north is a square area 100' x 100' containing 10,000 square feet. The shaded area is only one-half that amount or 5,000 square feet. The area to the south is a rectangular parcel 50' x 100' which contains 5,000 square feet. Hence, 5,000 square feet plus 5,000 square feet equals 10,000 square feet of area

3. Starting at the N.E. corner of lot 9 draw a line 100' due west; thence 100' due south, thence 50' due east, thence to the point of beginning. This parcel contains 7,500 square feet.

Calculation to determine square footage:

Divide the parcel into two separate areas as shown by the dotted line running through lot 9. To the left is a rectangular area 50' x 100' containing 5,000 square feet. To the right is a rectangular area of the same square footage, 5,000 square feet, but only one-half the area is shaded which would be 2,500 square feet. Hence, 5,000 square feet plus 2,500 square feet equals a total area of 7,500 square feet.

4. Starting at the N.E. corner of lot 14, draw a line 100' due south; thence 200' due west; thence 150' due north; thence 100' due east; and thence to the point of beginning. This parcel contains 27,500 square feet.

Calculation to determine square footage:

Lots 14 and 15 are completely shaded. They are both 100' x 100' which is 10,000 square feet in each lot. The shaded area of lot 10 is one-half the size of the entire lot which would be 5,000 square feet. "Square" one-half of lot 11 (with the dotted line) to find a total area of 5,000 square feet. The shaded portion is one-half the total or 2,500 square feet. Then summarize: 10,000 square feet, plus 10,000 square feet, plus 5,000 square feet, plus 2,500 square feet totals 27,500 square feet.

5. Starting at the N.E. comer of lot 12, draw a line 200' due south; thence 50' due west; thence 100' due north; and thence to the point of beginning. This parcel contains 7,500 square feet.

Calculation to determine square footage:

Using the dotted line, "square up" the area described in lot 12. The total area is 50' x 100' or 5,000 square feet. The shaded portion is one-half of the total of 2,500 square feet. In lot 13, there is a parcel 50' x 100' or 5,000 square feet shaded. Hence, 5,000 square feet plus 2,500 square feet will total 7,500 square feet.

KEY LOT

A key lot is a lot which is bounded on one of its sides by the rear end of lots which front on another street.

A key lot is the least desirable lot in a subdivision because a person living on a key lot has the back yard of his neighbor at the side of his house. If the lot is keyed back of business frontage, then the one living there has the unsightly rear of a business property alongside his front yard.

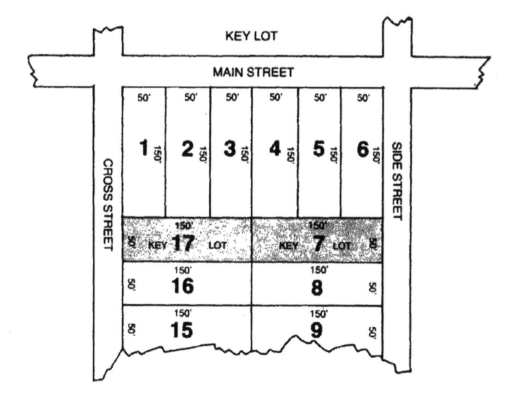

THE ARITHMETIC OF REAL ESTATE

A grade school level of education in arithmetic subjects is all that is required to compute the problems encountered in the majority of real estate transactions. Addition, subtraction, multiplication, long and short division present no difficulty to the average student, but he/she may have forgotten the rules for using these basic subjects in solving problems related to percentage, reducing fractions to decimals, and the placing of the decimal point.

Obviously, we cannot undertake to give complete instruction to the student who lacks education in primary arithmetic, but perhaps a review of some of the fundamentals concerning decimals will be helpful in recalling rules and formulas which, from long disuse, have been forgotten.

The fractions most commonly used in real estate concern percentage, such as 6-1/4 % or 6-1/2%, or you may have seen a percentage written as 7.1% or 7.8% and verbally expressed as "seven point one percent" or "seven point eight percent."

When a number is followed by a "%" sign, it indicates that it is not a whole number, but represents a certain part or "percent" of a whole number. To make it easier to multiply and divide by such numbers, they are usually reduced to decimals.

To reduce any number followed by a "%" sign to a decimal, place a decimal point or period two places to the left. Thus, 6-1/4% is written as .0625; 6-1/2% as .0650; 7.1% as .071; and 7.8% as .078.

The location of the decimal point determines the value of a number. Those to the left of the decimal point are whole numbers. Those to the right of the decimal point are parts of whole numbers.

The decimal system is based on the use of multiples of ten. Moving the decimal point one place to the right multiplies the figure by 10; two places to the right multiplies it by 100, and three places to the right by 1000. In reverse, moving the decimal point one, two or three places to the left decreases the value of the number in the same proportion.

The United States money system is a good illustration of decimals. The dollar is the basis of the system and stands for 100 units or cents, each unit or cent being one hundredth part, or 1% of a dollar, and is written $.01. If you have One Dollar and Twenty-five cents, it is written $1.25, the number to the left of the decimal point indicating one whole dollar, the number to the right indicating 25 parts or hundredths of a dollar, or in fractions; 1/4 of a dollar. Fifty cents would be 1/2 of a dollar, written $.50; seventy-five cents is 3/4 of a dollar, written $.75.

ADDING and SUBTRACTING DECIMALS. RULE: To add or subtract numbers containing decimals, write the numbers in columnar form so that the decimal points are directly under each other. Then add or subtract as with whole numbers, and place the decimal point in the answer directly under those in the column. The following examples illustrate the addition and subtraction of decimals.

Problem: ADD .625, .3325 and .50

Solution:	.625
Position by rule:	+ .3325
	+ .50
Point off by rule:	1.4575

Problem: ADD 17.254 and 1.35

	17.254
Solution:	+ 1.35
Point off by rule:	18.604

Problem: SUBTRACT 8.0276 from 11.37

Solution:	11.37
	- 8.0276
Point off by rule:	3.3424

Problem: SUBTRACT .37254 from 1.2675

Solution:	1.2675
Place by rule:	- .37254
Point off by rule:	.89496

MULTIPLICATION OF DECIMALS: RULE

To multiply decimals, mutiply as with whole numbers; then begin at right side of the answer and point off, to the left, as many decimal places as the *combined total* of decimal places in the numbers being multiplied.

PROBLEM: MULTIPLY .927 by .56
Solution   .927 multiplicand
Position by rule: x .56 multiplier
                              5562
                              4635
Point off by rule: .51912 (product)

Note: There are 3 decimal places in the multiplicand and 2 in the multiplier, or a total of 5 decimal places. Point off 5 decimal places from the right side of the product (answer).

PROBLEM: Assume that the tax rate is 1.125% of the assessed value (taxable value) of the property which is $125,000. Calculate the amount of the property taxes due on this property.

Change the tax rate stated as a percentage to a decimal by moving the decimal point two places to the left. Thus, 1.125% becomes 0.01125. Next, multiply the taxable value of the property by this decimal. In this problem multiply $125,000 by 0.01125.

Solution: $125,000
Position by rule: x 0.01125
                              625000
                              250000
                              125000
                              125000
Point off by rule: $1406.25000 tax bill

PRACTICE PROBLEMS - Work the following problems to see if you arrive at the correct answers as shown.

(a)	.35 x 4	(1.40 or 1.4)
(b)	.785 x 25	(19.625)
(c)	.287 x .356	(.102172)
(d)	.002 x .014	(.000028)
(e)	1.0034 x 2.503	(2.5115102)
(f)	32.25 x 2.376	(76.62600)

DIVISION OF DECIMALS: RULE

To divide decimals, they must first be converted into whole numbers in the following manner: 1. Move the decimal places in the "divisor" (the number by which you are dividing) TO THE RIGHT, as many places as necessary to create a whole number. 2. Move the decimal in the "dividend" (the number to be divided) by the EXACT NUMBER OF PLACES TO THE RIGHT, as with the divisor. 3. Before dividing, place a decimal point directly above the decimal point in the dividend so that it will be correctly placed in the answer (the quotient).

PROBLEM: Divide 82.57 by .27

Solution   .27/82.57
Set up division diagram
Step 1. Move decimal in the   27./82.57
divisor 2 places to the right
to make it a whole number.

Step 2. Move the decimal in
the dividend the same   27./8257.
number of places (2) to the
right.

Step 3. Place answer decimal
point directly above the decimal
in the dividend   27./8257.

DIVIDE   305.814
                          27./8257.000
                              81
                              157
                              135
                              220
                              216
                               40
                               27
                              130
                              108
                              22/27

Work the problem as indicated dividing as with whole numbers, putting the first number in the answer (quotient) above the number in the dividend where you begin to multiply the divisor. NOTE: that zeros are added in the dividend to carry out additional decimal places.

PROBLEM: DIVIDE   8.3726 by .055

SOLUTION:
Set up division diagram $.055\overline{)8.3726}$

Step 1. Move decimal in the divisor 3 places to the right to make it a whole number $055.\overline{)8.3726}$

Step 2. Move decimal in the dividend the same number of places (3) to the right. $055.\overline{)8372.6}$

Step 3. Place the decimal point for the answer directly above the one in the dividend $055.\overline{)8372.6}$

DIVIDE

```
        152.22
055./8372.60
     55
     287
     275
     122
     110
     126
     110
     160
     110
     50/55
```

PRACTICE PROBLEMS. Work the following problems to see if you arrive at the correct answers, as shown:

(a)   Divide 3.036 by .06   (50.6)
(b)   "   3.728 by .16   (23.3)
(c)   "   .864 by .024   (36)
(d)   "   10.044 by .36   (27.9)
(e)   "   .125 by 8000   (.0000156+)
(f)   "   2.34 by .211   (11.09+)
(g)   "   12 by .7854   (15.27+)

FACTORS IN PERCENTAGE PROBLEMS

Before working any arithmetic problem, it is important that you ANALYZE it carefully to determine and identify the factors involved so that you may apply the proper formula for solution.

There are three such factors in every percentage problem. You must learn to identify them. The three factors are:

(a) The amount *earned* or the amount MADE
(b) The amount *invested* or the amount PAID
(C) The rate of return or the PERCENT (%) of return

For simplification we shall call these factors MADE, PAID and PERCENTAGE.

RULES FOR PERCENTAGE PROBLEMS

The percentage problem arises when *one* of the three factors is missing and we are asked to find it. The three simple rules for finding the missing factor are:

1. To find amount MADE: Multiply PAID by %
2. To find amount PAID: Divide MADE by %
3. To find %   Divide MADE by PAID

FORMULA:

PAID		V(value)	
X	/ MADE or	X	/ I(income)
%		R(rate)	

DIRECTIONS: To find MADE, cover the word MADE and do the remaining problem.
To find PAID, cover the word PAID and do the remaining problem.
To find %, cover the % sign and do the remaining problem.

OTHER TERMS FOR:

MADE	PAID	% (ANNUAL)
return	investment	rate of return
profit	cost	rate of profit
commission	price	rate of commission
net income	value	rate of capitalization
interest	principal	rate of interest

IDENTIFYING THE FACTORS AND USING THE RULE

Let us see how these rules work with some very simple problems:

1. PROBLEM: Find the amount earned by an investment of $1,000 at 6% per annum. Here we have the factors of investment (PAID) and percent (%).

APPLY RULE ONE: MULTIPLY PAID by % to get MADE.

$1,000
X .06
$60.00 MADE

2. PROBLEM: $60 is 6% of what amount?

First, we identify the factors present. The missing one is our problem. Here it is evident that $60 is the amount earned (MADE) at the rate of 6%. The missing factor is the amount invested (PAID).

APPLY RULE TWO: Divide MADE by % to get PAID

$$\begin{array}{r} \$1000. \ \text{Paid} \\ .06 \overline{\smash{)}\ \$60.00.} \end{array}$$

60 divided by 6%

3. PROBLEM: What is the rate of interest on an investment of $1,000, showing a return of $60.00 per year?

Here the factors are the amount invested (PAID) and the amount earned (MADE) are present. We have to find percentage (%).

APPLY RULE THREE: Divide MADE by PAID to get %

$$\begin{array}{r} .06 = 6\% \\ \$1000 \overline{\smash{)}\ \$60.00} \end{array}$$

PROBLEMS REQUIRING APPLICATION OF RULE ONE

(1) A man bought a building for $120,000 and received a 6% annual return on this investment. What amount of money did he receive each year?

In this case we have the factors of investment (PAID) and the percentage of return on the investment (PERCENT - %). WHAT IS MADE? Apply Rule One to find MADE.

$$\begin{array}{r} \$120,000 \\ \underline{x \qquad .06} \\ \$7200.00 \quad \text{dollar return} \end{array}$$
received each year

(2) A real estate salesperson sold a house for $32,500. and received 60% of the total commission of 5% of the sales price. What did the salesperson receive?

In this case we have the factors of sales price (PAID) and the commission percentage for the office and the salesperson PERCENT (%). What is MADE? Apply Rule One to find MADE.

$$\begin{array}{r} \$32,500 \\ \underline{x \qquad .05} \quad (6\%) \\ \$1625.00 \quad \text{Broker's Commission} \end{array}$$

$$\begin{array}{r} \$1625 \\ \underline{x \qquad .60} \quad (60\%) \\ \$975.00 \quad \text{Salesperson's} \end{array}$$
Commission

(3) A real estate broker negotiated a five year lease at $650 per month and received a 5% commission on the total lease amount. What commission did the broker receive?

There we have the factor of total lease amount (PAID) and the percentage commission the broker is to receive (%). What is MADE? APPLY RULE ONE to find MADE

5 yrs = 5 x 12 mo. (per yr) = 60 months lease
60 mo. x $650 = $39,000 (PAID) TOTAL
LEASE PAYMENTS

$$\begin{array}{r} \$39000 \quad \text{total lease (PAID)} \\ \underline{x \qquad .05} \quad (5\%) \ (\%) \\ \$1950.00 \quad \text{Broker's Commission (MADE)} \end{array}$$

TYPES OF PROBLEMS REQUIRING APPLICATION OF RULE TWO

(1) $57.50 is 5% of what sum?

We identify the factors of MADE and %. We have to find PAID.

$$\begin{array}{r} \$1150. \text{ Paid} \\ \$57.50 \text{ divided by } 5\% = \quad .05/\$\ 57.50. \end{array}$$

(2) A return of $180 per month at 6% requires an investment of what sum?

Here we have the factors MADE and %. But note that $180 is a monthly figure. We also have %. We have a cardinal RULE: Everything in real estate arithmetic is worked on an ANNUAL BASIS.

> APPLY RULE TWO to find PAID
> DIVIDE MADE by % to get PAID

$180 per mo. x 12 mos. = $2160

$$\begin{array}{r} \$36000. = \text{ Amount invested (PAID)} \\ \$.06/\$\ 2160.00. \end{array}$$

(3) An owner purchased a lot for $2000. He is selling through a broker for a price that will give him a 10% profit, plus sales expenses of $99, a sum of $2299 for the owner. This does not include the broker's commission. In other words, the lot must sell at a price high enough to give the owner $2299 net and give the broker a 5% commission.

Here we are given the factor MADE which is the money for the owner. We have to find the % which this amount represents of the sales price. Then, we will discover the sales price of the lot. (PAID)

The Sales Price (PAID) will be 100% (the whole of anything). We know the broker is to receive 5% of that price as commission. If this is so, it also means that the owner will receive the money that represents 95% of the sales price. (100% - 5% = 95%). We have determined then that $2299 is 95% of what amount (PAID)?

We apply RULE 2 to find PAID.

$$\begin{array}{r} \$2420. \text{ The full sales price} \\ .95/\ \$2299.00. \qquad \text{(PAID)} \end{array}$$

(4) Falson acquired a parcel of real property for $17424. He is now listing it for sale with broker Kelly. He wants to sell the property at a price that will return him all of his original investment together with a 40% profit, after he has paid Kelly a 10% commission. The sales price in this instance would be approximately?

Here we must apply two rules to find our answer. In the first place: We have the factors PAID and %. They are $17,424 and 40% (.40) profit. We apply rule ONE to find MADE.

$17424 X .40 (40%) = $6969.60 owner's PROFIT.
$17424 + 6970 (rounded) = $24,394 money the owner wishes to receive. This does not include any commission for the broker.

At this point we have the factors MADE and %. We are seeking PAID.

Apply RULE 2 to find PAID. DIVIDE MADE x % to get PAID. The sales price we seek will be 100%. Of that sales price we know the broker is to get 10%. It follows, then, that 100% (sales price) -- 10% (broker's commission) = 90% of the seller's portion of the sales price.

$$\begin{array}{r} \$27,104. \text{ (PAID) sales price} \\ .90/\ \$24,394.00. \qquad \text{needed} \end{array}$$

PROBLEMS REQUIRING APPLICATION OF RULE THREE

1. An apartment house owner receives $4800 net income per year from his investment which was $60,000. What is the percentage return on his investment?

We have the factors PAID and MADE. Apply RULE THREE: DIVIDE MADE by PAID to get %.

$$\frac{.08}{\$60,000 / \$4800.00} = 8\% \text{ return on investment.}$$

2. A broker sold a building for $38,500 and received a commission check of $2310. What commission percentage did the broker receive?

Again, we have the factors PAID and MADE Apply RULE THREE - DIVIDE MADE by PAID to get %.

$$\frac{.06}{\$38,500 / \$2310.00} = 6\% \text{ broker's commission percentage}$$

3. A man purchases a building for $120,000. His gross income from this investment is $23,000 per year. His annual expenses are $11,000. What is the percentage return on his investment?

First $23000 (gross inc.) - $11,000 = $12,000 annual net income.

We now have the factors PAID and MADE. Apply RULE THREE - DIVIDE MADE by PAID to get %.

$$\frac{.10}{\$120,000 / \$12,000.00} = 10\% \text{ percentage return on investment}$$

4. An investor purchases two 75 ft. lots for $4500 each. He later divides them into three lots 50 ft. wide and sells each for $3600. What was the investor's percentage of profit?

3 50 ft. lots sell for $3600 x 3   = $10,800

2 75 ft. lots cost $4,500 each x 2 =   9,000
                                    $ 1,800
                                     Profit

We have the factors PAID x MADE. Apply RULE THREE. DIVIDE MADE by PAID to get %

$$\frac{.20}{\$9,000 / \$1,800.00} = 20\% \text{ percentage profit on investment}$$

LOAN COMPUTATIONS FOR PLUS AND INCLUDING INTEREST

1. $100 loan payable $10 per month PLUS 10% interest.

	PAYMENT BOOK			INTEREST WORKSHEET			
LOAN BALANCE	PRINCIPAL	INTEREST	PAYMENT	LOAN	%	YEAR	MONTH
$100.00	$10.00	$ .83	$10.83	$100.00	.10	$10.00	$ .83
90.00	10.00	.75	10.75	90.00	.10	9.00	.75
80.00	10.00	.666	10.67	80.00	.10	8.00	.666

2. $100 loan payable $10 per month INCLUDING 10% interest.

	PAYMENT BOOK			INTEREST WORKSHEET			
LOAN BALANCE	PRINCIPAL	INTEREST	PAYMENT	LOAN	%	YEAR	MONTH
$100.00	$ 9.17	$ .83	$10.00	$100.00	.10	$10.00	$ .83
90.83	9.24	.76	10.00	90.83	.10	9.08	.76
81.59	9.32	.68	10.00	81.59	.10	8.16	.68

TABLE OF MONTHLY PAYMENTS TO FULLY AMORTIZE $1,000 LOAN

Term of Years	5%	5-1/2%	6%	6-1/2%	6.6%	7%	7-1/2%	8%	8-1/4%	8-1/2%	8-3/4%	9%	9-1/4%	9-1/2%	9-3/4%	10%
5....	18.88	19.11	19.34	19.57	19.62	19.81	20.04	20.28	20.40	20.52	20.64	20.76	20.88	21.01	21.13	21.25
6....	16.11	16.34	16.58	16.81	16.86	17.05	17.30	17.54	17.66	17.78	17.90	18.03	18.15	18.28	18.40	18.53
7....	14.14	14.38	14.61	14.85	14.90	15.10	15.34	15.59	15.71	15.84	15.96	16.09	16.22	16.35	16.47	16.61
8....	12.66	12.90	13.15	13.39	13.44	13.64	13.89	14.14	14.27	14.40	14.52	14.66	14.78	14.92	15.04	15.18
9....	11.52	11.76	12.01	12.26	12.31	12.51	12.77	13.02	13.15	13.28	13.41	13.55	13.68	13.81	13.94	14.08
10....	10.61	10.85	11.11	11.36	11.41	11.62	11.88	12.14	12.27	12.40	12.53	12.67	12.80	12.94	13.08	13.22
11....	9.87	10.12	10.37	10.63	10.68	10.89	11.15	11.42	11.55	11.69	11.82	11.97	12.10	12.24	12.38	12.52
12....	9.25	9.51	9.76	10.02	10.08	10.29	10.56	10.83	10.96	11.11	11.24	11.39	11.52	11.67	11.81	11.96
13....	8.74	8.99	9.25	9.52	9.57	9.79	10.06	10.34	10.47	10.62	10.75	10.90	11.04	11.19	11.33	11.48
14....	8.29	8.55	8.82	9.09	9.14	9.36	9.64	9.92	10.06	10.20	10.34	10.49	10.64	10.79	10.93	11.09
15....	7.91	8.17	8.44	8.72	8.77	8.99	9.28	9.56	9.70	9.85	10.00	10.15	10.29	10.45	10.59	10.75
16....	7.58	7.85	8.12	8.40	8.45	8.63	8.96	9.25	9.40	9.55	9.69	9.85	10.00	10.15	10.30	10.46
17....	7.29	7.56	7.84	8.12	8.17	8.40	8.69	8.99	9.13	9.29	9.44	9.59	9.74	9.90	10.05	10.22
18....	7.04	7.31	7.59	7.87	7.93	8.16	8.45	8.75	8.90	9.06	9.21	9.37	9.52	9.68	9.84	10.00
19....	6.81	7.08	7.37	7.65	7.71	7.95	8.25	8.55	8.70	8.86	9.01	9.17	9.33	9.49	9.65	9.82
20....	6.60	6.88	7.17	7.46	7.52	7.76	8.06	8.37	8.52	8.68	8.84	9.00	9.16	9.33	9.49	9.66
21....	6.42	6.70	6.99	7.29	7.35	7.59	7.90	8.21	8.36	8.53	8.68	8.85	9.01	9.18	9.34	9.51
22....	6.26	6.54	6.84	7.13	7.19	7.44	7.75	8.07	8.22	8.39	8.55	8.72	8.88	9.05	9.21	9.39
23....	6.11	6.40	6.69	7.00	7.06	7.30	7.62	7.94	8.10	8.27	8.43	8.60	8.76	8.93	9.10	9.28
24....	5.97	6.27	6.56	6.87	6.93	7.18	7.50	7.83	7.99	8.16	8.32	8.49	8.66	8.83	9.00	9.18
25....	5.85	6.15	6.45	6.76	6.82	7.07	7.39	7.72	7.88	8.06	8.22	8.40	8.56	8.74	8.91	9.09
26....	5.74	6.04	6.34	6.65	6.72	6.97	7.30	7.63	7.79	7.96	8.14	8.31	8.48	8.66	8.83	9.01
27....	5.64	5.94	6.24	6.56	6.62	6.88	7.21	7.55	7.71	7.88	8.06	8.23	8.41	8.58	8.76	8.94
28....	5.54	5.84	6.16	6.48	6.54	6.80	7.13	7.47	7.64	7.81	7.99	8.16	8.34	8.52	8.70	8.88
29....	5.45	5.76	6.08	6.40	6.46	6.73	7.06	7.40	7.57	7.75	7.92	8.10	8.28	8.46	8.64	8.82
30....	5.37	5.68	6.00	6.33	6.39	6.66	7.00	7.34	7.51	7.69	7.87	8.05	8.23	8.41	8.59	8.78
35....	5.05	5.38	5.71	6.05	6.13	6.39	6.75	7.11	7.29	7.47	7.65	7.84	8.03	8.22	8.41	8.60
40....	4.83	5.16	5.51	5.86	5.93	6.22	6.59	6.96	7.14	7.33	7.52	7.71	7.91	8.10	8.30	8.49

Lesson Seven
Part Two
Study Questions

────────(Lesson Seven - Paragraph 2 – Question 1)────────

A commercial acre is:
(A) An acre of land on which only retail buildings are situated
(B) An acre less the amount of land dedicated for public improvements (sidewalks, alleys, etc.)
(C) An acre of land on which only industrial buildings are situated
(D) An acre of land used only for agricultural purposes

(B) A commercial acre is less than a full acre of 43,560 square feet. A commercial acre is the remainder of a full acre after improvements such as streets and sidewalks are deducted.

────────(Lesson Seven - Paragraph 8 – Question 1)────────

The term "megalopolis" refers to:
(A)   Shopping centers.   (B) Freeways.   (C) Cities.   (D)   Subdivisions.

(C) Megalopolis is a Greek word meaning "Great City." The dictionary describes it as an extensive, heavily populated, continuously urban area, including any number of cities.

────────(Lesson Seven - Paragraph 17 – Question 1)────────

A builder/contractor owns a parcel of real property on which he is about to complete a building. He is forced to use some backfill. This would be used:
(A) To fill in the space around the foundation, or a retaining wall and other excavations.
(B) To remove excess soil from the site caused by earlier excavations.
(C) To assist in landscaping the property.
(D) None of the above.

(A)   Backfill is dirt and other matter that are filled in around retaining walls, foundations, or other excavations.

────────(Lesson Seven - Paragraph 23 – Question 1)────────

The following is true regarding a bearing wall:
(A) It usually remains intact during remodeling.   (B)   Can be at any angle to a door.
(C) Usually contains stronger structural members. (D)   All of the above.

(D) A bearing wall is a wall that supports weight of the structure. It is intact during remodeling. You do not remove it. A bearing wall can be at any angle to a door that one wishes. Normally, your bearing wall is required to be of stronger construction than would be a partition that does not bear weight.

────────(Lesson Seven - Paragraph 23 – Question 2)────────

A bearing wall:
(A) Determines the direction the house faces. (B) Is a wall with no doors or windows.
(C) Is always at a right angle to a hallway.   (D) Is usually discovered in the course of remodeling.

(D) A bearing wall is a wall that supports the ceiling joists and the weight of the roof or floors above. The question is not asking for a definition but is making certain statements regarding a bearing wall. You generally cannot determine if a wall is a weight-bearing wall until you take off the plaster and expose the framing.

──────────**(Lesson Seven - Paragraph 24 – Question 1)**────────

The person most apt to use a "bench mark" in the practice of his profession would be:
(A) Lawyer.   (B) Carpenter.   (C) General contractor.   (D) Surveyor.

(D) A benchmark is a surveyor's mark made on a permanent landmark that has a known position.

──────────**(Lesson Seven - Paragraph 26 – Question 1)**────────

A board foot of lumber could be obtained from a piece of lumber that would be:
(A) Six inches wide, six inches long, and one inch thick.
(B) Six inches wide, twelve inches long, and one inch thick.
(C) Twelve inches wide, six inches long, and one inch thick.
(D) Six inches wide, twelve inches long, and twelve inches thick.

(D) A "board foot" of lumber is said to be a square foot of lumber one-inch thick. In reality, a board foot is any piece of lumber containing 144 cubic inches, regardless of shape. Of the choices given only (D) develops more than 144 cubic inches. 6" x 12" x 12" = 864 cubic inches.

──────────**(Lesson Seven - Paragraph 29 – Question 1)**────────

BTUs would indicate:
(A) Water output.   (B) Butane gas pressure. (C) Heating output.   (D) Electric resistance.

(C) "BTU" is the abbreviation for "British Thermal Unit" and is a measure of heat output.

──────────**(Lesson Seven - Paragraph 42 – Question 1)**────────

The minimum height of the "crawl space" that is required by the California State Housing Law is:
(A) 6 inches. (B) 12 inches. (C)   18 inches. (D)   20 inches.

(C) The minimum height for a crawl space is set at 18".

──────────**(Lesson Seven - Paragraph 42 – Question 2)**────────

The space between the first floor and the ground level used as an access area under the house not built on a cement slab known as:
(A) Crawl space. (B) A foundation. (C)   An attic. (D)   Air space.

(A) It is sometimes necessary for a plumber, repairman or termite inspector a get under a house to make repairs, installations or inspections, and an area known as the "crawl space" is provided for this purpose.

──────────**(Lesson Seven - Paragraph 47 – Question 1)**────────

When an air conditioning unit has a higher energy efficiency ratio (EER), it means that:
(A) The unit is less efficient.   (B) The unit is more efficient.
(C) It needs more wafts of electricity.   (D) The BTU's are larger.

(B) The higher the number in the EER, the more efficient the unit.

_____(Lesson Seven - Paragraph 47 – Question 2)_____

Air conditioning units are usually given an Energy Efficient Rating. Based on this rating system, the higher the EER the:
(A) More BTU's are produced. (B) Higher efficiency of the appliance.
(C) Lower efficiency of the appliance. (D) Higher the wattage energy used by the appliance.

(B) The higher the Energy Efficient Rating the higher or greater efficiency of the unit.

_____(Lesson Seven - Paragraph 52 – Question 1)_____

The metal piece in the valley of a roof designed to prevent water seepage is called:
(A) Drain pipe. (B) Flashing. (C) Curbing. (D) Matting.

(B) "Flashing" is sheet metal used to waterproof roof valleys or hips or the angle between a chimney and roof.

_____(Lesson Seven - Paragraph 53 – Question 1)_____

"Footing" would be best described as the following:
(A) Masonry course upon which the sill is fastened.
(B) Square blocks of concrete used to support floor joists.
(C) A slab of concrete in rear yard area utilized for recreational purposes.
(D) Heavy concrete course placed in ground upon which concrete foundation is set.

(D) A concrete footing used in conjunction with a raised foundation would look like this. The dictionary describes a footing as the base or bottom of a foundation, wall, pier or column.

_____(Lesson Seven - Paragraph 53 – Question 2)_____

A footing is:
(A) The spreading element that supports a pier, column, wall or foundation. (B) A concrete deck.
(C) A corner bracing. (D) The element to which the collar beam is attached.

(A) Footing is poured before the foundation. It is the element to support a pier, column, wall or foundation.

_____(Lesson Seven - Paragraph 66 – Question 1)_____

"One of a series of parallel beams to which the boards of a floor and/or ceiling laths are nailed," would be a:
(A) Joist. (B) Rafter. (C) Stud. (D) Brace.

(A)   This is a precise definition of a floor or ceiling joist.

_____(Lesson Seven - Paragraph 66 – Question 2)_____

The parallel beams to which boards of a floor or ceiling laths are nailed are called:
(A) Rafters. (B) Headers. (C) Joists. (D) None of the above.

(C) Again, this is a repeat of a classic question defining joists.

—————————(**Lesson Seven - Paragraph 66 – Question 3**)————

A joist is:
(A) A parallel beam to which boards of a floor or ceiling are nailed.
(B) The board placed on edge at the ride of the roof to support the upper ends of the rafters.
(C) The spreading element that supports a pier, column, wall or foundation.
(D) Sheet metal or other material used to protect a building from seepage of water.

(A) A joist is clearly defined by choice (A).

—————————(**Lesson Seven - Paragraph 66 – Question 4**)————

Parallel wooden members used to support floor and ceiling loads are called:
(A) Rafters.   (B) Joists.   (C) Headers.   (D) Studs.

(B) This is a classic question not to be confused with a question that asks for the members that support the roof. The roof supporting members are called rafters.

—————————(**Lesson Seven - Paragraph 67 – Question 1**)————

A kiosk is:
(A) Type of residential roof.
(B) Parallel beam to which boards of a floor or ceiling laths are nailed.
(C) Freestanding booth in a parking lot or shopping mall.
(D) Metal pipe in which electrical wiring is installed.

(C) A kiosk is a freestanding booth in a parking lot or a shopping mall. Camera film booths and key shops located in these areas are examples of kiosks.

—————————(**Lesson Seven - Paragraph 85 – Question 1**)————

The higher the R-rating is:
(A) The greater the efficiency of the hot water heater.
(B) The greater the resistance to the passage of heat (better heating insulator).
(C) The less the efficiency of a furnace.
(D) None of the above.

(B) The higher the R-rating, the greater the insulating quality of insulation material.

—————————(**Lesson Seven - Paragraph 85 – Question 2**)————

Recent heating and ventilating standards generally require that buildings be properly insulated. The "R" designation used to identify different types of insulating materials refers to:
(A) The type of roofing material used in the structure.
(B) The use of rockwool in the construction of the home.
(C) The degree of the materials' resistance to heat or cold.
(D) The refrigerant used in the air conditioning system.

(C) This is a definition.

_____(Lesson Seven - Paragraph 94 – Question 1)————

Soil pipe is used in:
(A) Irrigation. (B) Sewer system. (C) Agriculture. (D) Horticulture.

(B) Soil pipe is described as pipe carrying wastewater from the house to the main sewer line or to a septic tank where one is used.

_____(Lesson Seven - Paragraph 96 – Question 1)————

Generally, the maximum space between studs that is permitted by building codes is:
(A) 16" on center. (B) 24" on center. (C) 12" on center. (D) 6" on center.

(A) The State Housing Act sets the maximum space at 16" under most circumstances.

_____(Lesson Seven - Paragraph 101 – Question 1)————

You would least likely need or find a legal description in a:
(A) Preliminary title report. (B) Policy of title insurance. (C) Deed. (D) Real property tax statement.

(D) Real property bills do not require a legal description although many have such a description. Assessors may describe a property billed for taxes by means of Assessors Map, which is not the legal description.

_____(Lesson Seven - Paragraph 102 – Question 1)————

Each row of townships running north and south parallel to a true meridian is called a:
(A) Township. (B) Section. (C) Range. (D) Tier.

(C) Each row of townships running north and south parallel to a true meridian is called a range. Each row of townships running east and west parallel to the principal base line is called a tier.

_____(Lesson Seven - Paragraph 102 – Question 2)————

"The South half (S-1/2) of the Southeast quarter (SE-1/4) of the Northeast quarter (NE-1/4) of Section 4, Township 7 South (T. 7 S.) Range 14 East (R. 14 E.) Mt. Diablo Base & Meridian (M.D.B.&M.)" would be an example of a legal description known as:
(A) Metes & bounds.   (B) U. S. Government survey.
(C) Recorded map (lot book). (D) U. S. Surveyor's Association.

(B) Much of the land in the United States is surveyed by the Government into tracts, the largest of which is a township. These are established in reference to base and meridian lines. A legal description in which townships bear numbers in respect to base lines and meridians is known as a Government Survey description, or Section, Township & Range. A metes & bounds description outlines the boundaries of a parcel, usually an irregularly shaped piece of land. A Lot-Book description is usually used in describing land subdivided into lots.

_____(Lesson Seven - Paragraph 102a – Question 1)————

The following statement would be false with respect to townships:
(A) A township contains 36 sections.
(B) Townships are bounded by township or range lines.
(C) Townships are 36 square miles.
(D) The word township describes a particular parcel of land with certainty.

(D) Due to the curvature of the earth, townships in the northern portions of the United States will be smaller than those in the southern portions of the country. Hence, all townships are not physically, geographically the same size.

_____(**Lesson Seven - Paragraph 106 to 108 – Question 1)**_____

California has how many principal base and meridian lines?
(A) Only one. (B) Two. (C) Three. (D) Five.

(C) In California there are three intersections of base and meridian: Humboldt, Mt. Diablo, and San Bernardino. They may be remembered by H.M.S.: High, middle, and south.

_____(**Lesson Seven - Paragraph 110 – Question 1)**_____

A property description that makes reference to monuments is usually considered to be less desirable because:
(A) Of failure to give clear evidence of range line designations.
(B) Of the possibility of the destruction of the monuments.
(C) Of the fact that title practice does not permit monuments to be shown on the public record.
(D) Of the proximity of the monuments to appurtenances and other improvements.

(B) A metes and bounds description of property describes the perimeters of a parcel of land. The description tries to identify what would be permanent features (monuments) and describes the distances between the monuments from the point of beginning around the parcel and back to the beginning point. Since these monuments are often material, physical things, they could at some time be destroyed which could make it difficult to identify the parcel properly.

_____(**Lesson Seven - Paragraph 5 – Question 1)**_____

In the planning and engineering of a tract for subdivision purposes, a "cul-de-sac" is frequently employed. This term is used in reference to the installation of:
(A) Sewage disposal. (B) Drainage. (C) Streets. (D) Recreation areas.

(C) This French expression is used frequently in referring to a dead-end street.

Note: If your greatest fear is math, don't let it stop you from passing.

You do not have to do anything in a state exam about math. If all you do is put the most logical answer, you can do any problem. Only 2% to 4% of any state examination involves math. As a real estate agent, computers do it all, so don't worry! Concentrate on everything else and do this last. With the Lumbleau way, you will still pass. Many former students have reported no math problems. Using a battery powered hand-held calculator, do the balance of this exam passing assignment. We have attempted to group them into similar type problems.

TOWNSHIP PROBLEMS

1 township contains 23,040 acres
1 township is 6 miles square
1 township contains 36 square miles
1 township contains 36 sections
1 section contains 640 acres
1 section is one mile square
1 section contains one square mile
5280 feet 1 mile
320 Rods = 1 mile
640 acres 1 square mile

160 acres = ½ mile square
160 acres = 1/4 of a section
A square 40 acre tract = % mile square
A square 40 acre tract = 1320 feet by 1320 feet
43,560 square feet - 1 acre
208.71 x 208.71 feet = 1 square acre
27 cubic feet - 1 cubic yard
9 square feet = 1 square yard

_____(Lesson Seven - Logic – Question 1)————

The direction "West" on a map is usually:
(A) Toward the top. (B) To the left. (C) Toward the bottom. (D) To the right.

(B) Since North is always at the top of a map, than West is to the left and East is to the right.

_____(Lesson Seven – See Measurements Above – Question 1)_____

The following parcel would contain the largest area:
(A) 10% of township. (B) Two sections. (C) 2 miles square. (D) 5,280'x 10,560.

(C) Remember that a township contains 36 sections and each section is one mile square.
Analysis of each answer:
Step one: 10% of a township 36 sq. miles ÷ 10 = 3.6 sq. miles.
Step two: 2 sections = 2 sq. miles.
Step three: An area 2 miles square is 2 miles on each side 2 X 2 = 4 sq. miles
Step four: 5,280' (1 mile) x 5,280 = 1 sq. mile

_____(Lesson Seven – See Measurements Above – Question 2)_____

A parcel of land measuring 1/2 mile by 1/2 miles contains:
(A) 40 acres. (B) 120 acres. (C) 160 acres. (D) 320 acres.

(C) 160 acres.
Step one: A parcel of land measuring 1/2 mile (2,640 feet) by 1/2 mile includes 1/4 section.
Step two: A section contains 640 acres. 640 acres ÷ 4 = 160 acres in the parcel

TOWNSHIP AND RANGE PROBLEMS
_____(Lesson Seven –Township & Range Problems– Question 1)_____

The number of miles of fencing material needed to fully enclose the un-shaded area of Sect. 10 is:

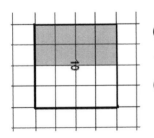

(A) 2.5 miles. (B) 4 miles. (C) 1 mile. (D) 3 miles.

_____

(D) 3 miles.

_____(Lesson Seven –Township & Range Problems– Question 2)_____

The listed price of the shaded area of section 2 is $43,200. If sold at this price it will represent a profit of 20% over what the seller originally paid for the property. The original cost per acre of the listed property was:

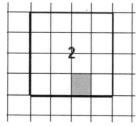

(A) $900 an acre. (B) $ 1,350 an acre. (C) $938 an acre. (D) $880 an acre.

(A) $900 per acre.

Step 1 - 100% originally paid + 20% profit = 120%
Step 2 - $43,200 ÷ 1.20 = $36,000 = price paid
Step 3 - $36,000 ÷ 40 acres = $900 per acre

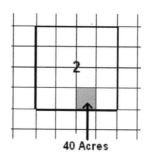

40 Acres

_____(Lesson Seven –Township & Range Problems– Question 3)_____

The total number of square feet contained in the shaded area of section 11 is:

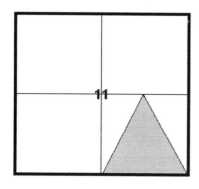

(A) 954,000. (B) 43,560. (C) 871,200. (D) 23,056.

(C) 871,200.

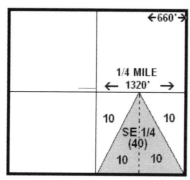

43.560 square feet per acre.

_____x 20 acres_____
871.200 square feet

____(Lesson Seven – Lot Measurement Problems – Question 1)____

Jones bought two adjoining parcels for $36,000 each. He divided the combined parcel into three parcels and sold them for $30,000 each. The profit he realized was:
(A) 10%. (B) 20%. (C) 25%. (D) 35%.

(C) 25%.

Step one: $36,000 x 2 lots = $72,000 original purchase price
Step two: $30,000 x 3 lots = $90,000 sales price
Step three: $90,000 - $72,000 = $18,000 profit from sale
Step four: $18,000 (profit) ÷ $72,000 = .25 (25%) percentage of profit

____(Lesson Seven – Lot Measurement Problems – Question 2)____

A parcel of land in Green County contains 395,340 square feet. Of this parcel, the County owns a parcel which measures 110' x 30' and Mr. Brown owns the remainder. If the property sells at a price of $5,250 per acre, Mr. Brown would receive:
(A) $47,250. (B) $47,650. (C) $47,000. (D) It is not possible to compute from the information given.

(A) $47,250.

Given: 395,340 sq. ft. is the total parcel size;
Step one: 110' x 30' = 3,300 sq. ft. is what the county owns;
Step two: 395,340 - 3,300 = 392,040 sq. ft. is what Mr. Brown owns;
Step three: 392,040 ÷ 43,560 = 9 acres
Step four: 9 x $5,250 = $47,250

____(Lesson Seven – Lot Measurement Problems – Question 3)____

A lot is 50 feet wide and 150 feet deep. It has a front setback of 20 feet and 4 foot setbacks on the sides and back of the lot. The buildable area is:
(A) 4260 sq. ft. (B) 5292 sq. ft. (C) 5460 sq. ft. (D) None of the above.

(B) 5292 sq. ft.

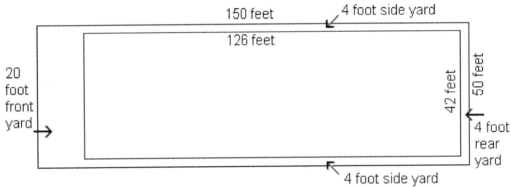

Step one: 20' + 4'   =   24 ft. total of front and rear set backs
Step two: 41+ 4'   =   8' side yard set backs (2)
Step three: Depth = 150'- 24'   =   126' buildable depth
Step four: Width = 50' - 8'   =   42' buildable width
Step five: 126 x 42'   =   5,292 sq. ft. buildable area
Interior building dimensions are 126' x 42' or 5,292 square feet.

_____(Lesson Seven – Commission Problems - Question 1)_____

An agent negotiates a 25-year lease on an industrial building. The rent for the property is $30,000 per year. He is compensated for his results by receiving a commission based upon a percentage of the rent for the building. He is to receive 7% of the first year's rent, 5% of the rent for the succeeding four years, 3% of the rent for the next 15 years and 1 % of the rent for the last 5 years of the period the property is leased. For the first 19 years of the lease the agent will receive a commission of:
(A) $15,550. (B) $20,700. (C) $21,600. (D) $23, 100.

(B) $20,700.

Step one: $30,000 (yearly rental income) x .07 (7%) = $2,100 commission for 1st year
Step two: $30,000 (yearly rental income) x .05 (5%) = $1,500 commission each of the next 4 years.
Step three: $30,000 (yearly rental income) x.03 (3%) = $900 commission each of the next 15 years.
To summarize:

$2,100 X 1	= $ 2,100	= 1 year lease commission @ 7% per year
$1,500 X 4	= $ 6,000	= 4 years lease commission @ 5% per year
$ 900 X 14	= $12,600	= 14 years lease commission @ 3% per year
	$20,700	= Lease commission for 19 years

_____(Lesson Seven – Commission Problems - Question 2)_____

The seller nets $91,049.66 at close of escrow after paying closing costs of $1,906.00 and a broker's commission of 6%. The selling price is:
(A) $98,533. (B) $96,513. (C) $96,861. (D) $98,889.

(D) $98,889.

Step one: $91,049.66 + $1,906.00 = $92,955.66. This is what the seller "made" after the broker received his 6% commission. Therefore, this would represent 94% of the sales price.
Step two: .94 (94%) ÷ 92,955.66 = $98,889.00

_____(Lesson Seven – Percentage on Notes Problems - Question 1)_____

Mr. Abrams paid his regular monthly payment on his home loan of $550. Of that amount $48.53 was applied to principal. The average balance owing on the note for that month was $56,500. The interest rate on the note was:
(A) 8 1/2%. (B) 9 3/4%. (C) 10.6%. (D) 12 1/2%.

(C) 10.6%.

Step one: $550-00 - 48.53 principal portion of payment = $501.47 interest portion of payment.
Step two: $501.47 x 12 mos. = $6,017.64 interest for one year.
Step three: $6,107.64 (interest) ÷ $56,500 (loan balance)= .108 or 10.8%

_____(Lesson Seven – Percentage on Notes Problems - Question 2)_____

The total interest earned on a straight loan of $26,500 for 20 years at the interest rate of 15 percent per annum is:
(A) $44,167. (B) $79,500. (C) $ 5,300. (D) $ 3,975.

(B) $79,500. This problem involves a straight note.
Step one: $26,500 x . 15 (15%) $3,975 interest for 1 year
Step two: $3,975 x 20 years $79,500 total interest over the 20 year period

__(Lesson Seven – Percentage on Notes Problems - Question 3)__

Jerry Hayfield borrows $5,000. The interest rate on the note is 11 % per annum. The note provides for equal monthly payments of $51.61 over a period of 20 years. The following amount of the first payment is amortization of the loan principal:
(A) $ 5.78. (B) $11.56. (C) $25.85. (D) $43.12.

(A) $5.78.

Given:	Original principal amount of note	= $5,000
Given:	Interest rate	= 11% per annum (.11)
Given:	Monthly payment on note	= $51.61

Step one: Interest for first year   5,000 x . 11 = $550.00
Step two: Interest for first month $550.00 ÷ 12 (months) = $45.84
Step three: Principle for first month $51.61 - $45.84 = $5.78

_____(Lesson Seven – Depreciation Problems - Question 1)_____

Jackson purchased an apartment property on 12/31/00. He paid $75,000. The value of the land was $15,000. He projected a 40-year useful life. Assuming Jackson is using the straight-line depreciation, the depreciated value of the property on December 31, 2009 would be:
(A) $13,500. (B) $46,500. (C) $75,500. (D) $61,500.

(D)$61,500.
Step one: $75,000 - $15,000 (land value)   = $60,000 (building value)
Step two: $60,000 ÷ 40 years   = $1,500 annual depreciation
Step three: 12/31/00 to 12/31/09   = 9 years.
Step four: $1,500 x 9   = $13,500 total depreciation.
Step five: $75,000 (original basis) - $13,500 (total depreciation) = $61,500 (12/31/09)

_____(Lesson Seven – Depreciation Problems - Question 2)_____

A house sold for $56,950, which was 11 % more than the cost of the house. The original cost of the house was most nearly:
(A) $49,980. (B) $50,200. (C) $50,900. (D) $51,255.

(D) $51,255.
Given: $56,950 is 11% greater than the cost of the property (100%) therefore:
Step one: $56,950 ÷ 1.11 (1.11%) = $51,306. This is most nearly (D), the original price.

_____(Lesson Seven – Capitalization Problems - Question 1)_____

Mr. Able had an income property and building of the freeway near his property caused him a loss of $180 per month in rent in an area where the capitalization rate was 10%. The property would suffer a value loss of:
(A) $1,800. (B) $2,160. (C) $18,000. (D) $21,600.

(D) $21,600.

Step one: $ 180 - monthly loss x 12 months = $2,160 - annual rent loss
Step two: $2,160 (loss) ÷ .10 (10% cap rate) = $21,600

_____(Lesson Seven – Capitalization Problems - Question 2)_____

Each of the units in a 4-plex rent for $412.50 per month. The appropriate vacancy rate is 5%, the operating expenses are expected to total $8,280 and the capitalization rate is 8%. The value of the property would be:
(A) $247,500. (B) $131,625. (C) $ 58,781. (D) $226,845.

(B) $131,625.

Step one:	$412.50 x 4	= $1,650 gross rent per month for 4 apts.
Step two:	$1650 x 12 months	= $19,800 gross scheduled annual income
Step three:	$19,800 x.05 (5% vacancy)	= $990
Step four:	$19,800 - $990	= $18,810 gross effective income
Step five:	$18,810 - $8,280 (operating expenses)	= $10,530 net operating income
Step six:	$10,530 (NOI) ÷.08 (8% cap. rate)	= $131,625 capitalized value

_____(Lesson Seven – Capitalization Problems - Question 3)_____

A road is being widened. This causes a decrease in the rent amounting to $400 per month. A capitalization rate of 12% is given. The resultant decrease in value of the property is:
(A) $ 3,333. (B) $ 4,800. (C) $40,000. (D) $48,000.

(C) A loss of income is capitalized in the same manner that additional income is capitalized. Annual figures must be used.
Step one: $400 (monthly loss) x 12 = $4,800 annual loss
Step two: $4,800 ÷ .12 (12% capitalization rate) = $40,000 (the loss in value that will occur)

_____(Lesson Seven – Cost Basis Problems - Question 1)_____

Carl Handley purchased a parcel of real property for a full price of $40,000. In doing so he paid $5,000 as a cash down payment and he assumed a loan from the seller with a balance of $35,000 at the time of the purchase. He did this with the knowledge and approval of the lender. In addition, he agreed to pay an existing street improvement assessment on the property of $1,200. For federal income tax purposes under present law, Handley's basis for this property would be:
(A) $40,000. (B) $ 5,000. (C) $41,200. (C) $35,000.

(C) $41,200. Cost or unadjusted basis is the amount attributable to the taxpayer's cost upon acquisition (including the amount of any mortgage loan taken either "subject to" or "assumed"). This amount may serve as a base figure in determining gain or loss at a later time. Hence, in this problem Handley's tax basis would be calculated:

Step one: $40,000 purchase price + $1,200 assumed improvement assessment lien = $41,200 cost basis or tax basis for this taxpayer.

_____(Lesson Seven – Cost Basis Problems - Question 2)_____

Reynolds paid $100,000 cash for a lot and constructed a $500,000 income producing building on the lot. The construction was financed by paying $100,000 cash and a $400,000 loan at 8% annual interest secured by a lien against the property. How much can Reynolds depreciate on future income tax returns:
(A) $100,000. (B) $350,000. (C) $400, 000. (D) $500,000.

(D) This is not a math question. The financing is nothing but a distracter. Reynolds can depreciate the entire $500,000 he paid to construct the building.

__(Lesson Seven – Return on Investment Problems - Question 1)__

An investor purchased a vacant parcel of land by making a down payment of 20% of the appraised value of the lot. The balance of the payment was a straight note that called for interest-only payments of $9,900 per year. The interest rate on the note was 11 % per annum. The appraised value of the property was:
(A) $ 90,000. (13) $112,500. (C) $108,000. (D) None of the above.

(B) $112,500.

Step one: To determine the principal amount of the promissory note, divide the annual interest payments of $9,900 by the interest rate of 11 %, obtaining $90,000.

Step two: The investor made a down payment of 20% of the purchase price. Therefore, the loan amounted to 80% of the purchase price.

Step three: To secure the price at which the property sold, divide the principal amount of the note by the percentage (80%) of the sales price that it represents.

Step four: $90,000 ÷ .80 = $112,500

__(Lesson Seven – Return on Investment Problems - Question 2)__

Jack Jones purchased 10 acres of land for $200,000 by making a down payment of $20,000 and borrowing the rest. The purchase contract provided that for every additional $20,000 payment that Jack made, the lender would release 1 acre free and clear. After one year Jack made a $40,000 payment to the lender and received free and clear title to 2 acres. The effect that would be that Jack's percentage of equity in the encumbered property:
(A) Increased. (B) Decreased. (C) Remained the same. (D) Was eliminated.

(A) Percentage of equity increased.

Step one: $200,000 ÷ 10 Acres = $20,000 per acre
Step two: $20,000 (down payment) ÷ $200,000 (price paid) = .10 = 10% (percent of equity)

After payment of $40,000 for release of 2 acres:

Step three: $200,000 - $40,000 = $160,000 (remaining acre value) for 8 acres
Step four: $20,000 (down payment) ÷ $160,000 (remaining acre value) =.12.5 or 12.5% equity

__(Lesson Seven – Business Investment Problems - Question 1)__

Crowell bought the contents of a store for $9,300. Crowell sold the goods for 33-1/3% more than they cost, but lost 15% of the selling price in bad debts. His profit on the venture was:
(A) 18-1/3%. (B) $1,240. (C) $1,860. (D) $3,1100.

(B) $1,240.

Step one: $9,300 x .3333 = $3,100 gross income
Step two: $9,300 + $3,100 = $12,400 gross sales price
Step three: $12,400 x.15 (15%) = $1,860 bad debt loss
Step four: $3,100 (gross income) - $1,860 (bad debts) = $1,240 net profit

(Lesson Seven – Documentary Transfer Tax Problems - Question 1)

A real property sells for $150,000. The documentary transfer tax is 55 cents per $500. $125,000 is subject to the documentary transfer tax. The tax would most nearly be:
(A) $165. (B) $163. (C) $143. (D) $138.

(D) $138.

Step one: $125,000 ÷ 100 = 125 times $1.10 per $1,000 = $137.50
Step two: 125 times $1.10 per $1,000   = $137.50
The possible responses all are stated in even dollars. Therefore, $138 is the best answer.

_____(Lesson Seven – Escrow Proration Problems - Question 1)_____

A developer purchased four lots in 1986. Ten years later he sold them for $10,000 a piece. His tax basis for each lot was $2,000. For federal income tax purposes the capital gain recognized in this sale would be:
(A) $8,000. (B) $32,000. (C) $40,000. (D) Not determinable from information given.

(B) $32,000.

Step one: $10,000 x 4   = $40,000 sales price for four lots.
Step two: $2,000 (basis per lot) x 4 lots   = $8,000 basis at time of sale.
Step three: $40,000 (sales price) - $8,000 (basis)   = $32,000 capital gain recognized

_____(Lesson Seven – Escrow Proration Problems - Question 2)_____

The personal residence of Jim Smith is valued at $100,000 for property tax purposes. If the property tax rate is 1.1 % and considering the homeowner exemption, the amount of property tax that Jim will have to pay for the year is:
(A) $1,000. (B) $1,023. (C) $1,100. (D) None of the above.

(B) $1,023.

Given: Sales price less homeowner's exemption   = Taxable value.
Given   Taxable value times tax rate   = Property tax
Given   1.1% tax rate   = .011
Step one: $100,000 - $7,000   = $93,000 taxable value
Step two: $ 93,000 x .011 (11%) tax rare   = $ 1,023 tax due

Lesson Seven
Part Three
Understanding Through Question Testing

 Log into your course at www.lumbleau.com.

STUDENT LOGIN
Login: [ ]
Password: [ ]

 On your student home page, click on the "State Exam Preparation".

STATE EXAM
PREPARATION

 Under the "Guided Lesson" tab click on the seventh of fourteen links: "Land Descriptions and Real Estate Arithmetic".

Real Estate Salesperson Course

Guided Lessons	Practice Exams	Progress Report	Success Video

Print Click	Questions
	HERE>>> 7. Land Descriptions and Real Estate Arithmetic 101

Here you will be tested on all of the questions you have been studying and learn the most recently added questions. It is essential, for maximum retention, that you eliminate all of the questions you can easily answer and "TAG" for study the questions with which you have difficulty.

LESSON 8

PUBLIC CONTROL
SUBDIVISIONS
RIPARIAN RIGHTS

Lesson Eight
Part One
Understanding Through Video Teaching

Lesson Eight
PUBLIC CONTROL

EMINENT DOMAIN

39   All property, whether it is real, personal, or mixed, is subject to the exercise of power of eminent domain and may be taken at any time by the state provided the property taken is intended for public use. The only requirements are: (1) The state or the public agency taking the property pays to the individual property owner the fair market value of the property taken. (2) The taking is necessary. (3) The taking is for the public good.

PROCEDURE

43   Formal condemnation action by the agency taking the title is usually preceded by negotiations with the property owner. If the negotiations are successful the agency and the owner enter into a purchase contract. If they are not successful, the taking of the title is accomplished by a court action called condemnation. The court must find affirmatively that the property is taken for a public use and that the taking is necessary. The court must also determine the just compensation to be paid the property owner. Just compensation today is determined by appraising the property to determine its fair market value. In arriving at market value the cost approach is rarely acceptable except where the property is so individualistic it is rarely traded on the market. Parties may agree to arbitration proceedings. The government even has the power to acquire riparian (water) rights by condemnation.

45   Sometimes public works are undertaken and damage to property results without condemnation action being filed by the public body. The property owner may sometimes initiate the suit himself in what is known as an "inverse" condemnation action. In the event inverse condemnation proceedings result in judgment or settlement in favor of plaintiff, costs must be paid by the government agency.

URBAN RENEWAL AND DEVELOPMENT

51   Blighting is caused by inharmonious elements, nonconforming uses, poor upkeep, divergent use of the property, vacant lots, and a serious disregard for the rights of property owners resulting in dangerous living conditions

POLICE POWER

55   Another of the rights of sovereignty is the exercise of the police powers. Those powers are the right to regulate the use of privately owned property for the health, safety, morals, welfare, convenience, and necessity of the public. Under these regulations the federal, state, or local government does not take title to the property as they do under eminent domain. No compensation need be paid to the property owner. The power to tax is not a police power nor is police power ever used for the good of one person.

56   A distinction must be made between police power regulations and deed restrictions as they operate separate and apart, although they may cover many of the same uses of property. Both are limitations on the use of property, but one is imposed by governmental regulation and the other is created by agreements, by deeds, or any form of written instrument executed by the owners of the land affected at the time they transfer the title to the property.

PLANNING AND ZONING

61   The State Conservation and Planning Law requires that each county and city has a "planning commission" or area planning commission. The planning commission has

responsibilities in the areas of zoning, approval of subdivisions, and generally for the physical development of the community.

62   In carrying out their responsibilities the planning commission devises a general plan (master plan). All elements and parts of a general plan must make up an internally consistent and compatible statement of policies for the city and/or county. This general plan provides guidelines for the future growth and development of the community in order that proper provision may be made for the promotion of safety and public welfare through flood control, parks and recreation, streets and highways, sewage disposal, drainage, subdivision design, open space areas and the setting aside of areas for residential, commercial and manufacturing.

ZONING

63   The local governing body (city council or county Board of Supervisors) has the power to pass ordinances establishing zones within which improvements must conform to certain use limitations and restricted locations on the lot. The right to zone comes under the rights defined under the police power of the government for the preservation and protection of public health, safety, morals, or general welfare.

64   "R" zoning indicates residential use and "M" zoning indicates manufacturing or industrial use.

REZONING AND VARIANCES

68   The zoning may be changed at any time by amending the existing ordinances. Frequently, the planning commission will initiate such a change when it is determined that it would best serve the community, or when a change is indicated, to carry out the general plan. Should a particular property in a rezoned area be substantially different than the use for which the new zoning is created, it is allowed to remain and referred to as a non-conforming use. Such a property is said to be 'grandfathered' into the variance and as long as the property is maintained the nature of the use of the property

will pass to the heirs of the owner. The only exception to this rule is when the zoning change is applied retroactively. Courts have held that non-conforming uses cannot be summarily eliminated by a retroactive ordinance unless the uses were such as to amount to a nuisance.

69   A zoning law cannot relieve land from lawful restrictions affecting the use of the land imposed by a prior recorded deed or by a prior recorded declaration of covenants, conditions, and restrictions. The deed restrictions will typically prevail.

70   If the planning commission decides to rezone an area from commercial to residential use, this kind of a change is identified usually as down zoning.

71   A zoning change may be initiated by the property owner on one or a number of parcels. The owner files a petition for rezoning with the local planning commission. This petition normally is referred to the planning commission that will hold public hearings after public notice and will refer the case to its technical staff for investigation and recommendation. If a vast majority of other property owners are already using their properties on a non-conforming way it is much easier for a new owner to obtain a variance on the acquired parcel. An adverse decision by a planning commission can be appealed to the local city council or Board of Supervisors.

72   Where only one lot is involved, a variance is more easily obtained.

HOUSING AND CONSTRUCTION

77   There are four laws that directly or indirectly affect the manner in which improvements upon real property may be constructed. The following laws control the construction of improvements:
(1) The State Housing Law.
(2) Local building codes.
(3) The Health and Safety Code.
(4) The State Contractors License Law.

STATE HOUSING LAW

78   This law is designed to provide minimum construction and occupancy requirements for all apartment houses, hotels and all other dwellings throughout the state. Construction regulations under this statewide act are handled by local building inspectors under the local planning commission.

LOCAL BUILDING CODES

79   In 1970 the legislature amended the State Housing Law to make uniform or national codes applicable in lieu of local building codes. The law now provides that the regulations of the Commission of Housing and Community Development under the State Housing Law shall impose substantially the same requirements as the most recent editions of these codes. Local government retains only the power to determine local use zone requirements, local fire zones, building setback, side and rear yard requirements, and property line requirements. Local variances are permitted when evidence exists that compliance with the uniform codes would be unsafe. If there is a conflict between this law and the State Housing Act, the most restrictive (highest degree of safety) would be enforced.

81   Construction regulations are administered by local building inspectors. Regulations concerning occupancy and sanitation are enforced by local health officers.

82   The procedure for new construction or building alterations requires initial application to the local building department for a building permit. The application must be accompanied by plans, specifications and a plot plan. When the application has been examined, revised where necessary, and approved, a building permit is issued once necessary fees have been paid. No construction or alteration can be commenced prior to issuance of a building permit. When construction has been completed, final inspection made, and construction has been approved, a "certificate of occupancy" is issued to the owner. Local ordinances may require use,

occupancy, and zoning reports from the city prior to transfer of title.

84   When there is any doubt as to whether or not the construction or alteration of an existing structure meets code specifications, the local building department will usually, for a fee, make an "occupancy survey" and report on the condition of the structure. If a construction permit was issued and the item was installed in the building in conformance with that permit, it would not be classified as substandard today provided it is fully functional and not a danger.

SUBDIVISIONS

92a   Subdividers, developers, and builders have realized large sums in profits by subdividing large land holdings into smaller tracts because of the nature of people. Basically, there are four factors that make subdividing both profitable and a necessity: (1) Industrialization, which happens as a civilization moves from an agrarian economy to an industrial economy. (2) Urbanization, which means the tendency to settle large numbers of people into close nit cities. (3) Migration, or the tendency of people to lift their roots and readily travel anywhere with little restraint. (4) Territorial settlement created when a government encourages people to populate frontier areas increasing the demand for land.

When selecting land for development, the developer often chooses suburban rather than urban land. The principal reason for this choice is that in an urban area, the development has been completed. The land costs are higher. The zoning and utilization of the land has been fairly well defined. Flexibility of uses is limited.

In a suburban area, the development costs are lower and the developer has the freedom to select the type of development he feels is best. He is not confined by the "strait jacket" of a preconceived city plan. He may plan self-contained communities complete with shopping centers, recreational, school and church facilities.

92b The most vital factor in planning a subdivision in which lots are to be sold for a profit, is a market analysis.

93 There are two laws in California, which control the development and sale of subdivisions: (1) The Subdivided Lands Act is found in the Business and Professions Code and (2) The Subdivision Map Act is found in the government code. According to the Subdivided Lands Act, a subdivision is generally defined as the division of any improved or unimproved land into five or more parcels for the purpose of sale, lease or financing, whether immediate or in the future. This includes such division as a condominium and community apartment project. The land to be divided may be a single or contiguous parcel. The law administered by the Real Estate Commissioner Subdivided Lands Act also includes a minimum of five parcels. A planned development and a stock cooperative are forms of subdivision.

SUBDIVISION MAP ACT

94 This law establishes that the regulation and control of the design and improvement of subdivisions are vested in the legislative bodies of local agencies. Each local agency, by ordinance, regulates and controls the physical aspects of subdivisions for which this law requires a tentative, final, or parcel map.

95 Under the provisions of the Subdivision Map Act the local authorities (planning commission) have approval over the general layout, zoning, streets, lot size and the improvements required in that particular area. This includes road surfacing, sidewalks drainage, sewage disposal, public utilities, and the dedication of land for recreational and educational facilities. The subdivider is responsible for the actual improvement of the dedicated areas. Dedication may also be required of access routes to public resources such as beaches, rivers and lakes. It will also include easements necessary for the inclusion and maintenance of sewers, lines, and cables over properties in the subdivision. The planning commission makes recommendations to the city council or Board of Supervisors.

95a If an easement over a particular property is taken by dedication, the original subdivider may obtain a release from the government if the public authority discontinues the use of the easement for the purpose it was granted.

96 The basic procedure for processing a subdivision of five or more lots, as set forth in the Subdivision Map Act, is as follows: Prepare a tentative map and file it with the city or county. Prepare a final map incorporating all changes required by the city or county. Get certificates from all persons having recorded interests in the property consenting to recordation of the final map and offering public areas for dedication. The subdivider then must enter into an agreement with the city or county for the improvement of streets and easements, supported by a performance bond. After a certificate of acceptance has been accepted, the final map is recorded.

97 Under the provisions of this Map Act, subdivisions of five or more parcels are exempt from the required tentative and final maps in the following circumstances:

98 (1) The land before division contains less than five acres and each parcel abuts upon a maintained public street or highway and no dedications or improvements are required.

99 (2) Any parcel divided into lots or parcels with each having an area of 20 acres or more and each having an approved access to a maintained public street or highway.

100 (3) Each parcel created by the division has a gross area of forty acres or more, or each is a quarter-quarter section or larger, or such other amount up to sixty acres, as specified by local ordinance.

101 The land consists of a parcel or parcels of land having approved access to a public street or highway which comprises part of a tract of land zoned for industrial or commercial development and which has the approval of the

governing body as to street alignments and widths.

104   The basic purpose of the Map Act is to give local authorities control over the physical development of subdivided property. This law is administered by the Real Estate Commissioner and protects the public against fraud, misrepresentation and deceit in the sale of subdivided property. To comply with this law, the subdivider must obtain the final public report from the Bureau of Real Estate prior to the sale, lease, or financing of any parcels whether located within California or outside of the state.

105   The normal method of obtaining this final public report is for the owner, his agent or subdivider of the proposed development, to file with the Bureau of Real Estate an application for a public report consisting of a "notice of intention."

SUBDIVIDED LANDS ACT

111   The subdivider is charged with handing any prospective buyer a true copy of the final public report and giving him a chance to read it so that he may become acquainted with the information the Commissioner has secured before he commits himself to the purchase. In addition, the subdivider must obtain a signed receipt for the copy and keep the receipts on file for the Commissioner's inspection for at least 3 years. Failure to do this may be a basis for stopping the sale of the subdivision and revoking the licenses of any sales agents involved. A final report is valid for five years unless renewed. Renewal becomes necessary if the subdivider rents the units and the five-year term expires. When the subdivider decides to sell, an amended report will be necessary.

112   If the public report is used for advertising, the whole report must be used. The report cannot be highlighted or used in part. It must be reproduced exactly as approved by the Commissioner.

113   A copy of the public report must now be given by the owner, subdivider or agent at any time, upon oral or written request to any member of the public. In addition, a copy of the public report and a statement advising that a copy of the report may be obtained from the owner, subdivider, or agent and shall be posted in a conspicuous place at any office where sales, leases, or offers to sell or lease lots within the subdivision are regularly made. The Real Estate Commissioner's office maintains a file of all subdivision final public reports. This information is available to the public.

114   Ordinarily the sale of subdivision lots is prohibited by the Commissioner until the subdivider has made a complete filing and a final public report is issued. However, the Commissioner may, due to unusual circumstances in some instances, issue a "preliminary public report" which permits the subdivider to take deposits in connection with advance lot reservations before he has completed his filing. The taking of a deposit does nothing but create a reservation. It is not a sale. It also must state the unilateral right of either the subdivider or the potential buyer to cancel the reservation at any time. The preliminary report is valid for one year or until the final report is issued, whichever occurs first. The preliminary report is frequently referred to as the "pink" report because it is published using pink paper stock.

MATERIAL CHANGES

122   The owner or developer of any type of real estate subdivision must report to the Commissioner the sale or lease of five or more parcels, or units to another person. The contract to option five or more units to a single person must also be reported. The new parties (owners in these instances) are potential subdividers and must obtain their own appropriate public reports.

DESIST AND REFRAIN ORDERS

125   Should the Commissioner find that any owner, subdivider, or other person is violating any of the provisions of the Subdivided Lands Act; the Commissioner may affect the immediate cessation of such violations or the immediate termination of selling or leasing of the property

by the issuance of an order to desist and refrain from such activity.

BLANKET ENCUMBRANCE

126   A blanket encumbrance is one that is secured by more than one parcel of property. This type of financing is often used in connection with construction loans to builders. One blanket mortgage (trust deed) covers the entire tract initially. As individual houses are sold to various buyers, a partial release (release clause) is usually obtained from the blanket loan holder. In California, the document usually used is a partial reconveyance deed. The buyer receives a grant deed and a separate loan is made to the new buyer and all or a portion of the proceeds of this new loan are paid by the seller against the blanket loan to obtain the release of the sold property. Until the release is actually recorded, the subdivider must maintain the buyer's money in a trust account.

127   Where there is no blanket encumbrance involved, the subdivider must protect the buyer's deposit by one of the following:
(1) Place all of buyer's money in a neutral escrow or trust account until title or other interest is delivered or default is made by either party, or the money is returned to the buyer.
(2) A bond is furnished to the state until title is delivered to the purchaser.
(3) An approved association of which the seller is a member furnishes a bond for protection of the buyer.
(4) Seller furnishes lien and completion bonds on improved residential land.
(5) All monies paid go into a neutral escrow and are paid out only for payments on construction for improvements on the land.

EXCEPTIONS

128   The law designates a subdivision as the dividing of property into five or more parcels with the intention of selling, leasing or financing, now or at any time in the future. It does not include divisions into parcels of not less than 160 acres which are designated by lot or parcel description by government survey, unless such division is for the purpose of sale for oil and gas purposes.

Nor does it apply to the leasing of apartments, stores or similar space within an apartment building, industrial building, or commercial building. Subdivisions limited to an area expressly zoned for industrial or commercial uses are exempted from the requirement of obtaining a public report.

COMMON OWNERSHIP SUBDIVISIONS

129   In today's circumstances where improved or unimproved lots are developed to be owned in common by many persons under some form of cooperative ownership, such development would be a subdivision under California statutes and would be subject to applicable subdivision laws.

130   Upon written request of the owner of a lot or unit in a common ownership subdivision, referred to in Section 11004.5 of the Business and Professions Code, the governing body of such subdivision must provide a copy of the declaration of restrictions, bylaws and articles of incorporation applicable at the time of the request, within ten days of the delivery of such request.

131   Planned development - Separately owned lots where one or more additional lots are owned in common or there are mutual, common, or reciprocal interests in the separately owned lots. The development must consist of five or more lots to be a subdivision and may involve title or leasehold interests. Since the planned development does not necessarily involve improved land, it could also be a land project.

132   Community apartment project - The ownership of an undivided interest in the land when coupled with the right of exclusive occupancy of any apartment thereon. To be classified as a subdivision, the community apartment project must be made up of five (5) or more units. The units are financed as one and the title insurance is issued on the entire project.

133   Stock cooperative - A corporation formed for the purpose of holding title, in fee, or as an estate for years, to improved real property where

the shareholders receive a right of exclusive occupancy to a portion of the real property.

134   Condominium – A estate in real property which consists of an undivided interest in common in a portion of real property coupled with a separate interest in space called a unit. The boundaries are described on a recorded final map, parcel map, or condominium plan in sufficient detail to locate all of its boundaries. The area within these boundaries may be filled with air, earth, water, or any combination thereof, and need not be physically attached to land, except by easements for access and, if necessary, support.

134a No amendments or alterations in the declarations of restrictions, which would materially change the rights or restrictions of any interest in a condominium, can be accomplished without written consent of the Real Estate Commissioner. This requirement does not have to be met after 3 years from the time the subdivider ceases to hold or directly control 1/3 of the votes that may be cast in any meeting concerning such a change.

136   A condominium "project" means the entire parcel of property, including the structures. "Unit" means the air space, earth, water and other elements which are not owned in common. "Common areas" means the entire project except the units.

138   The original owner-developer of a condominium project must record a declaration of restrictions that shall bind all owners of units in the project and are enforceable by any unit owner. The restrictions may provide for the management of the project by the owners, an elected agent, or a Board of Governors. Duties include amendment of restrictions by majority vote, independent audit of accounts, reasonable assessments for authorized expenditures, and subordination of liens securing such assessments. The management group of a condominium project may acquire, hold, and dispose of intangible personal property for the benefit of the condominium owners including contract rights, accounts payable, and accounts receivable.

139   Unpaid assessments by the management body become a lien against the unit when "notice" of it is recorded. Even if the unit is homesteaded, the lien may be foreclosed upon.

141   The "unit" (separate ownership) boundaries are the interior surfaces of the perimeter walls, floors, ceilings, windows and doors thereof, together with the intruding outlets (fixtures) of pipes, ducts and conduits from the walls, ceilings and floors. All other areas, equipment, utility installations, structures, bearing walls, and the land are the "common areas" in which each unit owner has a tenancy-in-common interest in equal shares with the other unit owners.

143   The owners and developers of lots or units in subdivisions which have commonly owned facilities (condominiums, planned developments, stock cooperatives) are required to give prospective purchasers copies of the C.C.&R's, articles of incorporation, and bylaws as soon as practical before the transfer of title or the completion of a real property sales contract.

144   A buyer of a condominium, other than the original buyer from the subdivider, must be given a copy of the articles, bylaws of the association, the most current financial statement, and the deed restrictions.

144a The term subdivision includes the conversion of existing improved property, such as an apartment house into condominiums. Under this special circumstance when the property to be subdivided is already occupied, the subdivider must give the existing tenants a minimum of 180 days notice of the start of the conversion.

FEDERAL SUBDIVISIONS

156   The "Interstate Land Sales Full Disclosure Act" became effective in 1969. Under federal law a subdivision is defined as "any development divided into 25 or more parcels or lots that are not improved with structures at the time of sale and are offered for sale by mail or interstate commerce." The regulatory agency established by the congress for land promotions

that are offered in interstate commerce or by mail is the Department of Housing and Urban Development (HUD).

158   This law does not apply to:

160   The sale or lease of improved land or the sale or lease of land under a contract obligating the seller or lessor to erect a building thereon within a period of 2 years.

162   All purchasers have the option to revoke a contract or lease in the subdivision until midnight of the seventh day following the signing of a contract or agreement, unless exempt.

164   Any developer subject to this law who in the judicial process is convicted of willfully violating the provisions of this law would be punishable by a fine of not more than $5,000, or by imprisonment of not more than 5 years, or both.

LAND PROJECTS

165   In 1969, State law introduced "land projects" into subdivision law in California. Land projects are defined as a development of 50 or more unimproved lots in a rural area with less than 1500 registered voters within the subdivision or within two (2) miles of the subdivision. The subdivision will not be subject to land project special regulations if all the lots are sold only to builders or developers, and if they are not sold with substantial direct mail advertising with no more than 10% of the price allowed for overhead and advertising and no more than conventional commissions. A land project is similar to a planned development inasmuch as the lot owners have access to all areas in common.

166   No public report on a land project will be issued unless the Commissioner is satisfied that completion bonds or impounded cash is available to assure completion, maintenance, and financing of roads, utilities, community facilities promised or other amenities in the offering. No bond or impounds will be required if all the improvements are completed and paid for, if no lien or assessment is imposed on any

lot for any cost of construction, and if the developer guarantees the preservation of each offsite improvement from damages not insurable under title policies. Once a public report has been issued on a land project type subdivision in California, a copy of that report must be given at any time to any member of the public upon oral or written request.

207   If a land developer offers a free prize to anyone who replies to his direct mail advertisement and visits the site of his subdivision where the subdivider requires the prize winner to attend a sales presentation at the subdivision site prior to awarding them the prize, the sales presentation is legal provided that the ad states the conditions to receive the prize. Failure to disclose that requirement, however, makes it illegal.

WATER RIGHTS

211   In California, the landowners have neither ownership of specific underground water nor absolute ownership of waters running across or bordering their property, such as a river or stream. In this state, the rights of an overlying landowner to use sub-surface (percolating) waters are correlative to the rights of fellow overlying owners to reasonable and beneficial use of those waters. The owner of land which touches upon a natural watercourse enjoys benefits known as "riparian rights," whereby he has the right along with other such owners to use such waters in a reasonable manner.

211a If a landowner holding riparian rights subdivides the property, those lots that do not abut the water will not convey the riparian rights previously held by the entire property.

212   Water in rivers changes its course often. If the boundary of a property is a metes and bounds description and the river or waterway is one of the boundary lines, then the owners on each side of the watercourse could either lose or gain property. Every student should know the following terms.

213   Alluvium - Deposits of earth made by the natural action of water.

214   Accretion - An addition to land from natural causes as, for example, from gradual action of the ocean or river waters.

215   Avulsion - A loss of land due to the tearing away of the banks next to a river or watercourse. This is also called erosion.

216   Tidelands are measured by the mesne (normal) high tide line. As the climate warms and the waters in the oceans increase, the mesne high tide line will go further inland. This is example of avulsion.

217   Because of the semi-arid climate, conservation of water resources is important in California. A vast body of detailed water laws has been enacted. Much litigation arises in connection with water rights and the courts are authorized to refer all such litigation to the State Division of Water Resources for investigation, hearings, and preliminary determination subject to final court approval, thus making use of the specialized knowledge and personnel of this agency. Should a litigant or other individual appealing to the board be awarded the rights to the use of non-abutting water, the action is called "appropriation of water." The person or entity receiving the appropriation gains the taking, impounding, or diversion of water flowing on the public domain from its natural course and the application of the water to some beneficial use, personal and exclusive to the appropriator (taker).

220   An "irrigation district" is a district created under a special law for the purpose of developing and furnishing water, primarily for agricultural purposes. It has many characteristics of other local governments, such as a municipal government. It is said to be a quasi-public corporation, that is, it is in the nature of a political subdivision. Bonds for development may be voted by residents of the district subject to a court.

221   The term "water table" denotes the distance from the surface of the ground to the depth to which groundwater has risen. Potable water refers to drinkable or purified water. Percolation is the act of water draining or passing through a porous substance such as the earth.

FLOOD CONTROL

226   Water overflowing a defined channel is considered "floodwater" and any land owner may protect himself from same by reasonable methods, such as building up the sides of the channel with a "dike," even though this might result in the overflow of the channel where it runs across another's land.

Lesson Eight
Part Two
Study Questions

_____(Lesson Eight - Paragraph 39 - Question 1)_____

The government may acquire title in all of these ways, except:
(A) Eminent domain. (B) Police power. (C) Escheat. (D) Grant.

_____

(B) Police Power gives the government the right to regulate the use of property. The other three methods names are used to gain title.

_____(Lesson Eight - Paragraph 39 - Question 2)_____

When a public agency takes private property for public use, it is an exercise of:
(A) Police power. (B) Eminent domain. (C) Neither A nor B.   (D) Both A and B.

_____

(B) Eminent domain is the right to take private property for public use. Police power is the right to regulate - not the right to take.

_____(Lesson Eight - Paragraph 43 - Question 1)_____

Police power and eminent domain give government authority the right to regulate the use of and the right to take private real property for the general public good. The police power would include all of the following, except:
(A) Condemnation. (B) Zoning.   (C) Building regulations.   (D) Subdivision controls.

_____

(A) Condemnation is the exercising, in court, of the power of eminent domain.

_____(Lesson Eight - Paragraph 43 - Question 2)_____

A condemnation action is a legal procedure associated with:
(A) Eminent domain proceedings.   (B) The Subdivided Lands Act.
(C) Zoning ordinances.   (D) The Subdivision Map Act.

_____

(A) Condemnation is an action to take private property for the common good under the power of eminent domain. The owner must be compensated for the taking

_____(Lesson Eight - Paragraph 45 - Question 1)_____

A municipal airport was expanded and a new runway constructed immediately adjacent to a tract of single-family residences. The resulting noise pollution caused a substantial decline in value of the homes. Subsequently, the homeowners sued and won a judgment against the airport for their loss of value. The court action they took is known as an:
(A) Environmental impact. (B) Inverse condemnation. (C) Abatement. (D) Injunction.

_____

(B) This is clearly a case of taking private property for a public use. Since the court action is initiated by the property owners, we have an inverse condemnation.

_____(Lesson Eight - Paragraph 51 - Question 1)_____
The following gives the least protection against blighting in an area of improved property:
(A) Changes in zoning ordinances. (B) A partially developed neighborhood.
(C) Natural and artificial barriers.   (D) A homogenous population with a sense of civic responsibility.

(B) The fact that an area is only partially developed offers little protection against blighting. The lack of development makes it more difficult to block out or deter the entrance of what are called inharmonious elements (non-conforming uses, poor upkeep and divergent use of property).

_____(Lesson Eight - Paragraph 55 - Question 1)_____
The following are requirements that must be satisfied for a valid use of the police power, except:
(A) Uniform in application. (B) Non-discriminatory. (C) Private good. (D) General public welfare.

(C) Police power can never be used for the private good of one person or company

_____(Lesson Eight - Paragraph 55 - Question 2)_____
All of the following are related to the police power authority of government, but one:
(A) Establish rent controls.   (B) Establish building codes.
(C) Establish planning commissions. (D) Establish reasonable tax rates.

(D) Establish reasonable tax rates. Choices (A), (B), and (C) identify actions that can be taken under the police power authority of the government (sovereign). Taxation is a separate power of government as is the power of eminent domain.

_____(Lesson Eight - Paragraph 61 - Question 1)_____
The following statement is true with respect to planning commissions:
(A) All members are elected.
(B) Members must have had real estate or subdivision experience.
(C) They are authorized to give advice to the city council on subdivisions.
(D) Must be real estate brokers.

(C) Members of the planning commission should be knowledgeable in the field of real estate and city planning, but this is not a prerequisite for being a member. The members are appointed and it is their job to develop a master plan to advise the city council in this area.

_____(Lesson Eight - Paragraph 61 - Question 2)_____
State law requires that every city or county create a planning commission:
(A) When funds have been appropriated by the local governing body.
(B) Without exception.
(C) After a master plan has been approved.
(D) Membership of which must be comprised of at least three members of the city council or county Board of Supervisors.

(B) The state requires that a master plan be created without exception. It therefore follows that state law mandates a planning commission. It is the duty of the planning commission to draft a master plan and to see that it is put into effect. The first step of course is to establish a planning commission. Funds to operate and enforce the master plan come after the creation of the commission.

_____(Lesson Eight - Paragraph 62 - Question 1)_____

The basic reason why state law in California requires that every city and county must adopt a comprehensive long-term general plan (master plan) within its jurisdiction is to guide the future development of:
(A) Proposed major thoroughfares and transportation routes.
(B) The general distribution and location and the extent of the uses of land for residential, commercial, and industrial purposes.
(C) The identification and appraisal of potential seismic hazards.
(D) All of the above.

(D) A master plan is a long-term plan of growth and development. It can be for 20, 30, or 40 years. In discussing and preparing for such a plan, planning officials concern themselves with all of the items presented in the question.

_____(Lesson Eight - Paragraph 63 - Question 1)_____

Zoning laws are made to:
(A) Promote safety and public welfare.
(B) Promote the conformity of houses.
(C) Establish minimum building standards.
(D) Keep from having too many similar commercial users.

(A) The purposes of the zoning laws that are enacted under the right of police power are to promote the safety and public welfare of the community.

_____(Lesson Eight - Paragraph 63 - Question 2)_____

The legal purpose for the creation and existence of zoning restrictions is:
(A) To keep all types of commercial property out of residential neighborhoods.
(B) The preservation of protection of public health, safety, morals, or general welfare.
(C) To keep the land uses in every area as closely similar as possible.
(D) To make available to the public sufficient amounts of recreational areas.

(B) Each of the other choices is limited to a specific use or uses. Zoning restrictions must have a broader purpose than any individual interest. The power to create such use restrictions should be employed for the benefit of the general welfare of the entire community, not private interests. Public health, safety, morals, welfare, convenience and necessity of the public are the basis for such police power regulations.

_____(Lesson Eight - Paragraph 68 - Question 1)_____

A restaurant is built in an undeveloped area. Later, the surrounding area is zoned for single-family residential use. If the restaurant were permitted to continue operations, it would be an example of:
(A) Split zoning. (B) Downzoning. (C) A non-conforming use. (D) Exclusive zoning.

(C) The use as a restaurant does not conform to the residential use now designated for the area.

_____(Lesson Eight - Paragraph 69 - Question 1)_____

When zoning laws permit a use of a certain property which is restricted by construction and use limitations contained in a prior deed, the following would prevail:
(A) Deed restrictions. (B) Master zoning laws. (C) Variance permit. (D) The owner's planned use.

(A) A zoning law cannot relieve land from lawful restrictions affecting the use of the land imposed by a prior recorded deed or by a prior recorded declaration of covenants, conditions, and restrictions. In this question the deed restrictions will prevail.

_____(Lesson Eight - Paragraph 70 - Question 1)_____

The planning commission recently rezoned a section of the city changing its lawful use for new development from commercial to residential. This type of change is often referred to as:
(A) A variance. (B) Downzoning. (C) A city referendum. (D) Redevelopment planning.

___

(B) Changing the zoning from commercial to residential usually decreases the value of the property and is referred to as "downzoning."

_____(Lesson Eight - Paragraph 70 - Question 2)_____

An area of a city that was previously zoned for commercial use has just recently been rezoned for R-1 residential uses. This would be an example of:
(A) Density zoning. (B) Spot zoning. (C) Downzoning. (D) Split zoning.

___

(C) Downzoning. The residential use of property would generally make the land less valuable than it would be if it were zoned for commercial use. This kind of a change is identified usually as downzoning.

_____(Lesson Eight - Paragraph 71 - Question 1)_____

Zoning changes may be initiated by:
(A) Subdividers. (B) Local authorities. (C) Individuals. (D) All of the above.

___

(D) We must emphasize the question is based upon the word "initiated." All of these agencies may initiate (start) procedures for zoning changes. However, if a question asks about who makes zoning changes, you would answer "local authorities."

_____(Lesson Eight - Paragraph 77 - Question 1)_____

The basic regulation and control of the housing and construction industries in California is accomplished through:
(A) Building codes. (B) State Housing Law. (C) State Contractors License Law. (D) All of the above.

___

(D) The State Housing Law sets minimum building standards for all construction and these standards are usually further strengthened at the local level by city or county building codes. All contractors are regulated by the state, making choices (A), (B), and C) all correct.

_____(Lesson Eight - Paragraph 79 - Question 1)_____

If a local building code and the Uniform Building Code are in conflict:
(A) The Uniform Building Code prevails.
(B) The local code prevails.
(C) Neither code prevails. The law is silent on the subject on which they differ.
(D) The code that provides for the highest degree of safety prevails.

___

(D) If there is a conflict between two building codes, the code that has the highest protection of safety will prevail.

_____(Lesson Eight - Paragraph 81 - Question 1)_____

In a city the State Housing Law is enforced by the:
(A) Chief administrative officer. (B) Police department.
(C) Planning department.   (D) Building inspector.

(D) The State Housing Act is a state building code but the local building department (inspector) enforces it.

_____(Lesson Eight - Paragraph 81 - Question 2)_____

In a city, compliance with the State Housing Act usually is enforced by the:
(A) City engineer. (B) Police department. (C) City planning commission. (D) Building inspector.

(D) The State Housing Act sets the minimum building standards, which usually are enforced by the local building department.

_____(Lesson Eight - Paragraph 82 - Question 1)_____

Which of the following would give permission prior to the construction of an office building:
(A) Local planning commission. (B) Local building department.
(C) Real Estate Commissioner. (D) Local Health Department.

(B) The local building department issues building permits.

_____(Lesson Eight - Paragraph 82 - Question 2)_____

A developer who desires to construct a residence would secure a building permit from:
(A) Federal Housing Administration. (B) Local building department.
(C) California Housing Commission. (D) Bureau of Real Estate.

(B) The local building department issues building permits.

_____(Lesson Eight - Paragraph 84 - Question 1)_____

When applying for a loan, the following would not cause the building to be labeled "substandard":
(A) The heating system is inadequate.
(B) Some of the rooms are damp.
(C) At the time the building was constructed a permit was pulled for the electrical system. Today it is fully functional, but does not conform to current code requirements.
(D) Exterior walls are not adequate to stop the entry of moisture.

(C) If a construction permit were issued and the item was installed in the building in conformance with that permit, it would not be classified as substandard if it is fully functional and not a danger.

_____(Lesson Eight – Paragraph 64 - Question 1)_____

The following zoning symbol would be used to identify property zoned for multiple family dwellings:
(A) A3. (B) C2. (C) M 1. (D) R3.

(D) The symbol "R" usually indicates a residential use.

_____(Lesson Eight – Paragraph 64 - Question 2)_____

A "for sale" sign states that a property is zoned "M." This indicates it is zoned for:
(A) Commercial use. (B) Agriculture use. (C) Multiple use. (D) Industrial use.

(D) "M" refers to an industrial use. Commercial is indicated by "C."

_____(Lesson Eight - Paragraph 92b - Question 1)_____

The most vital factor in planning a subdivision in which lots are to be sold for a profit is generally acknowledged to be:
(A) A site analysis.   (B) A market analysis.
(C) A community facilities analysis. (D) A construction cost analysis.

(B) Before subdividing land and constructing improvements, one must decide if there is a market for such property.

_____(Lesson Eight - Paragraph 93 - Question 1)_____

An individual purchased 9 one-acre parcels and plans to sell 3 acres a year. If he sells 3 acres this year he must comply with the:
(A) California Real Estate Law. (B) State Subdivision Map Act. (C) Both A and B. (D) Neither A nor B.

(C) A subdivision under the Map Act and Real Estate Law is defined as the division of land into five or more parcels for sale, lease or finance. Since this party has nine one-acre parcels and he plans to sell the nine, he has a subdivision and must comply with both laws.

_____(Lesson Eight - Paragraph 93 - Question 2)_____

An owner of land divided it into 8 parcels in 1994. He sold 2 lots in 1994, 2 lots in 1995, took an option to purchase one lot in 1996, and sold the balance in 1997. When was he legally classified as a subdivider?
(A) 1994.   (B) 1995   (C) 1996   (D) 1997

(A) A subdivision under the Map Act and Real Estate Law is defined as the division of land into five or more parcels for sale, lease or finance. Since this party has eight parcels and he plans to sell them he has a subdivision from the inception in 1994 and must comply with both laws.

_____(Lesson Eight - Paragraph 95 - Question 1)_____

The Subdivision Map Act in California would be administered by the:
(A) Real Estate Commissioner.   (B) Local planning commission.
(C) State Registrar of Contractors. (D) State Department of Housing Community Development.

(B) The question deals with the Subdivision Map Act. "Map" has to do with the physical aspects of the subdivision: streets, sidewalks, and sewers. This is under the jurisdiction of the local planning commission. Any question concerning the Real Estate Commissioner should state the subdivision law as applied by the Real Estate Commissioner.

_____(Lesson Eight - Paragraph 95 - Question 2)_____

The Subdivision Map Act requires that submissions for approvals be made to:
(A) The Real Estate Commissioner. (B) The Corporation Commissioner.
(C) Local government officials.   (D) State Lands Commission.

(C) The local planning commission, not the Bureau of Real Estate, administers the Subdivision Map Act. Local officials, city or county, approve the physical aspects of the subdivision such as streets, sewers, grading and drainage. The Real Estate Commissioner enforces the subdivision law and is concerned with fraud in the selling or advertising of subdivisions.

_____(Lesson Eight - Paragraph 96 - Question 1)_____

The Subdivision Map Act provides for:
(A) Submission of proposed sales contracts for subdivision lots to the governing body for approval.
(B) Execution of an improvement contract between subdivider and city.

(C) Delivery of a copy of the Real Estate Commissioner's report to all prospective purchasers.
(D) Release clauses in all blanket mortgages on subdivision property.

(B) The Map Act is designed to control the physical aspects of a new subdivision under the jurisdiction of the planning commission. To insure that subdividers will actually install the proposed streets, sewers and other promised improvements, the local government might demand evidence of good faith by the execution of an improvement contract between the subdivider and the city.

_____(Lesson Eight - Paragraph 104 - Question 1)_____
The Real Estate Commissioner supervises the sale and lease of subdivisions within and outside of the state. The laws and regulations dealing with these transactions are similar in most states in all the following ways, except in California with:
(A) Handling of deposits. (B) Financing arrangements.
(C) The registration.   (D) Ability of the subdivider to deliver the interest contracted for.

(C) The registration. A change in 1996, of the Real Estate code states: A person acting as a principal or agent who intends, in this state, to sell or lease or offer for sale or lease lots, parcels, or interests in a subdivision, as defined in Section 10249.1, situated outside of this state but within the United States, shall, prior to a sale, lease, or offer, register the subdivision with the commissioner. An application for registration shall be made on a form acceptable to the commissioner and include, together with a fee, a description of the offering, certification by the applicant that the subdivision is in compliance with all applicable requirements of the state or states wherein the project is located, evidence of this compliance, if applicable, and a consent to service as described in Section 10249.92 The commissioner, within 10 days of receipt of an application of registration, shall provide the applicant with notice of the completion of the registration or a notice of deficiency. If the bureau does not provide a notice within 10 days, the registration shall be deemed complete.

_____(Lesson Eight - Paragraph 111 - Question 1)_____
A subdivider purchased an acre of land and built 5 homes on the property. After receiving the Real Estate Commissioner's Final Subdivision Report, he rented all five homes to different tenants. Ten years later he decides to sell the homes to the tenants. In order to sell the homes he:
(A) Must secure a Real Property Security Dealer's License.
(B) Must hire a real estate broker to sell them.
(C) Does not have to do anything as the Commissioner has no further control over the sale.
(D) Must secure a new Subdivision Final Report from the Real Estate Commissioner.

(D) The Real Estate Commissioner's Final Subdivision Report is valid for only 5 years. Even if the original report gave the subdivider the right to sell or lease the homes, it is no longer valid. However, an amended report would still be necessary even if the original report was not five years old.

_____(Lesson Eight - Paragraph 111 - Question 2)_____
The effective term of a final Subdivision Public Report is limited to a period of:
(A) Five years. (B) Three years. (C) One year. (D) Indefinite.

(A) Once a subdivider has secured a final report, it is valid for a period of five years. If he changes the "set-up" of his subdivision (financing, tract name, etc.), then he must obtain an amended report.

_____(Lesson Eight - Paragraph 112 - Question 1)_____
A subdivider has secured the Real Estate Commissioner's Final Public Report on a new subdivision and believes that it would be a valuable means of advertising. If the subdivider uses the public report for advertising purposes:

(A) He may use only part of the report and does not have to use it in its entirety.
(B) He must use the entire report but can underscore and highlight the attractive items even though the original report did not do so.
(C) He must use it in its entirety making no alterations.
(D) He would be violating the Real Estate Law because it cannot be used in any way.

(C) The report cannot be highlighted or used in part. It must be reproduced exactly as approved by the Commissioner.

_____(Lesson Eight - Paragraph 113 - Question 1)_____
A copy of a public report on a subdivision must be given to:
(A) Anyone requesting it orally or in writing. (B) A bona fide purchaser ready to close escrow.
(C) A neighboring property owner.   (D) None of the above.

(A) The sales office in a subdivision sale must give a public report to anyone who requests one whether the request is oral or in writing.

_____(Lesson Eight - Paragraph 113 - Question 2)_____
A subdivider who is not a licensee is selling lots in a mountain area. A prospective buyer desires information regarding assessment liens, blanket encumbrances, utilities and responsibility for street maintenance. The best source for this information would be the:
(A) County recorder. (B) Real Estate Commissioner. (C) City engineer. (D) Local title company.

(B) The Real Estate Commissioner's office maintains a file of all subdivision final public reports. This information is available to the public. A report would furnish all of the information desired by the buyer. The title company would not have information regarding all the matters that would concern the buyer regarding street maintenance.

_____(Lesson Eight - Paragraph 114 - Question 1)_____
With respect to handling subdivided lands under the authority of a preliminary public report, all of the following statements are true, except:
(A) A real estate broker may take a listing on the subdivision parcels subject to the issuance of the final public report.
(B) The subdivider may give a listing on the lots to a licensed real estate broker for purposes of showing the parcels.
(C) May sell or offer to sell the parcels subject to the issuance of a final public report.
(D) May not offer the parcels for sale until issuance of the final public report.

(C) The subdivider until the issuance of the final public report may legally use no sales agreement of any kind. When the preliminary public report is issued, the subdivider (or his agents) may only take nonbinding reservations.

_____(Lesson Eight - Paragraph 114 - Question 2)_____
A preliminary subdivision public report terminates under which of the following conditions:
(A) Upon release of the final subdivision report. (B) At the end of one year.
(C) Upon any material change.   (D) In any of the above situations.

(D) All the stated choices will bring about the termination of a preliminary public report.

_____(Lesson Eight - Paragraph 125 - Question 1)_____
If the Real Estate Commissioner determines that a subdivider has done something wrong, he can:

(A) Seek an injunction in the superior court.   (B) Issue an order to desist and refrain.
(C) Prosecute the subdivider in the Supreme Court.   (D) Revoke the final permit.

(B) Issue an order to desist.

_____(Lesson Eight - Paragraph 126 - Question 1)_____

The maximum number of lots that a subdivider would cover under a single trust deed in order to avoid a blanket encumbrance would be:
(A) One lot. (B) Two lots. (C) Three lots. (D) Four lots.

(A) An encumbrance covering more than one parcel of real property is known as a blanket encumbrance.

_____(Lesson Eight - Paragraph 126 - Question 2)_____

A subdivider in Southern California received a grant deed on a subdivision that was covered by a blanket encumbrance in the form of a first trust deed with partial release clauses. A buyer purchased a lot from the subdivider paying all cash. In this instance, the buyer most likely received a:
(A) Warranty deed. (B) Trust deed. (C) Deed of partial reconveyance. (D) Grant deed.

(D) The subdivider receives a grant deed transferring title to him even though the property is covered with a blanket encumbrance. He in turn gives a grant deed to the purchaser when the cash purchase is made. When the debt is removed from the lot, the subdivider will receive a deed of partial reconveyance which, when recorded, will remove the lien from the public record.

_____(Lesson Eight - Paragraph 127 - Question 1)_____

A completion bond would be for the benefit of:
(A) Lender. (B) Subdivider. (C) Contractor. (D) Laborers and material men.

(A) A lender would insist on a completion bond whereas a subdivider or contractor may not. There is a protection for all listed in the question but the best answer is lender.

_____(Lesson Eight - Paragraph 128 - Question 1)_____

The division of 2,000 acres of land into parcels to be used for commercial or agricultural purposes will not come under the Real Estate Subdivision Laws if such subdivided parcels are not less than:
(A) 40 acres. (B) 120 acres. (C) 160 acres. (D) 140 acres.

(C) While the law designates a "subdivision" as the dividing of land into five or more parcels with the intention of selling, leasing or financing now or at any time in the future. It does not include divisions into parcels of not less than 160 acres unless such division is for the purpose of sale for oil and gas purposes.

_____(Lesson Eight - Paragraph 129 - Question 1)_____

The owner of a five-unit apartment house which is located within the city limits intends to convert the units into five condominium units and offer them for sale to the public. In this situation, the owner:
(A) Is exempt from the Subdivision Map Act and the Subdivision Lands Act.
(B) Must comply with the Subdivision Map Act and The Subdivided Lands Act.
(C) Must file a map with the city under the provisions of the Map Act.
(D) Must apply for a public report from the Real Estate Commissioner under the Subdivided Lands Act.

(C) A standard subdivision within the city limits having completed residential structures and other buildings for occupancy, or with financial arrangements to guarantee such completion satisfactorily to the city is exempt from the Subdivided Lands Act. All Subdivisions of two or more parcels must comply with the Subdivision Map Act.

_____(Lesson Eight - Paragraph 129 - Question 2)_____

A developer is converting five apartments to a form of common ownership. This results in separate ownership of the individual units and shared ownership of the common areas. Which would be true?
(A) This is a subdivision. (B) This is a community apartment project.
(C) This is a time share.   (D) All of the above are true statements.

(A) This question states that a condominium has been created. As it is five units or more, it is classified as a subdivision.

_____(Lesson Eight - Paragraph 131 - Question 1)_____

Under subdivision law administered by the Real Estate Commissioner a "planned development" would include:
(A) Lot purchasers that own areas in common with other lot owners.
(B) A lot purchaser required to pay a maintenance fee for recreational facilities in the development.
(C) Both (A) and (B) are correct.   (D) Neither (A) nor (B) are correct.

(C) Both (A) and (B) apply to the "planned development" type of subdivision.

_____(Lesson Eight - Paragraph 131 - Question 2)_____

A planned development project is a:
(A) Fully improved subdivision.
(B) Standard subdivision in which owners of separate lots own other lots in common
(C) Subdivision for which a final report has been issued.
(D) Community apartment in which each owner has a fractional interest in the whole.

(B) A planned development is similar to a standard type subdivision. In addition, it has lots or areas owned in common and reserved for the use of some or all of the owners of the separately owned lots.

_____(Lesson Eight - Paragraph 132 - Question 1)_____

Hall lives in a multiple residential structure without individual title policies. He owns an undivided interest in the land and building coupled with the right of exclusive occupancy to a specific unit. According to the Real Estate Law, this type of subdivision is known as a:
(A) Planned development project. (B) Stock cooperative project.
(C) Condominium project.   (D) Community apartment project.

(D) This question describes a community apartment project.

_____(Lesson Eight - Paragraph 132, 133 - Question 1)_____

Under the provision of California's Subdivided Lands Act, a condominium or a community apartment project must contain at least the following number of units to be a considered to be a subdivision:
(A) 1. (B) 2. (C) 4. (D) 5.

(D) California's Subdivided Lands Act establishes that a planned development, condominium, community apartment project and a stock cooperative must have 5 or more units to be a subdivision.

_____(Lesson Eight - Paragraph 134 - Question 1)_____
An undivided interest in common areas and a separate interest in a living area or a working area in an industrial, residential or commercial building or office building is best known as a/an:
(A) Community apartment project. (B) Condominium. (C) Personal property. (D) Subdivision.

(B) This is the concise definition of a condominium

_____(Lesson Eight - Paragraph 134 - Question 2)_____
A person who owns an undivided interest in common in a parcel of real property together with a separate interest in space in a residential, industrial or commercial building on such real property is said to have an interest in a:
(A) Community apartment project. (B) Planned development project.
(C) Condominium project.   (D) Stock cooperative project.

(C) Any private ownership of air space as well as a common ownership in the land usually falls into the condominium classification. It can be residential, industrial or commercial.

_____(Lesson Eight - Paragraph 134a - Question 1)_____
Which of the following would require the prior written consent of the Real Estate Commissioner?
(A) Transfer of a salesperson's license from an individual broker to a broker corporation.
(B) Changing the deed restrictions affecting a buyer's interest in a condominium project less than 3 years old.
(C) The formation of a partnership by two real estate brokers.
(D) Selling stock in an incorporated real estate syndicate.

(B) Paragraph #11018.7 of the real estate law provides, "No amendments, alterations in declarations of restrictions... which would materially change the rights ... or restrictions of any interest... without written consent of the Real Estate Commissioner." This requirement does not have to be met after 3 years from the time the subdivider ceases to hold or directly control 1/3 of the votes that may be cast in any meeting concerning such a change.

_____(Lesson Eight - Paragraph 136 - Question 1)_____
In a condominium project, the sidewalks are:
(A) Owned by the individuals that hold title to the condos that front on the sidewalk.
(B) Owned by the condominium association.
(C) Common area.
(D) Easements appurtenant.

(C) A condominium project is the whole development. The project consists of the separately owned units and the common area. The sidewalks of the condominium project are owned in common. The separate ownership is the airspace in the unit. All other items would be owned in common with the other owners.

_____(Lesson Eight - Paragraph 138 - Question 1)_____
Deed restrictions are placed on a subdivision development by:
(A) The Federal Housing Administration. (B) State and local ordinances.
(C) The developer.   (D) The permanent lender.

(C) The developer is the one putting together the subdivision and is usually the owner of the subdivided land. As the owner, he will create the restrictions he needs to maintain the subdivision. He will usually record a "declaration of restrictions" and make reference to these restrictions in the deeds to each parcel affected as it is sold.

_____(Lesson Eight - Paragraph 138 - Question 2)_____
C.C. & R's would most likely be contained in the following document:
(A) Lien. (B) Declaration of restrictions. (C) Exclusive right to sell. (D) Affirmation.

(B) The initials C.C. & R. represent the words covenants, conditions and restrictions and refer to items that are recorded in a declaration of restrictions for a subdivision.

_____(Lesson Eight - Paragraph 141 - Question 1)_____
The following would be considered to be a part of the "unit" in a condominium project:
(A) The bearing walls. (B) The central heating. (C) The elevator. (D) None of the above.

(D) The unit in space that constitutes the unit purchased consists only of these elements found within the inner walls of that unit. None of the suggested items are ordinarily part of a unit.

_____(Lesson Eight - Paragraph 141 - Question 2)_____
With respect to condominiums, the following is incorrect:
(A) A unit is the portion not owned in common with other condominium owners.
(B) They can be residential, industrial or commercial.
(C) The fact that there are no provisions for tax assessments for individual units is a disadvantage.
(D) "Common areas" means the entire project except units granted or reserved.

(C) An owner of a condominium unit owns the air space in his particular unit. He receives a grant deed to that unit and he will also receive separate tax assessments and levies. He can also apply for and acquire a title insurance policy for his unit. Each unit is owned separately from the condominium project and the common areas are owned as tenants-in-common by all the unit owners.

_____(Lesson Eight - Paragraph 144 - Question 1)_____
The buyer of a condominium other than the original buyer from the subdivider must be given a copy of the:
(A) CC & R's. (B) Bylaws.
(C) Most recent financial statement of the homeowners' association. (D) All of the above.

(D) Real estate law requires that owners provide all of these upon resale of the condominium unit.

_____(Lesson Eight - Paragraph 165 - Question 1)_____
The following could be similar to a planned development in California:
(A) A stock cooperative. (B) A land project. (C) A condominium. (D) A community apartment project.

(B) A planned development is a type of subdivision where the buyer, in addition to getting ownership of the land, also has rights outside the land (such as in a common area, golf course or a riding club). Among the choices, the planned development would be closest to a land project.

_____(Lesson Eight - Paragraph 165 - Question 2)_____
A land project is best defined as:
(A) Ownership of an undivided interest in land coupled with the right of exclusive occupancy of any apartment thereon.
(B) An area populated by more than 1, 500 registered voters within a two-mile area.
(C) 50 or more unimproved lots in a rural area.
(D) Ownership of an undivided interest in common in a portion of a property, together with a separate interest in space in a residential, industrial or commercial building

(C) A land project is defined as 50 or more unimproved lots in a rural area with less than 1,500 registered voters within two miles of the subdivision.

_____(Lesson Eight - Paragraph 166 - Question 1)_____
The Real Estate Commissioner would most likely deny a final report to a subdivider where he:
(A) Provides separate water systems for each lot.
(B) Makes use of private roads for access to the lots.
(C) Makes use of septic tanks for sewage disposal.
(D) Is financially unable to make proposed recreational improvements.

(D) The Real Estate Commissioner is primarily interested in protecting the public from fraud. In his case the public would not be receiving what had been promised in the subdivision public report. The Commissioner would be concerned about (A), (B), and (C) if they differed from what was proposed.

_____(Lesson Eight - Paragraph 207 - Question 1)_____
A land developer offers a free prize to anyone who replies to his direct mail advertisement and visits the site of his subdivision. The subdivider requires the prize winner to attend a sales presentation at the subdivision site prior to awarding them the prize. The sales presentation requirement was not mentioned in the subdivider advertisement. This type of promotion is:
(A) Legal if the prize is actually awarded
(B) Legal only if the prizewinner purchases a property
(C) Illegal because free prizes may not be offered as incentives to buy under any circumstances
(D) Illegal because it did not disclose the sales presentation attendance requirement

(D) Prizes are legal provided that the ad states the conditions to receive the prize require attendance at a sales presentation. Failure to disclose that requirement makes it illegal.

_____(Lesson Eight - Paragraph 211 - Question 1)_____
Riparian Rights:
(A) Give an absolute right to all adjacent waters.
(B) Are identified in the standard policy of title insurance policy.
(C) Are identified found in the County Recorder's files.
(D) Are none of the above.

(D) The owner of land that touches upon a lake or watercourse enjoys the right to reasonable use of such water with others. This is the doctrine of riparian rights. There cannot be absolute ownership of this water by any landowner. These rights run with the land and do not have to be recorded and would not be disclosed in a standard policy of title insurance.

_____(Lesson Eight - Paragraph 211 - Question 2)_____
An owner of real property is in doubt whether or not he has riparian rights. Riparian rights may be found:
(A) By searching the records of the county recorder. (B) Listed in the title policy.
(C) In the grant deed. (D) None of the above.

(D) Riparian rights are not a matter of record but are water rights that go with the land and do not have to be specified in any deed or document.

_____(Lesson Eight - Paragraph 214 - Question 1)_____
Title to land bordering a stream or river that was added through accretion is vested in the:
(A) Federal Government. (B) State Government. (C) Adjoining owners. (D) None of the above.

(C) By statute any land that forms upon the bank of a river or stream, either by accumulation of material (accretion) or recession of the water, belongs to the owner of the existing land along the banks of the river or stream.

_____(Lesson Eight - Paragraph 214 - Question 2)_____

The party that would benefit from an addition to land resulting from a gradual build-up of land by the flow of water in a natural river course by natural causes would be:
(A) Federal government. (B) State government. (C) Local government. (D) Land owner.

(D) Addition to land from a gradual buildup of natural causes is defined as accretion and this land that accretes from a river belongs to the adjoining landowner.

_____(Lesson Eight - Paragraph 215 - Question 1)_____

An owner can lose title to real property in the event of:
(A) Accretion. (B) Certiorari. (C) Erosion. (D) Either A or B.

(C) Land maybe lost by erosion. Through accretion it becomes the property of the person who owns the land on which it settles. Lose by erosion. Gain by accretion.

_____(Lesson Eight - Paragraph 215 - Question 2)_____

When a stream suddenly tears land away from its bank, this is called:
(A) Accretion. (B) Avulsion. (C) Absorption. (D) Alluvium.

(B) When a stream suddenly tears land away, this is called avulsion. This is distinguished from erosion that is the gradual removal of the soil by air or water.

_____(Lesson Eight - Paragraph 217 - Question 1)_____

A non-riparian rights owner of a farm who has been given permission by the state to take surplus water for beneficial use from a non-adjacent lake has received rights by:
(A) Percolation. (B) Accretion. (C) Estoppel. (D) Appropriation.

(D) Public interest requires that there be the greatest number of beneficial uses that the water supply can yield. Surplus water may be appropriated by the state for beneficial use subject to the rights of those who have a lawful priority.

_____(Lesson Eight - Paragraph 217 - Question 2)_____

An owner of land that does not abut a stream may gain rights to the use of excess waters from that stream through procedures established by the State Division of Water Resources by:
(A) Prescription. (B) Appropriation. (C) Accretion. (D) Avulsion.

(B) Basic doctrine on water usage establishes that, "Public interest demands that there be the greatest number of beneficial uses that the water supply can yield and surplus water may be appropriated for private beneficial use subject to the rights of owners and others who have a lawful priority (overlying owners, riparian owners).

_____(Lesson Eight - Paragraph 221 - Question 1)_____

Some cities or counties require an individual who is building a new home to secure a percolation test to obtain a building permit. This test would be used in relation to:
(A) Smog. (B) Water. (C) Sewage disposal. (D) Electricity.

(C) The word "percolate" means to pass or filter a liquid gradually through a porous substance. A septic tank must be built in an area where the soil is porous enough to drain off the accumulated water.

_____(Lesson Eight - Paragraph 221 - Question 2)_____
A percolation test is usually made to learn the:
(A) Necessary depth of footings.
(B) Quantity and potability of well water.
(C) Approximate size of a cistern needed to service a given sized house or farm building.
(D) Ability of the soil to absorb water.

(D) Percolation is the action of the water passing through the soil. Such a test would be very important, for example, when a person is installing a septic tank. The ability of the soil to absorb water will determine the required size a location of the septic facility.

_____(Lesson Eight - Paragraph 226 - Question 1)_____
The owner of a lot at the bottom of a hill during the rainy season directs floodwater onto a vacant lot next door. This action is:
(A) Legal if it protects his property.   (B) Illegal as the adjacent lot is vacant.
(C) Illegal - he should dam the water. (D) Illegal because he may not divert the water.

(A) Legal if it protects his property. Water overflowing a defined channel is considered floodwater and any land owner may protect himself from same by reasonable methods, such as building up the sides of the channel with a dike, even though this might result in the overflow of the channel where it runs across another's land.

_____(Lesson Eight - Paragraph 226 - Question 2)_____
The following would be true regarding floodwaters:
(A) Floodwaters are waters on the surface of the land but lower than the water table in the area
(B) Flood waters are deemed the enemy of every affected owner and owners may protect their property by employing any reasonable protective measure.
(C) Floodwaters are found below the water table, at the water table, and above the water table.
(D) Floodwaters refer to water in minor depths, either standing or flowing, which do not produce serious surfaces scars or leave deposits of silt.

(B) Floodwaters, meaning water from a downpour, or a river overflowing its bank. One may protect himself against such floodwater by building a dike, sand bagging, and other methods of diverting the water to other property owners.

Lesson Eight
Part Three
Understanding Through Question Testing

Log into your course at www.lumbleau.com.

STUDENT LOGIN

Login:
Password:

On your student home page, click on the "State Exam Preparation".

STATE EXAM PREPARATION

Under the "Guided Lesson" tab click on the eighth of fourteen links: "Public Control: Subdivisions".

Real Estate Salesperson Course

Guided Lessons	Practice Exams	Progress Report	Success Video

Print	Questions
Click	HERE>>> **8. Public Control: Subdivisions**

Here you will be tested on all of the questions you have been studying and learn the most recently added questions. It is essential, for maximum retention, that you eliminate all of the questions you can easily answer and "TAG" for study the questions with which you have difficulty.

Lesson Nine
Part One

Understanding Through Video Teaching

Lesson Nine

DISCRIMINATION IN THE SALE AND RENTAL OF RESIDENTIAL REAL ESTATE

1   Race restrictions in deeds prohibiting use or occupancy of real property because of a person's race, color, sex, religion, ancestry, marital status, national origin or physical handicap are not enforceable under both federal and state laws. They are in violation of the fourteenth amendment to the constitution.

FEDERAL REGULATIONS

2   The Civil Rights Act of 1968, which became fully operational in 1970 (Titles VIII, IX and X), is often referred to as the Open Housing or the Fair Housing laws. Congress attempted to establish that in the sale and rental of housing all persons are to be treated equally. All people are to be "color blind" in matters involving the sale or rental of such housing.

3   Should the U.S. Attorney General have reasonable cause to believe that any group of persons has been denied any of the rights granted by this law and where this denial raises an issue of general public importance, he may take action in the appropriate United States district court. If HUD reports a violation, the attorney general must take action.

4   In 1968 with the case of Jones vs. Mayer, the United States Supreme Court reaffirmed the constitutionality of the Civil Rights Act of 1866. This earlier legislation was founded on an interpretation of the Thirteenth Amendment to the United States Constitution that abolished slavery in this country.

5   The Open Housing Laws of 1968 gives administrative authority in matters involving discrimination in the sale and rental of housing to the Department of Housing and Urban Development (HUD). This federal law establishes that complaints of violations are to be made to HUD within 180 days of the alleged discriminatory act.

6   If the complaint is not acted upon within 30 days of being filed with the Secretary then the aggrieved party may commence a civil action in any appropriate United States district court against the party named in the complaint, as long as there would be no state or local fair housing laws which provide remedies similar to those provided by federal law.

7   This federal law also provides that the injured party may act to enforce the rights it bestows on private persons by initiating a civil action in any appropriate federal, state or local court to recover damages for the alleged discriminatory act. Under this federal law the aggrieved parties might recover such actual damages as they are found to have suffered, plus not more than $1,000 in additional punitive damages together with court costs and reasonable attorney fees. Since this is a civil action no criminal penalties are available.

8   Department of Housing and Urban Development (HUD) requests that all real estate agents display the identifying logo shown below as identification that they cooperate with the rules and regulations of the department.

EQUAL HOUSING OPPORTUNITY

8a   It should be noted that acts of discrimination should not be confused with acts of good business. For example: If a broker refuses to take a listing from a member of a minority group because the seller wanted to list the property well above the market, this would not be an act of discrimination.

8b   If an owner asks the listing broker the ethnic background of a person offering to buy the property, the broker is prohibited by law from disclosing this fact.

CREDIT GRANTING AGENCIES

11   In 1974, Congress passed another law in this subject area, the Equal Credit Opportunity Act. The purpose of this law is to forbid mortgage lenders from discriminating against borrowers in making loans because of the person's race, color, religion, national origin, sex, marital status, or because all or part of the applicant's income is from a public assistance program.

CALIFORNIA LAW

14   In California, the legislature's first attempt to legally eliminate racial discrimination in the workplace was to pass the Unruh Civil Rights Act of 1959. This law established that it is against public policy in the State of California for the proprietor of a business to discriminate in their business activity because of a customer's race, color, etc. It also establishes that the same business operators could not discriminate in the hiring and firing of their employees for the same or similar reasons.

15   This Unruh Act now provides that any violation of its provisions can be penalized by requiring the payment of:

16   (1) Actual damages suffered by the injured party.
17   (2) Punitive damages of three times the actual damages but not less than $250.
18   (3) Attorney's fees as determined by the court.

19   In 1963, the California legislature went further in this matter and passed what is called the Rumford Act. This law applies the principles established by the Unruh Act to the sale and rental of housing. Under this law, injured persons can file a complaint with the Fair Employment and Housing Commission within 60 days of the alleged discriminatory act.

20   If a hearing with the Fair Employment and Housing Commission finds the accused to be guilty of an unlawful practice they are to state their findings and issue an order requiring the accused person to cease and desist from such practices and to do one of the following:

21 (1) Complete the sale or rental of the housing accommodation if it is still available. This applies to the sale or rental of a like housing if one is available.

22 (2) Pay punitive damages not to exceed $1,000.

23 (3) Pay any actual damages suffered by the injured party.

24   The next step taken by the California legislature was to enact the Housing Financial Discrimination Act of 1977. Since 1982, this law is familiarly known as the Holden Act. Its purpose is to try to prevent lending institutions from making their lending decisions based upon the conditions, characteristics, and trends in the neighborhood or geographic area surrounding the property offered as security for the loan rather than on the value of the property itself and on the credit worthiness of the prospective borrower. In the real estate business such a practice is called "redlining." In effect, this law determined that the lending practice just described is against public policy in California and prohibited by law.

30   Under the provisions of this law the term "housing accommodation" means any improved or unimproved real property or portion of the same that contains not more than four dwelling units.

33 California law provides that it is unlawful for the owner of a publicly assisted housing accommodation to discriminate in the sale or rental of such accommodation because of a person's race, color, religion, sex, marital status, ancestry, or national origin. In this circumstance, a publicly assisted housing accommodation would include an improved property which is granted an exemption in whole or in part from taxes (except veterans), an improved property on which the improvements were constructed on land sold below cost by the state, or any of its political subdivisions or agency under the Federal Housing Act of 1949. This also applies to improved property which is financed in whole or in part by a government agency, or by the state, or any of its political subdivisions, or any agency thereof.

LENDING INSTITUTIONS

36 Lastly, you must understand another California Law, the Consumer Credit Reporting Agencies Act, which became law in 1970. The purpose of this law was similar to that of the federal Fair Credit Reporting Act of the same year. This California law established the means by which a person who is denied credit or denied an opportunity for employment because of information supplied by a credit reporting agency may proceed to correct the matter. The consumer must be given the name and addresses of the consumer credit reporting agency making the report. The consumer must also be told the nature and substance of adverse information.

37 Under this law any applicant who suffers damages as the result of a violation of the law may bring an action in court to recover the following:

38 Attorney's fees and when applicable, pain and suffering damages.

39 In the case of a willful violation:
(1) Actual damages as shown above.

(2) Punitive damages of not less than $100 nor more than $5000 for each violation as the court deems proper.

(3) Any other relief which the courts deem proper.

FEDERAL CONSUMER CREDIT PROTECTION ACT (Truth in Lending)

41 The Truth in Lending Act became effective July 1, 1969. The principal purpose of this act is to promote the informed use of consumer credit by requiring creditors to disclose credit terms in order to enable consumers to make comparisons between various credit sources. To implement the Act, the Board of Governors of the Federal Reserve System issued a regulation known as Regulation Z.

43 Under this law, the creditor is responsible for furnishing truth in lending disclosures to the consumer. Regulation Z now defines a creditor as any person who extends consumer credit more than 25 times a year or more than 5 times a year for transactions secured by a dwelling. The transaction is limited to loans repayable in five or more installments. The credit extended must be subject to a finance charge or be payable by written agreement in more than four installments. Another requirement is that the obligation be initially payable on its face or by agreement to the person extending the credit. Because of provisions in the Garn-St. Germain Depository Institutions Act of 1982, the Federal Reserve Board amended the revised Regulation Z by removing "arranger of credit" from the "creditor" definition. This action by the Board releases real estate brokers or other arrangers of credit from the responsibility for providing disclosures unless these persons otherwise come within the definition of creditors.

44 Credit report and appraisal fees - The Federal Reserve Board in Regulation Z specifically excludes these two items from the finance charges that are to be disclosed to the borrower on a real estate loan.

45   There are two basic types of transactions that are exempt from coverage under Regulation Z. The first is for credit extended primarily for a business, commercial or agricultural purpose. The second is for credit over $25,000. This dollar limitation does not apply if the loan is secured by real property or by personal property that is used, or expected to be used, as the consumer's principal residence including mobile homes.

46   Regulation Z requires all truth in lending (TIL) disclosures concerning the credit sale or loan to be grouped together and segregated from other information. In addition, it also requires that the terms "finance charge" and "annual percentage rate" be more conspicuous than other required disclosures. The portion of the sale or loan documents that contains these disclosures is commonly called "the federal box." Under the revised Regulation Z, the TIL disclosures must be separate from everything else, but may be continued from one page to another.

47   A creditor is only required to make those disclosures that are relevant to a particular transaction. The disclosure statement must have simple descriptive phrases next to five of the most important items disclosed. These items are: the amount financed, the finance charge, the annual percentage rate, the total of payments and, in credit sales, the total sale prices.

REAL ESTATE SETTLEMENT PROCEDURES ACT (RESPA)

48   Congress enacted the Real Estate Settlement Procedures Act in 1974. They later amended the law in 1976. The purpose of this legislation was to give consumers sufficient information at an early enough time to permit shopping in the marketplace for the best settlement services and costs in transactions involving the purchase of one-to-four family residential real estate. Creditors involved in residential mortgage transactions subject to RESPA are required to make

Regulation Z disclosures before consummation and deliver or place them in the mail within three (3) business days after receiving the consumer's written application, whichever is earlier. If the estimates turn out to be inaccurate, it may be necessary to make another disclosure at consummation. Two events occurring after consummation that require the creditor to make new disclosures are a refinancing or an assumption. The Federal Real Estate Settlement Procedures Act forbids those who must present the Disclosure Settlement Statement to their borrowers from charging a fee for the preparation of the form.

49   The consumer has the right to rescind until midnight of the third business day following the last of these events to occur:
(1) Consummation of the transaction.
(2) Delivery of all material TIL disclosures.
(3) Delivery of the notice of right to rescind.
A business day is any calendar day, except Sundays and federal legal holidays.

51   There are a number of important exceptions to this "right to rescind" applicable to residential real estate transactions. One exemption concerns "residential mortgage transactions." Under this exemption, the right of rescission does not apply to transactions made to finance the acquisition or initial construction of the consumer's principal dwelling and secured by that dwelling regardless of lien status. Hence, second mortgages for the purpose of financing an acquisition are no longer subject to the right of rescission. Another exemption is for refinancing by the same creditor of a loan already secured by the principal dwelling, provided no new money is advanced. If new money is advanced, the transaction is rescindable to the extent of the new money if the loan is secured by the consumer's principal dwelling.

53   One placing an advertisement for consumer credit must comply with the advertising requirements of the Truth-in-Lending Act and Regulation Z. Hence, real estate brokers and home builders who

advertise credit terms must comply even if they are not creditors in the financing being advertised. Disclosures in credit advertisements must be made "clearly and conspicuously." If the finance charge in a credit advertisement is expressed as a rate, it must be stated as an "annual percentage rate" using that term. Prices cannot be advertised as a percentage of a non-expressed value.

54   An advertisement for a variable rate with an initial annual percentage rate of 14% that may vary after settlement without any limit could be advertised as "14% annual percentage rate subject to increase after settlement." This may not be used in advertisements of graduated payment mortgages that have a fixed interest rate and payments that increase during the loan. Such mortgages involve different interest rates in effect during the life of the loan, all of which are known at settlement. This kind of mortgage note often creates a negative amortization increasing the amount of the loan instead of paying it off. A variable rate transaction involves future interest rates unknown at settlement.

55   If only the annual percentage rate is disclosed in advertising, additional disclosures are not required. If an advertisement contains any one of the following terms then the ad must also disclose other credit terms:
(1) The amount or percentage of any down payment.
(2) The number of payments or period of repayment.
(3) The amount of any payment.
(4) The amount of any finance charge.

56   However, an ad that states "100% financing" requires no further disclosures because no down payment is required.

57   The Federal Trade Commission is charged with the enforcement of the Truth-in-lending Act and Regulation Z with respect to real estate mortgage loan brokers and mortgage bankers. In the event of conviction for a violation, a creditor may be liable to a consumer for a statutory penalty of twice the amount of the finance charge with a minimum of $100 and a maximum of $1,000. This statutory liability applies only to seven specific violations.

58   A creditor is also subject to a fine of not more than $5,000 or imprisonment for not more than one year, or both, for willfully and knowingly violating the TIL Act or Regulation Z by giving false or inaccurate information, failing to provide required disclosures, or consistently understating the annual percentage rate.

REDLINING

59   When lending institutions attempt to limit their liability for loans by restricting their loans on real property only to those neighborhoods where the more affluent credit responsible homeowners are to be found, the practice is called redlining. The name comes from the practice of drawing a red line on a map and not making loans on the side they have determined to be racially or ethnically undesirable.

BLOCKBUSTING

60   This form of discrimination has been practiced since the early 1930's. It takes on many forms, the most basic of which is the persuasion of homeowners in a given neighborhood to sell because buyers of a different racial or ethnic heritage were moving into the area.

STEERING

62   Steering is the practice of driving a buyer only to neighborhoods where the homeowners were not bigoted about having a person of a different heritage live in the community. The agent literally steers his automobile into neighborhoods that are racially and ethnically mixed.

COVERED TRANSACTIONS

64   RESPA covers mortgages and trust deeds on 1 to 4 family homes including mobile homes, condominiums and cooperatives financed by a federally regulated lender as defined in the act. This includes loans made through FHA, VA or with other government assistance and loans from financial institutions with FDIC or FSLIC insurance on deposits.

SPECIAL INFORMATION BOOKLET GOOD FAITH ESTIMATES

81   The lender must give the borrower a special information booklet on settlement costs. This is a written estimate of the charges the borrower is likely to incur at settlement (other than for escrow, taxes, and insurance premiums) and must be given at the time of loan application or within three business days thereafter. If the lender requires that a settlement service be provided by a particular person or firm (legal services, title insurance, etc.), the lender must:
(1) Inform the borrower of the requirement.
(2) Provide cost estimates for the service.
(3) Disclose the name, address, and telephone number of each provider.
(4) Give a statement disclosing whether or not each provider has a business relationship with the lender.

82   A "settlement statement" must be delivered upon settlement with the following exceptions:

(1) Borrower may waive his right to receive the statement at settlement by executing a written waiver.
(2) When the borrower or his agent do not attend or are not required to attend the settlement.

84   "Kickback" or unearned fees - The law prohibits any person giving or accepting any type of compensation unless a service was actually performed to earn it. The law does not prohibit the payment of reasonable salary or compensation for services actually performed. Specifically permitted are payments pursuant to cooperative brokerage and referral arrangements between real estate brokers. Violators are subject to criminal penalties ($10,000 fine or one year's imprisonment) and liability up to three times the value of the illegal compensation in each suit, plus court costs and attorney's fees.

85   RESPA now prohibits a lender from requiring escrow impounds for taxes, insurance and other charges in excess of the amount of money needed to make a specific payment plus an amount equal to two months payments for such charges.

86   Election of title company - No seller (primarily builders and developers) may directly or indirectly require a buyer to purchase title insurance from a particular company. Violators are subject to a penalty of three times the charges for the insurance.

86a   The buyer has the right to select a specific loan provider.

REAL ESTATE INVESTMENT TRUSTS (REITs)

88   In 1960 the Real Estate Investment Trust Act was enacted by the U.S. Congress adding sections to the Internal Revenue Code. The Act became effective January 1, 1961. A real estate investment trust (REIT) is an unincorporated trust or association of at least 100 investors owning real property or mortgages. In actual fact, a real estate investment trust is an entity that is allowed to do business to some degree as if it were a corporation. Were it not for the tax exemption provided by law, the REIT would be taxed as a corporation. Investors become shareholders in these trusts. Although unincorporated, The Commissioner of Corporations has full supervisory powers over REIT's.

THREE TYPES OF REIT'S

91   Equity trusts - This type of trust is involved essentially in the ownership of real property and its chief source of income is rent and the offset of inflation through appreciation.

92   Mortgage trusts - In this case the assets are invested in short-term and long-term mortgages or other liens against real property. They lend money and receive income in the form of interest.

93   Combination trusts – These develop property, own property, lease property, provide mortgage financing, and make land development loans. Income is derived from both rent and interest.

REAL ESTATE SYNDICATION
GENERAL PROVISIONS

105   A typical real estate syndication combines the money of individual investors with the management of a sponsor and has a three-phase cycle: origination (planning, acquiring property, satisfying registration and disclosure rules, and marketing); operation (sponsor usually operates both the syndicate and the real property); and liquidation or completion (the resale of the property). A typical syndication is a limited partnership in which the investors providing the funds are the limited partners and the sponsor providing the management is the general partner. A general partnership would be inadvisable as all partners would become individually liable for the entire debts of the partnership.

SYNDICATION ADVANTAGES

106   Leverage is the key ingredient. One person joining others to invest in a large syndicate may receive a return on invested capital in excess of that which can be obtained through individual purchases.

107   By pooling limited financial resources with others who are similarly situated, a small-scale investor is afforded an opportunity to participate in ownership and operation of a piece of property that is too much to handle singly or in a joint venture with one or two others. This affords liquidity to participants because their shares are transferable on the market or through the trust.

108   Often more than one property is involved with a syndication. The "blind-pool" syndication buys and sells multiple properties with the investors having little or no knowledge of the properties being purchased or sold until the annual report is issued.

SYNDICATE FORMS

110   The entity selection involves practical as well as legal and tax considerations. Each of the available entities offers advantages as well as disadvantages. The corporate form insures centralized management as well as limited liability for the investors but is seldom utilized in modem syndicates because of its negative tax features. The general partnership (joint venture) avoids the double taxation normally involved in a corporate entity but the unlimited liability provision and lack of centralized management militate against its use. The limited partnership combines nearly all of the advantages of the corporate and partnership forms. It has the corporate advantages of limited liability, centralized management, and the tax advantages of the partnership. Consequently, the limited partnership form of organization is the one most frequently selected for real estate syndicates.

110a The application for the sale of real estate syndicate securities must be submitted to the Commissioner of Corporations and be accompanied by the appropriate fee.

LIMITED PARTNERSHIP

111   Under the California Limited Partnership Act, a limited partner is not liable as a general partner unless the limited partner is named as a general partner in the certificate of limited partnership or the limited partner participates in the control of the business. If the limited partnership agreement otherwise qualifies, the limited partnership is taxed as a partnership rather than as an association taxable as a corporation.

Lesson Nine
Part Two
Study Questions

_____(Lesson Nine - Paragraph 1 - Question 1)_____

Regarding the conveyance of a deed including race restrictions:
(A) The deed is valid, but race restrictions are unenforceable. (B) The deed is void.
(C) The deed is voidable. (D) The deed is valid and the race restrictions are enforceable.

(A) Race restrictions in a deed were declared to be unenforceable by the Supreme Court shortly after World War II. The deed is valid and conveys a proper title, but any restrictions as to race are totally unenforceable.

_____(Lesson Nine - Paragraph 1 - Question 2)_____

Able sold a property to Baker by grant deed. In the deed Able inserted a deed restriction stating, "the property conveyed by this deed may be resold only to members of the Caucasian race." Under these circumstances, the deed is:
(A) Valid and the restriction is enforceable because it does not discriminate against a particular ethnic or racial group.
(B) Valid, however, the restriction is unenforceable.
(C) Voidable at option of grantee.
(D) Void.

(B) A deed containing a race restriction is a valid conveyance of title, however, the restriction itself was declared to be unenforceable (the courts may not be used to enforce it or to sue for damages) by the U.S. Supreme Court in 1948, based upon the 14th Amendment to the U.S. Constitution (equal protection under the law.)

_____(Lesson Nine - Paragraph 2 - Question 1)_____

A prospect of Mexican-American ancestry asks to be shown three bedroom homes without specifying a particular area. As a licensee you should:
(A) Show his properties in a Mexican-American neighborhood only.
(B) Show him properties that are not located in a Mexican-American neighborhood.
(C) Refer him to a broker who specialized in properties for minorities.
(D) Treat him as you would any other prospect.

(D) A licensee must treat all prospects alike without preference for race, color, sex, religion or national origin.

_____(Lesson Nine - Paragraph 2 - Question 2)_____

The type of property an agent should show a Mexican-American if the Mexican-American does not ask to look at properties in a Mexican-American community is:
(A) Only homes in an Anglo community.
(B) Only homes in a Mexican-American community.
(C) Only homes in which the majority of the residents are members of a minority group.
(D) Any property that is available.

(D)   If any person asks to be shown property, you would treat that person as any other person and show any property that is available.

_____(Lesson Nine - Paragraph 2 - Question 3)_____
The Civil Rights Act, Title VIII, (commonly referred to as the Open Housing Law) applies in the sale or rental of which of the following types of housing:
(A)   Dwellings owned or operated by the federal government.
(B)   Dwellings provided in whole or in part with the aid of loans or advances made by the federal government under agreements entered into after November 20, 1962, unless payment thereon has been made in full prior to the date of enactment of this act.
(C)   Property financed by state funds generated through federal assistance after Nov. 20, 1962
(D)   All of the above.

___

(D)   The choices outline major provisions of this federal law.

_____(Lesson Nine - Paragraph 3 - Question 1)_____
Should there be a violation of the provisions of the Civil Rights Act of 1968 Title VIII Fair Housing, the aggrieved person may seek relief by:
(A) Filing a civil action in state court.
(B) Filing a civil action in a federal district court.
(C) Filing a complaint with the secretary of Housing and Urban Development.
(D) Any of the above.

___

(D) In a case of this nature federal law offers the aggrieved party the opportunity of choosing any one of the means suggested in seeking a remedy for the violation of law.

_____(Lesson Nine - Paragraph 3 - Question 2)_____
The United States Attorney General would prosecute a complaint lodged by two or three persons involving racial discrimination in housing at the direction of the following agency:
(A) Fair Employment Practices Commission.
(B) Federal Housing Administration.
(C) Secretary of Housing and Urban Development.
(D) Department of Human Resources.

___

(C) The Civil Rights Act of 1968 provides that the Attorney General of the United States shall conduct all litigation in which the Secretary of HUD participates as a party.

_____(Lesson Nine - Paragraph 4 - Question 1)_____
The following court case, which was ruled upon by the Supreme Court of the United States in 1968, has had far-reaching effects upon recent legislative actions and court rulings throughout the country regarding discrimination on the part of homeowners and their agents in the sale and rental of residential property:
(A) Pann vs. Lawrence.
(B) Jones vs. Mayer.
(C) Bidwell vs. Smith.
(D) Clav vs. Robertson.

___

(B) This case originated in the St. Louis, Missouri courts and the Supreme Court decision was handed down in July 1968. The decision prohibits discrimination because of race, color, religion or natural origin in the sale and rental of dwellings.

―――――――――(Lesson Nine - Paragraph 4 - Question 2)―――――――――

In a now famous court decision handed down in July 1968, the Supreme Court of the United States interpreted and applied a law enacted in 1866 prohibiting discrimination because of race, color, religion or national origin everywhere in the United States. The constitutionality of this decision was based upon:
(A) The First Amendment of the Constitution.
(B) The Thirteenth Amendment of the Constitution.
(C) An opinion of the National Association of Lawyers and Legislative Advocates.
(D) The Rumford Act.

(B) This decision rested its constitutionality on the Thirteenth Amendment of the Constitution of the United States - the amendment prohibiting slavery.

―――――――――(Lesson Nine - Paragraph 8 - Question 1)―――――――――

This symbol is used to identify which of the following:
(A) Equal opportunity employer.
(B) Equal housing opportunity.
(C) Plumber's and carpenter's union.
(D) Fair housing.

(B) The department of Housing and Urban Development (HUD) requires that all types of firms dealing with the sale or rental of housing units must display a poster dealing with discrimination. The poster is embellished with this symbol or logo and beneath it the statement, "Equal Housing Opportunity."

―――――――――(Lesson Nine - Paragraph 11 - Question 1)―――――――――

The Equal Credit Opportunity Act that was enacted in 1974 to:
(A) Set uniform interest rates on real estate loans in the country.
(B) Set minimum requirements to enable a person to make credit purchases.
(C) Prohibit discrimination based on the sex and marital status of the credit applicant in the extension of credit.
(D) Set uniform standards for the documents used in extending credit.

(C) This choice presents a brief statement of the legitimate reasons why this federal law was enacted.

―――――――――(Lesson Nine - Paragraph 11 - Question 2)―――――――――

The Equal Credit Opportunity Act that was enacted in 1974 to:
(A) Set uniform interest rates on real estate loans in the country.
(B) Set minimum requirements to qualify a person to make credit purchases.
(C) Forbid discrimination based on sex and marital status in the extension of credit.
(D) None of the above.

(C) The effect of this legislation was to ensure that lenders would give full credit to a woman's income when qualifying her for a loan.

_____(Lesson Nine - Paragraph 19 - Question 1)_____
An example of property that is controlled by the provisions of the government code that prohibits discrimination in housing is a:
(A) Twenty unit apartment building.
(B) Single family unencumbered residence.
(C) Single family FHA financed residence.
(D) Any of the above.

(D) The Rumford Act (in the government code) forbids discrimination because of the race, creed, religion, etc. in the sale or lease of any of the properties listed in the question.

_____(Lesson Nine - Paragraph 19 - Question 2)_____
Under the provisions of the California Fair Housing Legislation of 1963, the person filing a complaint with the proper authority must take action for the violation within:
(A) 30 days of the alleged violation.
(B) 60 days of the alleged violation.
(C) 180 days of the alleged violation.
(D) 1 year of the alleged violation.

(B) The complaint must be filed with the Fair Employment and Housing Commission within 60 days of the occurrence of the alleged violation under the provisions of the Fair Housing Laws of California (Govt. Code #12980).

_____(Lesson Nine - Paragraphs 20 to 23 - Question 1)_____
According to the provisions of the Fair Housing Law of California, known as the Rumford Act, discrimination includes all of the following kinds of actions, except:
(A) The refusal by the owner to rent an unencumbered single family residence to a member of a minority race.
(B) The refusal by the owner to negotiate for the sale of an unencumbered duplex because of the prospect's race or national origin.
(C) The refusal to rent a portion of an owner-occupied single-family house to a minority person as a boarder living within the household.
(D) The cancellation of a sales contract by the owner of an unencumbered fourplex because of the purchaser's religious beliefs.

(C) This is the one circumstance mentioned in the present version of the Rumford Act that is excluded in the law from being a discriminatory act.

_____(Lesson Nine - Paragraphs 21 to 23 - Question 1)_____
A real estate broker found guilty of discrimination in the leasing of an apartment may:
(A) Be liable for $250 for each offense. (B) Be charged actual damages.
(C) Have his license revoked.   (D) Subject to all of the above.

(D) A broker is subject to all of the stated penalties if he discriminates because of race, creed or ethnic origin.

_____(Lesson Nine - Paragraphs 21 to 23 - Question 2)_____
A property owner is charged with discrimination in the sale of housing accommodations. If, after a hearing the Fair Employment and Housing Commission finds that a violation did take place, it may:
(A) Order the sale of the property to the injured party if it is still available.
(B) Order the sale of a like accommodation if one is available.
(C) Order the payment of punitive damages not exceeding $1,000 and actual damages.
(D) Do any of the above

(D) All of these choices are remedies available to the Fair Employment Housing Commission.

_____(Lesson Nine - Paragraphs 21 to 23 - Question 3)_____
A subdivider was investigated by the Fair Employment and Housing Commission on a complaint that he had violated the California Fair Housing Act in the sale of a home. The commission decided he had violated the law. They may:
(A) Require the subdivider to go through with the sale of the home.
(B) Sell a similar home if the original is no longer available.
(C) Pay up to $500 in damages.
(D) Do any of the above.

(D) All of the answers listed are under the authority of the Fair Employment & Housing Commission.

_____(Lesson Nine - Paragraph 24 - Question 1)_____
The practice of denying mortgage loans or adversely varying the terms of such loans because of conditions, characteristics, or trends in a neighborhood or geographic area at or unrelated to the credit worthiness of the applicant or the value of the real property security is:
(A) Unlawful in California.   (B) Identified as "redlining."
(C) Against public policy in California. (D) All of the above.

(D) All of the above. This question is almost a direct quote from one of the provisions of the Holden Act that was known originally as the Housing Financial Discrimination Act of 1977.

_____(Lesson Nine - Paragraphs 36 to 39 - Question 1)_____
Mr. and Mrs. Robertson were denied a home loan due to an extremely critical credit report. They obtained a copy of the report and found that the grievous information contained in the report was false. They sent the credit reporting agency all the information necessary to disprove the false information and requested that they correct their records. Should the credit reporting agency fail to correct the information in their files, the Robertsons could file a court action and seek:
(A) Actual damages, plus court costs and attorney's fees. (B) Damages for pain and suffering.
(C) Punitive damages up to a maximum of $5,000.   (D) Any of the above.

(D) Failure of the credit reporting agency to correct false information contained in their files could lead to a law suit and could include all listed choices.

_____(Lesson Nine - Paragraph 41 - Question 1)_____
The Consumer Credit Protection Act affecting "truth in lending" for persons who seek consumer credit became effective:
(A) June 1, 1969.   (B) May 31, 1969.   (C) July 1, 1969. (D) June 30, 1969.

(C) This portion of the Consumer Credit Protection Act became effective July 1, 1969.

_____(Lesson Nine - Paragraph 43 - Question 1)_____

By the provisions of Federal Truth in Lending Law the required disclosures to people seeking certain forms of consumer credit must be made by people who "arrange" for the extension of credit. In the instance where a seller arranges to carry back a second trust deed note as part of the purchase price for the buyer's residence:

(A) This seller would be identified as an "arranger of credit" and must make the required disclosure.
(B) This seller would not be identified as an "arranger of credit" and need not make the required disclosures.
(C) The first trust deed lender would be required to make disclosures on all loans needed to complete the purchase.
(D) The first trust deed lender must make disclosures regarding the amount of the finance charge for the credit he happens to extend.

_____

(B) Under this law, the creditor is responsible for furnishing truth in lending disclosures to the consumer. Regulation Z now defines a creditor as any person who extends consumer credit more than 25 times a year or more than 5 times a year for transactions secured by a dwelling. This does not define a seller "carry back".

_____(Lesson Nine - Paragraph 45 - Question 1)_____

Federal truth in lending regulations does not require that certain disclosures be made by creditors to buyers seeking credit in the purchase of:

(A) Any industrial lot.
(B) Vacant land which he intends to hold for investment other than his residence.
(C) Vacant land on which he intends to construct improvements to produce future income.
(D) None of the above applies.

_____

(D) Regulation Z does not apply to extensions of credit to organizations including governments, business, or commercial purposes other than agricultural purposes.

_____(Lesson Nine - Paragraph 45 - Question 2)_____

Mr. John Hardwick purchased a parcel of land on which he planned to build a deluxe 4-unit apartment structure. When completed, the property had a projected value of $400,000. Mr. Hardwick did not plan to live at this location. In seeking the necessary first trust deed financing of approximately $200,000, the owner could be certain that:

(A) Federal truth in lending regulations does not apply to this financing as the buyer was not going to reside on the property.
(B) Federal truth in lending regulations does not apply because of the amount of the loan sought.
(C) Federal truth in lending regulations requires the broker involved to give a disclosure statement regarding the finance charges.
(D) Federal truth in lending regulations requires the lender to give a disclosure statement regarding the finance charges.

_____

(B) Federal truth in lending does not apply to loans for over $25,000 where the property is not to be used as a personal residence.

_____(Lesson Nine - Paragraph 48 - Question 1)_____

Under the provisions of the Real Estate Settlement and Procedures Act (RESPA), estimates of the amounts of all the following charges must be disclosed at the time of closing, except:

(A) Credit report.   (B) Loan document preparation.
(C) Appraisal fees.   (D) Uniform settlement statement preparation costs.

_____

(D) Uniform settlement statement preparation costs. Federal law prohibits charging a fee for the preparation of this document.

_____(Lesson Nine - Paragraph 48 - Question 2)_____
Federal law requires that lenders present borrowers a disclosure settlement statement prior to concluding loan arrangements involved in the purchase of certain residential real estate. For the preparation of the required form, the lender may charge the borrower:
(A) 1/2 of 1% of the loan. (B) Nothing. (C) I% of the loan. (D) $25.

(B) Nothing. The Federal Real Estate Settlement Procedures Act which became effective June 20, 1975, forbids those who must present the disclosure settlement statement to their borrowers from charging a fee for the preparation of the form.

_____(Lesson Nine - Paragraph 49 - Question 1)_____
Kelly borrowed $4,000 on a note secured by a second mortgage on his residence. The note was signed on May 2. The notice of right to cancel was given on May 3. The funds were deposited in escrow on May 4. The disclosure statement was delivered on May 5. Under these circumstances, the Truth in Lending Act gives Kelly the right to rescind the transaction until midnight of the third business day following the date:
(A) The note was signed.   (B) Escrow was signed.
(C) Funds were deposited in escrow.   (D) Delivery of the disclosure statement.

(D) Delivery of the required disclosures has been made. When the borrower has a right of rescission, the three-day period begins the date the transaction is consummated or the date the delivery of the required disclosures are made, whichever is later.

_____(Lesson Nine - Paragraph 51 - Question 1)_____
A lender would be exempt from the requirement of providing the borrower with a Federal Right to Rescind Notice in all of the following instances, except:
(A) When the borrower is refinancing his personal residence.
(B) When the loan is for business expansion.
(C) When the security for the loan is commercial property.
(D) When the loan is for more than $25,000 and it is not secured by the borrower's personal residence.

(A) A negative question. It states that all of the statements are exemptions except. Refinancing your personal residence is not an exemption and is fully covered by a three-day right of rescission. The other choices are all exempt from a right of rescission.

_____(Lesson Nine - Paragraph 51 - Question 2)_____
According to the provisions of the federal truth in lending regulations, should the purchaser of real property for his principal place of residence make use of a first trust deed loan to complete the purchase, he could:
(A) Rescind the agreement without penalty as his constitutional right.
(B) Not rescind the offer without liability for possible damages or other appropriate legal action by the seller.
(C) Rescind the offer within three business days after his offer.
(D) Rescind the offer within three business days after receiving the required disclosure statement.

(B) The Federal Reserve Board tells us that a first mortgage to finance the purchase of your customer's residence carries no right to rescind or cancel.

_____(Lesson Nine - Paragraph 51 - Question 3)_____

Jackson purchased a residence for his family using a first trust deed loan from a federally chartered bank to do so. He was given no written notification of his right to withdraw his offer to borrow the money. This was so because:

(A) Federal savings and loan associations are exempt from truth in lending regulations.

(B) This type of loan is exempt from the right of rescission required in truth in lending.

(C) The amount of the loan he obtained is not subject to the truth in lending statute.

(D) The written notice of right of rescission need be given to borrowers only on loans which would be the first such loan on that particular property.

(B) The pamphlet on truth in lending published by the Federal Reserve Bank states that, "A first mortgage to finance the purchase of a customer's residence carries no right to cancel or rescind."

_____(Lesson Nine - Paragraph 53 - Question 1)_____

According to the provisions of the truth in lending law, the following is an illegal advertisement regarding a real estate loan:

(A) 11% APR.

(B) Dial 1-800-For-Loan.

(C) 65% loan of what our appraiser states the property is worth.

(D) All of the above are prohibited by the truth in lending law.

(C) The truth in lending law concerning advertising contains what are known as "triggers". If you place in the ad a statement about the amount of down payment, then you must state all the facts: You must state the APR, the amount of the monthly payment, and the length of the loan. In this question, choice (C) is stating that the down payment is 35%. That statement alone is unlawful without also including all the facts of the loan: Monthly payment, APR, length. Choice (A) is proper. You may advertise the APR without a complete explanation of the financing. (B) - A phone number in the ad is not a trigger. Consequently (A) and (B) are not triggers, and (C) is.

_____(Lesson Nine - Paragraph 53 - Question 2)_____

The Federal Truth in Lending Act requires that lenders disclose to borrowers the annual percentage rate being charged on the loan. In this usage, annual percentage rate means:

(A) The complete direct and indirect costs of the loan to be paid by the borrower.

(B) The relative cost of the loan to the borrower expressed in percentage terms.

(C) The interest, time price differential and any discount paid by the borrower to obtain the loan.

(D) None of the above.

(B) The relative cost of the loan to the borrower expressed in percentage terms. It is described in this fashion by the Federal Reserve Board.

_____(Lesson Nine - Paragraphs 53 to 55 - Question 1)_____

When a real estate broker advertises properties he must make certain credit disclosures in his advertisements where financing is involved. All of the following must be disclosed, except:

(A) The amount of the cash price.

(B) A description of the property.

(C) The rate of the finance charges expressed as an annual percentage rate.

(D) The amount of the down payment or that none is required.

(B) A description of the property need not be given as far as truth in lending regulations is concerned. Disclosure of choices (A), (C), and (D) are required by federal law and in addition the advertiser must reveal the number, amount, and due date or period of payments scheduled to repay the indebtedness if credit is extended.

_____(Lesson Nine - Paragraph 54 - Question 1)_____

When a mortgage company is advertising a graduated mortgage, under the Truth in Lending Act the advertisement must include the:
(A) Name of the broker.
(B) Name of the lending institution.
(C) Difference in monthly payments.
(D) All of the above

(C) The truth in lending law requires an advertisement concerning a graduated payment loan to distinctly illustrate the increases in monthly payment.

_____(Lesson Nine - Paragraph 60 - Question 1)_____

The practice of making written or oral statements creating fear and alarm, and making written or oral threats, or warnings to induce, or attempt to induce the sale or lease of real property through any representation regarding the prospective entry of one or more persons of another race, color, sex, religion, ancestry, or national origin into an area or neighborhood is a violation of:
(A) California state law.   (B) Federal open housing legislation.
(C) Both (A) and (B).   (D) Neither (A) nor (B).

(C) Both (A) and (B). This question describes a practice generally called block busting or panic selling. Such practices are contrary to both federal and state statutes.

_____(Lesson Nine - Paragraph 60 - Question 2)_____

A licensee contacts owners of homes in an area indicating that they should list their homes for sale with him because African-Americans may be moving into the area. The following would not apply:
(A) Block busting. (B) Encouraging to panic sell.
(C) Illegal.   (D) Legal but unethical.

(D) This is a negative question and asks for the incorrect answer. Spreading rumors of certain ethnic groups or religions moving into an area is said to be block busting, panic selling, and is illegal against both federal and state law. (D) is incorrect because it states the action is legal.

_____(Lesson Nine - Paragraph 62 - Question 1)_____

An agent is showing a Mexican-American some single-family residences. In doing so, the agent avoids certain areas in which Caucasians reside. This is called:
(A) Steering. (B) Blockbusting. (C) Red lining. (D) Pyramiding.

(A)   If an agent, by his actions, deliberately avoids certain areas for certain clients, it is called steering which is a violation of both real estate law and federal law.

_____(Lesson Nine - Paragraph 64 to 66 - Question 1)_____

The Real Estate Settlement Procedures Act ("RESPA") applies to first trust deed loans made by a federally regulated lender for the purchase of:
(A) All residential property.   (B) All real property.
(C) All single family homes.   (D) All owner-occupied 1-4 unit residential properties.

(D) The Real Estate Settlement Procedures Act, RESPA applies only to federally related first trust deeds secured by owner-occupied one-to-four unit residential properties.

_____(Lesson Nine - Paragraph 64 to 66 - Question 2)_____
The Real Estate Settlement Procedures Act (RESPA) was passed to:
(A) Oversee home improvement loan applications.
(B) Control loan application processing.
(C) Establish uniform procedures regarding disclosures, pro-rations, etc. regarding 1-4 unit residential properties.
(D) Regulate non-federally regulated mortgages.

(C) RESPA was established by congress to make certain borrowers received sufficient information concerning costs in order to select the best loan. Again, RESPA applies only to first trust deeds on one-to-four unit residential properties.

_____(Lesson Nine - Paragraph 81 - Question 1)_____
The Real Estate Settlement Procedures Act requires lenders who grant loans under the jurisdiction of this federal law to make a good faith estimate of the cost of settlement services and give the borrower a copy of a "special information booklet" authorized by the Department of Housing and Urban Development to their borrowers:
(A) At least 12 days prior to the closing date of the loan transaction.
(B) On the day previous to the closing of the loan transaction.
(C) Within one week after the date the loan application is made.
(D) At the time of the loan application or within three business days following the loan application.

(D) At the time of the loan application or within three business days following the loan application. This is a specific requirement of the Real Estate Settlement Procedures Act.

_____(Lesson Nine - Paragraph 81 - Question 2)_____
Under the provisions of RESPA, a federally related lender makes a real estate loan for a person to purchase a home. The lender must furnish the borrower a copy of a special information booklet prepared by HUD no later than three business days from the date:
(A) The borrower requests a copy.
(B) The lender received the borrower's loan application.
(C) The uniform settlement statement is delivered to the borrower.
(D) Of the opening of escrow for the sales transaction.

(B) The Real Estate Settlement Procedures Act specifically requires the lender to furnish a copy of this information booklet and a good faith estimate of the anticipated closing costs within three business days of taking the borrower's application.

_____(Lesson Nine - Paragraph 82 - Question 1)_____
Under the provisions of the Real Estate Settlement and Procedures Act (RESPA), estimates of the amounts of all the following charges must be disclosed at time of closing, except:
(A) Credit report.   (B) Loan document preparation.
(C) Appraisal fees.   (D) Uniform Settlement Statement preparation costs.

(D) Uniform Settlement Statement preparation costs. Federal law prohibits charging a fee for the preparation of this document.

_____(Lesson Nine - Paragraph 82 - Question 2)_____

In the absence of a waiver by the borrower, the disclosure settlement statement must be delivered by the lender to the borrower as required by the Real Estate Settlement Procedures Act:
(A) Within 10 days of the submission of the loan application by the borrower.
(B) At least 3 days prior to the settlement date.
(C) On the day previous to the settlement date.
(D) On or before the settlement date.

_____

(D) On or before the settlement date. Federal law places this obligation upon the lender. The lender is not permitted to charge any fee for the preparation of this statement. The statement should be delivered by the lender to the borrower on or before closing the transaction.

_____(Lesson Nine - Paragraph 84 - Question 1)_____

A broker has discovered that one of his salespersons received a referral fee from a lender. The broker does only the following two things: He fires the salesperson and warns the rest of his office salespeople not to do the same thing. The effect of this would be that:
(A) There is no cause for disciplinary action by the Real Estate Commissioner.
(B) The salesperson is guilty of commingling.
(C) The broker is not guilty of anything because he had no prior knowledge and he discharged the salesperson.
(D) Both the salesperson and the broker are subject to disciplinary action by the Commissioner.

_____

(D) The real estate law requires a broker who discharges a sales person for a license violation must make a certified statement of the cause to the Real Estate Commissioner forthwith (immediately). In this question, both parties have violated real estate law. The salesperson violated law by accepting the referral fee and the broker violated real estate law by his failure to submit a statement.

_____(Lesson Nine - Paragraph 84 - Question 2)_____

A real estate broker sends all of his title insurance business to XYZ Title Company and receives a referral fee. This is:
(A) Acceptable, providing all parties to the transaction has been informed.   (B) Illegal.
(C) Acceptable, if broker has a listing and seller is paying for the title charges. (D) Good business.

_____

(B) RESPA prohibits any person giving or accepting any type of compensation unless a service was actually performed to earn it.

_____(Lesson Nine - Paragraph 85 - Question 1)_____

According to the provisions of the Real Estate Settlement Procedures Act, lenders who require monthly pro-rata payments for taxes and fire insurance in addition to the regular loan payments are limited in the amount of money they can require for such accounts. The limitation is based on what owes since the previous regular payment made, plus an amount equivalent to:
(A) One month's payment for these charges.   (B) Two month's payments for these charges.
(C) Six month's payments for these charges.   (D) None of the above.

_____

(B) Two month's payments for these charges. This is limited by RESPA.

_____(Lesson Nine - Paragraph 86 - Question 1)_____

Spencer, in selling property financed by a Federal Savings Bank, insisted that the buyer use ABC Title Company in purchasing the title insurance policy even though the purchase contract made it a condition of the sale that the buyer pays the cost of this policy. The purchase agreement has been signed and escrow has been opened. The agreement regarding the title insurance is:

(A) A violation of real estate law.
(B) A violation of federal law and the buyer can recoup.
(C) Not a violation of law as parties can agree to such a condition in a civil contract.
(D) Not a violation of law as the seller traditionally chooses the title company.

_____

(B) A violation of federal law and the buyer can recoup three times the costs for the title policy. This is a matter required under the provisions of the Real Estate Settlement Procedures Act (RESPA). Where a federally related mortgage loan is used in the purchase of a residence, the seller is denied the ability to require that the buyer use a specific title insurance company. Should a seller violate this law, he is liable to the buyer in an amount equal to three times all the charges made for the title insurance.

_____(Lesson Nine - Paragraph 88 - Question 1)_____

The following type of syndicate requires at least 100 participants:
(A) Corporation.   (B) Real estate investment trust.   (C) Limited partnership.   (D) Joint venture.

_____

(B) Specifically defined, a real estate investment trust is an unincorporated trust or association of at least 100 investors owning real property or mortgages.

_____(Lesson Nine - Paragraph 107 - Question 1)_____

Lack of liquidity is a disadvantage to real property ownership. It may be overcome by:
(A) Alienation. (B) Hypothecation. (C) Syndication. (D) Segregation.

_____

(C) One of the advantages claimed for the syndicate form of ownership is the easier and faster resale of shares of ownership in a limited partnership or corporation, as compared to an undivided interest in a fee ownership.

Notes

Lesson Nine
Part Three
Understanding Through Question Testing

 Log into your course at www.lumbleau.com.

STUDENT LOGIN
Login:
Password:

 On your student home page click on the first link to take existing courses.

HERE>>>» Click Take Existing Courses

 Another page will appear on your monitor.
Click on the link to take State exam passing lessons.

HERE>>>» Click State exam passing lessons

 Under the "Guided Lesson" tab click on the ninth of fourteen links:
"Discrimination and Syndication".

Real Estate Salesperson Course

Guided Lessons	Practice Exams	Progress Report	Success Video

Print Click	Questions
	HERE>>> 9. Discrimination and Syndication 123

Here you will be tested on all of the questions you have been studying and learn the most recently added questions. It is essential, for maximum retention, that you eliminate all of the questions you can easily answer and "TAG" for study the questions with which you have difficulty.

Lesson Ten
Part One

Understanding Through Video Teaching

Lesson Ten

CONTRACTS

40   A contract is defined as, "An agreement between two or more persons to do or not to do something that is judicially enforceable." It is a bilateral agreement expressing a meeting of the minds. What they promise to do or not to do may consist of the performance or non-performance of some act or the payment of money. Generally speaking in the field of real estate, one of the parties promises to pay money and the other promises to perform some act such as the transfer of title or, under an agency agreement, to procure a buyer or lessee.

REQUIREMENTS FOR A VALID CONTRACT

41   Every contract of whatever kind must meet four essential requirements before it comes into existence as a contract:

(1) Mutual consent.
(2) Consideration.
(3) Capacity.
(4) Legality.

41a   Performance is not necessary to create a contract. It may be a necessary ingredient to complete the terms of a contract, as in a listing.

42   Mutual consent - This requirement means that the parties to a contract must agree on the exact same thing. No contract would arise if one of the parties agreed to do one thing and the other party agreed to do something else. All terms and conditions of a contract must be drawn carefully so that there can be no misunderstanding or misinterpretation of exactly what the parties agreed.

43   Consideration - The consideration necessary to make a contract binding is not the payment of money or the performance of the act agreed to, but the consideration is the mutual promise in the contract to carry out its terms. A legal dictionary states consideration is, "An act of the promise from which the promisor derives a benefit or advantage." An illegal consideration would void the contract.

44   Capacity - Before a person may enter into a binding contract, he must have the legal capacity to do so. The law limits the capacity of certain persons to enter into a contract as with minors and incompetents. Contracts by such persons may be void or voidable depending on the circumstances in each case. Sometimes a purchaser of a property does not wish to disclose the other purchasers and will use the phrase "et alii" or "et aliae" which are Latin phrases that are commonly used in legal practice. They mean "and others." This phrase is abbreviated very often as "et al".

45   Legality - Before a contract can come into existence, the object of the contract must be legal or lawful. According to law, an agreement to do something prohibited by law cannot be a contract. Thus, an agreement to commit a criminal act is not enforceable. A person signing an agreement for another without the legal authority to do so would be forgery.

45a   Current real estate contracts explicitly state that the signer should read the contents of the agreement and indicate that he has done so. Where one signs a contract without reading it and where the failure to familiarize oneself with the contents of a written contract prior to its execution, is solely carelessness or negligence. The contract is valid. If such failure or negligence is induced by false representation or fraud of the other party to the contract so that its provisions are different than those set out orally, the court may reform the contract to reflect the true contract between the parties.

46 Three words constantly appear in real estate phraseology and must be understood to both enter the profession and work within the profession. The words are:

Valid - Having force or binding force, legally sufficient and authorized by law (enforceable).

Void - Having no force or effect.

Voidable - That which is unenforceable and capable of being adjudged void, but is not void unless action is taken to make it so. May be avoided is another way of expressing what voidable signifies.

47 Duress is unlawful constraint exercised upon a person whereby he is forced to do some act against his will. This creates a voidable contract.

NOVATION

48 "Novation" is the substitution of a new debt or obligation for an existing one. For example, if two men entered into a long-term real estate contract and after one year elapsed they decided to change the contract and a new contract was executed replacing the original one.

AMENDMENTS (RIDERS)

49 An amendment to a contract could be a rider attached to the contract intending it to be a part of the contract.

STATUTE OF FRAUDS

52 The requirements of a real estate contract are no different than those of any other contract except that most real estate contracts must be in writing. Thus, a real estate contract is said to have a fifth characteristic to be enforceable in court. Such contracts must be in writing. All of the requirements of contracts, in general, may be related to real estate contracts. There is one exception. In the exchange of real property, the statute of frauds makes an exception and allows oral contracts to be enforceable.

54 These terms must be drafted carefully so that they will state the agreements of the parties to avoid mistake or possibility of misinterpretation. If the parties enter into a contract with mutual consent as to the subject matter of the agreement, but there is a mistake as to a basic or material fact that induces one or both of the parties to enter into the contract, the contract is voidable. If a mistake does not concern a material element of the contract and does not vitally affect the facts on the basis of which the parties contracted, the mistake has no effect. The contract is valid. If a mistake is solely the result of negligence of one of the parties to a contract and there is absence of knowledge of the mistake by the other party, the courts have ruled the contract to be valid. If there is a mutual mistake as to the subject matter of a contract, it prevents the creation of a contract. Example: Buyer and seller of unimproved real property believed the purchase price included a lease on the property; however, later it was determined that the lease was not binding on the lessee. The court held that the buyer was entitled to void the contract because of mistake. If a term is stated indefinitely so that it may be interpreted in two ways, the contract becomes unenforceable on the basis that there is no mutual consent because the parties have not agreed on the same thing. If the terms give one party the right to perform or not to perform as he wishes, or are written in such a way that it cannot be clearly understood what the parties mean, the contract becomes "illusory" and unenforceable. For example: When a buyer agrees to obtain a loan, a mere statement that he will do so is not sufficient. The amount, method of payment, interest rate, type of loan, length, due date, purpose and disposition of the proceeds must be stated.

CONSIDERATION

55 The consideration that makes a real estate contract binding is the mutual promise of the parties. In an agency agreement, the principal agrees to pay a commission and the agent agrees to use his best efforts to procure a buyer, lessee, loan, or manage the property. This is called a bilateral executory contract. In a purchase agreement, the seller agrees basically to convey title while the buyer agrees to pay the purchase price. The same is true of a land contract. In a lease, the lessee promises to pay

the rent and the lessor to give possession to the lessee.

OFFER AND ACCEPTANCE

66   When a buyer or seller, or a party to an exchange agreement, makes an offer to buy, sell, or exchange, no contract arises until the person to whom the offer is made accepts the exact offer and the fact of acceptance is communicated to the person who made the offer. Only after acceptance or producing a buyer ready, willing, and able to buy, lease or rent, can a broker earn a commission.

68   The offer is, primarily, the beginning of the negotiations. The person to whom the offer is made may not find the terms of the offer acceptable and reject it. It may be rejected outright, or a counter offer may be made. The counter offer must, in turn, be accepted or rejected by the person making the original offer. If the parties finally agree on the same exact terms (mutual consent), they have both signed the contract and the one making the final offer is informed of the acceptance, a binding contract comes into existence.

EXECUTORY CONTRACTS

69   A distinction must be made between executory contract and executed contract. An executed contract is one the provisions of which have been fully performed. An executory contract is one the provisions of which have not been fully performed.

70   A contract may be executed (carried out) within a short period of time or it may be executory for years before it is fully performed. A purchase agreement is executory until the transfer of title and payment of money, which takes place usually within 30 to 90 days. A land contract or lease on the other hand, may take years to perform depending on how long the buyer is given to pay the purchase price or how

long the term of the lease may be. Should a broker render service or make improvements that are not in the original contract or agreed to by both parties, the costs for the improvements will be that of the broker and not the contracting parties.

78   In the event the buyer breaches the terms of the contract, the seller has legal remedies. The buyer may sue for specific performance and/or liquidated damages. In the case of the seller breaching an exclusive listing by unilaterally terminating the agreement, the seller may, if the broker is allowed to continue to show the property and produces a buyer at the listed price, be forced to pay a commission. The seller would not be forced to sell. For a party who contracts for the sale of real property to be able to sustain an action for specific performance there must be evidence of adequate valuable consideration.

86   The property description may include not only the legal description but also the nature of the interest being sold. For example: "An undivided one-third interest" or a "life estate," and enumeration of the encumbrances subject to which the property is being sold. In addition, personal property being transferred may be mentioned. Any description that can be used to validly locate the property is considered adequate in a listing or purchase agreement.

92   Contingencies - A contingency is a provision whereby one or more parties can be released from an obligation under a contract in the event some stated condition fails to materialize. For example: "Offer is contingent upon securing a trust deed loan for $10,000 payable, etc.," or, "Offer subject to securing a trust deed loan for $10,000." The contract is enforceable if the conditions are met.

94   Subject to and assume - These terms determine the obligations of a seller and buyer when the buyer is purchasing a parcel of real property that is already encumbered by a trust deed or mortgage. If the buyer takes the title subject to a certain loan, then he accepts no responsibility for payment of the note, he agrees merely that he will lose the property if he does

not make the payments. The seller remains responsible for payment. Under these conditions, the truth in lending laws would not apply because the seller remains fully responsible for the debt. If the buyer "assumes" the loan, he agrees to pay and guarantees that the loan will be paid in full.

95   The only practical difference between "subject to" and "assume" is when there is a foreclosure sale and a deficiency judgment is sought. In that case, if the buyer took title subject to the loan, he cannot be held responsible for the judgment. The seller remains primarily responsible. On the other hand, if the buyer assumes the loan (guarantees its payment), he would have to pay the judgment as he would be primarily liable. However, under an assumption agreement, the seller is not entirely relieved of his responsibility but remains secondarily liable unless specifically released by the lender.

96   Subordination clause - Used in a trust deed or mortgage. This clause states that some other trust deed or mortgage, dated and recorded subsequently, may take priority over it. Usually, the amount of the loan to be obtained, dated, and recorded later, is stated. Such agreements are written for the benefit of the borrower.

98   Liquidated damages clause - This is a contractual agreement predetermining the amount of damages for breach or failure to carry out a contract. In contracts for the sale of residential property containing 1 to 4 units with one to be occupied by the buyer, the following provisions will apply:

(1) The forfeiture of deposits that are paid and do not exceed 3% of the purchase price will be presumed valid unless the amount is proved to have been unreasonable.

(2) If the amount actually paid pursuant to the liquidated damages provision exceeds 3% of the purchase price, the provision is invalid. The seller will have to establish the reasonableness of the damage amount. In other sales contracts the forfeiture of deposits actually paid will be presumed valid regardless the amount. Terms of a subsequent sale will be evidence of the reasonableness of a liquidated damages provision. The law also requires that such clauses be prominently displayed and separately signed or initialed by each party to the contract.

98A   Protection clause - This clause is also referred to as the "safety clause". It provides that the agent is protected in his commission if the property is sold after the expiration of the listing term to a person with whom the agent has negotiated during the listing term. However, before it is operative, the agent must inform the seller of the names of such persons in writing and within the listing period. This period is often called the "safety period."

PEST CONTROL DOCUMENTATION
(Structural Pest Control Board)

99   Termites are the most destructive type of wood destroying insects. The subterranean type that lives in the soil and enters into the foundation of a home does more damage than the flying type known as the dry wood termite.

103   Whenever a licensee is an agent in a transaction in which the delivery of a structural pest control inspection report, notice of work completed, or certification is a condition of a contract affecting the transfer of the real property or a condition of financing the transfer, the licensee shall:

(1) Cause delivery of the appropriate documents to the transferee.
(2) Determine that the transferor has caused such delivery.
(3) Advise the transferee that Section 1099 of the Civil Code requires that the appropriate documents be delivered to the transferee by the transferor, fee owner, or his agent as soon as practical before transfer of title of any real property or the execution of a real property sales contract.

However, when a listing broker and a cooperating (selling) broker are involved in a real estate transaction, unless the transferor in the transaction has given written instructions to the listing broker to effect delivery of the documents, the responsibility is that of the broker who obtained the offer (selling broker).

Because the report may disclose damage to the structure it is advisable for the owner to have the report in advance and the work done to insure a smooth sale transaction.

105   Any person whether or not a party to a real property transaction, has a right to request upon payment of the required fee to the Structural Pest Control Board in Sacramento, a certified copy of all inspection reports and completion notices prepared and filed by any structural pest control operator during the preceding two years.

AUTHORIZATION TO SELL (Listing)

111   A "listing" is a promise for a promise. It is a bilateral employment contract between a principal and broker by which the principal employs the broker as his agent to sell, lease, and exchange or rent a property. As a rule, it is between a seller and broke but it could be between a buyer and broker as when a buyer employs a broker to locate a property for sale or lease. In either case, the broker as an agent has a fiduciary capacity to his client. The listing broker is the only broker ethically allowed to place a sign on the property. Listings are service contracts and, as such, cannot be recorded.

111a As a bilateral contract, the seller and broker are bound by its terms immediately upon execution. Repudiation by the seller indicating he will not perform the agreement constitutes an anticipatory breach of contract entitling the broker to his entire commission without proof of any effort to procure a purchaser.

112   A broker cannot exceed the authority given him by the seller under a listing agreement. The right of a principal to control the activities of his agent is an inherent part of the law of agency.

113   The usual term of reference is that of the contract between the seller and the broker, commonly known as an authorization to sell. In either case, it is an employment (service) contract and has nothing to do with the actual transfer of real property. Under this contract, the broker is an agent of the principal and is bound by the law of agency. He has certain obligations to his principal. Because the listing is a service (employment) contract, it is non-assignable and is canceled by the death of either party.

115   In case law, the state has asked a question that seems to differ with the principle that, "Any person signing a listing with a broker obligates himself to pay a commission if the broker performs, even though that person cannot or will not deliver the property." This may shock some students. If the contract calls for a forfeiture of the deposit to the seller and the seller accepts the forfeiture and releases the buyer, the broker has, by legal authority, not produced a buyer "ready, willing, and able" to buy and cannot force the seller to provide any part of the forfeited deposit. On the other hand, if the seller refused the forfeiture and sued for specific performance, the broker would be due the commission because the buyer was forced to buy. In either case, the broker does not have the right to bring an action in court on behalf of his principal.

115a If only one spouse signs a listing on community property and the broker performs, that spouse has obligated the community funds to pay the commission even though the other spouse refuses to accept the offer and the property cannot be delivered. The prudent broker will secure the signatures of both spouses when dealing with community property.

116   This would be true also where one party in a joint tenancy or tenancy-in-common signs a listing on the entire property. All parties to the tenancy must join in the sale and if one refuses to do so, the property cannot be sold. A co-tenant may sell his interest in the property, but not the entire holding without the consent of all parties. However, the party signing the listing may be held for the commission due the broker.

119   California now requires that any printed form or agreement which is intended to establish a right to compensation must contain this statement in not less than 10 point boldface type immediately preceding any provision of such agreement relating to compensation of the licensee.

Notice: The amount or rate of real estate commissions is not fixed by law. They are set by each broker individually and may be negotiable between the seller and the broker.

OPEN LISTING (Procuring Cause)

121   An "open listing" is the simplest form of employment contract. Usually, it sets forth a description of the property, price and terms of the sale. It may or may not provide a time limit for performance. The seller may give an open listing to a number of different brokers at the same time. The broker who first produces a buyer that meets the terms of the listing or whose offer is accepted by the seller, is the one who has earned the commission. As a rule, the owner is not required to notify the other brokers of the sale in order to prevent liability for paying more than one commission as the sale itself cancels the other listings automatically. In the event the owner himself finds a buyer, he is not obligated to pay a commission to any of the brokers holding open listings. For these reasons, brokers spend little money advertising an open listing. The only protection a broker has is to create a clause in the open listing creating a right to collect a commission if the broker notifies the owner in writing of the names of prospective buyers for the property. This gives the broker proof of being the "procuring cause" in case of a commission dispute.

EXCLUSIVE AGENCY LISTING

122   An "exclusive agency" listing is a contract by which a principal employs one broker as his exclusive agent to negotiate the sale of his property. If that broker, any other broker, or any other party finds a buyer and effects the sale, the one holding the exclusive agency listing is entitled to the commission. It should be noted that the listing refers to an "agency," and as the owner is not an agent, he may affect the sale himself without incurring liability for commission to the broker holding the exclusive agency listing.

EXCLUSIVE RIGHT TO SELL LISTING

123   In this type of listing the owner obligates himself to pay a commission to the broker to whom he has given an "exclusive right to sell" whether it is sold by that broker, any other broker, or by the owner himself. In other words, the owner excludes even his own right to sell his own property and must pay the listing broker his commission no matter who generates the sale. This type of listing places a special responsibility on the broker to spend time and money to find a buyer.

124   An exclusive listing (agency or right to sell) must have a termination date. Such a date may be for as little as one day or for as long as may be established in the agreement. A listing cannot, for example, run for a period starting with the date of the contract and continuing "until sold." It cannot state that it is effective "until canceled in writing," or "until a notice of cancellation is given." It may, however, provide that the broker be protected against sale by the owner to one of the broker's prospects for a definite period of time after the listing expires. Such a contract can be canceled, but the party so doing may be liable for damages as stated in the agreement. Most listings state that if the seller withdraws the property from sale, the broker is entitled to a full commission. Therefore, within the "four corners" of the contract, there is this agreement: You have the right to cancel, but if you do, you must pay a full commission.

124a   If the owner accepts an offer to buy under the terms of the contract and later refuses to sell, the broker may collect not only the commission due but also the damages and costs of defense against any action of the buyer to compel specific performance.

124b An exclusive agreement authorizing or employing a licensee to negotiate a loan secured directly or collaterally by a lien on real property shall be limited to a term of not more than 45 days.

NET LISTING

126   A net listing may be an open, exclusive agency or exclusive right to sell listing. It is one that permits the agent to retain as compensation all money received in excess of the selling price

set by the seller. The seller agrees to accept a certain set sum for his property and permits the broker to retain any excess over that amount as his compensation. Real estate law requires that the broker disclose the amount of his compensation in connection with a net listing to the owner prior to or at the time the principal binds himself to the transaction. This, of course, infers that he will get the owner to accept the entire contract that includes the broker's commission.

MULTIPLE LISTING SERVICE

129   The group provides a standard "multiple listing" form (usually an exclusive right to sell listing) which is used by all members requiring them to turn in all such listings to a central bureau from which they are distributed to all members. They all have the right to work on them. It is very effective in securing action for sellers and promotes business for the members.

132   The statute of frauds requires most of these agreements to be in writing to be enforceable. In the event a contract employing the broker is not in writing, it does not mean that it is an illegal contract but the contract could not be enforced in a court of law. It should be noted, however, that the statute of frauds also provides that a verbal agreement may be enforced if there is a sufficient memorandum in writing signed by the party to be charged. Thus, where there is a verbal listing to sell and the seller accepts an offer and signs a purchase agreement containing a clause agreeing to pay a commission, it should be a sufficient writing to satisfy the statute.

136   A broker completes his performance under the contract when, within its term, he delivers or tenders to the owner a valid, enforceable, written offer to purchase on the terms of the sale as listed and signed by a buyer able to comply therewith or to suffer damages if he fails to perform. The broker is not entitled to any commission, no matter how much time, money and effort he has expended, unless a customer is produced.

137   When a broker has found a customer who signs an offer to purchase, even though it may be on terms other than those stated in the listing, it is his duty to tender it to the seller for his acceptance or refusal. If the seller signs an acceptance of such an offer, the broker is entitled to a commission based upon the actual selling price.

138   In ordinary circumstances in real estate practice, the seller who gives a listing and agrees to pay the broker for his services is called the broker's client. The prospective buyer is referred to as the customer.

150   The words, "and to accept a deposit thereon," is the agent's authority to accept a monetary deposit as agent of the seller. The question arises as to whether an unqualified authorization to accept a deposit is in the seller's best interest. If so, and the broker loses or misappropriates the deposit, an express authorization to accept a deposit may place the risk of loss on the seller. In the absence of express authorization, the broker holds the deposit as agent of the buyer and the buyer bears the risk of loss.

DEPOSIT RECEIPT

160   The purpose of the deposit receipt contract (purchase agreement) is to secure a firm offer to purchase from a prospective buyer and to give a receipt for money given by him to a broker as a deposit or guarantee of his good faith in making the offer. Such deposits are sometimes called "earnest money." It is a contract between the seller and the buyer. Should there be a difference in the terms of sale set forth in a listing agreement from those in a purchase agreement, the latter will prevail.

161   Up to the time that such an offer to purchase is accepted by the seller, it remains merely an offer and may be withdrawn (rescinded) by the buyer at any time before it is accepted and the buyer has been notified of such acceptance within the specified time.

162   If a seller accepts the offer exactly as made and buyer is so notified, the purchase agreement constitutes a binding contract

between buyer and seller. If the seller changes any of the terms, he is in effect making a counter offer and the original offer is dead (revoked). If the buyer rejects the counter offer, the seller cannot reconsider and accept the buyer's original offer. The buyer would then have to make the offer again. If both buyer and seller decide following acceptance by both parties to rescind the transaction, the broker should restore all monies and draw a cancellation of the purchase agreement. This, in no way, affects the right of the broker to collect a commission.

165 Should the buyer or seller wish to contract for items not printed into the form or wish to change the wording of the printed matter, the handwritten entries would take precedence over any printed matter as evidence of the latest meeting of the minds of the parties.

168 If a seller misrepresents necessary facts and under the terms of a listing the broker produces a buyer ready, willing and able to buy, who after all papers are signed, refuses to buy because of the misrepresented facts:

(1) The buyer has the right to refuse.
(2) The broker would be due a full commission.

170 Matters of title, taxes, insurance premiums, rents, bonds, possession, and time limit for acceptance are usually taken care of in the printed clauses of standard forms. These clauses need to be read and studied as they bind the parties in many ways and are of great importance, not only for the state test, but to the buyer and seller in an actual transaction. They depend upon you, their real estate broker, to prepare the terms of their agreement properly.

UNIFORM VENDOR AND PURCHASER RISK ACT

171 It sometimes happens that after a contract is made for the purchase and sale of real property, a fire or other disaster destroys or seriously damages the property. Who shall take the loss? In 1947, California adopted the Uniform Vendor and Purchaser Risk Act, which provides a statutory answer.

172 If, when neither the legal title nor the possession of the subject matter of the contract has been transferred, all or a material part thereof is destroyed without fault of the purchaser, the seller cannot enforce the contract.

173 If, when either the legal title or the possession of the subject matter of contract has been transferred, all or any part thereof is destroyed without fault of the seller, the purchaser is not relieved from a duty to pay the price.

194 The clause stating, "Time is of the essence," requires that the parties perform their agreements within the times specified or they have breached the contract.

Lesson Ten
Part Two
Study Questions

_____(Lesson Ten - Paragraph 40 - Question 1)_____
Which of the following best fits the definition of a contract?
(A) Two or more persons entering into a legal agreement.
(B) Two or more competent persons entering into a legal agreement to do a legal act.
(C) Two or more competent persons entering into a legal agreement for a consideration to do or not to do a certain thing.
(D) Two or more competent persons entering into an agreement to do or not to do a certain thing.

(C) All are proper definitions of a contract. (C) incorporates the 4 requirements best.

_____(Lesson Ten - Paragraph 41 - Question 1)_____
Of the following, which is the least important factor in determining the validity of a contract?
(A) Performance. (B) Consideration. (C) Offer and acceptance. (D) Capacity.

(A) To be valid a contract must have four elements: 1. Legal Object. 2. Mutual consent. 3. Consideration. 4. Capacity of the parties. Performance is not one of these requirements.

_____(Lesson Ten - Paragraph 41 - Question 2)_____
The following are essential to form a contract, except:
(A) Consideration. (B) Performance. (C) Offer. (D) Acceptance.

(B) A contract has not been formed until there has been an offer and an acceptance. Further, the contract must contain the four essential elements of a contract: 1. Lawful object. 2. Mutual consent. 3. Lawful consideration. 4. Capacity of the parties. Actual performance is not necessary to make the contract valid.

_____(Lesson Ten - Paragraph 43 - Question 1)_____
All of the following are necessary elements of a contract except:
(A) Must have a legal object. (B) Competency of the parties.
(C) Payment of money. (D) Meeting of the minds.

(C) The payment of money is not an element of a contract. A contract must have consideration, but the consideration may be a promise to do something or not do something. Remember, the elements are mutual consent, also called a meeting of the minds, consideration of some type, competency of the parties, and a lawful object.

_____(Lesson Ten - Paragraph 43 - Question 2)_____
A contract based on an illegal consideration is:
(A) Valid. (B) Void. (C) Legal. (D) Enforceable.

(B) A contract to be valid must have the four essentials: Consent between the parties, consideration, capacity of the parties, and a lawful object. Therefore, if the consideration of a contract is unlawful, there is no contract. It is void.

_____(Lesson Ten - Paragraph 45 - Question 1)_____

A contract is signed by a party who, through fraud of the other party, is deceived as to the nature of the contents of the document. The contract is:
(A) Valid. (B) Voidable. (C) Void. (D) None of the above.

(C) There are two types of fraud concerning contracts: 1) Fraud in the inducement to sign which makes a contract voidable and, 2) "Fraud in the inception," which makes a contract void. This question illustrates "fraud in the inception" wherein a person does not know the nature of what he is saying.

_____(Lesson Ten - Paragraph 46 - Question 1)_____

A voidable contract is good until it is:
(A) Amended. (B) Rescinded. (C) Confirmed. (D) Notarized.

(B) A voidable contract is valid but able to be voided by one of the parties. When a voidable contract is terminated it is said to be "rescinded."

_____(Lesson Ten - Paragraph 46 - Question 2)_____

A voidable contract is:
(A) One that is illegal.
(B) One that is valid and enforceable.
(C) One that is valid on its face which can be avoided by an interested party for due cause.
(D) Not really a contract at all.

(C) This choice gives a clear description of the meaning of the word "voidable."

_____(Lesson Ten - Paragraph 47 - Question 1)_____

"Duress" is a term which is most closely associated to matters concerning:
(A) Easements. (B) Adverse possession. (C) Condemnation. (D) Contracts.

(D) "Duress" is defined as unlawful restrain exercised upon a person whereby he is forced to do some act that he otherwise would not have performed. It is most often used with reference to the unwilling entering into a contract.

_____(Lesson Ten - Paragraph 47 - Question 2)_____

A contract for the sale of real property made under duress is considered to be:
(A) Void. (B) Voidable. (C) Valid. (D) Illegal.

(B) Duress is a wrongful act of one person that compels an apparent assent by another to a transaction against his will. The person placed under duress may avoid his obligation if he wishes, or he may hold the other party to the contract (a voidable contract).

_____(Lesson Ten - Paragraph 48 - Question 1)_____

Novation is most closely related to:
(A) Modification of a contract.   (B) Substitution of a new contract for an old one.
(C) Creation of an existing agreement.   (D) Realization of an unexpected profit.

(B) Novation is a legal term to describe replacing an old contract with a new contract. A successful football coach after the super bowl might be called in and told to, "Tear up your old five-year contract, we are going to give you a new five-year contract at one million dollars a year." Novation is new for old.

_____(Lesson Ten - Paragraph 48 - Question 2)_____
Two men entered into a long-term real estate contract. After one year had elapsed they decided to change the contract and a new contract was executed replacing the original one. This would be an example of:
(A) Rescission. (B) Subrogation. (C) Novation. (D) Accession.

(C) "Novation" is the substitution of a new debt or obligation for an existing one.

_____(Lesson Ten - Paragraph 49 - Question 1)_____
As used in real estate practice, a rider:
(A) Is an amendment. (B) Is a person. (C) Is a lien. (D) Is a contract.

(A) An amendment to a contract could be a rider, typed and attached to the contract intending it to be a part of the contract.

_____(Lesson Ten - Paragraph 52 - Question 1)_____
To be enforceable in court, a listing agreement for the sale of real property must be:
(A) In writing. (B) Acknowledged. (C) Recorded. (D) All of the above

(A) Any contract employing a real estate licensee to find a buyer of real property or a lessee for a fee and the lease is for more than one year must be in writing to be enforceable by the broker.

_____(Lesson Ten - Paragraph 52 - Question 2)_____
An oral contract for the exchange of title to real property is:
(A) Enforceable.   (B) Enforceable by specific provision of the real estate law.
(C) Unenforceable most of the time. (D) Unenforceable.

(C) Section 1624 of the Civil Code in California, which is referred to as the statute of frauds, demands contracts dealing with real property must be written to be enforceable. Exceptions to this requirement have been applied in the case of an oral contract that has been partially performed by the vendee taking possession and making improvements or where the seller's fraud prevented the contract from being put in writing.

_____(Lesson Ten - Paragraph 54 - Question 1)_____
The parties enter into a contract with mutual assent as to the subject matter of the agreement, but there is a mistake as to a basic or material fact that induces one or both of the parties to enter into the contract. The contract is:
(A) Valid. (B) Voidable. (C) Void. (D) None of the above.

(B) Under the stated circumstances a contract has been created; however, it maybe avoided (is voidable) by the injured party.

_____(Lesson Ten - Paragraph 54 - Question 2)_____

A contract was freely entered into and the parties are in mutual agreement on the subject matter. Later, both parties become aware of a mistake concerning a collateral matter of the contract. Under these circumstances, the contract is:
(A) Valid. (B) Voidable. (C) Void. (D) None of the above.

(A) If a mistake does not concern a material element of the contract and does not vitally affect the facts on the basis of which the parties contracted, the mistake has no effect. The contract is valid.

_____(Lesson Ten - Paragraph 55 - Question 1)_____

In a bilateral contract an offered promise is given for receipt of a return promise. If a return promise is offered, this is treated as:
(A) Consideration. (B) Part performance. (C) An option. (D) More responsibility.

(A) One of the essentials of a legal contract is consideration. The offeror makes a promise expecting a return promise from the offeree. Consideration is not only the payment of money. It also might be the mutual promises stated in the contract by the parties to the agreement.

_____(Lesson Ten - Paragraph 55 - Question 2)_____

Contract is to consideration as:
(A) Assignment is to sublease.   (B) Holder in due course is to endorsement by maker.
(C) Grant deed is to signature of grantee. (D) None of the above.

(D) Analysis of answers: (A) - There is no assignment when subleasing. A lease is either assigned or possession is subleased. (B) - The maker of a note does not endorse it. The payee endorses. (C) - The grantee is not required to sign the deed, the grantor must sign. (D) - This must be the answer.

_____(Lesson Ten - Paragraph 69 - Question 1)_____

If a contract has been executed:
(A) Matters relating to the contract remain to be performed.
(B) Both parties have performed completely their obligations as provided by the contract.
(C) Only one party must perform.
(D) None of the above.

(B) In this sense the word "executed" in relationship and the context with contracts is defined by choice (B). When both parties have completely performed their obligations and promises in the contract, it is said to be executed. As an example, while a purchase contract is in escrow, the promises in the contract are executory, they have not all been performed including the promise to deliver a deed, the promise to obtain a pest control report, and the promise to deposit the money from a loan. When escrow is closed and all terms have been performed, the contract is said to be executed.

_____(Lesson Ten - Paragraph 78 - Question 1)_____

Consideration need not be major, but must be reasonable in order to require:
(A) Specific performance. (B) Damages. (C) Recession.   (D) Eminent domain.

(A) When suing on a contract and asking the court to order a party to perform specifically as promised in the agreement, the consideration to be given for this performance must be reasonable in order for the court to order one to perform.

_____(Lesson Ten - Paragraph 86 - Question 1)_____
A listing contract described the property for sale as, "A vacant lot at the northeast corner of 16th Street and Main Street, Los Angeles, CA." This description:
(A) Causes the contract to be void for lack of certainty.
(B) Would be grounds for license revocation of the licensee preparing the contract.
(C) Is an adequate description. The contract is valid.
(D) Would require that an amendment be made to the contract to provide an adequate description.

(C) An adequate description is one that describes no other property but the one in question. This clearly identifies the land. The description in the question serves this purpose, thus, the contract is valid.

_____(Lesson Ten - Paragraph 86 - Question 2)_____
An authorization to sell does not always contain what is generally referred to as a complete "legal description" of the property involved. Therefore, it is:
(A) A violation of the Civil Code. (B) A violation of the Real Estate Law.
(C) Unenforceable.   (D) None of the above.

(D) The listing is an employment agreement in which an owner hires the broker to be his representative. It should identify the property clearly but doesn't require a "legal description."

_____(Lesson Ten - Paragraph 92 - Question 1)_____
A purchase agreement in which the buyer's performance is conditioned upon his obtaining satisfactory leases is:
(A) An enforceable contract.
(B) Illusory.
(C) A combined bilateral and unilateral contract.
(D) An unenforceable contract because it violates the Statute of Limitations.

(A) An important Supreme Court case decided in 1958 hinged on the point raised in this question. The purpose of the condition (obtaining satisfactory leases) was to give the buyer the opportunity to obtain such leases of the shopping center buildings involved in the transaction prior to the time he was finally committed to pay the balance of purchase price and take title to the property. Even though the satisfaction of the purchaser as to such clauses cannot be measured by an objective standard, the duty of the promisor to exercise his judgment in good faith is an adequate consideration to support the contract. Therefore, it is not illusory.

_____(Lesson Ten - Paragraph 94 - Question 1)_____
The "truth in lending" requirements would very likely be applicable in all of the following instances, except :
(A) Where a homeowner advertises that the buyer can purchase subject to a mortgage.
(B) When a real estate broker advertises assumption of a loan at an annual rate.
(C) To financial institutions which advertise to promote consumer credit.
(D) Where a homeowner advertises that the buyer can assume an existing loan on certain stated terms.

(A) Truth in lending rules apply in those loan circumstances in which the buyer (borrower) becomes liable for the payment of the debt and in which the property of the borrower can become subject to a lien for the debt. In this choice the buyer (borrower) will purchase the property "subject to" the lien of the record (the existing loan). In purchasing "subject to" the buyer will get no such liability. The seller remains fully liable for payment of the debt involved.

_____(Lesson Ten - Paragraph 94 - Question 2)_____

If a seller wanted to relieve himself of the primary liability for payment of a trust deed and note, he must find a buyer who is willing to:
(A) Assume the trust deed and note liability.
(B) Sign a release agreement.
(C)Take title subject to the trust deed and note.
(D) Execute a subordination agreement.

(A) If the buyer "assumes" the loan he agrees to pay and guarantees that it will be paid in full.

_____(Lesson Ten - Paragraphs 94, 95 - Question 1)_____

Brown buys Greenacre from Black taking title to the property subject to the existing loan. The person primarily responsible for the repayment of the loan would be:
(A) Brown.
(B) Black.
(C) The beneficiary of the trust deed securing the existing loan.
(D) The trustee of the trust deed securing the existing loan.

(B) When taking title "subject to" the buyer assumes no liability on the note. He agrees to make the monthly payment. If the payments are not made the lender will foreclose. The foreclosure action will be against the original signer of the note. If a deficiency results after the foreclosure and a default judgment is rendered, it will be against the seller whose signature appears on the note.

_____(Lesson Ten - Paragraphs 94, 95 - Question 2)_____

If a seller wanted to relieve himself of the primary liability for payment of a trust deed and note, he must find a buyer who is willing to:
(A) Assume the trust deed and note liability.   (B) Sign a release agreement.
(C) Take title subject to the trust deed and note. (D) Execute a subordination agreement.

(A) If the buyer "assumes" the loan he agrees to pay and guarantees that it will be paid in full.

_____(Lesson Ten - Paragraph 95 - Question 1)_____

Jason Brown purchases his residence from Harold Smith. In doing so he assumed making the payments on Smith's existing FHA loan. Upon proper application for assumption of the loan, a substitution of responsibility for the loan was issued to the seller. In this event the following is true:
(A) Smith retains primary responsibility for repayment of the loan to the lender.
(B) Brown now has primary responsibility for repayment of the loan to the lender.
(C) Brown has primary responsibility for repaying the loan but Smith still retains a secondary responsibility.
(D) Smith retains the primary responsibility and Brown becomes secondarily responsible for repayment of the loan.

(B) A release from the liability to pay the FHA debt may be obtained by the seller providing the buyer makes application to the lender holding the FHA loan. The lender, in turn, submits to FHA a completed assumption form together with a completed FHA loan application for the buyer with the usual supporting verifications. If the FHA approves the application, it will issue a "substitution of responsibility" to the seller evidencing release of liability.

_____(Lesson Ten - Paragraph 95 - Question 2)_____

The Irvins made an offer to purchase the Grey's property. As part of the offer, the Irvins agreed to take title "subject to" an existing VA loan that the Greys obtained when they purchased the property in the approximate amount of $39,000. If the Greys sell to the Irvins under these conditions, which of the following is true concerning liability for a loss suffered by the government after a foreclosure on the VA loan:

(A) The Irvins will be primarily liable.
(B) The Greys and the Irvins will be equally liable.
(C) The Greys will be primarily liable.
(D) Neither couple is liable because the Irvins took title "subject to" the existing loan.

(C) The only practical difference between "subject to" and "assume" is when there is a foreclosure sale and a deficiency judgment is sought. In that case, if the buyer took title subject to the loan, he cannot be held responsible for such judgment. The seller is said to remain primarily responsible.

_____(Lesson Ten - Paragraph 96 - Question 1)_____

To subordinate means:
(A) To provide for the repayment of a loan before its maturity with an agreed penalty.
(B) An agreement by which a lien upon, or interest in, real property which would normally have priority, is made junior to a future encumbrance which, in the absence of such agreement, would be a junior lien or charge.
(C) To give the lender the right to call all sums owing to him to be immediately due upon the happening of a certain event.
(D) A stipulation that upon the payment of a specific sum of money to a holder of a mortgage, the lien on a specifically described lot or area shall be removed.

(B) Choice (A) describes a prepayment penalty agreement. Choice (C) describes an acceleration clause. Choice (D) describes a release clause.

_____(Lesson Ten - Paragraph 96 - Question 2)_____

A clause in a trust deed providing that the rights of the beneficiary are secondary to those of holders of subsequently recorded trust deeds is known as:
(A) Acceleration. (B) Alienation. (C) Subrogation. (D) Subordination.

(D) A subordination clause in a trust deed and a note agrees that the borrower may place an additional trust deed lien against the property in the future which will be prior in rights to this presently recorded trust deed. This creates an exception to the normal rule, "First to record is first in right." By agreeing to the subordination clause, the lender agrees that he will give up his recorded priority.

_____(Lesson Ten - Paragraph 98a - Question 1)_____

A real estate broker only has a right to earn a commission only when the property sells during the listing period except when the following is included in the listing agreement:
(A) Exculpatory clause.   (B) Broker's protection clause.
(C) Subordination clause. (D) None of the above.

(B) The broker's protection clause states that the broker is entitled to a commission if the property is sold to parties with whom he has negotiated during the term of the listing for a stated number of days after the listing expires.

_____(Lesson Ten - Paragraph 98a - Question 2)_____

Assume that Broker Brown had been negotiating with a prospective buyer but had been unable to close the transaction. However, on June 5, he telephoned the owner and informed him that he had been negotiating with the prospect during the term of the listing contract that expires on June 5. On June 6, the owner sold the property to the broker's prospect. According to the terms of the California Association of Realtors purchase agreement, the broker:
(A) Would be entitled to his actual expenses incurred in showing the property.
(B) Would be entitled to one-half his commission not to exceed the amount of the deposit.
(C) Would be entitled to the agreed upon commission.
(D) Would have no claim to a commission.

(D) The listing contract requires that the broker notify the owner in writing of his prospective buyer. Hence, the telephone conversation on June 5 did not protect the broker if the owner and the prospect come to agreeable terms of purchase and sale.

_____(Lesson Ten - Paragraph 99 - Question 1)_____

The wood destroying insect that causes the greatest amount of damage to real property is a:
(A) Beetle. (B) Silverfish. (C) Dry wood termite. (D) Subterranean termite.

(D) Termites are the most destructive type of wood destroying insects. The subterranean type that lives in the soil and enters into the foundation of a home does more damage than the flying type known as the dry wood termite.

_____(Lesson Ten - Paragraph 103 - Question 1)_____

State law requires a Pest Control Company:
(A) Provide a copy of the Structural Pest Control report to the buyer.
(B) Provide a copy of the Structural Pest Control report to the seller.
(C) Charge a nominal inspection fee.
(D) Provide a copy of the Structural Pest Control report only if there is damage from dry rot or termites.

(A) A pest control company is required by state law to provide a copy of the structural pest control report to the buyer.

_____(Lesson Ten - Paragraph 103 - Question 2)_____

A copy of a structural pest control inspection report prepared under the provisions of the Business and Professions Code must be delivered to the buyer:
(A) Only if required by the transferee.   (B) Only if required by the lender.
(C) If required by the transferee or the lender. (D) If there is visible evidence of infestation.

(C) § 1099 of the California Civil Code requires the delivery of structural pest control reports to the buyer before the close of the transaction. Either the buyer or the lender who is making the loan to complete the sale transaction can require a report.

_____(Lesson Ten - Paragraph 105 - Question 1)_____
As a licensee you would refer a person with a problem with a termite contractor to the:
(A) Behavioral Science Examiners Board. (B) Structural Pest Control Board.
(C) Veterinary Medicine Board.   (D) Board of Landscape Architects.

(B) The Structural Pest Control Board is the state agency that regulates licensed termite contractors.

_____(Lesson Ten - Paragraph 105 - Question 2)_____
Copies of termite reports that have been prepared by licensed termite inspectors during the 2 years previous to a request for such copy may be obtained from which of these:
(A) Real Estate Commissioners Office. (B) Structural Pest Control Board.
(C) State Bureau of Entomology.   (D) None of these.

(B) Licensed structural pest control operators must file a copy of each report they issue, whether or not corrective work is undertaken, with the Structural Pest Control Board in Sacramento, California.

_____(Lesson Ten - Paragraph 111 - Question 1)_____
The broker owner relationship that is established by a listing agreement generally is:
(A) Bilateral. (B) A promise for a promise. (C) An employment contract. (D) All of the above.

(D) This refers to a listing agreement and the type of contract being questioned. Answer (A) states "bilateral" and this is correct. Bilateral means "two sided." The two sides (two parties) to a listing are the owners of the property and a broker. A bilateral contract involves a promise for a promise. In the listing, the seller promises to pay a commission. He does not promise to sell the property. The broker promises to use his best efforts in attempts to seek a buyer. A listing is also described as an employment contract where the seller employs a licensed broker to represent him as an agent.

_____(Lesson Ten - Paragraph 111 - Question 2)_____
In an open, non-exclusive listing situation, the broker who most likely will be paid a commission is the one who has:
(A) Obtained a substantial deposit with an offer
(B) Secured acceptance to an offer
(C) Produced a person who would purchase under the terms of the listing.
(D) Communicated acceptance of an offer to the offeror.

(D) The presentation of an offer to purchase has three steps before becoming a binding contract. The first step is the presentation of the offer, the second step is the acceptance of the offer, and the third is the communication of such acceptance back to the offeror.

_____(Lesson Ten - Paragraph 112 - Question 1)_____
A real estate broker could be held liable to a buyer if the broker:
(A) Unknowingly makes a misrepresentation to the buyer based on false information given to him by the seller.
(B) Executes an agreement with the buyer on behalf of the seller under a power-of-attorney granted by the seller.
(C) Acts in excess of the authority given to him by the seller under a listing agreement.
(D) Retains the buyer's check at the seller's request after an offer has been accepted by the seller and acceptance has been communicated to buyer.

(C) A broker cannot exceed the authority given him by the seller under a listing agreement. The right of a principal to control the activities of his agent is an inherent part of the law of agency.

_____(Lesson Ten - Paragraph 113 - Question 1)_____

A contract is non-assignable when it is:

(A) For a period of more than one year. (B) A personal service contract.

(C) In writing. (D) Includes an alienation clause.

(B) When a contract involves personal services like that of a doctor or an artist, that contract may not be assigned to another person.

_____(Lesson Ten - Paragraph 113 - Question 2)_____

If in a transaction the amount made as a deposit is not sufficient to cover the monetary damages incurred by a party to the real estate sales transaction, the following could not file an action in a court of law:

(A) The seller. (B) The buyer.

(C) An attorney acting for his client. (D) A real estate broker acting as the agent for his principal.

(D) The question asks who may not file an action in court concerning a real estate transaction. The answer, "A real estate broker acting as an agent for the principal," is a special agent. The broker's powers are limited to acting in the sale of the property. He has no power to file a court action for his principal.

_____(Lesson Ten - Paragraph 116 - Question 1)_____

Assume the seller, without broker's knowledge, owned this property in joint tenancy with his wife. Broker produced a signed offer at the listed price and terms but the wife refused to sign. The broker claimed a commission but the wife pointed out that she had never signed the listing.

(A) Broker is wrong; he should not have accepted the listing.

(B) Broker has no basis for claiming a commission.

(C) Wife is wrong; husband obligated himself for the commission by signing the listing.

(D) The listing was voidable at the wife's option.

(C) A listing is a personal service contract and not an agreement to sell real property. The husband employed the broker for a specific purpose to produce a buyer. If broker performs the service, for which he was employed, he has earned the commission. The "ready, willing and able" buyer he produced may not be able to purchase the property because of the wife's refusal to sign the acceptance, but the broker has performed, as the buyer was financially "able" to buy.

_____(Lesson Ten - Paragraph 119 - Question 1)_____

The amount of commission that may be charged by a real estate broker is:

(A) Regulated by truth in lending laws.

(B) Limited to 6% on residential properties.

(C) Not limited in any manner.

(D) Normally established in the listing agreement between the broker and the principal.

(D) In order to have an enforceable claim to a commission, a broker must have a written agreement. This is normally the listing contract. His commission is not regulated by truth in lending nor is there a 6% limit on residential properties. (C) is an incorrect choice because it is too broad a statement. There is a limit on a broker's commission for negotiating a loan.

_____(Lesson Ten - Paragraph 121 - Question 1)_____

Brokers X and others each have an open listing on the property. Broker X showed the property to a buyer and carried on negotiations, but the buyer decided not to buy. Two weeks later, Broker Y contacted the same buyer and arranged a sale of the property. The seller is obligated to pay a commission as follows:
(A) The full amount to both broker X and Y.
(B) The full amount to broker Y only.
(C) 50 percent each to broker X and Y.
(D) The full amount to broker X who will have to settle with broker Y.

(B) Full amount to broker Y only. This is so because of the open listing. Broker Y in this case would be the procuring cause.

_____(Lesson Ten - Paragraph 121 - Question 2)_____

The term "procuring cause" is most often associated with the following:
(A) A lease.
(B) An offer to purchase agreement.
(C) An action for claiming a commission on an open listing.
(D) An action against a licensee for violation of the real estate law.

(C) When open listings are used; the broker who first procures a customer who is ready, willing and able to buy in accordance with the terms of the listing is the "procuring cause" of the sale and is entitled to a commission. He may have to submit such proof in court to actually obtain it.

_____(Lesson Ten - Paragraph 122 - Question 1)_____

Broker Brown has listed Sam Seller's home using a four-month exclusive agency listing agreement. He expends much time and effort marketing the home and much money advertising it for sale. Ten days before the listing expiration date, Sam sells the home to his own neighbor Ned. The following is the most likely result:
(A) Sam owes the broker a full commission.
(B) Sam owes the broker only the listing half of the commission.
(C) Sam owes the broker a commission only if escrow closes.
(D) Sam owes the broker no commission.

(D) The listing described is an exclusive agency. In this type of listing, the owner may sell the property himself without obligation for a commission. Therefore, Sam owes nothing.

_____(Lesson Ten - Paragraph 122 - Question 2)_____

Under an exclusive agency to sell contract, an owner is not obligated to pay the listing broker a commission if:
(A) The owner sells the property with the aid of another broker who was given an open listing
(B) The owner sells the property directly to a friend who has a house listed with another broker
(C) The owner sells the property through another broker who was given an exclusive listing
(D) The owner withdraws the property from sale so that he can sell it through another broker.

(B) An exclusive agency listing gives the owner the power to sell and transfer property to another without any obligation to pay the listing broker a commission if the services of another agent are not used.

_____(Lesson Ten - Paragraph 123 - Question 1)_____

A broker in court to collect commission must allege and prove all of the following, except:
(A) He acted in agency.
(B) The commissioner licensed him.
(C) In an exclusive right to sell listing, he introduced the buyer and seller.
(D) In an open listing, he introduced the parties to the contract.

(C) Under an exclusive right to sell listing no matter who sells the property, or if the property is leased or taken off the market, the broker receives his full commission and would not have to prove introduction of buyer and seller.

_____(Lesson Ten - Paragraph 123 - Question 2)_____

A broker licensee can legally claim a commission in the following:
(A) For a loan which he did not negotiate.
(B) For the sale of a property on which he had an exclusive authorization to sell with a definite termination date.
(C) For the sale by another of a property on which he had an open listing with a termination date.
(D) For the sale by another on which he had a net listing with a termination date.

(B) The question involves the definite termination date. In the exclusive listing, either exclusive agency or in the exclusive authorization to sell, there must be a definite termination date by real estate law. (B) states the conditions where the broker can claim a commission.

_____(Lesson Ten - Paragraph 124 - Question 1)_____

A real estate broker need not prove that he is the procuring cause when the following type listing is used:
(A) Open.   (B) Net.
(C) Exclusive right to sell. (D) The broker never need prove that he is the procuring cause.

(C) The exclusive right to sell listing has in it the words, "If this property is sold by you or by me, or any other cause, I am entitled to a commission." Consequently, the broker need only prove the property was sold during the term of the listing regardless of who was the procuring cause.

_____(Lesson Ten - Paragraph 124 - Question 2)_____

Owner signs an exclusive authorization and right to sell listing. Later, the owner cancels the agreement. Under these circumstances:
(A) The owner cannot cancel the listing agreement until its term expires.
(B) The owner can cancel the contract, but may be liable for the payment of damages under the agreement.
(C) The Real Estate Commissioner can order the owner to honor the listing agreement.
(D) The district attorney of the county in which the property is situated could file criminal charges against the property owner.

(B) A listing creates an agency contract that is a personal service contract. Such a contract can be canceled, but the party so doing may be liable for damages as stated in the agreement. Most listings state that if the seller withdraws the property from sale, the broker is entitled to a full commission. You have the right to cancel, but if you do, you must pay a full commission.

_____(Lesson Ten - Paragraph 126 - Question 1)_____
The following contract, although executed and performed, would be unenforceable:
(A) An open listing signed by the seller that did not contain a definite and final termination date.
(B) An oral listing obtained by a real estate broker for the lease of a residence for one year.
(C) A verbal listing taken by a real estate broker for the sale of a business opportunity.
(D) A net listing in which the broker failed to disclose the amount of his compensation to the seller.

(D) The Real Estate Commissioner does not welcome the use of net listings and makes it a violation of real estate law if the broker who uses one does not disclose his profit or commission at the time of sale. A final and definite date of termination is only required in an exclusive listing.

_____(Lesson Ten - Paragraph 129 - Question 1)_____
The type of listing used by members of a multiple listing service is usually:
(A) A net listing.　　　　　(B) An exclusive right to sell listing.
(C) An exclusive agency listing. (D) An open listing.

(B) To make certain that only members will have access to listing information carried by a multiple listing service and to make certain that unlicensed persons will not have access to this information during the listing period, listing services use the "Exclusive Authorization and Right to Sell" almost exclusively. In this situation the listing service will receive a fee to cover their expense of operation. The commission is divided by the listing and selling member in accordance with their established rules.

_____(Lesson Ten - Paragraph 129 - Question 2)_____
A listing is a written contract in which an owner of property appoints an agent. The following is a correct statement concerning a listing contract:
(A) An open listing may not be given to more than one agent.
(B) An open listing without a specified date of termination provides grounds for disciplinary action.
(C) A net listing may not be legally taken unless it provides for a definitely determined amount of commission.
(D) Most multiple listings are exclusive right to sale listings.

(D) A multiple listing is an exclusive right to sell listing used by brokers who belong to a multiple listing service or exchange. With respect to open listings there is no legal limit to the number of them that can be given by any owner. Law requires no specified termination because all would terminate with the sale of the property. Net listings may be used in California providing the licensee reveals his compensation to the seller before the deal is concluded.

_____(Lesson Ten - Paragraph 132 - Question 1)_____
To establish an enforceable agency for the purpose of selling real estate, one must have:
(A) Trust deed.　(B) Partnership.　(C) Written contract.　(D) None of the above.

(C) The listing agreement is the contract that establishes agency.

_____(Lesson Ten - Paragraph 137 - Question 1)_____

A licensee obtained a listing on a residence at a price of $65,000. The owner stated in the listing that the price was firm. Several days later the licensee received an offer of $38,000 for the property. The licensee should:
(A) Refuse the offer as it does not meet the terms of the listing.
(B) Hold the offer while awaiting a firm offer of $65,000.
(C) Present the offer to the seller.
(D) Make a counter offer of $65,000 to the offeror.

(C) The law of agency requires the agent to present all offers to his principal, even though they do not meet the terms of the listing. The seller should be made aware of the facts existing in the market place relative to his property.

_____(Lesson Ten - Paragraph 138 - Question 1)_____

In common practice, a prospective buyer is known to the real estate broker as a:
(A) Customer. (B) Fiduciary. (C) Grantor. (D) Vendor.

(A) A broker represents his client, the seller, and a fiduciary relationship would exist between them. The buyer is the customer and the seller is referred to as the client.

_____(Lesson Ten - Paragraph 150 - Question 1)_____

A real estate broker receives his authority to accept a deposit on behalf of his principal in the following contract:
(A) A purchase agreement. (B) A lease agreement. (C) A broker's loan statement. (D) A listing.

(D) It is a provision in the listing contract that normally gives the broker the authority to accept a deposit from a prospective buyer on behalf of the listing party.

_____(Lesson Ten - Paragraph 161 - Question 1)_____

Assume the broker secured an offer on the exact terms of this listing, together with a $500 deposit. He telephoned the seller and made a 4 o'clock appointment to get a signed acceptance. At 3:30 the buyer returned to the office saying he had decided not to buy the property and asked for the return of his deposit. The broker protested that he had not had an opportunity to present the offer to the seller and could not return the deposit until the seller had a chance to accept the offer. In your opinion:
(A) Broker was right in his position.
(B) Deposit money always belongs to the seller. Broker has no right to return it to buyer.
(C) Broker must return deposit to buyer upon demand as the buyer has withdrawn his offer.
(D) Buyer automatically forfeits deposit as he is not willing to complete the transaction..

(C) Remember that any offer may be withdrawn before it is accepted and buyer has been notified of such acceptance.

_____(Lesson Ten - Paragraph 161 - Question 2)_____

One who submits a written offer to purchase real property:
(A) Must accompany it with a financial statement of responsibility.
(B) May not withdraw it until the seller has had an opportunity to accept or refuse it.
(C) May withdraw it any time before it is accepted and a signed copy of the acceptance is delivered to the buyer.
(D) May not do so directly but only through a broker or agent.

(C) Regardless of the fact that buyer has set a time limit for acceptance of his offer by the seller, it does not mean that he will keep the offer open for the 7-day period. It only means that if the seller does not accept within the time limit, the offer will automatically be revoked at the end of seven days. The basic rule still applies: "Any offer may be revoked or withdrawn at any time before it is accepted and such acceptance is communicated to the buyer." On this particular form a further requirement is added: "And a signed copy of the acceptance delivered to him."

_____(Lesson Ten - Paragraphs 161, 162 - Question 1)_____
Which of the following terminates an offer?
(A) Revocation by the offeror.   (B) Rejection by the offeree.
(C) Conditional acceptance by the offeree.   (D) All of the above

(D) An offer may be revoked by the buyer (offeror) any time before acceptance and communication. An offer may be rejected by the offeree (seller). A conditional acceptance defines a counter offer and it also terminates the original offer.

_____(Lesson Ten - Paragraphs 161, 162 - Question 2)_____
All the following ways can terminate a purchase agreement, except:
(A) Failure to accept the offer within a prescribed period.
(B) Failure to communicate notice of revocation before the other party has communicated acceptance.
(C) A conditional acceptance of the offer by the offeree.
(D) Death or insanity of the offeror or offeree regardless of the notice thereof.

(B) Once an offeree's (seller's) acceptance of an offer has been communicated to the offeror (buyer), there is a binding contract between the buyer and the seller. The offeror (buyer) cannot withdraw after being told of the seller's acceptance without breaching the contract. In breaching the contract the buyer makes himself liable to the remedies available to the seller.

_____(Lesson Ten - Paragraph 162 - Question 1)_____
To be binding on a seller and a purchaser, an agreement for the transfer of title to real property must:
(A) Be recorded to be effective.   (B) Be acknowledged before a proper official.
(C) Contain and offer an acceptance. (D) Be signed by the purchaser.

(C) This deals with the agreement or transfer of title. This is known as the real estate purchase contract and the receipt for deposit. In order to be binding, this contract must contain a signed offer and term by the offeror and a signed acceptance of these terms by the offeree. The third step of communicating acceptance back to the offeror is done by mail or personally, depending on the contract.

_____(Lesson Ten - Paragraph 162 - Question 2)_____
After a valid offer and acceptance had been affected, the vendee decides he will not complete his written assignment to buy and so notifies the vendor. The vendor agrees to a recession. In order to accomplish this he would:
(A) By mutual agreement restore all monies and conditions that existed before the agreement.
(B) File a notice of recession in a newspaper of general circulation.
(C) Sue for specific performance.
(D) Keep the vendee's deposit.

(A) Recession is the act of restoring both parties to their original position, including money, and relieving them of performing any part of the duties of their contract.

_____(Lesson Ten - Paragraph 162 - Question 3)_____

If both parties to this contract were unhappy with the transaction after acceptance and arranged a meeting at which it was agreed in writing that the contract would be rescinded, and the broker was then notified of their decision:

(A) Broker would be entitled to keep at least half of the deposit money to compensate for the time and effort he has expended.

(B) The contract cannot be rescinded without the brokers consent.

(C) The broker must return the entire deposit to the buyer, but would have a legal claim for commission from the seller.

(D) Broker could sue both buyer and seller for specific performance.

(C) The broker is not a party to this purchase and sale contract and cannot enter into the matter in any way. He has earned the commission that the seller has agreed to pay according to the signed acceptance clause, but he cannot withhold any part of the money to insure its payment.

_____(Lesson Ten - Paragraph 165 - Question 1)_____

If there is a conflict between the handwritten and printed clause of a contract:

(A) The printed clause takes precedence.　　(B) The handwritten terms takes precedence.

(C) The contract would be void.　　(D) The contract would be unenforceable.

(B) Such a conflict would be interpreted in favor of the handwritten terms. The handwritten terms would be determined to have been entered later in time than the printing on the form.

_____(Lesson Ten - Paragraph 170 - Question 1)_____

Assume that both Mr. and Mrs. Jones in a purchase agreement specify that title is to be taken in the name of the wife alone, instead of both their names:

(A) This would make the contract invalid as the wife cannot hold title alone.

(B) The contract would be valid, even if the manner of taking title were not specified.

(C) Title in the name of the wife alone would create the presumption that it is separate.

(D) All property acquired after marriage must be held in joint tenancy.

(B) The title vesting clause is merely a memorandum to the escrow holder and is not relevant to the validity of the contract. Often, it is more practical in a purchase agreement to insert the statement, "The manner of vesting title will be determined in escrow."

_____(Lesson Ten - Paragraphs 172, 173 - Question 1)_____

Nate Samuels purchased a home using a land contract of sale in 1991. In 1996 a severe earthquake heavily damaged the property. Under the provisions of the Uniform Vender and Purchaser Risk Act of 1947, the following would best state the position of the buyer and seller in this case:

(A) The seller would be held liable to replace and restore the improvements on the property.

(B) Buyer is considered liable and must continue payments on the land contract.

(C) The law mentioned does not cover an instance of this type (earthquake).

(D) None of the above.

(B) Under the provisions of the code named (CC #1662) if the possession of the property has been legally transferred, the risk of loss is upon the buyer since he has sole right of possession. If possession has not been transferred, the risk of loss is with the seller.

Lesson Ten
Part Three
Understanding Through Question Testing

 Log into your course at www.lumbleau.com.

STUDENT LOGIN

Login:

Password:

 On your student home page click on the first link to take existing courses.

HERE>>>» Click Take Existing Courses

 Another page will appear on your monitor.
Click on the link to take State exam passing lessons.

HERE>>>» Click State exam passing lessons

 Under the "Guided Lesson" tab click on the tenth of fourteen links:
"Contracts in General".

Real Estate Salesperson Course

Guided Lessons	Practice Exams	Progress Report	Success Video

Print	Questions
Click	HERE>>> 10. Contracts in General 184

Here you will be tested on all of the questions you have been studying and learn the most recently added questions. It is essential, for maximum retention, that you eliminate all of the questions you can easily answer and "TAG" for study the questions with which you have difficulty.

LESSON 11

CONTRACTS - TWO
EXCHANGES
OPTIONS
SALES CONTRACTS
ESCROW
CLOSING STATEMENTS

Lesson Eleven
Part One

Understanding Through Video Teaching

Lesson Eleven
REAL PROPERTY SALES CONTRACT

23　A real property sales contract is a written statement in which a seller agrees to convey title to real property to a buyer after the buyer has met certain conditions specified in the agreement which does not call for the conveyance of title within one year of the execution of the contract. Assuming that the condition to be satisfied by the buyer is the payment of the purchase price, a land contract may be defined as a real property sales contract which provides that the seller (vendor) will act as the lender (by extending credit) and that he will hold the legal title to the property as security for the payment of the debt (the balance of the purchase price). The purchaser holds possession and "equitable title". There are no implied warranties in a land contract. Such an agreement is unenforceable unless it is in writing and signed by the party against whom enforcement is sought (seller) or by that party's agent.

24　This device is also known as:
    (1) Installment sales contract
    (2) Land sales contract
    (3) Land contract of sale
    (4) Agreement to convey
    (5) Conditional sales contract
    (6) Agreement for purchase and sale
    (7) Land contract

26　Real property sales contracts most often are used when the buyer does not have sufficient cash for a substantial down payment on the property. It is a "security device" in that the owner retains title to the property to insure the payment of the price. He may require that the buyer pay the amount in full before he will deliver a deed to the property (as is done in Cal Vet financing) or he may agree to give a deed when the buyer has paid in a sufficient amount to make the owner feel secure in giving title to the property, at which time

(according to agreement) the buyer signs a note and trust deed for the balance as in a regular sale.

28　Since the seller holds the legal title there is no guarantee clear marketable title will exist upon completion of the contract. The buyer or vendee, as he is referred to, only holds equitable title. This is why the contract is not considered a secure collateral by institutional lenders.

29　Since the existing contract does not prohibit a sale or assignment, the vendee may sell the property by assigning his interest in the contract, or sell his interest using another land contract between himself and the new purchaser. However, he is still personally obligated on his original contract unless he obtains a release of liability from the original vendor.

30　When the contract of sale is signed and the seller owes an outstanding obligation, the buyer's contract payments must be used to meet the seller's payments. It is also necessary that, should the buyer make impound payments for taxes, insurance, etc., to the seller, this money must be held in trust and used for no other purpose unless the seller receives the buyer's written consent to do so. Every seller of property under a real property sales contract who appropriates the payment for other than payment of the seller's obligation is guilty of a public offense punishable by a fine of not exceeding $10,000 or by imprisonment in state prison, or county jail for a term not exceeding one year, or by both such fine and imprisonment. In the event the seller transfers the title to another, he also must assign his interest in the land contract to that person. If he assigns his contract to another he also must transfer the title to the assignee.

31　Sometimes a land contract will contain a provision prohibiting the buyer from recording the contract. The courts have held that such a provision is not enforceable. The buyer should be entitled to record his contract for his own protection in the event seller should again contract to sell or take steps to mortgage the property. However, the seller's signature must be acknowledged by him to make the contract eligible for recording. When recorded the land contract becomes a cloud on the title to the property. This protects the title to property which is unoccupied by the buyer.

32 When selling a parcel of land under a real property sales contract which is not recorded, the seller is prohibited from otherwise encumbering the parcel to an aggregate amount exceeding the amount due under the contract without the written consent of the purchasing party. In addition, if after entering into the contract of sale, the seller should seek additional financing on the property his payments on such encumbrances may not exceed the amount of the buyer's contract payments without the buyer's written consent. In addition, the seller must transfer the title to the property which is the subject of the contract together with the contract and must assign the contract if he transfers the real property which is the subject of the contract.

34 The law requires that each sales contract relating to purchase of real property in a subdivision shall clearly set forth the legal description of the property. All of the existing encumbrances on the date of the contract and terms of the encumbrances must be set forth. Other than in a subdivision, contracts of sale are not held to the same degree of certainty in description as are deeds. Courts have allowed oral evidence to be admitted to complete a description in a contract of sale.

35 A buyer shall be entitled to prepay all or any part of the balance due on any real property sales contract with respect to the

sale of land which has been subdivided for not more than four families provided, however, that the seller, by an agreement in writing with the buyer, may prohibit prepayment for up to a 12 month period following the sale (Locked-in clause). Any waiver by the buyer of the provisions of this section shall be deemed contrary to public policy and shall be unenforceable and void. Any such waiver shall in no way affect the validity of the remainder of the contract.

35a One of the rights available to the vendor on a contract of sale is the "right of rescission." In the event of default of payments on the contract, in order to exercise this right, the vendor would inform the buyer of his intention to rescind and return everything of value he had received to the buyer on the condition that the buyer does the same. To effect a rescission of the contract, the purchaser must agree and is normally entitled to a refund of payments made under the contract.

35b Should a recession of contract be rejected by the buyer who is behind in payments, the buyer's position in a land contract is better defensively than in any other security device. According to the court decision in Barkus vs. Scott, the rule against forfeitures was sufficient barrier to harsh and unreasonable foreclosure proceedings.

35c In a qualified installment sale the taxability of the gain recognized on the sale is deferred until the actual receipt of the purchase price. The gain recognized is equal to the proportion of the cash received to the total sales price.

35d The broker is entitled to or has earned his or her compensation when the sales contract has been bound by the signatures of the parties. The question does not explore, as some think, the matter of the time the compensation would be payable.

EXCHANGE AGREEMENT

37 The printed clauses of an exchange agreement contain the consent of both parties to the broker(s) commission, as well as providing for all other terms, prorations, etc.

38 There are a number of good reasons for suggesting to a client that a trade may be advantageous and sometimes, as when there is a tight money market and financing is not readily available, it may be the only way of disposing of a property. If the equities of the owners are of the same approximate value, little cash outlay is required and the properties themselves constitute payment of the purchase price usually with no financing necessary.

40   Actually, in a trade, the owners exchange the equity in their respective holdings, each taking over the encumbrances existing on the newly acquired property. For example, the owner of a property with a fair market value of $135,000, which is subject to a first trust deed lien of $108,000, exchanges it for a property having fair market value of $155,000 and which is encumbered with a first trust deed lien of $122,000. The owner of the first property offers the equity of $27,000 in his property ($135,000 - $108,000) together with a $6,000 cash payment to satisfy the equity of $33,000 ($155,000 - $122,000) of the owner of the second property. Each party agrees to take over the loan obligation on the property that they acquire. In these circumstances there could be a workable exchange of properties assuming everything else is agreeable to the two parties.

OPTIONS

125 An option to buy is a contract by which an owner, in exchange for an actual consideration, gives another person the right to buy, and agrees to sell, a property within a certain time, for a specified price and upon specified terms. The optionee obtains no legal interest in the property, only a right to buy.

126 The practical effect of an owner giving an option is to keep the offer to sell open. Should the value of the property increase during the period of the option, that increased value would essentially go to the optionee. Effectively, this appears to indicate that the property is off the market but that is not necessarily the case. The owner (optionor) could sell the property to another, subject to the option. It is rare that such would ever happen, but it could take place. Since the option is still in effect the purchaser acquires title to the property subject to the right of the optionee to purchase.

127 The optionor must sell to the optionee at the price and terms agreed upon if the optionee elects to buy within the time limit of the option contract. If the optionee elects not to complete the purchase he simply forfeits the consideration given for the option. The optionor and optionee would be relieved of any further responsibility in the matter.

129 Conversely, an optionor may sell the property subject to the rights of the optionee.

130 When an optionee decides to buy the property (exercise his option), the option becomes a sales contract and both optionor and optionee are legally bound by its terms. It is important, therefore, that the option set out the details of the proposed purchase. If it merely states the total sales price, the optionee cannot insist upon terms.

132 The consideration given for an option may be money or anything of value, but it must be actual. It must pass from the optionee to the optionor, even though it may be only one dollar on a $100,000 property. A mere recital of the consideration is not sufficient.

133   One need not hold a real estate license to take an option on real property and sell either the option itself or the property at a profit. The amount of profit must be disclosed to the original seller. Both optionor and optionee are principals (seller and buyer). If a license is held, it must be reveled. It is always best to do this in writing.

ESCROWS

138 The use of an escrow company is not required in California by a broker who is handling the escrow on a transaction in which he is the broker. The escrow law establishes the criteria under which escrow officers must act. The owner of an escrow company is required to post a bond with the Commissioner of Corporations.

145   Should any conflict occur with respect to any document in an escrow it is the duty of the escrow officer to notify all parties to the escrow of such a conflict and gain agreement as to the resolution of differences. If a real estate broker opened the escrow to be certain that the deposit receipt understandings were translated exactly into the escrow instructions, the broker should also be notified to enable the broker to act as a mediating source to gain agreement to the

conflict. The broker cannot act unilaterally and cancel the escrow without agreement of all parties.

153 Escrow instructions are not a contract. They are merely instructions to a third disinterested party to carry out certain acts. Though not a contract within itself, the instructions will supersede the deposit receipt as a meeting of the minds of the parties because they are signed at a later date. When the instructions have been signed by the parties to the escrow, neither party may change escrow instructions to the detriment of the other. However, by mutual agreement between both parties, the escrow the instructions may be changed at any time. Escrow instructions may be modified at any time by escrow drawing up an amendment and having both parties sign their approval. One party may waive the performance of certain conditions. If in doing so, the waiver must not act as a detriment to the other parties to the transaction. Unlike the purchase agreement, escrow may have separate instructions for the buyers and sellers. These are called unilateral instructions. Instuctions may be bilateral and may be in the form of a formal business letter.

155 When no time limit is set forth in a purchase agreement the escrow officer will assume a "reasonable time". Such a time will be no less than 30 days and no more than the time it takes to clear title and be ready to record. When the time limit provided in the escrow agreement has expired and neither party to the escrow has performed in accordance with the terms of that agreement, good sense dictates that all the parties are entitled to a return of their respective documents and funds (if any) by the escrow holder. Another answer is if the parties refuse to have the escrow close in this fashion, is to have the escrow holder file an action in court called "interpleader." The court will determine the rights of the parties. Of course, an escrow instruction like any other contract can be dissolved by mutual consent of all parties.

REQUIREMENTS FOR ESCROW

157 The first step in an escrow is to "open" the escrow. This includes:

158 (1) Binding contract (real estate must be in writing) between parties.
159 (2) Conditions to be satisfied.
160 (3) Submit contract to neutral third person (escrow holder).

161 During this period the third person (escrow holder) is the dual agent (trustee) of the parties to the contract, but is not the agent of the broker. The escrow officer is also know as a "stakeholder". Escrow owes a fiduciary duty to both parties in an escrow (usually the buyer and seller). The escrow holder does not hold a fiduciary relationship to the broker involved. Therefore, the broker would have no power to change any of the agreements in an escrow unless both the buyer and the seller give the broker the authority to do so.

162 To Close an escrow:

163 All conditions must have been satisfied and all monies deposited. At this time the 3rd person (escrow holder) acts independently as an agent for:

164 (1) The buyer - to deliver the deed and other documents.
165 (2) The seller - to deliver the consideration from buyer.
166 (3) Report the selling price to the IRS. The IRS requires that the selling price of real property be reported to them. The primary responsibility for this report is the escrow officer.

CLOSING STATEMENTS

169 Some charges are the direct liability of one party because of contractual agreements with a third party, such as the seller's duty to pay his broker's commission as agreed in the listing agreement. The obligation of one party to pay these charges is seldom shifted to the other party by their agreement of sale or the escrow instructions. The following chart lists common

closing costs and indicates who typically pays such charge.

The final amount on each side of a closing statement is forced into balance by a differential to be paid in cash by either the buyer or seller. Rarely is the balance equal without the forced addition.

BASIC RULES

173 Recurring costs are costs that occur more than once on the property such as a tax impound.

176 Closing statements are made up in "debit" and "credit" form. If an item is owed by the seller, it is debited (charged) to him. If it is owed to the seller, it is credited. On the other hand, if the item is owed by the buyer, it is debited to him. If it is paid to the buyer, the buyer is credited.

180 Rents - When income producing property is involved, there will be rents to prorate. Rent is usually paid in advance and the buyer is entitled to the rent after the close of escrow. That rent is in the possession of the seller and must be turned over to the buyer. This payment to the buyer is accomplished by debiting the seller and crediting the buyer. The amount usually is a part of one month's rent. In the event the last month's rent on the lease has been paid to the seller, the amount debited and credited will be the last month's rent plus the proration of the current month.

181 Security Depostits and Prepaid Rents - In the event all or a portion of the property is leased and the seller is in possession of a security deposit from the lessee, the amount of the deposit must be turned over to the buyer for the reason that the security deposit is only held in trust and must be returned to the lessee at the termination of the lease. The buyer will be the lessor at that time. It is accomplished by debiting the seller and crediting the buyer. This is also true of any prepaid rents.

182 Propety Taxes - With the exception of a transaction closing on July 1st, the amount of real property taxes will always have to be prorated. Taxes may be in arrears or they may be paid in advance. If they are in arrears, the seller will be debited and the buyer credited. If paid in advance, the seller will be credited and the buyer debited. In determining the tax proration it may be said that if the taxes are paid up at the date of close of escrow the seller will be credited and the buyer debited. If taxes are not paid up at the close of escrow, the seller will be debited and the buyer credited.

RULES SUMMARY

185 Certain rules may be drawn from the above discussion:

186 1. Interest - Always paid in arrears. Debit seller, credit buyer, if taking over an existing loan.

187 2. Insurance - Always paid in advance. Credit seller, debit buyer, if taking over the existing policy. To "short-rate" the policy is to cancel the policy and credit the seller. To short-rate forces the seller to pay a high premium to cancel the policy prior to its maturity. Insurance companies do this in an attempt to cover their costs and induce the buyer to "take over" the remaining policy. The insurance company uses the short rate in an attempt to make the policy difficult to pay off. The insurance company wants to keep policies in force and will allow an assignment but only under the circumstances that both parties agree in writing to do so. During ownership, cancellation can occur only after a certain number of days specified in the policy related to notice of cancellation.

188 Rents - Usually paid in advance to seller. Debit seller and credit buyer.

Investor buyers may request to pay for a "binder" to be issued by their title company and paid for by the buyer in escrow. A binder (or interim binder) is a written agreement by the title insurance company to issue a title policy at a latter date. The cost of a binder policy is ten percent of the basic title insurance rate. Paying for the binder in advance of a future sale saves on the cost of buying another title policy.

PROPERTY TAX PRORATIONS.

194 To prorate taxes find the amount per month by dividing the annual tax amount by 12 months. To find one day's taxes, divide the monthly figure by 30 days, regardless of the month in question. Escrow companies use a 30-day month and tables based on the recording date of documents. All escrow prorations are based on a 30-day month or on a 360-day year. This kind of standard is referred to as a "banking year" in common practice.

LOAN CONSIDERATIONS

197 Existing Loan Amount - This amount will always be owed by the seller and will be a debit. It will be a credit to the buyer, if he is taking over the existing loan, as buyer will not be required to pay the amount in cash at close of escrow.

199 The buyer pays for recording the deed and other items of record that must be cleared to provide marketable title.

200 Purchase Price - The purchase price will always be debited to the buyer as he agrees to pay that amount and will always be credited to the seller, as the seller is entitled to receive that amount.

Lesson Eleven
Part Two
Study Questions

_____(Lesson Eleven - Paragraph 23 - Question 1)_____

When compared to a land contract of sale, the requisites of a grant deed differ with respect to:
(A) Warranties.   (B) Signatures of principals. (C)   Title. (D) All of the above.

(D) A grant deed and a contract of sale differ in the signatures of the principals. A grant deed requires only the signature of the grantor. The contract of sale requires the signatures of both the vendor and the vendee. They generally do not disclose the purchase price in a grant deed but must in the contract of sale as it is a contract. A grant deed has implied warranties; the contract has none.

_____(Lesson Eleven - Paragraph 23 - Question 2)_____

A land contract is a method of financing the sale of property. The following is a correct statement concerning such a contract:
(A) It is used when the seller wishes to convey title without using a trustee relationship.
(B) It is similar to a lease in that buyer has a right of possession but no rights in the title.
(C) The buyer has absolute assurance of receiving title upon performance of the contract.
(D) It is the least secure method of financing real property for the buyer, because the seller has retained the title and the buyer is merely the equitable owner.

(D) Do not be misled by choice (C). This is one of the hazards in using a land contract in financing the purchase of real property. If the seller neglects to make payments on an existing trust deed and foreclosures results, the buyer under a land contract could lose his equitable interest.

_____(Lesson Eleven - Paragraph 23 - Question 3)_____

The sale of real property by a contract of sale gives the buyers:
(A) Right of possession. (B) An estate of inheritance. (C) A freehold estate. (D) All of the above.

(A) The land contract of sale gives the purchaser the sole right of possession of the property. He gains an equitable interest in the property but does not acquire the interests suggested in choices (B) and (C).

_____(Lesson Eleven - Paragraph 23 - Question 4)_____

Duff sells property to Smith on a land contract. From a financing point of view the parties are most similar to:
(A) Mortgagee – mortgagor. (B)   Lessor - lessee. (C) Optionor - optionee.   (D) Grantor - grantee.

(A) From a financing point of view, the vendor and vendee would represent a lender and borrower - a mortgagee and mortgagor.

—————————**(Lesson Eleven - Paragraph 23 - Question 5)**—————————
The real estate financing instrument which transfers equitable title to real property, but retains legal title in the seller, is called:
(A) A security agreement.   (B) A mortgage.
(C) A real property conditional installment sales contract.   (D) A trust deed.
(C) A real property sales contract is a written statement in which a seller agrees to convey title to real property to a buyer after the buyer has met certain conditions specified in the agreement and which does not call for the conveyance of title within one year of the execution of the contract.

—————————**(Lesson Eleven - Paragraph 23 - Question 6)**—————————
A debtor who holds "equitable title" to real property could be:
(A) A vendee under a real property sales contract.   (B) A trustor as party to a trust deed.
(C) Either of the above. (D)   The beneficiary as party to a trust deed.

(C) Either of the above. The nature of the land contract is usually understood as a situation in which the buyer under the contract holds "equitable title". The trustor, who deeds "legal title" to the trustee in the deed of trust, is also looked upon as holding "equitable title" to the property until the time that the trustor receives reconveyance of his title upon paying the loan in full.

—————————**(Lesson Eleven - Paragraph 23 - Question 7)**—————————
A real estate financing device which a seller can use to transfer equitable title to a buyer, is known as:
(A) A mortgage.   (B)   A grant deed.
(C) A real property conditional or installment sales contract.   (D)   All of the above.

(C) The statement of the question identifies the legal conditions that exist in selling property by means of a land contract of sale.

—————————**(Lesson Eleven - Paragraph 23 - Question 8)**—————————
Financially speaking, the relationship between the seller and buyer under a land contract of sale is comparable to that of a:
(A) Grantor or grantee. (B) Beneficiary to trustor. (C) Lessor to lessee.   (D) Optionor to optionee.

(B) The land contract is a device for the seller to extend credit to the buyer in the sale of property. In a sense, the seller is financing the sale for the buyer, holding the title as security.

—————————**(Lesson Eleven - Paragraph 23 - Question 9)**—————————
In a legal sales contract, the seller is often referred to as the:
(A) Trustor.   (B) Devisor.   (C) Donor.   (D) Vendor.

(D) In a sales contract, also known as an installment sales contract, also known as a land contract, the parties to the contract are the vendor (the seller), and the vendee (the buyer).

—————————**(Lesson Eleven - Paragraph 23 - Question 10)**—————————
The party who holds legal title when a land contract is used is the:
(A) Mortgagee.   (B) Beneficiary. (C) Vendee. (D) Vendor.

(D)   A land contract, also called a real property sales contract, is a method of financing real property. It is done by a contract, not a deed. In the contract, the seller, also called vendor, gives possession of the property to the vendee, also called buyer. The vendor keeps the legal title and promises to deliver the legal title when the vendee fulfills his promise to pay.

_____(Lesson Eleven - Paragraph 23 - Question 11)_____

When compared to a land contract of sale, the requisites of a grant deed differ with respect to:
(A) Warranties. (B) Signatures of principals. (C) Title. (D) All of the above.

(D) A grant deed and a contract of sale differ in the signatures of the principals. A grant deed requires only the signature of the grantor. The contract of sale requires the signatures of both the vendor and the vendee. They generally do not disclose the purchase price in a grant deed but must in the contract of sale as it is a contract. A grant deed has implied warranties; the contract of sale has none.

_____(Lesson Eleven - Paragraph 23 - Question 12)_____

The party who holds legal title when a land contract is used is the:
(A) Mortgagee. (B) Beneficiary. (C) Vendee. (D) Vendor.

(D) A land contract, also called a real property sales contract, is a method of financing real property. It is done by a contract, not a deed. In the contract, the seller (vendor), gives possession of the property to the vendee (buyer). The vendor keeps the legal title and promises to deliver the legal title when the vendee fulfills his promise to pay the outstanding balance on the contract.

_____(Lesson Eleven - Paragraph 23 - Question 13)_____

Generally, a purchase of real property by means of a contract of sale or installment sale contract:
(A) Conveys legal title to the buyer.   (B) Conveys equitable title to the seller.
(C) Gives the right of possession to the buyer. (D) All of the above.

(C) When purchasing real property by contract of sale, the buyer receives the right of possession. The buyer is recognized as an equitable owner and the seller retains legal title. The contract of sale has many names, land contract is one.

_____(Lesson Eleven - Paragraph 23 - Question 14)_____

When a buyer purchases real property on an installment sales contract, he receives:
(A) Possession. (B) Legal title. (C) A freehold estate. (D) None of the above.

(A) A purchase by means of a contract of sale does not convey the legal title. The seller retains it. The buyer is given possession and use of the property and gains an equitable interest in the property.

_____(Lesson Eleven - Paragraph 23 - Question 15)_____

In the sale of real property, the following would allow the seller to retain legal title to the property being conveyed:
(A) Bill of sale. (B) Mortgage. (C) Contract of sale. (D) Grant deed.

(C) When selling real property by contract of sale, also called real property sales contract, also called a land contract, the seller (vendor) retains the "legal title to the property". The buyer receives the right of possession and a promise to a title in the future when the payments on the agreement are completed.

———————(Lesson Eleven - Paragraph 23 - Question 16)———————

A land contract generally conveys:
(A) Right of possession. (B) Estate of inheritance. (C) Freehold estate. (D) All of the above.

(A) The land contract, also called the real property sales contract, generally coveys the right of possession to the vendee, the buyer. However, the vendor (seller), retains the legal title to the property. Answer (B), an estate of inheritance, is a quality of the fee simple estate. (C) refers to a freehold estate. The fee simple and life estates are classified as freeholds. (A), the land contract as stated, generally conveys possession.

———————(Lesson Eleven - Paragraph 24 - Question 1)———————

Title in real property would pass to the purchaser under the following contract:
(A) Land contract of sale.   (B) Installment sales contract.
(C) Agreement of sale.   (D) None of the above.

(D) All of these contracts are conditional sales contracts whereby the seller retains title until the contract is paid off. At that time a deed is given and title passes to the contract purchaser.

———————(Lesson Eleven - Paragraph 26 - Question 1)———————

The contractual agreement for the purchase of real property which is ordinarily used when a buyer does not have a large down payment is called:
(A) A security agreement.   (B) A conditional sales contract.
(C) A deed of trust.   (D) An option agreement.

(B) The seller often uses the conditional sales contract, also called the land contract, when the seller carries the financing. It usually involves a small down payment.

———————(Lesson Eleven - Paragraph 26 - Question 2)———————

The following is a correct statement concerning a land contract:
(A) It is a security device.
(B) It is generally used when a transaction involves a third party lender.
(C) The vendor holds the equitable title until the terms of the contract have been completed by the vendee.
(D) If a default occurs, the vendor must give the vendee three months notice of default before instituting foreclosure action.

(A) The agreement of sale form is used when the seller is, in effect, financing the transaction himself, and the buyer is not providing the financing by borrowing from a lending institution. From the lender's point of view it is treated as a "security device." Choice (B) would make use of a trust deed or mortgage. Choice (C) is the reverse of what is true. The vendee has equitable title until the contract is paid in full. The vendor has legal title until such time as the installment payments are made in full.

———————(Lesson Eleven - Paragraph 26 - Question 3)———————

With relation to the operation of a land contract, which of the following answers most closely resembles the relationship of the parties?
(A) An option. (B) A security agreement.   (C) A mortgage.   (D) A third party contract.

(B) A security agreement is another name for a land contract. The owner sells the property by contract and finances the sale using the contract as security for the loan.

_____(Lesson Eleven - Paragraph 28 - Question 1)_____

All of the following statements concerning the "land contract" method of financing the purchase of real property are true, except:
(A) Death of the seller might force litigation to obtain title.
(B) Lending institutions consider land contracts to be poor collateral.
(C) There is a possibility that the buyer would not get clear title.
(D) The buyer is assured of obtaining title to the property upon completion of the terms of the contract.

_____

(D) Since the seller holds the legal title there is no guarantee clear marketable title will exist upon completion of the contract. The buyer or vendee, as he is referred to, only holds equitable title. That is why the contract is not considered secure collateral by institutional lenders.

_____(Lesson Eleven - Paragraph 29 - Question 1)_____

You have been asked to take a listing on a single family residence and find that your client is purchasing the home under a land contract of sale. In reviewing the contract, if you find that there is no acceleration clause and no clause prohibiting a sale or assignment, the following is correct:
(A) Your seller could sell the home and take back a purchase money trust deed as long as he keeps up the payments on the land contract.
(B) Your seller must pay off the land contract before he can sell his interest.
(C) Your client can assign his interest in the land contract, but must obtain permission from the title holder to be relieved of his obligations.
(D) Your client can sell and give a grant deed if he obtains written permission from the titleholder.

_____

(C) Since the existing contract does not prohibit a sale or assignment, the vendee may sell the property by assigning his interest in the contract, or sell his interest using another and contract between himself and the new purchaser. However, he is still personally obligated on his original contract unless he obtains a release of liability from the original vendor. Answers (A) & (D) are incorrect because the vendee (new seller) does not have the full legal title that would be required to give a grant deed. Since he cannot transfer legal title to his buyer, the buyer could not transfer bare legal title to a trustee with a trust deed.

_____(Lesson Eleven - Paragraph 29 - Question 2)_____

The best course to follow when an owner is selling a property that he is buying on a land contract would be to:
(A) Issue a grant deed.   (B) Issue a warranty deed.
(C) Issue a trust deed.   (D) Obtain the seller's consent to assign your responsibility.

_____

(D) When buying on a land contract the vendee is responsible to the vendor for the performance of the contract. If he assigns his interest in the contract he must obtain the seller's consent to assign his responsibilities on the contract.

_____(Lesson Eleven - Paragraph 30 - Question 1)_____

Jeff Dennis sold his home to Ray Bell under a real property sales contract. Neither of them is a real estate licensee. Bell makes pro-rata payments to Dennis for taxes and insurance. The following statement is correct:
(A) Dennis may use these funds until a tax or insurance payment is due.

(B) Dennis should credit these payments to amount due on the contract.

(C) Dennis must hold such payments in trust for payment of taxes and insurance only.

(D) Dennis may place these payments in his personal bank account as long as the balance of said account does not fall below the amount of taxes and insurance due semiannually.

(C) This is a specific requirement imposed on land contract agreements by provisions of the Civil Code of California.

_____(Lesson Eleven - Paragraph 30 to 32 - Question 1)_____

Concerning real property sales contracts, the following is a correct statement:

(A) The vendor may not assign a real property sales contract unless accompanied by transfer of the real property subject to the contract.

(B) Real property subject to a real property sales contract may not be transferred unless accompanied by an assignment of the contract.

(C) Real property subject to a real property sales contract may not be encumbered unless approved by the buyer and the income pays the mortgage payments.

(D) All of these are correct statements.

(D) All are legal requirements binding upon the vendor in a real property sales contract. They state essentially: 1. The vendor may not assign a contract without also transferring the title. 2. He may not transfer title to the property without also assigning the contract. 3. If the vendor owes money on the property, he must make payment on the debt from the payment he receives on the contract.

_____(Lesson Eleven - Paragraph 31 - Question 1)_____

Two people entered into a land contract for the purchase of a home and the contract was recorded. A few months later, the vendee abandons the property and defaults on the contract. If the vendee refuses to execute and record some form of release, it will:

(A) Result in a mortgage foreclosure. (B) Result in a trustee's foreclosure.

(C) Result in a deficiency judgment. (D) Create a cloud on the title.

(D) A recorded land contract shows an equitable interest in the property. When the vendee (buyer) defaults and abandons the property the land contract becomes a "cloud on the title" until either a quitclaim deed or quiet title action removes it.

_____(Lesson Eleven - Paragraph 31 - Question 2)_____

All of the following are correct statements concerning a land contract, except:

(A) Title must be passed with performance of an act.

(B) Conveyance of title is not required within one year.

(C) Need not be acknowledged by buyer or seller.

(D) Must contain a requirement prohibiting recording.

(D) The contract not only need not contain a clause prohibiting recording, such an agreement in a contract would be unenforceable.

_____(Lesson Eleven - Paragraph 31 - Question 3)_____

A real property sales contract that has been recorded offers:

(A) An advantage to the seller.

(B) An absolute assurance to the buyer that he will receive title upon performance of the contract.

(C) An advantage to the buyer if he does not occupy the property.

(D) Can only be done with permission of the seller.

(C) If a buyer does not occupy the property, he is not providing actual notice of his equitable title to the property. Therefore, it is to his advantage to record the contract to provide constructive notice of his interest.

_____(Lesson Eleven - Paragraph 31 - Question 4)_____

Which of the following is most likely to cause a cloud on the title to real property?
(A) A locked-in clause in promissory note. (B) A recorded real property sales contract.
(C) A recorded homestead. (D) Private deed restrictions.

(B) A recorded real property sales contract. A cloud on title can be described as an outstanding claim or encumbrance which, if valid, could impair or adversely affect the title of the owner of a particular estate making such estate unmarketable. Choice (A) mentions a note but a note is not a charge against property; hence, not applicable. A recorded homestead (B) protects the interest of the owner of an estate; hence, does not apply. Choice (D) does not apply as restrictions. If applicable, the restriction would limit only a portion of an estate but not an entire estate. The recordation of a land contract places a cloud on the vendor's title that, on the vendee's default, requires the vendor to take some appropriate legal action to make his title marketable.

_____(Lesson Eleven - Paragraph 37 - Question 1)_____

You would generally find the names of all the parties to the transaction, including the broker, in the preparation of the following instrument involving the services of a real estate broker:
(A) An agreement of sale. (B) An option contract.
(C) A lease for commercial property. (D) An exchange agreement.

(D) The exchange agreement generally calls for the names of the principals, the buyers and the sellers, and also the broker agreeing to the commission arrangement.

_____(Lesson Eleven - Paragraph 37 - Question 2)_____

A real estate broker most commonly would receive a commission from more than one party in a transaction when:
(A) Selling a business opportunity. (B) Holding an open listing.
(C) Negotiating a long-term lease. (D) Negotiating an exchange.

(D) An exchange involves the transfer of title of two properties. A principal to the transaction is the transferor of title to one property and the transferee of another. Clauses in the exchange contract authorize the broker to be a dual agent and to collect a fee for each property. Therefore, it would be more common for a broker to receive commissions from more than one party in an exchange transaction than in one of the other transactions listed.

_____(Lesson Eleven - Paragraph 37 - Question 3)_____

Under certain circumstances a real estate broker acts for more than one party in a transaction. A broker would most likely act as an agent for both parties when:
(A) Negotiating the sale of investment properties.
(B) Holding an option to purchase, together with a listing on the same property.
(C) Negotiating an exchange of real properties.
(D) Selling real property securities to the public.

(C) Generally, when negotiating an exchange, the broker acts as agent of both and collects a commission from both parties.

_____(Lesson Eleven - Paragraph 38 - Question 1)_____
When times are hard and money for financing new purchases is scarce, a real estate salesperson would have a better chance of earning a living if he specialized in:
(A) The sale of industrial property.   (B) Negotiating real estate loans.
(C) The sale of residential property. (D) Exchanges of properties.

(D) Buyers and sellers have a difficult time when there is no financing available for purchasing property. The parties interested in exchanging properties can do so quite easily without the need of new financing. The salesperson that can spot this possibility and can bring buyers and sellers together can still negotiate sales through exchanges.

_____(Lesson Eleven - Paragraph 125 - Question 1)_____
An option is best defined as:
(A) An offer to enter into a contract.
(B) A contract in which to make an offer within a specified period.
(C) A contract to purchase real property.
(D) A contract to keep an offer to sell open for a specified period of time.

(D) An offer to purchase or sell can be withdrawn anytime prior to its being properly accepted. A method of making the offer irrevocable is to enter into an option contract. Consideration must be given by the optionee to the optionor for his promise to keep the offer open for an agreed period.

_____(Lesson Eleven - Paragraph 125 - Question 2)_____
A contract to keep an offer open for a specified period of time is:
(A) An option. (B) A trust deed. (C) An open-ended agreement. (D) A periodic agreement.

(A) This is a precise definition of an option. Remember, an offer to purchase may be revoked or rejected at any time before acceptance and communication. If one wants to keep an offer open for a period of time, they must give consideration to the optionor. This creates a contract with consideration. The promise of the optionor is to keep his offer open for a definite period of time.

_____(Lesson Eleven - Paragraph 126 - Question 1)_____
With respect to options:
(A) The terms of the option must be rewritten upon exercise of the option.
(B) The optionor may cancel the option.
(C) The optionee has the right to any increase in value of amenities occurring during the option period if he exercises the option.
(D) All of the above.

(C) An option gives the recipient (the optionee) the exclusive right to buy at an established price during the period of the option. If the value of the property should increase for any cause whatsoever, the optionee in exercising the option would benefit from such an increase.

_____(Lesson Eleven - Paragraph 127 - Question 1)_____
All of the following are correct statements concerning an option, except:
(A) The optionee must perform if the optionor exercises his option within the period specified.
(B) The optionor must perform if the optionee exercises his option within the period specified.
(C) The consideration for granting the option must be actual.
(D) To exercise the option, the buyer must pay the amount specified in the option.

(A) The question is a negative question asking for the false statement concerning options. Answer (A) states that the "optionee must perform" which is false. The optionee receives and the optionor must perform. "If the optionor exercises his option" is false. The optionee is the one who exercises the option. Answers (B), (C), and (D) are all correct. Regarding answer (C), there must be some consideration. It may be money or an act. In a lease option it often states that there is the option to purchase the property for $100,000. The consideration is the leasing of the property. The leasing of the property is sufficient consideration upon the part of the optionee. An option must contain all the terms of the purchase similar to a deposit receipt. At the time of exercise, all that the optionee must do is state "I will buy according to the option terms".

_____(Lesson Eleven - Paragraph 129 - Question 1)_____

The distinguishing characteristic of an option is the initial lack of mutuality in the obligation created. All of the following are true, except:
(A) The optionor is bound to sell to the purchaser if the latter elects to purchase.
(B) The option, if exercised, cuts off intervening rights acquired with knowledge of its existence
(C) The optionee may reject the offer contained in the option.
(D) A purchase from the optionor with notice of the option would take title free and clear of any obligation created by the option.

(D) A purchase from an optionor with notice of the option would take title subject to the right of the optionee to exercise his right and require a conveyance of title to the land. The other choices are true statements.

_____(Lesson Eleven - Paragraph 130 - Question 1)_____

The following statement regarding options is incorrect:
(A) The optionee who does not exercise the option, loses the money given for the right.
(B) The optionee must surrender a valuable consideration to the optionor
(C) Should the optionee elect to buy the property within the option period, to be legally bound he must enter into a written sales contract with the optionor before the expiration of the option period.
(D) An option can be used in conjunction with the right to purchase a business opportunity separate from the real estate owned by the business.

(C) Although this would be a good way of giving notice to the optionor of the optionee's election to exercise the option, it is not the only means. If the option is written clearly and provides some other means of giving the optionor notice, then any method will do as long as the optionor is notified within the option period.

_____(Lesson Eleven - Paragraph 132 - Question 1)_____

The following statement is true with the respect to options. An option is:
(A) Valid without consideration.
(B) Valid if the consideration is exactly $10.00 but is not delivered.
(C) Valid if consideration is delivered even if it is less than $10.00.
(D) Not valid if the delivered consideration is less than $10.00.

(C) An option, to be valid, must have actual consideration and the consideration must be delivered. The amount does not matter, as long as it is delivered.

_____(Lesson Eleven - Paragraph 133 - Question 1)_____

A broker who has a written option agreement to purchase a parcel is now dealing with a potential buyer of that property. In this situation, the broker must reveal to the buyer that he is acting as:

(A) A licensee. (B) An optionor. (C) A fiduciary. (D) A principal.

(D) A principal. Since the broker is a licensee and since as a licensee the broker is ordinarily expected to be the representative of another or others, the broker must be careful when acting in his own interest. The broker must make others aware of the fact that he is acting in his personal interest.

_____(Lesson Eleven - Paragraph 138 - Question 1)_____

A real estate broker may contact one of the following state agencies for information and advice concerning the given subject matter. The correct statement is:
(A) State Personnel Agency concerning personnel problems in his office.
(B) State Land Commission concerning an agricultural problem.
(C) Franchise Tax Board concerning a fraudulent escrow.
(D) Department of Corporations concerning a fraudulent escrow.

(D) Escrow companies are under the supervision and regulation of the Department of Corporations.

_____(Lesson Eleven - Paragraph 138 - Question 2)_____

Under the provisions of the Financial Code of the State of California, all escrow companies must be incorporated and licensed to operate by the Corporations Commissioner. Some exceptions are permitted. With respect to escrow activity, all of the following statements are true, except:
(A)   A real estate broker can handle an escrow for separate compensation in a transaction for which his license is required.
(B)   A real estate broker can handle an escrow for no compensation in a transaction for which his license is required.
(C)   A real estate broker can handle an escrow in a transaction for which his license is not required.
(D)   A licensed attorney not engaged in an escrow business may handle an escrow.

(C) The Financial Code provides that escrow operators must be incorporated to be able to be licensed. This code describes an escrow agent as any person (legal) in the business of receiving escrows for deposit or delivery for compensation. Choices (A), (B) and (D) are specifically exempted from the requirement of obtaining the license issued by the Corporations Commissioner to escrow agents.

_____(Lesson Eleven - Paragraph 145 - Question 1)_____

An escrow officer receives two pest control reports, prepared on different dates, with one requiring more corrective action than the other does. The escrow officer should:
(A) Rewrite the escrow instructions providing that seller pick the one to use.
(B) Rewrite the escrow instructions providing that buyer pick the one to use.
(C) Send them both back to the pest control companies asking which is the most current.
(D) Notify the buyer and seller that they need to agree which one to use.

(D) The escrow officer is not to make decisions for the principal but to follow instructions. In this case the discrepancy should be reported to the buyer and seller and let them make the decision.

_____(Lesson Eleven - Paragraph 153 - Question 1)_____

When all of the instruments for a real property sale have been deposited in escrow and the escrow instructions, signed by both parties, contain terms in conflict with the original purchase agreement, the following is true:
(A) Escrow instructions will control.
(B) The original contract will prevail.

(C) A new contract must be drawn up between buyer and seller.
(D) Buyer could demand that his deposit be refunded.

(A) Escrow instructions signed by both parties constitute a valid contract and would control, even though the terms may differ from the purchase agreement. The escrow instructions are signed at a later date than the purchase agreement.

_____(Lesson Eleven - Paragraph 153 - Question 2)_____

Where a buyer of a residence, after signing a valid agreement of sale, asks the broker for permission to move into the property before the sale closes, the broker should:
(A) Deny the buyer permission.
(B) Grant the buyer oral permission.
(C) Have the buyer sign a temporary lease for the property.
(D) Obtain written consent from owner.

(D) In view of the emotional nature of the purchase of a residence (real estate), prudence and the statute of frauds dictate that such a rental agreement should be in writing.

_____(Lesson Eleven - Paragraph 153 - Question 3)_____

Smith sold a property to Jones. An escrow was opened and all documents deposited. Just before escrow was to close, Smith decided to postpone the sale for tax reasons and asked the escrow holder to return his deed. The escrow holder should:
(A) Return the deed.   (B) Arbitrate the matter between buyer and seller.
(C) Terminate the escrow. (D) Not return the deed.

(D) Where parties to an escrow deposit documents to be held, the escrow holder may not return to one party to a document without the consent of the other party. If the escrow holder receives conflicting demands from the parties, he is not required to decide the controversy. He may compel them to litigate their claims in court.

_____(Lesson Eleven - Paragraph 155 - Question 1)_____

No mention is made in a deposit receipt as to the time for the escrow period. In such a circumstance the following would generally be used:
(A) 30 days. (B) 60 days. (C) A reasonable time. (D) Unlimited time.

(C) Where escrow does not express a definite time limit for performance; a reasonable time would be implied. In the eyes of the law 30 days is acceptable as a reasonable period of time.

_____(Lesson Eleven - Paragraph 155 - Question 2)_____

During escrow, if an unresolved dispute should arise between the seller and buyer preventing the close of escrow, the escrow holder may legally:
(A) Arbitrate the dispute as a neutral party.
(B) Rescind the escrow and return all documents and monies to the respective parties.
(C) File an interpleader action in court.
(D) Do any of the above.
(C) If the two parties to an escrow disagree, the escrow holder has a right to file an action in court called "interpleader." The court will determine the rights of the parties.

_____(Lesson Eleven - Paragraph 161 - Question 1)_____

In an instance in which a buyer and a seller have entered into an agreement to purchase and sell a parcel of real property and they have put the matter in the hands of an escrow agent, the broker involved can change the time of performance of the agreements within:
(A) 3 days. (B) 5 days. (C) 30 days. (D) The broker cannot change these agreements.

(D) The broker would have no power to change any of the agreements in an escrow unless both the buyer and the seller authorize him to do so.

_____(Lesson Eleven - Paragraph 161 - Question 2)_____
An escrow may be terminated under all of the following conditions, except:
(A) By mutual agreement of the parties to the escrow.
(B) By expiration of the specified time limit under the escrow.
(C) By instructions of the real estate broker to the escrow agent.
(D) Performance of the terms by the parties to the escrow.

(C) We are looking for the false statement. The broker cannot extend or terminate an escrow.

_____(Lesson Eleven - Paragraph 161 - Question 3)_____
Ordinarily, the escrow officer, in performing the normal escrow services, is acting as/a:
(A) An independent contractor. (B) An advocate. (C) An agent. (D) A consultant.

(C) In fact the escrow officer is usually a dual agent and acting for the benefit of the buyer and the seller.

_____(Lesson Eleven - Paragraph 161 - Question 4)_____
During the escrow period, the escrow holder acts as:
(A) An independent contractor.   (B) An employee.
(C) An agent for buyer and seller. (D) A counselor.

(C) The escrow holder is sometimes called a "stake holder". He is the agent of the respective parties until the time escrow is closed and then he becomes a trustee for the money and the documents until they are distributed in accordance with the escrow instructions.

_____(Lesson Eleven - Paragraph 161 - Question 5)_____
The escrow agent usually is the agent of:
(A) Buyer. (B) Seller. (C) Buyer and seller. (D) Buyer, seller and third parties.

(C) The escrow agent is an agent of both buyer and seller.

_____(Lesson Eleven - Paragraph 163 - Question 1)_____
An escrow agent is authorized to do the following:
(A) Obtain a termite report and authorize repairs to correct problems noted in it.
(B) Give suggestions to the buyer regarding financing for the property.
(C) Arrange financing for the property.
(D) Call for the funds to close the escrow.

(D) An escrow agent is an agent acting according to instructions. The agent can issue a demand or call for funds from the lender to close the escrow, but the agent does not do actions (A), (B), and (C), which are actions of the principal.

(Lesson Eleven - Paragraphs 163 to 165 - Question 1)

Concerning escrow procedures, the following is correct:

(A) After the conditions of the escrow instructions have been performed, the escrow agency changes from a dual agency to one of a separate agency for each party.

(B) The escrow agent is a mediator and counselor between the parties.

(C) A real estate broker may conduct escrows for compensation only in connection with other broker's transactions.

(D) When the escrow holder receives a binding contract between the parties it is said to be a "complete" escrow.

(A) After the conditions of the escrow have been performed (delivery of deed by seller and deposit of purchase price by buyer), the escrow agent is now a separate agent for each party. He is holding the deed for the buyer and may not return it to the seller. He is holding the purchase price for the seller and may not return it to the buyer. (B) Incorrect - he is an agent. (C) Incorrect - he can conduct escrows only when he is the agent. (D) Incorrect - an escrow is "complete" when all of the terms of the binding contract have been met.

(Lesson Eleven - Paragraphs 163 to 165 - Question 2)

When an escrow is in progress, at the time when all the conditions in the escrow agreement have been satisfied, the escrow officer becomes:

(A) A counselor to both the buyer and the seller

(B) An advocate to safeguard the interest of the principles.

(C) The independent agent for each of the parties to the escrow.

(D) None of the above.

(C) This question deals with a fact of escrow. As soon as all the conditions of the escrow have been met, such as the lender has agreed to lend the money or the termite inspection has been made, then the escrow agent becomes an independent agent for both the buyer and the seller.

(Lesson Eleven - Paragraph 166 - Question 1)

The party who is primarily responsible for reporting a real estate transaction to the Internal Revenue Service is:

(A) The buyer's agent. (B) The seller's agent. (C) The buyer. (D) Escrow.

(D) The recent law requiring the reporting of proceeds of a real estate sale to the Internal Revenue Service has placed this responsibility primarily on the escrow agent.

(Lesson Eleven - Paragraph 173 - Question 1)

In an escrow closing statement recurring costs would include:

(A) Escrow costs. (B) An appraisal fee. (C) Impounds. (D) A title insurance premium.

(C) Recurring cost as used in FHA financing are costs that occur more than once on the property such as tax impounds. The other choices all reflect a one-time cost at close of escrow. Escrow fees, appraisal fee, and title insurance premium are all one-time costs.

_____(Lesson Eleven - Paragraph 173 - Question 2)_____
A recurring item on an escrow closing statement would be:
(A) The points charged. (B) The escrow fee. (C) The appraisal fee. (D) Impounds.

(D) A recurring item is one that would be charged again to the party involved. Impounds are paid by the borrower (buyer) at the time he initiates the loan. He will also be required to make monthly payments to the loan impound account, sometimes called trust account. These impounds are pre-payments for future taxes and fire insurance obligations.

_____(Lesson Eleven - Paragraph 182 - Question 1)_____
Able sells Blackacre to Baker. Escrow closed on February 1. Taxes on Blackacre for the entire year are $1,200. Baker had made the first half property tax payment. Under these circumstances Able will be debited in escrow the following sum:
(A) $100. (B) $200. (C) $300.   (D) $400.

(A) Taxes paid to Jan. 1 and escrow closed Feb. 1. Seller owes 1 month; $1200 ÷ 12 = $100.

_____(Lesson Eleven - Paragraph 194 - Question 1)_____
The number of days in a year used by escrow in prorating is usually:
(A) 365 days. (B) 360 days. (C) 355 days. (D) 350 days.

(B) Escrow normally uses a 30-day month for proration; 12 x 30 = 360 days per year.

_____(Lesson Eleven - Paragraph 194 - Question 2)_____
A buyer purchased a property for $88,000, paying $8,000 cash and securing a new first trust deed and note for the balance of the purchase price. If the escrow closed on September 30, 2013 and the seller had paid the taxes for the tax year 2013-14:
(A) The seller owed the buyer 3 months taxes.   (B) The buyer owed the seller 3 months taxes.
(C) The seller owed the buyer 9 month taxes.   (D) The buyer owed the seller 9 months taxes.

(A) The 2013-14 tax year runs from July 1, 2013 to June 30, 2014. The seller paid the taxes for this period. Since the sale was concluded September 30, 2014, he has owned the property three months into a new tax year. He owes the buyer the taxes for three months.

_____(Lesson Eleven - Paragraph 197 - Question 1)_____
"A" sells property to "B" who assumes the existing trust deed in purchasing the property. In the closing statement on this sale, this loan would be treated as a:
(A) Credit to the seller.   (B) Debit to the buyer.   (C) Credit to the buyer.   (D) None of the above.

(C) The closing statement reflects the cash the buyer must give the seller to complete the purchase successfully. A buyer assumes the loan of a seller. He would not have to produce cash for the loan amount. The buyer's statement would show a credit of the amount of the loan being assumed. On the other hand, the same loan amount would be debited in the account of the seller.

_____(Lesson Eleven - Paragraph 200 - Question 1)_____
The item that would always appear as a debit in a buyer's closing statement is:
(A) Prepaid rent collected by the seller.
(B) Accrued interest on the seller's loan that is to be assumed by the purchaser.
(C) A 1911 Street Improvement Act assessment lien.
(D) The purchase price.

(D) The buyer will always be charged (debited) for the purchase price. Choices (A) and (B) are usually credits to the buyer. Choice (C) is not an item for proration. There usually is a separate contractual agreement for assessments to be paid off by the seller or to be assumed by the buyer.

_____(Lesson Eleven - Paragraph 200 - Question 2)_____

On a closing statement, the following is always a debit to the buyer:
(A) Interest. (B) Purchase price. (C) Bonds and assessments. (D) All of the above.

(B) The purchase price of the property is a debit to the buyer on his bill. The purchase price would be a credit to the seller indicating that the seller is to receive the purchase price less other charges against him.

_____(Lesson Eleven - Paragraph 200 - Question 3)_____

Which of the following is least likely to appear as a debit on the buyer's closing statement?
(A) Closing points on a new FHA loan.   (B) The interest on a assumed loan.
(C) Prorations on an existing insurance policy. (D) Proration of property taxes.

(B) Any proration appears on both the buyers and sellers closing statement based on the closing date and the date the item is paid. This is commonly referred to as either a credit or debit to the party. Points on a FHA loan are negotiable so either party may be debited. Interest on an assumed loan is debited to the seller at the close of escrow.

Notes

Lesson Eleven
Part Three
Understanding Through Question Testing

 Log into your course at www.lumbleau.com.

STUDENT LOGIN
Login:
Password:

 On your student home page click on the first link to take existing courses.

HERE>>>» Click Take Existing Courses

 Another page will appear on your monitor.
Click on the link to take State exam passing lessons.

HERE>>>» Click State exam passing lessons

 Under the "Guided Lesson" tab click on the eleventh of fourteen links:
"Real Property Sales Contracts and Options".

Real Estate Salesperson Course

Guided Lessons	Practice Exams	Progress Report	Success Video

Print	Questions
Click	HERE>>> **11. Real Property Sales Contracts and Options 124**

Here you will be tested on all of the questions you have been studying and learn the most recently added questions. It is essential, for maximum retention, that you eliminate all of the questions you can easily answer and "TAG" for study the questions with which you have difficulty.

Lesson Twelve

Part One

Understanding Through Video Teaching

Lesson Twelve

INCOME TAXES

45   Both the state and federal governments impose an annual tax upon income received by taxpayers each year. This tax is a progressive tax, the amount of tax increases in some proportion to the amount of net income earned by the taxpayer. The income tax method of taxation is based on marginal tax rates. That is, there is a sliding scale of tax rates: 10%, 15%, 25%, 28%, 33%, 35%, and 39.6% with the highest rate depending upon the total amount of your taxable income (2014 single filers). The highest marginal bracket used to determine one's tax liability depends on the next dollar of your income. One can be taxed on a portion of their income at a 10% tax rate up to the current upper bracket amount of $9,075. The next dollar earned would put them in the 15% tax bracket. For example, if you earned $100,000 in 2014 you would be taxed at the following rates:

$9,075 x 10%   = $907.50
27,825 x 15%   =   5,081.25
52,450 x 25%   =   18,193.75
10,650 x 28%   =   2,982.00

$100,000 income = $27,164.50 tax

45a Often, a person with a real estate broker's license will buy and sell real estate on their own account. This action would involve the broker in dealing with what for him would be inventory. All income or profit would be treated as ordinary income for tax purposes since the broker would be a "dealer" in real property.

46   Tax consciousness should start prior to the acquisition of real property, continue during ownership and through its ultimate disposition.

48 Income or loss from real property comes from three main sources:

(1) Rental operation of improved real estate.
(2) Capital gains.
(3) Exchanges.

RENTAL OPERATION OF IMPROVED REAL ESTATE

54 Prepaid rent becomes deferred income. For income tax purposes, advance rental is income when receive regardless of the taxpayer's accounting method.

56   In a cash operating statement, taxes and fire insurance premiums would be identified as a fixed expense. These expenses do not increase or decrease significantly with changes in the level of sales activity conducted on the site.

57   Operating losses from rental income property can be deducted against ordinary income but is limited by the IRS. Capital losses from a residence are not deductible expenses.

58   Property used in a trade or a business is said to be a "section 1231 asset," and consequently receives more favorable treatment. Such property has the normal advantages of investment property, such as deducting all expenses of care and maintenance, depreciation and capital gain treatment. It has an added advantage when the property is sold at a loss if the property is used in a trade or business, the taxpayer is entitled to deduct the entire net loss as an ordinary loss against current income as opposed to investment property which is limited by the IRS.

60   The most common use of the term tax shelter is to describe the circumstances in which an operating loss and depreciation from rental real property is used to offset the taxpayer's taxable income from other sources, thus reducing tax liability.

BASIS OF PROPERTY

62 Cost basis - When property is purchased, its cost is the money you pay, the debt for which you become obligated, and the fair market value of other property or services you provided in the transaction.

Example: A property was purchased on the following terms:

Cash	$10,000
Assumption of Existing Loan	60,000
Assumption of Sewer Lien	5,000
Closing Costs	500
Unadjusted Cost Basis	$75,500

63 Adjusted basis - Once the cost basis is established, certain adjustments can be made to it before gain or loss on sale can be determined. When all the additions and subtractions to basis have been made, the result is what is known as the adjusted basis of the property. Basis must be increased by the cost of any permanent improvements to the property. This includes adding a room, putting up a fence, installing a new roof, paving a driveway or installing a swimming pool. The basis of property must be reduced by the amount of depreciation claimed or allowable each year. Any depreciation which is not claimed when it is due is lost and cannot be claimed later by the taxpayer. Principle payments on a loan increase the equity in the property but have nothing to do with basis.

CAPITAL GAINS

64 Holding period profits or losses from sale of investment property held one year or less are classified as short-term capital gains or losses.

65 For investors "in the business" (buying and selling real property) there are no tax advantages provided for capital gains under present law. This would apply to subdividers and investors who "flip" properties. They must be included with other forms of ordinary income and are taxed accordingly. On the other hand, a capital loss on property held for investment may be deducted from other ordinary income.

65a Raw land held for investment cannot be depreciated. The only income tax consequences available are in the capital gain or loss treatment at the time of sale.

PRINCIPAL RESIDENCE PROPERTY
(IRC Section 1034)

66 Residence property is defined as the owner's principal place of residence. If it is a single-family home, it is entirely residence property. If it is a unit in a multiple unit dwelling, the proportionate part of the property in which the owner resides is the taxpayer's principal residence property

67 The owner of a residence is limited to income tax deductions for real property taxes, interest on the loans, and any uninsured casualty losses. Prepaid interest (points) may be fully deductable in the year paid, but are otherwise deducted porportionaltely over the life of the loan. If the owner decides to pay off the loan early, the prepayment penalty can be deducted as interest.

67a The capital loss on the sale of a personal residence is not deductible for income tax purposes.

68 The tax on the gain that a taxpayer realizes from the sale of his principal residence is considered a capital gain. It is taxed only to the extent that the gain exceeds $250,000 in the case of a single person and $500,000 if married.

69 The $250,000 or $500,000 can be excluded from profits above basis once every two years. There are no limits on the number of two-year sales periods wherein this can occur.

INSTALLMENT SALES

71   Federal law permits the taxpayer who sells under a land contract and retained title to the property to receive payment from the sale of real property (seller) over a period of years and to pay the taxes due on the capital gain as it is received each year. He does not have to pay the tax on the entire gain in the year of the sale. This provision is moot because of the large $250,000 and $500,000 capital gain exclusions in most cases.

TAX DEFERRED EXCHANGES
(IRC Section 1031)

72   If you trade investment or business property for other investment or business property of a like kind, you postpone tax on the gain or postpone deduction of the loss until you dispose of the property you receive in the exchange. This is commonly referred to as a "tax free" exchange.   However, the following conditions must be met:

73   The property you trade and the property you receive both must be held by you for business or investment purposes. Neither property may be held for personal purposes such as your residence.

BOOT

76   If you receive cash or unlike property in addition to the "like" real property received in the trade, you are said to have received "boot." Under these circumstances you are taxed on the gain realized in the exchange, but only to the extent of the cash and fair market value of the unlike property you receive. For example, if 'A' exchanges an 8 unit apartment with an adjusted basis of $90,000 for a duplex with a fair market value of $190,000 and also receives $10,000 cash and a note with a fair market value of $5,000. Calculations:

$190,000 Fair market value of duplex
 $90,000 Adjusted basis of 8 units given
$100,000 Difference = realized gain

Part of realized gain that is taxable:
$10,000 Cash received
 5,000 Unlike property received (note)
$15,000 Recognized as taxable gain
The basis of the property obtained is $90,000 plus the recognized gain of $15,000 or $105,000 total.

MORTGAGE RELIEF

77   In addition to boot in the form of cash and unlike property such as notes and personal property, the exchange may also involve a form of boot known as "mortgage boot" or "mortgage relief." When another party to the exchange assumes a liability of the taxpayer or acquires property subject to a liability as part of the consideration to the taxpayer, the relief of such liability is considered as boot received (mortgage boot). Potential gain from the transaction is taxable to the extent of boot received unless offset by boot given.

79 If a property is taken by a local government under eminent domain, the money received from the condemnation is an involuntary conversion.

DEPRECIATION

80   Care must be taken when discussing depreciation of real property. The concept of depreciation is different when applied to the appraisal of property than when used in the context of the income tax considerations of property.

81   When appraising real property, depreciation is determined by an estimated actual loss of value from any cause.   The three chief causes of depreciation are physical deterioration, functional, and economic obsolescence.

When determining depreciation for income tax purposes, a cost recovery system is presently used. Each new owner establishes new period of time and their own method to be used.

81a   Residential property, no matter where it is located, does not qualify for depreciation deductions in income tax matters. Land also is not depreciable. A property improved for investment would be depreciable as far as the improvements are concerned.

82   When determining depreciation for income tax purposes a cost recovery system is presently used. Each new owner establishes a new period of time and their own method to be used.

83   Depreciation allows the owner to recover the cost of improvements over a fixed recovery period. The length of the recovery period varies according to the type of the property.

84   From the accountant's viewpoint, depreciation is a mathematical calculation that is taken as an income tax deduction and accrued each year. "Book value" is an accounting value of an asset based upon its original cost plus capital additions minus accrued depreciation. A depreciation deduction is allowed only for improvements. Land may not be depreciated. When the property is fully depreciated, its book value consists of the original land cost only as the improvements have been fully written off the books (expensed).

103   It should be pointed out that the interest paid on the loans that encumber the home, as well as the real property taxes are also a tax shelter because they are deducted from ordinary income in the calculation of both state and federal income tax.

104   On the other hand, the homeowner (as opposed to the tenant) must weigh these tax benefits against the loss of income from the investment of his money as well as real property taxes not paid as a tenant.

105   Another great advantage of ownership is leverage. Leverage is the use of credit (borrowed money) to purchase a property. When a property is 80% leveraged, it means a debt on the property of 80% of its value. The owner's equity is 20%. The lower the down payment and the longer the loan (reduced payments) the greater the leveraged position. "Trading on equity" is just another term used to describe what we usually identify as "leverage." For leverage to be fully effective, the appreciation from the property must be greater than the cost of the debt.

PORTFOLIO ACTIVITY

118   Investments such as stocks and bonds create portfolio income. Interest, dividends, royalties, annuity income, and capital gain or loss resulting from the sale of portfolio assets are examples of portfolio income.

PASSIVE ACTIVITY

121   A major change in real estate investment has been introduced by the TRA 86 rule that annual tax losses from passive activities may be used as an offset against passive income only. Passive losses may not be used to offset ordinary income, except for the $25,000 real estate rental property rule which states that passive investment losses of up to $25,000 that result from rental income property can be deducted by the taxpayer, provided the party's adjusted gross income is less than $100,000 and the party "materially participates" in the management of the property.

PROPERTY TAXATION

128   In taxation there is no contractual relationship between the state and the property owner. There is no limitation on the right of the state to impose taxes, except that the taxes levied shall be uniform. The right of the federal government to impose income taxes was granted by an amendment to the constitution. The form of tax imposed on property is called "Ad Valorem"- "According to value."

REAL PROPERTY TAXES

129 The tax on real property is one of the oldest forms of taxation. Historically, local taxing powers chose land as the principal source of tax revenue since the amount of land owned by a person gave an indication of his proportionate wealth and ability to pay. Another reason for taxing land is the fact that it is easily accessible and cannot be concealed from the tax collector. Whether the property be residential, vacant land, or income producing, outside of mortgage interest, real property taxes are the highest operating expense.

129a The assessment of taxes play an important part in the economic health of a community. Any community will suffer from the effects of a property tax rate that is inordinately high. New ventures would be discouraged by the prospect of the future tax burden. If established firms could find relief by moving to a new location, they would do so. Under these circumstances, new assessment bonds would be difficult to market. Investment money would be turned away as the prospects of making a profitable return would be more difficult.

132 In California, property taxes become a lien on the first day in January prior to the fiscal year in which they become due. The amount is not yet known and will not be known until the owner receives his tax bill some months later.

STEPS IN TAXING REAL PROPERTY

134 Step 1: The total assessed value (market value) of all properties subject to taxation in each county is determined through the work of the county tax assessor. The tax rate is now one percent (1%) of the market value of each parcel of real property at the time of transfer. By special vote approved by the voters this may be increased for specific purposes. A legal description is not necessary to have a valid tax bill.

135 The assessed value is subject to adjustment any time that new construction is added to the property or that a change of ownership takes place.

136 Using the pool of assessed value developed by the tax assessor; the Board of Supervisors determines the tax rate (and therefore the tax bill) for the coming tax year that will produce the needed revenue to meet the county (city) budgetary requirements. The base tax rate, per Prop. 13, cannot be greater than 1% of the parcel's market value at time of sale and the tax payment cannot increase more than 2% per year thereafter.

EXEMPTIONS

141 Homeowner's exemption - Every owner of an owner occupied single-family residence, condominium, multiple dwelling unit, and cooperative apartment may be eligible for a $7,000 exemption from the property's assessed value.

142 Veteran's exemption - Every qualified veteran who was a resident of California upon entering the service or a resident of the state prior to November 3, 1964 is entitled to an exemption of $4,000 of the assessed value.

143 California law permited persons 62 years of age or older and persons who are blind or disabled to defer payment of taxes on their personal residences. These programs depend on current funding and were not funded in 2013.

TAX CALENDAR AND PROCEDURE

144 January 1 - (Prior to the fiscal tax year) Taxes become a lien on the property on this date each year. The person to be assessed is the owner of the property on that date.

146 July to August - The Board of Supervisors of each county is required by law to sit as the county board of equalization for at least three weeks beginning on the first Monday of July. It has the power to adjust

assessed values of property upon appeal by the taxpayer. This does not apply in counties using Assessment Appeal Boards.

148 In counties that have Assessment Appeals Boards, taxpayers may appeal their assessed value. The board may grant a reduction and the taxpayer who has paid the taxes (due November 1st) may obtain a refund upon which interest may be paid.

149 November 1st - The first installment (one half the real property taxes plus personal property taxes, if applicable) of the taxes becomes due. If the taxpayer desires to pay the total tax he may do so.

150 December 10th - The first installment becomes delinquent if not paid by 5:00 p.m. at which time a penalty of 10% is added to the first installment.

151 February 1st - The second installment becomes due.

152 April 10th - The second installment becomes delinquent if not paid by 5:00 p.m. at which time a penalty of 10% is added to it.

152a. A good way to remember these dates is the phrase: "No Darn Fooling Around." November 1st is the due date for the first installment. December 10th is the delinquent date. February 1st. Is the due date for the second installment and April 10th is the delinquent date.

153 June 8th - Annually, on or before June 8th, the tax collector publishes a notice of impending default for failure to pay taxes on real property which will be unpaid by the close of business on the final day of the fiscal year. On or before June 30th at the time fixed in the notice of impending default, the taxes and assessments which are unpaid shall by operation of law and declaration of the tax collector be in default. In an instance in which property taxes are delinquent more than one year, it is declared to be in default. The tax collectors "stamp sale" establishes

the beginning date of the legally established delinquency redemption period. Such property will be designated "tax defaulted property." (Formerly, the property was said to be "sold to the state" at this point even though no transfer actually took place.) Finally, on or before September 8th, the tax collector publishes an affidavit stating that the real property on which the taxes and assessments are unpaid and are in default together with a list of all such properties.

154 The tax collector will transmit a proper copy of this list to the State Controller. Under current law, five years after the property becomes tax-defaulted, the tax collector has the power to sell such property or any portion of it, as he sees fit. He then publishes a notice to this effect. Any person may purchase the property at such a sale. (During the five-year redemption period such taxpayers are not disturbed in the possession of their property.)

REDEMPTION OF TAX DEFAULTED PROPERTY

155 Tax defaulted property may be redeemed by the owner or his successor upon payment of taxes, interest, costs, and penalties, including "redemption penalties." The redemptioner may receive a certificate of redemption as evidence of payment. Delinquent taxes and penalties may be paid in five annual installments and redemption is then complete, providing current taxes are paid as they become due.

EXEMPTIONS

160 Certain personal property is exempt from taxation, such as household furnishings and personal effects.

SPECIAL ASSESSMENT TAX

161 Whenever there is a public improvement that improves the value of or benefits privately owned property, the property owners so benefited are required to pay for such

improvement. Improvements may consist of a variety of things such as street paving, street lighting, and public parks. The law permits the county tax assessor to prepare and file in his office maps showing parcels of land designated by number or letter. Land may be described by a reference to such map for assessment purposes. Such improvements are often referred to as "offsite" improvements.

161a Assessments of this nature are considered to be capital improvements to the property and increase the basis of the owner. The Revenue and Taxation (R & T) Code of California states that such assessments become a lien when they are fixed by the governing body.

162 The tax may be imposed through an Assessment District or directly upon the properties benefited. Whatever the method, the district, city or county will issue "improvement bonds" in order to raise the necessary funds and give them to the contractor involved, or sell them directly to investors. The bonds become a lien on the property when they are known and fixed. They are payable along with the real property tax bill over a period of years, depending upon the particular improvement act itself. Usually, the taxpayer is presented with a bill in the amount assessed against his property. If it is not paid within 30 days it becomes a lien on the property and is said to have "gone to bond." There are many state laws that provide for making these assessments, the first being passed in 1885. They have to do mostly with street and road improvements.

162a Assessment bonds "run with the land." They do not need to be paid off at the time of sale but may be assumed by the property buyer.

165 Street Improvement Act of 1911 - This law is used frequently to finance street and highway improvements. Again, property owners are charged per front foot with a share of the costs. The amount depends upon how much they are benefited. This is the most commonly used special assessment law.

166 Direct assessment - A direct assessment is one levied against individual parcels of land and becomes a lien upon such parcel. Customarily, if an assessment is under the sum of $150, it is due and payable when levied. If it is over $150 and not paid in 30 days, a bond is issued against the individual parcel of land.

BOARD OF EQUALIZATION

167 A function of the State Board of Equalization is to appraise properties owned by public utility corporations and allocate the assessed values between the counties involved with these huge and scattered properties.

168 The State Board of Equalization also has the function of collecting the sales tax on the sale of tangible personal property. All records of unremitted sales taxes will be found by requesting that information from this source.

BUSINESS LICENSE TAX
(Gross Receipts Tax)

170 Some cities and counties impose a tax on all persons engaged in a business venture or a professional practice within its boundaries.

172 The conveying deed is required to be taxed if the consideration or value of the interest or property conveyed exclusive of the value of any liens or encumbrances, exceeds $100. The tax is computed at the rate of 55 cents for each $500 of consideration or fraction thereof.

179 Under federal tax law, the tax basis of property acquired by heirs as an inheritance, bequest, or devise is the fair market value of the property the day prior to the death of the decedent.

CALIFORNIA SALES AND USE TAX PROVISIONS

180 Upon the sale of any business holding a sales tax permit, it is necessary to pay a sales tax on the furniture, fixtures, and equipment sold. It is essential for buyer and seller to understand that this is paid by the seller on his final sales tax return, but the cost is paid by the buyer. It is evident that considerable trouble can arise if the purchaser does not fully understand this. Usually it is necessary to get a final clearance form from the State Board of Equalization to close the escrow. The broker should inform the seller to attend to such matters as soon as possible to avoid delay in closing.

181 Successor's liability - The requirement that a successor or purchaser of a business or stock of goods withhold a sufficient amount of the purchase price to cover the tax liability of the seller to pay sales tax due at the time of sale.

188 The purchaser of the business or stock of goods will be released from further obligation to withhold the purchase price if he obtains a certificate from the board (clearance receipt) stating that no taxes, interest, or penalties are due from a predecessor.

189 All persons or firms in the business of selling tangible personal property in California must secure a "sellers permit" from the State Board of Equalization, frequently referred to as a "resale number."

189a Use tax - A liability of the purchaser that he must pay to the state unless the retailer has collected the tax as a sales tax under the provisions of the sales tax law. The law also states that any sales or use tax must be listed separately on any sales document.

193 There are many documents that may be recorded. Some documents, in order to be effective, must be recorded. Documents which must be recorded to be effective include: Mechanic's liens, notices of completion, notices of non-responsibility, abstracts of judgment, homestead declarations, declarations of abandonment of a homestead, subdivision maps, attachments, tax deeds, certificates of discharge, reconveyance deeds, notices of default, notices of sale, and a number of others.

195 When one records a document, he is simply making that document a part of the public record maintained in that particular county. Documents relating to real property transactions are recorded, generally, in the county in which the affected property is located. A legal description is essential to assure a correct filing.

CONSTRUCTIVE NOTICE

196 Recording of an instrument imparts "constructive notice." Instruments affecting real property must be recorded in the county in which the property is located in order to give such notice.

197 Every citizen has a right under the freedom of information laws to inspect the public records.

ACTUAL NOTICE

198 Actual notice is said to consist of "express information of a fact." There are two general circumstances which give rise to "actual notice."

(1) Where a person does in fact know that a certain transaction has taken place.
(2) Where circumstances exist which indicate that the person should have had knowledge of the fact.

RECORDING INDEX

199 When a document is filed for recording in the county recorder's office it is stamped with the date, time and document number, as well as the book and page number where the copy of the document may be found in the records. The recorder may combine the

general index of grantors and the general index of grantees into a single index which shall alphabetically combine the grantors and grantees. Where such a combined index is used, the names of the grantors shall be distinguished from the names of the grantees by an easily recognizable mark or symbol.

199a Government code states: "Before acceptance for recording, in addition to every deed or instrument executed to convey fee title to real property, shall have noted across the bottom of the first page thereof the name and address to which future tax assessments may be mailed."

PRIORITIES OF RECORDING

201 From a practical standpoint, the subject of priorities of recording is concerned with the order in which they have a claim upon the property with reference to the time when "constructive notice" of each claim is made.

202 While it is true that the instruments themselves may be valid in the order in which they were executed, the recording system of California provides that an instrument executed first in time may not take precedence over subsequent claimants if the subsequent parties have acted in good faith, for a valuable consideration, and recorded their interest first. It would seem, therefore, that the general rule of priority might be that those who are first to record are first in right.

203 Although it may be said that this is the general rule, there are four important exceptions:

    (1) Taxes and assessments.
    (2) Mechanic's liens.
    (3) Agreements.
    (4) Actual notice.

ACKNOWLEDGMENT

205 An acknowledgment is a declaration that a person has executed (signed) an instrument and that it is done of his own free will. An acknowledgment must be declared before someone authorized by law to take acknowledgments, usually a Notary Public. A fingerprint, usually the right thumb print of the signing party, is now required on many documents including deeds.

206 An agreement for sale, option agreement, deposit receipt, commission receipt, affidavit, and such instrument claims that affects any interest in real property, shall be executed and acknowledged. In the matter of a trust deed, it is the trust deed itself that is recorded, not the note that evidences the debt.

207 The person who executes or signs a document alienating his interest in real property is the one who makes the acknowledgment of his signature. An official "witness" is required and this person takes the acknowledgement.

AFFIDAVIT

212 An affidavit is a statement or recital of circumstances made in writing to which a person takes an oath that they are true. For instance, a person may swear to an affidavit stating that he saw a certain person, in a certain place, at a specified time.

AFFIRMATION

213 An affirmation is a solemn declaration made by a person whose religious beliefs prohibit him from taking an oath.

TITLE INSURANCE
ABSTRACT OF TITLE

215 An abstract of title is a digest of all recorded instruments affecting title to the property and tracing that title back, in summary, from the last recorded deed or encumbrance to the patent or grant from the sovereign power. The instruments involved are called a "chain of title."

POLICY OF TITLE INSURANCE

219 The name itself indicates that title insurance companies come under the jurisdiction of the Insurance Commissioner of the State of California. The wording of this law must be interpreted carefully. The Insurance Commissioner is granted regulatory powers over those licensed in the title insurance business. Title insurers are to compete for public business in this state within the regulatory authority of the Insurance Commissioner. They must submit schedules of their rate charges to the commissioner at least 30 days before new fee schedules go into effect.

221 Today, policies of title insurance are used almost exclusively in California, largely in the standardized form prepared by the California Land Title Association.

222 Title insurance procedures include the investigation of innumerable public records, their interpretation, and the issuance of an insurance policy protecting the insured against specified types of risks in the chain of title. It can be said, generally, that title insurance assures protection against most risks which are a matter of public record and against some non-recorded risks. The number of the latter being dependent upon the type of policy ordered.

224 Title plant - Title insurance companies previously maintained a "plant" consisting of copies of all county recordings made each day which affect title to property. It is from this "plant" that searches are made for title insurance. Title companies will "post" these recorded documents by legal description. In contrast the county recorder will index recorded documents in alphabetical order.

226 A preliminary title report is usually issued at the beginning of the escrow period. This report will reveal any defects found in the chain of title and which need to be cleared prior to the transfer of title and the issuance of the final title insurance policy. The purpose is obvious. If "clouds" on the title need to be removed, they should be found at the beginning of escrow and removed as a part of the escrow process.

OWNER'S STANDARD COVERAGE POLICY (CLTA Policy)

227 The risks normally insured against under this policy are the following:

(1) Most matters disclosed by the public records.
(2) Lack of capacity of parties, such as minors and incompetents.
(3) Forgery in the chain of title.
(4) Lack of authority of parties (agents, corporations and fiduciaries)
(5) Lack of, or defective delivery of, instruments of title.
(6) Cost of defending title, if necessary.

228 The risks not normally insured against under this policy are matters not disclosed by public records including zoning, water and mineral rights, and defects that are actually known to the insured at the time the policy is issued but not disclosed to the title company.

EXTENDED COVERAGE LENDERS POLICY - ALTA (American Land Title Association)

229 To meet the demands of non-resident lenders who could not inspect the physical condition of the premises personally, the "ALTA" policy was devised. It generally covers anything requiring a physical inspection of the property. Encroachments would be a good example. It expands the risks normally insured against under the standard policy to include:

(1) Unrecorded mechanic's liens.
(2) Unrecorded physical easements.
(3) Facts a correct survey would show.
(4) Water and mineral rights.
(5) Rights of parties in possession (tenants).
(6) Cost of defending title, if necessary.

231 Risks not normally insured against under any type of policy are: Zoning regulations and defects actually known to the insured at the time the policy is issued but not disclosed to the title company.

FRANCHISING

233 Franchising is a marketing or distribution system under which a large business firm (franchisor) awards an exclusive dealership to a purchaser or investor (franchisee).

235 The Franchise Investment Law exempts from registering the offer and sale of a franchise if the franchiser:

(1) Has a net worth on a consolidated basis according to its most recent audited financial statement of not less than five million dollars.

(2) Has a net worth according to its most recent audited financial statement of not less than one million dollars and is at least 80% owned by a corporation which has a net worth on a consolidated basis, according to its most recent audited financial statement, of not less than five million dollars.

235a Another exemption in the Corporations Code provides that after sale of a franchise by a franchisee for his own account, or the offer or sale of the entire area franchise owned by a sub-franchisor for his own account, is exempted from the requirements of the Franchise Investment Law.

238 The intent of the law is to compel a franchisor to furnish a prospective franchisee with sufficient information to enable the franchisee to make an intelligent decision on that being offered. This protects against fraud or a likelihood that the franchiser's promises would not be fulfilled and to protect the franchisor by providing a better understanding of the relationship between the franchisor and franchisee with regard to their business relationship.

239 There are three separate and distinct categories of persons authorized to sell nonexempt franchises under Section 31210 of the Corporations Code. They are:

(1) A person listed in a franchise application registered with the Commissioner of Corporations for an offering in California.

(2) A person licensed by the California Bureau of Real Estate as a real estate broker or a salesperson.

(3) A person licensed by the Commissioner of Corporations as a broker-dealer or agent under the Corporate Securities Law of 1968.

BUSINESS OPPORTUNITY

249 From a study published under the auspices of the Bureau of Real Estate, we learn that it could take: 1,000 families to support an appliance store, 1,100 families to support a liquor store, 300 families to support a restaurant, 1,900 families to support a shoe store. It is important that a neighborhood survey be taken before the election to open a competing business within a given community.

HANDLING BUSINESS OPPORTUNITY TRANSACTIONS

253 The purchase may include the rehiring of existing employees. The broker should be aware that if several employees have not received their vacations, the closing should insure that this item is the seller's expense to be handled personally or in the closing.

TRANSFER OF TITLE

258 The "bill of sale" is to chattels what the deed is to real estate. It is the instrument or document used to certify the transfer of title to personal property.
258a From person to person, most personal property is sold without anything written. The sale is legal but difficult to prove.

APPLICATIONS OF DIVISION 6

260 Of particular importance to real estate licensees are the requirements of Division 6 of the Uniform Commercial Code pertaining to "bulk transfers" of goods in this state. The broker who handles the sale of a business should see that the seller and buyer observe these statutory provisions designed to warn the transferor's creditors of the impending transfer so they may obtain payment of their claims or to protect their rights before the assets are disposed of or encumbered. Recordation and publication achieve this purpose.

261 When a retail or wholesale merchant (a baker, owner of a cafe or restaurant, garage, or of a cleaning service) desires to transfer in bulk, other than in the ordinary course of the transferor's business, a substantial part of his material, supplies, merchandise, or inventory.

271 Note that this list did not include the purchase price of the business nor the purchaser's name.

UNIFORM COMMERCIAL CODE

274 When personal property is made security for a loan under a chattel mortgage or security agreement, it is said to be "hypothecated" (given as security without relinquishing actual possession). When title is transferred to another person it is "alienated."

274a Often, personal property is delivered as security for a loan. Such an agreement is called a "bailment". It is a contract where personal property is delivered by one party to another, held for a purpose, and later returned (such as a pawnbroker).

275 Although a written agreement is not necessary when collateral (personal property security) is in the possession of the secured party as in a pledge (and there are other exceptions). In all other cases a security interest is not enforceable unless there is a written security agreement signed by the debtor which describes the collateral. Sometimes a compensating balance is placed with the lender. Interest from this sum of money on deposit with the lender is an income to compensate them for making the loan.

276 In contrast to the trust deed or mortgage with which real property is made security for an obligation (debt), a security agreement is the instrument commonly used to create a security interest in personal property. To protect or "perfect" the interest created by the security agreement against other security interests, lien creditors, or subsequent purchasers, a financing statement must be filed in connection with personal property security transactions.

278 The financing statement (form UCC1) is ordinarily filed with the Secretary of State's office in Sacramento. The filing will take place at the County Recorder's Office in the county of the debtor's residence on transactions involving some consumer goods, farm equipment, farm crops growing or to be grown, timber to be cut, or minerals and the like (including oil and gas) with limited exceptions. Exceptions are goods if they are primarily used for personal, family or household purposes.

EXCERPTS FROM ALCOHOLIC BEVERAGE CONTROL ACT

292 The consideration that may be paid or received for an on-sale or off-sale general license depends upon the number of years that have elapsed since the license was originally issued. During the first five years of the license life, the amount shall not exceed the original amount paid to the state. After five years there is no limit for which it may be sold.

ADDITIONAL PROVISIONS CONDENSED

297 On-sale general licenses will be issued to public premises, bona fide public eating places, and to a bona fide club providing such club has at least 100 members, has been in existence for at least 1 year, and is a nonprofit organization. On-sale general licenses may also be issued to seasonal resort locations, clubs, boats, airplanes, and trains.

BUSINESS OPPORTUNITY ACCOUNTING

302 The "balance sheet" is a statement showing the financial condition of a business and lists the firm's assets, liabilities and net worth as of a given date.

303 Assets - Things of value owned by the firm (personal property, prepaid expenses).

304 Liabilities - Debts or expenses still owing or unpaid (accounts and notes payable, accrued expenses).

306 Accounts Payable - A running record of business transactions showing the amounts of money owed. They are considered as liabilities.

309 Liquidity - Current liabilities less cash on hand equals liquid assets. This is a test of the ability of a merchant to obtain a loan.

310 Depreciation reserve - Used to provide protection for invested capital. It would show that the venture not only produces return on investment (income) but in addition, a return of the initial investment.

310a Specific items shown on a firm's books indicate the total accumulated figures. Items

are identified as: (A) Assets; (L) Liabilities; (I) Income; (C) Cost; (E) Expenses. These identifications will not be shown in examination circumstances. You will note that "goodwill" is not listed because it is not a tangible item the value of which can be ascertained outside of the above asset price a willing buyer will pay for a business.

NOTICE OF INTENDED SALE

311 After a sales contract has been entered into on a business, the next step is to put the transaction in escrow. Many brokers who specialize in business sales handle their own escrows, which has its advantages and disadvantages.

312 Twelve business days before the bulk transfer is to be consummated or the sale by auction is to be commenced. The "Notice to Creditors of Bulk Transfer" must be:

(1) Recorded in the county recorders office in which the property is located.
(2) Published in a newspaper of general circulation in the judicial district in which the property is located.
(3) Personally delivered or sent by registered or certified mail to the county tax collector of the county or counties in which the property to be transferred is located.

The above actions are required by law or the new owner can become responsible for any unpaid accounts of the old owner. Although it is the seller's responsibility to have the notice published, it is the duty of the broker to protect the buyer from any such "successor's liability." Failure to accomplish the above does not void the sale but it does place a cloud on the rights of the buyers.

Lesson Twelve
Part Two
Study Questions

──────────**(Lesson Twelve - Paragraph 45 - Question 1)**──────────

A marginal tax rate:
(A) Determines the minimum income tax a person must pay.
(B) Determines the average income tax rate a person pays.
(C) Determines the tax rate on the next dollar earned.
(D) None of the above.

──

(C) The income tax method of taxation is said to have a marginal tax rate. There is a sliding scale of taxes depending upon the amount of your taxable income. The bracket that your tax liability comes under depends on the next dollar of your income. One can be taxed on a portion of their income at 10% tax rate. The next dollar earned would put them in the 15% tax rate.

──────────**(Lesson Twelve - Paragraph 46 - Question 1)**──────────

Income tax consciousness should begin:
(A) Prior to the close of escrow in the purchase of real estate.
(B) After acquiring property.
(C) Upon contemplation of purchasing the property.
(D) After disposing of the property.

──

(C) Since the income tax consequences of purchasing real property are complex and extensive, income tax consciousness should begin prior to acquisition of the property.

──────────**(Lesson Twelve - Paragraph 54 - Question 1)**──────────

In November, 1995 a property owner sold a property and leased it back for a two-year period so that he could continue to operate his grocery store business. In doing so, he paid rent for the last two months of the lease period at close of the sale escrow. In preparing his federal income return he will treat the payment of the last two months rent by:
(A) Prorating the two months rent over the two year lease period
(B) Take it as a deduction in 1995
(C) Take it as a deduction in 1997
(D) It will have no effect on the seller's income tax.

──

(B) When paying the rent for 1995 in 1997, he may take this as a deduction in 1995. If the tenant put up a deposit for payment of rent, he would not be allowed to take it as a deduction in 1995. The tenant would, reporting on a cash basis, be allowed to deduct the payment as an expense.

_____(Lesson Twelve - Paragraph 54 - Question 2)_____

It often happens that the lessee prepays one months rent at the outset of his lease period. In normal accounting procedures the prepaid rent is treated as:

(A) Accrued income for the lessor.
(B) Accrued expenses for the lessee.
(C) Deferred income of the lessor.
(D) Deferred income for the lessee.

_____

(C) In accounting, income that has been received prior to the performance of the service or delivery of goods is defined as deferred income. Accrued income is the opposite as services are performed prior to receipt of income. An accrued expense is an expense incurred but not yet paid.

_____(Lesson Twelve - Paragraph 56 - Question 1)_____

In a cash operating statement, taxes and fire insurance premiums would be identified as:
(A) Operating expenses. (B) Capital expenses. (C) Fixed expenses. (D) Other expenses.

_____

(C) The regular recurring costs or charges required in the holding of a property or for the guarantee of the unimpairment of capital invested therein are designated fixed expenses. Real estate taxes and fire insurance costs are in this category.

_____(Lesson Twelve - Paragraph 57 - Question 1)_____

Should an owner taxpayer sell residential property at a loss, he could report the loss on his federal income tax return:

(A) If it was used as a business property but only if a profit realized in the year of sale.
(B) If it is used as rental income property.
(C) If it is used as the taxpayer's residence.
(D) If the taxpayer had capitalized the property taxes.

_____

(B) A capital loss can only be reported in the federal tax return with investment property and with property used in the taxpayer's trade or business. The only choice that fits is the rental income property.

_____(Lesson Twelve - Paragraph 58 - Question 1)_____

The person that is finally given the most favorable treatment for federal income tax purposes would be an owner of:

(A) Investment property. (B) Income property.
(C) Single family residential property. (D) Property held for use in a trade or business.

_____

(D) Property used in a trade or a business is said to be a "section 1231 asset" and consequently receives more favorable treatment. Such property has the normal advantages of investment property, such as deducting all expenses of care and maintenance, depreciation and capital gain treatment. However, it has an added advantage when the property is sold at a loss as the property is used in a trade or business since the taxpayer is entitled to deduct the entire net loss as an ordinary loss against current income. On the other hand, the deduction for a capital loss on income or investment property is limited by the IRS.

_____(Lesson Twelve - Paragraph 60 - Question 1)_____
When a broker uses the term "tax shelter" he is most likely referring to:
(A) Real estate property tax. (B) Cash flow. (C) Interest income. (D) Depreciation.

(D) Certain types of income property offer investors great tax savings by allowing the owner to deduct depreciation of the improvements from otherwise taxable income. This is what is meant by tax shelter.

_____(Lesson Twelve - Paragraph 60 - Question 2)_____
Depreciation has which of the following effects?
(A) Increases value. (B) Decreases cost basis. (C) Creates a lien. (D) None of the above.

(B) The unadjusted cost basis of real property is its original cost. The cost basis is adjusted in future years. Depreciation taken decreases the cost basis of your property. Improvements added to the property increase the cost basis. A property is said to be fully depreciated when the original cost of improvements has been taken as depreciation. If one paid $100,000 for an investment property: the land valued at $20,000, the improvements valued at $80,000, when the improvements have been fully depreciated to 0, the adjusted cost basis remains at $20,000, the value of the land. Land may not be depreciated.

_____(Lesson Twelve - Paragraph 62 - Question 1)_____
Smith bought a home at a price of $380,000. It is assessed at $370,000 and appraised at $390,000. The basis of the property for federal income tax purposes is:
(A) $370,000. (B) $380,000. (C) $390,000. (D) None of the above.

(B) The cost of a property establishes its unadjusted (original) basis for income tax purposes. Since the property cost $380,000, the original basis of it is $380,000.

_____(Lesson Twelve - Paragraph 62 - Question 2)_____
The unadjusted cost basis of a property would include:
(A) Original sales price.
(B) Original sales price plus capital improvements.
(C) Original sales price plus capital improvements minus depreciation.
(D) Original sales price plus capital improvements and depreciation.

(A) The unadjusted cost basis is the original sales price of the property. Starting at that point, the cost basis can be adjusted upwards for improvements such as a swimming pool or added rooms. If it is investment property, the cost basis is decreased by the depreciation taken for income tax.

_____(Lesson Twelve - Paragraph 63 - Question 1)_____
With respect to the "basis" of real property:
(A) It is the original cost of the property less the cost of the land.
(B) It may never be increased.
(C) It is generally the original cost of the property adjusted upward for capital improvements and downward for depreciation.
(D) It is not affected by depreciation.

(C) This is a good general definition of the "basis" of real property.

_____(Lesson Twelve - Paragraph 63 - Question 2)_____

The following could not add to the basis of a property for income tax purposes:
(A) Addition of a concrete patio.   (B) Broker's commission.
(C) Mortgage principal payment. (D) Miscellaneous acquisition costs.

(C) Principal payments do not add to the basis of property. Principal payments amount to taking money out of one pocket and putting it into another. As you pay principal, you are increasing your asset equity in the property.

_____(Lesson Twelve – Paragraphs 64, 65 - Question 1)_____

Smith purchased a 16-unit apartment building on January 10, 2008. He resold it to Hansen on August 8, 2008. When filing his federal income tax return for 2008, any profit he made would be reported as a:
(A) Long-term capital gain. (B) Short-term capital gain.
(C) Deferred capital gain.   (D) Investment tax credit.

(B) A short-term capital gain. Current federal income tax law establishes that profits or losses from the sale of: 1. Properties held for 12 months or less are short-term capital gains or losses. 2. Property held for more than 12 months are long-term capital gains or losses. Smith owned the property for approximately 8 months when he sold the apartment building.

_____(Lesson Twelve – Paragraphs 64, 65 - Question 2)_____

Under the provisions of federal income tax rules and regulations, a taxpayer may not deduct a loss on the sale of residential real property, except:
(A) When the loss exceeds 25% of the taxpayer's adjusted gross income
(B) When the taxpayer has a capital gain that would be offset by the loss in the sale
(C) When the property was acquired as an investment that was rented or leased to others
(D) When the property was used for trade or business purposes and showed a profit for at least five years.

(C) The question deals with a negative. One may not deduct a loss on the sale of residential real property except when property which is residential is acquired as an investment and not as your personal residence. A capital loss may be taken upon sale.

_____(Lesson Twelve - Paragraph 65 - Question 1)_____

When unimproved property is being held for investment purposes, the following may be deducted for income tax purposes by one who is itemizing deductions:
(A) Annual depreciation.   (B) Loss incurred through sale.
(C) Carrying charges, if capitalized. (D) All of the above.

(B) When investment property is sold at a loss, it is classified as capital loss. The capital loss may be applied against capital gains. If capital losses exceed capital gains, the excess loss may be deducted from ordinary income to a limit set by the IRS. Remember that a loss incurred in the sale of an owner-occupied residence is not deductible and has no effect on your income tax.

_____(Lesson Twelve - Paragraph 66 - Question 1)_____

A property sold recently which the owner used partially as his personal residence and partially as a business location. For federal income tax purposes the sale of this property will be treated as:

(A) A single sale with one-half of the proceeds allocated to the owners personal tax account and one-half of the proceeds to the business tax account.

(B) Two sales, allocating one-half of the proceeds to the owners personal tax account and one half of the proceeds to the owner's business tax account.

(C) A single sale with the proceeds allocated to the owners personal and business tax accounts in any proportion chosen at the option of the owner.

(D) A single sale with the proceeds allocated to the owner's personal and business tax accounts in the proportion in which the property was used during ownership period.

(D) One may sell their personal residence in which he maintains an office. The proceeds of the sale are allocated proportionately to the area for personal use and business use.

_____(Lesson Twelve - Paragraph 67 - Question 1)_____

In lending money to a purchaser of a residence using VA financing, the lender charged the seller 4 points. Considering the income tax aspects from the lender's point of view, these charges would be considered as:

(A) A prepayment penalty.   (B) Prepaid interest.
(C) An expense of making the loan. (D) None of the above.

(B) The points are income to the lender and would be considered prepayment of interest on the loan.

_____(Lesson Twelve - Paragraph 67 - Question 2)_____

The following would be allowed as a deduction for federal income tax purposes involving the owner of a residence:

(A) Remodeling.   (B) Painting a bedroom.
(C) Depreciation. (D) Uninsured loss by theft of a garage door.

(D) The homeowner cannot deduct either repairs (A), (B) or depreciation (C). If he is unfortunate and has a casualty loss (D), he is able to deduct the amount of the casualty above an amount fixed by law.

_____(Lesson Twelve - Paragraph 69 - Question 1)_____

In May 2013, a 71 year old gentleman sells his home in which he has lived for the last 12 years for $86,000. Costs and commissions for the sale amounted to $6,500. In selling at this price he realized a long-term capital gain of $32,500. In figuring his tax obligation for 2013, he would include as taxable income as a result of this sale:

(A) $26,000. (B) $32,500. (C) $ 6,500. (D) Nothing.

(D) The July 1, 1997 $250,000 capital gains tax exclusion would eliminate the need to pay tax.

_____(Lesson Twelve - Paragraph 69 - Question 2)_____

At what age can a taxpayer sell his principal home in prescribed circumstances and receive some income tax benefit?
(A) Any age. (B) Age 60. (C) Age 62. (D) Age 65.

(A) The taxpayer who sells the principal home in these circumstances:
1. The taxpayer has lived in the home for two of the past five years.
2. The $250,000 single or $500,000 married tax exclusion has not been used in the previous two years.

_____(Lesson Twelve - Paragraph 71 - Question 1)_____

Johns sold a property in November 2004 accepting $40,000 as the full sale price. The buyer gave him $11,600 and contracted to pay John's monthly payments of $120 plus interest. The interest rate was 12% per annum. Under current federal income tax rules regarding installment sales, the following would be true:
(A) He could accept payments of interest only.
(B) He could accept payments of principal and interest.
(C) He could accept payments of principal only.
(D) He could do any of the above.

(D) He could do any of the above. Any taxpayer who receives payments in a sales agreement in other than the year of sale will use the installment method of reporting the tax on the capital gain he receives in the sale. He will pay the tax on the gain as he receives it. The question is moot because of the $250,000 and $500,000 capital gains deductions created in 1997 for a personal residence.

_____(Lesson Twelve - Paragraph 71 - Question 2)_____

For federal income tax purposes, an advantage to the vendor in a sale of real property using a land contract of sale would be:
(A) Taking profit in the year of the sale.
(B) Spreading the tax on the gain over a period of years.
(C) The contract is readily acceptable by banks and other lending institutions as security.
(D) Deferring gain until the completion of the contract.

(B) In the sale of property in which a sizeable capital gain is realized, the taxpayer can defer payment of the tax by using the installment method of handling the sale. He is required to pay the tax on the capital gain as he gets it over the life of the contract. He doesn't have to pay the entire tax in the year of the sale. The question is moot because of the $250,000 and $500,000 capital gains deductions created in 1997 if the property is a personal residence.

_____(Lesson Twelve - Paragraph 72 - Question 1)_____

An investor would least likely be liable for income taxes when:
(A) Trading up. (B) Trading down. (C) Trading unlike properties. (D) Selling income property.

(A) "Trading up" would be exchanging a $50,000 property for a $100,000 property and giving $50,000 in boot. There is no tax on boot given. However, trading down would involve exchanging the $100,000 property and taking $50,000 in boot. There is tax due on boot received.

—————————(Lesson Twelve - Paragraph 72 - Question 2)—————

Hadley enters into an agreement to exchange investment real estate he owns which has a fair market value of $330,000 and an adjusted basis of $220,000. He is exchanging this property for other investment property that he agrees has a fair market value of $360,000. Both properties were owned free and clear of any encumbrances and no boot is given or received by either party. Hadley's basis on his new property would be:
(A) $110,000. (B) $140,000. (C) $220,000. (D) $330,000.

(C) $220,000. In a tax-deferred exchange of like properties, the basis of the property disposed of becomes the basis of the property acquired. To that basis the taxpayer would add any new investment needed to make the exchange. In the question at hand there was no added capital used to make the exchange. Hence, the basis of the new property will be $220,000.

—————————(Lesson Twelve - Paragraph 72 - Question 3)—————

The term "tax free exchange" most nearly means:
(A) No gain realized.   (B) Deferred tax transaction.
(C) Exchanging parties transfer tax responsibility.   (D) No tax identifiable on the transaction.

(B) "Tax free exchange" sounds good but is not a fact. The taxpayer does not have to pay any taxes due in the year of the exchange. He is permitted to defer payment of any tax owed until a later tax year.

—————————(Lesson Twelve - Paragraph 73 - Question 1)—————

Mr. Jones owns a commercial building having a fair market value of $660,000 and a basis of $440,000 exchanges it for an apartment house having a fair market value of $730,000. His basis in the property being acquired would be:
(A) $410,000. (B) $440,000. (C) $ 20,000. (D) $730,000.

(B) $440,000. Mr. Jones is effecting an I.R.C. § 1031 exchange. By doing this, he delays the paying of income tax on the capital gains he realizes. His basis in the property being acquired (his "up leg") is his basis in the property he is giving in the exchange plus any other valuable consideration he is giving (cash or other unlike property including additional debt). No other such consideration is mentioned in the question. Therefore, the basis of Mr. Jones in the apartment house is $440,000, the same basis he had in the commercial building in the exchange.

—————————(Lesson Twelve - Paragraph 73 - Question 2)—————

A broker attempting to set up an exchange would most likely seek out the following type of prospect:
(A) An owner of subdivided land.
(B) An owner of a new apartment.
(C) An owner of a building with ten years depreciation.
(D) Another broker with a number of single family residence listings.

(C) An apartment with ten years depreciation would probably have a large capital gain liability if the building is sold. By arranging an exchange, the possibility of deferring this capital gain tax liability would be a strong motivation.

_____(Lesson Twelve - Paragraph 73a - Question 1)_____

An individual who owned a 20-unit apartment building wants to exchange his property and qualify for a tax deferred exchange. In order to accomplish this, he could complete all the following transactions except:
(A) For another apartment and receive boot.
(B) For another apartment building and assume a much larger loan and receive no boot.
(C) For a personal residence and receive boot.
(D) For another apartment building of equal value and assume a smaller existing loan.

(C) A personal residence does not qualify for a 1031 tax-free exchange.

_____(Lesson Twelve - Paragraph 76 - Question 1)_____

Boot is used:
(A) In determining the amount of backfill needed.
(B) When evicting a lessee.
(C) In computing the federal income tax due when real property is exchanged.
(D) In computing the amount of depreciation that can be taken on real property.

(C) The term "boot" relates to an exchange. Generally, income tax is due on the amount of boot that is recognized as gain in the exchange.

_____(Lesson Twelve - Paragraph 76 - Question 2)_____

The term "boot" is used in reference to:
(A) Income taxes. (B) Depreciation. (C) Value. (D) Appreciation.

(A) It is difficult to find properties of exact values to exchange. Usually, one party contributes cash or other property in addition to the real property being exchanged. This unlike property is designated boot. Receiving boot may make the exchange taxable to some degree.

_____(Lesson Twelve - Paragraph 77 - Question 1)_____

Which of the following would be an example of "boot" for income tax purposes?
(A) A decrease in basis.   (B) Debt relief from a mortgage in the exchange.
(C) A decrease in real estate property taxes. (D) An increase in deductible depreciation.

(B) When another party to the exchange assumes a liability of the taxpayer or acquires property subject to a liability as part of the consideration to the taxpayer, the relief of such liability is considered as boot received (mortgage boot). Potential gain from the transaction is taxable to the extent of mortgage boot received unless offset by boot given by the taxpayer.

_____(Lesson Twelve - Paragraphs 77 - Question 2)_____

An individual who owned an apartment wants to exchange his property and avoid paying any income tax at this time. In order to defer this tax, he could exchange his apartment:
(A) For a principal residence property with equal equity.
(B) For another apartment and assume a smaller mortgage loan and receive no cash.
(C) For another apartment at equal value and equal equity and receive some cash.
(D) For another apartment and assume a larger mortgage loan and give some cash to the other owner.

(D) In order to exchange property and defer any income tax, he must trade on an "even" or "up" basis for a similar property and receive no "boot" or "mortgage relief."

_____(Lesson Twelve - Paragraph 79 - Question 1)_____

An owner receives money for property that was either destroyed or condemned for public use. For federal income tax purposes such an occurrence can be treated as:
(A) Subrogated redemption.　　　(B) An involuntary conversion.
(C) Extinguishment of conveyance. (D) Depreciable obsolescence.

(B) This is identified as an involuntary conversion. It is treated like a sale or exchange of property. The taxpayer is given a period of time to convert the money received into a like property. If property is converted involuntarily into other property similar in nature and use, no gain will be recognized on the exchange. The taxpayer (owner) transfers his basis over to the new property in the conversion as if nothing had happened. If the property was a capital asset or was used in the owner's trade or business, the owner can take the holding period for his old property onto the new.

_____(Lesson Twelve - Paragraphs 80, 81 & 82 - Question 1)_____

An accountant and an appraiser look at depreciation in a different manner. The following best illustrates this difference in viewpoint:
(A) An appraiser concerns himself with historical costs only.
(B) An accountant is unrealistic in his approach to depreciation.
(C) An accountant utilizes the straight-line method only while the appraiser uses accelerated methods of depreciation.
(D) An accountant is interested only in the book depreciation of the property while the appraiser is interested only in the effect actual depreciation has on value.

(D) This choice is a textbook statement of the relative positions of an accountant and an appraiser with respect to depreciation. The (A) choice is incorrect in that the appraiser concerns himself with present costs most particularly. The (B) choice might have a grain of truth from the appraiser's point of view, but not from the income tax consideration which concerns the accountant. The (C) choice is the opposite of the truth. The accountant can use accelerated methods of depreciation while the appraiser generally uses straight-line depreciation.

_____(Lesson Twelve - Paragraph 81a - Question 1)_____

A man owns several pieces of investment property. For federal income tax purposes, he could not claim a depreciation deduction on:
(A) An apartment house. (B) A home he leased to a friend.
(C) A vacant duplex.　　　(D) Income producing land.

(D) Apartments, houses, stores or any improvement which is appurtenant to land has a limited economic life and which is used for investment purposes or business purposes is eligible for depreciation deduction under present tax law. Land cannot be depreciated.

_____(Lesson Twelve - Paragraph 83 - Question 1)_____

Mr. Smith purchased vacant land, paying $100,000 in cash. Later he spent $500,000 to construct an income-producing building on the property. He financed the construction by securing a $400,000 loan and paying the rest in cash. The basis upon which he can take an income tax deduction for depreciation will be:
(A) $320,000. (B) $400,000. (C) $500,000. (D) $600,000.

(C) The basis for depreciation is the original cost of the improvements. Land cost may not be depreciated. The stated cost of the building is $500,000. Therefore, this is the basis for depreciation.

_____(Lesson Twelve - Paragraph 84 - Question 1)_____

The principal reason for investing in real estate as compared with stocks, bonds, and other investment opportunities is the potential for:
(A) Appreciation.   (B) Depreciation.
(C) Favorable capital gains treatment. (D) A positive return during the period of investment.

___

(B) One of the major investment advantages of real estate, as compared with stocks, bonds, and other paper investments, would be the fact that you may take depreciation as an expense, even though no cash is involved. In some cases you can pass over this loss created into other income. Depreciation is not permitted on stocks, bonds, and many other investments. All investments may appreciate and capital gains treatment is available for all these investments.

_____(Lesson Twelve - Paragraph 84 - Question 2)_____

The owner of which would obtain the least return of investment a:
(A) Farm.   (B) Commercial property.
(C) Industrial property. (D) Residential property.

___

(A) "Return of investment" is a term indicating depreciation. Depreciation is allowed on improvements, not on land. Inasmuch as a farm has the lowest ratio of improvements to total value, it will provide the least amount of depreciation. (Note: ROI = Income/Investment).

_____(Lesson Twelve – Paragraphs 103, 104 - Question 1)_____

The following is considered to be an expense or cost to a homeowner in owning a residence:
(A) Interest lost on equity investment in the home. (B) Reduction in the value to the lot.
(C) Appreciation due to painting.   (D) Increase in amenities.

___

(A) Interest that the homeowner might have earned from a bank savings account on his cash down payment and subsequent payments on the principle (his equity) are rightfully considered a cost of home ownership. If the value of the lot decreased, however, he has suffered a loss but such a loss is not considered to be an expense of home ownership.

_____(Lesson Twelve - Paragraph 104 - Question 1)_____

Which of the following is a cost of home ownership?
(A) Land depreciation.   (B) Amenity value.
(C) Improvement appreciation. (D) Interest lost on owner's equity.

___

(D) The cost of home ownership is the return the owner could receive on the equity in the home if it were invested in anything which would render a yield (savings).

_____(Lesson Twelve - Paragraph 104 - Question 2)_____

Among the costs of home ownership are:
(A) Tax shelter. (B) Loss of interest on equity. (C) Appreciation. (D) All of the above.

___

(B) When one owns their home and has equity of $100,000, that equity is not earning interest. It could be invested in government bonds, stock, or CDs. Therefore, it is called one of the costs of owning your home.

_____(Lesson Twelve - Paragraph 105 - Question 1)_____
When a purchaser of real property is utilizing leverage he is:
(A) Using the maximum amount of his money to purchase the property.
(B) Using the maximum amount of borrowed money to purchase property.
(C) Making the maximum down payment for the property.
(D) None of the above.

(B) Leverage is the use of credit (borrowed money) to purchase a property. When a property is 80% leveraged, it means a debt on the property of 80% of its value. The owner's equity is 20%.

_____(Lesson Twelve - Paragraph 105 - Question 2)_____
An apartment building was purchased for $200,000 by making a down payment of $50,000. One year later its market value was 10% higher than the purchase price, causing the owner's equity to increase by 40%. This is an example of how an owner can profit because of:
(A) Escalation. (B) Discounting. (C) Leverage. (D) Liquidity.

(C) The apartment owner profited because of leverage. At the end of one year the value of the apartment building increased to $220,000. Therefore, the owner's equity in the property increased to $70,000 from the $50,000 he had at the time he purchased it. Thus, the 4:1 leverage ($200,000 $50,000) enabled the owner to earn a 40% return on investment from the 10% increase in the value of the property. Escalation means "going up." Discounting is purchasing something for less than the asked price. Liquidity is a measure of the ease that an asset can be converted to cash.

_____(Lesson Twelve - Paragraph 118 - Question 1)_____
In terms of portfolio risk management, lenders would be concerned about:
(A) Diversification. (B) Liquidity. (C) Reserves. (D) All of the above.

(D) In managing the risk on their portfolios of investments, lenders are concerned with all of these things.

_____(Lesson Twelve - Paragraph 118 - Question 2)_____
In portfolio risk management, a lender considers:
(A) Liquidity. (B) Reserves. (C) Diversification. (D) All of the above.

(D) In portfolio risk management, a lender determines what type of loans to have in his portfolio. These factors involve the following: How quickly can I sell these loans? What are my reserves? How diversified are these loans? Are they all business? All they all residential? Are they a mixture?

_____(Lesson Twelve - Paragraph 121 - Question 1)_____
A school teacher with a total income of less than $50,000 owned an apartment that showed a $3,000 operating loss for the year. For income tax purposes, he:
(A) Could deduct $1,000 per year.
(B) Must apply the loss against capital gains.
(C) Can take the entire $3,000 as a deduction against ordinary income.
(D) May take 50% of the loss in the year in which it was incurred.

(C) This type of loss is classified as an ordinary loss in income tax usage. An ordinary loss is deductible against other income.

_____(Lesson Twelve - Paragraph 128 - Question 1)_____

Ad valorem most nearly means:
(A) The price at which a property could be expected to sell when it has been on the market for a reasonable period of time, neither the seller nor the buyer is under undue pressure to sell or buy and financing is normal.
(B) Income taxes.
(C) According to value.
(D) None of the above.

_____

(C) Ad valorem is a Latin term meaning "according to value."

_____(Lesson Twelve - Paragraph 134 - Question 1)_____

The main duty of the county tax assessor is to:
(A) Set the amount of tax to be paid by each property owner.
(B) Set the proportionate share of tax to be paid by each property owner.
(C) Set the tax rate to be applied to the assessed value of each property.
(D) Determine how taxes can be reduced on real property.

_____

(B) The county tax assessor determines the value of all property and by that act the proportionate share of tax to be paid by each property owner.

_____(Lesson Twelve - Paragraph 134 - Question 2)_____

The annual residential tax obligation is determined by the:
(A) State Board of Equalization.   (B) The County Board of Supervisors.
(C) The County Assessor's Office. (D) The State Treasurer's Office.

_____

(C) The County Assessor's Office determines the annual residential tax obligation.

_____(Lesson Twelve - Paragraph 135 - Question 1)_____

Real property is reassessed:
(A) Upon sale. (B) Annually. (C) Semi-annually. (D) When it is refinanced.

_____

(A) Since Proposition 13 real property is reassessed upon its sale.

_____(Lesson Twelve - Paragraph 135 - Question 2)_____

All of the following transfers would trigger a reappraisal of real property for property tax purposes, except:
(A) Ownership acquired in the purchase of real property.
(B) Any grant from another as a gift or inheritance.
(C) Abbot grants property to Abbot and Benson as husband & wife as joint tenants.
(D) Creation of a leasehold interest in taxable real property for a term of 35 years or more.

_____

(C) Re-appraising property for tax purposes was established in Proposition 13. When property is resold the assessor will reappraise it and send a supplemental tax bill to the new owner. In answer (C) the owner sold the property to himself and his spouse. This does not constitute a transfer of ownership under Proposition 13.

_____(**Lesson Twelve – Paragraphs 141, 142 & 143a - Question 1**)___

In California all of the following would be eligible for some form of property tax exemption, except:
(A) Eligible veterans.   (B) Homeowners.
(C) Senior citizens.   (D) Residents in low income housing developments.

(D) The question is a negative asking for the false answer. Tax exemptions are given to (A), (B), and (C): eligible veterans, homeowners, and senior citizens. There is no tax exemption for (D), residents in low-income housing.

_____(**Lesson Twelve - Paragraph 144 - Question 1**)_____

Simons sold a ranch to Bayless. The current fiscal year real estate taxes:
(A) Are attached to the purchase price Simons received for the sale of the property.
(B) Became a personal obligation for Simons.
(C) Became a personal obligation for the buyer.
(D) Are a lien on the property.

(D) They are a lien on the property until paid.

_____(**Lesson Twelve - Paragraph 144 - Question 2**)_____

Real estate taxes become a lien on the property:
(A) July 1st of the applicable tax year. (B) First Monday of November of the fiscal tax year.
(C) If not paid by December 10 of the tax year. (D) January 1st of each year.

(D) This is a memory fact. The lien date of taxes is January 1st, preceding the beginning of the tax year on July 1st. Taxes for the fiscal year, 2013-2014 become a lien on January 1, 2013.

_____(**Lesson Twelve - Paragraphs 146 & 148 - Question 1**)_____

An owner is concerned that his home is valued too high for property tax purposes. If he wants to correct the situation, he would seek action by the:
(A) Real Estate Commissioner.   (B) Assessment Appeals Board or Board of Supervisors.
(C) State Board of Equalization. (D) Tax Collector.

(B) When contesting tax appraisals, one would apply to the Assessment Appeals Board.

_____(**Lesson Twelve - Paragraphs 146 & 148 - Question 2**)_____

When a property is over-assessed, the owner can appeal to the:
(A) Real Estate Commissioner.   (B) Board of Supervisors.
(C) Assessment appeals board or Board of Supervisors (D) Tax collector.

(C) On an over-assessment of your property, each county must have either an Assessments Appeals Board or a Board of Supervisors to which a real property owner may appeal.

_____(**Lesson Twelve - Paragraph 149 - Question 1**)_____

The due date for the payment of the first installment of real property taxes is:
(A) July 1. (B) November 1. (C) December 1. (D) March 1.

(B) Don't forget "No Darn Fooling Around." November 1st is the due date for the first installment. December 10th is the delinquent date. February 1st is the due date for the second installment and April 10th is the delinquent date.

_____(Lesson Twelve - Paragraphs 151, 152 - Question 1)_____

The second property tax payment is due and delinquent:
(A) November 1 and December 10. (B) February 1 and March 10.
(C) February 1 and April 10.   (D) March 1 and July 1.

(C) Remember N.D.F.A. The first installment is due on November 1st and delinquent on December 10th. The second installment is due on February 1 and delinquent on April 10.

_____(Lesson Twelve - Paragraph 154 - Question 1)_____

When an owner becomes delinquent in the payment of his real estate taxes, he:
(A) Must vacate the property.
(B) Must pay rent to the State of California.
(C) Under the law may remain in the property undisturbed.
(D) Must pay rent to the county where the property is situated.

(C) When delinquent on real property taxes, the owner has 5 years to redeem the property from the delinquency. His possession is undisturbed for the five years.

_____(Lesson Twelve - Paragraph 154 - Question 2)_____

With reference to delinquent taxes and redemption rights, the following is a true statement:
(A) The important effect of a "tax delinquent property" declaration by the tax collector is to start the redemption period running but the delinquent owner's possession is undisturbed.
(B) After one year, if tax-sold property is not redeemed, it is deeded to the state.
(C) Delinquent property taxes along with accrued penalties may be paid in monthly installments.
(D) The redemption period of tax delinquent property is automatically terminated if the delinquent owner alienates the property.

(A) This is a matter of fact. The redemption period runs five years. If after that period the property has not been redeemed, it is sold at the discretion of local authorities. The privilege of redemption is extended to anyone so long as the property is unsold. The owner's possession is undisturbed during the redemption period and until the property is sold.

_____(Lesson Twelve - Paragraph 160 - Question 1)_____

The taxpayer would ordinarily have to pay property taxes on all of these, except:
(A) A condominium interest.   (B) Intangible personal property.
(C) Public tax exempt land under a lease. (D) An easement over the land of another.

(B) The taxpayer does not have to pay taxes on intangible personal property. Intangible personal property would be such things as accounts receivable or a right to insurance proceeds in an insurance policy. These are not taxed. The other choices are subject to property taxes.

—————————(Lesson Twelve - Paragraph 161 - Question 1)—————————

The difference between property taxes and assessments is that:
(A) Assessments always are only applied to the land portion of the property's value.
(B) Assessments are for local improvements.
(C) Assessments always are only applied to the improvement portion of the property's value.
(D) The rate for assessments always is less than the property tax rate.

(B) This is the difference between your general property taxes and assessments that are both on your tax bill. General property taxes are for police, fire, parks and recreation, whereas assessments are for specific improvements in your local area such as street lighting, storm drains and widening the street.

—————————(Lesson Twelve - Paragraph 161 - Question 2)—————————

The county tax assessor may describe real estate for property tax assessment by:
(A) Owner's name and street address.   (B) California Coordinate System.
(C) Quadrant map.   (D) Parcel number.

(D) The law permits the county tax assessor to prepare and file in his office maps showing parcels of land designated by number or letter. Land may be described by a reference to such map for assessment purposes.

—————————(Lesson Twelve - Paragraph 165 - Question 1)—————————

A developer can use the Street Improvement Act of 1911 for all of the following purposes, except:
(A) Purchasing land for subdividing. (B) Constructing streets.
(C) Constructing sewers.   (D) Improving streets.

(A) The street improvement act of 1911 is used even today for special assessments in an area. If one wants street lamps or wants to widen the street, you will agree to assess yourself with bonds. However, the correct answer, (A), prohibits the use of this act for the purchasing of land for subdividing.

—————————(Lesson Twelve - Paragraph 166 - Question 1)—————————

The Street Improvement Act of 1911 allows land developers to use the money obtained under the authority of this Act for all of the following purposes, except:
(A) Put in off-site improvements in their developments.
(B) Buy additional land for development into future subdivisions.
(C) Put in sewers and provide for proper storm drainage.
(D) Provide for certain public utilities in their development.

(B) Funds obtained under the Street Improvement Act of 1911 may not be used for the buying of additional land to be developed into subdivisions.

—————————(Lesson Twelve - Paragraph 166 - Question 2)—————————

Under the provisions of the Street Improvement Act of 1911 you have received notice of an assessment lien against your property for street improvements. The owner of property to prevent the matter from going to bond, you will have to make payment within:
(A) 30 days. (B) 60 days. (C) 90 days. (D) 120 days.

(A) The lien must be satisfied in 30 days of notice of assessment or it will go to bond.

_____(Lesson Twelve - Paragraph 167 - Question 1)_____

The State Board of Equalization:
(A) Equalizes the flow of mortgage funds throughout California.
(B) Appraises all public utility real estate for property tax purposes.
(C) Appraises all real property wherein there is a liquor license.
(D) Is the board to which one appeals in case of an excessive tax assessment of his property.

(B) The State Board of Equalization appraises real property owned by public utilities as they own property in many counties. These appraisals are for tax assessments. They also equalize the assessments between the counties.

_____(Lesson Twelve - Paragraph 170 - Question 1)_____

An example of a gross receipts tax would be the:
(A) Business license tax. (B) Sales tax. (C) Use tax. (D) Income tax.

(A)   The fee for a business license in many counties in California is based upon the gross receipts of the business. The higher the gross the higher the tax.

_____(Lesson Twelve - Paragraph 172 - Question 1)_____

If a property sold for $100,000 and the buyer assumed an existing $40,000 first trust deed, the documentary transfer tax would be:
(A) $44.00. (B) $55.00. (C) $66.00. (D) $110.00.

(C) Documentary Transfer Tax is only calculated on "new money' in the transaction. Any existing loan assumed by the buyer is not used to calculate documentary transfer tax. The conversion rule is $1.10 per thousand dollars or .55 cents for every $500, or any fraction thereof. Therefore, $100,000 minus the assumed loan of $40,000 = $60,000 new money. Multiply $1.10 by 60 (number of units in $60,000) = $66.00

_____(Lesson Twelve - Paragraph 172 - Question 2)_____

State and county law require that the documentary transfer tax be paid at the time a deed to transfer ownership is recorded, except:
(A) When the value of the property being transferred, excluding any lien or encumbrance remaining thereon at the time of sale, does not exceed $100.
(B) When the grantee is a veteran entitled to a tax exemption on $4,000 of assessed value.
(C) When no cash is involved in the transfer by an exchange of properties.
(D) When buyer executes a purchase money encumbrance for all or part of the consideration.

(A) Documentary transfer tax need not be paid at the time a deed is recorded if the consideration or value of the interest or property conveyed, exclusive of the value of any liens or an encumbrance remaining thereon does not exceed $100.

_____(Lesson Twelve - Paragraph 180 - Question 1)_____

In the sale of a business opportunity that includes the sale of fixtures:
(A) The buyer must pay a sales tax on the fixtures.
(B) The seller must collect a sales tax.
(C) The seller must remit the sales tax to the State Board of Equalization.
(D) All of the above are correct.

(D) Sales tax must be paid on the fixtures and furniture of a business when sold to a new owner. This tax is paid by the purchaser to the seller. It is then reported and paid by the seller to the State Board of Equalization.

_____(Lesson Twelve - Paragraph 180 - Question 2)_____
In the event of a sale of a retail business, it is necessary to pay sales tax on:
(A) Furniture and fixtures sold. (B) Goodwill. (C) Stock transferred. (D) None of the above.

(A) Sales tax is charged on that portion of the selling price of a retail business that represents value of the furniture and fixtures sold. There is no tax on the value of the goodwill or inventory that will later be sold at retail.

_____(Lesson Twelve - Paragraph 188 - Question 1)_____
To protect a purchaser against "successors liability" for taxes incurred in the operation of the business by the former owner, a "clearance receipt" should be obtained from the State Board of Equalization by the:
(A) Transferee. (B) Mortgagor. (C) Vendor. (D) Mortgagee.

(C) The "clearance receipt" is issued to the seller and shows that his sales tax account is in proper order. The seller for the buyer's protection should place this receipt in escrow. If the purchaser of a business fails to see to it that the seller's sales tax account is in order, the purchaser can be held liable up to the purchase price. This is referred to as "successor's liability."

_____(Lesson Twelve - Paragraph 189 - Question 1)_____
The California sales tax is:
(A) An ad valorem tax.   (B) A tax on real and personal property.
(C) A tax on tangible personal property. (D) A tax on prescription medicines.

(C) Most items purchased at the store are subject to a sales tax charge. These items are moveable, hence they are personal property. Sales tax is never included in the sales price. It must be calculated on the sales price and separately shown and added to the sales price.

_____(Lesson Twelve - Paragraph 196 - Question 1)_____
A grant deed that is recorded provides which of the following to subsequent purchasers of the property named in the grant deed:
(A) Actual notice.   (B) Constructive notice.
(C) Both actual and constructive notice (D) Neither actual nor constructive notice.

(B) Recording a document, such as a grant deed at the Hall of Records, is said to provide constructive notice. It is construed to be notice because it is there for a title company employee or the public to check.

_____(Lesson Twelve - Paragraph 197 - Question 1)_____
The following persons may examine the records at the county recorder's office without being accompanied by an employee of such office:
(A) Bank employees.   (B) Employees of the County Recorders office.
(C) Any interested citizens. (D) Any of the above.

(D) All documents in the county recorder's office are public records and available to the public during business hours. The clerks in the office do not accompany individuals in their search of the records but they will show anyone wishing to know how they should use the files and records.

_____(Lesson Twelve - Paragraph 198 - Question 1)_____

All of the following would be considered to be equivalent to constructive notice, except:
(A) A stranger in possession with an unrecorded deed.
(B) Power lines across a tract of land.
(C) An unrecorded easement in the form of a paved driveway.
(D) Actual knowledge of a person, not in possession, but holding an unrecorded deed.

(D) Actual notice is notice expressly and actually given, and then brought home to the party directly. Constructive notice is information or knowledge of a fact implied by law (although the person may not actually have it) because he could have discovered by diligent inquiry. Choices (A), (B), and (C) are examples of constructive notice.

_____(Lesson Twelve - Paragraph 198 - Question 2)_____

Adam sold his home to Baker. Baker moved into the home but failed to record his deed. Adam offered to sell the same home to Charles. Charles examined the records at the county recorder's office. He did not, however, look at the property. Charles bought the property from Adam and recorded his deed. Considering these circumstances:
(A) Priority of recordation prevails.   (B) Baker and Charles have equal rights.
(C) Charles has a vested title.   (D) Baker maintains title.

(D) Under these circumstances, Charles is not a subsequent holder of a recorded deed without notice. Even though Baker did not record his deed, he took possession of the property. Baker's possession of the property gave notice to Charles that he had rights in the property. If a person buys property without inspecting it, he should protect himself by purchasing an extended policy of title insurance. The title company will inspect the property and inform him of the party in possession.

_____(Lesson Twelve - Paragraph 199 - Question 1)_____

The county recorder must:
(A) Microfilm all recorded documents.
(B) File documents by a phone & system.
(C) Index grant deeds alphabetically by grantor and grantee.
(D) Record sales tax returns submitted by business proprietors.

(C) The county recorder must keep a record of all documents with an adequate filing and index system but does not file phonetically nor does he have to keep a copy of the documents on microfilm. Sales tax returns are filed with the State Board of Equalization.

_____(Lesson Twelve - Paragraph 201 - Question 1)_____

Priority of liens is generally established by the:
(A) Amount of the liens.   (B) Dates of the liens.
(C) Dates of the judgments. (D) Recording dates of the liens.

(D) Priority of liens (money encumbrances) is generally established by date and time of recording.

_____(Lesson Twelve - Paragraph 201 - Question 2)_____

A property with a $7,000 first trust deed and a $12,000 second trust deed against it was purchased for $32,000. The buyer paid $25,000 down and agreed to assume the first trust deed. The appropriate documents to be recorded and the order of their recording in this transaction would be:

(A) A grant deed - then reconveyance deed. (B) A trust deed - then grant deed.
(C) A grant deed - then trust deed. (D) A reconveyance deed - then grant deed.

(D) The buyer is paying cash to the existing 1st trust deed and, therefore, desires a title free from the lien of the existing second trust deed. Consequently, a reconveyance deed would be recorded to remove the lien of the second trust deed and then the grant deed to the buyer would be recorded.

_____(Lesson Twelve - Paragraph 202 - Question 1)_____

A voluntary lien on real property takes priority when it is:
(A) Executed. (B) Acknowledged. (C) Recorded. (D) Witnessed.

(C) When one creates a voluntary lien on his property such as a trust deed, it generally takes priority by the date and time of recording.

_____(Lesson Twelve - Paragraph 202 - Question 2)_____

Bob Brown bought an unimproved lot from Sam Green. Brown did not record his deed. Later, Green sold the same lot to Bill White. White had no knowledge of the previous transaction and recorded his deed. A suit was instituted to determine who owned the property. The court would hold that the deed to Brown was:

(A) Valid depending on the recovery by White's payment to Green. (B) Valid and effective.
(C) Void as against the rights of White. (D) Void as between Brown and Green.

(B)   This is an illustration of the principal that an unrecorded deed is void as to the holder of a subsequent recorded deed without notice (White), but valid between the parties (Brown and Green). White has the title, but Brown may sue Green for his wrongdoing.

_____(Lesson Twelve - Paragraph 203 - Question 1)_____

When unpaid property taxes are liened, they are:
(A) Superior to a prior recorded trust deed.
(B) Have parity with a prior recorded trust deed.
(C) Inferior to a prior recorded trust deed.
(D) Inferior to a prior recorded mechanic's lien.

(A) Unpaid taxes become a lien on January 1. The real property tax lien is of equal priority to assessment liens. Both are superior to all other liens.

_____(Lesson Twelve - Paragraph 203 - Question 2)_____

Able sold a home to Baker. A title report obtained by Baker disclosed several existing liens on the property. The following would be the most senior lien:
(A) A trust deed executed on March 27 and recorded on March 29.
(B) A trust deed executed and recorded on March 28.
(C) A street improvement assessment declared on April 15.
(D) A mechanic's lien recorded on March 27.

(C) Improvement assessment liens have priority as though they were real property tax liens. They have priority over all other liens without regard to the time they became effective.

_____(Lesson Twelve - Paragraphs 205 & 207 - Question 1)_____
Before a lease can be recorded, it must be acknowledged by:
(A) A notary public. (B) The lessee. (C) The lessor. (D) The tenant.

(C) Before a document affecting title to real property will be recorded, the county recorder requires assurance that the owner of the property has knowledge of its contents and how it will affect his holding. This assurance is given in the form of an "acknowledgment" signed by the owner (in this case, the lessor) in the presence of a duly authorized officer, usually a notary public, that he has executed the instrument and that such execution is his own act and deed.

_____(Lesson Twelve - Paragraphs 205 & 207 - Question 2)_____
If a notary must acknowledge a document, the following person can take it when properly commissioned:
(A) The mortgagee. (B) The grantor.
(C) The grantee. (D) The member of a corporation who has no interest in the property.

(D) The question asks which person, when properly commissioned (meaning they have the designation of a notary), could take an acknowledgment. A person who was a notary and has an interest in the transaction may not be involved as a notary in the transaction. In this question, a member of a corporation with no interest in the property could take the acknowledgment. As in banks, an employee of the bank may be commissioned as a notary public. Consequently, they may acknowledge or take the acknowledgment of a person involved in a loan transaction. The other three choices all disclose parties with an interest in the transaction.

_____(Lesson Twelve - Paragraph 212 - Question 1)_____
A statement in writing which is sworn to or affirmed before a person who has authority to administer an oath or affirmation is known as:
(A) An acknowledgment. (B) An affidavit. (C) A verification. (D) An abstract.

(B) This is a definition.

_____(Lesson Twelve - Paragraph 212 - Question 2)_____
A declaration by one who is averse to taking an oath which is reduced to writing and is affirmed before an officer who has authority to administer such an act is called:
(A) An affidavit. (B) A verification. (C) An acknowledgment. (D) An abstract.

(A) The Bureau of Real Estate reference book defines an "affidavit" as a "statement reduced to writing that is sworn to or affirmed before an officer with authority to take an oath or affirmation."

_____(Lesson Twelve - Paragraph 215 - Question 1)_____
The document which summarizes the history of all the significant instruments used in transferring property from one owner to another, as well as the mortgages, leases, restrictive covenants and other agreements affecting the title or use of property is known as:
(A) A title insurance policy. (B) An abstract of title. (C) A chain of title. (D) A title report.

(B) An abstract of title is a short account of the state of the title of a parcel of real estate, or a synopsis of the instruments which show title history.

_____(Lesson Twelve - Paragraph 215 - Question 2)_____
A history of conveyances and encumbrances affecting the title to real property from as far back as records are available is called a:
(A) Chain of title. (B) Cloud of title. (C) Title report. (D) Policy of title insurance.

(A) "Chain of title" aptly describes a report or history of all important documents, deeds, liens, etc., affecting title to a parcel of real property from the beginning of recorded history until the present. An "abstract of title" is a summary of the most important instruments found in the "chain of title."

_____(Lesson Twelve - Paragraph 221 - Question 1)_____
In California, the abstract of title has been replaced by:
(A) Certificate of title. (B) Title insurance. (C) Claim of title. (D) Color of title.

(B) Title insurance policies have almost universally replaced the abstract of title that is a written summary of all the conveyances, transfers and other facts relied on as evidence of title.

_____(Lesson Twelve - Paragraph 222 - Question 1)_____
A title company employee would be most interested in a:
(A) Chain of title. (B) Title report. (C) Title search. (D) Preliminary title report.

(A) The chain of title is defined as the recorded history of title from its original existence. When a title employee searches the chain of title to complete a title report, he is most interested in the recorded chain of title.

_____(Lesson Twelve - Paragraph 222 - Question 2)_____
The persons most likely involved in an examination of a chain of title are:
(A) An escrow employee and a real estate broker.
(B) A real estate broker and title company employee.
(C) An attorney and an escrow employee.
(D) A title company employee and an attorney.

(D) The chain of title is the history of the transfer of title and encumbrances on the title in the public records, including deeds, wills, divorces, and court judgments. Attorneys and title company employees have the skills to search the records and prepare abstracts of title.

_____(Lesson Twelve - Paragraph 222 - Question 3)_____
A title company searches the records of:
(A) County recorder. (B) County clerk. (C) Federal court clerk. (D) All of the above.

(D) Title companies search many forms of records. They will search the county recorder for items recorded against the property. They will search county and federal records for judgments, divorces and original land grants.

_____(Lesson Twelve - Paragraph 224 - Question 1)_____

A title plant is a:
(A) Policy of title insurance.   (B) Grant deed.
(C) Collection of real estate records. (D) Conventional lender.

(C) A title plant is a title company's accumulation of all recorded documents. They keep duplicates of almost all documents filed or recorded with the county recorder to have them available for their own use and reference at all times.

_____(Lesson Twelve - Paragraph 224 - Question 2)_____

The primary reason for including a legal description in a real estate sales contract is:
(A) Because the owner might have other property in the area in which it is situated.
(B) So real estate brokers can find the property to show it to prospective purchasers.
(C) So the title company can locate the property.
(D) So a lender can locate the property.

(C) The legal description is required by the title company in order for them to make a title search before they issue title insurance. The other choices all involve situations involving a street address, not the legal description.

_____(Lesson Twelve - Paragraph 226 - Question 1)_____

Davis is buying a home from Brown. Brown purchased the home in 1974, using FHA financing. A preliminary title report will not show:
(A) Title vests in Davis.
(B) Certain information that will be the same as a future policy of title insurance for Davis.
(C) Details of a trust deed executed by Brown.
(D) Title vests with Brown.

(A) Since Davis is buying a home, he will not receive title until the purchase is consummated. The preliminary title report would show title to be vested in Brown and the trust deed executed by Brown would be of record. Any C.C. & R's of record would be found in the preliminary report.

_____(Lesson Twelve - Paragraph 227 - Question 1)_____

The standard coverage title insurance policy protects against the following defect:
(A) Private deed restrictions.   (B) Forgery in the chain of title.
(C) Undisclosed liens.   (D) Defects known to the insured.

(B) A forgery in the chain of title is one of the unrecorded risks that are covered by the standard policy of title insurance.

_____(Lesson Twelve - Paragraph 227 - Question 2)_____

The California "standard form" policy of title insurance on real property insures against loss occasioned by:
(A) A forgery in the chain of recorded title.
(B) Liens or encumbrances not disclosed by official records.
(C) Rights of parties in possession of the property.
(D) Actions of governmental agencies regulating the use or occupancy of the property.

(A) The "standard form" of title insurance insures against recorded matters, forgery in the chain of title, defective deliveries, and incompetent parties. It does not insure against unrecorded matters, rights of parties in possession, or zoning regulations.

_____(Lesson Twelve - Paragraphs 227 & 230 - Question 1)_____
A policy of title insurance on real property:
(A) Can be either extended or standard.   (B) Does not guarantee title to the buyer.
(C) Is an ALTA policy and is coverage for buyer only. (D) None of the above.

(A) A policy of title insurance is either standard or extended, does guarantee the title to the buyer and an ALTA policy is for the lenders benefit.

_____(Lesson Twelve - Paragraph 228 - Question 1)_____
Generally, any policy of title insurance covers all of the following, except:
(A) Forgery and matters of public record. (B) Lack of signatures of both husband and wife.
(C) Zoning laws.   (D) Capacity of parties.

(C) Most title policies cover risks disclosed by public records and competency of the parties. However, zoning laws are not covered by general title policies. To obtain this protection one must pay for a special endorsement in the policy.

_____(Lesson Twelve - Paragraph 228 - Question 2)_____
A standard policy of title insurance would establish all of the following, except:
(A) The amount of insurance.   (B) That a survey was made on the property.
(C) The capacity of the parties. (D) Lack of forgery in the chain of title.

(B) A standard title insurance policy would not concern itself with a survey. The ALTA type policy or the extended coverage policy offers this type of protection.

_____(Lesson Twelve - Paragraph 229 - Question 1)_____
The following would be covered by an American Land Title Association policy but not by a California Land Title Association property:
(A) Forgery.   (B) Zoning.
(C) An encroachment on the adjoining property. (D) None of the above.

(C) The American Land Title Association (ALTA) does cover facts that would be disclosed by a proper survey of the property. An encroachment is defined as an adjoining landowner constructing improvements on your property. This risk is not covered under the CLTA policy. Forgery in the chain of title is covered in the ALTA policy. Zoning is not covered in either policy without a special endorsement and an additional fee.

_____(Lesson Twelve - Paragraph 229 - Question 2)_____
The following is covered by an American Land Title Association Lenders Policy but not by the California Land Title Association Standard Policy:
(A) Survey of boundaries. (B) Forgery. (C) Incompetent parties. (D) Recorded deeds.

(A) The American Land Title Association policy (ALTA) does offer insurance as if the property was surveyed and corresponds to legal description of the property. Answer (A) is not covered by the CLTA policy. Both policies, ALTA and CLTA, do cover (B), (C), and (D).

_____(Lesson Twelve - Paragraph 231 - Question 1)_____

ALTA policies protect against all of the following except:
(A) Rights of parties in possession.   (B) Unrecorded easements.
(C) Zoning.   (D) Unrecorded mechanics liens.

(C) Zoning is not covered by a title policy, if one wants insurance that the zoning is proper for a development, an endorsement must be purchased at extra cost.

_____(Lesson Twelve - Paragraph 231 - Question 2)_____

The CLTA Policy of Title Insurance protects against all the following risks:
(A) Forgery in the chain of title.   (B) Expenses incurred in defending a title.
(C) Lack of intent to deliver a deed. (D) Governmental regulations on occupancy and use.

(D) CLTA (Calif. Land Title Association) standard policy insures against (A) and (C). The title company agree to provide legal defense if there is a lawsuit concerning the marketability of the title. Insurance that the zoning laws will permit an intended use is not included in the standard policy. This risk may be covered in a specific policy, however.

_____(Lesson Twelve - Paragraph 233 - Question 1)_____

The person who for payment of a fee acquires the right to offer, to sell, or to distribute goods and/or services to others under a marketing plan prescribed by another, is known as a:
(A) Limited partner. (B) Franchisee. (C) Joint venturer. (D) Licensee.

(B) Franchisee. This question is based upon the description of a franchisee found in the Franchise Investment Law (paragraph 31005 of the California Corporation Code.)

_____(Lesson Twelve - Paragraph 238 - Question 1)_____

The intent of the legislature in creating the Franchise Investment Law was to:
(A) Safeguard those members of the public who would buy from the franchisees.
(B) Establish the interests of the franchisor.
(C) Protect the interests of prospective franchisees.
(D) Safeguard the respective interests of the parties to the franchise agreement.

(C) The Franchise Investment Law was passed to protect purchasers of new franchises. The law requires that persons selling franchises to investors provide information and a prospectus concerning the franchise. The Corporations Commissioner regulates the sales of such franchises.

_____(Lesson Twelve - Paragraph 238 - Question 2)_____

The Franchise Investment Law protects:
(A) The purchaser upon the resale of an existing franchise.
(B) Buyers in contemplation of the purchase of a new franchise.
(C) Government in processing taxes.
(D) Lessors in the purchase of a business opportunity.

(B) The purpose of the sections of the Corporations Code of California, called the Franchise Investment Law, is to provide each prospective franchisee (buyer) with the information necessary to make an intelligent decision regarding franchises being offered for sale or lease. This law concerns itself with sales of new franchises by a franchisor and is not concerned with the sales by an owner of a franchise (a franchisee) to a new owner of the already existent franchise.

_____(Lesson Twelve - Paragraphs 239 - Question 1)_____
Other than a person identified in an application registered with the Commissioner of Corporations for an offering of a franchise in California, the following could sell non-exempt franchises in California:
(A) A person licensed by the Securities and Exchange Commission.
(B) A person licensed by the Federal Trade Commission.
(C) A person licensed by the Real Estate Commissioner or the Corporations Commissioner.
(D) A person licensed by the Franchise Tax Board.

(C) Section 31210 of the Corporations Code distinctly identifies three categories of persons authorized to sell non-exempt franchises in California. They are:
1. A person identified in the application registered with the Corporations Commissioner for an offering of a franchise.
2. A person licensed as a real estate broker or a real estate salesperson.
3. A person licensed by the Commissioner of Corporations as a broker-dealer or agent under the Corporate Securities Law of 1968.

_____(Lesson Twelve - Paragraphs 239 - Question 2)_____
If you are engaged to sell a franchise venture and you are not identified in an application on file with the Commissioner of Corporations, you must be licensed by:
(A) The Franchise Tax Board
(B) Either the Commissioner of Corporations or the Real Estate Commissioner
(C) The Commissioner of Corporations or the Franchise Tax Board
(D) Either the Security and Exchange Commissioner or the Commissioner of Corporations.

(B) The question deals with selling new franchises and deals with the fact that one is not identified in the application as a principal. The seller of the franchise would have to be licensed by the Corporation Commissioner or the Real Estate Commissioner.

_____(Lesson Twelve - Paragraph 258 - Question 1)_____
The ownership of personal property is transferred by using a:
(A) Grant deed. (B) Bill of sale. (C) Financing statement. (D) Trust deed.

(B) Personal property is transferred by a document called "bill of sale."

_____(Lesson Twelve - Paragraph 258 - Question 2)_____
To transfer an interest in trade fixtures at the end of a lease, the lessee would use:
(A) A chattel real. (B) A bill of sale. (C) A financing statement. (D) None of the above.

(B) Trade fixtures define fixtures that have been used in a trade or business; therefore, they are not classified as real property. Title to such trade fixtures such as machinery, a barber chair, and a shampoo bowl would be transferred by a bill of sale in the sale of a business opportunity.

_____(Lesson Twelve - Paragraph 260 - Question 1)_____

The procedure in handling the sale of a business in bulk is governed by the following law:
(A) The Real Estate Law.   (B) The Civil Code.
(C) The Business and Professions Code. (D) The Uniform Commercial Code.

(D) The sale of a business in bulk is called a "bulk sale" and is governed by laws contained in the Uniform Commercial Code.

_____(Lesson Twelve - Paragraph 260 - Question 2)_____

A "bulk sale" would be conducted under the provisions of the:
(A) Uniform Commercial Code.
(B) Business and Professions Code.
(C) Real Estate Commissioner's Regulations.
(D) Corporation Commissioner's Regulations.

(A) The U.C.C. regulates the sale of, "A substantial part of the inventory other than in the ordinary course of business." This is a bulk sale.

_____(Lesson Twelve - Paragraph 274 - Question 1)_____

A lender who possesses a chattel mortgage may:
(A) Alienate it. (B) Hypothecate it. (C) Assess it. (D) All of the above.

(D) This re-emphasizes a prior question concerning these terms: Alienate, hypothecate, and assess. A chattel mortgage is a mortgage secured by personal property. Such a mortgage may be sold to another, hence, alienated. Such a mortgage may be used as security for an additional loan. When property is put up as security for a loan and one retains possession, it is said to be hypothecated. Personal property may be assessed for personal property taxes and/or federal estate taxes.

_____(Lesson Twelve - Paragraph 275 - Question 1)_____

James Coleman sought a loan of $85,000 for a one-year term at 14% annual interest. In agreeing to make the loan, Rainbow Bank required that Coleman maintain a balance in his savings account with the institution of at least $8,000 for the term of the note. This balance would be called:
(A) Loan commitment insurance. (B) A compensating balance.
(C) Prepayment insurance.   (D) None of the above.

(B) A compensating balance. This should be interpretable from the information given. This sum of money on deposit with the lender is a source of income to compensate them for making the loan.

_____(Lesson Twelve - Paragraph 276 - Question 1)_____

The instrument used to encumber growing crops as security for a loan is a:
(A) Bill of sale. (B) Security agreement. (C) Trust deed. (D) Mortgage.

(B) When growing crops are used as security they are considered to be personal property. The Uniform Commercial Code defines the document used to create the security interest in personal property as the security agreement.

————(Lesson Twelve - Paragraph 276 - Question 2)————

The instrument used to secure a loan on personal property is called a:
(A) Bill of sale. (B) Trust deed. (C) Security agreement. (D) Bill of exchange.

(C) When using personal property as security for a loan, such as in the sale of a business opportunity where the seller carries back financing on the trade fixtures (refrigerators, stoves, cash registers, tables, and chairs). The document used to put these up as security is called a security agreement.

————(Lesson Twelve – Paragraphs 276 & 278 - Question 1)————

A parcel of real property is purchased using personal property to secure a loan. When doing so, the forms that would be used would be:
(A) Note, security agreement, U.C.C.1 financing statement.
(B) Trust deed, note, and security agreement.
(C) U.C.C.1, U.C.C.2, U.C.C.3
(D) Promissory note, trust deed, notice of intent.

(A) The question involves placing a lien on personal property. The documents used in encumbering personal property are: 1 - A note for the amount of money; 2. A security agreement which creates a security interest in personal property; 3. UCC1 financing statement, which is mailed to Sacramento and the Secretary of State to file notice of a lien against the personal property. The public may search those records to ascertain if a lien exists.

————(Lesson Twelve - Paragraph 278 - Question 1)————

When you research a chattel lien you would go to the:
(A) County recorder's office.   (B) Office of the Secretary of State.
(C) Either A or B.   (D) Neither A nor B.

(C) Since a chattel lien could be evidenced by a chattel mortgage (county recordation) or by a security agreement with its financing statement (recorded with Secretary of State), a person would have to examine either file, depending upon the type of chattel.

————(Lesson Twelve - Paragraph 292 - Question 1)————

In selling his restaurant business in 1996, the owner who obtained an original on-sale general liquor license from the Alcoholic Beverage Control Board in 1994 may obtain no more than the following amount of money for the sale of that liquor license:
(A) No more than originally paid to the state.   (B) $12,000.
(C) $20,000.   (D) Not limited by law as it is a bona-fide eating place.

(A) In the sale of an on-sale general liquor license or an off-sale general liquor license originally issued on or after June 1 1961, the seller can receive no more than he originally paid to the state. After five years from the date of the original issuance of the license there is no limit on the fee charged for the sale of such a license.

_____(Lesson Twelve - Paragraph 297 - Question 1)_____

An on-sale general liquor license can be issued to all of the following, except:
(A) A boat docked in San Francisco County.   (B) A cafeteria just completed.
(C) A hotel finished one year ago.   (D) A club in existence for six months.

(D) In order to be classified as a non-public premises, a club must be in existence for at least one year, not six months. The three other choices are all correct. Liquor licenses may be obtained for boat docked like the Queen Mary, etc. A cafeteria is not a club and can obtain a liquor license. A hotel can obtain a liquor license.

_____(Lesson Twelve - Paragraph 297 - Question 2)_____

The Dept. of Alcoholic Beverage Control will not issue an on-sale general or off-sale license to:
(A) An alien.
(B) A corporation operating a seasonal business.
(C) A cafeteria or hotel that has been in operation for only six months.
(D) A bona fide club that has been lawfully operated for six months.

(D) A bona fide club that has been legally operated for six months cannot get such a license. Such a club must have 100 or more members and must have operated for more than a year to be capable of filing for the on-sale general liquor license.

_____(Lesson Twelve - Paragraph 312 - Question 1)_____

A sells a business to B but the latter fails to record a proper "Notice of Intended Sale" and publish such notice as required by law. This sales agreement would be:
(A) Void. (B) Voidable as to the creditors. (C) Unenforceable. (D) Valid.

(D) Of itself, the sales agreement is a valid agreement between A and B. The Uniform Commercial Code was enacted to protect the interest of the seller's creditors and not for the principals. To say that this agreement is void is saying too much. To say that the agreement is voidable as to the creditors is not going far enough. The law is interpreted that it is void as to creditors. In saying that the agreement is unenforceable is also too general a statement.

_____(Lesson Twelve - Paragraph 312 - Question 2)_____

A notice to creditors of bulk transfer would contain all of the following, except:
(A) Names and addresses of all creditors. (B) Names of transferor and transferee.
(C) Date of sale.   (D) Location of property to be transferred.

(A)   The transferee (buyer) publishes and records the notice of sale to give recorded notice to any and all creditors of the transferor (seller). He would have no knowledge of their names and addresses.

Notes

Lesson Twelve
Part Three
Understanding Through Question Testing

1 Log into your course at www.lumbleau.com.

STUDENT LOGIN

Login:

Password:

2 On your student home page click on the first link to take existing courses.

HERE>>>» Click Take Existing Courses

3 Another page will appear on your monitor.
Click on the link to take State exam passing lessons.

HERE>>>» Click State exam passing lessons

4 Under the "Guided Lesson" tab click on the twelfth of fourteen links: "Specialized Services".

Real Estate Salesperson Course

Guided Lessons	Practice Exams	Progress Report	Success Video

Print	Questions
Click	HERE>>> 12. Specialized Services 277

Here you will be tested on all of the questions you have been studying and learn the most recently added questions. It is essential, for maximum retention, that you eliminate all of the questions you can easily answer and "TAG" for study the questions with which you have difficulty.

Lesson Thirteen

Part One
Understanding Through Video Teaching

Lesson Thirteen
FINANCING REAL ESTATE PURCHASES

19 In the realm of real estate financing, comparisons are often made between the many kinds of property used as security for loans. When comparing a lender's attitude in making a loan on an apartment house or on a motel, interest rates often run ½ to 1½ percent higher for motel loans than for apartment and office buildings. They also have a normal loan-to-value ratio of less than ½ of appraised value. There is greater competition for motel loans because of nationwide and regional chains of motels that have been established and the large supply of land upon which to erect the establishments. It can readily be shown that interest rates charged on the financing of extensive commercial property ventures, such as office buildings and shopping centers, are usually lower than that charged in other real estate ventures even though they are sometimes subject to greater risk. The advantages to the institution making this type of loan is the reduced cost of establishing and servicing the loan which may produce a higher than average yield over the term of the loan. For the balance of this lesson we will be dealing with interest rates as they affect the average real estate agent working with residential properties.

19a One should understand that if everyone had to pay cash to purchase a home there would be little home ownership. Financing is essential to purchasing a home on a "pay as you go" purchase plan rather than outright home ownership. There are many good reasons other than the simple fact that homebuyers don't have the savings to pay cash. Some of these are:

(1) Savings remain as more liquid assets for use in sudden or emergency needs.
(2) Mortgage amortization payments constitute a regular and consistent form of savings in the form of increased equity.
(3) A home can be more readily sold, if the need arises, if it is subject to mortgage debt and is currently financed at available low rates of interest. The only advantage to 100% equity ownership is the use of the spendable monthly cash that would, otherwise, be used to pay off a loan.

19b In its simplest form, a secured real property loan, most often referred to as "the mortgage," consists of the note (evidence of the debt) and the security for the note (deed of trust). The deed of trust, when recorded, creates a voluntary lien against the property.

EQUITY

20 The greater a down payment a person places on a property the larger is that person's equity position (difference between mortgage indebtedness and market value of the property). Should the value of the property increase during the period held, the amount of the equity will increase since the loan remains the same or decreases. The reverse is also true as most California homeowners realized during the first half of the 1990's and again from 2007 to 2012. As the value of property decreases the equity will decrease since the loan remains the same or declines slightly due to payments. If the owner decides to pay off part of the loan, the consequence would be an increase in equity. Conversely, should an owner borrow more money on their property by taking out an equity loan, their equity in the property would decrease.

22 The larger the equity or cash a borrower has in a property, the more secure will be the lenders position and the lower will be the interest charged by the lender. This is stated as the loan-to-value ratio. The lower the loan-to-value ratio, the larger the owner's equity. The higher the loan-to-value, the smaller the owner's equity.

22a The companies that are in the business of making loans where real estate is the security would offer the lowest loan-to-value ratio on industrial real estate. In view of the highly specialized use of an industrial property, lenders are normally most cautious in making loans. In general, lenders give the lowest loan-to-value consideration to the property itself. More consideration is given to the profitability of the industrial venture.

23   Most buyers want a low down payment and a large loan to value ratio because:

(1) The buyer does not have to liquidate his savings account and make a fixed investment.

(2) The amortized payments are a good form of forced savings.

(3) If the value of the home goes up, he will profit from the increase by a higher valuation of property.

(4) The loan-to-value ratio makes a subsequent loan assumption more desirable.

The opposite of these advantages also occur. In liberalizing loan terms, the lender makes it possible for borrowers with lower incomes to be able to borrow.

24   Lenders want as much security as possible for every loan. To find this security they:

(1) Look for a large down payment (high equity). The borrower is the first to lose money in a loan transaction and the higher the borrower's equity in the property the lower the loan-to-value ratio, the better the security. Lenders also feel that a substantial equity tends to foster greater pride in ownership.

(2) Look to the borrower's ability to pay the monthly payments. A borrower's high income with low other expenses increases a borrower's ability to pay, further adding security.

(3) Look to the guarantees given by the federal government through VA, FHA, Freddy Mac, Fanny Mae and Ginny Mae.

24a Real estate lending is a long-term venture. The present condition of the economy will generally have little effect upon what will be the case in five or ten years.

25   The process of determining the borrower's ability to repay the debt is referred to as a "loan or mortgage evaluation".

25a In the case of industrial property, it is because of the relatively large supply of land suitable for industrial use and because of buildings already in existence that loans on industrial properties are made primarily on the basis of the financial strength of the industrial user - not the estimated value of the land and improvements.

26   The interest rate agreed upon and named in the loan (nominal rate) depends, to a degree, upon these factors.

27   The need that the borrower has for the money lent is of little or no significance in the determination of the borrower's ability to repay the loan.

MORTGAGE MARKETS

31   The "secondary mortgage market" is one in which existing mortgage loans or trust deed loans are bought, sold, or borrowed against.

32   "Primary financing" is an expression used to indicate the first or "prime" loan on a property such as a first trust deed. The value of the property is of prime consideration because the "prime" lender must have a certified appraisal if the loan is to be sold.

33   "Secondary financing" is the term used to refer to loans that are subordinate to a first loan (second trust deeds, third trust deeds, etc.). Secondary financing is always involved with the homeowner's equity in the property. The higher the amount of equity the greater ability to obtain secondary financing. Most secondary financing comes from hard money "equity loans" and from

sellers taking back a loan to assist the purchaser by lowering the down payment.

34   Today, practically all residential real estate loans made by institutional lenders are fully amortized loans. These are loans that are repaid in equal or level installments of principal and interest over the term of the loan. Understand that the terms "to amortize" or "amortization" mean to repay (liquidate) debt or obligation on the installment plan. It has nothing to do with the security device used to protect the lender. The interest is payable after the period during which the money was used (in arrears). The principle payments increase each month as the interest payment is reduced because interest is always paid on the remaining unpaid balance of the loan.

34a   Service debt or debt service is the amount of the monthly mortgage payment. If the monthly payment is not sufficient to cover the interest amount of the loan, the non-paid interest will be added to the principal amount of the loan. This will increase the principal amount of the loan and is referred to as negative amortization.

37   Some real estate loans are "straight loans." This means that the entire debt or obligation is to be paid at one fixed time. In this kind of a loan there would be no installment payments of principal at all and no periodic payments of interest unless this is provided for by the terms of the note. Ordinarily, the entire obligation, principal, and interest is cleared by a single payment.

CONVENTIONAL LOANS

46   This form of financing is known as "conventional financing." This means that the lender assumes the risk without any governmental guarantees against loss to support the credit of the borrower. Broadly speaking, it is any real property loan which is not insured or guaranteed by a government agency. With the influence of government purchases, guarantees and insurance loans of this type are usually made by financial institutions known as institutional lenders. These include:

(1)   Life insurance companies.
(2)   Banks.
(3)   Savings banks whose loan practices are controlled by law and by adopted policy.
These loans are referred to as institutional and purchase-money, since they are usually arranged for an original purchase.

DEBT-INCOME RATIO

52   "Debt-income ratio" is a loan qualification tool that indicates the fraction that your loan payment on the property is relative to the net income from the property. This is used by lenders when qualifying a person for an income property loan and measuring their margin of safety. If your annual debt payment of principal and interest is $10,000, and the net income from the property is $15,000, then the income is 1½ times the debt payment. This is expressed as:

$$\frac{\text{Annual Debt Service}}{\text{Net Operating income}} = \frac{\$10,000}{\$15,000} = 1.5$$

54   Lenders charge points or origination fees for many reasons. The fees cover risks to a lender in making a loan to a less stable borrower and compensates for foregoing higher yields obtainable from other types of investments. Investors, on the other hand, are sometimes willing to pay premium points for attractive mortgage loans. "Discount points" charged on a loan are paid by the seller to the lender from the sale proceeds. This is income to the lender and is considered to be 'prepaid interest' for the lender. Points increase the overall yield because they lower the total amount of money actually lent but not the amount eventually received back.

56   In effect, the word "discount" means a reduction in value or the difference between face value and cash value. The term "discount points" is ordinarily used when the seller is being charged a specific number of points to compensate the lender for contracting to make the buyer a lower-than-market interest rate mortgage loan, or when the investor is bidding for a seasoned loan as an investment and offers less than the unpaid principal balance based

upon the risk involved or yield acquired. Discounting any kind of a loan increases its effective yield to the buyer of the note.

57   A seasoned loan is one that has been in existence for a period of time sufficient for a loan payment history to be seen as a normal method of payment for that particular loan.

59   Most institutional lenders also require that the borrower make payments for 1/12th of the annual insurance premiums and 1/12th of the annual taxes along with their monthly payments. These payments are placed into an "impound account." This practice guarantees the lender that the borrower makes these payments The borower is not hit with a major layout of money once each year. Fire insurance is demanded by most lenders as a safeguard for the money they have invested in the property.

59a It is an expression that one should have sufficient fire insurance so that the insured would neither gain money, nor lose money if the insurance proceeds are given in case of a total loss.   If a home has an insured value of $100,000, and carries a $200,000 insurance policy, the company will accept your premium on the $200,000 but in the event of a total loss you would receive $100,000 to replace the current value of the improvements. If you under insure the property, planning to take advantage of small losses only, then the insurer will require you to be a co-insurer. If the insured value is $100,000 and you insure for only 50% of value and then have a loss of $20,000, you would be a co-insurer for 50% of the $20,000 loss and receive only $10,000 in insurance proceeds.

59b Conventional loans are currently offered in fixed rate loans and variable rate loans. The reason behind these two packages being offered on the market is because the lending institutions were caught in the early 1980's with all fixed rate loans at around 8%. When the interest rates climbed into the 15% to 20% range, the lenders lost billions of dollars because of their portfolio of fixed rate loans at low interest rates. The variable rate loan offers a much lower interest

rate to start. This allows more people to buy because payments are based on a lower rate making the monthly payment lower. The rate then changes either up or down according to market conditions and is set by a precise index. The federal government created a law that makes the loan subject to a maximum rate no higher than 5% of the original rate set on the loan.

INSTITUTIONAL LENDING AGENCIES
INSURANCE COMPANIES

61   Life insurance companies prefer to make long-term loans on large, high quality properties such as large shopping centers. For the most part, mortgage companies solicit borrowers for insurance company loans.

62   The lending characteristics of an insurance company include:

(1) Many long-term loans.
(2) Many residential loans but a number of commercial and industrial loans.
(3) Make medium sized loans relative to value.
(4) Prefer large loans.
(5) Buy loan packages.
(6) No geographic limitations but are selective as to neighborhoods.
(7) Usually low interest rate.
(8) Almost no construction loans.
(9) Borrower's ability to repay a major concern.
(10) Seeks to avoid administration of a loan.

PENSION FUNDS

64a In the past few decades private pension funds have accumulated billions of dollars. In recent years, a trend has developed where these funds invest not only in large-scale real estate financing investments, but also invest in portfolios of FHA and VA backed mortgages.

SAVINGS BANKS

65   For many years, these lenders accounted for the greatest share of home loans. They

include both federally chartered and state chartered banks. They are regulated by the Federal Home Loan Bank that lends money to re-loan on the open market. These lenders are corporations that have their stocks traded by the major exchanges. For this reason, they are accountable to their stockholders to make large profits and would be less likely to make lower interest rate loans.

66   Federal savings banks are members of the Federal Home Loan Bank System and are subject to its supervision. In California there are many state-chartered institutions that operate under the provisions of the Financial Code of California. The principal function of savings banks is to gather the savings of as many people as possible and to lend these savings to other people principally for the purpose of building, buying, improving, or refinancing residential real property.

68   Although the Federal Home Loan Bank Board requires that the loan-to-value ratio shall not exceed 90% of the value of the security property, it does allow a loan-to-value ratio not to exceed 95% of the value of the security property in special cases.

COMMERCIAL BANKS

69   Commercial banks prefer loans secured by property in close proximity to its office, prefer to have had a prior relationship with the borrower, and prefer to make short term loans. Federal banks are regulated by federal statutes. State banks are governed by state laws that limit their activities.

MUTUAL SAVINGS BANKS

71   Mutual savings banks are located mainly in the northeastern states. They serve the same purpose of the savings banks in the states in which they function.

MORTGAGE COMPANIES

73   Mortgage companies are usually privately owned firms that have limited funds for outright

mortgage lending.   Ordinarily, mortgage companies can be either mortgage brokers or mortgage bankers, or they can be both. Mortgage brokers arrange loans as correspondents for life insurance companies, mutual savings banks, pension funds, etc. Mortgage bankers originate, finance, and close first mortgage loans. Then they sell these loans to institutional investors. After the loans are sold, typically, they are serviced by the mortgage broker under a contractual relationship with the beneficiary.   In addition, they are actively engaged making short-term construction loans. Many mortgage companies actively solicit, by email, direct mail, radio and television advertising, short-term equity loans on existing properties. On most loans made through mortgage companies, they will continue to collect the payments and make additional income from the service charges collected for this service.

MORTGAGE COMPANIES

74   Mortgage companies are established under individual state laws and in California they must have a real estate broker license to operate. It is the policy of mortgage companies to be active in the one-to-four family loan market, either conventional, FHA insured, and VA guaranteed loans that are readily marketable in the secondary mortgage market. They sometimes act as middlemen by seeking permanent loan commitments for developers and investors and then arrange for construction financing with other lenders.

75   It is the duty of the mortgage company before arriving at a commitment to make the loan to consider the value of the property, the amount of the loan in relation to that property, and the ability and history of a borrower to repay the loan.

CONSTRUCTION FINANCING

76   A construction loan is made to complete the improvements on real property. An interim loan is another name for a construction loan. A progressive payment loan is the name of a type

of construction loan. A commercial bank or mortgage company, situated in the area of the construction, can supervise the project at a lower cost. This type of lender tends to make short-term loan transactions such as construction loans. The money is rarely if ever paid in advance. As each phase of construction is completed the contractor receives a percentage of the loan or the amount of money used during that phase. These are referred to as obligatory advances. The maturity date of the loan is measured from the date of the note. With FHA construction loans, on the other hand, maturity is computed from the date of the first payment made by the borrower.

77 It is the practice of these short-term construction loan lenders to "hold back" 10% of the money due the contractor until the lien period for mechanics has expired. At this time the contractor would receive his final payment. Construction financing is usually paid off after the building has been completed by refinancing the property on a long-term loan. The lender on the construction financing is taken out of the picture with the new loan.

77a   Standby commitments - This type of loan commitment is used in two possible circumstances:
  (1) Also called gap financing. Is employed in the event a contingency in a take-out loan commitment is not met. The standby would be used until the contingency is satisfied.
  (2) The borrower who does not have a take-out loan commitment is looking for a more favorable permanent loan from still another lender. If more favorable circumstances do not develop, the permanent loan will be closed by the lender who made the standby commitment.

78 Lenders who prefer to make long-term loans are savings banks and insurance companies. If the lender likes the proposed property he would prefer to agree to make the long-term loan rather than the construction loan. To accomplish this the lender would issue a take-out loan commitment often called a take-out letter. This letter assures both the contractor and the construction loan provider that the money is ready when the construction is complete and the last payment on the interim financing has been provided to the contractor.

78a Participation Loan - Inflationary tendencies have brought increased use of a number of debt equity combinations in real estate finance. These "piece of the action" types of plans can be arranged in many ways. They are usually referred to as a "participation" by the lender. An example is when the interest rate stated was 9% per annum and the builder asked the lender to reconsider the terms of the loan and give him a lower annual interest charge. The insurance company suggested that they would lower the interest rate 1/2% per year if the builder would grant it a 2% equity position in the ownership of the project.

FARM LOANS

84 According to the percentage of farm loans made, lenders would be identified as follows:
  (1) Individuals and others 37%
  (2) Federal Land Bank and other federal agencies 36%
  (3) Life insurance companies 13.9%
  (4) Commercial banks 13.1%. Land bank loans are serviced through the National Farm Loan Association.

84b Since its creation in 1917, the Federal Land Banks (12 in all) have made all of their loans through more than 1000 national farm loan associations throughout the country. These associations are wholly owned by their farmer members. They exist for the purpose of supplying the needed amounts of mortgage financing and are not institutions for the deposit of money. The Farmers Home Administration is a government agency that makes loans and/or guarantees loans for specific agricultural purposes.

FEDERAL HOUSING ADMINISTRATION (FHA)

85 The main purpose of the FHA program and, incidentally, also the VA program, has been to meet the housing needs of all citizens through a flow of money and credit. These federal housing programs have had a sizeable influence in expanding the housing market.

ADVANTAGES OF FHA FINANCING

86 Among the advantages of FHA financing are:
  (1) Monthly, budgeted payments suited to the borrower's financial ability to pay.
  (2) Elimination of short-term financing that removes the need for expensive refinancing.

  (3) A high loan-to-value ratio.
  (4) Protection for the lender.
  (5) Prepayment of loan without penalty.
  (6) Improvement in housing standards due to FHA minimum property requirements (M.P.R.). For example, all staircases must have at least one handrail.
  (7) Lower interest rates than conventional financing because of the protections and insurance.
  (8) Interest rates will be lower for owner occupied properties than non-owner occupied properties.
  (9) A maximum loan service fee of 1%.
      a. This fee is a nondeductible fee for
      b. I.R.S. purposes.

87 FHA does not make loans. It insures loans made by lending institutions such as banks, savings and loan associations, life insurance companies, independent mortgage companies, and state agencies. FHA considers a supervised lender to be any lending institution subject to periodic examination by a government agency, whether state or federal. Independent mortgage companies and some life insurance companies are called non-supervised lenders. An individual person may not become a FHA approved mortgagee. Pension fund investors usually are active as investing mortgagees.

90 A borrower does not apply directly to HUD or FHA for a mortgage loan. Instead, application is made for a mortgage insurance commitment to a HUD/FHA approved mortgagee. The mortgagee takes the application and submits it for mortgage insurance to HUD/FHA on prescribed forms.

95 With FHA insured loans the mortgage loan may bear interest at any rate agreed upon between the lender and the borrower. HUD does not set interest rates for FHA backed loans. Interest must be paid in monthly installments on the principal amount outstanding.

FHA LOAN ASSUMPTION

97 The FHA Commissioner has established that for a period of 12 months (owner occupied) or 24 months (non-owner occupied), the credit worthiness of the prospective borrower (buyer) must be established.

MORTGAGE INSURANCE PREMIUM

100 FHA requires both up-front and annual mortgage insurance premiums. The up-front premium is to be paid at the close of the escrow. The up-front premium can be paid by anyone. If the buyer desires to finance the premium in the loan that is being made, then the premium will be added to the loan. When adding the premium to the base loan, that loan will be called the "gross loan." The monthly payments and the interest and discount points will all be based on the gross loan. The annual mortgage insurance premium will be paid monthly with the regular payment. The authorized maximum loan amount can be exceeded if the excess is for the mortgage insurance premium. This premium may not be considered as an acquisition cost for the purpose of computing the down payment. This money goes directly to FHA. Annually, if there are surplus monies remaining after expenses have been paid the surplus monies might be distributed to the qualified F.H.A. borrowers who paid off their loans during that year and applied for the unused portion of their insurance.

100a The down payment must be acquired from the buyer's personal assets. FHA does not allow the undisclosed and unapproved borrowing of money to create or be a part of a down payment.

102 The application fee (origination fee) is associated with expenses of obtaining the loan. It is not a deductible item for income tax purposes since it is considered to be a cost for services rendered not interest on borrowed money.

102a Every financial institution that makes loans upon the security of real property containing a one-to-four family residence and located in this state or which purchases obligations secured by such property (secondary money market) and receives money in advance for payment of taxes and assessments on the property for insurance, or for other purposes relating to the property, shall pay interest on the amount so held to the borrower. The interest on such amounts shall be at the rate of at least two percent (2%) simple interest per annum. Such interest shall be credited to the borrower's account annually or upon termination of the contract, whichever is earlier.

103 HUD provides insurance for low income housing and works with local governments to assure that this form of housing is built in neighborhoods that will insure that the development will maintain its value and the tenants are placed into affluent school districts. Often, HUD provides the insurance for the money for local governments to rehabilitate existing low-income housing. A turnkey property is a specific term used by HUD in providing low-income housing. It describes a property that has been completely rehabilitated and is ready for the subsidized tenant to move in.

DEPARTMENT OF VETERANS AFFAIRS
(G.I. Loans)

105 The method is similar to FHA loans in such items as monthly budgeted payments, low interest rates, high loan-to-value ratio, and prescribed appraisal techniques. Unlike FHA, the Veterans Administration usually guarantees rather than insures the loan.

ADVANTAGES OF V.A. LOANS

107 Some of the advantages which VA loans still have include:

(1) No mortgage insurance premium is charged.

(2) A maximum loan service fee of 1%. This fee is a non-tax deductible fee for I.R.S. purposes.

(3) No down payment if the price does not exceed CRV (Certificate of Reasonable Value) up to the amount of the maximum permissible loan. In other words, one hundred percent financing.

(4) No maximum limitation on purchase price. If loan is at the VA appraised value or less, the buyer may pay the additional amount.

(5) Amortization Plan - Loans may be amortized under any generally recognized plan such as equal, increasing or decreasing payments.

(6) Prepayment of loan without penalty.

(7) Appraisal methods used are similar to FHA. The VA appraiser determines (CRV) as a fair price given prevailing conditions.

107a Purpose of loan - In addition to home loans where the veteran must intend to occupy the home, VA loans can be made for the purchase of a farm residence to be occupied by the veteran as a home. This includes the purchase of a mobilehome with or without the lot and to refinance existing mortgage liens or other liens of record on a dwelling occupied by the veteran. Loans are only for owner occupied dwellings.

107b In more recent years, the VA has adopted regulations that give them control over such features as streets, utilities, lot size, construction standards, and set-backs of subdivisions that utilize VA financing.

CERTIFICATE OF REASONABLE VALUE

108   The appraisal of the property made by VA is known as a "certificate of reasonable value" (CRV) and sets the maximum loan amount to the veteran. If the veteran desires to pay a price above the CRV, he may do so but must pay cash for the excess. Therefore, there is no maximum sale price only a maximum loan amount. If the cash payment is borrowed, it must be shown in the financial statement used to qualify for the loan. Anyone attempting to circumvent this regulation is subject to federal penalty.

109   The VA guarantees most loans and insures the rest for qualified lending institutions that maintain a lender's insurance account. The VA guarantee to the lender is 25% of the loan. If there is a default on a guaranteed loan, the VA pays the lender a specified maximum amount, which is reduced proportionately as the loan is paid. On insured loans, the VA will pay the net loss of the lender up to the amount of the insurance account. If there is a default on a guaranteed V.A. loan, the veteran's eligibility is charged with the amount of the deficiency that has to be paid because of the guarantee.

CALIFORNIA FARM AND HOME PURCHASE ACT (Cal-Vet)

115   Cal-Vet provisions require owner occupancy. The whole nature of the transaction is different in Cal-Vet financing in that it involves a contract of sale with the title remaining with the state. Because of this, no discount points are involved. A California veteran must apply to the California Department of Veterans affairs for a Cal-Vet loan within 30 years following release from active military duty to qualify for such a loan. However, those who are wounded or disabled from war service or were prisoners of war have an indefinite period in which to apply.

117   Interest rates are less than either FHA or VA. The Cal-Vet rate under both the 1943 Act and the 1974 Act is a floating rate. The rate changes from time to time but this does not affect the amount of monthly payment, merely the length of time necessary to pay off the contract. The borrower must take out disability and life insurance under a plan that guarantees clear title to the property for survivors of the veteran purchaser without further payment if he dies. The Department of Veterans Affairs holds the title of the property. The borrower may not transfer, assign, encumber, or rent the property without the written consent of the state.

118   Funds for the operation of the Cal-Vet plan are derived from the sale of bonds voted by the public. The State Department of Veterans Affairs handles the financing transaction.

119 The Department may lend a qualified veteran up to $521,250 for the purchase of a single-family residence or a mobile-home placed on a foundation on a lot he owns. ($125,000 if the mobilehome is placed on leased land.) The Department may lend up to $200,000 to a qualified veteran for the purchase of a farm. On home loans where the amount of the loan is $35,000 or less, the Department may lend up to 97 percent of the appraised value of the property. Where the loan amount exceeds $35,000, the maximum loan is 95 percent of the appraised value. Loans on mobilehomes and farms cannot exceed 95 percent of the Department's appraised value.

123   Any verteran younger than 17 years old may purchase his residence using the Cal-Vet loan program. This variation of the legal real property purchasing restraints on minors is exclusive to this program and is found in the Military and Veterans Code of California law, paragraph #986.10.

FEDERAL GOVERNMENT AND REAL ESTATE ECONOMIC ACTIVITY

126   Economic forces are difficult to measure directly even though they exert their influence anywhere people live. Because of this, we resort

to certain measures of economic activity (indexes). The most common and most important measures at the national level are:

127 (1) Gross Domestic Product (GDP) - In terms of dollar value, the sum total of all goods and services produced or, viewed from a different perspective all goods and services consumed, saved and invested by all economic units in a nation.

129 (2) Consumer price index (CPI) - Statistics for these measures may be compared from one time to another and, except for GNP/GDP, for one community or area to another at both regional and local levels. When the consumer price index increases, the value of the dollar decreases.

129a   Some economists use the phrase "cost of living" in reference to an index. A rise in the index would indicate that the value of the dollar is weakened, thus more dollars would be necessary in an inflationary period to buy the same amount of commodities than could be acquired for a lesser monetary sum in a period that had a lower cost of living index.

130   As economic activity increases, unemployment decreases. This again influences prices because of the increase in the income of all potential buyers. This would influence a non-homeowner to leave those ranks and become a homeowner.

131   Lenders loan money to realize income. The rate of interest indicates the rate of return they expect to receive on their investment. Purchasers of income property also are interested in earning money on their investments and their rate of return is reflected by capitalization rates. Investors usually demand a higher rate of return than do commercial lenders. When commercial lenders increase the rate of return (interest rate), investors also increase their rates (capitalization rates).

131a In times of inflation, the value of real property will tend to increase as rents increase. If a tenant is on a fixed long-term rental not tied

to an economic index, the value of the total property and the corresponding equity of the owner will tend to decrease. Conversely in a time of deflation, as seen in the greater part of California during the period 1989-1997 and 2007-2012, the value of the dollar increases allowing the purchase of a greater valued property for less money.

132   Many loans are influenced by the economic activity as shown by these indicators. The "Variable Interest Rate" loans will have their rates increase or decrease based on these indexes and on the influence of the Federal Reserve System. These loans are provided by every major type of lender in the marketplace. Remember that real estate loans are "long term investments." In a market where people demand liquidity (cash or its equivalent), real estate funds tend to dry up. When liquidity is desired, funds are invested in short-term commercial notes or government securities.

132a Most investors, during an inflationary period, fear erosion of capital from escalating interest rates and turn to short-term investments which usually provide a higher yield.

133   The "Prime Rate", which increases or decreases immediately following an action by the Federal Reserve system, influences the money rates that affect all borrowers. If interest rates go down, the monthly payment on a real estate loan goes down in proportion and the number of potential buyers entering the market increases. Conversely, as interest rates increase, the number of buyers capable of qualifying for a loan at the higher monthly payments decreases.

133a In times of relative economic stability, large numbers of people place their savings in financial institutions (banks, savings banks, and credit unions) which invest these funds for their mutual profit. Periodically, economic conditions change to such a degree that it becomes more profitable for investors to withdraw their savings from the depository type institutions and invest directly in securities (stocks, bonds) and other financial assets. In the periods during which we see shifts in the flow of investment funds out of financial institutions into the market for other financial assets, we experience what is called financial disintermediation. In the years when it is more advantageous for investors to give their dollars to financial institutions for investment, we are said to be experiencing what is called financial intermediation.

134 Many studies of economic activity have been maintained by a number of professional companies over the years. These studies reveal a rhythmic change from booms to depressions interspersed by minor periods of prosperity and minor business recessions. The regularity of periodic business swings from boom to bust has led to the belief in a business cycle which is described as "depression - recovery - prosperity - recession," and which is subject to minor changes and disturbances that will inevitably repeat itself in swings or business cycles.

134a Specific government intervention, other than the actions of the Federal Reserve System, rarely have any lasting effect on the business cycle. An example is the government placing low income housing in major metropolitan areas.

135 There is also a housing market cycle to take into consideration. The housing market cycle is a major factor in the economics of the nation. Builders build without conferring with one another about how much construction their company does as a part of the total amount of construction needed to be purchased to satisfy the buying demand of the time. Usually they, within six years, forget the last over-building cycle and again overbuild for the buying demand. It takes from 12 to 18 months to reduce the overbuilt inventory until the supply again meets the demand. Builders then slowly start to build and increase the number of houses built and sold until another six to eight years passes and they again overbuild. This overbuilding cycle occurred in 1958, 1966, 1972, 1981, 1989 and 2006. At these points, the overbuilt market was, within a short time, decreased by the consistent demand for housing. Because of this constant demand, virtually every single-family residence in

California during this entire period increased in value. This increase in the buyer's equity created a strong position for the lenders.

138 Always remember that the purpose of owning a single family residence is to eventually pay off the loans and have a place "rent free" to retire. Real estate is a long-range investment and, as such, whether prices go up or down, if the property is maintained the investment is sound. This is the primary reason for home ownership. Speculation should only be considered as a secondary purpose. There is no reason to refinance a home lest it be that the existing financing has a "due date" and forces the refinance, or mortgage interest rates become so low that a refinance would appreciably benefit a savings in interest both in the short term and, including refinance costs, in the long term.

142 Seller's Market - A period of time in the economy when interest rates are low and real estate prices are increasing because of demand. This places the seller in a favorable position to negotiate a higher price on a property.

FEDERAL DEREGULATION

143 Deregulation indicates the reduction of control in financial institutions. In the 1980's when the federal government deregulated the saving and loans industry they were permitted to make loans secured by assets other than real estate such as junk bonds, restaurant chains, and racehorses.

MONITORING THE MONEY SUPPLY

148 Reserve Requirements - By establishing reserve requirements the Fed increases or decreases the amount of money in circulation. Member banks must set aside and keep a certain percentage of each deposit received as reserves. An increase by the Fed in reserve requirements means banks have less money to lend, interest rates increase, and borrowing and spending slows. A decrease in reserve requirements increases money the banks have to lend, interest rates may decrease, and

borrowing and spending increases. This brings more buyers into the market eventually driving up the price of homes. Conversely, during a "tight money policy" period the Federal Reserve Board demands a higher reserve, shrinking the money supply, and driving up interest rates. This lowers the total loans provided by lenders.

149   During the early eighties, to drastically reduce a heavy inflation, the Federal Reserve Board took the tight money policy attitude to the point that the availability of long-term loans dried up almost completely, or were at extremely high interest rates with heavy discount points. Lending institutions were unable to make loans. The real estate community responded with "creative financing" including "wrap around" loans and second and third trust deeds taken back by owners.

150 The prime rate is the minimum interest rate a commercial bank is willing to lend their most creditworthy clients.

151 A discount rate is the interest rate a bank must pay to the Fed when the bank borrows money from its bank. A decrease in the discount rate will encourage bank borrowing. Bank borrowing increases deposits at the bank and allows it to lend more. A boost in the discount rate does the opposite. Discount rates obviously affect the interest rate that the average homebuyer will pay for new financing.

152 Open Market Operations - The Fed also uses the tactic of open market operations (buys and sells government securities) to influence the amount of available credit. When the Fed buys government securities from the public it stimulates the economy because the cash it pays the sellers is deposited into seller's bank accounts which increases the bank's reserves and with the additional funds on deposit the banks may extend more credit to borrowers.

153 However, if the Fed is selling securities the opposite occurs since buyers withdraw funds from their banks for payment, thefore reserves in the buyer's banks decrease and less credit and lending is available through the banking system.

153a If the frequency of the business cycle increases with an accompanying rapid change in business and money conditions, flexibility to meet changing financial conditions is wise. Long-term investments restrict such flexibility. In such times money flows to highly liquid sources.

FEDERAL HOME LOAN BANK

154   The Federal Government took another step in its effort to stabilize economic conditions by establishing the Federal Home Loan Bank in July 1932. The Home Loan Bank Board is the federal government's regulatory agency for all federal savings banks across the country. It operates for the savings bank industry in much the same way the Fed operates for the commercial banks in the country. This Home Loan Bank System is made up of 12 District Federal Home Loan Banks operating in 12 separate districts throughout the country.

OTHER GOVERNMENT INFLUENCES

157   A more direct way in which the federal government can influence the economy is by making changes in the federal income tax laws. We have experienced the effects of such changes in the last several years. Very simply, by increasing federal income taxes – other things being equal - the supply of money at the disposal of the average citizen will certainly diminish. The opposite would be true if the tax rates were lowered. In that event, there would be greater sums of money at the disposal of the ordinary taxpayer.

MORTGAGE OPERATIONS OF FEDERAL GOVERNMENT AGENCIES:

163   Federal National Mortgage Association – "Fannie Mae" was originally organized in 1938 under Title III of the National Housing Act of 1934 to create a secondary market for Title II FHA insured mortgages. However, in retrospect,

the agency's real objective was to provide liquidity for government insured mortgage loans issured at high loan-to-value ratios and at relatively low rates of interest. The association, in effect, was to provide funds for the stimulation of new construction by purchasing mortgage obligations insured up to 100% of loan value by another government agency. It was intended that associations of this type would be organized by private individuals and operate under federal charter and supervision. Until 1938 no such associations were organized unitl the Federal National Mortgage Association (FNMA) was created.

164   In 1948, FNMA was rechartered to allow the purchase of VA guaranteed loans. In 1972, under congressional authority, "Fannie Mae" was permitted to enter the secondary market for the purchase of some conventional home mortgages. Consequently, FNMA is now authorized to purchase FHA, VA and conventional loans. FNMA increases the credit available in the mortgage market for residential financing by attracting new funds through sales of notes it issues. Fannie Mae is presently operated as a private corporation and its stock is held by private investors. However, FNMA operations are under the supervision of the secretary of the Department of Housing and Urban Development.

GOVERNMENT NATIONAL MORTGAGE ASSOCIATION

167   GNMA (Ginnie Mae) does not purchase mortgages, as do Fannie Mae and Freddie Mac, but simply adds its guarantee to mortgage backed securities issued by approved lenders. Mortgage bankers, savings institutions, commercial banks and other approved types of financial institutions are securities issuers and because of the federal warranty (pledge of full faith and credit of the U.S. Government) and uniformity of the securities, these GNMA instruments are considered by many to be as safe, as liquid, and as easy to hold as treasury securities. Underlying the securities are mortgages which are used by "Ginnie Mae" as collateral for the guarantee. The issuer is

responsible for acquiring and servicing the mortgages and for marketing the securities it issues.

168   "Ginnie May" also performs certain special assistance functions on behalf of the federal government. Under these programs GNMA purchases particular kinds of mortgages to accomplish two statutory objectives: Provide support for types of housing for which financing is not readily available, such as housing for low-income families and for the elderly, and to counter declines in mortgage lending and housing construction.

THE FEDERAL HOME LOAN MORTGAGE CORPORATION

171   Institutional lenders (mortgagees) may sell existing mortgages to FHLMC. "Freddie Mac" may then either resell the mortgages directly or sell securities on the open capital market that are backed by the mortgages they have purchased.

ARTICLE 5 -- TRANSACTIONS IN TRUST DEEDS AND REAL PROPERTY SALES CONTRACTS (Land Contracts)

182   "Any real estate licensee who undertakes to service a promissory note secured directly or indirectly by a lien on real property or a real property sales contract, shall have a written authorization from the borrower or lender or holder of the contract.

184   Where a licensee sells, exchanges or negotiates the sale or exchange of an existing trust deed or sales contract, he shall cause a proper assignment to be executed and recorded, naming the purchaser or nominee as assignee, within 10 working days after funds are received from buyer or after close of escrow, or he shall deliver such contract or trust deed to purchaser with a written recommendation an assignment be immediately recorded.

ARTICLE 7 - LOAN BROKER LAW

198   A mortgage loan broker is a person holding a real estate broker's license who specializes in loans and charges a commission for making or selling a loan. The real estate law has long required the licensing of one who negotiates a loan secured by real property for another for compensation. Article 7 is referred to as the Real Property Loan Law and the Mortgage Loan Broker Law, and applies to loans secured by first trust deeds under $30,000 and by junior trust deeds under $20,000.

199   The mortgage loan disclosure statement, also referred to as the mortgage loan broker's statement, is at the heart of the real property loan law. Its purpose is to provide a prospective borrower with information concerning all salient features of a loan to be negotiated for the borrower (trustor). A real estate licensee, negotiating a mortgage loan subject to Article 7, must present a completed broker loan disclosure statement to the prospective borrower and obtain the borrower's signature on the statement prior to the time that the borrower becomes obligated to complete the loan. The real estate licensee must furnish this disclosure statement to the borrower regardless of the amount of the loan negotiated. In addition, the licensee must certify in the statement that the loan in question is in compliance with the provisions of Article 7. The form must also be signed by the loan broker or his agent. If the licensee is negotiating a loan to be made by an institutional lender (banks, savings banks and life insurance companies) and the licensee does not charge the borrower a commission in excess of 2% of the principal amount of the loan, a mortgage loan disclosure statement is not required.

200   The form of the statement must be approved by the Commissioner. The Commissioner has, by regulation, established an approved form of the statement in Section 2840 of his regulations.

201   Contrary to general belief, the borrower's credit rating does not appear on the statement. A true and correct copy of the statement must be kept on file by the broker for four years from the date the instrument was signed by the borrower.

201a   In the Real Estate Commissioner's regulations, we learn that publication, distribution or use of advertising containing any of the following shall be considered to be false, misleading or deceptive: The use of terms such as "guaranteed," "insured," "secured," "bonded," "sure," "positive," or other terms relating to the security of funds of lenders or purchasers without fully explaining the extent or conditions to which such funds or rate of return are secured. Also, any statement relating to an absence of loss to lenders or purchasers without stating the period of time such statements cover.

201b   The fraudulent act of working with a buyer and seller to increase the selling price to raise the amount of the loan is conduct that will be disciplined by the Real Estate Commissioner under paragraph #10176 (1) which states that, "any other conduct which constitutes fraud or dishonest dealing" is grounds for disciplinary action.

COMMISSIONS AND OTHER CHARGES WHEN LIMITS APPLY

202   A real estate broker negotiating mortgage loans subject to Article 7 is limited by law in the amount that may be charged as commission for arranging the loan and as to the "costs and expenses" of making the loan. These limitations do not apply in the case of a first loan with a principal of $30,000 or more nor to a junior loan the principal of which is $ 20,000 or more.

LEGAL LIMITS

203   The commission maximum for loans subject to Article 7 are as follows:

First Trust Deeds (under $30,000) - 5 percent of the principal of a loan of less than 3 years.10 percent of the principal of a loan of 3 years or more.

Second or other Junior Trust Deeds (Under $20,000) - 5 percent of the principal of a loan of less than 2 years.10 percent of the principal of a loan of at least 2 years, but less than 3 years.15 percent of the principal of a loan of 3 years or more.

CHARGES OTHER THAN COMMISSION

211   Costs and expenses of making the loan, including appraisal fees, escrow fees, notary and credit investigation fees (but excluding actual title charges and recording fees) charged to the borrower cannot exceed 5 percent of the principal of the loan, provided, however, that if 5 percent of the loan is less than $390, the broker may charge up to that amount. Regardless of the size of the loan, the borrower cannot be charged more than $700 for costs and expenses, provided that in no event shall maximum amount exceed actual costs and expenses paid, incurred or reasonably earned. The regulations of the Commissioner preclude the broker from charging, as part of the costs and expenses of making the loan, a fee that exceeds that customarily charged for the same or comparable service in the community where the service is rendered. It is most important to recognize that there is no circumstance where the charges billed to the borrower can exceed the actual costs incurred in obtaining the loan.

ADVANCES ON AN EXISTING LOAN

211a   "With respect to a further advance on a note, the charges shall not exceed the charges for an original loan in the same amount as the further advance and made for a term equal to the remaining term of the note on which the further advance is being made."

SUMMARY

216   If the loan is never consummated due to failure of the borrower to disclose prior liens, the borrower is liable for all costs and expenses and for one-half of the commission.

216a An exclusive agreement authorizing a licensee to negotiate a loan secured by a lien on real property shall be limited to a term of not more than 45 days.

219   If the property securing the loan is an owner-occupied dwelling, a balloon payment is not permissible if the term of the loan is 6 years or less. As in the case of the 3-year balloon payment provision, the restriction does not apply to a promissory note given back to the seller by the purchaser of the dwelling place on account of the purchase price.

223   A late charge may not be imposed more than once for the same late payment of any installment. Also, a late charge may not be imposed on any installment which is paid or tendered in full within 10 days after its scheduled due date, even though an earlier payment or a late charge on a previously scheduled payment has not been paid in full. Finally, this law establishes that a payment or tender of a payment made within 10 days of a scheduled installment due date is to be treated as paid or tendered for payment of the installment due.

Lesson Thirteen
Part Two
Study Questions

_____(Lesson Thirteen - Paragraph 19b - Question 1)_____
Which of the following defines a "mortgage loan":
(A) An instrument that is used only in the exchange of real property.
(B) A financial obligation which is unsecured but is used to buy a building.
(C) A promissory note that is unpaid.
(D) A loan collateralized with real estate.

(D) In its simplest form a mortgage loan is a loan collateralized by a trust deed.

_____(Lesson Thirteen - Paragraph 19b - Question 2)_____
In California a secured real property loan usually consists of:
(A) Financing statement and trust deed.   (B) The debt (note) and the lien (deed of trust).
(C) FHA or PMI insurance.   (D) Security agreement and financing statement.

(B) A secured real property loan consists of the note which is evidence of the debt they promise to pay and the security for the note (deed of trust). The deed of trust, when recorded, creates a voluntary lien against the property.

_____(Lesson Thirteen - Paragraph 20 - Question 1)_____
Equity in real property is the:
(A) Cash flow value of the property.
(B) Total of all mortgage payments made to date.
(C) Difference between mortgage indebtedness and market value of the property.
(D) Appraised value of the property.

(C) Equity indicates ownership as opposed to debt. The owner's equity in a property is the total value of the property less any indebtedness against the property. A property with the market value of $100,000 with a total debt of $90,000, the equity would be $ 10,000.

_____(Lesson Thirteen - Paragraph 20 - Question 2)_____
Equity is best defined as the:
(A) Means of clearing a cloud on title.   (B) Purchase price of a property less the loans on it.
(C) Fair market value of a property less the loans on it.   (D) All of the above.

(C) Equity, as used in real estate terminology, defines the fair market value of a property less any loans that are against it.

_____(Lesson Thirteen - Paragraph 22 - Question 1)_____
The often used term "loan to value ratio" indicates the following relationship:
(A) Loan to sales price.   (B)   Loan to appraised value.

371

(C) Assessed value of property to the market value. (D) Loan to assessed value of the property.

(B) The phrase "loan to value ratio" merely designates the percentage of the appraised value of the property that the loan can be. Institutional lenders are required by either federal or state law to limit their loans in relation to the appraised value.

_____(Lesson Thirteen - Paragraph 22 - Question 2)_____
The lender would be best protected by:
(A) A low interest rate.   (B) Low monthly payments.
(C) Appreciation.   (D) A downturn in the economy.

(C) The down payment a person places in a property the larger is that person's equity position (difference between mortgage indebtedness and market value of the property). During the period of holding, should the value of the property increase since the loan remains the same, the amount of the equity will increase. The larger the equity a borrower has in a property the more secure will be the lender's position.

_____(Lesson Thirteen - Paragraph 23 - Question 1)_____
In residential real estate lending, when lenders liberalize the terms under which loans are made, such as lowering qualifying ratios and giving longer terms of repayment, the following would be true:
(A) Overall financing costs tend to increase.
(B) Overall financing costs tend to decrease.
(C) Overall financing costs tend to remain the same.
(D) Overall financing costs would not be affected.

(A) In liberalizing loan terms, the lender makes it possible for the borrowers with lower incomes to be able to borrow money. In the long run, however, the loan costs will actually grow larger with more total interest due to the longer terms and other loan charges.

_____(Lesson Thirteen - Paragraph 24 - Question 1)_____
If "A" bought a home and made a larger down payment than "B," how would the lending institution view "A's" purchase:
(A) He would probably be more reliable in making payments.
(B) He would probably take better care of the property.
(C) They would probably give him a lower interest rate on the loan.
(D) All of the above.

(D) A person putting a large down payment on property has more at stake and would do more to protect the investment. For this reason, the lender would consider the risk of the borrower would be lessened. They would be more apt to give a lower interest bearing loan due to the greater security.

_____(Lesson Thirteen - Paragraph 24a - Question 1)_____
The best way to insure that a borrower will not default on a real estate loan is to have a:
(A) Low interest rate on the loan. (B) Low monthly payments.
(C) Low down payment.   (D) High equity in the property.

(D) The best defense against default is a high equity in the property by the borrower. In this case, the borrower is not likely to allow the property to go into foreclosure.

_____(Lesson Thirteen - Paragraph 24a - Question 2)_____

With respect to equities, lending institutions would consider the following to be in their best interest:
(A) Lower equity would be better since the lender makes a maximum loan.
(B) Greater equity would not allow lender to get maximum profit return.
(C) Greater equity would provide the lender with greater security.
(D) Minimum equity provides a hedge against inflation.

(C)   (A) and (B) say the same thing and (D) is obviously wrong. A lending institution is interested in the buyer's equity so it would ordinarily increase his desire to meet his payment schedule. The lender has a smaller investment in the property.

_____(Lesson Thirteen - Paragraph 24c - Question 1)_____

Lenders are more inclined in recent years to make 95% loans on single family residential properties because of:
(A) Freddy Mac's activity in the marketplace.   B) Credit life insurance.
(C) Private mortgage insurance.   (D) The activity of Ginny Mae.

(C) Private mortgage insurance gives the lender making a loan an added source of security. He would be secured not only by the real estate itself but also the insurance company issuing the mortgage insurance policy. With such added protection lenders are sometimes willing to make higher loan-to-value ratio loans.

_____(Lesson Thirteen - Paragraph 26 - Question 1)_____

Jane Jackson secures a loan from the Last Western Bank. The loan is secured by a second deed of trust on her condominium. Her boyfriend asks her what the nominal and effective rates are for this promissory note. Jane is knowledgeable concerning real estate and finance; therefore, she would state to him that:
(A) The nominal and effective rates are the same, being different names for the same thing.
(B) The effective rate is the interest that she pays; the nominal rate is the rate named in the note.
(C) The nominal rate is the interest that she pays; the effective rate is the rate named in the note.
(D) The nominal rate is the return to the lender; the effective rate is the cost to the borrower.

(B) This deals with the terms "nominal rate" and "effective rate." The nominal rate is the rate stated on the face of the note. The effective rate is the rate of return computed on the discounted amount paid for the loan.

_____(Lesson Thirteen - Paragraph 26 - Question 2)_____

What is the nominal rate of interest you would pay on a conventional loan?
(A) Interest with discount points so it will be more than the simple interest rate.
(B) The maximum amount of interest allowed by law.
(C) The legal rate of interest.
(D) The amount of interest agreed upon in the contract.

(D) Nominal rate means named rate and would be the rate named or agreed upon in the contract.

_____(Lesson Thirteen - Paragraph 27 - Question 1)_____

Which of the following would least likely be taken into consideration in granting a loan for the purchase of real property?
(A) Credit rating. (B) Wife's salary. (C) Husband's overtime. (D) Financial need of the borrower.

(D) The borrower's need for the money is the least concern of the lender. His ability to repay the loan is of great concern. Everyone can show a need for money but it is more difficult to demonstrate the ability to repay the loan.

_____(Lesson Thirteen - Paragraph 27 - Question 2)_____

Large firms that lend money secured by real estate mortgages would least likely be concerned with the following factor when granting such loans:
(A) Availability of other investments.   (B) The financial need of the borrower.
(C) Overtime earnings of the borrower.   (C) Credit risk of the borrower.

(B) Factors (A), (C) and (D) are all considered by the lender prior to granting a loan and would have more influence on their decision than the need of the borrower. How badly one needs the money generally does not influence the lender's decision.

_____(Lesson Thirteen - Paragraph 31 - Question 1)_____

Which of the following is not a secondary mortgage market lender?
(A) The Federal Housing Administration.
(B) The Federal National Mortgage Association.
(C) The Government National Mortgage Association.
(D) The Federal Home Loan Mortgage Corporation.

(A) FHA insures new loans, which may be sold in the secondary market at a later date.

_____(Lesson Thirteen - Paragraph 33 - Question 1)_____

From a lender's point of view, the following would be a disadvantage to the holder of a note secured by a second deed of trust:
(A) It denies the holder the right to a deficiency judgment.
(B) The interest rate is generally lower than that on a first trust deed note.
(C) It denies the holder any right to notice should foreclosure proceedings be started upon the primary lien.
(D) The risk to the holder of the junior lien is greater than the risk to the holder of the first lien.

(D) This is a great example of how to use true/false to eliminate the wrong answers. (A), (B) & (C) are all false. (D) is true.

_____(Lesson Thirteen - Paragraph 33 - Question 2)_____

A primary source of secondary financing for junior loans is:
(A) Savings and loan associations. (B) Insurance companies.
(C) Private (individual) lenders.   (D) All of the above.

(C) A primary source of secondary financing, meaning second and third trust deeds as opposed to first trust deeds, would be from private lenders who are not institutional lenders, but do make more risky loans at higher rates or interest.

_____(Lesson Thirteen - Paragraph 34 - Question 1)_____

Amortization does not apply to:
(A) A lease.   (B) A trust deed.   (C) A loan.   (D) Depreciation.

(B) Amortization means the liquidation of a financial obligation on an installment basis. It also means recovery over a period of time - which refers to a lease, a loan and depreciation. A trust deed is the security for a note, not the note itself.

_____(Lesson Thirteen - Paragraph 34 - Question 2)_____

When liquidating a financial agreement on the installment plan, you are:
(A) Accelerating. (B) Conveying. (C) Amortizing. (D) Leveraging.

(C) Amortizing. This question presents the textbook definition of amortization: "The liquidation of a financial obligation on an installment basis."

_____(Lesson Thirteen - Paragraph 34a - Question 1)_____

When the service debt of the loan is not sufficient to cover the interest amount of the loan, the result will usually be:
(A) A larger down payment. (B) Additional principal payments.
(C) Negative amortization.   (D) A shorter term.

(C) Service debt (debt service) is the amount of the monthly mortgage payment. If the monthly payment is not sufficient to cover the interest amount of the loan, the non-paid interest will be added to the principal amount of the loan. This will increase the principal amount of the loan and is referred to as negative amortization.

_____(Lesson Thirteen - Paragraph 37 - Question 1)_____

A note on which only interest is paid during its term is called:
(A) A straight note. (B) An amortized note. (C) An installment note. (D) Void .

(A) In contrast to amortized loans, recall that some real estate loans are straight loans. This means that the entire debt or obligation is to be paid at one fixed time. In this kind of a loan there would be no installment payments of principal at all and no periodic payments of interest unless this is provided for in the terms of the note. Ordinarily, the entire obligation is cleared in a single payment.

_____(Lesson Thirteen - Paragraph 52 - Question 1)_____

When lenders refer to the term "debt-income ratio" they mean:
(A) A requirement of the Federal Government.   (B) A loan qualifying tool.
(C) A formula used in appraising property.   (D) A part of the closing costs.

(B) "Debt-income ratio" indicates the fraction that your loan payment on the property is in relation to the net income from the property. Lenders use this when qualifying a person for an income property loan and measuring their margin of safety. If your annual debt payment of principal and interest is $10,000, and the net income from the property is $15,000, then the income is 1 and 1/2 times the debt payment. This is expressed as:

Net operating income = $15,000 = 1.5

Annual debt service $10,000

_____(Lesson Thirteen - Paragraph 54 - Question 1)_____

A lender would charge points:

(A) To close a gap between fixed and market rates.   (B) To increase effective yields.

(C) To help defray the costs of the loan.   (D) All of the above.

(D) A point is defined as 1%. When a lender charges points, he is charging 1% of the loan amount. This charge can be for several purposes. If the points are involved in a VA loan, it is to increase the yield to the lender to counter the difference between the VA fixed rate and whatever the market rate might be. If the VA fixes 8%, and the lender may make 81/2% on the conventional market, the lender most likely would charge 4 points to increase the 8% yield stated on the note to an effective yield of 81/2%. A rule of thumb being that 1 point in advance effectively increases the nominal rate of interest by 1/8%. Receiving four points (4/8), would increase the interest rate by 1/2 %. Lenders also charge points, a percentage of the loan, to defray the processing cost. A lender might charge 4 discount points to increase the yield and charge a 1 point loan processing fee. All of the choices are correct.

_____(Lesson Thirteen - Paragraph 54 - Question 2)_____

When discount points are paid in connection with a V.A. insured loan, from the lender's point of view they are equivalent to:

(A) Pro-rated taxes.   (B) Prepayment penalty. (C) Discount to buyer. (D) Prepaid interest.

(D) "Discount points" charged on a V.A. loan are paid by the seller to the lender from the sale proceeds. This is income to the lender and is considered to be prepaid interest for the lender.

_____(Lesson Thirteen - Paragraph 56 - Question 1)_____

A note secured by a second deed of trust having a remaining balance of $50,000 is sold for $35,000. This transaction is an example of:

(A) Leverage.   (B) Foreclosure.   (C) Discounting.   (D) Devaluating.

(C) This is discounting, the buying of a note for less than the remaining principal amount. By buying a note at a discount its purchaser increases the yield he will receive. The buyer will receive the interest on the remaining principal. Also, at the maturity date of the note, the buyer will be paid the face value of the remaining principal (if any remains). Leverage occurs when the buyer of a property acquires it by using borrowed funds in addition to equity monies. Foreclosure is the process by which a holder of a security interest (trust deed or mortgage) in a property can cause the property to be sold because the creator of the security device (trustor or mortgagor) has not performed as promised. Devaluating refers to the reduction in value of an asset.

_____(Lesson Thirteen - Paragraph 56 - Question 2)_____

The beneficiary of a trust deed and note found himself in a position requiring immediate cash. He, therefore, sold his note for less than its face value. This is known as:

(A) Liquidating.   (B) Depreciating.   (C) Discounting.   (D) Subrogating.

(C) When a loan note is sold for less than its remaining value, it is said to be sold at a discount.

_____(Lesson Thirteen - Paragraph 57 - Question 1)_____

Black held a seasoned note in his investment portfolio. This term "seasoned" refers to:
(A) The time of year in which the note originated.   (B) The maturity date of the loan.
(C) The qualifications of the borrower.   (D) A history of prompt payments on the note.

(D) A "seasoned" note is a note that has a favorable history of prompt payments on the note by the borrower. Such evidence is a reasonable indication that the borrower will continue to pay the note through to the end.

_____(Lesson Thirteen - Paragraph 59 - Question 1)_____

A man purchased a home on a FHA approved loan. About one year later he was informed by the lender that his monthly payment will be increased $4.00. This would be a result of:
(A) A reappraisal of the property that showed the loan to value ratio to be inadequate.
(B) An interest rate increase.
(C) The borrower's credit had deteriorated.
(D) A property tax increase.

(D) A FHA loan payment includes monthly impounds for 1/12 of yearly property taxes. If property taxes increase or decrease, the monthly payment would reflect the change.

_____(Lesson Thirteen - Paragraph 59 - Question 2)_____

In real estate finance the term "impounds" most nearly means:
(A) Moratorium. (B) Reserves. (C) Attachments. (D) Penalties.

(B) The term "impounds" or "impound account" designates the reserves set aside by the lender for the future payment of taxes and/or insurance.

_____(Lesson Thirteen - Paragraph 61 - Question 1)_____

A life insurance company making real estate loans would normally create them with the assistance of a/an:
(A) Mortgage banker. (B) Real estate agent. (C) Commercial bank. (D) Savings bank.

(A) Life insurance companies must invest millions of dollars daily that they receive as premiums on insurance. To do this, they use the services of mortgage bankers who act as loan correspondents.

_____(Lesson Thirteen - Paragraph 61 - Question 2)_____

Life insurance companies not willing to deal directly with mortgagors or trustors usually pay a loan servicing and preparation fee to:
(A) FHA or VA. (B) Savings banks. (C) Mortgage companies. (D) All of the above.

(C) Life insurance companies collect premiums daily in the millions of dollars. These premiums must be invested. The insurance companies use mortgage companies throughout the country to process and service loans at a fee.

_____(Lesson Thirteen - Paragraph 62 - Question 1)_____
A portfolio of long-term amortized loans would be most attractive to which of these:
(A) Individual lenders. (B) Savings banks. (C) Insurance companies. (D) Credit unions.

(C) One reference work lists these as the lending characteristics of an insurance company:
1. Many long-term loans.
2. Many residential loans but a number of commercial and industrial loans too.
3. Make medium sized loans relative to value.
4. Prefer large loans and loan packages.
5. No geographic limitations but selective as to neighborhoods.
6. Usually low interest rate.
7. Almost no construction loans.
8. Borrower's ability to repay a major concern.
9. Usually seek to avoid administration of loan.

_____(Lesson Thirteen - Paragraph 65 - Question 1)_____
In a tight money market, savings banks would prefer not to make V.A. loans because they consider:
(A) Competition from other lenders. (B) Dividends to investors.
(C) Impaired security for the loan. (D) Lack of demand.

V.A. loans usually have an interest rate that is lower than the market interest rate. As money becomes more scarce (tight money), lenders who have to account to their stockholders would be less likely to make lower interest rate loans.

_____(Lesson Thirteen - Paragraph 65 - Question 2)_____
A principal lender of money for financing the purchase of residential property is:
(A) Savings banks. (B) Commercial banks.
(C) Insurance companies. (D) Federal National Mortgage Association.

(A) Savings banks that may be state or federally chartered are principal lenders in the financing of residential property.

_____(Lesson Thirteen - Paragraph 66 - Question 1)_____
Lending institutions that specialize in granting loans to homebuyers, obtain most of the money they lend from:
(A) Corporation savings. (B) Non-corporation savings. (C) F.N.M.A. (D) Household savings.

(D) Savers have the ability to choose how they invest their savings: 1. Invest directly in goods. 2. Buy credit instruments such as notes or bonds. 3. Invest in financial institutions that in turn loan out their savings. Most household savings (personal savings) are invested in financial institutions such as savings banks, banks, or insurance companies.

_____(Lesson Thirteen - Paragraph 66 - Question 2)_____
A principal lender of funds for financing the purchase of residential property would be:
(A) The Federal Home Loan Bank. (B) The Federal Deposit Insurance Corporation.
(C) The Savings banks. (D) The Federal Housing Administration.

(C) Savings banks are the prime lenders of residential financing.

_____(Lesson Thirteen - Paragraph 69 - Question 1)_____

A lender that (1) prefers loans secured by property in close proximity to its office; (2) prefers to have had a prior relationship with the borrower; and (3) prefers to make short-term loans, most likely would be a:
(A) Mortgage company. (B) Life insurance company. (C) Savings bank. (D) Commercial bank.

(D) The stated characteristics are those of a commercial bank. Life insurance companies prefer to make long term loans on large, high-quality properties, such as large shopping centers. Savings banks make the greatest number of loans to enable persons to purchase homes. Mortgage companies can be either mortgage brokers or mortgage bankers, or they can be both. Mortgage brokers arrange loans as correspondents for life insurance companies, mutual savings banks, pension funds, etc. Mortgage bankers originate, finance and close first mortgage loans and sell such loans to institutional investors. After the loans are sold, typically, they are serviced by the mortgage broker under a contractual relationship with the beneficiary.

_____(Lesson Thirteen - Paragraph 69 - Question 2)_____

The lender that grants smaller loans for shorter terms, to well known borrowers in close proximity
to the same office is a:
(A) Commercial bank. (B) Insurance company. (C) Mortgage company. (D) Savings bank.

(A) The question is an exact description of the normal lending policies of a commercial bank.

_____(Lesson Thirteen - Paragraph 71 - Question 1)_____

In the United States, the greatest numbers of mutual savings banks are in the:
(A) Southeastern section. (B) Northwest section. (C) Northeast section. (D) Southwest section.

(C) Mutual Savings Banks are established in the northeast section of the United States. This is also true of a number of the older institutions operating in this country. Historically, this type of lending institution has not spread elsewhere throughout the country.

_____(Lesson Thirteen - Paragraph 71 - Question 2)_____

Mortgage companies acting as loan correspondents for institutional lenders:
(A) Prefer loans that are saleable in the secondary market.
(B) Are federally organized and under rigorous supervision.
(C) Do not service the loans they arrange.
(D) Are not active in the negotiating of government insured loans.

(A) Mortgage companies make loans and usually sell them off to lending institutions or they get a commitment form a lending institution and earn the points charged for the loan. Mortgage companies are not federally organized, but deal in government insured loans as an approved lender. On most loans made through mortgage companies, they will continue to collect the payments and make additional income from the service charges collectable for this service.

_____(Lesson Thirteen - Paragraph 73 - Question 1)_____

The lender who: 1. Makes construction loans. 2. Generally does not lend their own funds. 3. Services loans. 4. Actively solicits loans, would most likely be:
(A) Mortgage company.   (B) Commercial bank.
(C) Savings and loan association. (D) Life insurance company.

(A) The listed attributes describe most nearly the activities of a mortgage company. Generally, these firms act as correspondents for life insurance companies, and service loans made with Life Insurance Company funds. Also, they are actively engaged making short-term construction loans. Many mortgage companies actively solicit by classified and direct mail advertising short-term equity loans on existing properties.

_____(Lesson Thirteen - Paragraph 74 - Question 1)_____
Mortgage companies acting as loan correspondents for institutional lenders:
(A) Prefer loans that are saleable in the secondary market.
(B) Are federally organized and under rigorous supervision.
(C) Do not service the loans they arrange.
(D) Are not active in the negotiating of government insured loans.

(A) Mortgage companies make loans and usually sell them off to lending institutions or they get a commitment form a lending institution and earn the points charged for the loan. Mortgage companies are not federally organized, but deal in government insured loans as an approved lender. On most loans made through mortgage companies they will continue to collect the payments and make additional income from the service charges collectable for this service.

_____(Lesson Thirteen - Paragraph 74 - Question 2)_____
Banks and others, are usually regulated by:
(A) Federal law. (B) State law. (C) County ordinances. (D) Federal Housing Administration.

(B) Mortgage companies operating primarily as mortgage loan correspondents are not considered to be institutional lenders and are not subject to the same controls. Organized under state laws, they are under control of the state in which they operate, and are subject to minimum supervision.

_____(Lesson Thirteen - Paragraph 75 - Question 1)_____
A lending officer coordinates the borrower, loan and property to arrive at:
(A) Property appraisal. (B) Loan commitment. (C) Credit rating. (D) Statement of liability.

(B) Before arriving at a commitment to make the loan, a lending officer has to consider the value of the property, the amount of the loan in relation to that property, and the ability and history of a borrower to repay the loan.

_____(Lesson Thirteen - Paragraph 76 - Question 1)_____
The following pair of terms are synonymous:
(A) Take-out loan - interim loan.   (B) Construction loan - interim loan.
(C) Construction loan – take-out loan.   (D) Take-out loan - progressive payment loan.

(B) A take-out loan is considered the final or long-term loan. A construction loan is made to complete the improvements on real property. An interim loan is another name for a construction loan. A progressive payment loan is the name of a construction loan.

_____(Lesson Thirteen - Paragraph 76 - Question 2)_____
The following institutional lender most likely would make interim loans:
(A) A mutual savings bank. (B) A savings and loan association.
(C) A commercial bank.   (D) A pension trust fund.

(C) A commercial bank situated in the area of the construction can supervise the project at lower cost. Therefore, this lender tends to make short-term loan transactions such as construction loans.

_____(Lesson Thirteen - Paragraph 77 - Question 1)_____
A contractor obtained a construction loan, and the loan funds are to be released in a series of progress payments. Most lenders disburse the last payment when the:
(A) Building is completed.   (B) Notice of completion is filed.
(C) Buyer approves the construction.   (D) Period to file a lien has expired.

(D) On a construction loan, if a notice of completion has been recorded, the subcontractors and workmen have 30 days to file a mechanics' lien. If they do not, their right to a mechanic's lien is lost forever. The general contractor has 60 days from the date of the notice of completion to file his mechanic's lien. Therefore, the final payment will be held back until this 60-day period has expired. At that time, the lender knows he is free from the risks of mechanic's lien.

_____(Lesson Thirteen - Paragraph 77 - Question 2)_____
When a contractor negotiates a construction loan with the agreement to receive progress payments from the lender, the contractor will receive the final payment:
(A) At the time of the completion of the building.
(B) At the time of recording the final notice of completion.
(C) When the lien period has expired.
(D) When the buyer approves the construction.

(C) It is the practice of lenders to "hold back" 10% of the money due the contractor until the lien
period has expired. At this time the contractor would receive his final payment.

_____(Lesson Thirteen - Paragraph 78 - Question 1)_____
The purpose of a take-out loan is to:
(A) Obtain the necessary funds to complete the construction of a new subdivision.
(B) Maintain the necessary funds to continue to operate the project at a loss.
(C) Obtain long term financing to repay interim or short term financing.
(D) All of the above.

(C) The take-out loan is the long-term loan - generally 25 or 30 years - that the purchaser obtains. The developer uses the proceeds to pay off the short-term construction loan. Take-out is long term. Construction loan is interim.

_____(Lesson Thirteen - Paragraph 78 - Question 2)_____
Lending institutions are limited as to the amount that they can lend, the types of loans and the length of the loans. Because of certain limitations, some lenders are not interested in giving or

are unable to give construction loans, but are willing to issue long-term financing after the construction is completed. Long term loans to be issued by one lender upon completion of the interim construction financing by another lender are known as:
(A) Discount loans. (B) Take out loans. (C) Redemption loans. (D) Renewal loans.

(B) Construction financing is usually paid after the building has been completed by refinancing the property on a long-term loan. The lender on the construction financing is taken out of the picture with the new loan.

_____(Lesson Thirteen - Paragraph 85 - Question 1)_____
Many companies and organizations are known by the initials or abbreviations used in their name. e following would be incorrect:
(A) FNMA (Federal National Mortgage Association).   (B) VA (Veterans Administration).
(C) NAR (National Association of Realtors).   (D) FHA (Federal Housing Association).

(D) FHA stands for Federal Housing Administration.

_____(Lesson Thirteen - Paragraph 85 - Question 2)_____
The Federal Housing Administration (FHA) was created primarily to provide:
(A) A market for home mortgages. (B) Insurance for bank depositors.
(C) A flow of money and credit.   (D) Insurance for home loans made by approved lenders.

(C) The main purpose of the FHA program, and the VA program, has been to meet the housing needs of all citizens through a flow of money and credit. These federal housing programs have had a sizeable influence in expanding the housing market.

_____(Lesson Thirteen - Paragraph 86/3 - Question 1)_____
A couple purchased a home at a full price of $94,000. They used a FHA insured loan to complete the purchase. All of the following would be advantages created by this transaction, except:
(A) Enforced savings. (B) Conserving working capital. (C) Liquidity. (D) Budgeted payments.

(C) Real estate investment is generally considered to be more fixed than other forms of investment. Real estate is the least liquid of available forms of investment opportunity.

_____(Lesson Thirteen - Paragraph 86/4 - Question 1)_____
FHA financing provides the buyer with all of the following advantages, except:
(A) Providing long-term financing geared to monthly payments the purchaser can afford.
(B) Eliminating short-term financing.
(C) Providing low cost insurance that protects the borrower.
(D) Promoting better building standards.

(C) FHA Mutual Mortgage Insurance is for the protection of the lender, not the borrower. (A), (B) & (D) are correct answers applicable to FHA financing.

_____(Lesson Thirteen - Paragraph 86/7 - Question 1)_____
All of the following are correct statements concerning FHA insured loans, except :
(A) Monthly budgeted payment suitable to the buyer's pocket.
(B) "Level payments" is the usual method of amortization.

(C) Equal monthly payments of taxes and insurance.
(D) Provides for maximum building standards.

(D) FHA established certain minimum property requirements for the protection of the buyer. These minimal building standards are credited with a general improvement of standards throughout the country.

_____(Lesson Thirteen - Paragraph 86/7 - Question 2)_____
Besides the provisions of the California Subdivision Map Act, land development is regulated by:
(A) Zoning laws. (B) Health and safety codes.
(C) FHA minimum housing standards. (D) All of the above.

(D) All of the above. State and local building standards must be adhered to in developing land. State and local health standards and local land use ordinances (zoning) also must be followed. Federal control is felt in the application of minimum housing standards when FHA or VA financing is used.

_____(Lesson Thirteen - Paragraph 86/9 - Question 1)_____
Interest rates on a conventional loan are usually:
(A) The same as FHA. (B) More than FHA.
(C) The same, no matter the source of the money. (D) The maximum allowable by law.

(B) The primary reason for using FHA insured loans is because of the lower interest rates.

_____(Lesson Thirteen - Paragraph 86/9 - Question 2)_____
A bank might make a government insured or guaranteed loan when with the same money it could make a conventional loan at a higher interest rate because:
(A) A deficiency judgment would be barred on the FHA loan. (B) FHA will collect the payments.
(C) Of the lesser risk of losing money should the borrower default. (D) It is a longer term loan.

(C) Institutional lenders are encouraged to make FHA or VA loans that can be at lower interest rates because government loans are either insured or guaranteed. This means that such loans offer a lesser degree of risk and they are also readily saleable to FNMA (Fanny-Mae) in the secondary money market.

_____(Lesson Thirteen - Paragraph 86/8 - Question 1)_____
With respect to government financing of real estate, the following are true, except:
(A) The Department of Veterans Affairs requires the veteran to obtain written permission prior to his renting a property financed under their program.
(B) FHA makes no distinction between loans for an owner-occupant and a borrower who is not the occupant of the property.
(C) FHA will insure a loan for the purchase of a duplex.
(D) The Veterans Administration will not guarantee a loan to finance the purchase single-family residence the veteran intends to rent.

(B) This is the incorrect statement the question seeks. When the borrower is not the owner--occupant under FHA regulations, the loan will be somewhat less than the amount available to an owner occupant. (A), (C), and (D) are all correct statements.

_____(Lesson Thirteen - Paragraph 87 - Question 1)_____
If a person borrows money to purchase a personal residence, the loan most likely would be insured by:
(A) VA.
(B) FHA or private mortgage insurer.
(C) Federal National Mortgage Association, Federal Home Loan Mortgage Corporation and Government National Mortgage Association.
(D) The lender.

(B) Insurance on loans called mortgage insurance is generally obtained from FHA or a private mortgage insurer.

_____(Lesson Thirteen - Paragraph 87 - Question 2)_____
A prospect for a property wants to purchase it with a FHA loan. You, as a real estate licensee, would refer him to:
(A) An approved bank, insurance company or savings & loan association.
(B) The Federal Housing Administration.
(C) California Department of Veterans Affairs.
(D) A licensed loan broker.

(A) The Federal Housing Administration does not lend money. It insures loans made by banks, insurance companies, and other qualified institutional lenders.

_____(Lesson Thirteen - Paragraph 95 - Question 1)_____
The interest rate on a new FHA loan is determined by the:
(A) Lender. (B) Trustee. (C) Federal Reserve Bank. (D) Federal Housing Administration.

(A) The law permits the lender to determine the rate on FHA loans. VA interest rates are still established by the Veteran's Administration.

_____(Lesson Thirteen - Paragraph 97 - Question 1)_____
The following would not be permitted in an FHA insured loan and would ordinarily be included in
a conventional loan agreement:
(A) Subordination clause. (B) Release clause. (C) Alienation clause. (D) Acceleration clause.

(C) The question refers to a clause that is not permitted in an FHA insured loan and would ordinarily be in a conventional loan. The FHA insured loan does not permit an alienation clause. Recent legislation does permit HUD to make a credit check on a resale of the property. After the credit check, if approved, the buyer must agree to assume the FHA loan and pay it in full.

_____(Lesson Thirteen - Paragraph 100 - Question 1)_____
The person would most likely pay a premium for mutual mortgage insurance is:
(A) A homeowner with a VA home loan.

(B) A homeowner with a home loan from a life insurance company.
(C) A homeowner who wishes to insure both real and personal property.
(D) A homeowner who assumed an FHA loan.

(D) The FHA insurance program is called mutual mortgage insurance. Earlier, FHA borrowers paid an insurance premium as part of their monthly loan payment. Current FHA borrowers either pay a one-time lump sum payment at the time they get the loan or the mortgage insurance premium is financed as part of the loan. This FHA insurance protects the lender from loss in the event the borrower defaults in making payments on the loan.

_____(Lesson Thirteen - Paragraph 102 - Question 1)_____
On a FHA insured loan, the lender is permitted to charge the buyer a one percent fee as an initial service fee. FHA refers to this fee as:
(A) An accommodation fee. (B) An application fee. (C) An acceleration fee. (D) An origination fee.

(B) This fee is generally called an origination fee. However, FHA refers to it as an "application fee."
_____(Lesson Thirteen - Paragraph 103a - Question 1)_____
A turnkey property is:
(A) A low-income housing project subsidized by the federal government.
(B) A vacant lot for which there is building plans.
(C) A subdivision project completely finished (ready to move in).
(D) An illegal subdivision.

(A) A turnkey property is a specific term used by HUD in providing low-income housing. it describes a property that has been rehabilitated and is ready for the subsidized tenant to move in.

_____(Lesson Thirteen - Paragraph 107/3 - Question 1)_____
Of the following loans, which offers the highest loan to value ratio?
(A) A VA guaranteed loan.   (B) An FHA insured loan.
(C) A California Veterans Farm and Home Purchase Loan. (D) A conventional loan.

(A) The VA guaranteed loan may be 100% of the reasonable value. This is as high as a loan-to-value ratios go.

_____(Lesson Thirteen - Paragraph 107/3 - Question 2)_____
The type of financing with which a person could buy a home with no down payment would be:
(A) FHA. (B) Conventional. (C) Cal-Vet. (D) VA.

(D) The VA loan permits the lender to issue a no down payment loan up to the CRV. The other choices, FHA, conventional, and Cal-Vet require a down payment.

_____(Lesson Thirteen - Paragraph 107a - Question 1)_____
There are many ways in which FHA insured loans differ from VA guaranteed loans. With respect to these loans, all of the following statements are true, except :
(A) VA loans may be obtained in the purchase of a mobile home with or without the lot.
(B) VA loans are made on residential property that the veteran will occupy.

(C) FHA loans may be obtained in the purchase of business property.
(D) FHA loans can be made on property that is to be owner-occupied or rented to others.

(C) FHA loans may only be used for residential properties. The properties need not be owner-occupied. VA loans may be used in the purchase of owner-occupied properties of 4 units or less, or for the purchase of a mobilehome with or without the lot, or to refinance loans, or other liens of record on the dwelling owned by the veteran.

_____(Lesson Thirteen - Paragraph 107a - Question 2)_____
FHA provides loans for, but VA will not provide loans for which of the following?
(A) Agricultural land.   (B) Farming equipment.
(C) A duplex purchased for a rental. (D) A business property.

(C) A VA loan can never be used for the purchase of rental properties. Therefore, a duplex or multiple units can never be purchased using a VA loan. FHA loans allow the purchase of one-to-four residential property for rental purposes.

_____(Lesson Thirteen - Paragraph 107b - Question 1)_____
The Veterans Administration, with its program of guaranteeing loans to eligible purchasers of residential property, indirectly influences the development of many subdivisions in California. The VA has adopted direct subdivision regulations:
(A) Where the VA plans to subsidize rents or loan payments to the people occupying the property.
(B) That are applicable only within incorporated areas.
(C) To control developments where home sites are to be acquired by veterans under the GI Bill.
(D) Adhering to a policy of laissez-faire.

(C) In more recent years the VA has adopted regulations that give them control over such features as streets, utilities, lot size, construction standards, and setbacks of residential subdivisions that utilize VA financing. Laissez-faire is an expression meaning a government policy of deliberately abstaining from interference with individual freedom of choice and action.

_____(Lesson Thirteen - Paragraph 108 - Question 1)_____
You have a customer that is interested in purchasing a home using his GI benefits. You have located a most desirable home for which the owner is asking $120,000. The VA has appraised it for $118,000. If the customer wants to purchase the home and use his GI benefits, you should advise him that:
(A) He can get a VA loan of $118,000 and can finance the balance by using a second trust deed.
(B) He can pay more than $118,000 and use GI benefits but must pay cash for the excess above
the $118,000.
(C) You will reduce your commission in half and have the owner reduce his price to $119,000 and
take back a second trust deed of $1000.
(D) He can do any of the above.

(B) The VA permits a veteran to purchase a home for a price that exceeds the CRV, but he must pay cash for the amount in excess of the CRV. Secondary financing may be used but the purchase price may not exceed the CRV.

_____(Lesson Thirteen - Paragraph 108 - Question 2)_____

Generally speaking FHA insures loans and VA guarantees loans. Which of the following is a correct statement?
(A) The maximum VA loan is limited to the CRV.
(B) FHA insured loans are only available to purchase of owner-occupied residences.
(C) FHA and VA protect the borrower from loss if a foreclosure sale does not bring enough to satisfy
the lien.
(D) Both FHA and VA permit a borrower to pay in excess of the appraised value to purchase a home.

(D) Both FHA and VA permit a borrower to pay in excess of the appraised value to purchase a home. The VA and the FHA are not concerned with the price a person actually pays for a property. An appraisal is made and the loan, insurance, and guarantee are based upon that appraisal. The purchaser may pay over the appraised amount without affecting his ability to obtain the financing.

_____(Lesson Thirteen - Paragraph 109 - Question 1)_____

If a lender granted a qualified veteran a $110,000 loan under the VA loan program, the loan guarantee given by the Veterans Administration would be:
(A) The CRV. (B) $47,500. (C) $36,000. (D) $44,000.

(C) The VA guarantee to the lender is 40% of the loan but not to exceed $36,000. $110,000 x .40 (40%) = $44,000. The maximum VA guarantee would be called for in this case.

_____(Lesson Thirteen - Paragraph 115 - Question 1)_____

The following party would pay the discount points in obtaining a Cal-Vet loan:
(A) The State Department of Veterans Affairs. (B) The veteran. (C) The lender. (D) Nobody.

(D) There are no discount points involved in a Cal-Vet loan. The state buys the property and resells to the veteran on a land contract.

_____(Lesson Thirteen - Paragraph 115 - Question 2)_____

When a home is financed under the California Veterans Farm and Home Purchase Plan, which of
the following documents is used:
(A) A mortgage. (B) A deed of trust. (C) A bill of sale. (D) A real property purchase contract.

(D) Cal-Vet provisions require owner-occupancy. However, the whole nature of the transaction is
different in that it involves a contract of sale (also called a land contract, or a real estate purchase contract) with the title remaining in the State.

_____(Lesson Thirteen - Paragraph 117 - Question 1)_____

The interest rate on outstanding loans is subject to periodic redetermination on which of the following types of financing:
(A) Cal-Vet. (B) FHA. (C) VA. (D) None of the above.

(A) Cal-Vet financing utilizes a variable interest rate. The rate change does not change the monthly payments but instead changes the length of the contract.

_____(Lesson Thirteen - Paragraph 117 - Question 2)_____
Of the following, the loan that permits a variable amortization period is:
(A) The California Veterans Farm and Home Purchase Program loan.
(B) The Veterans Administration guaranteed loan.
(C) The FHA Title 11 insured loan.
(D) The Title 1 FHA home improvement loan.

(A) The Cal-Vet loan is an open-end loan in which the period of the loan can vary from 25 to 40 years in different circumstances.

_____(Lesson Thirteen - Paragraph 118 - Question 1)_____
Money used by the State of California to finance the Farm and Home Purchase Plan is provided by:
(A) State funds and guaranteed by the federal government.
(B) Institutional lenders and guaranteed by the state government.
(C) The sale of state general obligation bonds and revenue bonds.
(D) Low interest loans from government retirement funds.

(C) The California Farm and Home Purchase Plan, also known as Cal-Vet, is financed with the sale of state bonds. The sale of these bonds is authorized by ballot of the general voting public.

_____(Lesson Thirteen - Paragraph 126 - Question 1)_____
The following would ordinarily be used to measure the relative purchasing power of the dollar:
(A) Treasury bills. (B) Price indices. (C) The gold standard. (D) Interest rates.

(B) The higher prices are in general, the less each dollar will purchase. As prices decline, your dollar will buy more.

_____(Lesson Thirteen - Paragraph 126 - Question 2)_____
A person wishing to determine the relative value of the dollar at any given time would ordinarily refer to (consult):
(A) U.S. Treasury Bond interest rates.   (B) Price indexes.
(C) The gold standard.   (D) The prime rate charged their customers by commercial banks.

(B) Price indexes (sometimes spelled indices). One of our reference texts says: "Economic forces are difficult to measure directly, even though they exert their influence anywhere people live. Thus, we resort to certain measures of economic activity. The most common and most important measures at the national level are: 1) Gross national products (GNP); 2) Employment and unemployment; 3) Consumer price index (CPI) and per capita personal income. Statistics for these measures may be compared from one time to another and, except for GNP, for one community or area to another at both regional and local levels." We believe the quote is pertinent to this question asking about the relative value of money at any given time. The only reference identified in this quote would be price indexes. The other suggestions are too limited in their application as general economic indicators.

_____(Lesson Thirteen - Paragraph 127 - Question 1)_____

The measurement of the total goods and services produced annually in the United States is called:
(A) Budget. (B) Amortization. (C) Gross national product. (D) Subordination.

(C) This statement is a precise definition of the term "gross national product."

_____(Lesson Thirteen - Paragraph 129 - Question 1)_____

In a period of recession or decline in the economy as a whole, a general decline in the prices of commodities would result in:
(A) A general decline in sales.   (B) A decrease in the value of the dollar.
(C) An increase in the value of the dollar. (D) The value of the dollar would remain the same.

(C) If prices should decline the dollars available would purchase more commodities than they could previously. This would increase the value of the dollar. The dollar could buy more in the marketplace.

_____(Lesson Thirteen - Paragraph 129a - Question 1)_____

During inflationary periods the value of the dollar is weakened. This would be evidenced by:
(A) Cost of living index rising from 112 to 135. (B) Cost of living index dropping from 108 to 90.
(C) An increase in points for loans.   (D) A drop in the prime interest rate.

(A) Some economists use the phrase "cost of living" in reference to an index. A rise in the index would indicate that more dollars would be necessary in an inflationary period to buy the same amount of commodities than could be acquired for a lesser monetary sum in a period that had a lower cost of living index.

_____(Lesson Thirteen - Paragraph 130 - Question 1)_____

In times when the Gross National Product grows (increases) and unemployment declines, the following would be true:
(A) Houses would tend to increase in value.   (B) New home sales would tend to advance.
(C) Sales of resale homes would tend to increase. (D) All of the above are true.

(D) The Gross National Product, GNP is the sum total of all the products and services that are produced in the country in a year. If the GNP is up, all three choices would be true.

_____(Lesson Thirteen - Paragraph 130 - Question 2)_____

The following does not have a direct impact upon mortgage interest rates:
(A) Inflation. (B) Demand. (C) Unemployment rates. (D) The discount rate.

(C) This is a negative question. Unemployment rates do not have a direct impact upon mortgage interest rates though they do have an indirect effect because as economic activity increases unemployment decreases this influences prices because of the increase in the income of potential buyers. This would influence a non-homeowner to leave those ranks and become a homeowner. Choices (A), (B), and (D), all have a direct impact.

_____(Lesson Thirteen - Paragraph 131 - Question 1)_____
A tight money market generally forces the "Prime" rate of interest to increase. If interest rates increase, capitalization rates generally:
(A) Increase. (B) Decrease. (C) Remain the same. (D) None of the above.

(A) Lenders loan money to realize income. The rate of interest indicates the rate of return they except to receive on their investment. Purchasers of income property also are interested in earning money on their investments and we base their rate of return on capitalization rates. Investors usually demand a higher rate of return than do commercial lenders. When commercial lenders increase the rate of return (interest rate), investors also increase their rates (Cap Rate).

_____(Lesson Thirteen - Paragraph 131a - Question 1)_____
When the general level of prices decreases:
(A) It has no effect on the value of money.   (B) The value of commodities increases.
(C) The value of money increases.   (D) The value of money decreases.

(C) When prices decrease, the value of the dollar increases. If the price of a quart of milk is 2 cents, as it was in 1934, then the dollar is worth 50 quarts of milk.

_____(Lesson Thirteen - Paragraph 131a - Question 2)_____
How would a serious inflation trend in the economy affect the equity of a landlord who has leased his property at a fixed income?
(A) Increase his equity.   (B) Decrease his equity.
(C) Have no effect on his equity. (D) Remain the same.

(B) Decrease his equity. In times of inflation the value of real property will tend to increase as rents increase. If a tenant is on a fixed long-term rental not tied to an economic index the value of the total property and the corresponding equity of the owner will decrease.

_____(Lesson Thirteen - Paragraph 132 - Question 1)_____
A lender would consider the following in establishing the interest rate on a proposed real estate loan:
(A) The credit rating from the borrower.   (B) Long-term economic trends.
(C) The location of the property securing the loan. (D) All of the above.

(D) Prudent lending institutions would investigate thoroughly the suggested areas in choices (A), (B), and (C) to establish the interest rates to be applicable for prospective real estate loans.

_____(Lesson Thirteen - Paragraph 132 - Question 2)_____
The terms of some real estate loans provide that the interest rate may be increased or decreased depending on money market conditions. This type of loan is:
(A) An interim loan.   (B) A loan which is secured by a short term land contract.
(C) A variable interest rate loan.   (D) A fluctuating market condition loan.

(C) Many loans are influenced by the economic activity as shown by these indicators. The "variable interest rate" loans will have their rates increase or decrease based on these indexes and on the influence of the Federal Reserve System.

_____(Lesson Thirteen - Paragraph 133 - Question 1)_____

All of the following would tend to indicate that there is an increase in the supply of money available for real estate mortgages, except:
(A) The desire of people to provide for retirement income.
(B) The desire to invest in liquid assets.
(C) The desire to increase personal savings.
(D) The mortgage loan insurance and guarantee policies of the Federal Housing Administration and the Veterans Administration.

(B) Real estate loans are usually of a long-term and lack liquidity when compared with other investments. When liquidity is desired, funds are invested in short-term commercial notes or government securities.

_____(Lesson Thirteen - Paragraph 134 - Question 1)_____

Depression - recovery; Recession - stability; refer to which cycle:
(A) Real estate. (B) Capital. (C) Mortgage market. (D) Business.

(D) Many studies of economic activity have been maintained by a number of professional companies over the years. These studies reveal a rhythmic change from major booms to major business depressions interspersed by minor periods of prosperity and minor business recessions. The regularity of the periodic business swings from boom to bust and has led to the belief in the existence of a business cycle.

_____(Lesson Thirteen - Paragraph 134 - Question 2)_____

An economic trend is the result of:
(A) A series of changes brought about by a chain of causes and effects. (B) Population growth.
(C) Purchasing power. (D) Price levels.

(A) This is a good definition of an economic trend.

_____(Lesson Thirteen - Paragraph 134a - Question 1)_____

The following would least likely affect the business cycle:
(A) Erratic spending by government, public and business people.
(B) The government creating new loans for low income housing in a major metropolitan area.
(C) New innovations in industrial production.
(D) Fluctuations in interest rates and changes in lending policies by the major lending institutions.

(B) This would affect the housing market more than the business cycle. The other choices are more related to business and industry.

_____(Lesson Thirteen - Paragraph 135 - Question 1)_____

Mr. Jones recently purchased a residence using a loan that required a small down payment. The following factor would afford the lender the greatest protection against a loss because of default on this type of loan:
(A) A low interest rate. (B) An economy where incomes and housing prices are rising.
(C) A low monthly payment. (D) Proper servicing of the loan by a loan officer.

(B) Risks in a loan with a low down payment are greater in the first five years. The risks are greatly influenced by the state of the economy. When incomes and housing price are rising, even the poorest of loans succeed as the lender has the security of a higher equity value in the property.

_____(Lesson Thirteen - Paragraph 135 - Question 2)_____
Lenders have greater risks with no down payment loans. A lender's greatest protection against default would be:
(A) Low monthly payments on the loan. (B) Low interest rate on the loan.
(C) Appreciation of the property.   (D) Computerized monthly loan payments.

(C) The greatest protection against default over the last from the great depression to 1990 has been the constant appreciation of the property. Time has healed loan problems as property values have exceeded loan amounts. When this process reverses, as it has done during the years 1990-1995 and 2006-2012 when values of property fell below many the loan amount owed, it creates a substantial increase in foreclosures.

_____(Lesson Thirteen - Paragraph 138 - Question 1)_____
The principal economic characteristic of real property would be:
(A) It is a long-term investment. (B) Its immobility.
(C) Its indestructibility.   (D) Its durability.

(A) The keyword in this question is economic characteristic. Other than choice (A), the choices mention physical characteristics.

_____(Lesson Thirteen - Paragraph 138 - Question 2)_____
As a general rule, financial enhancement and speculative possibilities in the purchase of a home
would receive the following consideration:
(A) Exclusive.   (B) Primary.
(C) Secondary.   (D) None of the above.

(C) In the purchase of a home, the buyer's primary concern should be the shelter that is needed for the buyer's family. Any other considerations should come after the shelter need has been satisfied.

_____(Lesson Thirteen - Paragraph 142 - Question 1)_____
In the field of real estate, a seller's market is said to exist when:
(A) Competition between sellers is increasing.
(B) A multiple listing service is functioning, collecting, and distributing information about properties for sale.
(C) In the marketplace sellers outnumber buyers.

392

(D) Fewer properties are offered for sale to an increasing number of prospects with the ability to buy.

(D) A seller's market exists when demand and supply factors favor the seller receiving the highest price for his property. This is when the demand is high and supply is low. Thus, (D) is the best response. Responses (A) and (C) are identical and the opposite of what exists in a seller's market. Response (B) is not relevant to the condition of the marketplace.

_____(Lesson Thirteen - Paragraph 142 - Question 2)_____
If the real estate market changes from a "buyer's market" to a "seller's market":
(A) Interest rates on home mortgages will increase.
(B) Interest rates on home mortgages will decrease.
(C) Prices of homes will increase.
(D) Prices of homes will decrease.

(C) When the market goes to a seller's market, this indicates more buyers than there are sellers. Because of this increased demand, sellers generally increase the asking price of their property.

_____(Lesson Thirteen - Paragraph 143 - Question 1)_____
Federal deregulation means:
(A) No limit on interest rates banks can pay on deposits.
(B) No governmental regulation of banks and savings and loan associations.
(C) No enforcement of regulations pertaining to financial institutions.
(D) A relaxing of controls that federal governmental agencies exercise in regard to the operation of
financial institutions.

(D) Deregulation indicates the reduction of control in institutions. The saving and loans, for example, were permitted to make loans secured by assets other than real estate such as junk bonds, restaurant chains, and racehorses.

_____(Lesson Thirteen - Paragraph 148 - Question 1)_____
Money available for real estate loans normally would increase, except when:
(A) One desires to save for old age.
(B) There is in increase in the interest rate paid on corporate and government bonds.
(C) Personal savings are high.
(D) The savings-to-consumption ratio increases.

(B) The question deals with an increasing supply of money for real estate loans. (A) is true. When people want to save for old age, they save money and increase the money supply. (B) is the correct answer. When there is an increase in interest in corporate and government bonds, people place their money in government bonds and remove it from depositories of real estate lenders, therefore lessening the money supply. When savings are high there is more money for real estate loans.

_____(Lesson Thirteen - Paragraph 148 - Question 2)_____
If the Federal Reserve Bank increases the reserve requirements for member banks:
(A) More construction will result.

(B) More loans will be made.
(C) Less funds will be available to make loans.
(D) Lower interest rates will result.

(C) This re-emphasizes that when the Federal Reserve Bank increases reserve requirements for member banks, they must borrow additional funds for reserves, increasing their costs, or they must liquidate certain loans to meet the higher reserve requirements. Therefore, fewer funds will be available to the banks to make loans.

_____(Lesson Thirteen - Paragraph 149 - Question 1)_____
When there is a scarcity of money available for loans on real property, we refer to this period as a "tight money market." During this time:
(A) Buyer would have to pay more points to obtain VA financing.
(B) Seller would have to pay more points to obtain a VA loan.
(C) Points would not be affected at all since the Home Loan Bank sets these.
(D) Points are usually lower.

(B) "Tight money" indicates there is little money available for the mortgage market and, as a result, mortgage money will be more costly. This cost is reflected in more points and higher interest rates. Since the buyer cannot pay more than (1) one point "loan origination fee" on VA loan, the seller is required to pay the "discount points."

_____(Lesson Thirteen - Paragraph 149 - Question 2)_____
In a tight money market the following would be true regarding conventional loans:
(A) The buyer will pay a lower origination fee.   (B) The buyers will pay more points.
(C) The seller will pay greater discount points.   (D) The seller will pay a higher origination fee.

(B) A tight money market indicates that loans are difficult to obtain, therefore, money is difficult to find for the financing of property. Lenders will demand more points for the loan in this period than in loose money markets.

_____(Lesson Thirteen - Paragraph 150 - Question 1)_____
The interest rate charged by commercial banks on loans to borrowers with the highest credit qualifications is commonly referred to as:
(A) The discount rate. (B) The compound rate. (C) The prime rate. (D) The principal rate.

(C) The interest rate charged by your large commercial banks to their prime borrower their best credit risks is called the prime rate. Other loans to less credit-worthy borrowers will be charged an interest rate higher than the prime rate, often described as 2 points above prime, or 5 points above prime.

_____(Lesson Thirteen - Paragraph 151 - Question 1)_____
The Federal Reserve Bank advances money to its member banks from time to time to assist them in maintaining required reserve amounts. The rate of interest charged by the Federal Reserve for making such loans is designated as:
(A) The demand rate. (B) The discount rate. (C) The standard rate. (D) The prime rate.

(B) The Federal Reserve Bank makes loans to its member banks. These member banks use these loans as reserves against which they make loans. The rate of interest on these loans is said to be "the discount rate."

_____(Lesson Thirteen - Paragraph 151 - Question 2)_____
If the Federal Reserve Bank increases the discount rate, then:
(A) More discounts will be made.   (B) Fewer loans will be made.
(C) The money supply will increase. (D) The market rate will decrease.

(B) When the discount rate is increased, the cost of money to member banks increases. As a result, the member banks must increase the interest rate and fewer loans will be made.

_____(Lesson Thirteen - Paragraphs 151 & 153 - Question 1)_____
The Federal Reserve wants to tighten the money market. To accomplish this it would:
(A) Decrease the discount rate and buy government bonds.
(B) Increase the discount rate and buy government bonds.
(C) Increase the discount rate and sell government bonds.
(D) Decrease the discount rate and sell government bonds.

(C) When the Federal Reserve wishes to "tighten" the money market, it increases the discount rate they charge member banks to borrow funds from them. This in turn increased the cost to member banks and they in turn must raise interest rates to the public. When the Federal Reserve sells government bonds on the open market, people who buy them write checks against their bank account reducing the bank's reserve and requiring the banks to borrow additional money from the Federal Reserve or to cease making loans.

_____(Lesson Thirteen - Paragraph 164 - Question 1)_____
The following entity is involved in the secondary mortgage market:
(A) Federal Deposit Insurance Corporation. (B) Federal Reserve Bank.
(C) Federal Housing Administration.   (D) Federal National Mortgage Association.

(D) FNMA, "Fannie Mae", is a private organization that purchases existing FHA, VA and conventional loans. This is an example of the secondary mortgage market. The primary mortgage market is that in which lenders make loans to borrowers.

_____(Lesson Thirteen - Paragraph 164 - Question 2)_____
The Federal National Mortgage Association (FNMA), originally created under Title III of the National Housing Act of 1934, and now a privately owned venture, operates for the primary purpose of:
(A) Buying title I FHA loans.
(B) Lending money on FHA Title H loans when banks will not.
(C) Buying FHA, VA and conventional loans from lending institutions in order to stimulate the mortgage market.
(D) Advancing funds to builders and developers of large tracts of residential property in or near metropolitan centers.

(C) The major purpose of FNMA is to assure a secondary market for FHA insured mortgages and trust deeds, VA guaranteed loans, and conventional loans. Lending agencies, which have lent the limit of their money available for this purpose, sell these notes to FNMA to secure more cash to make more loans. FNMA purchases these loans at discount according to current market conditions and resells them to other institutions having money to invest.

_____(Lesson Thirteen - Paragraph 168 - Question 1)_____

Lenders are more inclined in recent years to make 95% loans on single-family residential properties because of:

(A) Freddie Mac's activity in the market place. (B) Credit life insurance.

(C) Private mortgage insurance . (D) The activity of Ginny Mae.

(C) The risk involved in making a loan with a small (5%) down payment is that if the buyer stops making the payments and the lender must have the house sold at a trustee's sale, it might not sell for a price sufficient to return to the bank all of the money loaned. Private mortgage insurance insures against that specific risk by paying the lender the difference between the price at the trustee's sale and the loan amount (within the limits of the policy amount.)

_____(Lesson Thirteen - Paragraph 182 - Question 1)_____

Broker Rowe is servicing a trust deed loan for his client Steele:

(A) He would have to be involved in the transaction in which the trust deed was created.

(B) He would have to have the client's written consent to do this.

(C) He would have to have a Securities Dealer's license.

(D) He would have to have a trust account to deposit the payments.

(B) Real estate license law (B&P Code #10233) requires that the loan broker get written consent from the borrower or lender to service a loan or land contract.

_____(Lesson Thirteen - Paragraph 182 - Question 2)_____

Mr. Traveler calls a real estate broker in his neighborhood and indicates he is going on an extended vacation. He asks the broker to service a trust deed note that he had taken as part of the price of real property he sold. To do this, the broker must:

(A) Obtain a securities dealer's license.

(B) Obtain a permit to do so from the Department of Real Estate.

(C) Obtain the written permission of the owner of the note to perform this service.

(D) Obtain a license to do this from the Corporations Commissioner.

(C) Real Estate Law states, "Any real estate licensee who undertakes to service a promissory note secured directly or indirectly by a lien on real property or a real property sales contract, shall have a written authorization from the borrower or lender or holder of the contract."

_____(Lesson Thirteen - Paragraph 184 - Question 1)_____

Realtor Jones is the beneficiary of a promissory note that is secured by a first trust deed on real property. He has held the note for a number of years and decides to sell it. When he sells the note it is his duty to see to it that the security instrument is:

(A) Assessed and reconveyed. (B) Assigned and recorded.

(C) Assigned and acknowledged. (D) assigned and estopped.

(B) Whenever a broker is involved in the resale of an existing note secured by a lien on real property, either as principal or as agent, real estate law requires that he execute and record a proper assignment of the deed of trust to the purchaser of the note. He must do this within 10 working days of taking the purchaser's money.

——————(Lesson Thirteen - Paragraph 198 - Question 1)—————
You are employed by a life insurance company to solicit loans that will be secured by real property.
You will receive a commission for each loan you obtain. You must:
(A) Possess a real estate broker's license.   (B) Post a $5,000 bond.
(C) Obtain a permit.   (D) All of the above.

(A) Soliciting loans that are secured by real property requires a real estate broker license.

——————(Lesson Thirteen - Paragraph 198 - Question 2)—————
To operate legally in California the following person must be properly licensed:
(A) A principal selling three lots.
(B) A resident manager of an apartment house.
(C) A mortgage loan broker.
(D) A trustee.

(C) A mortgage loan broker is a licensed real estate broker who specializes in negotiating and arranging loans for a commission.

——————(Lesson Thirteen - Paragraph 201 - Question 1)—————
Certain requirements have been imposed on brokers engaged in the business of negotiating mortgage loans, including the requirement of securing a borrower's signature on a mortgage broker's loan statement. The period of time during which he must keep this statement on file for inspection is?
(A) 90 days after the transaction is completed and the funds distributed to the borrower.
(B) Four years from date the borrower signed the instrument.
(C) One year from the date the loan was secured.
(D) Three years from the date originally fixed for the termination of the note.

(B) A real estate broker must retain most all documents for a period of three years. There is one exception to this rule that applies to a broker acting as a loan broker. Some loan brokerage forms must be retained four years.

——————(Lesson Thirteen - Paragraphs 203- Question 1)——————
A broker negotiates a second trust deed loan for $20,000, charging $1,600 commission to which all parties agree. Under the real property loan brokerage law, such transaction is:
(A) Permissible. (B) Usurious. (C) Illegal. (D) Void.

(A) The Loan Brokerage Law applies to junior liens of less than $20,000 only. Commission on this loan is a matter of agreement.

——————(Lesson Thirteen - Paragraph 203- Question 2)—————
Under the mortgage loan broker law, a broker is limited in the amount of commission he may charge for negotiating a loan depending upon the type of encumbrance and the time of maturity. Assume a broker negotiated a third trust deed for $2,000, payable in five semi-annual installments. The maximum rate of commission allowable would be:
(A) 5% (B) 10% (C) $ 1,000 (D) nothing.

(B) A third trust deed is a "junior lien." The maximum commission to be paid for negotiating a junior loan for less than $10,000 for a term of 2 years or more, but less than 3 years, is 10%.

_____(Lesson Thirteen - Paragraph 203 - Question 3)_____
A real estate broker negotiates a $7,000 second trust deed note secured by real property. The loan was to be paid in full in five years. The most the broker could charge as a commission for his services would be:
(A) 3%   (B) 6% (C) 15% (D) 10%

(C) The commission is limited to 15% for a junior trust deed less than $30,000 for a term of 3 years or more.

_____(Lesson Thirteen - Paragraph 216 - Question 1)_____
A real estate broker can be reimbursed for his costs and expenses and one-half of his commission in representing his principal, even though no contact is consummated, in which of the following:
(A) When negotiating a loan.   (B) When selling industrial properties.
(C) When exchanging real property. (D) When selling a business property.

(A) In negotiating a loan the broker's costs and expenses would be reimbursable if the borrower failed to disclose all outstanding liens of record on the current vested title that is material to the security for the loan. The borrower would also be liable in this instance for 1/2 of the commission chargeable. In all the other cases the broker would risk these expenses for the possibility of earning a commission.

_____(Lesson Thirteen - Paragraph 216 - Question 2)_____
A broker would be entitled to one-half of his commission and certain expenses in the following circumstances:
(A) The buyer's recession of a purchase agreement.
(B) The borrower's non-disclosure of a second trust deed resulting in a loan not being consummated.
(C) The seller's rejection of an offer to purchase a residence.
(D) A borrower failing to meet credit requirements resulting in the failure of a loan to be consummated.

(B) Real Estate Law, §10243, provides that the two charges mentioned in the statement of the question would be the borrowers responsibility if he failed to disclose all liens of record against the property. The question refers to a loan broker even though it does not specify. Do not confuse this with the acceptance clause in the deposit receipt that states that the broker may be entitled to half of any deposit retained by the seller if the buyer breaches the contract.

_____(Lesson Thirteen - Paragraph 216a - Question 1)_____
An exclusive agreement authorizing a licensee to negotiate a loan secured by a lien on real property must be limited to 45 days if the loan is:
(A) Any amount. (B) Less than $6,000.   (C) Less than $12,000. (D) $2,000 or less.

(A)   An exclusive agreement authorizing a licensee to negotiate a loan in any amount regulated by the loan broker law can be for a period of no more than 45 days.

─────────**(Lesson Thirteen - Paragraph 219 - Question 1)**─────────

Section 10244.1 of the Real Estate Law states: "Notwithstanding the provisions of Section 10244, on a loan secured directly or collaterally by a lien on real property comprising an owner-occupied dwelling, for a term of six years or less, no installment shall be greater than twice the amount of the smallest installment." A correct statement is:

(A) It applies to all real property loans.

(B) It requires monthly payments on loans secured by real property.

(C) It does not apply to a loan of more than six years.

(D) It requires a mortgage loan broker license to negotiate such a loan.

───

(C) This law applies to loans secured by an owner occupied residence. A term of six years or less may not have a balloon payment. This law does not apply to loans of more than 6 years.

─────────**(Lesson Thirteen - Paragraph 223 - Question 1)**─────────

The monthly payment on a mortgage loan is, by statute, late when received by the lender:

(A) 3 days after the due date.   (B) 5 days after the due date.

(C) 10 days after the due date.   (D) More than 10 days after the due date.

───

(D)   A late charge may not be imposed on any installment which is paid or tendered in full within 10 days after its scheduled due date.

Lesson Thirteen
Part Three
Understanding Through Question Testing

 Log into your course at www.lumbleau.com.

STUDENT LOGIN

Login: [   ]

Password: [   ]

 On your student home page, click on the "State Exam Preparation".

STATE EXAM
PREPARATION

 Under the "Guided Lesson" tab click on the thirteenth of fourteen links: "Real Estate Finance".

Real Estate Salesperson Course

| Guided Lessons | Practice Exams | Progress Report | Success Video |

Print	Questions
Click	HERE>>> **13. Real Estate Finance**

Here you will be tested on all of the questions you have been studying and learn the most recently added questions. It is essential, for maximum retention, that you eliminate all of the questions you can easily answer and "TAG" for study the questions with which you have difficulty.

Lesson Fourteen

Part One
Understanding Through Video Teaching

Lesson Fourteen

The Appraisal Process

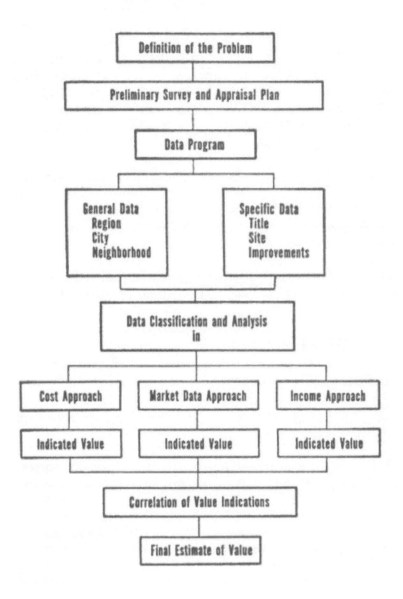

THE APPRAISAL PROCESS

38 Strip Development - Commercial development in which the main thoroughfares of a city are bordered by an almost continuous row or strip of retail stores and allied service establishments. This also includes any shopping area that consists of a row of stores.

43 Vacancy - An allowance for the percentage of vacant units must be calculated when arriving at the gross operating income.

45 An appraisal (or valuation) is an estimate or opinion of value for a stated purpose as of a given date. It is not an exact science, rather it rests upon the appraiser's knowledge of appraisal techniques and his experience in the field. The first step in any appraisal is to determine its purpose. In today's society, investors have learned to rely more and more on the advice of professional appraisers rather than acquiring property by their own experience. Lenders demand it and will not loan on a property without an adequate appraisal. Governments today are demanding a certified appraisal before guaranteeing, purchasing or insuring a loan.

47 This process is an orderly program by which the problem is defined, the work necessary to solve the problem is planned, and the data involved is acquired, classified, analyzed, and interpreted into an estimate of value. It is a dependable method of making a thorough and accurate appraisal in an efficient manner. It can also serve as the outline of the appraisal report.

DEFINITION OF APPRAISAL

48 What a person pays for a property has nothing to do with its appraised value unless the property is new. The appraiser must be independent of the owner's thinking and must determine the value as of a given date.

PURPOSES AND USES OF APPRAISALS

49 Appraisals are needed for:
(1) Transfer of ownership of property.
(2) An appraisal assures the seller that he is receiving a fair market value if he sells at the appraised value.
(3) The listing agent needs an estimate of value of the property before accepting a listing from the owner. Generally, an owner over-values his property.

50 Lessor's interest consists in his rights to the income established in the terms of the lease contract. This factor is capitalized to a value of the lessor's interest. At the termination of the lease contract, both the land and building will revert to the control of the lessor. The lessor has a reversionary interest in the land and building, including the value of future rental income. All are taken into consideration in an appraisal.

TYPES OF APPRAISAL REPORTS

51 The appraiser would be most concerned in directing his appraisal efforts to the date his client, buyer or seller would sign the agreement to purchase the property being appraised. The appraiser must give the report only to the employing client. The report will be furnished to the client in one of three forms.

54 Narrative report - This type is the longest and most complete report. It includes all pertinent information about the area and the subject property as well as the reasons and computations for the value conclusions. It includes maps, photographs, charts, elevation, foundation, floor and plot plans. A foundation plan is the plan that discloses piers, footings, and columns. A plot plan includes lot dimensions and improvements drawn to scale and in proportion to boundary lines. A floor plan includes all dimensions of interior and porch spaces. An elevation plan depicts the architectural style by a drawing from the north, southeast, and west sides of the building. It is written for court cases and out-of-town clients who need all the factual data.

NATURE OF VALUE IN APPRAISING

55   Value is a word of many meanings. Because the word has so many different applications, it cannot be defined simply. One very common definition is: "Value is a relationship between the thing desired and the potential purchaser." Relationship is the key word in this definition. It indicates that the value of a thing relates to something outside the thing itself. The value of a home is established by what interested purchasers are willing to pay. This leads to another definition of value: "Value is in the eyes of the beholder," implying that the value of a thing is relative to the needs, desires, and purchasing power of the individual. It, in the "eyes of the buyer," is subjective in nature.

ELEMENTS OF VALUE

56   An object cannot have value unless it has utility. This means it must arouse the desire for possession and have the power to give satisfaction. Functional Utility is the sum of a property's attractiveness and usefulness. These characteristics are found more in the property itself than in the minds of the occupants.

57   The four elements of value are utility, scarcity, demand, and transferability. No one of these alone can create value. All must be present to maintain value.

59   Scarcity - If an object is useful, but in great supply, its value will be diminished. For example, the over-building of homes to the point where there is an oversupply on the market is a form of economic obsolescence and will result in lower values.

60   Demand - There must be demand for an object for it to have value.   Utility creates demand. Demand, to be effective, must be implemented by purchasing power.

Transferability - Although the other elements of value may be present a property will have no value unless the current owner is free to transfer use to others wanting to utilize it for some purpose.

63   Cost - The past expenditure of dollars for the acquisition or improvement of residential real property. It should be noted that cost is not one of the essential elements of value. A home constructed twenty years ago at a cost of $10,000 may have a present value of $50,000 or $5,000, depending on current market factors.

63a   Another theory put forth by appraisers is that there are other significant forces influencing value. The four forces are:
   (1) Physical characteristics.
   (2) Social ideals, attitudes, and standards.
   (3) Economic adjustments.
   (4) Political regulations.

VALUE DESIGNATIONS MARKET VALUE

73   Generally, when speaking of the value of real property, the reference is to market value. Market value is also referred to as "value in exchange" or "objective value" since it is not determined by or subject to the restrictions of an established project. It has been variously defined as follows:

74   "The highest price estimated in terms of money which a property will bring if exposed for sale in the open market, allowing a reasonable time to find a purchaser who buys with knowledge of all the uses to which it is adapted."

75   The price at which a willing seller would sell and willing buyer would buy with neither being under abnormal pressure.

83   Price - What one pays for a commodity regardless of pressure, motives, or intelligence of the seller or buyer. Usually it is considered to be the amount of money involved in a transaction. Whether we receive in value more or less than what we pay will depend on how sound our judgment is in the appraisal. Some factors that tend to cause price to differ from value are:

(1) Favorable financing.
(2) Distress sale.
(3) Forced purchase.
(4) Uninformed buyer or seller.
(5) High-pressure salesmanship.

BASIC PRINCIPLES AFFECTING THE VALUE OF REAL PROPERTY

85 Supply and Demand - Demand for a commodity is created by its scarcity and it is limited by the financial ability of people to satisfy their desires and needs. The greater the supply of a commodity available the lower its value.
(1) Scarcity influences supply.
(2) Desire influences demand.
(3) Desire, to be effective, must be
(4) backed by purchasing power.

86 Change - Nothing remains static. The future rather than the past is of primary importance in estimating value. The appraiser must observe the stage of development which a neighborhood has reached and define the phase of its life cycle. In the life cycle of a neighborhood, appraisers identify three stages:
(1) Integration (development)
(2) Equilibrium (static state)
(3) Disintegration (decline or decay)

87 Substitution - This principle affirms that the maximum value of a property tends to be set by the cost of acquiring a substitute property of equal utility and desirability.

91 Highest and Best Use - The available use and program of future utilization that produces the highest present land value. Maximum utilization of resources states another way of saying "highest and best use."

92 It is the use that will provide the greatest return to the land. For example, short blocks in a subdivision devote more land for street use. Long blocks are more economical in utilizing land.

92a When selecting land for development the developer often chooses suburban rather than urban land. The principal reason for this choice is the completeness of development in an urban area. The land costs are higher. The zoning and utilization of the land has been fairly well defined. Flexibility of uses is limited. In a suburban area the development costs are lower; however, the developer has the freedom to select the type of development he feels best and is not confined by a "strait jacket" of a preconceived city plan. He may plan self-contained communities, complete with shopping centers, recreational, school and church facilities.

94 Return sometimes takes the form of amenities. An open wooded area in a city, for example, may have its highest and best use as a park or the amenities of a private residence may outweigh the advantages of rental income potentially available on the rental market. The location of a private residence is considered an amenity. For example, a residence located in the center of other similar residences versus the same residence located on a main street.

96 Labor (Wages) - By law and nature, labor is the first agent that must be paid.

97 Coordination (Management) - Operating expenses such as utilities, supplies, repairs, taxes, and insurance must be paid next.

98 Capital Investment – Money allocated for the building and equipment.

99 Land - The remainder of the gross income goes to satisfy capital and land.

99a Productivity - The highest and best use is that use which is most likely to produce the greatest net return over a given period of time. Productivity is understood in relation to highest and best use, utility, or use. It employs all four agents.

103 Contribution - This principle may be said to be the principle of increasing and decreasing returns as it applies to some portion of improvement. This principle would be applied in the feasibility study of a proposed

modernization or remodeling project. Contribution can positively or negatively impact the value of a property. A new swimming pool may impact value more than its cost. On the other hand, asbestos found in a building constructed prior to 1953, would have a major negative effect on value. Gasoline stations constructed in the 1950's and earlier can negatively impact a site because the underground storage tanks have created a toxic waste problem. Appraisers are always on the lookout for these negative elements of contribution. They will not only include them in the final report, they will depreciate their appraisal by the amount calculated to eliminate the toxic waste in a "Toxic Waste Report" issued by a company in the business of cleaning up these conditions. The appraiser will also notify the proper authorities.

103a The appraisal manual defines remodeling as, "Changing the plan, form, or style of a structure to correct functional or economic deficiencies."

104 The Principle of Diminishing Returns - Also called increasing and decreasing returns, states that increasing an investment in one of the agents of production labor, management, land, or building will eventually reach the point where any added investment will actually decrease the return on the investment. As previously stated increasing an investment in an apartment by adding a $15,000 swimming pool that does not result in a corresponding increase in rents will actually lessen the owner's return on his investment. Increasing rents in a neighborhood above the comparative rates of competitive apartments will create vacancies and form another type of diminishing returns.

105 Conformity - The principle of conformity holds that maximum value is realized when there is a reasonable degree of architectural homogeneity and where land uses are compatible. In a shopping center this would mean that the major stores occupy the center. In a residential neighborhood this principle also

applies to the income of those in the population.

106 When there are largely varied incomes in an area, those with the greater income can afford to improve their property where those with a smaller income cannot.

108 Dwellings in a residential neighborhood should conform in size, age, condition, and style for maximum value. A neighborhood of single-family residences would be adversely affected by the introduction of boarding houses. Owner-occupied properties certainly lessen the possibility of property turnover as this type of owner is rooted to the present circumstances. Maximum property value would be maintained for the long term by owner occupancy.

110 A misplaced improvement (the wrong type of structure) is a direct violation of conformity. It is considered economic obsolescence.

111 Regression - This principle holds that where a neighborhood consists of dissimilar properties, the value of the better properties will be adversely affected by the presence of the properties of lesser value. For example, in a neighborhood of $150,000 to $180,000 properties the value of a $300,000 property tends to regress towards the value of the price level typical of the neighborhood.

112 Progression - This is the reverse of the principle of regression. It states that property of lesser value will be enhanced by proximity to better properties. For example, a $150,000 property in a neighborhood of $250,000 to $300,000 homes might sell for more than $150,000 because there are people who will pay a premium to live in a higher priced neighborhood.

INFLUENCES
ON THE VALUE OF REAL PROPERTY

121 An economic trend is a series of changes brought about by a chain of causes and effects. The appraiser must be alert to past and

present economic trends. He must consider the direction of the trend and its probable limit.

PHYSICAL FACTORS

124 Action of the Sun - The south and west sides of business streets are, as a rule, preferred by merchants because the pedestrian traffic seeks the shady side of the street in warm weather, and merchandise displayed in the windows is not damaged by the sun. This is referred to as orientation.

125 Amenities - These add value to residential income property as well as to single-family dwellings. Proximity to markets, transportation, amusement parks, shopping centers, and churches are factors of value. Certain locations will appeal to potential tenants and the rents will be higher in these than in similar buildings in different locations. Upgrades over the neighborhood standard are also considered amenities, such as granite kitchen counters when other homes have Formica or tile tops.

125a Location - Barron Hilton once said the three most important considerations in appraising the desirability of a property are location, location, and location. Though a bit exaggerated, location is important and is significant. Before a developer spends time and money developing a shopping center, the location comes into play. A neighborhood shopping center requires 5,000 - 10,000 population at minimum within a one-mile radius. A community shopping center requires 30,000 population within a four-mile radius, and a regional shopping center requires 100,000 population within a six-mile radius in order to exist financially. It also requires a major "triple A" tenant to secure the financing to construct the facility and draw the largest number of shoppers. A one hundred percent location is said to be the best possible location in that city for that place of business.

Note that a broker would normally locate a new office in an area which he is familiar or has built a reputation and clientele.

126 Building Restrictions and Zoning - These sometimes operate to depress values and at other times to increase values. For example, there may be a vacant lot on a residential street that will sell for only $50 a front foot for residence use, but would sell for $300 per front foot as an apartment site. On the other hand, a vacant lot in a zoned area may sell for more per front foot as a business site because of the supply of business sites being restricted by zoning. Industrial areas, depending on size, would best be valued by the acre or square foot.

130 Cost of Construction - This is subject to frequent adjustments to compensate for changes in the cost of lumber and other building materials as well as the wage scale of carpenters, plumbers, electricians, painters, and others. A thorough knowledge, or at least a very authentic source of current information on construction costs and fluctuations, is necessary for the appraiser. "Means" cost data is a useful compilation with which to be familiar.

130a Construction costs are classified as direct and indirect. A building permit is classified as indirect as it does not enter into the construction of the building but is an overhead item. Direct costs could be the consideration of whether the land is hilly or flat (topography), the architectural type of home in demand by the purchasers in that area, and if the highest and best use of the land would be to build a one or two story property. For example, it costs less to construct 2,000 square feet of living space in a two-story house than a one-story house because there is half the foundation, half the lateral plumbing lines, half the roof area and half the heating ducts...and half the land. These items are usually the most costly portions of a structure.

Another classification one finds is hard and soft costs. Hard costs are those that enter into a modification of the site such as grading, material costs, and sewer lines. Soft costs are all the related project costs such as architectural fees, permit costs, and project supervision.

132   Highest and Best Use - Another factor used in appraising. It means creating the greatest value for a lot by improving it with buildings or using it in a way that will produce the greatest net income. A lot value may actually be depreciated by the wrong improvement.

134   Plottage - The added value of several parcels of land when brought under one ownership making possible a higher utility than could be found for the parcels when considered separately.

135 Size - The width and depth often determine the possibilities and the character of use. A series of factors called a "depth table" is often used to estimate relative value of commercial lots that vary from a normal depth. The depth table rule is stated as the 4-3-2-1 rule. This means that the first 25% of the depth contains 40% of the value, the second 25% contains 30%, the third 25% contains 20% and the fourth 25% contains 10%. 40% + 30% + 20% + 10% = 100% of value. There are two general rules of behavior concerning square foot and front foot units of value:
(1) As the depth increases the front foot value increases; however, the square foot value decreases.
(2) As the depth decreases, the front foot value decreases; however, the square foot value increases.

138 Unearned Increment - This is an increase in the value of property not anticipated by the owner that is due primarily to the operation of social or economic forces rather than to the personal efforts, intelligence, skill, or initiative of the owner. Usually, but not necessarily, this is applied to land.

DEPRECIATION CONCEPTS

139 Depreciation from the viewpoint of the appraiser may be defined as:

(1) "Loss in value from any cause whatever."
(2) "A loss from upper limits of value."
(3) "An effect caused by deterioration and obsolescence."

140 Depreciation, to an appraiser, is actual. This is far different than the depreciation as viewed by an accountant. An accountant is interested only in the book depreciation of the property for financial reporting or income tax purposes; while the appraiser is interested only in the actual effect depreciation has on value.

142 Depreciation makes a structure not only lack value; it can become a burden to the land. A residence, constructed in 1910 still standing on a lot that would be valued at $100,000 if vacant, will reduce the value of the lot by the cost of demolishing and clearing the structure.

143 A. Huxley, an accountant, said all assets are on, "an inexorable parade to the junk heap" because of depreciation. Depreciation is the almost inevitable companion of an improved property over its economic life. It is never a deduction applied to the land wither for appraisal or income tax purposes.

144 Economic life is the period over which a property will yield a return on the investment over and above the economic or ground rent due the land. The economic life of a structure should not be confused with its physical or chronological life. This is used to determine depreciation.

145 Physical life is the estimated period during which a physical thing may be capable of use if normally maintained. An apartment house may have a physical life expectancy of 100 years. However, its economic life expectancy may be only 40 to 50 years. Economic life can never exceed physical life and is generally shorter than physical life.

ACCRUED DEPRECIATION

146 In appraisal, accrued depreciation is defined as the actual loss of value existing in a

property at a given date. Accrued depreciation has already occurred.

148 Curable depreciation refers to items that are customarily repaired or replaced by a prudent owner. A curable depreciation item is one that may be cured on the date of valuation which if immediately accomplished would put the building in optimum condition. Examples of curable items of depreciation would be the replacement of a worn out roof or inadequate or old fashioned fixtures.

ACCRUED DEPRECIATION

149 Incurable depreciation refers to those items of depreciation that are not economically feasible or profitable to replace or cure on the date of appraisal. Examples of incurable depreciation are major structural changes to foundations, girders, or extensive changes in architectural design.

CAUSES OF DEPRECIATION

151 Physical Deterioration - A loss of value brought about by wear and tear, disintegration, use in service, and the action of the elements constitutes physical deterioration. It is said to be inherent to the property. Physical deterioration may result from:
(1) Wear and tear.
(2) Negligent care (sometimes defined as "deferred maintenance").
(3) Damage by dry rot, termites, or other infestation.
(4) Severe changes in temperature.
(5) Action of the elements.

152 Physical deterioration usually occurs first in the lower price ranges. They are usually constructed with cheaper materials, and consequently will deteriorate faster than costly structures.

153 Deferred maintenance is a form of physical deterioration. When normal maintenance has not been performed and a lump sum expenditure is required to correct deficiencies in paint, screens, and landscaping,

this lump sum amount is classified as deferred maintenance and is deducted from the building value.

153a Rehabilitation is referred to as necessary maintenance or accrued maintenance. Regardless of the term, it is the cost to restore the property to a competitive level. This does not mean the anticipation of repairs in advance or sustaining an unnecessarily high degree of maintenance. It simply means completing necessary repairs.

154 Functional Obsolescence - Probably the greatest cause in the decline in a property's value is the passage of its physical life. This includes a loss of value brought about by such factors as over-capacity, inadequacy, and changes in the art that affect the property. It is also defined as the inability of a structure to perform adequately the function for which it is currently employed. It is said to be inherent to the property (within property lines). It is usually "curable".

154a There are times when functional obsolescence could be termed incurable. When an improvement that has over-capacity and super-adequate facilities suffers a loss of value due to functional obsolescence, it is incurable. For example, when a builder constructed an office building containing 100 separate offices for lease, he attempted to sell the property and discovered that he could not recover his cost of construction because the area would presently support only 20 additional office units and that he had installed oversized heating, cooling, plumbing and electrical systems.

Functional obsolescence results from:
(1) Poor architectural design.
(2) Lack of modern facilities.
(3) Out-of-date fixtures.
(4) Changes in style of construction.
(5) Changes in construction methods and materials.
(6) Changes in utility demand (one car garage, one bathroom home).
(7) Massive cornices.

For example, a building's corridors are twelve feet wide. In today's market, over six feet of width is considered functionally obsolete space. The appraiser's primary measure of the efficiency of an office building plan is the ratio of net rentable area to gross floor area. The net rental area of office space is considered as the rental space between the outside wall and the corridor wall. Extra wide corridors reduce net rentable space, thus the value.

154b Improperly locating a residence on its lot is a factor inherent in the property itself. Hence, the value loss would be identified as functional obsolescence.

156 Economic obsolescence is also referred to as social obsolescence and defined as impairment of desirability arising from economic forces such as changes in highest and best use, legislative enactments, and changes in supply-demand relationships. It is the most difficult kind of value loss for the owner of the affected property to correct. Economic obsolescence may result from:
  (1) Misplacement of improvements.
  (2) Over-improvement of property.
  (3) Zoning and legislative restrictions.
  (4) Detrimental changes in supply and demand.
  (5) Proximity to noxious odors and fumes.
  (6) Proximity to freeways, major highways, and airports.
  (7) Major industries leaving an area.
  (8) Unreasonable tax rates.
  (9) Over-supply of like properties.

METHODS OF ESTIMATING ACCRUED DEPRECIATION

157 Accrued depreciation is the sum total of the depreciation that has occurred since the building was first constructed. There are five general methods of estimating accrued depreciation:

Indirect Methods
(1) Capitalized income.
(2) Market.

Direct Methods
(3) Straight line (age-life).
(4) Engineering (observed condition).
(5) Breakdown.

159 The straight-line method (age-life) assumes the value declines in equal amounts of depreciation each year until it reaches zero. Using this method, a building with an economic life of 50 years would depreciate 1/50th in value each year. Note that depreciation on a 50-year life can also be expressed at 2% a year (100% ÷ 50 years. 2% per year). This is the method most used by appraisers.

160 In some cases when using the age-life method, an appraiser will use an age other than the actual age of the building. This is known as the effective age. Effective age is defined as the number of years of age that is indicated by the condition of the building. If a building has had better than average maintenance, its effective age may be less than the actual age. If there has been inadequate maintenance, it may be greater. A 50-year old home may have an effective age of 20 years after rehabilitation and modernization.

ACCRUAL FOR DEPRECIATION

163 Accrual for depreciation or future depreciation is the loss in value that has not yet occurred but will come in the future and is of significance in the capitalization approach. In the income approach to valuation (capitalizing the net income), it is based on the remaining economic or useful life during which time provision is made for the recapture of the value of the improvements as they wear out.

164 In other words, an accrual for depreciation provides for a return of the investment in the building during its estimated useful life. It may be figured either by the "straight-line" method, or by the "sinking-fund" method.

165 The straight-line method contemplates that a definite sum be written off or deducted from the income each year during the total

estimated economic life of the building in order to replace the building.

APPRAISAL METHODS

171   The appraiser always determines the value of a whole property "free and clear" from any encumbrances. Should an appraiser be called upon to appraise a part of a property, an interest in the property, or the value encumbered by a low interest loan, the appraisal of the whole property unencumbered by partial interests or money liens would be made first. After the appraisal, the value of the interest would be determined.

METHOD CONSIDERATIONS

174   Reproduction Cost - This approach computes the current cost of reproducing the improvements with an added value for the land, arrived at by comparison with other lands. Deductions are made for depreciation from any cause. In the mechanics of preparing the facts of the reproduction cost approach, the process of bringing together the depreciated building value and the land value is the summation step in the procedure.

174a   Replacement Cost - A theoretical difference between the reproduction cost and the replacement cost approaches to value. The replacement cost approach is replacing the property being appraised with an equally useful property without using exact materials used in the structure as it stands. It is the final estimate of the value if all else fails.

175   Capitalization is the calculation of the present value of future benefits. The process simply put, "converts income into value." Using this method on income property, the present value is established by considering the prospective future annual net income of the property. Capitalization converts this net income stream into an estimate of the present worth of the property. This is done by dividing the annual net income by an appropriate interest rate (cap rate). The interest rate referred to as the overall rate includes both the return on investment (net Income), and return of investment (recapture rate).

Note that land is never capitalized because it alone does not produce a net income.

176   For example, if the economic life of the building is 25 years and the interest rate is 11%, you would add the depreciation rate of 4% (equivalent to 25 year life) to the interest rate 11% to give the overall "cap rate" of 15%.

177   If interest rates rise, new investors will require greater rates of return on invested capital. This means that properties with a fixed income will have income capitalized by an increasingly higher rate of return (cap rate) which decreases the value of the property. Conversely, when interest rates decline, the effect on income producing property value is to have it increase. As compared to stocks and other forms of investing, real estate has a slower capital turnover.

179   Though it is incumbent upon the appraiser to use any and all methods of appraisal to complete and validate the work, the final solution is always one of judgment. Never does an appraiser justify the solution by combining the answers arrived at by the use of each method independently and averaging the total.

TYPES OF PROPERTY

182   Service Property - Any property that does not fit the characteristics of other classifications is known as a service property. Such properties are churches, schools, and public buildings. There is no active sales market to provide an indication of value. Thus, the comparison approach cannot be used. There is no net income to capitalize, eliminating the use of the capitalization approach. Therefore, the only method remaining is the cost of reproduction approach.

THE COMPARISON APPROACH

184   Also known as the market-data or comparative analysis approach is the oldest method of appraisal known. This method is particularly adaptable for use by real estate brokers and salespersons. It lends itself readily to the appraisal of land, buildings, and residences that have a high degree of similarity and amenities. It is also a good check against the other methods of appraisal. This approach concerns itself with today's immediate market. The value achieved has nothing to do with what an owner originally paid for a property. The appraiser uses recent sales of comparable property by checking public records and by directly acquiring this information from buyers and sellers of comparable property. Appraisers also look at multiple listing board data. The listed prices tend to set the upper limit of value because sellers usually ask for more than they expect to receive. Selling prices tend to set the market value of similar properties.

184a   In the determination of value within a given neighborhood, offers to purchase property received by brokers will tend to set the floor of what prices can be expected in the neighborhood. Sellers list high whereas buyers generally offer to pay less than they might have to agree to pay. In a bargaining circumstance, asking prices establish the upper limit for prices in the area while offers to purchase will set the lower limit to which prices might fall.

185   As stated in the basic textbook of the American Institute of Real Estate Appraisers, "The primary concern in the appraisal analysis of any residential property is its degree of marketability, or acceptability, when offered for sale. Marketability and acceptability by the public is the ultimate test of style and design (functional utility).

187 A residential neighborhood is best defined as a grouping of individuals with similar social and economic status. Another definition is: "A homogenous grouping of individuals within or as part of a community." Neighborhoods are not fixed. In character they are always changing. The boundaries of a neighborhood vary in size, but they are generally homogeneous in some respect. These boundaries are both natural and economic. Examples: A natural barrier, such as a hill, or a man-made barrier, such as a main traffic artery, a distinct change in type of land use or in the character of inhabitants. A more or less unified area is a neighborhood with a fairly homogeneous population that has a community of interests. Appraisers use all of these boundaries.

188   The procedure used in the comparison approach is to assemble data concerning sales and other market data of comparable properties. The greater the number of good comparisons used the better the conclusions that may be drawn from them. The approach is based on the assumption that property is worth what it will sell for in the absence of undue stress if reasonable time is given to find a buyer. For this reason the appraiser should examine other sales and transfers to ascertain what influences may have affected sale prices. Obviously, the more active the market (the higher number of sales), the more valid the appraisal.

189   Proper comparisons between properties should be based on actual and thorough inspection of such properties. For nearly comparable properties, penalties should be assessed for poor repair, freakish design, and nuisances. Conversely, additional values should be allowed for attractive view, special features, better condition, higher quality of materials, landscaping, and the like. Unless the sales being compared are of recent date, consideration also must be given to adjusting value in keeping with the general economic worth of the dollar as of such dates. The average of the adjusted price for all selected comparable sales usually provides a measure of value for the property being appraised.

190   The comparison of unimproved land first requires a site analysis. In the matter of site analysis, excess land is land which exceeds that which is needed to serve the existing

improvements on the site, or identified with sites which are larger than other marketable lots in the area, or such that it may or may not be an addition to the estimated value of the site.

COST APPROACH

191   When a property is new or when there is no active market for a property and where market data is lacking and it has no monthly income to consider, the appraisal approach most likely to be employed would be the cost approach. In its simplest form the cost approach determines the cost to reproduce the improvements, subtracts the depreciation, and adds the value of the land. The cost approach is an estimate of the investment that would be required to duplicate a property in its present condition. Ordinarily, since people will not pay more for a property than it would cost to replace the structure at the time, or to obtain an equally satisfactory substitute property, the cost approach tends to set the upper limit of value. This approach is almost never used on old structures with functional deficiencies.

192   Though weighted heavily with a depreciation factor based upon the current age, a fire insurance appraiser will use the cost of reproduction approach to obtain the replacement value of a property.

193   The first step of this approach is to make an independent estimate of the value of the land. This is always the current market value of the land as if vacant and available now for improvement to its highest and best use. The comparison approach is used in this valuation.

193a   When the property has been improved with trees, shrubs, lawns, fences and sidewalks, the appraiser would always value these items separately. These items may be considered as part of the improvements or as part of the earth itself. However, when comparing different sites, they must be treated as separate items for comparative value. The appraiser would make a dollar adjustment for the value of landscaping, fences, and sidewalks.

196   The third step in the cost approach method is to determine the existing depreciation of the property. The amount must be deducted from the replacement cost as new to determine the present value of all improvements. The difficulties of estimating depreciation correctly tend to increase with the age of the property. Determining how much depreciation has occurred requires skill, experience, and good judgment. A value determined by using the cost approach is no more reliable than is the estimate of depreciation.

197   The last step is to add the estimated value of the land to the remaining depreciated value of the building to arrive at the total value of the property. This is referred to as the "improved" value.

METHODS OF DETERMINING COST NEW

198   There are several methods of determining the cost of improvements new (second step above). They are:

199   Quantity Survey - This is the most accurate (and most difficult) method. It involves detailed estimates of the quantities of raw materials used, such as lumber, brick, and cement. The price of such materials and the labor costs give an accurate and detailed cost of reproduction. Most experienced estimators use this method.

200   Unit-Cost-In-Place - Estimating the cost of erecting each component part of the structure such as foundations, floors, walls, windows, and roofs. These estimates include labor and overhead; therefore, the shape of a structure would influence the cost of construction.

201   Comparative Unit Method - The comparative method involves square and cubic footage. The actual cost of similarly constructed buildings is divided by the number

of square or cubic feet arriving at a dollar amount per square or cubic foot. Obviously, the use of cubic over square feet to determine value will be more accurate. Using square or cubic footage is called the unit of comparison method. It is probably the easiest to use.

202   Square footage is calculated by measuring the maximum length by the width of a structure then subtracting any deviations from this space caused by indentations in the exterior walls. When using the number of square feet in your residential unit comparison method, it is assumed that ceiling heights are a constant height.

203   Cubic footage simply multiplies the square footage obtained by the height of the interior walls. A warehouse may contain varied numbers of ceiling heights. A warehouse is appraised for the number of cubic feet it has for storage.

INCOME (CAPITALIZATION) APPROACH

204   The income approach is concerned with the present worth of future benefits which may be derived from the property. This method is particularly important in the valuation of income property. The income method is also defined as the capitalization method. Capitalization is a procedure by which the value of a property can be estimated from the quantity, quality, and durability of its net income. Inwood and Hoskold are well known in the field of appraising for the work they have done in perfecting the income approach to the valuation of real property. The past history of the property is not used. Only the anticipation of future income is employed.

204a   Maturity - In the language of real estate professional persons, a property is said to have reached "maturity" when the overall operation of the property is beginning to show a profit for the owners.

205   Management is never over-looked by a professional appraiser. It is the most likely item to be overlooked in the purchase of an income

producing property. Good management begins as an assist to the appraiser before the property is purchased. Urbanization, technological development in building construction, and absentee ownership make good property management a necessity. Property management may be said to be twofold in scope:
(1) To maintain the investment (income) in the property.
(2) To maintain the physical aspects of the property at a point of optimum efficiency and economy. A good management company will return to the investor far more in savings than the cost of management. The purchasing power of in labor and materials is returned to the owner in savings. The ability of the management company to maintain rents and lower vacancies, because of their advertising prowess, maintains high levels of income.

205a   The Administrative Code of the State of California requires that a responsible person reside upon the premises and have charge of every apartment house in which there are 16 or more apartments. A good on-premises manager creates a happy tenancy and a profitable investment.

209   The appropriate gross income that should be used is the expected future gross income, also known as scheduled gross income. The gross scheduled is that income based upon all units being rented all the time. The realities are that there will be some vacancies and rent collection losses over the economic life of the property. Therefore, when you subtract a factor for vacancies and rent losses, the remainder is called "effective gross income".

211   Expenses are classified as "fixed and operating". Fixed expenses, such as taxes and insurance, seldom vary. Operating expenses tend to fluctuate with the usage level. The result of gross income, minus expenses, is called "net operating income."

212   A selection is made of an appropriate capitalization rate.   This rate is the rate of

return which investors actually demand before they will be attracted to the investment.

212a Capitalization rates are often provided in reciprocal numbers. When multiplied together, reciprocal numbers have a product of one (1). Hence, since a capitalization rate is always a fraction, its reciprocal will always be a whole number (1 ÷ .08 = 12.5 Proof 12.5 x .08 = 1).

213 The final step to be accomplished after having determined the net income and the capitalization rate is to capitalize the income. This is merely a mathematical calculation of dividing the net income by the appropriate rate.

214 For example, a net income of $10,000 and a cap rate of 10% would result in a capitalized value of $100,000 ($10,000 ÷ .10 (10%) = $ 100,000).

This indicates that if the investor paid $100,000 for the property, he would receive 10% on his capital investment ($100,000 x .10 (10%) = $10,000).

SELECTION OF CAPITALIZATION RATES

215 The selection of capitalization rates is one of the most important tasks of the appraiser. Rates must be selected with utmost care based upon market experience. A variation in the rate can produce a wide variation in the resulting value. For example:

Net Income Rate Value
$6,000 ÷ .06 = $100,000
$6,000 ÷ .08 = $ 75,000

216 This illustrates a basic rule of capitalization rates. Given a fixed income amount, "The higher the rate, the lower the value and the lower the rate, the higher the value."

217 Rate Selection By Comparison - The appraiser collects data concerning a sufficient number of examples of property sales in the open market. He then determines the rate of return developed by each property and

establishes an average overall rate acceptable to typical investors. A typical analysis is:

Comparable	#1	#2	#3	#4	#5
True Net Inc.	$10,500	$10,160	$10,400	$11,000	$10,000
Selling Price	$125,000	$119,950	$122,000	$130,000	$126,600
Cap Rate	.084	.0847	.0852	.0846	.079

218 Rate Selection By Band of Investment Theory – The band of investment method is a combination of mortgage and equity rates which market data discloses as existing on comparable properties. The rate developed is a weighted average, the weighting consisting of the percentages of value occupied by the mortgages and the equity owner. For example, an apartment house has the following mortgage and equity investment:

	% of Value		Rate		Product
1st Trust Deed	50%	x	6%	x	3.0%
2nd Trust Deed	25%	x	8%	x	2.0%
Equity Investor	25%	x	10%	x	2.5% 7.5%

219 Gross Multiplier - Often investors use a factor of the gross income to place a property in a price range. For example:

Selling Price		Annual Gross Income		Gross Multiplier
$100,000	÷	$10,000	=	10
$90,000	÷	$10,000	=	9
$80,000	÷	$10,000	=	8

Note that this method is never used by a qualified appraiser. Only real estate agents and investors apply this method as a fast "first look" judgment.

CASH FLOW - SPENDABLE INCOME

222 The appraiser is concerned with developing reasonable estimates of gross income, effective gross income, expenses, and net income. He does not include in the appraisal process mortgage payments of principal and interest, sometimes referred to as "debt servicing costs." However, debt service is used by an investor to determine the spendable income generated by a property with a given amount of financing.

PROPERTY RESIDUAL INCOME

224 For this method, the depreciation allowed on the improvements is calculated separately and is then deducted from the estimated net income before depreciation to determine the net income for the entire property (true net income). The residual (left over) income amount is attributable to the property (land and buildings) and is then capitalized into the value of the property as a whole.

LAND RESIDUAL INCOME

226 In this method the building is valued separately. The net income is derived by determining the economic rent or the amount of income that the space would bring in the open market at the time of an appraisal. Contract rent is the rent that has been bargained for. Economic rent is rent determined by comparison to other similar properties and assumes that the property is being employed to its highest and best use. The fair annual net return on the building value (includes capitalization or return rate and recapture or depreciation rate) is deducted from the net income of the entire property before depreciation allowances. The residual amount (left over) is said to be earned by the land alone and is capitalized into a value for the land.

226a Development Method - This method is applied by an appraiser in his evaluation of land under development in which he projects the land as fully developed in its highest and best use and determines the value of the site by deducting the costs of development. The appraisal manual defines the anticipated use or development method of valuing a site in exactly this way.

227 If the net income of a property before depreciation was $25,300 annually, the building being valued separately at $180,000, the capitalization rate was 8% and the recapture rate was 2½% annually, we would proceed as follows:

Net income from property before depreciation	$25,300
Return & recapture of building $180,000 x .105 (8% + 2.5%)	-18,900
	$6,400
$6,400 divided by .08 (8% Capitalization Rate) = $80,000 =	Value of Land

APPRAISAL PRACTICE

231 After studying the technical aspects of real estate appraisal including its terminology and its procedures, you should know that throughout the United States a great deal of honest concern and inquiry has been focused on this specialized segment of the real estate industry. The most widely accepted appraiser has either one or both professional designations, M.A.I. (Member American Institute) or SREA (Society of Real Estate Appraisers founded in the 1930's). Membership in any other organization is not necessary to receive these designations.

LEGISLATIVE CONCERN

232 Many in government and elsewhere in the business of real estate lending, have voiced the opinion that some effort should be made to regulate or license real estate appraisers in some way. Because of the rash of lending institution failures an accusing finger has been pointed at real estate appraisal practitioners as the real cause for much of the financial difficulty lenders have suffered with the implication being that the appraisal work done was questionable, to say the least. Today, an appraiser must comply with stringent laws, as well as qualify by taking pre-licensing courses, become licensed and have apprentice experience. No one can appraise for a fee for a lending institution, appraise as an independent fee appraiser, nor can anyone have their work accepted by any court or governmental agency without meeting these requirements

A "CERTIFIED APPRAISAL"

234 As with real estate professionals, disclosure is of paramount importance in the

appraisal profession. If the appraiser has any interest in the property or is a relative of the person requesting the appraisal, a disclosure of these facts must be made to everyone that is affected by the appraised value. No kickbacks or undisclosed referrals are permitted. As with the profession of real estate all discriminatory practices are prohibited.

241 A certified appraisal report must be presented in clear and unequivocal terms with sufficient information to enable the user of that report, or any other person who may be expected to rely on the report, to understand it properly and in such a manner as to avoid being misleading. There are no fixed fees applied to a certified appraisal.

Lesson Fourteen
Part Two
Study Questions

_____(Lesson Fourteen - Paragraph 38 - Question 1)_____
A major thoroughfare has a line of store buildings built along the sides of the street. This kind of development is known as:
(A) A line commercial zone.   (B) A cluster development.
(C) A strip commercial development. (D) A neighborhood shopping center.

(C) The development described in the statement has come to be known as a "strip commercial" type of project.

_____(Lesson Fourteen - Paragraph 45 - Question 1)_____
In performing his task of determining the worth of a parcel of real property for a specific reason as a definite date, the real estate appraiser is making:
(A) An evaluation. (B) A valuation. (C) A determine of highest and best use. (D) None of these.

(B) In appraising, the term "valuation" is used to describe an appraisal. "Evaluation", a wrong choice, does not apply to appraising.

_____(Lesson Fourteen - Paragraph 45 - Question 2)_____
An appraiser intends that the estimate of market value disclosed in his appraisal report on a property will be valid:
(A) As of the date of the appraisal.
(B) For a period of three months after the appraisal date.
(C) For a period of six months after the appraisal date.
(D) For a period of one year after the appraisal date.

(A) Appraisals are always developed for a certain date. Since the value of property can vary by time the date is most important.

_____(Lesson Fourteen - Paragraph 47 - Question 1)_____
The first step in the approach to an appraisal assignment is to:
(A) Define the problem. (B) Determine the fee. (C) Collect the data. (D) Correlate the values.

(A) The first step in the appraisal process is to write a concise statement of the problem in the assignment.

_____(Lesson Fourteen - Paragraph 48 - Question 1)_____
Definitions of market value are least concerned with:
(A) Material cost. (B) Value in exchange. (C) Objective value. (D) An open market.

(A) Material cost. Market value is determined by the comparison technique. Comparison depends on everything except the original cost of construction or the cost of construction new less depreciation.

————————(Lesson Fourteen - Paragraph 48 - Question 2)————————
The least important factor in applying the cost approach is:
(A) Original cost of property. (B) Current value of land.
(C) Accrued depreciation on the improvements. (D) Cost of reproduction.

(A) The price an owner pays for a property has little if anything to do with its present value.

————————(Lesson Fourteen - Paragraph 49 - Question 1)————————
When an appraiser makes a comparative analysis of listed prices of older homes in an area, he considers the listed prices as establishing the:
(A) Ceiling on price. (B) Floor on price. (C) Fair market price. (D) Value in use.

(A) Listing prices usually reflect a price that is higher than the willing seller will actually accept on the whole. Properties sell for less than listed prices. Consequently, an appraiser considers listing prices as reflecting the ceiling on prices.

————————(Lesson Fourteen - Paragraph 51 - Question 1)————————
In the rather detailed activity required of a person making a real estate appraisal, the following item would be of most importance to the appraiser:
(A) The date the deed is signed. (B) The date the sale is put in escrow.
(C) The date the agreement to purchase is signed. (D) The date the deed is recorded.

(C) The appraiser would be most concerned in directing his appraisal efforts to the date his client, buyer or seller, would sign the agreement to purchase the property appraised. On signing such an agreement, the buyer is committed to buy and the seller is obligated to sell.

————————(Lesson Fourteen - Paragraph 51 - Question 2————————
Jones hired an appraiser at a fee of $100 to determine the value of Brown's property. The appraiser should disclose the results of his appraisal to:
(A) Brown. (B) No one. (C) Anyone who is interested in the property. (D) Jones.

(D) The American Institute of Real Estate Appraiser's Code of Ethics states: "It is unethical for an appraiser to reveal the findings of his appraisal to anyone other than his client, unless he is required to do so by due process of law, or authorized to do so by his client."

————————(Lesson Fourteen - Paragraph 54 - Question 1)————————
The builder's plan, which displays the piers, footing and columns within a structure, is called a:
(A) Floor plan. (B) Elevation plan. (C) Foundation plan. (D) Plot plan.

(C) The foundation plan is the plan that discloses piers, footings, and columns. These all deal with the foundation of a structure.

————————(Lesson Fourteen - Paragraph 54 - Question 2)————————
An elevation drawing (plan) discloses:
(A) Lot dimensions and lot improvements drawn to scale.

(B) Exterior sides of a building after all structural work have been completed.
(C) Essential detail concerning size of footings, size and dimensions of piers, and subfloor areas.
(D) Wall to wall measurements, room sizes and exposures, and placement of doors, windows, fireplace, cabinets and attached garage.

(B) This choice an exact definition of an elevation plan. Answer (A) defines a plot plan, answer (C) a foundation plan, and answer (D) a floor plan.

_____(Lesson Fourteen - Paragraph 55 - Question 1)_____
To an appraiser, value means:
(A) A desirous thing and a person desiring it.
(B) A commodity that will bring money or another commodity in exchange for it.
(C) The present use of future benefits arising out of ownership of a property.
(D) Any of the above.

(D) Value for the appraiser can mean several things. The answers suggested here express some of them: (A) suggests what might be called value in use or inherent value, (B) suggests what is called value in exchange, (C) suggests value an interpretation of future income in terms of present dollars. Hence, any of the choices is correct. The value in the appraisal of property may be said to be the present worth of all benefits that may accrue in the future from the use of it.

_____(Lesson Fourteen - Paragraph 55 - Question 2)_____
The relationship between "the thing desired and the potential purchaser" is best defined as:
(A) The economic man. (B) Utility as an element of value.
(C) Value.   (D) The present worth of future income.

(C) This question is taken directly from appraiser's handbook of terminology. Value is described as the relationship between a thing desired and a potential purchaser.

_____(Lesson Fourteen - Paragraph 57 - Question 1)_____
In property appraisal, the following are considered to be essential elements of value:
(A) Utility, scarcity, demand, desirability.   (B) Accessibility, scarcity, demand, transferability.
(C) Utility, scarcity, demand, transferability. (D) Scarcity, utility, accessibility, desirability.

(C) The essential elements of value are utility, scarcity, demand and transferability. This is strictly a memory item. Remember "USDT" as the United States Demands Taxes.

_____(Lesson Fourteen - Paragraph 60 - Question 1)_____
Demand is one of the four elements of value. In order for demand to be effective, it must be implemented by:
(A) Conspicuousness. (B) Objectivity. (C) Purchasing power. (D) Reliability.

(C) Unless there are buyers with the necessary borrowing power and equity investment there is no demand.

_____(Lesson Fourteen - Paragraph 74 - Question 1)_____
There are numerous and various types of value. The type of value that is the highest would be:

(A) Book value. (B) Market value. (C) Intrinsic value. (D) Mortgage loan value.

(B) "The price at which a willing seller would sell and willing buyer would buy neither being under abnormal pressure," constitutes the highest price and defines market value.

————————(Lesson Fourteen - Paragraph 74 - Question 2)————————
The following best describes market value:
(A) An appraiser's report in which the future net income from the property is interpreted by computation in terms of present dollar value.
(B) The value attributable to a property by the process of reproducing the improvements with a substitute structure and making proper allowance for allowable depreciation.
(C) The highest price that could be expected exposed for sale in the open market allowing a reasonable time with both he buyer and the seller having full knowledge of local conditions at the time of sale.
(D) Any of them.

(C) (A) is a description of capitalized value, (B) is a description of replacement or reproduction value, and (C) is the definition of market value.

————————(Lesson Fourteen - Paragraph 75 - Question 1)————————
The following statement would be most closely related to the idea of the market value of real property:
(A) The asking price of a property that is for sale in the market place.
(B) The price offered by a knowledgeable buyer to purchase a parcel of real property.
(C) The price actually paid for a property by a buyer in the open market.
(D) The price at which a property is offered for sale by a fully informed owner.

(C) The idea of "market value" deals with the price actually paid for a property in an open market.

————————(Lesson Fourteen - Paragraph 85 - Question 1)————————
Under the usual competitive circumstances, the vacancy rate attributable to a particular apartment property is fundamentally the result of:
(A) The schedule of rents and the number of the units in the apartment building.
(B) The cost of money and the costs of construction.
(C) Housing supply and demand in that particular area.
(D) Employment fluctuation in the community.

(C) This is an example of the general economic principle of supply and demand.

————————(Lesson Fourteen - Paragraph 86 - Question 1)————————
Integration - equilibrium - disintegration - all refer to the principle of:
(A) Progression - regression. (B) Change. (C) Competition. (D) Supply and demand.

(B) The age-cycle of a neighborhood area is said to go through three stages:
    1. Integration (growth & development).
    2. Equilibrium (static and stable).
    3. Disintegration (deterioration & decline).

_____(Lesson Fourteen - Paragraph 86 - Question 2)_____

"Regression and progression" and "integration and disintegration" relate to the following principal:
(A) Change. (B) Balance. (C) Highest and best use. (D) Contribution.

(A) Nothing material remains static. An appraiser making his value determination must recognize the point of development that the property and the neighborhood in which it is situated have reached at the time the appraisal is made.

_____(Lesson Fourteen - Paragraph 87 - Question 1)_____

When applying the principle of substitution the homebuyer would consider:
(A) Use. (B) Earnings. (C) Structural design. (D) All of the above.

(D) The principle of substitution is the heart of appraising. You must take the value of the known sales and substitute them for the unknown property that you are appraising. In making this substitution you would substitute one use for another. If you were appraising an income property you would substitute for other income properties. You substitute the earnings of one property or property with comparable earnings of other properties. With a structural design, you attempt to substitute a property with the same design. All of these will be considered in the principle of substitution.

_____(Lesson Fourteen - Paragraph 87 - Question 2)_____

1. The value of a replaceable property tends to be indicated by the value of an equally desirable substitute property
2. The value of a property tends to coincide with the value indicated by the actions of informed buyers in the market for comparable properties.
3. The cost of producing, through new construction, an equally desirable substitute property usually sets the upper limit of value.
All of the above statements are in reference to the principle of:
(A) Highest and best use.
(B) Substitution.
(C) Conformity.
(D) Supply and Demand.

(B) All three statements refer to the principal of substitution when applied to each of the three appraisal methods:
1. Comparison. 2. Income. 3. Cost.

_____(Lesson Fourteen - Paragraph 91 - Question 1)_____

The principal of "highest and best use" refers to the use:
(A) That produces the largest gross income.
(B) That produces the greatest net income attributable to the land.
(C) Of improvements best adapted to the architectural style and design of the neighborhood.
(D) That is best suited to the environment.

(B) Highest and best use refers to use of land. It is defined as that use of the land that will produce the greatest net income that is designated and credited to the land.

_____(Lesson Fourteen - Paragraph 91 - Question 2)_____

When appraising an undeveloped parcel, an appraiser would use site analysis to determine:
(A) Highest and best use.   (B) Soils and subsoil conditions.
(C) Applicability of zoning laws.   (D) Contour and dimensions.

(A) When you are appraising undeveloped land you must determine the highest and best use of the land. Site analysis describes the process by which you determine the highest and best use.

─────────(Lesson Fourteen - Paragraph 92 - Question 1)─────────
All of the following are correct statements concerning a subdivision, except:
(A) Parcels of land irregular in shape cannot be developed as advantageously as rectangular.
(B) Short blocks afford the most economical use land.
(C) Streets intersecting at other than 90-degree angles are wasteful of land.
(D) Wider lots are more in demand in recent subdivisions.

(B) This is the false answer. Short blocks utilize more land area than do long blocks.

─────────(Lesson Fourteen - Paragraph 92 - Question 2)─────────
Subdividers consider all of the following as correct, except:
(A) Lots that are too deep are wasteful.
(B) Side streets should enter major streets at right angles for the most economical use of land.
(C) Short blocks result in the most economical use of the land.
(D) Lots with sharp angles create an engineering problem.

(C) Short blocks devote more land for street use. Long blocks are more economical in utilizing land than short blocks.

─────────(Lesson Fourteen - Paragraph 94 - Question 1)─────────
A developer produces the same house in each of the following locations:
1. One house across the street from a shopping center. 2. One house adjacent to a bus stop on a heavily traveled thoroughfare. 3. One house in the center of the subdivision. 4. One house on a key lot in the subdivision.
These various properties could all be purchased for the same price. As a knowledgeable real estate licensee, you would advise a homebuyer to purchase the house:
(A) Across from the shopping center.   (B) Near the bus stop on the heavily traveled street.
(C) In the center of the subdivision.   (D) On the key lot.

(C) If a buyer were looking for a home, the most desirable home location would be in the center of the development as it should afford the most pleasant living conditions.

─────────(Lesson Fourteen - Paragraph 96 to 99 - Question 1)─────────
In the evaluation of income and worth of real property, four agents are generally recognized as contributing factors. The following would not be one of their agents:
(A) Depreciation. (B) Labor. (C) Capital. (D) Coordination.

(A) The four agents that influence income production and value of real property are identified as: labor, coordination, land and capital. Depreciation is certainly not one of these.

─────────(Lesson Fourteen - Paragraph 103 - Question 1)─────────

An appraiser considers the addition of a swimming pool to a property and increases the property's value more than the cost of the swimming pool. This is an example of the principle of:
(A) Contribution. (B) Regression. (C) Progression. (D) None of the above.

(A) The principal of contribution states that an improvement made to property should contribute more value than the cost of the improvement. If not, it is not a wise investment.

—————(Lesson Fourteen - Paragraph 103 - Question 2)—————
An owner is considering modernizing an income-producing building. In making this decision, he would rely most on:
(A) Cost. (B) Vacancy history. (C) Potential increase in property tax. (D) Effect on net income.

(D) The criterion for modernizing an income-producing building is: What positive effect will it have on increasing net income? The appraiser uses the principal of contribution in making this report.

—————(Lesson Fourteen - Paragraph 104 - Question 1)—————
Peter is considering purchasing a commercial property to be used in Peter's business. This use will involve significant remodeling of the building and will result in the building being inappropriate for any other purpose. In considering the purchase price of the property and the dollars necessary to bring the building into a useable state, Peter will consider the factor of:
(A) Value in exchange. (B) Diminishing returns. (C) Reproduction value. (D) Book value.

(B) The principle of diminishing returns, also called increasing and decreasing returns, states that increasing an investment in one of the agents of production (labor, management, land or building) will reach the point where any added investment will actually decrease the return on the investment. Peter must consider this factor in his original investment.

—————(Lesson Fourteen - Paragraph 104 - Question 2)—————
When developing a property there is a proper amount that should be invested in the improvements on a specific site, a proper amount of management efforts to be expended, and a proper expenditure for furnishing a building. This illustrates the application of the principle of:
(A) Conformity. (B) Change. (C) Supply and demand. (D) Diminishing returns.

(D) The principle of diminishing returns, also called increasing and decreasing returns, states that increasing an investment in one of the agents of production (labor, management, land or building) will reach the point where any added investment will actually decrease the return on the investment. For example, increasing an investment in an apartment by adding a $50,000 swimming pool that does not result in a corresponding increase in rents will actually lessen the owner's return on his investment.

—————(Lesson Fourteen - Paragraph 105 - Question 1)—————
A developer who tries to maintain a certain amount of uniformity but attempts to keep the development from being monotonous is said to be applying the principle of:
(A) Change. (B) Progression. (C) Accretion. (D) Conformity.

(D) A developer would want land utilized in conformity with the standards governing the area in which it is located. Zoning regulations are often times made to maintain conformity. Accretion is an addition to land from natural causes and an example of progression would be the building of a $300,000 home in a neighborhood of $400,000 homes.

_____(Lesson Fourteen - Paragraph 105, 106 - Question 1)_____
What best maintains value in an area of single-family dwellings:
(A) An area with 20% income property.
(B) People having approximately the same income.
(C) An area where no down payment is required.
(D) Some families with low income and some families with high income.

(B) Value is best maintained by property when owners in a given area have an income of approximately the same amount. When you have largely varied incomes in an area, the large income homeowner can afford to improve their property where a smaller income homeowner cannot.

_____(Lesson Fourteen - Paragraph 105, 106 - Question 2)_____
Of the following circumstances the least effective in preventing the loss of value to property in a residential neighborhood would be:
(A) Some homes of average quality, some of high quality.
(B) A population of the same ethnic and religious background.
(C) A population with the same income level.
(D) All the homes of better than average or good quality.

(A) Homes of different quality would be a violation of the principle of conformity and would be the least effective in preventing a loss of value.

_____(Lesson Fourteen - Paragraph 112 - Question 1)_____
A lower priced home located in a neighborhood of more expensive homes would benefit according the principle of:
(A) Regression. (B) Progression. (C) Increasing returns. (D) Decreasing returns.

(B) In appraisal theory and practice, progression simply stated is, "the worth of a lesser object is enhanced by association with better objects."

_____(Lesson Fourteen - Paragraph 112 - Question 2)_____
In the event a person constructed a high quality home costing $300,000 in a neighborhood where the other homes were valued at $100,000, he would suffer a downward trend in value due to:
(A) Regression. (B) Supply and demand. (C) Progression. (D) Contribution.

(A) This is an example of economic obsolescence based upon the principal of regression. The value of his $300,000 home tends to come closer to the value of other homes in the area. Since this is downward, it regresses. Supply and demand is not a factor since the demand may exist for this home but the purchasing power is usually lacking in such an area.

_____(Lesson Fourteen - Paragraph 124 - Question 1)_____

The placement of a house regarding exposure to the rays of the sun, prevailing winds, and privacy from the street is referred to as:
(A) Orientation. (B) Plottage. (C) Elevation. (D) Topography.

(A) The question gives an exact description of the term orientation.

─────────(Lesson Fourteen - Paragraph 124 - Question 2)─────────
Considering the action of the sun and the comfort and habits of pedestrian shoppers, the sides of the street best suited for retail business purposes would be:
(A) North or east side. (B) South or east side. (C) South or west side. (D) North or west side.

(C) Buildings on the west side of a street (facing east) would receive sunshine only in the morning. As the sun travels from east to west, such buildings (and those on the south side, facing north) cast deep shadows making pedestrian shopping much more comfortable. The north and east sides would be the least desirable.

─────────(Lesson Fourteen - Paragraph 126 - Question 1)─────────
The unit of measurement ordinarily used in the appraisal of urban industrial areas would be:
(A) Acre/square foot. (B) Acre/front foot. (C) Square foot/front foot. (D) Square foot/unit foot.

(A) Front foot considerations are most important in commercial properties (and to some extent, on ocean or lake front properties). Though all properties may be compared in this way Industrial properties are usually sold by the acre or by square footage.

─────────(Lesson Fourteen - Paragraph 130 - Question 1)─────────
Expenditure of dollars for the construction of improvements of residential real property is:
(A) Cost. (B) Price. (C) Value. (D) Investment.

(A) This question presents a definition of cost.

─────────(Lesson Fourteen - Paragraph 130a - Question 1)─────────
A subdivider and developer must be aware of many cost factors in developing new property. The following would be considered in estimating his development costs:
(A) Topography. (B) Zoning Laws. (C) Trend of construction. (D) All of the above.

(D) A subdivider must consider whether the land is hilly or flat (topography) and what type of structure can be built according to local zoning laws. The other important consideration is the architectural type of home in demand by the purchasers in that area.

─────────(Lesson Fourteen - Paragraph 130a - Question 2)─────────
The topography of land is the defining of its surface features. A subdivider must give consideration to the topography of the proposed subdivided lands because:
(A) Some irregularities in the surface are desirable.
(B) Hilly or irregularly shaped lots reduce the cost of construction.
(C) A rolling terrain is more monotonous than a flat terrain.
(D) Elevated lots are subject to inundation in the winter.

(A) Irregularities refer to hills or slopes on the land. Homes with a view or at least not on the same level as the other homes in the same neighborhood usually are more desirable.

—————(**Lesson Fourteen - Paragraph 134 - Question 1**)————

An increase in utility of land through the annexation of contiguous lots by the same owner is called:
(A) Joint purchase. (B) Plottage. (C) Demurrage. (D) Combined value sale.

(B) The merging of contiguous properties by the same owner is called plottage or sometimes referred to as assemblage. This can be done for many reasons and when it is done so that there is an increase in the overall value of the entire property the term "plottage" is used.

—————(**Lesson Fourteen - Paragraph 134 - Question 2**)————

Two properties are combined to make one property that is more valuable that the sum of the two separately. This is an example of:
(A) Subdividing. (B) Plottage. (C) Inflation. (D) Leverage.

(B) The term plottage is an appraisal term meaning the increasing in value of joining two separate parcels into one. If parcel A is worth $ 10,000 and parcel B is worth $10,000, but when sold together they are worth $30,000, that is said to be plottage by joining them. As you've increased the property value the plottage value is the added $10,000 in value.

—————(**Lesson Fourteen - Paragraph 135 - Question 1**)————

An appraiser would likely make use of a "depth table" in preparing an appraisal report for:
(A) Residential property.   (B) Multiple unit residential property.
(C) Retail commercial property.   (D) None of the above.

(C) A depth table is used by an appraiser to correlate the value of a retail commercial property with a greater depth than adjoining properties of the same front footage. When using a depth table we are concerned with front footage. Front footage is related to retail commercial property.

—————(**Lesson Fourteen - Paragraph 138 - Question 1**)————

When real property increases in value because of an increase in population this would be classified as:
(A) Economic value. (B) Economic obsolescence. (C) An unearned increment. (D) None of the above.

(C) The correct definition for of "unearned increment" is a value increase due to social forces rather than to the personal effort of the owner.

—————(**Lesson Fourteen - Paragraph 138 - Question 2**)————

In the appraisal of real property, the term "unearned increment" would apply to:
(A) A value increase due to population increase.
(B) A value decrease due to social forces rather than personal effort.
(C) A decrease in property taxes.
(D) Depreciation.

(A) In this problem the most correct answer is a value increase due to population increase. Be careful! The correct definition for "unearned increment" is a value increase (not decrease) due to social forces rather than to the personal effort of the owner.

_____(Lesson Fourteen - Paragraph 139 - Question 1)————
The following is the best definition of depreciation:
(A) Physical deterioration.   (B) Functional obsolescence.
(C) Economic obsolescence.   (D) Loss in value for any reason.

(D) Depreciation has many causes for loss of value including physical, functional, and economic. However, the best definition of depreciation is a loss of value from any reason whatsoever.

_____(Lesson Fourteen - Paragraph 139 - Question 2)————
Depreciation is all of the following, except:
(A) The wearing out of the property.
(B) Buildings placed on the parcel which cause the value of the property to decrease.
(C) A decrease in value due to an increase in property taxes.
(D) Inherent in the property and not due to external factors.

(D) This is a negative question that asks for the false statement. (D) is false because depreciation can be caused by external factors such as adverse zoning changes, recessions, or airport flight patterns.

_____(Lesson Fourteen - Paragraph 140 - Question 1)————
An accountant and an appraiser look at depreciation in a different manner. The following best illustrates this difference in viewpoint:
(A) An appraiser concerns himself with historical costs only.
(B) An accountant is unrealistic in his approach to depreciation.
(C) An accountant utilizes the straight line method only while the appraiser uses accelerated methods of depreciation.
(D) An accountant is interested only in the book depreciation of the property while the appraiser is interested only in the effect actual depreciation has on value.

(D) This choice is a textbook statement of the relative positions of an accountant and an appraiser with respect to depreciation. The (A) choice is incorrect in that the appraiser concerns himself with present costs most particularly. The (B) choice might have a grain of truth from the appraiser's point of view, but not from the income tax consideration which concerns the accountant. The (C) choice is the opposite of the truth. The accountant can use accelerated methods of depreciation while the appraiser generally uses straight-line depreciation.

_____(Lesson Fourteen - Paragraph 142 - Question 1)————
An appraiser determines that the building on a parcel adds no value to the land. Considering the highest and best use of the property in determining its value, he would:
(A) Ignore the building completely.
(B) Add the salvage value of the building to the value of the land.
(C) Subtract the cost of demolishing the building from the value of the land.
(D) Add the cost of demolishing the building to the value of the land.

(C) When appraising property, its highest and best use requires the demolition of the building. The cost of demolishing and removing the building is subtracted from the market value of the land.

_____(Lesson Fourteen - Paragraph 143 - Question 1)_____
All of the following are depreciable, except:
(A) Buildings. (B) Land. (C) Fixtures. (D) Sidewalks in the common area of a condominium project.

(B) This is a negative question asking which is not depreciable. Land is not depreciable. There is no depreciation deduction used either by appraisers or by the Internal Revenue Service for land.

_____(Lesson Fourteen - Paragraphs 144, 145 - Question 1)_____
When considering the value of the improvements, which is the most important?
(A) Effective age. (B) Physical age. (C) Future physical life. (D) Remaining economic life.

(D) Effective age would refer to the past existence of the structure. Physical age, whether present or future, would indicated its actual period of existence. Remaining economic life is the period of time (years) from the date of appraisal to the date when the improvements become economically valueless. This would generally be less than the projected or physical life.

_____(Lesson Fourteen - Paragraph 149 - Question 1)_____
While gathering information about a particular building, an appraiser discovers that several places in the substructure of the building show evidence that the beams supporting the structure as they connect with the foundation show signs of more than ordinary deterioration. This type of defect would be classified as:

(A) Physical deterioration curable.   (B) Functional obsolescence curable.
(C) Functional obsolescence incurable. (D) Physical deterioration incurable.

(A) A curable depreciation item is one that may be readily curable as of the date of the valuation. This would include all items of rehabilitation or accrued maintenance that, if immediately corrected, would place the building in optimum condition. All other building components are treated as incurable because it is not economically profitable to replace or cure the condition as of the date of the appraisal.

_____(Lesson Fourteen - Paragraph 151 - Question 1)_____
The following are examples of economic obsolescence, except:
(A) Worn out fixtures.
(B) A decrease in the gross payroll of companies in the area that causes apartment rents to decrease.
(C) The widening of a freeway which causes a reduction in the rent of a nearby commercial structure.
(D) An increase in property tax levies.

(A) This is a negative question. It is asking which is not economic obsolescence. (A) describes physical depreciation. The other choices are examples of economic obsolescence.

————————(Lesson Fourteen - Paragraph 151 - Question 2)————————

The following should not be considered to be evidence of obsolescence:
(A) Wear and tear.
(B) Misplaced improvements.
(C) Out-of-date equipment.
(D) Change of locational demand.

(A) Wear and tear is physical deterioration. Misplaced improvements and a change in locational demand are economic obsolescence. Worn out equipment is functional obsolescence.

————————(Lesson Fourteen - Paragraph 152 - Question 1)————————

For the appraiser, the following would be an example of wear and tear:
(A) An encroachment into the area by a use foreign to that area.
(B) The over-improvement of a particular property.
(C) A driveway that is cracked and crumbling.
(D) None of the above.

(C) A cracked driveway falls into this category.

————————(Lesson Fourteen - Paragraph 152 - Question 2)————————

In a new tract of homes the following would suffer the fastest loss of value due to wear and tear:
(A) Low cost homes in the $52,000 to $64,000 range.
(B) Average cost homes in the $114,000 to $115,000 range.
(C) Medium quality homes in the $170,000 to $192,000 range.
(D) High quality homes in the $223,000 to $225,000 range.

(A) It is generally a recognized fact that structures in the lower price ranges are usually constructed with cheaper materials and consequently will deteriorate faster than more costly structures.

————————(Lesson Fourteen - Paragraph 153a - Question 1)————————

An apartment building owner fixed up the property in such a way that he didn't alter the interior or exterior design. This is an example of what is called:
(A) Remodeling. (B) Reclamation. (C) Rehabilitation. (D) Modernization.

(C) Rehabilitation is the restoration of property to satisfactory condition without changing the plan, form or style of a structure.

————————(Lesson Fourteen - Paragraph 154 - Question 2)————————

The following would be interpreted by an appraiser as functional obsolescence:
(A) A cracked and broken driveway.
(B) A residence with a single car garage.
(C) Neighborhood surroundings considerably altered.
(D) Visible evidence of dry rot and termite damage.

(B) Evidence of physical deterioration would be a cracked driveway, dry rot and the termite damage. Neighborhood surroundings would indicate economic obsolescence. A residence with a one-car garage would be an example of functional obsolescence.

_____(Lesson Fourteen - Paragraph 154a - Question 1)_____

The appraiser's primary measure of the efficiency of an office building plan would be:
(A) The ratio of net rentable area to gross floor area.   (B) Corridor widths.
(C) Elevator capacity.   (D) Parking.

(A) The appraiser's primary measure of the efficiency of an office building plan is the ratio of net rentable area to gross floor area. The net rental area of office space is considered as the rental space between the outside wall and the corridor wall.

_____(Lesson Fourteen - Paragraph 156 - Question 1)_____

The most difficult form of depreciation to cure is:
(A) Functional obsolescence.
(B) Physical wear and tear.
(C) Physical depreciation.
(D) Economic obsolescence.

(D) Economic obsolescence is extraneous to the property and not under the control of the property owner to correct. Examples of economic obsolescence to keep in mind are adverse zoning, recessions, misplaced improvement, and major industry leaving the area.

_____(Lesson Fourteen - Paragraph 156 - Question 2)_____

Economic obsolescence would ordinarily be considered to be:
(A) Curable (B) Incurable   (C) Functional in the use of the property.   (D) Inherent in the property itself.

(B) Normally, economic obsolescence is neither curable nor incurable as it is not under the control of the owner of the property. However, in these circumstances we would have to select incurable as the owner has no control over outside causes of value loss.

_____(Lesson Fourteen - Paragraph 159 - Question 1)_____

An appraiser when using straight capitalization with straight-line recapture, assumes:
(A) Land value will remain constant and income imputable to land is level in perpetuity.
(B) The market value of the buildings will decline at a fixed annual rate based upon remaining life.
(C) Income imputable to buildings will decline at a fixed annual rate.
(D) all of the above.

(D) Choices (A), (B) and (C) are all assumptions of the straight-line method of capitalization as stated in the American Institute of Real Estate Appraiser's text on appraisal practice.

_____(Lesson Fourteen - Paragraph 160 - Question 1)_____

An appraiser has been requested to place a value on a residential home. He finds that the home when originally built had an estimated total economic life of 40 years. At this time the home is 10 years old. In viewing the home, however, he finds that it has been exceptionally

well card for and maintained in such a lovely manner that he plans to consider its age as only 6 years. This age is known as the:
(A) Actual age. (B) Effective age. (C) Undepreciated age. (D) Remaining life.

(B) Effective age is defined as the number of years of age that is indicated by the condition of the building. If a building has had better than average maintenance, its effective age may be less than the actual age. If there has been inadequate maintenance, it may be greater. A 50-year old building may have an effective age of 20 years after rehabilitation and modernization

————————**(Lesson Fourteen - Paragraph 160 - Question 2)**————————
A house is 19 years old. Because of good maintenance it looks like it is 6 years old. It has an estimated life of 40 years. In appraising the property using the cost approach, the appraiser most likely would use:
(A) Chronological age of the improvements. (B) Effective age of the improvements.
(C) Physical age of the improvements. (D) Economic age of the improvements.

(B) When an appraiser uses an age other than the actual age of a home, that age is known as the effective age.

————————**(Lesson Fourteen - Paragraph 163 - Question 1)**————————
Future depreciation is taken into consideration in using which of the following techniques:
(A) Cost. (B) Income. (C) Comparative rent. (D) Fixed rent.

(B) The term "recapture of capital" (accruals for depreciation) is associated with future depreciation and refers to the amount which is charged against expected net income to provide for the probable depreciation which will take place in the future. In real estate appraising, such accruals for future depreciation generally are used in connection with the income approach to provide for recapture of the cost imputed to the improvement.

————————**(Lesson Fourteen - Paragraph 164 - Question 1)**————————
When appraising income property and selecting a capitalization rate, the appraiser considers "return on" and "return of" the investment. "Return of" the investment refers to:
(A) Depreciation. (B) Appreciation. (C) Income. (D) Yield.

(A) An investor, in addition to making a profit on his investment, would also expect to recover his original investment over the life of the investment. With a long-term investment such as real estate, the investor (appraiser) earmarks a portion of the annual net income not only for a return on his investment (income on) but also some return of his original investment. The former is identified using a capitalization rate (return on), the latter is identified using a depreciation rate (return of).

————————**(Lesson Fourteen - Paragraph 171 - Question 1)**————————
When using the income approach in the appraisal of an apartment building, the appraiser would consider all of the following to determine net income, except:
(A) Mortgage interest. (B) Allowance for vacancies.
(C) Electricity expense. (D) Replacement reserves.

(A) Financing costs such as principal and interest payments are not deducted in arriving at net income. These items are deducted from net income to arrive at spendable income or cash flow.

————————(Lesson Fourteen - Paragraph 171 - Question 2)————————
For an accurate appraisal of residential real property, the appraiser must assume that:
(A) The payments on the loan will not be too high for the buyer.
(B) That the buyer can obtain a FHA loan.
(C) That the buyer is paying all cash.
(D) That some kind of loan can be arranged by the buyer.

(C) The appraiser, as he performs his task, ignores the facts of the financing involved in purchasing the property. He assumes that the property is owned free and clear.

————————(Lesson Fourteen - Paragraph 174a - Question 1)————————
In the appraisal process, the "replacement cost approach" represents:
(A) The original cost. (B) The cost new.
(C) The cost new of the exact replica. (D) Not important in determining an appraisal.

(B) The "replacement cost" uses the cost of the improvements new on the date of the appraisal, then deducts the accrued (past) depreciation to establish the value.

————————(Lesson Fourteen - Paragraph 175 - Question 1)————————
In making an appraisal of a shopping center, the appraiser would most likely make use of the:
(A) Market data approach. (B) Income approach.
(C) Cost of reproduction approach. (D) Cost to cure approach.

(B) The income approach is best used to determine the value of property that produces income and is most likely used in appraising a shopping center.

————————(Lesson Fourteen - Paragraph 175 - Question 2)————————
In the appraisal of real property the following approach would put the greatest emphasis on the present worth of future benefits:
(A) The market approach (B) The reproduction cost approach.
(C) The summation of estimates. (D) The income approach.

(D) The appraisal approach that places the greatest emphasis on the present worth of future benefits is the income approach. When buying an income property such as a shopping center or apartment house, one does not buy for pride of ownership, but buys for the value of the future income stream over the economic life of the property. It may be 10, 20, or 30 years.
————————(Lesson Fourteen - Paragraph 176 - Question 1)————————
Given straight-line income, 25 year remaining economic life, and an 11% interest rate, what will be the capitalization rate to find the indicated building value?
(A) 4%. (B) 8%. (C) 11%. (D) 15%.

(D) Since the building in this question is depreciable and earns income also we must use what is called the overall rate to capitalize and find value. The interest rate 11 % is added to the depreciation rate 4% (equivalent to 25 year life) to give the overall rate of 15%. This would be the capitalization (overall) rate for the building and the answer to this question.

_____(Lesson Fourteen - Paragraph 177 - Question 1)_____

The following statement most adequately characterizes the rate of capital turnover in real estate investments as compared with other forms of investment:
(A) Faster investment return than other commodities.
(B) Average investment return when compared with other commodities.
(C) Slightly slower than average when compared with stocks.
(D) Much slower.

(D) Real estate is an income-producing asset and is characterized by a slow capital turnover. This means that even under favorable circumstances, many years are required before the aggregate annual gross income derived from a property equals or returns the total capital investment. On the average, most forms of real estate investment require five to ten years for the capital "turnover" once. Other forms of personal or corporate assets represented by merchandise inventory (both hardware and software) turnover weekly, monthly or at least several times during a given year.

_____(Lesson Fourteen - Paragraph 177 - Question 2)_____

When an appraiser finds it necessary to raise a capitalization rate, it would imply an increase in the:
(A) Value of the subject property.   (B) Risk of the income for the property.
(C) Amenities in the area.   (D) Cost of the property.

(B) The riskier the venture the higher the rate of return demanded. Cap rates increase as risk increases.

_____(Lesson Fourteen - Paragraph 179 - Question 1)_____

The final step in the appraisal process is to correlate the results of the three approaches to value and arrive at a single estimate of value. This correlation is accomplished by:
(A) Adding the three value estimates and dividing by three.
(B) After reviewing each of the approaches, the appraiser should weigh the relative significance of each and place the most significance on the approach which, in his judgment, is most applicable.
(C) Both A and B are correct.
(D) Neither A nor B are correct.

(B) Keeping in mind that an appraisal is an opinion or estimate of value as of a specific date, this opinion cannot be based solely on arithmetic procedures. An appraisal opinion is a matter of judgment based on facts discovered in the appraisal process.

_____(Lesson Fourteen - Paragraph 182 - Question 1)_____

The appraisal method that has the greatest weight when appraising a public library is:
(A) Market data.   (B) Cost of reproduction.   (C) Capitalization of income.   (D) Gross rent multiplier.

(B) A public library is a service property (single use). The cost method of appraisal would be used in arriving at its value. There is no rent or income from public libraries and it is difficult to ascertain.

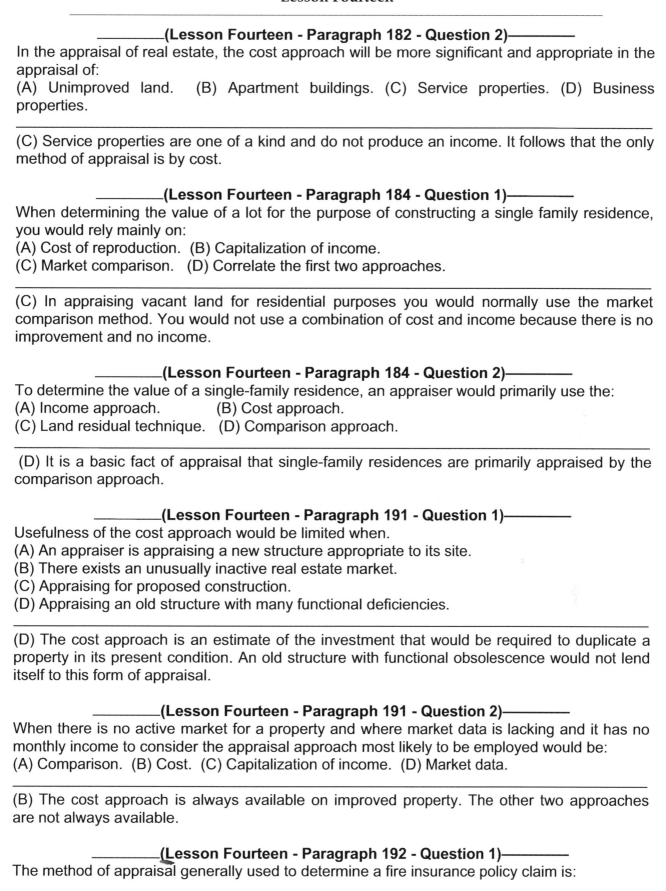

————————(Lesson Fourteen - Paragraph 182 - Question 2)————————
In the appraisal of real estate, the cost approach will be more significant and appropriate in the appraisal of:
(A) Unimproved land.   (B) Apartment buildings. (C) Service properties. (D) Business properties.

(C) Service properties are one of a kind and do not produce an income. It follows that the only method of appraisal is by cost.

————————(Lesson Fourteen - Paragraph 184 - Question 1)————————
When determining the value of a lot for the purpose of constructing a single family residence, you would rely mainly on:
(A) Cost of reproduction. (B) Capitalization of income.
(C) Market comparison.   (D) Correlate the first two approaches.

(C) In appraising vacant land for residential purposes you would normally use the market comparison method. You would not use a combination of cost and income because there is no improvement and no income.

————————(Lesson Fourteen - Paragraph 184 - Question 2)————————
To determine the value of a single-family residence, an appraiser would primarily use the:
(A) Income approach.   (B) Cost approach.
(C) Land residual technique. (D) Comparison approach.

(D) It is a basic fact of appraisal that single-family residences are primarily appraised by the comparison approach.

————————(Lesson Fourteen - Paragraph 191 - Question 1)————————
Usefulness of the cost approach would be limited when.
(A) An appraiser is appraising a new structure appropriate to its site.
(B) There exists an unusually inactive real estate market.
(C) Appraising for proposed construction.
(D) Appraising an old structure with many functional deficiencies.

(D) The cost approach is an estimate of the investment that would be required to duplicate a property in its present condition. An old structure with functional obsolescence would not lend itself to this form of appraisal.

————————(Lesson Fourteen - Paragraph 191 - Question 2)————————
When there is no active market for a property and where market data is lacking and it has no monthly income to consider the appraisal approach most likely to be employed would be:
(A) Comparison. (B) Cost. (C) Capitalization of income. (D) Market data.

(B) The cost approach is always available on improved property. The other two approaches are not always available.

————————(Lesson Fourteen - Paragraph 192 - Question 1)————————
The method of appraisal generally used to determine a fire insurance policy claim is:

(A) Direct market comparison. (B) Cost of reproduction. (C) Income capitalization. (D) Land residual.

(B) Fire insurance claims are based upon the cost of repairing or reproducing the damaged improvements.

―――――――(Lesson Fourteen - Paragraph 192 - Question 2)―――――――
In figuring the value of a residential duplex for fire insurance purposes, an appraiser would place the most emphasis on the:
(A) Cost approach.　　(B) Comparison approach.
(C) Income approach.　(D) None of the above.

(A) An insurance company would be interested in replacing the building at today's costs; hence, it would place most emphasis on the reproduction cost approach.

―――――――(Lesson Fourteen - Paragraph 192 – Question 3)―――――――
The amount of fire insurance coverage a prudent homeowner would carry is:
(A) So that in the event of a fire he will incur a loss.
(B) So that in the event of a fire he will have a gain.
(C) So that in the event of a fire he will have neither a gain nor a loss.
(D) As much as he can afford.

(C) It is an expression that one should have sufficient fire insurance so that the insured would neither gain nor lose money if the insurance proceeds are given in case of a total loss. If a home has an insured value of $100,000 and carries a $200,000 insurance policy, the company will accept your premium on the $200,000 but in the event of a total loss, you would receive $100,000 to replace the current value of the improvements. If you under insure the property planning to take advantage of small losses only, then the insurer will require you to be a co-insurer. If the insured value is $100,000 and you insure for only 50% of value and then have a loss of $20,000, you would be a co-insurer for 50% of the $20,000 loss and receive $10,000 in insurance proceeds.

―――――――(Lesson Fourteen - Paragraph 193 - Question 1)―――――――
All of the following are acceptable methods of valuing unimproved land, except:
(A) Comparison approach.　(B) Development method.
(C) Equity method.　　　　(D) Abstraction or allocation method.

(C) This is a negative question indicated by the word "except." All of these choices are methods of valuing unimproved land except the equity method. The equity method is a distracter it has nothing to do with appraising.

―――――――(Lesson Fourteen - Paragraph 193 - Question 2)―――――――
In determining the value of a lot on which a worthless building is situated and considering the highest and best use of the parcel, an appraiser would:
(A) Deduct the cost of demolition of the building.　(B) Ignore the building completely.
(C) Figure the replacement cost of the building.　(D) Include the salvage value of the building.

(A) In his appraisal, the appraiser cannot ignore the building to be removed. He must make a charge against the land to provide for its removal.

————————(Lesson Fourteen - Paragraph 196 - Question 1)————————

The following would be considered a difficulty in using the cost approach in appraising an older building:

(A) Building code changes.　(B) Changes in material costs.

(C) Changes in labor costs.　(D) Estimating depreciation.

(D) The first three answers can be looked up in books because the data is available. Depreciation is a judgment call. Therefore, depreciation is the most difficult.

————————(Lesson Fourteen - Paragraph 196 - Question 2)————————

The reproduction cost method of appraisal would be less accurate in valuing an older property as compared with the new property because of:

(A) Changes in the building codes.　(B) Changes in the cost of materials.

(C) Changes in the cost of labor.　(D) The difficulty in estimating depreciation.

(D) Estimating depreciation is not an exact science, consequently the older the property, the more chance of error. The statements in (A), (B) and (C) have no real effect on the cost approach as the appraiser uses current costs and the current building code.

——————(Lesson Fourteen - Paragraphs 198 to 201 - Question 1)——————

Cost estimating methods presently used by architects, builders and appraisers are:

(A) Capitalized cost of replacement.

(B) Capitalization of residual income.

(C) Unit-in-place, quantity survey, declining balance.

(D) Quantity survey, unit-in-place, comparative square or cubic foot.

(D) The three methods in common use using the cost approach to estimate value are: 1. Quantity survey. 2. Unit-in-place cost. 3. Comparative square foot or cubic foot.

——————(Lesson Fourteen - Paragraphs 198 to 201 - Question 2)——————

In determining the value of improvements to be made on an existing real property, many times the building contractor, the architect, and the real estate appraiser make use of the same techniques. Which of the following best approximates the methods that could be used by all three individuals?

(A) Market, capitalization, unit methods.

(B) Capitalization, quantity survey and cubic footage methods.

(C) Comparative, unit-in-place cost, and quantity survey methods.

(D) Square foot, cubic foot, residual and quantity survey methods.

(C) When determining the cost "new" to replace improvements, the appraiser, architect and building contractor make use of three techniques: 1. Comparison method (comparing square foot or cubic foot costs). 2. Unit-in-place cost. 3. Quantity survey method.

————————(Lesson Fourteen - Paragraph 199 - Question 1)————————

In determining the reproduction cost of a building new today the following method would be the most difficult:

(A) Unit-in-place cost.　(B) Quantity survey. (C) Square foot unit method. (D) Cubic foot unit method.

(B) The quantity survey method of appraising fits the description exactly. The technique is seldom used by appraisers but contractors use it in projecting cost of building any type of improvement.

_____(Lesson Fourteen - Paragraph 199 - Question 2)————

In determining property value, the quantity survey method is used in the:
(A) Income approach.   (B) Comparison approach.   (C) Cost approach.   (D) Land residual technique.

(C) The cost approach has three steps: 1. Determine the present value of the land. 2. Determine the cost of replacement of the improvements. 3. Determine the total depreciation that the existing improvements have suffered in order to obtain the current depreciated value of the improvements. 4. Add these two values together. This is called the summation of value. When performing the second step to determine the cost of replacement at current cost, there are several methods. The quantity survey method is the most complex and difficult. It involves rebuilding the structure as a contractor would, starting with grading, foundation, and so forth. The other two methods of step two would be the unit-cost-in-place method, and the square foot or cubic foot unit methods.

_____(Lesson Fourteen - Paragraph 201 - Question 1)————

The quickest and easiest method used by an appraiser to determine the replacement cost of a building would be:
(A) Comparative unit method.   (B) Quantity survey method.
(C) Unit-cost-in-place method. (D) Economic residential method.

(A) The reproduction cost per square foot in a given community is easily used as a yardstick to obtain the approximate cost of a comparable building.

_____(Lesson Fourteen - Paragraph 201 - Question 2)————

The easiest method to determine cost of reproduction is:
(A) Unit-in-place.   (B) Quantity survey.
(C) Comparative square foot or cubic foot unit cost.   (D) Original cost modified by an index.

(C) There are fewer mathematical calculations involved in using the comparative square foot or cubic foot cost method of determining building value new today. It also involves less research in making the value determination.

_____(Lesson Fourteen - Paragraph 203 - Question 1)————

To be able to determine the cubic footage of a house the appraiser would make use of this formula:
(A) Length x width x height = cubic footage.
(B) Length x width x height + 3 = cubic footage.
(C) Length x width x height ÷ 2 = cubic footage.
(D) Length x width x height x 3 = cubic footage.

(A) This is the exact formula.

_____(Lesson Fourteen - Paragraph 203 - Question 2)————

The most appropriate method of measuring space in a warehouse is:
(A) Square feet.   (B) Front foot.   (C) Cubic feet.   (D) Relation of size of building to size of the parcel.

(C) A warehouse may contain varied numbers of ceiling heights. A warehouse is considered for the number of cubic feet it has for storage. When using the number of square feet in your residential unit comparison method, it is assumed that ceiling heights are a constant height.

————(Lesson Fourteen - Paragraph 204 - Question 1)————
The appraisal of income property is most appropriately based upon the use of the:
(A) Capitalization approach.   (B) Comparison approach. (C) Cost approach.   (D) Gross rent multiplier.

(A) Although all four methods might be used in appraising income property (capitalization approach, comparison approach, reproduction cost approach and gross multiplier), the capitalization approach is considered the best for income-producing property since it is based on the net income that the property can produce.

————(Lesson Fourteen - Paragraph 204 - Question 2)————
When valuing a parcel of real property, an appraiser takes into consideration the quantity, quality and durability of the property's projected net income. This appraisal is known as:
(A) The Q.Q.D. approach.   (B) The market data approach.
(C) The capitalization approach.   (D) Marginal utility analysis.

(C) The appraiser would be using the income or capitalization approach.

————(Lesson Fourteen - Paragraph 205 - Question 1)————
The following item of expense is most likely to be overlooked in the purchase of a business building:
(A) Size of building. (B) Management costs. (C) Prospective income. (D) Unusable floor plan.

(B) Property management may be said to be two-fold in scope:
1. To maintain the investment (income) in the property.
2. To maintain the physical aspects of the property at a point of optimum efficiency and economy.
Unless the purchaser of income property is able to recognize the existence of such an expense in the operation of the property, he could easily overlook the matter in identifying expenses. The ordinary purchaser more readily recognizes the other suggested choices. An appraiser on the other hand would never establish a capitalization rate without including property management as an expense when arriving at the net income.

————(Lesson Fourteen - Paragraph 205 - Question 2)————
Good property management begins:
(A) Before the property is acquired.
(B) After the property is acquired.
(C) After expenditures are made for improvements on the property.
(D) After the period of construction.

(A) Good management includes a complete survey of the property and the surrounding area to indicate a demand for space, maximum rents available, and other such items which should be made before acquisition to help in deciding whether it should be acquired or not.

———————(Lesson Fourteen - Paragraph 209 - Question 1)————————
When an appraiser looks at effective gross income, one important factor is:
(A) Vacancy. (B) Depreciation. (C) Mortgage costs. (D) Principal and interest.

(A) An appraiser would be interested in the vacancy factor and the costs of collection in order to determine the effective gross income.

———————(Lesson Fourteen - Paragraph 209 - Question 2)————————
In calculating net income for evaluation purposes, an appraiser would use:
(A) Reserve for depreciation. (B) Federal income taxes.
(C) Vacancy allowance.   (D) Amortization of the liens.

(C) This question concerns an appraiser arriving at a net income.

———————(Lesson Fourteen - Paragraph 211 - Question 1)————————
When determining net income mathematically, an appraiser would take into account:
(A) Mortgage, interest and amortization. (B) Capital additions.
(C) Allowance for depreciation.   (D) Real property taxes.

(D) Real property taxes are classified as an expense and are deducted by appraisers in determining annual net income. The other choices are not considered by the appraiser when determining net income.

———————(Lesson Fourteen - Paragraph 211 - Question 2)————————
To arrive at the net operating income, you would calculate the:
(A) Gross scheduled income less vacancies and collection losses, less operating expenses.
(B) Gross rent multiplier minus vacancies and operating expenses.
(C) Gross income minus operating expenses and depreciation.
(D) Any of the above.

(A) This is a precise definition of NOI, the net operating income.

———————(Lesson Fourteen - Paragraph 212a - Question 1)————————
The reciprocal for a capitalization rate of 8% would be:
(A) 1.25 (B) .0125 (C) 12.5 (D) .125

(C) Two numbers which when multiplied together have a product of one (1) are reciprocal numbers. Since a capitalization rate is always a fraction, its reciprocal will always be a whole number.
$1 \div .08 = 12.5$ Prove $12.5 \times .08 = 1$
Other examples: $1 \div .5 = 2$ $2 \times .5 = 1$ $1 \div .4 = 2.5$ $2.5 \times .4 = 1$

———————(Lesson Fourteen - Paragraph 213, 214 - Question 1)————————

If a property was valued at $200,000 at a time when a 6% capitalization rate was applicable and the capitalization rate is now 8% and the income remains the same, the property would be worth:
(A) $170,000. (B) $120,000. (C) $150,000. (D) $180,000.

(C) Using the formula: Value x Rate = Income, $200,000 x .06 = $12,000. To determine the value of a $12,000 income using an 8% capitalization rate we use the formula: Income ÷ Rate Value, $12,000 ÷.08 (8%) = $150,000 projected value.

_____(Lesson Fourteen - Paragraph 213, 214 - Question 2)_____
If an appraiser finds that the fair rent for a vacant parcel of land is $700 per month and the interest rate is 11%, the approximate indicated land value would be:
(A) $ 54,545. (B) $ 69,280. (C) $ 76,360. (D) $105,000.

(C) $76,360 is approximately correct.
$700 (monthly income) x 12   = $8,400 yearly income from land.
$8,400 ÷.11 (11 % cap rate)   = $76,363 value of the land.

_____(Lesson Fourteen - Paragraphs 215 to 218 - Question 1)_____
The most critical and vital consideration when using the income approach to valuation is:
(A) Adjusting the sales prices of comparables to make them like the subject property.
(B) Determining accrued depreciation.
(C) Calculating operating expenses.
(D) Selecting an appropriate capitalization rate.

(D) The question emphasizes the most critical and vital consideration in the income approach which is selecting the proper capitalization rate for the property under appraisal. An error in a capitalization rate could magnify an error in value. The capitalization rate on a property varies according to the quantity of the income (how much), the quality of the income (how good). For example, the type of tenants, the terms, and length of leases (week to week vs. five or ten year leases). The capitalization rate depends upon the duration of the income. Does this building have a remaining economic life of 10 years or 50 years?

_____(Lesson Fourteen - Paragraph 218 - Question 1)_____
A capitalization rate can be determined by:
(A) Subordination. (B) Liquidation. (C) Rationalization. (D) The band of investment theory.

(D) The band of investment theory is a method of calculating a capitalization rate. This method involves a weighted average. The return demanded on the first trust deed, junior loans, and the investor are weighted according to degrees of value and then averaged.

_____(Lesson Fourteen - Paragraph 218 - Question 2)_____
The following may be used by a real estate appraiser to determine a capitalization rate for an investor:
(A) The 4-3-2-1 rule.   (B) Band of investment theory.
(C) Bank managers in the locality.   (D) Property residual technique.

(B) Appraisers and sometimes assessors in valuing lots of different depths have used the 4-3-2-1 rule. The banks could only give a limited amount of evidence as to a capitalization rate.

The band of investment theory is an accepted method of calculating the capitalization rate required by an individual investor.

————————(Lesson Fourteen - Paragraph 219 - Question 1)————————
The gross rent multiplier that is sometimes used in estimating the value of income properties is determined by:
(A) Dividing the sales price by the gross income.
(B) Dividing the market price by the gross income.
(C) Multiplying the sales price by the gross income.
(D) Multiplying the market value by the gross income.

(A) This is a matter of fact.

————————(Lesson Fourteen - Paragraph 219 - Question 2)————————
The fair market value divided by its gross income is called:
(A) Capitalization rate. (B) Equity. (C) Unearned increment. (D) Rent multiplier.

(D) When the fair market value of a property is divided by its gross income, the result is a rent multiplier. If a property sells for $100,000 and its annual gross income from rental is $10,000, by dividing the $10,000 into the $100,000, the quotient is 10. Therefore, the property sold for ten times its gross income.

————————(Lesson Fourteen - Paragraph 219 - Question 2)————————
An appraiser examines a rental property earning $125 a month and by comparison with like properties establishes this to be a proper income figure. He also located comparable properties that sold recently that were properly valued at $18,000. What monthly gross multiplier would he use in making further projections?
(A) 1.25 (B) 125 (C) 144 (D) .0068

(C) A multiplier is a figure that, times the income, produces an estimate of value. If income is multiplied by the figure it is called a gross income multiplier. Appraisers, where it is meaningful, will use either monthly gross rental figures or annual gross rental figures. In this question we have the gross monthly income ($125.00) and we have the reasonable value of the property ($18,000). We are seeking the multiplier that applies.

125 x 12 (months) = $1,500.00 per year
18,000 - 1,500 = 12 gross income multiplier or 144 (12 x 12 mths.) monthly gross multiplier.

————————(Lesson Fourteen - Paragraph 222 - Question 1)————————
You have a customer that is interested in purchasing a business for investment purposes. The average investor would be most interested in knowing the following information about the business:
(A) Gross income. (B) Net income. (C) Operating expenses. (D) Pedestrian count.

(B) An investor is interested in his return on the investment. This is the net income after deducting expenses from the property's gross income.

————————(Lesson Fourteen - Paragraph 222 - Question 2)————————

A prospective investor in an apartment house asked a licensee to determine his spendable income. The licensee should:
(A) Deduct from the gross income an allowance for vacancies and collection losses.
(B) Deduct from the gross income an allowance for vacancies and collection losses and the operating expenses.
(C) Deduct from the net income the operating expenses.
(D) Deduct from the net income the principal and interest payments.

(D) Spendable income (also called cash flow) is a trade term and has no precise legal definition. Spendable income may be used to mean spendable before income taxes or spendable after income taxes. In normal use, when speaking of an investment without a particular investor in mind, the spendable income refers to spendable before income taxes. On the other hand, when working out the spendable income for a particular investor, his tax bracket can be determined and his spendable income reflects the deduction of his income tax liability created by the added income.

_____(Lesson Fourteen - Paragraphs 224 & 226 - Question 1)_____
In appraising an income-producing property, the appraiser would make use of:
(A) Land residual technique.   (B) Building residual technique.
(C) Property residual technique.   (D) Any of the above.

(D) The land residual method, the building residual method, and the property residual method are all recognized ways in which to appraise income-producing properties. These methods are used by professional appraisers and require highly qualified people to estimate value accurately.

_____(Lesson Fourteen - Paragraph 226 - Question 1)_____
When appraising a property where the value is well established, the appraiser would least likely use:
(A) Building residual - straight line.   (B) Land residual - straight line.
(C) Property residual - with capitalization of net income. (D) Property residual - without reversion.

(B) The land residual technique is used when land value is difficult to determine from other sources. Hence, it would least likely be used in valuing the type property indicated here.

_____(Lesson Fourteen - Paragraph 226 - Question 2)_____
In the evaluation of real property the land residual technique is ideal to determine the:
(A) Land value. (B) Building value. (C) Net income. (D) Capitalization.

(A) The value of unimproved land can be learned by determining the net income from several hypothetical land uses. The income from the highest and best use is capitalized into an estimate of the value of land.

_____(Lesson Fourteen - Paragraph 227 - Question 1)_____
In order to evaluate a vacant commercial site, an appraiser decides to use the land residual technique. Here is the information the appraiser gathered: Cost new of a proper building is $250,000, estimated net income before recapture is $32,800 per year, interest rate is 8.5%

and the estimated remaining economic life of building is 40 years. The approximate estimated value of the land using this technique would be:
(A) $31,000. (B) $47,000. (C) $48,182. (D) $62,353.

(D) $62,353. The building in this question must be interpreted with the overall rate which takes into account both income and depreciation rates. The overall rate in this case is 11%. The income rate of .085 (8.5%) is combined with the depreciation rate of .025 (2.5% = 40 years) to give .11 (11 %). $250,000 x .11 (11 %) = $27,500 annual income for building. $32,800 (property income) - $27,500 (bldg. income) = $5,300 annual income for land. $5,300 (land income) ÷ .085 (8.5%) = $62,353 value of the land. We do not use the overall rate in capitalizing the land income since land is not depreciable.

(Lesson Fourteen - Paragraph 227 - Question 2)

In the appraisal of residential real property the appraiser, after using all three techniques, would arrive at his value estimate by:
(A) Adding the 3 estimates and dividing by 3.
(B) Weighing each of the three estimates and dividing by 3.
(C) Both A and B.
(D) Neither A nor B.

(D) In correlating the value estimates projected by each of the appraisal techniques (comparison, cost, income), the professional appraiser will not make his final judgment using a mathematical process. His final estimate will be a decision based on his judgment and not based solely on his mathematical calculations.

(Lesson Fourteen - Paragraph 227 - Question 3)

Concerning the appraisal of residential properties, all of the following are correct statements, except:
(A) A rental multiplier may be used for a quick indication of value.
(B) Zoning ordinances and zoning variances definitely influence the value of such properties.
(C) The reproduction cost method is a valid method in appraising such properties.
(D) All three methods of appraising may be used and the sum of the results divided by three to obtain value.

(D) It is never permissible to average results obtained from the different methods of appraisal. You may use all three, but then you must choose the value indicated by the one method most appropriate to the property.

(Lesson Fourteen - Paragraph 231 - Question 1)

The American Institute of Real Estate Appraisers and the Society of Real Estate Appraisers:
(A) Are international in scope. (B) Were founded in the early 1930's.
(C) Evaluate residential and income properties. (D) All of the above.

(D) All are correct statements concerning these two organizations.

(Lesson Fourteen - Paragraph 231 - Question 2)

In California a real estate appraisers:
(A) Must be licensed by the Bureau of Real Estate.
(B) Must be a California resident for at least one year.

(C) Must reckon his fee as a percentage of the appraised value.
(D) May display a certificate of membership in any professional organization of appraisers without being a member of the National Association of Realtors.

(D) There is no requirement to belong to any other organization to hold membership in either appraisal society.

────────(Lesson Fourteen - Paragraph 232 - Question 1)────────
A fee appraiser is a/an:
(A) Full-time employee of a lender.
(B) Employee of the Department of Transportation.
(C) Employee of the federal government.
(D) Appraiser who prepares appraisals for the payment of a fee.

(D) A fee appraiser is one who appraises independently for a fee, as opposed to employees of a lender, the state, or the federal government who work for a salary.

────────(Lesson Fourteen - Paragraph 234 - Question 1)────────
The following act of an appraiser would not be in violation of the Code of Ethics of the American Institute of Real Estate Appraisers:
(A) Performs an appraisal and collects a fee for his services on a property in which he has an interest which fact had been disclosed to his client in his report.
(B) Performs an appraisal and bases his fee upon a percentage of the value estimate.
(C) Accepts an assignment without previous experience or knowledge of a character to qualify him to accept the assignment.
(D) Pays a fee to another for referring clients to him for appraisal assignments.

(A) This is a negative question as it asks what is not a violation. The Code of Ethics does permit an appraiser to charge a fee for appraising a property in which he has an interest as long as this interest is disclosed to his client. Choices (B), (C), (D), are all violations of the appraisers Code of Ethics.

────────(Lesson Fourteen - Paragraph 241 - Question 1)────────
In reference to appraisal reports, all of the following are true, except:
(A) They can be oral or written.
(B) Certified appraisers charge standardized fees for similar appraisal reports.
(C) The subject property must be adequately described.
(D) The report must be dated.

(B) This is a negative question and (B) is the negative answer. Certified appraisers do not charge standard fees. They charge according to their skills and experience.

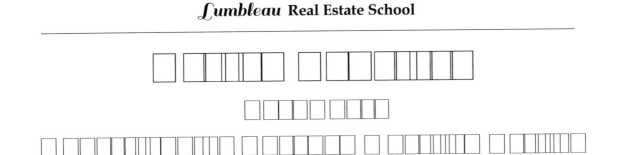

Log into your course at www.lumbleau.com.

STUDENT LOGIN

Login:

Password:

On your student home page, click on the "State Exam Preparation".

STATE EXAM
PREPARATION

Under the "Guided Lesson" tab click on the fourteenth of fourteen links: "Real Estate Appraisal and Valuation".

Real Estate Salesperson Course

Guided Lessons	Practice Exams	Progress Report	Success Video

Print	Questions
Click	HERE>>> **14. Real Estate Appraisal and Valuation**

Here you will be tested on all of the questions you have been studying and learn the most recently added questions. It is essential, for maximum retention, that you eliminate all of the questions you can easily answer and "TAG" for study the questions with which you have difficulty.

Made in the USA
San Bernardino, CA
15 October 2015